PHILIPPINE ETHNOGRAPHY
A Critically Annotated and Selected Bibliography

1/11/74

East-West Bibliographic Series

Editorial Committee   Joyce Wright, Chairman
G. Raymond Nunn
Shiro Saito
Stanley West

1. China and America: A Bibliography
of Interactions, Foreign and Domestic
compiled by James M. McCutcheon

2. Philippine Ethnography: A Critically
Annotated and Selected Bibliography
by Shiro Saito

Philippine Ethnography
A Critically Annotated and Selected Bibliography
by

Shiro Saito

The University Press of Hawaii
Honolulu

To Frank Lynch, S.J.

TABLE OF CONTENTS

INTRODUCTION

BACKGROUND: In 1968 I distributed a <u>Preliminary Bibliography of Philippine Ethno-</u><u>graphy</u> to about 60 Philippine specialists for their comments and annotations. That edition was the result of a year's work in the Philippines in 1967/68 and over two years' work prior to that. This project has throughout been largely a labor of love, pursued as my time permitted, which delayed until now the comple- tion of the successor work, <u>Philippine Ethnography</u>, revised, enlarged and con- taining the ratings and annotations provided by the specialists.

Originally I had intended to include only those titles rated by the con- tributors 3 (good) or higher on the five-point scale, ranging from 1 (poor) to 5 (excellent primary data), used in the <u>Outline of Cultural Materials</u>.[1] This plan had to be revised when some of the annotators who had agreed to participate were unable to do so because of the pressure of work or change of plans. Since without their contributions bibliographic coverage of some categories would have been incomplete, it was decided, after consulting with Philippine specialists, to include titles which had not been rated and annotated by contributors and to update the information by including 1967 and 1968 publications, which had not been in the <u>Preliminary Bibliography</u>. These titles were selected on the basis of the authority of the author, appropriateness of the publication or, in some subject and group areas, because of the scarcity of available literature.

PURPOSE: The primary purpose of this bibliography is to provide bibliographic guidance to researchers who are conducting initial literature searches for references outside their immediate interests, or to graduate students embarking on their first search, and to assist librarians in locating Philippine materials for their clientele, non-specialist as well as other.

SCOPE: In American usage, ethnology is considered a part of cultural anthropology and distinct from physical anthropology. In conformity with this, titles in physical anthropology have been excluded, with the exception of those that deal with a specific cultural-language group. Folklore and linguistics, normally included in a bibliography of ethnography and ethnology, have been de-emphasized since publications on both have already been listed by other bibliographers, notably Manuel, Welsh and Landé.[2] However folklore titles are cited if the myths, legends or proverbs contribute substantially to the cultural setting. Entries under Language and Literature are largely non-technical linguistic essays with the exception of some which refer to cultural-linguistic groups.

Types of materials included are books, journal articles, mimeographed papers, and official publications published in the major western languages from the early Spanish period to 1968 inclusive. The following have been excluded: films, one-page articles, newspaper articles, textbooks for high schools, and publications about the Filipinos in the United States.

---

[1]Human Relations Area Files, inc. <u>Outline of Cultural Materials</u>, by George Murdock and others. Fourth revised edition. New Hampshire, 1965. 164 p.

[2]E. Arsenio Manuel. <u>Philippine Folklore Bibliography; A Preliminary</u> <u>Survey</u>. Quezon City, Philippine Folklore Society. 1965. 125 p. (Paper Number 1)
Doris V. Welsh. <u>Checklist of Philippine Linguistics in the Newberry</u> <u>Library</u>. Chicago, 1950. 176 p.
Nobleza Asuncion [Landé]. <u>Bibliography of Philippine Linguistics</u>. 1964? Mimeographed.

ARRANGEMENT: The bibliography is divided into four parts. In Part I the entries are arranged by subjects, the headings adapted largely from those in the Outline of Cultural Materials (OCM). Very often several OCM categories have been combined into one heading. The OCM category numbers are included, where appropriate in the Guide to Subject Headings on p. xxii.

Parts II (Luzon), III (The Bisayas and Palawan), and IV (Mindanao and Sulu) are each divided into two sections, the first arranged by subject and the second by cultural-linguistic group. The geographical arrangement generally follows the official ten-region division used during and since the Philippine census of 1960.

LIMITATIONS: Since some major compilations on the history and ethnology of the Philippines are already well-indexed, references to them are not numerous in this bibliography. Notable among these sources are Blair and Robertson's The Philippine Islands, Beyer's Philippine Ethnographic series, and the 25 titles which have been indexed, paragraph by paragraph, by Helen R. Tubangui and Aurora N. Corvera.[3]

Although annotators suggested many additional titles for my preliminary edition, I am certain omissions will be apparent to specialists who use this bibliography. I would appreciate being informed of them so that they can be included in my next edition. I consider this bibliography to be a working research tool for scholars, students and librarians. As a result of dialogue with such users I hope to produce in the near future an edition which will respond to their requirements and satisfy their needs.

GUIDE TO USE: To make the most effective use of this bibliography one should consult both the subject and the cultural-linguistic sections within the appropriate Parts. For example, if one needs information on the family structure of the Ifugao, he should look in the Table of Contents under "Ifugao-Family and Kinship," and also under "Luzon, Northern - Family and Kinship." To be certain of obtaining all pertinent references, he should also consult Part I, under "Family and Kinship."

---

[3]Emma H. Blair and James A. Robertson. The Philippine Islands 1493-1898. Cleveland, Arthur H. Clark, 1903-1909. 55 volumes. Vols. 54 and 55 = Index.
    University of Chicago. Philippine Studies Program. Beyer Library: Typescripts on Philippine Ethnography, Folklore, Customary Law, and Archaeology. Compiled under the direction of E. D. Hester, by the Staff of the Asia Foundation-Beyer Project. [Chicago], 1962. 187p.
    E. Arsenio Manuel. "The Beyer Collection of Original Sources in Philippine Ethnography." ASLP [Association of Special Libraries of the Philippines] Bulletin. Vol. 4, nos. 3-4 (September-December 1958), pp. 46-66.
    Helen R. Tubangui. "Manila Area Study," Philippine Historical Review, Vol. 1, no. 1 (1965), pp. 334-364.
    Frank Lynch and Helen R. Tubangui. Basic Bibliography Project; Preliminary Subject Index. Quezon City, Ateneo de Manila University.
        Sources 1-7. 1963. 70p. (IPC Manila Area Study Series, no. 1)
        Sources 8-14. 1963. 97p. (IPC Manila Area Study Series, no. 2)
        Sources 15-20. 1963. 103p. (IPC Manila Area Study Series, no. 3)
        Sources 21-25. 1964. 102p. (IPC Manila Area Study Series, no. 4)

If a user is looking for an elusive subject for which he finds no entry in the Table of Contents, he should obtain the Outline of Cultural Materials and consult its index. For example, if he wants references on sorcery in the Philippines, by consulting the index to the Outline, he will be referred to OCM classification "754," which is a subsection of "75 - Sickness." Upon consulting "Sickness" in "Guide to Subject Headings" in this Bibliography he will be led to "Health and Sickness," the subject under which references on sorcery are indexed in this Table of Contents.

For a sample entry and for an explanation of the coding system, see pp. xxviii-xxix. In some instances an item annotated by several contributors has been assigned different time periods, since in one annotator's judgment a work emphasizes a given period while another considers that it deals with more than one and has so indicated in the coding.

When a citation has not been verified, either by personal examination or in standard bibliographical sources such as the Library of Congress printed catalogs, I have indicated the source of the reference.

If an article appeared in a journal of limited accessibility in the United States and if it has been reprinted, that information, when available, has been included. Articles, for example, which appeared in Philippine Magazine and were later reprinted in the Journal of East Asiatic Studies have been indicated.

For the convenience of the users, references which occur under more than one heading are cited in full instead of by item number.

When a user requires more comprehensive coverage than is afforded by this bibliography, the four bibliographies of bibliographies (item nos. 484-487) should be consulted. Depending on the topic or material needed, the following bibliographies should also be examined:

Edralin, Josefa S. and Vicenta C. Rimando
   Local Government in the Philippines; A Classified Annotated Bibliography. Manila, Joint Local Government Reform Commission, 1970. 236p.

Morco, Erlinda S.
   Philippine Business Literature, A Bibliography. Quezon City, Division of Business Research, College of Business Administration, University of the Philippines, 1971. 427p.

Nemenzo, Catalina A.
   The Flora and Fauna of the Philippines, 1851-1966: An Annotated Bibliography. Natural and Applied Science Bulletin (University of the Philippines), vol. 21, nos. 1 & 2, January-June 1969. 307p.

Philippines. University. Institute of Planning.
   An Annotated Bibliography of Philippine Planning. Padre Faura, Manila, 1968. 203p.
   _____. _____. Supplement I. Quezon City, 1970. 141p.

Philippines. University. Library.
   Filipiniana 1968. A Classified Catalog of Filipiniana Books and Pamphlets in the University of the Philippines Library as of January 1, 1968. Diliman, Rizal, 1969.
      Part I. General References. Social Sciences. pp. 1-674.
         II. Humanities. Science. Military and Naval Science. Indexes, pp. 674-1380.

Philippines. University. Library.
   U.P. Theses and Dissertations Index: 1956-1968. Diliman, Rizal, 1969. 397p. (Research Guide No. 6)

Philippines (Republic) National Science Development Board.
   Compilation of Graduate Theses Prepared in the Philippines, 1913-1960. Manila, [1964] 437p.

Tiamson, Alfredo T.
   Mindanao-Sulu Bibliography; Containing Published, Unpublished Manuscripts and Works-In-Progress. A Preliminary Survey and W.E. Retana's Bibliografia de Mindanao (1894). Davao City, Ateneo de Davao, 1970. 344p.

Ward, Jack H.
   A Bibliography of Philippine Linguistics and Minor Languages (With Annotations and Indices Based on Works in the Library of Cornell University). Ithaca, New York, Southeast Asia Program, Dept. of Asian Studies, Cornell University. 1971. 539p. (Data Paper: Number 83)

Zamora, Mario D. and Jose Y. Arcellana, Editors.
   A Bibliography of Philippine Anthropology. Verge, A Journal of Thought (University of the Philippines At Baguio), vol. 3, no. 2 (June 1971), Supplementary Series One. 164p.
   This publication was listed in the Cormosea Newsletter (December 1971) which I received on March 16, 1972.

ACKNOWLEDGMENTS: It gives me great pleasure to acknowledge the support and help I received in completing this bibliography. I am grateful to the U.S. Educational Foundation for a Fulbright research grant which enabled me to go to the Philippines to complete the preliminary edition; to the Asia Foundation for a grant which provided a staff of two and funds for printing and distributing the preliminary edition; and also to the University of Hawaii Research Council for a grant to complete the present publication.

For individual assistance I am indebted to Father Robert J. Suchan, Director of Libraries, Ateneo de Manila, who provided me with an office and extended countless courtesies; and to Miss Marina G. Dayrit, University Librarian, University of the Philippines, for assisting me in many ways at the U.P. Library. I am very grateful to the 62 annotators who took time from their busy schedules to participate in this project for, without their active support and encouragement, this bibliography would not have been completed. Their names and their institutional affiliations at the time of the submission of their annotations are listed on p.xxx . Harold Conklin devoted many hours to the bibliogra-

phy giving special attention to the subject and cultural-linguistic headings but
any shortcomings or errors in either are mine, since I was able to incorporate
only a few of his valuable suggestions. I hope to include other recommendations
of his in my next edition. Lawrence Reid also helped me to classify some of the
references in their proper cultural-linguistic groups. Thomas McHale suggested
many titles for inclusion. Stanley West and Virginia Crozier provided support
and encouragement during the project. Diana Chang went over most of the
references and made many helpful suggestions. Ethel Ito assisted me from the
very beginning to the completion of this project, for which I am greatly indebted.
Fred Riggs and Richard Barber made it possible for the Social Science Research
Institute, University of Hawaii, to type the bibliography. Thanks are due to
Freda Hellinger for the supervision of the typing and especially to Mary Chong,
who typed meticulously from a most difficult manuscript. Lastly, I am most
grateful to Father Frank Lynch to whom this work is dedicated and who provided
most of the initial impetus for this project and furthered its development by
his continued support, guidance and suggestions.

Honolulu   Shiro Saito
April 1972

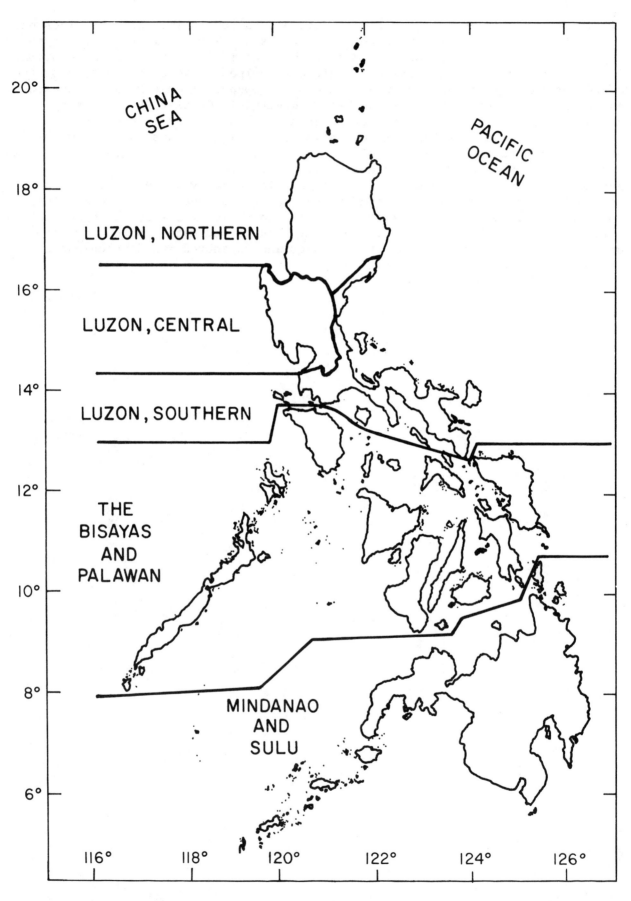

CHINA
SEA

PACIFIC
OCEAN

LUZON, NORTHERN

LUZON, CENTRAL

LUZON, SOUTHERN

THE
BISAYAS
AND
PALAWAN

MINDANAO
AND
SULU

GEOGRAPHICAL ARRANGEMENT

Luzon (Part II)

Northern: Abra, Batanes, Cagayan, Ilocos Norte, Ilocos Sur, Isabela, La Union, Mountain Province and Nueva Vizcaya.

Central: Bataan, Bulacan, Nueva Ecija, Pampanga, Pangasinan, Rizal, Tarlac, Zambales and Metropolitan Manila (Manila, Quezon, Pasay, Caloocan, Makati, Mandaluyong, Navotas and San Juan).

Southern: Albay, Batangas, Camarines Norte, Camarines Sur, Cantanduanes, Cavite, Laguna, Marinduque, Quezon and Sorsogon.

The Bisayas and Palawan (Part III)

Alkan, Antique, Bohol, Capiz, Cebu, Iloilo, Leyte, Masbate, Negros Occidental, Negros Oriental, Occidental Mindoro, Oriental Mindoro, Palawan, Romblon, Samar and Southern Leyte.

Mindanao and Sulu (Part IV)

Agusan, Bukidnon, Cotabato, Davao, Lanao del Norte, Lanao del Sur, Misamis Occidental, Misamis Oriental, Surigao del Norte, Surigao del Sur, Sulu, Zamboanga del Norte and Zamboanga del Sur.

GUIDE TO SUBJECT HEADINGS
Adapted from the Outline of Cultural Materials
(OCM Category Number in Parenthesis)

General

Adolescence, Adulthood and Old Age (88)

Adornment *see* Clothing, Adornment and Materials

Agriculture and Animal Husbandry (24, 23) [Part I only]

Agriculture and Food (24, 22, 23,25, 26) [Parts II - IV]

Anthropology [Part I only]

Archaeology (172)

Armed Forces and Warfare (70, 71, 72)
     Including weapons

Behavior Process and Personality (15)
     Including hiya, value system

Bibliography of Bibliographies

Buildings, Equipment and Tools (33, 34, 35, 40, 41)

Childhood *see* Infancy and Childhood

Clothing, Adornment and Materials (29, 30, 28)

Communications [Part I only]

Community and Community Development (62) [Parts I - II]

Community Development and Territorial Organization (62, 63) [Parts II - IV]

Culture Change *see* History and Culture Change

Death *see* Religion

Demography (16) [Part I only]
     see also Geography and Demography [Parts II - IV]

Drink, Drugs and Indulgence (27)

Economics (44, 45, 47)
     Economic Development [Part I only]

Education (87)
     Education, Higher [Part I only]

Equipment and Tools *see* Buildings, Equipment and Tools

Ethnic Influences
    Americans   Japanese
    Chinese   Spanish
    English   Other
    Indians

Exact Knowledge (81, 80, 82) [Part I only]

Family and Kinship (59, 60, 61)

Fine Arts (53)

Folklore and Mythology [Parts I - II]
    see also Religious Beliefs and Practices [Parts II - IV]

Food (22, 25, 26) [Part I only]
    see also Agriculture and Food [Parts II - IV]

Geography and Demography (13, 16, 36) [Parts II - IV]
    Including city and regional planning, cities, ethnobotany, fauna and flora,
        housing, land utilization, land tenure (*see also* Property and Exchange),
        land value, urbanization and place names

Health and Sickness (74, 75)

Heavy and Light Industries (31, 32, 37, 38, 39) [Part I only]
    see also Industries [Parts II - IV]

History and Culture Change (17)

Industries (31, 32, 37, 38, 39) [Parts II - IV]
    see also Heavy and Light Industries

Infancy and Childhood (85, 86)

Interpersonal Relations (57)
    Including cultural conflicts, ethics, intellectuals, manners, and
        utang na loob

Kinship *see* Family and Kinship

Labor (46)

Land Tenure and Land Reform [Part I only]
    see also Geography and Demography [Parts II - IV]
    see also Property and Exchange [Parts II - IV]

Language and Literature (19, 20)

Law and Justice (67, 68, 69) [Part I only]

Local Government and Territorial Organization *see* Political Science

Total Culture (18)
     Including cultural heritage, characteristics of culture, ethnology,
          national characteristics, social organization and social structure

Transportation (48, 49, 50)

Warfare *see* Armed Forces and Warfare

Women

JOURNAL ABBREVIATIONS

AA	American Anthropologist
AP	Asian Perspectives
AQ	Anthropological Quarterly
AS	Asian Studies (University of the Philippines)
AUFSR	American Universities Field Staff Report
B & R or Blair & Robertson	Blair, Emma H. and James A. Robertson. The Philippine Islands 1493-1898. Cleveland, Arthur H. Clark, 1903-1909. 55 volumes.
CC	Church and Community
CEU. GFS	Centro Escolar University. Graduate and Faculty Studies
CS	Contemporary Studies
DR	Diliman Review
ERJ	Economic Research Journal
EQ	Educational Quarterly (University of the Philippines)
FEUFJ	Far Eastern University Faculty Journal (Manila)
FTY	Fookien Times Yearbook
GEJ	General Education Journal (University of the Philippines)
HB	Historical Bulletin (Philippine Historical Association)
HO	Human Organization
JAS	Journal of Asian Studies
JEAS	Journal of East Asiatic Studies (University of Manila)
JH	Journal of History (Philippine National Historical Society)
JSEAH	Journal of Southeast Asian History
NASB	Natural and Applied Science Bulletin (University of the Philippines. College of Arts & Sciences)
PA	Philippine Agriculturist
Pac. Aff.	Pacific Affairs
PCARFB	Philippine Christian Advance and Rural Fellowship Bulletin

PEB	Philippine Economy Bulletin
PEJ	Philippine Economic Journal
PGJ	Philippine Geographical Journal
Phil. Stat.	Philippine Statistician
PJE	Philippine Journal of Education
PJHE	Philippine Journal of Home Economics
PJN	Philippine Journal of Nursing
PJP	Philippine Journal of Psychology
PJPA	Philippine Journal of Public Administration
PJPH	Philippine Journal of Public Health
PJS	Philippine Journal of Science
PL	Philippine Labor
PM	Philippine Magazine
PMAJ	Philippine Medical Association. Journal
PQ	Philippine Quarterly
PRBE	Philippine Review of Business and Economics
PS	Philippine Studies
PSR	Philippine Sociological Review
PSSHR	Philippine Social Sciences and Humanities Review
SGMB	Sociedad Geográfica de Madrid. Boletín
SJ	Silliman Journal
SLQ	Saint Louis Quarterly
SMJ	Sarawak Museum Journal
SR	Science Review
Stat. Rept.	Statistical Reporter (Philippines [Republic] Office of Statistical Coordination and Standards)
SW	Social Work (Philippine Association of Social Workers)
SWJA	Southwestern Journal of Anthropology
ZE	Zeitschrift für Ethnologie

ABBREVIATIONS

Jan.	January	Ms	manuscript
Feb.	February	no.	number
Mar.	March	n.s.	new series
Apr.	April	o.s.	old series
Aug.	August	p	paging
Sept.	September	U.P.	University of the
Oct.	October		Philippines
Nov.	November	univ.	university
Dec.	December		

SAMPLE ENTRY

Lieban, Richard W. Cebuano sorcery; malign magic in the Philippines. Berkeley, Univ. of California Press, 1967. 163 p.

Sibley:[1] Lieban has done extensive and excellent work on sorcery and folk medical practice in Central Philippine Islands.[2]

E[3] 5[4] 6[5]

1. Annotator's name   4. Annotator's rating
2. Annotation   5. Time period covered by item
3. Author's specialization

CODING SYSTEM

Author's Specialization:*

A - Archaeologist, Antiquarian
B - Folklorist
C - Technical Personnel
(engineers, agricultural experts,
Point Four advisors, etc.)
D - Physician, Physical
Anthropologist
E - Ethnologist, Social
Anthropologist
F - Foreign Resident
G - Government Official
(administrator, soldier,
foreign diplomat)
H - Historian
I - Indigene
J - Journalist
K - Geographer
L - Linguist
M - Missionary, Clergyman
N - Natural or Physical Scientist
O - Lawyer, Judicial Personnel
P - Psychologist, Psychiatrist
Q - Humanist (philosopher, critic,
editor, writer, etc.)
R - Artisan (artist, musician,
architect, dancer)
S - Social Scientist (other than
those designated)
T - Traveler (tourist, explorer)
V - Political Scientist, Propagandist
W - Organizational Documents and
Reports (constitutions, law
codes, government or UN reports
and documents, censuses)
X - Economist, Businessman
Y - Educator (teacher, school
administrator)
Z - Sociologist

Annotator's Rating:*

1 - Poor
2 - Fair
3 - Good, useful sources but
not uniformly excellent
4 - Excellent secondary data
(e.g., compilations and/or
interpretations of original
data and primary documents)
5 - Excellent primary data
(e.g., traveler's accounts,
ethnological studies, etc.,
as well as primary docu-
ments such as legal codes,
legal documents, autobio-
graphies, etc.)

Time period covered by item:

1 - Pre-Spanish (before 1521)
2 - Spanish I (1521-1749)
3 - Spanish II (1750-1898)
4 - American (1898-1941)
5 - World War II (1941-1945)
6 - Post World War II (1945-)
7 - General (more than one of
the periods 1-6)

*Outline of Cultural Materials. 4th rev. ed.

LIST OF ANNOTATORS*

Almanzor, Angelina	Philippine Women's University
Amyot, Jacques	Chulalongkorn University
Anderson, James N.	University of California, Berkeley
Arce, Wilfredo	Ateneo de Manila
Arens, Richard	Fu Jen, Taipei
Bello, Moises	University of the Philippines
Bulatao, Jaime	Ateneo de Manila
Coller, Richard W.	Kauai Community College
Doherty, John F.	Ateneo de Manila
Eggan, Fred	University of Chicago
Felix, Alfonso	Manila, Philippines
Frake, Charles	Stanford University
Geoghegan, William	University of California, Berkeley
Goodman, Grant	University of Kansas
Gowing, Peter	Silliman University
Grossholtz, Jean	Mount Holyoke College
Guthrie, George	Pennsylvania State University
Hart, Donn V.	Syracuse University
Hunt, Chester L.	Western Michigan University
Intengan, Carmen	National Institute of Science & Technology, Philippines
Jocano, F. Landa	University of the Philippines
Legarda, Benito	Central Bank of the Philippines
Liao, Shubert S. C.	University of the East
Llamzon, Teodoro	Ateneo de Manila
Luna, Telesforo	University of the Philippines
McMillan, Robert	Falls Church, Va.
Maceda, Marcelino	University of San Carlos
Madigan, Francis	Xavier University
Maher, Robert	Western Michigan University
Manalang, Priscilla	University of Pittsburgh
Moore, Grace Wood	Human Relations Area Files
Nimmo, Harry	California State College at Los Angeles
Nurge, Ethel	University of Kansas
Onorato, Michael	California State College at Fullerton
Peterson, Warren	University of Hawaii
Pfeiffer, William	University of Hawaii
Phelen, John	Univeristy of Wisconsin
Polson, Robert	Cornell University
Rixhon, Gerald	Notre Dame of Jolo College
Sals, Rev. Florent	St. Louis College
Sta. Iglesia, Jesus	University of the Philippines
Scheans, Daniel	Portland State College
Schlegel, Stuart	University of California, Santa Clara
Sibley, Willis	Washington State University
Solheim, Wilhelm G.	University of Hawaii
Spencer, Joseph	University of California, Los Angeles
Stauffer, Robert	University of Hawaii
Stone, Richard	California State College at Long Beach
Thomas, William	California State College at Hayward
Tiglao, Teodora	University of the Philippines
Trimillos, Ricardo	University of Hawaii

Tweddell, Colin   Western Washington State College
Valdepeñas, Vicente   Ateneo de Manila
Villanueva, Buenaventura   United Nations
Wallace, Ben   University of California, Santa Barbara
Ward, Jack   University of Hawaii
Warren, Charles   University of Illinois at Chicago Circle
Weightman, George   Hunter College
Wernstedt, Frederick   Pennsylvania State University
Wickberg, Edgar   University of British Columbia
Wulff, Inger   Nationalmuseet, Copenhagen
Yengoyan, Aram   University of Michigan

*Affiliations shown in this list are those held at the time annotations were submitted.

PART I
GENERAL

GENERAL WORKS

1. ALGUÉ, JOSÉ, ed. El archipiélago Filipino. Washington, Impr. del gobierno, 1900. 2v.

2. BARRANTES Y MORENO, VICENTE. Apuntes interesantes sobre las Islas Filipinas, que pueden ser utiles para hacer las reformas convenientes y productivas el país y para la nación. Escritos por un español de larga experiencia en el país y amante del progreso. Madrid, Impr. de el Pueblo, 1869. 281p.

3. BELLO, WALDEN F. and ALFONSO DE GUZMAN II., eds. Modernization: its impact in the Philippines III. Quezon City, Ateneo de Manila Univ. Press, 1968. 153p. (Institute of Philippine Culture. Papers, no. 6)

4. _____ and MARIA CLARA ROLDAN, eds. Modernization: its impact in the Philippines. Quezon City, Ateneo de Manila Univ. Press, 1967. 133p. (Institute of Philippine Culture. Papers, no. 4)

5. BERREMAN, GERALD D. The Philippines: a survey of current social, economic, and political conditions. Ithaca, N.Y., Southeast Asia Program, Dept. of Far Eastern Studies, Cornell Univ., 1956. 52p. (Data papers, no. 19)
    Polson: A good introductory statement that focuses on the inter-relations of problems.
               E   4   6

6. BLAIR, EMMA H. and JAMES A. ROBERTSON. The Philippine islands, 1493-1898. Cleveland, Ohio. Arthur H. Clark Co., 1903-1909. 55v.
    Felix: Insufficient from 1750-1898.
               H   5   2/3
    LeRoy: "Invaluable and monumental collection of source material for the history of the Philippines before and during the Spanish regime." American Historical Review, Oct. 1903, p.149.
    Onorato: G/H/Y 5   7

7. BOWRING, JOHN. A visit to the Philippine Islands. London, Smith, Elder and Co., 1859. 434p.
    Felix: The personal observations are excellent.
               G   5   3
    Onorato: G   3   3

8. BUSS, CLAUDE A. The Philippines. (In: Mills, Lennox A., ed. The new world of Southeast Asia. Minneapolis, University of Minnesota Press, 1949. p.18-78)
    Onorato: G/H/Y 3   7

I. GENERAL. GENERAL WORKS

9. BUZETA, MANUEL and FELIPE BRAVO. Diccionario geográfico, estadístico, histórico, de las Islas Filipinas. Madrid [Impr. de J.C. de la Pena] 1850-51. 2v

10. CARPENTER, FRANK GEORGE. ... Through the Philippines and Hawaii. Garden City, N.Y., Doubleday Page & Company, 1925. 314p.
    Onorato: T/V   3   7

11. CARROLL, JOHN J. Changing patterns of social structure in the Philippines, 1896-1963. Quezon City, Ateneo de Manila Univ. Press, 1968. 236p.

12. COLIN, FRANCISCO. Labor evangélica, ministerios apostolicos de los obreros de la Compania de Jesus, fundacion, y progressos de su provincia en las islas Filipinas. Madrid, 1663. 2nd ed. by Pablo Pastells. Barcelona, Impr. y litografia de Henrich y compania, 1900-1902. 3v.

13. DOHERTY, DAVID H. Paper on the conditions in the Philippines. Feb. 1904. (58th Congress. 2d Session. Senate Document No. 170. 20p.)

14. EGGAN, FRED, EVETT D. HESTER, and NORTON S. GINSBURG, supervisors. Area handbook on the Philippines. Preliminary ed. Chicago, Univ. of Chicago for the Human Relations Area Files, 1956. 4v. (HRAF Subcontractor's monograph, 16, Chicago-5)
    Onorato: E/Y   5   7
    Warren: E   5   7

15. Filipino appeal for freedom: the Philippine Parliamentary Mission's statement of actual conditions in the Philippine Islands and a summary of Philippine problems. Washington, 1923. 90p. (67th Congress, 4th Session House. House Document, no. 511)

16. FOREMAN, JOHN. The Philippine Islands; a political, geographical, ethnographical, social and commercial history of the Philippine Archipelago, embracing the whole period of Spanish rule, with an account of the succeeding American insular government... Third ed., rev. and enl. ... New York, Charles Scribner's Sons, 1906. 668p.

17. GEMELLI CARERI, GIOVANNI FRANCESCO. Giro del mondo. In Napoli, Nella stamperia di G. Roselli, 1699-1700. 6v.
_____. Another edition, 1719. in 9v. v.5 covers the Philippines. [Churchill, Awnsham] comp. A collection of voyages and travels, some now first printed from original manuscripts, others now first published in English....3d ed....London, Printed by assignment from Mess. Churchill, for H. Lintot...1744-1747. 6v. v.4 covers the Philippines.

18. _____. A voyage to the Philippines; with an introduction and notes by Mauro Garcia, and an appendix of the chapters on the Philippines in The Travels of Fray Sebastian Manrique. Manila, Filipiniana Book Guild, 1963. 210p. (Filipiniana Book Guild publications, 2)
    Felix: Excellent reports based on personal observation.
          T   5   2

19. GREENE, F. V. Memoranda concerning the situation in the Philippines on August 30, 1898. Washington, 1899. (55th Congress, 3rd Session. Senate. Senate Document No. 62, Part 2, p.404-429)

20. GUTHRIE, GEORGE, ed. Six perspectives on the Philippines. Manila, Bookmark, 1968. 279p.

21. _____, FRANK LYNCH and WALDEN F. BELLO. Modernization: its impact in the Philippines II. Quezon City, Ateneo de Manila University Press, 1967. 172p. (Institute of Philippine Culture. Papers, no.5)

22. HART, DONN V. Filipiniana in the Overland Monthly Magazine (1868-1935) JEAS 6, no. 1 (Jan. 1957), 95-100.

23. HAYDEN, J. RALSTON. The Philippines, a study in national development. New York, Macmillan Co., 1942. 984p.
      Grossholtz: The basic study of political development during the
                       American period and government and politics of the
                       Commonwealth.
                       V/G   4   4
      Onorato: V/Y   4   7
      Polson: The best descriptive and analytical work on the American
                       period.
                       V   5   4

24. HOWARD, JOSEPH T., FELIX REGALADO and IRENE ORTIGAS. Society and culture in rural Philippines. Iloilo City, Central Philippine University, 1967 [c1965] 383p.

25. JAGOR, FEDOR. Die Philippinen und ihre Bewohner. ZE 2 (1870), 148-151.

26. _____. Reisen in den Philippinen. Berlin, Weidmann, 1873. 381p.
      Felix: T   5   3

27. _____. Travels in the Philippines... (In: Craig, Austin: The former Philippines thru foreign eyes. New York, D. Appleton and Company, 1917. p.1-356)

28. JENKS, MAUD HUNTLEY. Death stalks the Philippine wilds; letters of Maud Huntley Jenks. Minneapolis, Lund Press, 1951. 206p.
      Coller: Informal, insightful descriptions written by the great an-
                       thropologist's wife during her stay in the field--delightful
                       and informative.
                       T   5   4

29. JORDANA Y MORERA, RAMON. Bosquejo geográfico é histórico-natural del archipiélago Filipino. Madrid, Impr. de Moreno y Rojas, 1885. 461p.
      Luna: Descriptive analytical study.
                       N   4   7

30. KOLB, ALBERT. Die Kulturschichtung auf den Philippinen. Geographische Zeitschrift 48, nos. 1/2 (1942), 1-20.

31. LA GIRONIÈRE, PAUL PROUST DE. Aventures d'un gentilhomme breton aux îles Philippines, ... Paris, Au Comptoir des Imprimeurs-Unis, Lacrois-Comon, 1855. 458p.
      Also published under title: Vingt années aux Philippines. Paris, 1853.
      Felix: Fact mixed with egotism.
                       F   3   3

32. _____. Twenty years in the Philippines. New York, Harper and Brothers,
     1854. 371p.
          Onorato: F/T   3   3

33. LE GENTIL DE LA GALAISIÈRE, GUILLAUME J. H. Voyage dans les mers de l'Inde
     ... Paris, De l'imprimerie royale, 1779-1781. 2v.
          Felix: Excellent.
                         F   5   3

34. _____. A voyage to the Indian seas. Translated from the French by l'Inde
     Frederick C. Fischer ... Introduction by William A. Burke Miailhe. Manila,
     Filipiniana Book Guild, 1964. 235p. (Filipiniana Book Guild publications,
     no. 5)
          Felix: Excellent.
                         F   5   3

35. LEROY, JAMES ALFRED. The Americans in the Philippines; a history of the
     conquest and first years of occupation, with an introductory account of the
     Spanish rule. Boston and New York, Houghton Mifflin Company, 1914. 2v.
          Onorato: G   3   4

36. _____. Philippine life in town and country. New York and London, G. P.
     Putnam's Sons, 1906 [c1905]   311p.
          Onorato: G   3   4

37. Youth and social change: a symposium for students-background and basis.
     Exchange (U.S. Educational Foundation in the Philippines) no. 35 (second
     quarter, 1965), 2-7.
          Bulatao: Essays by insightful students at a conference.
                         W   5   6

38. LODGE, HENRY CABOT. (From the Committee on the Philippines.) The Philip-
     pine Islands, a brief compilation of the latest information and statistics
     obtainable on the numbers, areas, population, races and tribes, mineral
     resources ... Feb. 1900. (56th Congress 1st Session. Senate. Document
     No. 171)

39. LYNCH, FRANK and MARY R. HOLLNSTEINER, eds. Understanding the Philip-
     pines: a study of cultural themes. 7th revision. Quezon City, Institute
     of Philippine Culture, Ateneo de Manila, 1967. Various paging.
     ("This course is a production of the multidisciplinary staff and associates
     of the Institute of Philippine Culture.")

40. MACMICKING, ROBERT. Recollections of Manila and the Philippines, during
     1848, 1849, and 1850. London, R. Bentley, 1851. 320p. Reprinted in 1967
     by Filipiniana Book Guild, Manila. (Filipiniana Book Guild, Publications,
     no. 11)
          Felix: An excellent report on Manila since 1850.
                         F/X   5   3

41. MADRID. EXPOSICIÓN GENERAL DE LAS ISLAS FILIPINAS, 1887. Catálogo de la
     Exposición general de las islas Filipinas, celebrada en Madrid...el 30 de
     Junio de 1887. Madrid, Estab. Tip. de Ricardo Fé, 1887. 732p.

42. MARTÍNEZ DE ZÚÑIGA, JOAQUÍN. Estadismo de las islas Filipinas; ó mis

viajes por este país. Ed. by W. E. Retana. Madrid, Impr. de la viuda de M. Minuesa de los Ríos, 1893. 2v.
Suggested by Wickberg.

43. MAS Y SANS, SINIBALDO DE. Informe sobre el estado de las islas Filipinas en 1842. Madrid, 1843. 2v.
v.3. Informe secreto de Sinibaldo de Mas. Spanish original with an English translation by Carlos Botor. Rev. by Alfonso Felix, Jr. and an introduction, and notes by Juan Palazon. Manila, Reprinted by Historical Conservation Society, 1963. 215p. "The third volume of Sinabaldo de Mas' Informe sobre el estado de las islas Filipinas en 1842 was originally intended for restricted circulation among Spanish ministers and other highranking officials." From verso of title page.
Excerpts in Blair and Robertson.

44. METZGER, JOHN A. The Filipino; his customs and character. American Philosophical Society. Proceedings 44, no. 179 (Jan./Apr. 1905), 6-31.

45. MONTERO Y VIDAL, JOSÉ. El archipiélago Filipino y las islas Marianas, Carolinas y Palaos; su historia, geográfica y estadistica. Madrid, Impr. y fundación de Manuel Tello, 1886. 511p.

46. OCAMPO, GALO B. The National Museum as the center of the educational, scientific and cultural activities of the community. SR 7, no. 9 (Sept. 1966), 21-28.

47. OSIAS, CAMILO. The Filipino way of life: the pluralized philosophy. Boston; New York [etc.] Ginn and Company, 1940. 321p.

48. PARKER, LUTHER. The last of the Lakans. PM 27, no. 10 (Mar. 1931), 628-629.

49. PHILIPPINE ISLANDS. EXPOSITION BOARD. LOUISIANA PURCHASE EXPOSITION, ST. LOUIS, MO., 1904. Official handbook of the Philippines and catalogue of the Philippine exhibit. [Pt. 1, Compiled in the Bureau of Insular Affairs, War Dept., Washington, D.C. Revised and completed with the aid of chiefs of bureaus and experts of the Philippine government] Manila, Bureau of Printing, 1903. 449p.

50. _____. INDEPENDENCE COMMISSION. The social integration of the Philippines, by various authors. Manila, Bureau of Printing, 1924. 91p. incl. tables. (Philippine Information pamphlets v. 1, no. 1)

51. PIGAFETTA, ANTONIO. Magellan's voyage around the world. The original text of the Ambrosian ms., with English translation, notes, bibliography and index by James Alexander Robertson. Cleveland, Arthur H. Clark, 1906. 2v. Italian and English on opposite pages. "Of this work only 350 copies were published." "Bibliography of Pigafetta manuscripts and printed books." v.2, p. [241]-313. Also in Blair and Robertson v.33:25-366. v.34:11-180.

52. PLAUCHUT, EDMOND. L'archipel des Philippines. Revue des Deux Mondes Part I. 3. période. 20 (Mar. 15, 1877), 447-464. Part II. 3. période. 20 (Apr. 15, 1877), 896-913.
   Felix: Good reporting.
             F   5   3

I. GENERAL. ADOLESCENCE, ADULTHOOD AND OLD AGE

53. RAVENHOLT, ALBERT. A note on the Philippines; the land, the people, and the politics. AUFSR. Southeast Asia Series 10, no. 8 (Mar. 1962), 13p. (AR-2-'62)

54. U.S. BUREAU OF INSULAR AFFAIRS. A pronouncing gazetteer and geographical dictionary of the Philippine islands, United States of America, with maps, charts, and illustrations. Also the law of civil government in the Philippine islands passed by Congress and approved by the President July 1, 1902, with a complete index...Washington, Govt. print. off., 1902. 933p.

55. _____. CONGRESS. SENATE. Special report of Wm. H. Taft, Secretary of War, to the President on the Philippines. Jan. 27, 1908. 60th Congress, 1st Session, S. Document No. 200, Washington, 1908.
Cited in U.S. Surgeon General's Office. Library. Index catalogue. Authors and subjects. 3rd series.
   Onorato: W   4   4

56. WHITE, JOHN ROBERTS. Bullets and bolos; fifteen years in the Philippines. New York, London, Century Co., [1928] 348p.
   Onorato: G   3   4

57. WORCESTER, DEAN C. The Philippine islands and their people. New York, Macmillan, 1909, (c1898). 529p.
   Onorato: G/E   4   7

ADOLESCENCE, ADULTHOOD AND OLD AGE

58. BARTOLOME, C. C. The problem of aging among Filipinos. PSSHR 26, no. 2 (June 1961), 219-232.

59. BULATAO, JAIME. Social change: its effects on youth. CC 4, no. 3 (May/June 1964), 9-15.
   Bulatao: Urban, family life from a clinician's viewpoint.
                 P   4   6

60. HERRADURA, ELMA S. The ideals and values of Filipino adolescents. Berkeley, 1962. Thesis (Ph.D.) - Univ. of California.

61. MIAO, EMILY. A study of parental attitudes in child and adolescent development. 1965. 140p. Thesis (M.A.) - Ateneo de Manila Univ.
   Guthrie: P   5   6

62. STOODLEY, BARTLETT H. Normative attitudes of Filipino youth compared with German and American youth. American Sociological Review 22, no. 5 (Oct. 1957), 553-561.
   Bulatao: Basic cross-cultural data on attitudes.
                 E   5   6

63. ULGADO, ANTONIO VICTOR. The adolescent in the Westernized Filipino family. Hemisphere 11, no. 11 (Nov. 1967), 30-31.

AGRICULTURE

Agriculture and Animal Husbandry

64. ABIJAY, FRANCISCO. One way to prevent "kaingin" in public forest.
     Forestry Leaves 11, no. 4 (1959), 55-56.
          Luna: Descriptive prescriptive article.
                          C   3   6
          Spencer: Very brief note, though primary.
                          G   5   6

65. ALLISON, WILLIAM W. A compound system of swidden ("Kaiñgin") agriculture.
     PGJ 7, no. 3 (July/Sept. 1963), 159-172.
          Sta. Iglesia: Highly useful descriptive research.
                          Y   5   6

66. _____. Interdisciplinary research: the Kaingin project. U.P. Research
     Digest 3, no. 1 (Jan. 1964), 2-5.
          Luna: Descriptive analytical study.
                          E   5   6

67. ALUNAN, JULIO A. An economic analysis of beef cattle production in the
     Philippines, 1966. 1968. 157p. Thesis (M.S.) - U.P. College of Agricul-
     ture.
     Suggested by Sta. Iglesia.
          Sta. Iglesia: Highly useful descriptive and analytical research.
                          Y   5   6

68. ANTONIO, DOROTEO U. Some suggested measures to solve kaingin menace.
     Forestry Leaves 16, nos. 2/3 (1965), 23-25, 46.
          Luna: Descriptive prescriptive article.
                          C   3   6

69. AZIZ, UNGKU. The interdependent development of agriculture and other
     industries. PJPA 3, no. 3 (July 1959), 303-315.
          Luna: Statistical analytical study with general application.
                          X   4   6

70. BARTLETT, HARLEY HARRIS. Fire in relation to primitive agriculture and
     grazing in the tropics: annotated bibliography. Ann Arbor, Univ. of
     Michigan Botanical Gardens, 1955-61. 3v.
     Suggested by McHale.

71. BERNAL-TORRES, E. and P. R. SANDOVAL. Landlord participation in the farm
     business. PA 51, no. 1 (June 1967), 65-76.

72. BRADFIELD, RICHARD. Toward more and better food for the Filipino people and
     more income for her farmers. New York, Agricultural Development Council,
     1966. 7p. (A/D/C/ Paper, Dec. 1966)
          Spencer: Chiefly a statement of problems to be faced.
                          C   4   6

73. BRENTON, THADDEUS REAMY. Farming to music in the Philippines. Asia
     (New York) 34, no. 4 (Apr. 1934), 244-246.
          Trimillos: Only mention of this kind of music.
                          Y   5   4

74. BROWN, WILLIAM HENRY. Vegetation of Philippine mountains, the relation be-
    tween the environment and physical types at different altitudes. Manila,
    Bureau of Printing, 1919. 434p. (Philippine Islands. Department of Agri-
    culture and Natural Resources. Bureau of Science· Manila. Publication
    no. 13)
        Luna: Descriptive pictorial analytical study.
                         N   5   4
        Spencer: Basic field study.
                         N   5   4

75. CASTRO, AGUSTIN T. The retailing of farm products through roadside markets.
    PA 36, no. 4 (Sept. 1952), 195-209.
        Luna: Descriptive analytical study.
                         C   3   6
        Sta. Iglesia: Highly useful descriptive research.
                         G   5   6

76. CATER, SONYA DIANE. The Philippine Federation of Free Farmers, a case study
    in mass agrarian organizations. Ithaca, N.Y., Southeast Asia Program, Dept.
    of Far Eastern Studies, Cornell Univ., 1959. 147p. (Data paper no. 35)
        Grossholtz: Based on documents, interviews and observation.
                         V   4   6
        Polson: An excellent study of the national FFF.
                         V   4   6
        Spencer: Good study in political science, revision of M.A. thesis.
                         V   4   6
        Stauffer: A balanced analysis of problems facing those attempting
                         to organize peasants. Data drawn from early years of FFF.
                         V   4   6

77. CENABRE, AGAPITO L. Forest policy on Kaingin in the Philippines. Forestry
    Leaves 8, nos. 2/3 (Nov. 1955), 17-20.
        Luna: Descriptive informative article.
                         C   4   6

78. COPELAND, EDWIN B. Spanish agricultural work in the Philippines. Philippine
    Agricultural Review 1, no. 8 (Aug. 1908), 307-318.
    Suggested by McHale.

79. CUTSHALL, ALDEN. Regionalism in Philippine agriculture. Journal of Geog-
    raphy 61, no. 7 (Oct. 1962), 290-296.
        Luna: Descriptive analytical study.
                         K   4   6
        Spencer: Accent on regional crop variations.
                         K   4   6
        Warren: K   5   6

80. DALISAY, AMANDO M. Development of economic policy in Philippine agriculture.
    Manila, Phoenix Publishing House, 1959. 251p.
        Luna: Historical descriptive analytical study.
                         X   4   6
        Sta. Iglesia: Valuable description and analysis.
                         Y(G) 5   6

81. _____. Price policy and the problems of agricultural marketing. PA 45,
    no. 8 (Jan. 1962), 421-454.

Luna: Descriptive statistical analytical study.
X   4   6
Sta. Iglesia: Useful observations.
Y/G   3   6

82. DAVID, ISIDORO P. Development of a statistical model for agricultural surveys in the Philippines. 1966. 109p. Thesis (M.S.) - U.P. College of Agriculture.
Luna: Statistical prescriptive analytical study.
C   4   6

83. DAWSON, OWEN L. Philippine agriculture, a problem of adjustment. Foreign Agriculture 4, no. 7 (July 1940), 383-456.
Spencer: Good summary report.
G   4   4

84. DEPOSITARIO, WILLIE G. Why kaingineros insist on destroying our forest reserves. U.P. Research Digest 4, no. 2 (Apr. 1965), 31-33.
Luna: Descriptive informative article.
C   3   6

85. DIA, MANUEL A. Filipino farmers' image of government: a neglected area in developmental change. PJPA 9, no. 2 (Apr. 1965), 153-166.
Luna: Descriptive analytical study.
S   4   6

86. Educational leadership in the improvement of agriculture. EQ 3, no. 3 (Nov. 1955), 78-96.
Luna: Describes patterns and characteristics of farming with recommendations for improvement.
W   4   6

87. EMERSON, J. P. Agriculture progress for the Philippines. JEAS 1, no. 3 (Apr. 1952), 11-14.
Luna: Descriptive informative essay.
J   3   6

88. ESTANISLAO, J. A note on the ratio between value added and gross value from agricultural crops. PRBE 2, no. 1 (May 1965), 34-41.

89. FELICIANO, GLORIA D. The farm and home development project: an evaluation. 1968. Quezon City, Community Development Research Council, U.P. 364p. (Study series no. 30)

90. _____. The human variable in farm practice adoption: Philippine setting. U.P. College of Agriculture. Department of Agriculture Information and Communication, Los Baños, 1964. Mimeographed.
Cited in Mario Zamora, ed. Studies in Philippine anthropology. 1967.
Luna: Descriptive statistical analytical study.
Z   4   6
Sta. Iglesia: Highly useful descriptive and analytical research.
Y   5   6

91. FONOLLERA, RAYMUNDO E. Labor and land resources in Philippine agriculture; trends and projections. 1966. 395p. Thesis (M.S.) - U.P.

I.   GENERAL. AGRICULTURE. Agriculture and Animal Husbandry

        Luna: Descriptive statistical analytical study with maps and
                           graphs. Emphasis is on current conditions.
                           X   4   7
      Sta. Iglesia: Highly useful descriptive and analytical research.
                           Y   5   6

92. FUJIMOTO, ISAO. Some considerations on a cultural majority: the Filipino
     farmer and agricultural development. (In: Zamora, Mario D., ed. Studies
     in Philippine anthropology (In honor of H. Otley Beyer). Quezon City,
     Alemar-Phoenix, 1967. p. 343-365)

93. GONZALEZ, B. M. Iwahig penal colony: the largest farm in the islands. PA
     21, no. 3 (Aug. 1932), 147-150.
        Luna: Descriptive informative essay.
                         Y/C   3   4

94. GUTIERREZ, JOSE S. Agricultural productivity and population increase: The
     Philippine case. (In: Philippines. Univ. Population Institute. First Con-
     ference on Population, 1965. Quezon City, 1966. p. 469-492)
        Luna: Descriptive statistical study.
                         C   4   6
      Madigan: N   3   6

95. _____. Objective yield estimation studies and surveys in the Philippines;
     with emphasis on the proposed 1959-1960 Palay crop-cutting survey. Stat.
     Rept. 4, no. 1 (Jan. 1960), 1-9.
        Luna: Statistical projective study.
                         C   4   6

96. GUZMAN, LEOPOLDO P. DE. An economic analysis of the methods of farm finan-
     cing used on 5,144 farms. PA 41, no. 8 (Jan. 1958), 460-478.
        Luna: Descriptive statistical analytical study.
                         X   4   6
      Sta. Iglesia: Highly useful descriptive and analytical research.
                           Y   5   6

97. HAINSWORTH, REGINALD GEORGE and RAYMOND T. MOYER. Agricultural geography of
     the Philippine islands. U.S. Department of Agriculture, Office of Foreign
     Agricultural Relations. Washington, D. C., Dec. 1945. 72p.
        Luna: Descriptive analytical study with maps.
                      C and K 4   4
       Spencer: Cartographic summary of 1939 Census on agriculture.
                       G   4   4

98. HART, DONN V. The Philippine cooperative movement. Far Eastern Survey
     Part I. 24, no. 2 (Feb. 1955), 27-30. Part II. 24, no. 3 (Mar. 1955),
     45-48.

99. HERRIN, ALEJANDRO N. Changing receptivity to innovation as a by-product of
     employment on a progressive farm. PSR 15, nos. 1/2 (Jan./Apr. 1967), 29-34.

100. HOFILEÑA, CRISTOBAL P. Towards social justice for the farm laborer. PS 3,
     no. 2 (June 1955), 157-163.

Luna: Descriptive expository analytical article.
                 X   3   6

101. HUKE, ROBERT E. A challenge to Philippine agriculture. PGJ 4, nos. 2/3
      (Apr./Sept. 1956), 55-62.
          Luna: Descriptive expository article.
                           K   3   6

102. JACOBY, ERICH H. Agrarian unrest in Southeast Asia. New York, Columbia
      Univ. Press, 1949. 287p. Chapter 6: The Philippines, p. 167-222.
          Spencer: Secondary study--resumé of literature.
                       X   4   7

103. JAMIAS, JUAN F. The effects of belief system styles on the communication
      and adoption of farm practices. 1964. 100p. Thesis (Ph.D.) - Michigan
      State Univ.
          Sta. Iglesia: Highly useful descriptive and analytical research.
                         Y   5   6

104. JENKS, A. E. Terrace agriculture in the Philippines. (In: Kroeber, Alfred
      L. and Waterman, T. T., comp. Source book in anthropology. rev. ed. New
      York, Harcourt, Brace and Company, 1931. p. 222-227)
          Luna: Descriptive analytical study.
                           E   5   7

105. [KAUT, CHARLES and OTHERS]. Chapter 16. Agriculture. (In: Human Relations
      Area Files, Inc. Area handbook on the Philippines. Chicago, University of
      Chicago for the Human Relations Area Files, Inc., 1956. v.3, p.1300-1408)
          Luna: Historical descriptive analytical study.
                           E   4   7
          Warren: E   5   6

106. KEARL, C. DELMAR. Prices of Philippine farm products. PA 39, no. 4 (Sept.
      1955), 218-225.
          Luna: Descriptive graphical study.
                           X   4   6
          Sta. Iglesia: Highly useful descriptive and analytical research
                         Y   5   6

109. LIAO, S. H., S. C. HSIEH and P. R. SANDOVAL. Factors affecting adoption of
      improved farm practices on rice farms. PA 52, no. 5 (Oct. 1968), 256-267.

110. _____. Factors affecting productivity in selected areas of Philippine rice
      farms. PA 52, no. 5 (Oct. 1968), 241-255.

111. MCMILLAN, ROBERT T. The Filipino farmer. FTY (1955), 139, 141-142.
          Luna: Descriptive informative article.
                           Z   4   6

112. _____. Problems on agricultural statistics. Phil. Stat. 1, no. 2 (Dec.
      1952), 49-54.
          Luna: Descriptive analytical study.
                           Z   4   6

113. MAKANAS, ELPIDIO D. Application of sampling in the 1960 censuses of

population and agriculture in the Philippines. Phil. Stat. 8, no. 1 (Mar. 1959), 12-24.

Luna:	Statistical methodological study.		
	C	4	6
Madigan:	S	4	6

114. MANUEL, CANUTO G. Observations on the Philippine weaver, Munia Jagori Martens, II: Foods and feeding habits. PJS 53, no. 4 (Apr. 1934), 393-419. One text figure.

Intengan:	Economic relation of this specie of bird to agriculture is given. Stomach examination of adult birds was method most used.		
	C	5	4

115. MONTEMAYOR, JEREMIAS U. The Federation of Free Farmers. PS 3, no. 4 (Dec. 1955), 373-388.

Luna:	Descriptive analytical study.		
	O	4	7

116. _____. Social justice and the agrarian workers. Solidarity 1, no. 3 (July/Sept. 1966), 56-62.

Luna:	Descriptive expository article.		
	O	4	7

117. MYERS, WILLIAM I. Agriculture and industry in the Philippines. PA 41, no. 9 (Feb. 1958), 479-485.

Luna:	Descriptive analytical article.		
	C	3	7

118. NANO, JOSÉ F. Kaingin laws and penalties in the Philippines. Philippine Journal of Forestry 2, no. 2 (1939), 87-92.

119. NASOL, RAMON L. The supply response of pork production in the Philippines. PA 51, no. 1 (June 1967), 77-88.

120. ORACION, TIMOTEO S. Research on Kaingin and needs for research. Forestry Leaves 15, no. 3 (1964), 25-30.

Luna:	Review of the literature on Kaingin and suggestions for further research.		
	E	4	6

121. PELZER, KARL J. Pioneer settlement in the Asiatic tropics; studies in land utilization and agricultural colonization in Southeastern Asia. American Geographical Society. 1945 (Special Publication no. 29) Chapter 4. Landless Filipinos, p. 81-114.

Luna:	Descriptive statistical analytical study with maps and illustrations.		
	K	4	4
Spencer:	Excellent study of settlement activities in Mindanao.		
	K	5	7
Wernstedt:	Survey of resettlement programs in Philippines and Indonesia.		
	K	5	4/5

122. PHILIPPINES (COMMONWEALTH). DEPT. OF AGRICULTURE AND COMMERCE. Facts and

figures about the Philippines. Manila, Bureau of Printing, 1939. 102p.
   Spencer: Dated statistical summary.
                   G   4   4

123. _____ (REPUBLIC). OFFICE OF STATISTICAL COORDINATION AND STANDARDS. Methodology of agricultural sector accounts and related statistics in the Philippines. Manila, 1963. 11p. (Its OSCAS monograph no. 3).
      Luna: Analysis of agricultural statistics and methods of collec-
                  tion and projection.
                  W   4   6

124. QUINTANA, VICENTE U. An economic analysis of straight agricultural loans
granted by the branches of the Development Bank of the Philippines in Nueva
Ecija and Isabela, 1962. Columbus, Ohio. 1964. 155p. Thesis (Ph.D.) -
Ohio State Univ.
      Sta.Iglesia: Highly useful descriptive and analytical research.
                  Y   5   6

125. _____. A study on the demand for medium-and long-term agricultural credit
for small farmers in 20 rural banks. PA 49, no. 8 (Jan. 1966), 603-642.
      Luna: Descriptive statistical analytical study.
                  X   4   6
      Sta. Iglesia: Highly useful descriptive and analytical research.
                  Y   5   6

126. QUINTOS, ROLANDO N. The Marxist view of agrarian reform. Solidarity 2,
no. 8 (July/Aug. 1967), 17-29.

127. RAVENHOLT, ALBERT. A bamboo pump--whose technology for progress? AUFSR.
Southeast Asia Series. 6, no. 2 (Mar. 10, 1958), 10p. (AR-2-'58)

128. _____. "Hacienda Ideal"--a Philippine sugar cane plantation. AUFSR.
Southeast Asia Series. 3, no. 16 (June 28, 1955), 18p. (AR-8-'55)

129. _____. New trends in Philippine agriculture. AUFSR. Southeast Asia
Series. 3, no. 24 (Sept. 7, 1955), 11p. (AR-10-'55)

130. RUTTAN, VERNON W. Growth stage theories and agricultural development policy.
Stat. Rept. 9, no. 3 (July/Sept. 1965), 1-12.
      Luna: Discusses growth stage models vis-a-vis the formulation
                  of agricultural plans of development: analytical.
                  X   4   7

131. SALITA, DOMINGO C. Agricultural problems: ownership, tenancy, and credit.
(In: Huke, Robert E., ed. Shadows on the land. Manila, Bookmark, 1963.
p. 190-211)
      Luna: Descriptive analytical study which should have included
                  1960 census data.
                  O/C 4   7
      Spencer: Scholarly review of issues.
                  K   4   7

132. SANDOVAL, PEDRO R. and ERNESTO P. ABARIENTOS. Some aspects of poultry farm
management and marketing. PA 42, no. 7 (Dec. 1958), 303-318.

Sta. Iglesia: Highly useful descriptive and analytical research.
Y   5   6

133. STA. IGLESIA, JESUS C. Review of farm management work in the Philippines.
PA 45, no. 9 (Feb. 1962), 517-532. Appendix I. Bibliography of published
studies in farm management in the Philippines arranged by year of publica-
tion. (53 studies are cited)
Sta. Iglesia: Useful perspective.
Y   3   7

134. SIBLEY, WILLIS E. Forestry (In: Human Relations Area Files, Inc. Area
handbook on the Philippines. 1956. v. 4, p. 1577-1592)
Luna: Historical descriptive study.
E   4   7

135. SIONIL, JOSE F. The Philippine agrarian problem. Comment 9, (Third Quarter
1959), 85-143.
Luna: Historical descriptive statistical analytical study.
J/H   4   7

136. SPENCER, JOSEPH E. Land use in the upland Philippines. (In: Institute of
Pacific Relations. International Secretariat. The development of upland
areas in the Far East. New York, 1949, v. 1, p. 26-57.
Spencer: Basic study of upland land use.
K   4   7

137. _____. Shifting cultivation in Southeastern Asia. Berkeley, Univ. of
California Press, 1966. 247p. (Univ. of California publications in geogra-
phy, v. 19)
Spencer: Includes Philippines in area of study.
K   4   7

138. SYCIP, FELICIDAD CHAN. Factors relating to the acceptance or rejection of
innovations in poultry and swine production in rural areas. Quezon City,
Community Development Research Council, U.P., 1960. 176p.

139. TABLANTE, NATHANIEL B. An appraisal of agricultural problems and policies
in the Philippines. Lafayette, Indiana, 1956. 356p. Thesis (Ph.D.) -
Purdue Univ.

140. _____. Implications of credit institutes and policy for savings and capital
accumulation in Philippine agriculture. PEJ 3, no. 2 (second semester 1964),
208-225.
Luna: Descriptive statistical analytical study.
X   4   6

141. UMALI, DIOSCORO L. The role of the Univ. of the Philippines in agricultural
development. (In: The role of the Univ. of the Philippines in the socio-
economic development of the country. Seminar on President Macapagal's Five-
Year integrated socio-economic program. Proceedings. U.P. June 27, 1962.
p. 29-39)
Suggested by Polson.
Polson: Description of the University's present and prospective
role.
Y   4   6

142. U.S. DEPT. OF AGRICULTURE. Report of the Philippine-United States agricul-
tural mission. Washington, D.C. Headed by Leland E. Call. June 1947. 50p.
(International agricultural collaboration series no. 3.)
  Luna: Describes agricultural patterns and characteristics with
                     recommendations for improvement.
                     W   4   7
  Spencer: Summary review of problems and proposals for solution.
                     C   4   7

143. _____. ECONOMIC RESEARCH SERVICE. The Philippines: long-term projection
of supply of and demand for selected agricultural products. ERS-Foreign-34
(contract S-621-fa-984) (AGRIC). Jerusalem: Israel Program for Scientific
Translations, 1962.
Cited in Wernstedt and Spencer, The Philippine island world...1967.
  Luna: Statistical projective analytical study.
                     W   4   6
  Spencer: Abstruse quantitative economic manipulations.
                     C   4   7

144. _____. ECONOMIC SURVEY MISSION TO THE PHILIPPINES. Report on agriculture,
fishing and forestry. 1950. 26p.
  Luna: Describes levels of agricultural, fishery and forestry
                     development, and recommendations for improvement.
                     W   4   6

145. VELMONTE, JOSE E. Some aspects of Philippine rural economy. (In: Rivera,
Generoso F., and Robert T. McMillan, eds. The rural Philippines; United
States Mutual Security Agency. Office of Information, Mutual Security
Agency, 1952. p.214-216)
  Luna: Descriptive informative essay.
                     X   4   7

146. VENEGAS, ERNESTO C. Interactions between labor intensity, cultural practices and yields in rice production. PA 51, no. 1 (June 1967), 32-54.

147. VERGARA, NAPOLEON T. The kaingin problem: proposals for its solution.
Forestry Leaves 13, no. 1 (1961), 37-38, 40.
  Luna: Descriptive prescriptive article.
                     C   4   6

148. VON OPPENFELD, HORST. The pilot study in farm development: general report
(July 1958-March 1960). A cooperative research project of the Dept. of
Agricultural Economics, College of Agriculture, Univ. of the Philippines and
the Bureau of Agricultural Extension of the Dept. of Agriculture and Natural
Resources. Manila, 1960. 23p. Mimeographed.
Suggested by Sta. Iglesia.

149. _____ and OTHERS. The pilot study in farm development. Los Bános, Laguna,
U.P. College of Agriculture. 1964. 112p.
Suggested by Sta. Iglesia.
  Sta. Iglesia: Highly useful descriptive and analytical research.
                     Y/C   5   6

150. _____. Farm management, land use and tenancy in the Philippines. Laguna.
College of Agriculture, U.P., Central Experiment Station Bulletin, no. 1.

Aug. 1957. 168p.
Cited in Pal, Rural sociology... Current sociology 8, no. 1 (1959).
    Luna: Historical descriptive statistical analytical monograph.
                   X   4   7
    Polson: A good profile.
                   X   5   6
    Spencer: Good status report; a how to do it guide.
                   C   4   7
    Sta. Iglesia: Highly useful descriptive and analytical research.
                   Y   5   6

151. WATTERS, R. F. The nature of shifting cultivation: a review of recent re-
      search. Pacific Viewpoint 1, no. 1 (Mar. 1960), 59-99.
          Luna: Evaluation of recent research in Kaingin with diagrams
                         and other illustrations.
                         K   4   6
          Spencer: Marginal reference to the Philippines.
                         K   4   6

152. WEBB, William L. Development of incentive control of shifting cultivation.
      Forestry Leaves 15, no. 3 (1964), 9-16, 20.
          Luna: Descriptive prescriptive study.
                         C   4   7

153. WESTER, P. J. The food plants of the Philippines. Third, revised edition.
      Manila, Bureau of printing, 1924. x, 236p. (Philippine Islands, Bureau
      of agriculture, Bulletin no. 39)
          Spencer: Good descriptive summary review, now slightly out of
                         date.
                         E   4   4

Agricultural Industries

154. ACAYAN, DOLORES S. and H. FAIRFIELD SMITH. Variability of palay production
      per farm in the 1956 Philippine crop survey. Phil. Stat. 7, no. 2 (June
      1958), 62-79.
          Luna: Statistical analytical study.
                         C   4   6

155. ADAMS, DOROTHY INEZ. The role of rice ritual in southeast Asia. Thesis
      (Ph.D.) - Columbia Univ. 1940.
          Luna: Historical descriptive analytical study.
                         E   5   7

156. ADRIANO, F. T. The Philippine mango and its utilization. PM 31, no. 1
      (Jan. 1934), 15-16, 40-42.
          Luna: Descriptive informative article.
                         C   3   4

157. AFRICA, ANGEL A. A preliminary survey of the comparative costs of different
      methods of harvesting rice. PA 8, no. 8-9 (Mar./Apr. 1920), 277-292.

1 plate.
    Luna: Descriptive analytical study.
                    C   5   4

158. APACIBLE, ALEJANDRO R. The sugar industry of the Philippines. PGJ 8, nos. 3-4 (July/Dec. 1964), 86-100.
    Luna: Descriptive statistical, analytical study.
                    C   4   7
    Spencer: Excellent summary study of sugar production system.
                    C   4   6

159. _____. Sugar's role in Philippine industry. PGJ 5, nos. 1/2 (Jan./June 1957), 14-20.
    Luna: Descriptive analytical study.
                    C   4   7
    Spencer: Excellent survey of role of sugar industry in Philippine Islands industry as a whole.
                    C   4   6

160. ARENS, RICHARD. Animism in Philippine rice ritual. Eastern World 11, no. 9 (Sept. 1957), 36-37.
    Luna: Descriptive analytical study.
                    M/E   5   7

161. _____. Thanksgiving ceremonies of the Philippine rice farmer. Mission Bulletin 8, no. 2 (Feb. 1956).
    Luna: Descriptive analytical study.
                    M/E   5   7

162. BARKER, R. and A. J. NYBERG. Coconut-cattle enterprises in the Philippines. PA 52, no. 1 (June 1968), 49-60.

163. BAUTISTA, BASILIO R. The general practice of lowland rice farming in the Philippines. Philippine Journal of Agriculture 8, no. 1 (1937), 105-119. 7 plates.
    Spencer: Good review of cropping practices.
                    C   4   6

164. BRATTON, C. A. An economist's view of rice and corn improvement. PA 37, nos. 1/2 (June/July 1953), 1-8.
    Luna: Descriptive analytical study.
                    X   4   6
    Sta. Iglesia: Useful observations.
                    Y   3   6

165. CAMUS, JOSE S. Rice in the Philippines. Manila, Bureau of Printing, 1921. 87p. Department of Agriculture and Natural Resources, Bureau of Agriculture, Bulletin No. 37.
    Luna: Historical descriptive statistical analytical study.
                    C   4   7
    Spencer: Basic study; now dated and out of date, but valuable still.
                    C   5   4

166. CORPUZ, EDUARDO G. An economic analysis of rice yields in the Philippines,

with emphasis on policy and development aspects. Honolulu, 1963. 156p. Thesis (M.S.) - Univ. of Hawaii.
    Sta. Iglesia: Highly useful descriptive and analytical research.
        G   5   6

167. COVAR, PROSPERO R. The Masagana/Margate system of planting rice: a study of an agricultural innovation. Quezon City, 1960. 150p. (Community Development Research Council, U.P. Study Series no. 5)
    Coller: Well-done report on the obstacles to acceptance of a new farming technique.
        Z   5   6
    Luna: Descriptive analytical study.
        C   4/5   6
    Polson: A good study on the problems of risk and credit.
        Z   5   6
    Spencer: Good report of agricultural innovation in rice growing.
        C   4   6
    Sta. Iglesia: Y   5   6

168. CRUZ, DALMACIO A. Retailing rice in selected areas. PA 44, no. 4 (Sept. 1960), 197-209.
    Luna: Descriptive analytical study.
        C   5   6
    Sta. Iglesia: Highly useful descriptive research.
        Y   5   6

169. CUTSHALL, ALDEN. The Philippine sugar industry: status and problems. Journal of Geography 60, no. 1 (Jan. 1960), 5-9.
Suggested by Warren.
    Warren: K   5   6

170. _____. Tobacco production in the Philippines. Illinois State Academy of Science.Transactions 52, nos. 1/2 (1959), 33-44.
    Warren: K   5   6

171. DE DIOS, M. B. Some aspects of the rice policy of the Philippines with emphasis on the economic rationale of rice imports. Phil. Stat. 14, no. 1 (Mar. 1965), 68-76.
    Luna: Descriptive graphical analytical study.
        C   4   6

172. DRILON, J. D. Rice price stabilization and the rice and corn administration. PJPA 11, no. 3 (July 1967), 230-243.

173. GOLAY, FRANK H. and MARVIN E. GOODSTEIN. Philippine rice needs to 1990: output and input requirements. Manila, U.S. AID Mission Report, 1967. 137p.
    Luna: Descriptive statistical projective analytical study.
        X   4   6

174. GUTIERREZ, JOSE S. Rice marketing in the Philippines: problems and related government programs. ERJ 12, no. 3 (Dec. 1965), 202-224.
    Luna: Descriptive statistical analytical study.
        C   4   6

175.   _____. Rice production and consumption requirements. Philippine Agricul-
        tural Situation 1 (1960), 13-33.
        Cited in Wernstedt and Spencer. The Philippine island world...1967.
            Luna: Descriptive statistical analytical study.
                            C   4   6

176.   _____. Theories of choice in relation to the Philippine rice farmers' deci-
        sions. Stat. Rept. 11, no. 3 (July/Sept. 1967), 11-17.

177.   GUZMAN, LEOPOLDO P. DE, H. VON OPPENFELD and E. U. QUINTANA. The effect of
        management on incomes of rice farmers. PA 42, no. 5 (Oct. 1958), 173-189.
            Luna: Comparative study of effects of management on resources
                            and incomes of single and double cropped farms.
                            X   4   6

178.   HARGREAVES, GEORGE H. Areas in the Philippines where rice can be grown
        without irrigation. PGJ 4, nos. 2/3 (Apr./Sept. 1956), 69-71.
            Luna: Descriptive graphical analytical study.
                            C   4   6
            Spencer: Very brief note, but effective map.
                            C   4   6
            Sta. Iglesia: Highly useful description and analysis.
                            C   5   6

179.   HESTER, EVETT D. and OTHERS. Some economic and social aspects of Philip-
        pine rice tenancies. PA 12, no. 9 (Feb. 1924), 367-444.
            Anderson: Remains the outstanding research survey on Philippine
                            land tenure written during the American period. Re-
                            quired reading for every student of the subject.
                            X   4   4(3)
            McMillan: A penetrating, coldly objective analysis--one of the
                            best!
                            X   4   7
            Sta. Iglesia: Highly useful descriptive research.
                            X   5   4

180.   HICKS, GEORGE L. The Philippine coconut industry; growth and change, 1900-
        1965. [Washington, D.C.] Center for Development Planning, National Plan-
        ning Association, 1967. 215p. (Field work report, no. 7)

181.   _____. The Philippine export sector, 1900-1967; a bibliography. [Washing-
        ton, D.C.] Center for Development Planning, National Planning Association,
        1967. 54p. (Field work report, no. 23)

182.   _____. The Philippine sugar industry, 1900-1965; a bibliography. [Washing-
        ton, D.C.] Center for Development Planning, National Planning Association,
        1967. 23p. (Field work report, no. 18)

183.   HOUSTON, CHARLES O. Customs associated with rice cultivation in the Philip-
        pines. JEAS 3, no. 3 (Apr. 1954), 287-296.
            Luna: Descriptive informative article.
                            H   3   7
            Spencer: The following seven articles are good studies by an eco-
                            nomic geographer, using historical data.

184. _____. Other Philippine crops and industries: 1934-1950. JEAS 4, no. 1 (Jan. 1955), 15-39.
    Luna: Descriptive informative article.
                    H   3   7
    Spencer: K   4   7

185. _____. The Philippine abaca industry, 1934-1950. JEAS 3, no. 4 (July/Oct. 1954), 408-415.
    Luna: Descriptive informative article.
                    H   3   7
    Spencer: K   4   7

186. _____. The Philippine coconut industry, 1934-1950. JEAS 3, no. 2 (Jan. 1954), 153-181.
    Luna: Descriptive informative article.
                    S   3   7
    Spencer: K   4   7

187. _____. The Philippine sugar industry: 1934-1950. JEAS 3, no. 4 (July/Oct. 1954), 370-407.
    Luna: Descriptive informative article.
                    H   3   7
    Spencer: K   4   7

188. _____. The Philippine tobacco industry: 1934-1950. PGJ 2, nos. 1/2 (Jan./June 1954), 12-21.
    Luna: Descriptive informative article.
                    H   3   7
    Spencer: K   4   7

189. _____. Rice in the Philippine economy, 1934-1950. JEAS 3, no. 1 (Oct. 1953), 13-85.
    Luna: Descriptive informative article.
                    H   3   7
    Spencer: K   4   7

190. HUKE, ROBERT E. Abaca production in the Philippines. PGJ 7, no. 1 (Jan./Mar. 1963), 18-35.
    Luna: Descriptive analytical study with maps.
                    K   4   7
    Spencer: Statement of problems to be faced.
                    K   4   6
    Sta. Iglesia: Highly useful description.
                    K   4   6

191. KALAW, MAXIMO M. The coconut industry - report on a special coconut mission abroad in pursuance of resolution. National Assembly, Manila, Bureau of Printing, 1940. 140p.
    Luna: Descriptive statistical analytical study.
                    G   4   4
    Spencer: Good report.
                    G   3   4

192. KEARL, C. D. The rice needs of the Philippines. PA 38, no. 8 (Jan. 1955), 542-547.

Luna: Descriptive analytical study.
                  X   4   6
Sta. Iglesia: Highly useful description and analysis.
                  Y   4   6

193. LU, HSUEH-YI. Some socio-economic factors affecting the implementation at
the farm level of a rice production program in the Philippines. 1968.
313p. Thesis (Ph.D.) - U.P. College of Agriculture.
Suggested by Sta. Iglesia.
       Sta. Iglesia: Highly useful descriptive and analytical research.
                  Y   5   6

194. MCHALE, THOMAS R. Early technological innovation in sugar cane agriculture
and sugar making techniques in the Philippines. (Abstract). Pacific
Science Congress. 9th, Bangkok, 1957. Proceedings. Bangkok, 1963. 3,
237-238.

195. MANGAHAS, MAHAR, AIDA E. RECTO and VERNON W. RUTTAN. Market relationships
for rice and corn in the Philippines. PEJ 5, no. 1 (First semester 1966),
1-27.
       Sta. Iglesia: Highly useful descriptive and analytical research.
                  Y   5   6

196. MAULIT, DIMAS A. Palay harvest and the supply of rice. Phil. Stat. Part I
6, no. 2 (June 1957), 94-112. Part II 6, no. 3 (Sept. 1957), 159-185.
       Luna: Descriptive statistical analytical study.
                  X   4   7

197. MILLER, HUGO. Abaca. Philippine Craftsman 1, no. 2 (Aug. 1912), 120-140.
15 plates.
Cited in Helen Butengko, JEAS, Oct. 1953, p.116.
       Luna: Descriptive analytical study.
                  K   3   7

198. NYBERG, ALBERT J. The Philippine coconut industry. Ithaca, N.Y. 1968.
258p. Thesis (Ph.D) - Cornell Univ.

199. _____. The Philippine coconut industry in economic perspective. PA 52,
no. 1 (June 1968), 1-48.

200. OBAYASHI, TARO. The cultivation of taro in the Philippines. Memoirs of the
Institute for Oriental Culture. Tokyo 23 (1961), 215-276.
       Spencer: Summary historical study.
                  C   4   7

201. OCAMPO, LAZARO A. Irrigation and the rice problem of the Philippines. Phil.
Stat. 14, no. 1 (Mar. 1965), 77-107.
       Luna: Descriptive statistical analytical study.
                  G   4   6
       Spencer: Statistical review.
                  C   4   7

202. PELZER, KARL J. The future of the Philippine abaca industry: peasant or
plantation crop? Pacific Science Congress. 7th, 1949. Proceedings v. 7:
Anthropology (1953), 190-195.

Warren: K   5   6

203. PEREDO, BENJAMIN D. Marketing corn at the farm level in the Philippines, 1956-1957. PA 42, no. 10 (Mar. 1959), 431-453.
    Sta. Iglesia: Highly useful descriptive and analytical research.
    Y/G   5   6

204. POBLADOR, NICETO S. The Philippine sugar industry: a case study in government control. PRBE 1, no. 2 (Oct. 1964), 1-20.

205. PRANTILLA, EDMUNDO B. The supply response of sugar in the Philippines. 1968. Thesis (M.S.) - U.P. College of Agriculture.
Suggested by Sta. Iglesia.
    Sta. Iglesia: Highly useful descriptive and statistically analytical research.
    Y   5   6

206. QUINTANA, EMILIO U. Resource productivity estimates for five types of Philippine farms. 1960. 204p. Thesis (Ph.D.) - Purdue Univ.

207. _____, B. D. PEREDO and E. P. MARIANO. The present situation and outlook of the rice marketing facilities with emphasis on their implications on the present rice problem of the country. Phil. Stat. 14, no. 1 (Mar. 1965), 1-54.
    Luna: Descriptive statistical analytical study.
    X   4   6
    Spencer: Statistical treatment.
    G   4   6

208. _____, B. N. DE LOS REYES and J. M. MARASIGAN. Farm business management of coconut farms. PA 42, nos. 8/9 (Jan./Feb. 1959), 374-389.
    Sta. Iglesia: Highly useful descriptive and analytical research.
    Y   5   6

209. _____, J. C. STA. IGLESIA and H. VON OPPENFELD. The farmer's cost of producing palay. PA 40, no. 8 (Jan. 1957), 393-398.
    Sta. Iglesia: Highly useful descriptive and analytical research.
    Y   5   6

210. RAVENHOLT, ALBERT. Ramie--new crop and textile for the tropics. AUFSR. Southeast Asia Series 3, no. 15 (June 10, 1955), 7p. (AR-7-'55)

211. RECTO, AIDA E. The response of Philippine rice and corn farmers to price. PSR 14, no. 4 (Oct. 1966), 232-242.
    Luna: Descriptive analytical study.
    X   4   6
    Sta. Iglesia: Highly useful descriptive and analytical research.
    Y   5   6

212. RODRIGUEZ, FILEMON C. The rice situation. PGJ 10, nos. 1/2 (Jan./June 1966), 2-6.
    Luna: Descriptive informative analytical article.
    G/C   3   6
    Spencer: Dated status report, statistical.
    G   4   6

I. GENERAL. AGRICULTURE. Agricultural Industries

213. SACAY, FRANCISCO M. Farm investment and income of rice farm owner-operators
and tenant-operators. PA 39, no. 9 (Feb. 1956), 505-509.
　　　Luna:　　　　　　　Comparative study of rice farm owner-operators and tenant-
　　　　　　　　　　　　operators. Descriptive analytical study.
　　　　　　　　　　　　C　　　4　　　6
　　　Sta. Iglesia:　Highly useful descriptive and analytical research.
　　　　　　　　　　　　Y　　　5　　　6

214. SANDOVAL, PEDRO R. and G. W. HEDLUND. Problems of supporting prices of farm
products. PA 40, no. 8 (Jan. 1957), 389-392.
　　　Sta. Iglesia:　Useful observations.
　　　　　　　　　　　　Y　　　4　　　6

215. SCHUL, NORMAN W. A Philippine sugar cane plantation: land tenure and sugar
cane production. Economic Geography 43, no. 2 (Apr. 1967), 157-69.

216. SELGA, MIGUEL. Historical notes on the cultivation of wheat in the Philip-
pines. PA 20, no. 4 (Sept. 1931), 239-245.
　　　Luna:　　　　　　　Historical descriptive informative article.
　　　　　　　　　　　　M　　　3　　　7

217. SPENCER, JOSEPH E. The Philippine rice problem. Far Eastern Survey 18,
no. 11 (June 1, 1949), 125-128.
　　　Luna:　　　　　　　Descriptive analytical article.
　　　　　　　　　　　　K　　　4　　　7
　　　Spencer:　　　　　Dated status report.
　　　　　　　　　　　　K　　　4　　　7

218. SUMAGUI, JUAN O. Cost of agricultural production of selected crops--rice,
corn, tobacco, abaca and coconut: 1956. Phil. Stat. 7, no. 4 (Dec. 1958),
202-259.
　　　Luna:　　　　　　　Descriptive statistical analytical study.
　　　　　　　　　　　　C　　　4　　　6
　　　Spencer:　　　　　Statistical cost summaries.
　　　　　　　　　　　　C　　　4　　　7

219. TIONGSON, FABIAN A. Improved merchandising of selected farm products. Que-
zon City, Community Development Research Council, U.P. 1964. 377p.
　　　Sta. Iglesia:　Highly useful descriptive and analytical research.
　　　　　　　　　　　　Y　　　5　　　6

220. UMALI, DIOSCORO L. The Rice Dilemma: its causes, effects and suggested
remedies. PA 45, no. 8 (Jan. 1962), 395-420.
　　　Luna:　　　　　　　Descriptive prescriptive analytical study.
　　　　　　　　　　　　Y/C　　　4　　　7

221. VENEGAS, ERNESTO C. Improving the estimation of Palay yields and production.
PA 51, no. 1 (June 1967), 55-64.

ANTHROPOLOGY

222. AMYOT, JACQUES. The problem of values in social anthropology. PSR 7,
      no. 4 (Oct. 1959), 1-6.
           Guthrie: E   4   6

223. ANTONIO, CELIA M. and ALLEN L. TAN. A preliminary bibliography of Philippine
      cultural minorities. Quezon City, Rep. of the Philippines, Commission on
      National Integration, 1967. 34p.

224. BAILEN, JEROME B. Studies in physical anthropology on the Philippines. (In:
      Zamora, Mario D., ed. Studies in Philippine anthropology (In honor of H.
      Otley Beyer). Quezon City, Alemar-Phoenix, 1967. p. 527-558)

225. BARNETT, MILTON L. Anthropology, home economics, and rural development. GEJ
      12 (2nd Semester), 1966-1967, 150-161.

226. BARROWS, DAVID P. Circulars of information, instructions for volunteer field
      workers. The Bureau of Non-Christian Tribes. Manila, The Museum of Ethnol-
      ogy, Natural History and Commerce, Dec. 1901. 16p.

227. [BARTON, ROY FRANKLIN: 1883-1947] [Obituary] By Alfred L. Kroeber. AA 51,
      no. 1 (Jan./Mar. 1949), 91-95.
           Jocano: A good source for Barton's contribution to Philippine
                           anthropology.
                           E   5   4

228. [BEAN, ROBERT BENNETT: 1874-1944] [Obituary] Robert Bennett Bean, 1874-
      1944, by R. J. Terry. AA 48, no. 1 (Jan./Mar. 1946), 70-74.

229. BEYER H. OTLEY. Anthropology at the Manila congresses, 1953. Polynesian
      Society Journal 63, nos. 3/4 (Sept./Dec. 1954), 247-250.

230. _____. A checklist of the writings of H. Otley Beyer, by E. Arsenio Manuel.
      (In: Zamora, Mario D., ed. Studies in Philippine anthropology (In honor of
      H. Otley Beyer). Quezon City, Alemar-Phoenix Publishing, 1967. p. 31-47)

231. _____. H. Otley Beyer: his researches and publications, by E. Arsenio
      Manuel. (In: Zamora, Mario D., ed. Studies in Philippine anthropology (In
      honor of H. Otley Beyer). Quezon City, Alemar-Phoenix Publishing, 1967.
      p. 23-30)

232. BRINTON, DANIEL G. Professor Blumentritt's studies of the Philippines. AA
      1, no. 1 (Jan. 1899), 122-125.

233. CASIÑO, ERIC S. Ethnographic art of the Philippines: an anthropological
      approach. GEJ, no. 12 (Second Semester 1966-1967), 230-267.

234. _____. The Future of anthropology in the Philippines. Solidarity 2, no. 9
      (Sept./Oct. 1967), 16-23.

235. CHICAGO. UNIVERSITY. PHILIPPINE STUDIES PROGRAM. Beyer Library: type-
      scripts on Philippine ethnography, folklore, customary law, and archaeology.
      Compiled under the direction of E. D. Hester, by the Staff of the Asia Foun-
      dation-Beyer Project. 1962. 187p.

236. [COLE, FAY-COOPER: 1881-1961] [Obituary] By Fred Eggan. Bibliography of
Fay-Cooper Cole, compiled with the assistance of E. Arsenio Manuel. AA 65,
no. 3, part 1 (June 1963), 641-648.
      Jocano: A good appraisal of early worker in Philippine anthropol-
                         ogy.
                         E   3   4

237. EGGAN, FRED. Fay Cooper Cole, architect of anthropology. Science 135,
no. 3502 (Feb. 9, 1962), 412-413.
      Jocano: An excellent view of Cole's contribution to ethnology.
                         E   5   7

238. _____. Notes and Comments: The Philippine Studies Program, Univ. of Chicago.
JEAS 3, no. 3 (Apr. 1954), 325-327.

239. _____ and R. F. BARTON. Anthropology during the war. Report no. IX. The
Philippines. (The Committee on International Cooperation in Anthropology,
National Research Council. AA 49, no. 3 (July/Sept. 1947), 532-533.
      Jocano: Useful material on anthropology's contribution to other
                         fields.
                         E   5   5

240. HOUSTON, CHARLES O. Anthropology in the Philippines. JEAS 1, no. 3 (Apr.
1952), 65-66.
      Jocano: H   4   7

241. JOCANO, F. LANDA. The relevance of anthropology to nutrition research. Philippine Journal of Nutrition 20, no. 4 (Oct./Dec. 1967), 202-210.

242. KROEBER, ALFRED L. Anthropology of the Philippines. Pan-Pacific scientific
conference, 1st session, Honolulu, 1920. Proceedings. Honolulu, 1921.
Pt. 1, 91-97. (Bernice P. Bishop Museum. Special Publication, no. 7,
part 1) Also published in Mid-Pacific Magazine 23 (Mar. 1922), 228-231.
      Jocano: E   4   7

243. [KROEBER, ALFRED LOUIS: 1876-1960] [Obituary] By Julian H. Steward. A Bibliography of the publications of Alfred Louis Kroeber by Ann J. Gibson and
John H. Rowe. AA 63, no. 5, part 1 (Oct. 1961), 1038-1087.
      Jocano: Useful notes on Kroeber's contribution to Philippine
                         anthropology.
                         E   4   7

244. LORRIN, ROSARIO DE SANTOS B. Anthropology and literature. GEJ, No. 12
(Second Semester, 1966-1967), 225-229.

245. LYNCH, FRANK. Henry Otley Beyer 1883-1966. PS 15, no. 1 (Jan. 1967), 3-8.

246. _____ and MARY R. HOLLNSTEINER. Sixty years of Philippine ethnology. A
first glance at the years 1901-1961. In Philippines (Republic) National
Science Development Board. Inter-Disciplinary Symposia Proceedings, National
Science and Technology Week, Nov. 20-26, 1961. Theme: "State of and Trends
in Science and Technology in the Philippines." Area VI-Social Sciences.
Manila, [1963?] 106p. Mimeographed. Bibliography: 30p. Table 1: Preliminary list of ethnologists studying Philippine peoples. By Cultural-linguistic
areas covered 1901-1961. 13p. Table 2: Preliminary data on ethnologists

studying Philippine Peoples 1901-1961. 15p.
> Jocano: Excellent initial assessment of ethnographic work in
> Philippine Islands.
> E   4   7

247. MANUEL, E. ARSENIO. The Beyer Collection of original sources in Philippine ethnography. ASLP Bulletin 4, nos. 3/4 (Sept./Dec. 1958), 46-66.

248. MELENDEZ, PEDRO and JOSEPHINE CACCAM. The U.P. Department of Anthropology: 1914-1965. (In: Zamora, Mario D., ed. Studies in Philippine anthropology (In honor of H. Otley Beyer). Quezon City, Alemar-Phoenix, 1967. p. 6-22)

249. ORACION, TIMOTEO S. The anthropology of religion and general education. GEJ, no. 12 (Second Semester, 1966-1967), 189-206.

250. PHILIPPINE ISLANDS. DIVISION OF ETHNOLOGY. Directions for ethnographic observations and collections ... Manila, Bureau of Printing, 1908. 224p.

251. PHILIPPINES (REPUBLIC) NATIONAL MUSEUM. Ethnographic collection. Manila, 1953. 44, 3, 4p.
> Jocano: G   5   7

252. RAHMANN, RUDOLF and GERTRUDES R. ANG, eds. Dr. H. Otley Beyer, dean of Philippine anthropology; a commemorative issue. Cebu City, Philippines, University of San Carlos, 1968. 124p. (San Carlos publications. Series E. Miscellaneous contributions in the humanities, no. 1)

253. RAVENHOLT, ALBERT. Dr. H. Otley Beyer; pioneer scientist on the frontier in Asia. AUFSR. Southeast Asia Series 12, no. 4 (May 1964), 13p. (AR-4-'64)
> Coller: Account of the highlights in the biography of this outstanding man.
> J   5   7

254. SALCEDO, JUAN, JR. H. Otley Beyer: Anthropology and the Philippines. (In: Zamora, Mario D., ed. Studies in Philippine anthropology (In honor of H. Otley Beyer). Quezon City, Alemar-Phoenix, 1967. p. 1-5)

255. SCHEERER, OTTO. Alexander Schadenberg, his life and work in the Philippines. PJS 22, no. 4 (Apr. 1923), 447-457. 1 plate.
> Jocano: L   4   7

256. TANGCO, MARCELO. Anthropology and the Philippines. ("Sketch of the history of anthropology in the Philippines.") PSSHR 12, no. 3 (Aug. 1940), 189-211.
> Jocano: A good background of the history of anthropology in the
> Philippine Islands.
> E   4   7

257. TUGBY, DONALD J. Ethnological and allied work on southeast Asia, 1950-1966. Current Anthropology 9, no. 2/3 (Apr./June 1968), 185-206. Publications arising out of fieldwork, 1950-1966. Philippines: 202-204.

258. TUGBY, ELSIE. The distribution of ethnological and allied fieldwork in southeast Asia, 1950-66. Current Anthropology 9, no. 2/3 (Apr./June 1968), 207-214. Philippines: 213-214.

I. GENERAL. ANTHROPOLOGY

259. VANOVERBERGH, MORICE. A suggested anthropological field method. Primitive
Man 9, no. 2 (Apr. 1936), 24-27.
    Jocano: Many of his suggestions are not acceptable to the annota-
                    tor.
                    M   3   7

260. WARREN, CHARLES P. Anthropology in the Philippines: a report. Unpublished
typescript manuscript, U.S. Educational Foundation in Manila. 1950. 15p.
    Jocano: An informative note.
                    E   4   7
    Warren: E   3   6

261. WHITE, WILLIAM LAWRENCE. The Panamin [Private Association for National Minori-
ties] Foundation: research opportunities among the national minorities. U.P.
Anthropology Bulletin 3, no. 1 (First semester 1967/1968), 16-17, 29.

262. YABES, LEOPOLDO Y. Observations on some aspects of Philippine scholarship and
H. Otley Beyer. SR 6, nos. 7/8 (July/Aug. 1965), 13-18.
    Jocano: Y   3   7

263. _____. Observations on some aspects of Philippine scholarship and H. Otley
Beyer. (In: Zamora, Mario D., ed. Studies in Philippine anthropology (In
honor of H. Otley Beyer). Quezon City, Alemar-Phoenix, 1967. p.48-60.)

264. _____. Philippine scholarship and H. Otley Beyer. Solidarity 1, no. 2
(Apr./June 1966), 9-14.
    Jocano: Y   3   7

265. ZAMORA, MARIO D., ed. Studies in Philippine anthropology (In honor of H. Otley
Beyer). Quezon City, Alemar-Phoenix Publishers, 1967. 656p.

266. _____. The U.P. anthropological department and research. U.P. Research
Digest 4, no. 1 (Jan. 1965), 31-33.
    Jocano: E   4   7

267. _____. The U.P.-national museum memorandum of agreement: a historic context. AS 3, no. 1 (Apr. 1965), 155-157. Document of understanding between
the National Museum's Division of Anthropology and the U.P.'s Department of
Anthropology. AS 3, no. 1 (Apr. 1965), 158-160.

ARCHAEOLOGY

268. ABAYA, CONSUELO. Recent Chinese pottery finds in the Philippines. FTY (1967),
299-301, 314-316.
    Liao: A   4   1

269. ADDIS, J. M. The dating of Chinese porcelain found in the Philippines: a
historical retrospect. PS 16, no. 2 (Apr. 1968), 371-380.

270. AGA-OGLU, KAMER. Blue and white porcelain plates made for Moslem patrons.
Far Eastern Ceramic Bulletin 3, no. 3 (Sept. 1951), 9-12. 3 plates.
    Solheim: Data paper.

I. GENERAL. ARCHAEOLOGY

A   5   1/2

271. _____. Early blue and white pot excavated in the Philippines. Far Eastern
Ceramic Bulletin, no. 10 (June 1950), 64-71. 1 plate.
      Solheim: Data paper.
                      A   5   1

272. _____. Ming export blue and white jars in the University of Michigan collection. Art Quarterly 11, (1948), 201-217. 12 figs.
      Solheim: Data paper.
                      A   4/5   1/2

273. _____. Ming porcelain from sites in the Philippines. Chinese Art Society
of America. Archives. 17 (1963), 7-19. 21 figs. Abbreviated version in AP
5, no. 2 (Winter 1961), 243-252. 5 plates.
      Petersen: A   3   1
      Solheim: A   4/5   1/2

274. _____. The relationship between the Ying-Ch'ng, Shu-Fu and early blue and
white. Far Eastern Ceramic Bulletin, no. 8 (Dec. 1949), 27-33. 3 plates.
      Solheim: A   4   1

275. _____. The so-called 'Swatow' wares: types and problems of provenance.
Far Eastern Ceramic Bulletin 7, no. 2 (June 1955), 1-34. 24 plates.
      Solheim: A   5   1/2

276. _____. Ying Ch'ing porcelain found in the Philippines. Art Quarterly 9,
(1946), 315-326. 11 figs.
      Solheim: A   5   2/3

277. ALGUÉ, JOSÉ. El archipiélago Filipino. Washington, ... gobierno, 1900. 2v.

278. BEAN, ROBERT BENNETT. Paleolithic man in the Philippine Islands, Homo Phil-
ippinensis. PJS 5-D, no. 1 (June 1910), 27-31. 8 plates.

279. BEYER, H. OTLEY. Archaeological and historical sources connecting the Philippines both with the mainland of eastern and southeast-Asia and with the
Pacific islands region. International Association of Historians of Asia,
1st, Manila, 1960. Proceedings ... Manila, 1962. p. 315-320.
      Peterson: A short bibliography relating Philippine archaeology to
                      that of Southeast Asia and portions of the Pacific.
                      A   4   1
      Solheim: A   4   1

280. _____. Ceramic wares found in the Philippines. Vol. I. First edition of
180 typewritten pages in 20 copies. Manila, 1930.
Cited in Charles O. Houston, A preliminary bibliography of Philippine anthropology ... JEAS, Jan. 1953.
      Solheim: Valuable source material.
                      A   5   1-3

281. _____. New finds of fossil mammals from the Pleistocene strata of the Philippines. National Research Council of the Philippines, Bulletin no. 41 (Feb.
1957), 220-239. 6 plates.
      Solheim: Report on H. R. Von Koenigswald's fieldwork in northern

Luzon.
A   4   1

282. _____. Notes on the archaeological work of H. R. Van Heekeren in Celebes
and elsewhere (1937-1950). JEAS 1, no. 3 (Apr. 1952), 15-31. 4 plates.
    Peterson: A statement of the relevance of Celebes archaeological
                    materials to Philippine prehistory.
                    A   4   1
    Solheim: Important for the history of archaeology in Southeast
                    Asia.
                    A   4   4/5

283. _____. Outline review of Philippine archaeology by islands and provinces.
PJS 77, nos. 3/4 (July/Aug. 1947), 205-374. 22 plates. 2 text figures.
    Peterson: A survey of the types of archaeological materials to be
                    found in the Philippines.
                    A   5   1
    Solheim: The major summary of prehistoric sites and artifacts known
                    in the Philippines up to 1947.
                    A   4   1/2

284. _____. Philippine and East Asian archaeology, and its relation to the origin
of the Pacific Islands population. Quezon City, Phil., National Research Council of the Philippines, 1948. 130p. (Bulletin no. 29) 37 plates.
    Peterson: Beyer's interpretation of the prehistory of the Philip-
                    pines: this work incorporates much original data.
                    A   4   1
    Solheim: The primary reconstruction of the "stone ages" in the
                    Philippines.
                    A   4   1

285. _____. Philippine archaeology and its relation to the origin of the Pacific
Islands population. Proceedings of the Sixth Pacific Science Congress 4
(1940), 157-164.
    Peterson: Beyer's interpretation of the prehistory of the Philip-
                    pines: this work incorporates much original data.
                    A   4   1
    Solheim: A preliminary rendering of above.
                    A   4   1

286. _____. Philippine tektites. (In: Galang, Zoilo, ed. Encyclopedia of the
Philippines, 2nd ed. 1957. v. 13, p.221-227)
    Solheim: Interesting for the history of tektite studies.
                    A   4/5   1

287. _____. Philippine tektites. A contribution to the study of the tektite
problem in general, in the light of both past and recent discoveries. Published by the office of the Research Coordinator. Quezon City: U.P. Philippine Tektites, 1, Parts I and II, 1961, 1-290. 20 plates.
    Peterson: A   3   7
    Solheim: The major review of Philippine tektite studies; of histor-
                    ical interest to tektite studies in general.
                    A   4/5   1

288. _____. Philippine tektites. PM 32, no. 11 (Nov. 1935), 542-543, 581-582.

```
                Peterson:      A     3     7
                Solheim:       Of historic interest.
                               A     4/5   1
```

289. _____. Philippine tektites and the tektite problem in general. Smithsonian Institution. Annual report, 1942. Washington, 1943. p. 253-259.
```
     Peterson:      More relevant to geology than to archaeology.
                    A     5     7
     Solheim:       Of historic interest; superseded by his Philippine
                    Tektites.  U.P., 1961.
                    A     4/5   1
```

290. _____. A prehistoric iron-age in the Philippines. PM 25, no. 5 (Oct.
1928), 253-255.
Cited in Charles O. Houston, A preliminary bibliography of Philippine anthropology ... JEAS, Jan. 1953.
```
     Peterson:      A short statement on the presence of an Iron Age in the
                    Philippines.
                    A     4     1
     Solheim:       Of historic interest.
                    A     4     1
```

291. _____. Recent discoveries in Philippine archaeology, Proceedings of the
Third Pan-Pacific Science Congress 2 (Oct./Nov. 1926), 2469-2491.
```
     Peterson:      A statement of the progress of archaeological work in the
                    Philippines.
                    A     3     1
     Solheim:       The first and only report by Beyer on his own fieldwork
                    in archaeology.
                    A     3     1
```

292. _____. The relation of tektites to archaeology. Proceedings of the 4th
Far-Eastern Prehistory and the Anthropology Division of the 8th Pacific
Science Congresses combined. Part I. (Second Fascicle: Section 1, p.371-
415. 12 plates.) Quezon City, National Research Council of the Philippines, Univ. of the Philippines, 1956.
```
     Peterson:      Explanation of the relevance of tektites to stratigraphic
                    excavation in the Philippines.
                    A     4     1
     Solheim:       A     3     1
```

293. _____. Supplementary illustrations to the "Outline review of Philippine
archaeology by islands and provinces." "Supplement No. 1." With a few critical bibliographic notes and preliminary data on new finds. Manila, Author,
1949. 18p. 18 plates.
Cited in Charles O. Houston, A preliminary bibliography of Philippine anthropology ... JEAS, Jan. 1953.
```
     Solheim:       Source material and information of interest to the history
                    of Philippine archaeology.
                    A     4/5   1/2
```

294. _____. A tribute to Van Stein Callenfels. JEAS 1, no. 1 (Oct. 1951), 77-
81.
```
     Solheim:       Important for history of Southeast Asian archaeology.
                    A     4     4
```

295.   _____ and E. D. Hester. Preliminary catalog of the Hester collection of
ceramic wares (Nos. H-1 to H-824). Typescript, Chicago Natural History Museum and the Univ. of Michigan Museum of Anthropology, 1937.
Cited in Stuart A. Schlegel, Preliminary bibliography of Philippine culture
history.
        Solheim: Source material.
                        A   5   1/2

296.   _____. Supplement to the preliminary catalog of the Hester collection of
ceramic wares (Nos. H-825 to H-855). Typescript, Chicago Natural History
Museum and the Univ. of Michigan Museum of Anthropology, 1941.
Cited in Stuart A. Schlegel, Preliminary bibliography of Philippine culture
history.
        Solheim: A   5   1/2

297.   _____ and WALTER ROBB. New data on Chinese and Siamese ceramic wares of the
14th and 15th centuries. PM 27, no. 3 (Aug. 1930), 150-153, 200-204, no. 4
(Sept. 1930), 220-223, 250, 252, 254. 33 figs.
        Peterson: An early comment on porcelains in the Philippines.
                        A   5   1
        Solheim: Valuable source material.
                        A   5   1-3

298.   COLE, FAY-COOPER and BERTHOLD LAUFER. Chinese pottery in the Philippines.
Chicago, 1912, 47p. (Field museum of natural history. Publication 162, Anthropological ser. vol. xii, no. 1) 22 plates. Cole: p.1-16; Laufer: p.17-
47.
        Peterson: A   3   1
        Solheim: First major publication on this field, data presented
                        still useful.
                        E   5   1/2

299.   DIXON, ROLAND BURRAGE. Recent archaeological discoveries in the Philippines
and their bearing on the prehistory of Eastern Asia. American Philosophical
Society. Proceedings 69, no. 4 (1930), 225-229.
        Peterson: A   3   1
        Solheim: Report on Beyer's discoveries from 1926-1929; of historic
                        interest.
                        E   3   1/2

300.   ERDBERG-CONSTEN, ELEANOR VON. The Manila trade pottery seminar. PS 16,
no. 3 (July 1968), 545-557.

301.   EVANGELISTA, ALFREDO E. H. O. Beyer's Philippine neolithic in the context
of postwar discoveries in local archaeology. (In: Zamora, Mario D., ed.
Studies in Philippine anthropology (In honor of H. Otley Beyer). Quezon
City, Alemar-Phoenix, 1967. p.63-87)

302.   _____. Identifying some intrusive archaeological materials found in Philippine proto-historic sites. AS 3, no. 1 (Apr. 1965), 86-102. 7 plates.
        Solheim: A   3?   2/3

303.   _____. The incipient and emergent periods in Philippine culture-history.
Philippine Educational Forum 15 (July 1966), 15-31.
        Solheim: A   4?   1

304. _____. Intimations of iron. Paper read in the lecture series, Philippine
Perspective, Lectures on the Prehistory and History of the Philippines, Nov.
20, 1963. Ateneo de Manila, Manila, 1964. 15p. Mimeographed.
    Peterson: A useful summary of what is known of the Iron Age in the
                     Philippines.
                     A   4   1

305. _____. Philippine archaeology up to 1950. SR 3, no. 9 (Sept. 1962), 17-
22.
    Solheim: History of Philippine archaeology.
                     A   4   7

306. _____. Regional Reports: Philippines. AP 4, no. 1/2 (Summer/Winter 1960),
85-88.
    Solheim: Report on current archaeological work.
                     A   4   1

307. _____. Regional Reports: Philippines. AP 5, no. 1 (Summer 1961), 67-70.
    Solheim: Report on current archaeological work.
                     A   4   1

308. _____. Regional Reports: Philippines. AP 6, no. 1/2 (Summer/Winter 1962),
46-47.
    Solheim: Report on current archaeological work.
                     A   4   1

309. _____. Regional Reports: Philippines. AP 7, no. 1/2 (Summer/Winter
1963), 52-56. 1 plate.
    Solheim: Report on current archaeological work.
                     A   4   1

310. _____. Shell artifacts from Philippine archaeological sites. Philippine
International 17, no. 10 (1963)
Cited by Tugby. Current Anthropology v.9 (Apr./June 1968), p. 202.
    Solheim: A   4/5?   1

311. _____ and ABDULLAH T. MADALE. Latest clues to our forgotten past. Chronicle
Yearbook (1961), 74-76, 78-80.
    Solheim: A   3   1/3

312. EVANS, IVOR H. N. Notes on the relationship between Philippine iron-age
antiquities and some from Perak. Federated Malay States Museums. Journal.
Kuala Lumpur 12, part 7 (June 1929), 189-196.
    Solheim: Report based on a letter from Beyer.
                     A/E   4   1

313. FERNANDEZ, JULITA G. and AMELIA O. ROGEL. Digging in the past. Esso Silangan 13, no. 3 (Mar. 1968), 6-11.

314. FOX, ROBERT B. Ancient Filipino communities. (In: Symposium on the impact
of man on humid tropics vegetation, Goroka, Territory of Papua and New Guinea,
September, 1960 ... Canberra, A. J. Arthur, Commonwealth Government printer
1962. p.380-387.
    Solheim: A/E   4   1

315. _____. The archaeological record of Chinese influences in the Philippines. PS 15, no. 1 (Jan. 1967), 41-62.

316. _____. Chinese pottery in the Philippines. FTY, (1962), 40-41, 248-258.
    Peterson: Excellent article on Chinese porcelains found in the
                 Philippines.
                 A   4   1

317. _____. Philippine prehistory and carbon-14 dating. SR 4, no. 10 (Oct. 1963), 4-8.
    Peterson: A presentation of relevant C-14 dates in the Philippines.
                 A   3   1

318. _____. The Philippines in prehistoric times. SR 3, no. 9 (Sept. 1962), 1-16. Reprinted: (In: Alip, Eufronio M., ed., The Philippines of yester-years. Manila, Alip, 1964. p.283-317. 2 plates)
    Peterson: A   3   1

319. _____. The Philippines since the beginning of time. (In: Abella, Pedro F., ed. Philippines (Republic) National Museum. Glimpses of Philippine Culture. Manila, 1964. p.15-44)

320. _____. The pre-historic Filipino village. Progress (1960), 162-166.
    Peterson: A good reconstruction of prehistoric Philippine village life.
                 A   4   1

321. _____. The prehistoric foundations of Philippine culture. Solidarity 3, no. 2 (Feb. 1968), 69-93.

322. _____. Pre-history of the Philippines. Manila, 1967. 20p. (Aspects of Philippine Culture, 1) "First in a series of lectures presented by the National Museum and sponsored by Ambassador and Mrs. William McC. Blair, Jr."

323. _____. The prehistory of the Philippines. Hemisphere 12, no. 10 (Oct. 1968), 10-16.

324. _____. The Tabon caves excavation. Manuscript. (Published in 1970 as: The Tabon caves. Archaeological explorations on Palawan Island, Philippines. Manila, National Museum. 197p. (Monograph of the National Museum, no. 1)
    Suggested by Peterson.
    Peterson: Probably the most significant work done in the archae-
                 ology of the Philippines.
                 A   4   1

325. _____ and AVELINO LEGASPI. Pottery treasures of the national museum. Esso Silangan 13, no. 3 (Mar. 1968), 14-17.

326. GUTHE, CARL E. Distribution of sites visited by the University of Michigan Philippine Expedition, 1922-1925. Michigan Academy of Science, Arts and Letters. Papers 10 (1929), 79-89.
    Peterson: A check-list of sites found by Guthe.
                 A   3   1

I. GENERAL. ARCHAEOLOGY

        Solheim: Important for the history of Philippine archaeology.
                     A   3   7

327. _____. The University of Michigan Philippine expedition. AA n.s. 29, no. 1 (Jan.-Mar. 1927), 69-76.
        Solheim: Important for the history of Philippine archaeology.
                     A   4   7

328. HARRISSON, TOM. Ceramic crayfish and related vessels in Central Borneo, the Philippines and Sweden. SMJ n.s. 15, nos. 30/31 (Dec. 1967), 1-9.

329. _____. Gold: West Borneo and Philippine crafts compared. SMJ 16, nos. 32/33, n.s. (July/Dec. 1968), 77-84.

330. HOUSTON, CHARLES O. Progress in Philippine archaeology: 1953-1957. JEAS 5, no. 2 (Apr. 1956), 213-228.
        Peterson: H   3   1

331. JANSE, OLOV R. T. An archaeological expedition to Indo-China and the Philippines (Preliminary Report). Harvard Journal of Asiatic Studies 6, no. 2 (June 1941), 247-267. 32 plates.
        Solheim: Of interest for the history of Philippine archaeology.
                     A   3   1/2

332. _____. Archaeology of the Philippine Islands. Smithsonian Institution. Annual Report, 1946, Washington, D.C. Government Printing Office, 1947, 345-360. 15 plates.
        Solheim: A   3   1/2

333. _____. Notes on Chinese influences in the Philippines in pre-Spanish times. Harvard Journal of Asiatic Studies 8, no. 1 (Mar. 1944), 34-62. 17 plates.

334. JOCANO, F. LANDA. Beyer's theory on Filipino prehistory and culture: an alternative approach to the problem. (In: Zamora, Mario D., ed. Studies in Philippine anthropology (In honor of H. Otley Beyer). Quezon City, Alemar-Phoenix, 1967. p.128-150)

335. _____. The new stone age. Philippine Perspective; lectures on the prehistory and history of the Philippines. Ateneo de Manila, Manila, Nov. 13, 1963. 14p. Mimeographed.

336. KOENIGSWALD, G. H. R. VON. Fossil mammals from the Philippines. Proceedings of the 4th Far-Eastern Prehistory and the Anthropology Division of the 8th Pacific Science Congresses combined. Part I. (Second Fascicle: Section 1, p.339-362. 7 plates. Quezon City, National Research Council of the Philippines, U.P., 1956.
        Peterson: Descriptive account of fossil Pleistocene mammals found in the Philippines.
                     A   5   1
        Solheim: Preliminary report on fossil mammals collected by author in the Philippines.
                     D   5   1

337. LOCSIN, CECILIA Y. Lead-glazed wares excavated in the Philippines. [Manila] Research Foundation in Philippine Anthropology and Archaeology [1968] 24p.

36

I. GENERAL. ARCHAEOLOGY

(Manila trade pottery seminar. Introductory notes)

338. LOEWENSTEIN, JOHN. Neolithic stone gouges from the Malay archipelago and their northern prototypes. Anthropos 52, fasc. 5/6 (1957), 841-849.
      Peterson: Comparative data on stone adzes from elsewhere in Southeast Asia.
                         A   5   1

339. LOOFS, H. H. Aspects matériels d'un complexe mégalithique aux Philippines. Archéocivilisation n.s. 1, nos. 3/4 (1967), 40-42. 13 plates.

340. _____. Some remarks on "Philippine Megaliths." AS 3, no. 3 (Dec. 1965), 393-402.

341. MATTHEWS, J. The Kerubong hoard. PS 10, no. 3 (July 1962), 386-433.
      Solheim: Report on a hoard found in Malaya containing porcelains similar to porcelain found in the Philippines.
                         A   5   2/3

342. MILES, W. K. The Jar burial people and their place in Philippine history. Unpublished paper, Department of History, Graduate School, U.P., Quezon City, 1951.
      Cited in Stuart A. Schlegel, Preliminary bibliography of Philippine culture history, 11p.
      Solheim: H/A   3   1/2

343. PHILIPPINES (REPUBLIC) NATIONAL MUSEUM. DIVISION OF ANTHROPOLOGY. 50,000 years of Philippine pre-history. Esso Silangan 13, no. 3 (Mar. 1968), 12-13. Chart.

344. _____. UNESCO NATIONAL COMMISSION. The Philippines in pre-historic times; a handbook for the first National Exhibition of Filipino Pre-history and Culture. By Robert B. Fox. Manila, 1959. 40p. 20 plates. "Sponsored by the UNESCO National Commission of the Philippines with the cooperation of the National Museum."
      Solheim: A popular summary of Philippine prehistory.
                         A/E   4   1/2

345. RAHMANN, RUDOLF and ROSA C. P. TENAZAS. A brief review of the archaeological field work undertaken by the Department of Anthropology, University of San Carlos, Philippines, during the years 1961-64. Taipei, Formosa. University. Department of Archaeology and Anthropology. Bulletin. nos. 23/24 (Nov. 1964), 46-51.

346. ROCES, ALFREDO R. Philippine jewelry - pre-historic ornaments. Esso Silangan 13, no. 3 (Mar. 1968), 18-23.

347. ROXAS-LIM, AURORA. Chinese pottery as a basis for the study of Philippine proto-history. (In: Felix, Alfonso, ed. The Chinese in the Philippines, 1570-1770. v.1., Manila, Solidaridad Pub. House, 1966, p.223-245)
      Felix: Excellent study on a little researched subject.
                         Y   4   1
      Wickberg: Y   3   1

348. SCHEANS, DANIEL J. The evolution of the potter's wheel: the Philippines

data. AA 67, no. 6, pt. 1 (Dec. 1965), 1527-1529.
    Peterson: Archaeological and ethnographic evidence on the develop-
                     ment of the wheel in Philippine pottery.
                     A   4   7
    Solheim: A   3   7

349.   _____. A new view of Philippines pottery manufacture. SWJA 22, no. 2
(Summer 1966), 206-219.

350.   SCOTT, WILLIAM HENRY. Prehispanic source materials for the study of Philippine history. Manila, Univ. of Santo Tomas Press, 1968. 156p.

351.   SOLHEIM, WILHELM G., II. Archaeology in the Philippines. JEAS 1, no. 3
(Apr. 1952), 63-64.
        Peterson: A   3   7
        Solheim: Of interest for the history of archaeology in the Philip-
                     pines.
                     A   3   7

352.   _____. The functions of pottery in Southeast Asia--from the present to the
past. (In: Mason, Frederick R., ed. Ceramics and Man. New York, Viking
Fund Publications in Anthropology, No. 41, 1965. p.254-273)
        Peterson: Interesting discourse on the uses to which pottery has
                     been put in Southeast Asia.
                     A   4   7
        Solheim: A general study, making considerable use of Philippine
                     data.
                     A   4   7

353.   _____. Oceanian pottery manufacture. JEAS 1, no. 2 (Jan. 1952), 1-39.

354.   _____. Paddle decoration of pottery. JEAS 2, no. 1 (Oct. 1952), 35-45.
9 figs.
        Peterson: Description of the technique of paddle decoration and its
                     distribution.
                     A   3   7
        Solheim: Little data from the Philippines but of theoretical impor-
                     tance to the study of Philippine pottery, past and present.
                     A   4   7

355.   _____. Philippine archaeology. Archaeology 6, no. 3 (1953), 154-158.
        Peterson: A useful summary of Philippine
                     A   4   1
        Solheim: A general and popular summary of Philippine archaeology
                     through 1952.
                     A   3   1/2

356.   _____. Philippine notes. AP 7, nos. 1/2 (Summer/Winter 1963), 138-143.
2 plates.
        Solheim: New data and interpretation.
                     A   4/5   1

357.   _____. Pottery and the Malayo-Polynesians. Current Anthropology 5, no.5
(Dec. 1964), 360, 376-384.

I. GENERAL. ARCHAEOLOGY

> Spencer: Revision of ideas on regional pottery making, archae-
> ologic data.
> A   4   1

358. _____. Regional reports: Philippine Islands. AP 1, nos. 1/2 (Summer 1957),
101-107.
> Solheim: Report on current archaeological work.
> A   4   1

359. _____. Regional reports: Philippines. AP 2, no. 1 (Summer 1958), 62-63.
> Solheim: Reports on current archaeological work.
> A   4   1

360. _____. Regional reports: Philippines. AP 3, no. 1 (Summer 1959), 47-50.
> Solheim: Reports on current archaeological work.
> A   4   1

361. _____. Sa-huýnh related pottery in Southeast Asia. AP 3, no. 2 (Winter
1959), 177-188. 3 plates.
> Peterson: An attempt to interpret some similarities in pottery found
> generally in Southeast Asia.
> A   3   1
> Solheim: Relatively little Philippine data but of importance for
> demonstrating relationships between Philippines and South-
> east Asia.
> A   4/5   1

362. _____. Two major problems in Bornean (and Asian) ethnology and archaeology.
SMJ 9, nos. 13/14 n.s. (July/Dec. 1959), 1-5.
> Solheim: The report is concerned with the problems of two different
> pottery traditions--their distribution, relationships, etc.
> --found in the Philippines and widely in Southeast Asia.
> A   4   1

363. SULLIVAN, MICHAEL. Archaeology in the Philippines. Antiquity 30, no. 118
(June 1956), 68-79.
> Peterson: One of the best summaries of Philippine archaeology.
> A   4   1
> Solheim: A general and popular summary of Philippine archaeology
> through 1955.
> H/Q   3   1/2

364. VANOVERBERGH, MORICE P. und R. HEINE-GELDERN. Der Megalithkomplex auf der Philippinen-Insel Luzon. Anthropos 24, Fasc. 1/2 (Jan./Apr. 1929), 317-321.

365. VIRCHOW, RUDOLF. Ueber die Schädel der älteren Bevölkerung der Philippinen,
insbesondere über künstlich verunstaltete Schädel derselben. ZE 2 (1870),
151-158.

ARMED FORCES AND WAR

366. BACON, RAYMOND F. Philippine arrow poisons. PJS 3A, no. 1 (Feb. 1908), 41-44.

367. BAQUIRIN, BIENVENIDO V. Sociometric choice in school as a prediction of officer success. PSR 15, nos. 3/4 (July/Oct. 1967), 123-135.

368. GATES, JOHN M. An experiment in benevolent pacification: the U.S. Army in the Philippines, 1898-1902. Durham, North Carolina, 1967. 409p. Thesis (Ph.D.) - Duke Univ.

369. HERBELLA Y PÉREZ, MANUEL. Manual de construcciones y de fortificación de campaña en Filipinas. Madrid, Impr. del Memorial de ingenieros, 1882. 400p.

370. KRIEGER, HERBERT W. The collection of primitive weapons and armor of the Philippine Islands in the United States national museum. Washington, Government Printing Office, 1926. 128p. 21 plates. United States National Museum Bulletin 137.

371. TAYLOR, GEORGE E. The challenge of mutual security. (In: American Assembly. The United States and the Philippines, edited by Frank H. Golay. Englewood Cliffs, Prentice-Hall, 1966. p. 67-94)

BEHAVIOR PROCESS AND PERSONALITY

372. AGUILA, NORMA ALAMPAY. Cultural patterns and values in the Filipino community. Journal of Educational Research (Manila, Philippine Christian College). 2 (Mar. 1966), 138-143.
(Source: Index to Periodicals (U.P. Library. Filipiniana Section)
Guthrie: Y   3   6

373. _____. Fiestas and hospitality. CC 5, no. 6 (Nov./Dec. 1965), 23-26.
Bulatao: Simple but accurate.
                M   4   6

374. ALDABA-LIM, ESTEFANIA. The application of psychology to industrial management. SR 4, no. 3 (March 1963), 5-8.
Guthrie: For larger public.
                P   3   6

375. _____. Our increasing mental health problems. Progress (1959), 170-173.
Bulatao: P   3   6
Guthrie: General
                P   3   6

376. _____. The role of the psychologist in manpower development. SR (Jan. 1966), 12-18.
Guthrie: Application of general principles to Philippines.
                P   3   6

377. _____ and Gloria V. Javillonar. Achievement motivation in Filipino entrepreneurship. International Social Science Journal 20, no. 3 (1968), 397-
411.

378. The anatomy of Philippine psychology. Unitas 38, no. 4 (Dec. 1965), 477-575.
Contents:
Is there a Filipino psychology? by Jesus M. Merino.
Oriental traits and the psychology of the Filipinos, by Jesus Merino.
Influence of Spanish culture of the Filipinos, by Vicente Rosales.
The Child in the Fil-American setting, by Fernando Hofilena.
Typologies and the Filipino temperament, by Emmanuel Vit. Samson.
Inferiority complex - a Filipino trait? by Josefa G. Estrada.
Peculiar patterns of behaviour in Filipino setting, by Jose A. Samson.
Religiosity and nationalism among the Filipinos, by Jesus Merino.
The Ningas Kugon and the Mañana habit, by Adoracion Ariona.
The hospitality and loyalty of the Filipinos, by Josefa G. Estrada.
Understanding the Filipino character and the prevention of crime, by
Eliseo Vibar.
Modern changes in behavioral patterns and future directions in the
Filipino psychology, by Emmanuel Vit. Samson.
Bulatao: -   3   6
Guthrie: History and present status of psychology.
                -       3   6

379. BARNETT, MILTON L. Hiya, shame and guilt: preliminary consideration of the
concepts as analytical tools for Philippine social science. PSR 14, no. 4
(Oct. 1966), 276-282.
Bulatao: Tentative criticisms of a current concept.
                E   4   6
Guthrie: One of a small number of significant papers on this topic.
                E   5   6

380. BATESON, MARY CATHERINE. Insight in bicultural context. PS 16, no. 4 (Oct.
1968), 605-621.

381. BLUMENTRITT, FERDINAND. Völkerpsychologisches in der Philippinenfrage.
Deutsche Rundschau 25, heft 8 (Mai 1899), 234-241.
Jocano: A   3   3

382. BULATAO, JAIME. Changing social values. PS 10, no. 2 (Apr. 1962), 206-214.
Guthrie   P   5   6

383. _____. Conflict of values in home and school. Guidance and Personnel Jour-
nal. Manila, Philippine Guidance and Personnel Association, no. 1 (Nov. 1965),
50-53.
Reprint: EQ 13, no. 4 (Apr. 1966), 16-22.
Bulatao: Analysis of one aspect in Philippine culture change.
                P   4   6
Guthrie: P   4   6

384. _____. Guidance trends in the Philippines. PAGE (Philippine Association for
Graduate Education) Yearbook No. 1 (1963), 117-122.
Cited in Ateneo de Manila University, Faculty publications as of February,
1967. p.18.

Bulatao: Evaluative report on situation of guidance and counsel-
                  ling.
                  P   4   6
Guthrie: P   4   6

385. _____. The Hiya system in Filipino culture. Philippine Educational Forum
14, no. 1 (Mar. 1965), 14-28.
Cited in Index to Philippine periodicals. v.10, p.34.
     Bulatao: A working out of concepts enunciated in earlier articles.
                       P   4   6
     Guthrie: P   4   6

386. _____. Hiya. PS 12, no. 3 (July 1964), 424-438.
     Bulatao: Source for phenomenological data and analysis.
                       P   5   6
     Guthrie: A definitive paper.
                       P   5   6

387. _____. The new Filipino. Manila. Far Eastern University. Faculty Journal
11, no. 2 (2nd Quarter 1966/67), 18-22.

388. _____. New psychological concepts and their application to nursing. Proceedings of the First Convocation on Nursing and the Behavioral Sciences,
(Quezon City, U.P., 1960).
Cited in Ateneo de Manila University, Faculty publications as of February,
1967. p.18.
     Bulatao: P   3   6
     Guthrie: P   3   6

389. _____. Personal preferences of Filipino students. PSR 11, nos. 3/4 (July/
Oct. 1963), 168-178.
Reprint: Symposium on the Filipino Personality (Manila: Psychological Asso-
ciation of the Philippines, 1965), p. 7-16.
     Bulatao: Hard data from tests comparing U.S. and Philippine samples.
                       P   5   6
     Guthrie: P   4   6

390. _____. Personalism versus efficiency in business. Scholar 18, no. 3
(1966), 31, 32, 49.
Cited in Ateneo de Manila University, Faculty publications as of February,
1967. p.19.
     Bulatao: Has become classical reading for business students.
                       P   4   6
     Guthrie: P   5   6

391. _____. Philippine values I: The manileño's mainsprings. PS 10, no. 1
(Jan. 1962), 45-81.
Reprint: PSR, vol. 10, nos. 1/2 (Jan./Apr. 1962), 7-26.
Reprint: Four Readings on Philippine Values, IPC Papers No. 2, (Quezon City:
Institute of Philippine Culture, 1964), p. 50-86.
     Bulatao: Original projective test data on Manila thinking.
                       P   5   6
     Guthrie: A classic paper.
                       P   5   6

392. _____. Psychotherapeutic attitudes and techniques in nation building. SR 6, nos. 1/2 (Jan./Feb. 1965), 3-7.
  Bulatao: Application to Philippines of modern group techniques.
        P   4   6
  Guthrie: P   3   6

393. _____. Self-discovery in the Filipino. SR 9 (May/June 1968), 24-27.

394. _____. The society page and its value system. PSR 12, nos. 3/4 (July/Oct. 1964), 139-151.
  Bulatao: Survey of attitudes to high society and society page.
        P   5   6
  Guthrie: Very original.
        P   5   6

395. _____. Sociological aspects in the utilization of research findings. (In: Research in the Philippines: a critical evaluation. A symposium sponsored by Gamma Sigma Delta, Honor Society of Agriculture, Society for the Advancement of Research in Cooperation with the National Science Development Board. p.88-91)
  Bulatao: P   4   6

396. _____. Some assumptions underlying a testing program. Proceedings of the Workshop-Conference on Guidance and Counseling, (San Pablo City: Sept. 1962), 28-30.
Cited in Ateneo de Manila University, Faculty publications as of February, 1967. p.18.
  Bulatao: P   3   6
  Guthrie: P   3   6

397. _____. Split-level Christianity (comments on Dr. F. Landa Jocano's paper on "Conversion and the patterning of Christian experience in Malitbog, Central Panay, Philippines." PSR 13, no. 2 (Apr. 1965), 119-121.
  Bulatao: P   3   6
  Guthrie: P   5   6

398. _____. Split-level Christianity. p.1-18. Quezon City, Ateneo de Manila Univ. Press, 1966. 73p.
  Bulatao: An essential element in the analysis of Filipino personality and behavior.
        P   4   6

399. _____. Unfolding the mystery: a social-psychological view of the Philippine church. Home Life (Manila, St. Paul Publications) (Apr. 1965), 41-47.
Cited in Ateneo de Manila University. Faculty publications, 1967. p.18.
  Bulatao: A good overview of the dynamics of development of the Philippine church.
        P   4   7
  Guthrie: P   3   6

400. _____ and ISABEL REYES-JUAN. Intellectual and creativity test factors in high school. PJP 1, no. 1 (Nov. 1968), 42-52.

401. CALDERON, AURELIO B. An analysis of Steinberg's use of walang hiya to explain Filipino elite collaboration in World War II. PSR 15, nos. 3/4 (July/Oct.

1967), 141-150.

402. CARREON, MANUEL LINGAD. Philippine studies in mental measurement. Yonkers-on-Hudson, New York, World Book Company, 1926. 175p.
    Guthrie: Classic work.
                  Y   5   4

403. CARROLL, JOHN and SALVADOR A. PARCO. Social organization in a crisis: the Taal disaster; a research report submitted to the Asia Foundation. Manila Philippine Sociological Society, 1966. 59p. (PSS Special papers, 1)
    Bulatao: A very scholarly gathering of data and analysis.
                  Z   5   6
    Guthrie: E   4   6

404. CORDERO, FELICIDAD V. Contemporary Philippine value orientation. Manila. University of the East. College of Liberal Arts and Sciences. Journal 3, no. 2 (1966/67), 85-102.

405. CORTEZ, OLIMPIO C. The compadre system. CC 5, no. 6 (Nov./Dec. 1965), 19-22.
    Bulatao: Simple but accurate.
                  M   4   6

406. COSTA, HORACIO DE LA. The concept of progress and traditional values in a Christian society. (In: Bellah, Robert N., ed. Religion and progress in modern Asia. New York, Free Press [1965], p.15-29)
    Bulatao: Good analysis.
                  H   4   7
    Guthrie: H   4   6

407. _____. The need for a social conscience. Heritage 1, no. 1 (July 1967), 6-11.

408. COVAR, PROSPERO R. Trends of change in the Filipino family. CC 5, no. 6 (Nov./Dec. 1965), 12-18.
    Bulatao: Simple but accurate.
                  M   4   6

409. CUYUGAN, RUBEN SANTOS. Changing social values in the Philippines. Philippine Educational Forum 11, no. 2 (June 1962), 1-10.
    Cited in Index to Philippine Periodicals. v.7, p. 94.
    Guthrie: Z   4   6

410. DONAHUE, ELIZABETH ANN. A study of the psychological characteristics of three sub-groups in a religious congregation of women as revealed by a battery of standardized tests. 1963. 177p. Thesis (M.A.) - Ateneo de Manila Univ.
    Doherty: Very interesting study.
                  Z   3   7

411. ENVERGA, TOBIAS Y. The comparative role expectations of Filipino and American teachers with regard to the administrator. Chicago, 1954. Thesis (Ph.D.) - Univ. of Chicago.

412. ESTOLAS, JOSEFINA V. Relationship of nicknames to Filipino children's self-perception. Lincoln, Nebraska, 1964. 88p. Thesis (Ed.D.) - Univ. of Nebraska

Teachers College.

413. FELIPE, ABRAHAM I. Social desirability and endorsement on the EPPS: prelimi-
      nary findings. PJP 1, no. 1 (Nov. 1968), 62-67.

414. FLORO, CHARLOTTE. Group Rorschach method: preliminary studies on Filipinos.
      1965. 187p. Thesis (M.A.) - U.P.
           Bulatao: Carefully collected data on the Rorschach test.
                           P   5   6
           Guthrie: P   3   6

415. FOX, ROBERT B. The Filipino concept of self-esteem. (In: Human Relations
      Area Files, Inc. Area handbook on the Philippines. 1956. Univ. of Chicago
      for the Human Relations Area Files, Inc. v.1, 430-436)
           Bulatao: E   5   6
           Guthrie: E   5   6

416. GAVINO, JASMIN A. A comparison of responses to personality test items of
      English-speaking Filipinos in English and in Filipino. PJP 1, no. 1 (Nov.
      1968), 68-70.

417. GODUCO-AGULAR, C. and R. WINTROB. Folie à famille in the Philippines. Psychi-
      atric Quarterly 38, no. 2 (Apr. 1964), 278-291.

418. GOROSPE, VITALIANO R. Christian renewal of Filipino values. PS 14, no. 2
      (Apr. 1966), 191-227.
           Bulatao: Q   3   6

419. _____. Selected bibliography on Filipino values. PSR 14, no. 3 (July 1966),
      173-179.
           Bulatao: Useful. Missed some of the more technical items.
                           Q   4   6

420. GUERRERO, SYLVIA H. and GELIA T. CASTILLO. A preliminary study on alienation.
      PSR 14, no. 2 (Apr. 1966), 85-93.

421. GUIANG, HONESTA F. A comparison of expressed values of prospective teachers
      in American and Philippine cultures. 1963. 146p. Thesis (Ph.D.) - Syracuse
      Univ.
           Guthrie: Y   3   6

422. GUTHRIE, GEORGE M. Cultural preparation for the Philippines. (In: Textor,
      Robert B., ed. Cultural frontiers of the Peace Corps. Cambridge, Mass.,
      M.I.T. Press, 1966. p.15-34)

423. _____. The Philippine temperament. (In: Guthrie, George M., ed. Six per-
      spectives on the Philippines. Manila, Bookmark, 1968. p.49-83)

424. _____. The primary mental abilities in the Philippines. Paper read at the
      Tenth Pacific Science Congress, Honolulu, Hawaii, Aug. 20/Sept. 6, 1961.
      13p. Mimeographed.
           Bulatao: P   5   6

425. _____. Structure of abilities in a non-Western culture. Journal of Educa-
      tional Psychology 54, no. 2 (Apr. 1963), 94-103.

I. GENERAL. BEHAVIOR PROCESS AND PERSONALITY

        Bulatao: Pioneer work in an important area in education.
                      P   5   6
        Guthrie: P   5   6

426. _____ and FORTUNATA M. AZORES. Philippine interpersonal behavior patterns. (In: Bello, Walden F. and Alfonso de Guzman II, eds. Modernization: its impact in the Philippines, III. Quezon City, Ateneo de Manila Univ. Press, 1968. p.3-63) IPC Papers No. 6.

427. _____ and PEPITA J. JACOBS. Child rearing and personality development in the Philippines. Univ. Park, Pennsylvania State Univ. Press, 1966. 223p.
        Guthrie: P   5   6
        Nurge: Limited to Manila and surrounding suburbs.
                      P   3   6
        Polson: A rich study on child-rearing attitudes and some suggestive hypotheses on the relation of child rearing to personality development.
                      P   5   6

428. GUTHRIE, HELEN A., GEORGE M. GUTHRIE and AMANDA TAYAG. Nutritional status and intellectual performance in a rural Philippine community. PJP 1, no. 1 (Nov. 1968), 28-34.

429. HARE, A. PAUL. Factors associated with peace corps volunteer success in the Philippines. HO 25, no. 2 (Summer 1966), 150-153.
        Guthrie: Z   5   6

430. HARTENDORP, A. V. H. Eastern and Western psychology. PM 33, no. 7 (July 1936), 340-342.
        Guthrie: J   4   4

431. _____. Results of the application of the Otis group intelligence scale to Filipino school teachers. PJE 3, no. 3 (Sept. 1920), 54-64.
        Guthrie: Some of the earliest psychological research.
                      P   5   4

432. _____. Some results with intelligence tests in the Philippine Islands. PJS 20, no. 3 (Mar. 1922), 287-307.
        Guthrie: P   5   4

433. HAYDEN, DAVID LEE. Factors of intelligence of college students in the Philippines as determined by the Otis Quick-Scoring Mental Ability Test, Gamma, FM, and the measure of intellectual maturation. 1968. 145p. Thesis (Ph.D.) - Catholic Univ.

434. HERRADURA, ELMA SISON. The ideals and values of Filipino adolescents. Berkeley, 1962. 168p. Thesis (Ph.D.) - Univ. of California.

435. HOFILEÑA, FERNANDO P. The role of the special child study center in mental hygiene in the Philippines. Unitas 37, no. 4 (Dec. 1964), 584-589.
        Guthrie: D   4   6

436. HOLLNSTEINER, MARY R. Philippine organizational behavior: personalism and group solidarity. Philippine Library Association. Bulletin n.s. 1, no. 2 (June 1965), 75-82.

Guthrie: Z   4   6

437. _____. Social control and Filipino personality. PSR 11, nos. 3/4 (July/
Oct. 1963), 184-188.
     Bulatao: E   5   6
     Guthrie: Z   5   6

438. _____. Social structure and reciprocity. Paper read at a symposium on "Aspects of Lowland Philippine Social Structure," Tenth Pacific Science Congress,
Honolulu, Aug. 21/Sept. 6, 1961.
     Bulatao: E   5   6
     Guthrie: Classic paper.
                E   5   6

439. HORSLEY, MARGARET W. Sangley: the formation of anti-Chinese feeling in the
Philippines--a cultural study of the stereotypes of prejudice. 1950. 239p.
Thesis (Ph.D.) - Columbia Univ.
     Wickberg: Shows how the Spanish experience with the Moors and Jews in
               Spain conditioned their attitudes toward the Chinese.
               E   4   2

440. HUNT, CHESTER L. Cultural barriers to point 4. Antioch Review 14, (Summer
1954), 159-167.
     Coller: Acute, terse "memo" on basic points often overlooked.
               Z   4   6
     Guthrie: Z   4   6

441. _____. Variation, group behavior, and the social self. (In: Hunt, Chester
L. and others. Sociology in the Philippine Setting. Rev. ed. Quezon City,
Phoenix Publishing House, 1963. p.38-54)
     Guthrie: Z   5   6

442. _____ and RICHARD W. COLLER. Philippine cultural values. (In: Hunt,
Chester L. and others. Sociology in the Philippine Setting. Rev. ed. Quezon City, Phoenix Publishing House, 1963. p.55-71)
     Guthrie: Z   5   6

443. JESUS, JOSE P. DE. Self-acceptance and creativity among college freshmen.
PJP 1, no. 1 (Nov. 1968), 18-27.

444. KRAPF, E. EDUARDO. A survey of mental health conditions in the Philippines.
Manila, World Health Organization. 1960. 22p. Mimeographed.
     Guthrie: D   4   6

445. LAPUZ, LOURDES V. Resistances in the Filipino to economic progress.
Comments by Francis Parisi and Concepcion Rodil-Martires. (In: Madigan,
Francis C., ed. Human factors in Philippine rural development. Cagayan de
Oro City, Xavier University. 1967. Xavier University Studies. Study no. 1.
p. 112-124)

446. LAWLESS, ROBERT. The foundation for culture-and-personality research in the
Philippines. AS 5, no. 1 (Apr. 1967), 101-136.

447. LUMBERA, BIENVENIDO. Literary notes on the Filipino personality. PSR 11,
nos. 3/4 (July/Oct. 1963), 163-168.

I. GENERAL. BEHAVIOR PROCESS AND PERSONALITY

> Bulatao: Analysis of Filipino personality from Philippine literary forms.
> Q   5   7

448. LYNCH, FRANK, comp. Four readings on Philippine values. 2d rev. ed. Quezon City, Ateneo de Manila Univ. Press, 1964. 113p. (IPC Papers, no. 2)
> Contents:
>   Social acceptance, by Frank Lynch.
>   Reciprocity in the lowland Philippines, by Mary Hollnsteiner.
>   The Manileño's mainsprings, by Jaime C. Bulatao.
>   Filipino entrepreneurship in manufacturing, by John J. Carroll.
> Bulatao: A classic, basic reader in Philippine ethnography.
>   E   5   6
> Coller: A compilation which is interdisciplinary--it drew attention to needed areas of study by its pilot studies on "what makes Filipinos tick."
>   E   5   6
> Guthrie: A basic reference book.
>   E   5   6

449. _____. Philippine values II: Social acceptance. PS 10, no. 1 (Jan. 1962), 82-99.
> Bulatao: E   5   6
> Guthrie: E   5   6

450. _____. Social acceptance (In: Lynch, Frank, compiler, Four readings on Philippine values. 2d rev. ed. Quezon City, Ateneo de Manila Univ. Press, 1968. Rev. ed. p.1-21) (IPC Papers, no. 2)
> Bulatao: E   5   6
> Guthrie: E   5   6

451. MADIGAN, FRANCIS C. The farmer said no; a study of background factors associated with dispositions to cooperate with or be resistant to community development projects. Diliman, Q. C., Community Development Research Council, U.P., 1962. 359p.
> Bulatao: Research very carefully done and interpreted.
>   Z   5   6
> Coller: Sophisticated analysis done in Mindanao using field study plus sample statistical techniques.
>   Z   5   6
> Guthrie: Important book.
>   Z   5   6
> Polson: Research report on a competent study of resistance to change.
>   Z   5   6
> Villanueva: Excellent statistical analysis of a social-political phenomenon.
>   Z   5   6

452. MAGUIGAD, L. C. Psychiatry in the Philippines. American Journal of Psychiatry 121, no. 1 (July 1964), 21-25.
> Guthrie: D   4   6

453. MIÑOZA, AURORA ABEAR. Relationship of physical, socio-economic, and attitudinal factors to elementary school training and academic achievement of secondary pupils. 1957. 114p. Thesis (Ph.D.) - Univ. of Michigan.
> Guthrie: P   5   6

454.   PACANA, HONESTO CH.   Notes on a Filipino rule of conduct: non-interference.
       PSR 6, no. 1 (Jan. 1958), 29-30.
          Guthrie: Z   5   6

455.   PADILLA, SINFOROSO G. and ESTEFANIA ALDABA-LIM.   Psychology in the Philip-
       pines. SR 2, no. 11 (Nov. 1961), 6-10.
          Guthrie: P   4   6

456.   _____.   State and trends in psychology in the Philippines.   (In: Philip-
       pines (Republic) National Science Development Board. Inter-Disciplinary
       Symposia Proceedings, National Science and Technology Week, Nov. 20-26, 1961.
       Theme: "State of and Trends in Science and Technology in the Philippines."
       Area VI- Social Sciences. [1963?] 106p. Mimeographed. p.87-95, Discussion:
       p.96-106)
          Bulatao: One of few histories of Philippine Psychology.
                          P and P 4   6
          Guthrie: Excellent summary.
                          P and P 5   6

457,   PANLASIGUI, ISIDORO.   The psychology of the Filipino people.   Far Eastern Eco-
       nomic Review 21, no. 25 (Dec. 20, 1956), 811-813.
          Guthrie: P   4   6

458.   PASCASIO, EMY M.   Codes of behavior: the relations between linguistic and
       nonlinguistic behavioral patterns. PSR 11, nos. 3/4 (July/Oct. 1963), 243-
       250.
          Guthrie: L   5   6

459.   PEABODY, DEAN.   Group judgments in the Philippines: their evaluative and de-
       scriptive aspects.   (In: Bello, Walden F. and Alfonso de Guzman II, eds.
       Modernization: its impact in the Philippines, III. Quezon City, Ateneo de
       Manila Univ. Press, 1968, p.114-128) IPC Papers, No. 6. Also published in
       Journal of Personality and Social Psychology 10, no. 3 (Nov. 1968), 290-300.

460.   PELAEZ, EMMANUEL.   Traditional values in Philippine society as deterrents to
       progress.   (In: Madigan, Francis C., ed. Human factors in Philippine rural
       development. Cagayan de Oro City, Xavier Univ., 1967. Xavier Univ. Studies,
       Study No. 1. p.4-10)

461.   PSYCHOLOGICAL ASSOCIATION OF THE PHILIPPINES.   Symposium on the Filipino per-
       sonality. Manila, n.p. 1965. 45p. Also published in PSR 11, nos. 3/4 (July/
       Oct. 1963)
          Bulatao: A basic compilation of studies on Filipino personality.
                          P   5   6
          Guthrie: Important.
                          P   5   6

462.   RABIN, A. I. and JOSEFINA A. LIMUACO.   A comparison of the connotative meaning
       of Rorschach's inkblots for American and Filipino college students. Journal
       of Social Psychology 72, second half (Aug. 1967), 197-203.

463.   REYES, BALTAZAR and LOURDES LAPUZ.   The practice of psychiatry in the Philip-
       pines. Internal Medicine; Official Journal of the Philippine College of Phy-
       sicians 1, no. 3 (July/Sept. 1963), 161-165.
          Bulatao: P   4   6

464. ROMUALDEZ, NORBERTO. The Psychology of the Filipino; lecture delivered in the hall of the Ateneo de Manila on Feb. 13, 1924. Baguio, Mt. Province, Catholic School Press, 1925. 74p.

465. ROSALES, VICENTE. The influence of Spanish culture on the psychology of the Filipino. Unitas 38, no. 4 (Dec. 1965), 498-504.

466. SAMSON, EMMANUEL V. Modern changes in behavioral patterns. Unitas 38, no. 4 (Dec. 1965), 570-575.
     Guthrie: P   4   6

467. _____. Typologies and the Filipino temperament. Unitas 38, no. 4 (Dec. 1965) 511-516.
     Guthrie: P   4   6

468. _____ and JOSE A. SAMSON. The applicability of the Minnesota multiphasic personality inventory to Filipino subjects. Unitas 33, no. 3 (July/Sept. 1960), 610-620.
     Guthrie: P   4   6

469. SAMSON, JOSE A. Is there a Filipino psychology? Unitas 38, no. 4 (Dec. 1965), 477-487.
     Guthrie: P   4   6

470. _____. Peculiar patterns of behavior in Filipino setting. Unitas 38, no. 4 (Dec. 1965), 524-536.
     Guthrie: P   4   6

471. _____. The Rorschach technique applied to Filipinos. Unitas 33, no. 4 (Oct./Dec. 1960), 878-894.
     Guthrie: P   4   6

472. _____. Schizophrenia among Filipino children. Unitas 38, no. 2 (June 1965), 298-310.
     Guthrie: P   4   6

473. SCHUH, ALLEN J. and CARMENCITA C. QUESADA. Attitudes of Filipino and American college students assessed with the semantic differential. Journal of Social Psychology 72, Second Half (Aug. 1967), 301-302.

474. SECHREST, LEE. Symptoms of mental disorder in the Philippines. PSR 11, nos. 3/4 (July/Oct. 1963), 189-206.
     Bulatao: One of few such studies in its field.
                     P   5   6
     Guthrie: Important.
                     P   5   6

475. SINGH, TEJ PRATAP. Some impressions on Indian and Filipino value systems. PSR 13, no. 4 (Oct. 1965), 210-215.

476. SOLIS, M. M. A pilot study of the SCRIT (Safran Culture Reduced Intelligence Test) in the Philippines. Alberta Psychologist 8, no. 4 (1968), 8-31. Cited in Perceptual Cognitive Development, Dec. 1968, p.1330.

477. STONE, RICHARD L. Private transitory ownership of public property: one key

to understanding public behavior: I-the driving game. (In: Bello, Walden F. and Maria Clara Roldan, eds. Modernization: its impact in the Philippines. Quezon City, Institute of Philippine Culture, Ateneo de Manila Univ. Press, 1967. Papers, No. 4, p.53-63)

478. STOODLEY, BARTLETT H. A cross-cultural study of structure and conflict in social norms. American Journal of Sociology 65, no. 1 (July 1959), 39-48.
      Bulatao: Z   5   6
      Guthrie: Z   5   6

479. TIRYAKIAN, EDWARD A. Occupational satisfaction and aspiration in an underdeveloped country: the Philippines. Economic Development and Cultural Change 7, no. 4 (July 1959), 431-444.
      Guthrie: Z   5   6
      Polson: A suggestive paper on a thinly studied topic.
                     Z   5   6

480. UNITED CHURCH OF CHRIST IN THE PHILIPPINES. Special issue on: Filipino personality and social change. CC 5, no. 6 (Nov./Dec. 1965).
      Contents:
          Social control and Filipino personality, by Mary R. Hollnsteiner, p.5-11.
          Trends of changes in the Filipino family, by Prospero R. Covar, p.12-18.
          The Compadre system, by O. C. Cortez, p.19-22.
          Fiestas and hospitality, by Norma Alampay-Aguila, p.23-26.
      Bulatao: Simple but accurate.
                     M   4   6

481. VARIAS, RODOLFO R. Mental hygiene for the Philippines. Philippine Journal of Public Health 8, no. 1 (Jan./Mar. 1963), 16-26.
      Guthrie: D   3   6

482. _____. Psychiatry and the Filipino personality. PSR 11, nos. 3/4 (July/Oct. 1963), 179-184.
      Guthrie: D   3   6

483. VARIAS DE GUZMAN, JOVITA and RODOLFO R. VARIAS. Psychology of Filipinos; studies and essays. Manila, Vilfran, 1965. 239p.
      Guthrie: P   5   6

BIBLIOGRAPHY OF BIBLIOGRAPHIES

484. BERNARDO, GABRIEL A. Bibliography of Philippine bibliographies: 1593-1961. Edited by Natividad P. Verzosa. Quezon City, Ateneo de Manila Univ., 1968. 192p. (Occasional Papers of the Department of History. Bibliographical series no. 2)

485. BLAIR, EMMA H. and JAMES A. ROBERTSON. The Philippine Islands, 1493-1898. v.53: Bibliography. Cleveland, Ohio, Arthur H. Clark Co., 1908. 433p.

486. HOUSTON, CHARLES O. Philippine bibliography. I. An annotated preliminary bibliography of Philippine bibliographies (since 1900). Manila, Philippines,

The University of Manila, 1960. 69,21p.

487. SAITO, SHIRO. The Philippines: a review of bibliographies. Honolulu, Hawaii, East-West Center Library, East-West Center, 1966. 80p. (Occasional Papers No. 5)

BUILDINGS, TOOLS AND EQUIPMENT

488. CONCEPCIÓN, LEONARDO. Architecture in the Philippines. Manila, 1967. 16p. (Aspects of Philippine Culture, 2)
"Second in a series of lectures presented by the National Museum and sponsored by Ambassador and Mrs. William McC. Blair, Jr."

489. DIAZ-TRECHUELO SPINOLA, MARÍA LOURDES. Arquitectura española en Filipinas, 1565-1800. Prólogo del Excmo. Sr. Dr. D. Diego Angulo Iñiguez. Sevilla, 1959. 562p. (Publicaciones de la Escuela de Estudios Hispano-Americanos de Sevilla, 117)

490. HARTENDORP, A. V. H. Philippine regional architecture. PM 31, no. 6 (June 1934), 231-232.

491. LOCSIN, LEANDRO V. A 20th Century view of Philippine folk architecture. Philippine Quarterly 2, no. 2 (1962), 6-9.
Cited by Casiño in General Education Journal 12 (1966-67), p.265.

492. MANAWIS, MARIANO D. Adoy builds a house. PM 36, no. 1 (Jan. 1939), 21-22, 27-28.

493. OCAMPO, GALO B. Cultural patterns in Philippine architecture. SR 6, nos. 9/11 (Sept./Nov. 1965), 21-24.

CLOTHING, ADORNMENT AND MATERIALS

494. BARNEY, CHARLES NORTON. Circumcision and flagellation among the Filipinos. Association of Military Surgeons of the U.S. Journal (1903), 158-161.

495. BELEN, HERMOGENES F. Philippine creative handcrafts with some illustrations by Paciente B. Udan. Manila, Philippine Education Co., 1952. 246p.

496. BEYER, H. OTLEY. Notes on the types of spinning and weaving apparatus in use in the Philippines and the possibility of making a collection of the same. General Philippine Ethnography, v.4 (1916), Paper 107.
Cited by Manuel, in Zamora, Studies in Philippine anthropology, 1967, p.33.
        Spencer   E   4   7

497. DICHOSO, FERMIN. Notes on barbershop culture in the Philippines. (Anthropica: Gedenkschrift zum 100. Geburtstag von P. Wilhelm Schmidt) Studia

Instituti Anthropos 21 (1968), 79-85.

498. GALANG, RICARDO E. Filing and blackening of teeth among some Philippine ethnic groups. PJS 75, no. 4 (Aug. 1941), 425-431. 2 plates.
    Intengan: Describes the erstwhile widespread practice of filing and blackening of teeth among some Philippine ethnic groups.
                    C   3   5

499. GUTHE, CARL EUGEN. Gold-decorated teeth from the Philippine Islands. Michigan Academy of Science, Arts and Letters 20 (1935), 7-22. 2 plates.

500. HARRISSON, TOM H. The "palang", its history and proto-history in west Borneo and the Philippines. Royal Asiatic Society, Malaysian Branch. Journal 37, pt. 2, no. 206 (Dec. 1964), 162-174. 2 plates.

501. Hartendorp, A. V. H. The Philippine decorative design contest. PM 29, no. 8 (Jan. 1933), 352-353, 378-379.

502. MACEDA, GENEROSA S. Some methods of circumcision in the Philippines. PJS 58, no. 4 (Dec. 1935), 513-519. 2 plates.
    Intengan: Paper describes some methods of circumcision employed in different regions of the Philippines and its historical background.
                    C   4   4

503. MILLER, HUGO H. Philippine hats. Manila, Bureau of Printing, 1910. 61p. (Philippine Islands. Bureau of Education. Bulletin No. 33)

504. _____. Some commercial notes on baskets. Philippine Craftsman 2, no. 7 (Jan. 1914), 485-505.
    Intengan: An article on Philippine basket industry, indicating that such products are bought on account of their utility, durability and beauty.
                    C   3   4

505. _____ and OTHERS. Philippine baskets. Philippine Craftsman 1, no. 1 (July 1912), 1-47. 39 plates.

506. _____ and _____. Philippine mats. Philippine Craftsman. Part I. 1, no. 3 (Sept. 1912), 157-203. 33 plates. Part II. 1, no. 4 (Oct. 1912), 277-322. Plates 34-58. Part III. 1, no. 5 (Nov. 1912), 401-426. Plates 59-79.

507. MINTON, FRANK L. The Philippine shoe industry. PM 27, no. 11 (Apr. 1931), 678-679, 700-701.

508. PARKER, LUTHER. Some common baskets of the Philippines. Philippine Craftsman 3, no. 1 (1914), 1-25.
    Cited in HRAF, Area Handbook on the Philippines. 1956. v.4, p.1813.
    Intengan: An illustrated article on some common baskets of Christian Filipinos in several ethnic groups which should interest teachers and students of basketry.
                    C   4   4

509. REYES, CONRADO DE LOS and GUILLERMO MENDOZA. Revival of handicraft training in schools. Commerce (Manila) 48 (June 1952), 10-11.

I. GENERAL. CLOTHING, ADORNMENT AND MATERIALS

Source: Index to Periodicals (U.P. Library. Filipiniana Section)
Intengan: A brief account of handicraft work in the Philippines since
the time of Magellan.
C   4   6

510. ROBINSON, C. B. Philippine hats. PJS 6C, no. 2 (June 1911), 93-131. 8
plates.
Intengan: An extensive article on Philippine hats giving description
and botanical classification of materials used, history,
origin, kinds, etc.
C   4   4

511. SCHNEIDER, E. E. Dental decoration. AA 23, no. 3 (July/Sept. 1921), 379-
380.

512. STIFEL, LAURENCE DAVIS. The textile industry; a case study of industrial
development in the Philippines. Ithaca, New York. Southeast Asia Program,
Department of Asian Studies, Cornell University, 1963. 199p. Southeast Asia
Program, Data Paper, No. 49.

513. WALLACE, LYSBETH. Hand-weaving in the Philippines, prepared for the Government
of the Philippines. New York, United Nations Technical Assistance Program,
1953. 94p. (United Nations. [Documents] ST/TAA/K/ Philippines/3)
Spencer: Art and economic summary of handicraft industries.
C   4   7

COMMUNICATIONS

514. ALBERT, LEO N. and OTHERS. Developmental book activities and needs in the
Philippines. New York, Wolf Management Services, 1966. 134p.

515. CARLOTA, DAISY J. Primacy and recency in impression formation as a function
of the timing of communications and measures. PJP 1, no. 1 (Nov. 1968), 71-
78.

516. CASTRO, JOSE LUNA. Press. (In: Feliciano, Gloria D. and Crispulo J.
Icban, Jr., eds. Philippine mass media in perspective. Quezon City, Capitol
Publishing House, 1967. p.1-21)

517. CRUZ, ANDRES CRISTOBAL. Book publishing. (In: Feliciano, Gloria D. and
Crispulo J. Icban, Jr., eds. Philippine mass media in perspective. Quezon
City, Capitol Publishing House, 1967. p.231-248)

518. DE YOUNG, JOHN E. Target: barrio; a study of communication problems on the
barrio level. Quezon City, Social Science Research Center, U.P., 1955. 101p.
Mimeographed.
Coller: Z   5   6

519. _____ and CHESTER HUNT. Communication channels and functional literacy in
the Philippine barrio. Journal of Asian Studies 22, no. 1 (Nov. 1962), 67-77.

I. GENERAL. COMMUNICATIONS

Coller:	Shorter version of monograph done on this study. Analysis and interpretation make it a useful source.	
	Z 5 6	
Spencer:	Good study of how barrio folk learn the news.	
	Z 5 6	
Ward:	Evaluates different languages as means of communications. No language data as such is given.	
	Z 3 6	
Warren:	Z 5 6	

520. FELICIANO, GLORIA D. and CRISPULO J. ICBAN, JR. Communication research. (In: Feliciano, Gloria D. and Crispulo J. Icban, Jr., eds. Philippine mass media in perspective. Quezon City, Capitol Publishing House, 1967. p.249-281.

521. _____ and _____, eds. Philippine mass media in perspective. Quezon City, Capitol Publishing House, 1967. 352p.

522. JAMIAS, JUAN F. The effects of belief system styles on the communication and adoption of farm practices. 1964. 100p. Thesis (Ph.D.) - Michigan State Univ.
　　　Sta. Iglesia: Highly useful descriptive and analytical research.
　　　　　　Y 5 6

523. LENT, JOHN A. Book publishing in the Philippines. Unitas 41, no. 2 (June 1968), 261-275.

524. _____. Philippine mass communications bibliography; first cumulation of sources on areas of advertising, journalism, newspaper, magazine, public relations, radio, television, movies, by John A. Lent. Fort Worth, Tex., Distribution in U.S. through the Dept. of Journalism, Texas Christian University [1965 or 6]. 102p.
Reprint from SJ 12, no. 3 (1965)

525. _____. Philippine radio--history and problems. AS 6, no. 1 (Apr. 1968), 37-52.

526. _____. The press of the Philippines: its history and problems. SJ 14, no. 1 (First Quarter, 1967), 67-90.

527. MAGSAYSAY, JOSE P. Advertising. (In: Feliciano, Gloria D. and Crispulo J. Icban, Jr., eds. Philippine mass media in perspective. Quezon City, Capitol Publishing House, 1967. p.179-203)

528. PAL, AGATON P. Channels of communication with the barrio people. PJPA 1, no. 2 (Apr. 1957), 160-164.

529. PEDROCHE, C. V. Public information. (In: Feliciano, Gloria D. and Crispulo J. Icban, Jr., eds. Philippine mass media in perspective. Quezon City, Capitol Publishing House, 1967. p.219-230)

530. RAVENHOLT, ALBERT. A. V. H. Hartendorp; Manila's doughty seventy-one-year-old American editor. AUFSR. Southeast Asia Series 12, no. 13 (Dec. 1964), 18p. (AR-9-'64)

531. _____. Philippine public opinion in the making. Rafael Yabut. AUFSR.

Southeast Asia Series 1, no. 2 (Jan. 17, 1953), 7p. (AR-2-'53)

532. [SMITH, GEORGE]. Communications. (In: Human Relations Area Files, Inc. Area handbook on the Philippines. Chicago, Univ. of Chicago for the Human Relations Area Files, Inc., 1956. v.3, Chapter 11, p.996-1101)

533. TIGLAO-TORRES, AMARYLLIS. The effects on inoculated beliefs of persuasive communications attributed to specific sources. PJP 1, no. 1 (Nov. 1968), 35-41.

534. TRINIDAD, FRANCISCO "KOKO". Broadcasting. (In: Feliciano, Gloria D. and Crispulo J. Icban, Jr., eds. Philippine mass media in perspective. Quezon City, Capitol Publishing House, 1967. p.51-84)

535. TY, LEON O. Periodicals. (In: Feliciano, Gloria D. and Crispulo J. Icban, Jr., eds. Philippine mass media in perspective. Quezon City, Capitol Publishing House, 1967. p.23-35)

COMMUNITY AND COMMUNITY DEVELOPMENT

536. ABUEVA, JOSE V. Focus on the barrio; the story behind the birth of the Philippine community program under President Ramon Magsaysay. Manila, Institute of Public Administration, U.P., 1959. 527p. (Studies in Public Administration, no. 5)

Coller: The author's access to most of the chief actors in this movement gives this book particular value.
V 4 6
Grossholtz: Useful insights into Magsaysay's political style and organization.
V 3 6
McMillan: A fairly objective history of the Philippine community development movement.
V 3 6
Polson: The standard reference on the origin and early days of the Philippine Community Development Program.
V 4 6
Villanueva: Excellent case study.
V 5 6

537. _____. Formulation of the Philippine community development program. Ann Arbor, 1959. 724p. Thesis (Ph.D.) - Univ. of Michigan.
Polson: The thesis version of Focus on the Barrio.
V 4 6

538. _____. The interrelations between local governments and community development. PJPA 5, no. 1 (Jan. 1961), 52-58.
Polson: A good discussion of the problem of dependence and decentralization.
V 4 6
Villanueva: V 4 6

539. BALMACEDA, CORNELIO. Community development in relation to social work. SW 5 (May/June 1960), 323-324+

540. _____. [Rural improvement.] (In: Philippines (Republic) National Science Development Board. Interdisciplinary Symposia of the National Science and Technology Week, Manila, 1961. Theme: "State of and Trends in Science and Technology in the Philippines." Area I-Agriculture. Manila, [1963?]. Mimeographed. p.74-88)
       Spencer: Rambling speech, outlines a government department program in rural development.
                      G   3   6

541. BINAMIRA, RAMON P. The Philippine community development program. Manila: Presidential Assistant on Community Development, 1957. 24p.

542. CABREROS LAYA, JUAN. Little democracies (of Bataan). 2d ed. Manila, Inang Wika Pub. Co., 1951. 241p.
       Coller: The factually-based exhortation which sparked the community school movement on Luzon.
                      Y   4   6
       McMillan: One man's dream or vision that was never quite realized.
                      Y   3   6
       Polman: Description of a school-sponsored community development program.
                      Y   4   6

543. CARPIO-LAUS, REMIGIA. Coordination of agencies in the community development program. Quezon City, Community Research Council, U.P., 1960. 130p. (Study series, no. 9)

544. CASTILLO, GELIA TAGUMPAY and OTHERS. A development program in action: A progress report on a Philippine case. AS 2, no. 1 (Apr. 1964), 37-66.
       Polson: An excellent account of the introductory period of an experimental developmental program in eight Laguna Province barrios.
                      Z   5   6

545. CHADWICK, EDWARD R. Planning and execution of community development programmes in the Philippines. Manila, Philippines. United Nations Technical Assistance Program, 1958. 100p. (TAA/PHI/6)
Suggested by Polson.
Verified in Cordero, An annotated bibliography on community development in the Philippines from 1946-1959. p.13.
       Polson: An excellent paper on the early days of the PACD.
                      C   5   6

546. CLARE, DONALD A. Organizational control in the PACD. PJPA 11, no. 2 (Apr. 1967), 138-149.

547. _____. Organizational power: influence and control in a Philippine community development organization. Corvallis, 1965. 204p. Thesis (Ph.D.) - Univ. of Oregon.

548. COLLER, RICHARD W. An analysis of the social effects of donated radios on barrio life. Quezon City, Community Development Research Council, U.P.,

1961. 94p. (Study series, no. 11)
   Villanueva: Very insightful.
                Z   5   6

549.   CORDERO, FELICIDAD V. An annotated bibliography of community development in the Philippines from 1946-1959. Diliman, Rizal, U.P., Community Development Research Council, 1965. 3v. (Special Research Project, no. 4)
       Coller: A massive work which is unlikely to be superseded for many years.
                      Z   4   6
       Polson: A comprehensive bibliography on community development and related topics.
                      Z   4   6

550.   DALISAY, AMANDO M. Assessing the contribution of investment in human resources to agricultural and community development. PEB 2, no. 6 (July/Aug. 1964), 5-28.

551.   DE YOUNG, JOHN E. The characteristics of rural communities in the Philippines. EQ 2, no. 1 (Aug. 1954), 168-170.
       Warren: Z   5   6

552.   _____ and CHESTER L. HUNT. Communication channels and functional literacy in the Philippine barrio. Journal of Asian Studies 22, no. 1 (Nov. 1962), 67-77.
       Coller: Shorter version of monograph done on this study. Analysis and interpretation make it a useful source.
                      Z   5   6
       Spencer: Good study of how barrio folk learn the news.
                      Z   5   6
       Ward: Evaluates different languages as means of communications. No language data as such is given.
                      Z   3   6
       Warren: Z   5   6

552a. ESPIRITU, SOCORRO C. and CHESTER L. HUNT, eds. Social foundations of community development; readings on the Philippines. Manila, R. M. Garcia Pub. House, 1964. 684p.
       Coller: Good source for many articles that are now out-of-print and unobtainable elsewhere.
                      Z   4   6

553.   Excerpts from a colloquium on community development and culture change -
                Robert Fox p.58-61
                Buenaventura Villanueva . . . p.62-66
                Ruben Santos-Cuyugan p.66-73
   EQ 8, no. 4 (Apr. 1961).

554.   FIRMALINO, TITO C. Political activities of barrio citizens in Iloilo as they affect community development. Quezon City, Community Development Research Council, U.P., 1959. 266p. (Study series, no. 4)
       Grossholtz: Survey data on political communication and local, provincial and national linkages.
                      V   3   6

I. GENERAL. COMMUNITY AND COMMUNITY DEVELOPMENT

> Polson: Useful survey data on political attitudes and activities.
>   V   5   6
> Villanueva: Very insightful.
>   V   5   6

555. FLAVIER, JUAN M. Some human obstacles to rural development. Summary of Paper
Presented at the Seminar by Juan M. Flavier.
Comments by Ernesto M. Maceda and R. Eugene Moran. (In: Madigan, Francis C.,
ed. Human factors in Philippine rural development. Cagayan de Oro City,
Xavier Univ., 1967. Xavier Univ. Studies. Study no. 1. p.256-288)

556. FUJIMOTO, ISAO. The process of community differentiation: an insight into
development. PSR 13, no. 4 (Oct. 1965), 199-210.
> Polson: Z   5   6

557. HARE, A. PAUL. Factors associated with peace corps volunteer success in the
Philippines. HO 25, no. 2 (Summer 1966), 150-153.
> Guthrie: Z   5   6

558. HESTER, E. D. Random notes on community development with special reference
to the Philippines and "How ugly is the ugly American?" Chicago, Philippine
Studies Program, Univ. of Chicago. 14p. Ms.
Cited in Univ. of Chicago. Philippine Studies Program. Sixth Annual Report:
1958/59.
> Warren: X   5   6

559. HIDALGO, MARIANO O. The Philippine community development movements as a
power of change. PJE 37, no. 2 (July 1958), 82-83, 127.
Cited in Index to Philippine periodicals, v.3, p.178.
> Polson: A general statement about some of the problems facing com-
>   munity development.
>   -   3   6

560. HOLLNSTEINER, MARY R. Social action in urban and rural settings. CS 3,
no. 3 (Sept. 1966), 182-189.

561. HUNT, CHESTER L. The rural community. (In: Hunt, Chester L. and others.
Sociology in the Philippine setting. Rev. ed. Quezon City, Phoenix Publishing House, 1963. p.258-283)

562. JOSE, SIONIL. Revolution for the barrio. Comment, no. 13 (Second Quarter
1961), 3-27.

563. KELSEY, LINCOLN D. Some problems of training. Community Development Bulletin
10, no. 4 (Sept. 1959), 74-77.
> Polson: Observations of an experienced community development con-
>   sultant.
>   Y   4   6

564. LAWLESS, ROBERT. Village-community studies in general education. GEJ, no. 12
(Second Semester 1966-1967), 162-171.

565. LYNCH, FRANK. A Philippine village: report from the field. Anthropology
Tomorrow 6, no. 2 (June 1958), 13-29.
> Warren: E   5   6

I. GENERAL. COMMUNITY AND COMMUNITY DEVELOPMENT

566. _____. The Philippines peace corps survey. SLQ 5, nos. 1/2 (Mar./June 1967), 67-76.

567. _____ and OTHERS. The Philippines peace corps survey: final report. Honolulu, Hawaii. International Programs and Social Science Research Institute, Univ. of Hawaii, 1966. 336p. of Appendixes: A-W.

568. MCKENDRY, JAMES M. and SALVADOR A. PARCO. A community development rating scale for Philippine poblaciones. Science Park, State College, Pa. HRB-Singer, Inc., 1967. 30p. (Technical Report 857-R-4)

569. MCMILLAN, ROBERT T. Major rural problems of the Philippines and suggested solutions. Soil Science Society of the Philippines. Journal 4, no. 2 (Second Quarter 1952), 101-109.

570. _____. Organization of resources for community development. EQ 4, no. 2 (Sept. 1956), 196-203.

571. _____. Some operational aspects of community development in the Philippines. ERJ 2, no. 2 (Sept. 1955), 47-52.

572. MADIGAN, FRANCIS C. The farmer said no; a study of background factors associated with dispositions to cooperate with or be resistant to community development projects. Diliman, Quezon City, Community Development Research Council, U.P., 1962. 359p. (Study series, no. 14)

Bulatao:	Research very carefully done and interpreted. Z 5 6
Coller:	Sophisticated analysis done in Mindanao using field study plus ample statistical techniques. Z 5 6
Guthrie:	Important book. Z 5 6
Polson:	Research report on a competent study of resistance to change. Z 5 6
Villanueva:	Excellent statistical analysis of a social-political phenomenon. Z 5 6

573. _____, ed. Human factors in Philippine rural development. Proceedings of the anniversary seminar on economic development of the rural Philippines held July 22-July 25, 1966 at Xavier Univ. Cagayan de Oro City, Philippines, Xavier Univ., 1967. 318p. (Xavier Univ. Studies, Study no. 1)

Madigan:	Excellent papers on sociology, psychology, and anthropology of development work in the Philippines by a multidisciplinary group. Z 4/5 6

574. MASA, JORGE O. Rural folkways in relation to rural improvement. PSR 2, no. 2 (July 1954), 12-17.

Coller:	Early effort at analysing the dysfunctional aspects of fiestas. Later works strive for greater balance. S 3 6
Polson:	An interesting note on views of time as reflected in major Filipino languages. Y 3 6

575. NEAL, ERNEST E. Community development in the Philippines. Community Development Review, no. 6 (Sept. 1957), 24-44.
>   Polson: Description of the establishment period by a U.S. AID advisor.
>   C   4   6

576. NGUYEN, THI HUE. Training for community development: a comparative study of national programs in Ghana, India, and the Philippines, Ann Arbor, 1961. 287p. Thesis (Ph.D.) - Univ. of Michigan.
>   Polson: Focuses on the structure of recruitment and pre-service training.
>   V   4   6

577. OREN, PAUL. The myth of painless metamorphosis: community development. SJ 5, no. 1 (Jan./Mar. 1958), 5-14.
>   Polson: A valuable article that serves as a realistic counter-statement to much community development propaganda.
>   -   4   6

578. PAL, AGATON P. Barrio institutions and their economic implications. PSR 7, nos. 1/2 (Jan./Apr. 1959), 51-63.
>   Polson: Good description of prenda and its relationships to other economic practices.
>   Z   4   6

579. _____. Ideal patterns and value judgments in development program planning. SJ 7, no. 2 (Apr./June 1960), 134-152.
>   Polson: An argument for cultural sensitivity in program formulation and implementation.
>   Z   4   6

580. PARCO, SALVADOR A. In-service training needs of barrio development workers in the Philippines. PSR 14, no. 2 (Apr. 1966), 93-109.
>   Polson: A good evaluation based on survey data.
>   Z   5   6

581. PELZER, KARL J. Rural problems and plans for rural development in the Republic of the Philippines. International Institute of Differing Civilizations. Compte Rendu. Programmes and plans for rural development in tropical and subtropical countries. Record. 28th meeting. Brussels, 1953. p.257-270.
>   McMillan: Excellent description of rural problems, especially land tenure.
>   K   4   7

582. PHILIPPINES (REPUBLIC) NATIONAL ECONOMIC COUNCIL. Report on the Philippine Community Development Program; a joint project of the National Economic Council of the Republic of the Philippines and the International Cooperation Administration of the United States of America. Manila. 1957- .

583. _____ PRESIDENTIAL ARM ON COMMUNITY DEVELOPMENT. Barrio development plan. Prepared by the Operations and Field Training. Manila, 1966. 24p.

584. _____. Focus of PACD operations. Prepared by the Operations and Field Training Division. Manila, 1963. 17p.

I. GENERAL. COMMUNITY AND COMMUNITY DEVELOPMENT

585. _____. PACD barrio Magsaysay urban community development research project. Prepared by the Operations and Field Training Division. Manila. 1966. 31p.

586. _____. The Philippine community development program. 1v. (various pagings) Manila? 1962? Mimeographed papers.

587. _____ PRESIDENTIAL ASSISTANT ON COMMUNITY DEVELOPMENT. Community development: the war against want, hunger, illiteracy and disease. Manila. 1959. 101p. Cited in Biblio. of Asian Studies. 1960. p.726.
   Polson: The standard PACD Presidential Assistant on Community Development) piece on the goals of the community development program.
               W   3   6

588. _____. What municipal mayors say about local autonomy and community development. (Seminar on Local Autonomy and Community Development, Los Baños, Laguna, April 3-5, 1959) Manila, 1959. 64p.
   Polson: Report of a conference organized to generate pressure for greater municipal powers.
               W   3   6

589. PHILIPPINES. UNIVERSITY. Community Development Research Council. PSR 6, no. 2 (Apr. 1958), 39-41.

590. POLSON, ROBERT A. Community development in the Philippines: observations and comments. PSR 4, no. 4 (Oct. 1956), 7-14.

591. QADIR, SYED ABDUL. Adoption of technological change in the rural Philippines; an analysis of compositional effects. 1966. 159p. Thesis (Ph.D.) - Cornell Univ.

592. REYNOLDS, HUBERT. We saw "community development." Philippine Christian 13, no. 4 (Apr. 1961), 40.
   Source: Index to Periodicals (U.P. Library, Filipiniana Section)

593. RIVERA, GENEROSO F. The characteristics of rural communities in the Philippines. EQ 2, no. 1 (Aug. 1954), 161-167.

594. _____ and ROBERT T. MCMILLAN. The rural Philippines; a cooperative project of the Philippine Council for United States Aid and the United States Mutual Security Agency. Manila, Reproduced by the Office of Information, Mutual Security Agency, 1952. 217p.
   Coller: The basic survey which fueled post-World War II efforts at rural development.
               Z   5   6
   McMillan: First-rate analysis of rural communities in the Philippines in the early 1950s.
               G & Z   4   6
   Polson: An influential survey of socioeconomic conditions including excellent vignettes of 13 barrios.
               C   5   6
   Villanueva: Provides good backdrop for social and economic reform programs.
               C & G   4   6

595. ROMANI, JOHN H. The Philippine barrio. Far Eastern Quarterly 15, no. 2 (Feb. 1956), 229-237.
      Coller: Pulls together various sources to provide an overview. Recent materials are more useful due to accumulated research.
                    V   3   6

596. RONDUEN, PEDRO. Pattern of community living in Philippine villages and urban areas. Manila, UNESCO National Commission, 1963. 26p. illus. (UNESCO Philippines. v.2, no. 10, Oct. 1963)

597. ROY, DAVID P. and OTHERS. The Philippines peace corps survey final report. (In: Bello, Walden F. and Maria Clara Roldan, eds. Modernization: its impact in the Philippines. Quezon City, Institute of Philippine Culture, Ateneo de Manila Univ. Press, 1967. Papers, no. 4. p.87-105)

598. SABER, MAMITUA. Problems of community development among cultural minorities. PSR 8, nos. 3/4 (July/Oct. 1960), 52-59.

599. SIBLEY, WILLIS E. Observations on barrio culture and barrio teaching. PJE 44, no. 2 (Aug. 1965), 98-100, 142-143.

600. TADENA, ROMUALDO B. Some postulates in the evaluation of the Philippine community development program. PJPA 12, no. 4 (Oct. 1968), 361-376.

601. THOMAS, M. LADD. The Philippine rural development program. Social Research 22, no. 2 (Summer 1955), 223-230.

602. TIGLAO, TEODORA V. Health practices in a Philippine rural community. Quezon City, Community Development Research Council, U.P., 1964. 232p. (Study series no. 23)
      Coller: One of the best reports yet on actual, detailed behavior in this area of life. Very careful work, bringing forth original and essential data.
                    S   5   6
      Villanueva: Interpretation of health data over a time period for empirical purposes.
                    S   4   6

603. U.S. DEPT. OF STATE. INTERNATIONAL COOPERATION ADMINISTRATION. Report on community development programs in India, Pakistan, and Philippines, Oct. 5, 1956; by Team no. 1, Harold S. Adams and others. 88p.

604. VIBAR-BASCO, CARMEN. Two Bago villages: a study. JEAS 5, no. 2 (Apr. 1956), 125-212.

605. VILLANUEVA, BUENAVENTURA M. The barrio people and barrio government: experiences, attitudes, resources, values, cultural matrix, and barrio government. Quezon City, Community Development Research Council, U.P., 1959. 41p. (Abstract series, no. 1)
      Polson: Summary statement of A Study of the Competence of Barrio Citizens · · ·
                    V   5   6
      Villanueva: V   5   6

606. _____. The community development program of the Philippine government. PJPA 1, no. 2 (Apr. 1957), 144-153.
       Villanueva: V   5   6

607. _____. Non-governmental programs in community development. v.1. The Philippine rural reconstruction movement. Quezon City, Community Development Research Council, U.P., 1961. 147p.

608. _____. Rural leadership patterns. SR 1, no. 4 (Sept. 1960), 10-13.
       Villanueva: V   5   6

609. _____. A study of the competence of barrio citizens to conduct barrio government. Quezon City, U.P., Community Development Research Council, 1959. 223p. (Study series, no. 1)
       Polson: Excellent study of political attitudes and behavior.
                    V   5   6
       Stauffer: Baseline monograph drawing on survey data from a national sample of barrio residents. Behavioral and attitude variables probed.
                    V   5   6
       Villanueva: A good evidence of barrio peoples capability for political development.
                    V   5   6

610. _____. The training program, PACD. Quezon City, Community Development Research Council, U.P., 1966. 95p.
       Polson: Good study based on survey data.
                    V   5   6

611. _____, FELICIDAD V. CORDERO and ROSALINA A. CONCEPCIÓN. The YMCA of the Philippines Summer Youth Work Camp Project and other non-Governmental Entities in Community Development. Rizal, U.P., Community Development Research Council, 1965. 284p. (Community Development Research Council. U.P. Special Study Series, no. 9)
       Polson: Good analytic study of private organizational activities in rural development.
                    V   5   6
       Villanueva: V   5   6

612. VILLANUEVA, PATROCINIO (SANTOS). Some socio-economic effects of rural roads. Quezon City, U.P., Community Development Research Council, 1959. 14p. (Abstract series, no. 2)
       Villanueva: V   5   6

613. _____. The value of rural roads. Quezon City, Community Development Research Council, U.P., 1959. 74p.
       Coller: Provides documentation of outcomes that were too often taken for granted.
                    V   5   6
       Luna: Descriptive semi-technical statistical analytical study.
                    V   4/5   6
       Polson: A good study on a topic about which there is little hard data.
                    V   5   6
       Villanueva: V   5   6

614. XAVIER UNIVERSITY. RESEARCH INSTITUTE FOR MINDANAO CULTURE. STAFF. Background and assessment of the current state of rural development in the Philippines.

> Introduction.
> Human factors in economic progress: a statement of the Research Institute for Mindanao Culture relating to rural economic development in the Philippines.
> Replies of participants and other scholars to the "background and assessment."
> The assessment: a preliminary analysis and comment upon the viewpoints on rural development of the seminar participants, by Francisco Claver.

(In: Madigan, Francis C., ed., Human factors in Philippine rural development. Cagayan de Oro City, Xavier Univ., 1967. Xavier University Studies. Study no. 1, p. 11-55)

615. _____. Some hints for rural development projects from applied social anthropology.
Comments by F. Landa Jocano, Lourdes R. Quisumbing, Vincent G. Cullen. (In: Madigan, Francis C., ed. Human factors in Philippine rural development. Cagayan de Oro City, Xavier Univ., 1967. Xavier University Studies. Study no. 1, p.207-225)

616. YEN, Y. C. JAMES. Back to the barrio - greatest challenge facing P.I. today. (In: Liao, Shubert S. C., ed. Chinese participation in Philippine culture and economy. Manila, 1964. p.196-203)
> Polson: A statement of the philosophy underlying the PRRM by its articulator.
> Y   4   6

DEMOGRAPHY

Census and Statistical Reports

617. ARAGON, YLDEFONSO DE. Estados de la población de las Islas Filipinas correspondiente á el año de 1818. Lo da ad público el Excmo. Ayuntamiento del M. N. Yl. ciudad de Manila. Manila, Imprenta de D. M. M. por D. Anastacio Gonzaga, 1820.
> Luna: Historical reference.
> -   3   3

618. AROMIN, BASILIO B. The demographic situation in the Philippines. Stat. Rept. 2, no. 3 (July 1958), 1-6.
> Luna: Descriptive, statistical study of population characteristics, trends, etc.
> S   4   6
> Madigan: S   3   6

619. _____. The trend of mortality in the Philippines: 1903 to 1960. Stat. Rept. 5, no. 3 (July 1961), 1-7.

<table>
<tr><td>Luna:</td><td>Descriptive, statistical study.</td></tr>
<tr><td></td><td>S   4   7</td></tr>
<tr><td>Madigan:</td><td>S   3   6</td></tr>
</table>

620. AYCARDO, MANUEL MA. On infant mortality in the Philippines. Phil. Stat. 2, no. 1 (1953), 22-54.

> Luna: Descriptive, statistical analytical study.
> N   4   7

621. _____. The 1953 trend of mortality in the Philippines. Phil. Stat. 4, no. 2 (June 1955), 83-91.

> Luna: Descriptive, statistical analytical study.
> N   4   6

622. BELARMINO, ISAGANI C. Some notes on population age grouping in the Philippines. Stat. Rept. 9, no. 4 (Oct./Dec. 1965), 1-14.

> Luna: Descriptive, statistical study.
> N   4   7
> Madigan: S   3   6

623. BEYER, H. OTLEY. Population of the Philippine Islands in 1916 (Población de las islas Filipinas en 1916) English-Spanish edition. Manila, Philippine Education Co., Inc., 1917. 95p.

> "Part One: Statistical tables."
> "Part Two: Brief descriptions, in alphabetical order, of each of the recognized Philippine ethnographic groups, with mention of physical types, languages, dialects, and bibliographical references."
> Part Two reprinted in Encyclopedia of the Philippines, Zoilo, M. Galang, ed. Manila, Exequiel Floro, 1957.
> Vol. 16: History. "Filipino Ethnographic Groups" p.37-109. Includes also "Bibliographical References" on p.86-109.

> Luna: Population estimates.
> E   3   4
> Warren: E   5   4

624. BLUMENTRITT, FERDINAND. Eine Studie zur Bevölkerungs-Statistik der Philippinen. Globus 41, no. 22 (1882), 343-345
>   41, no. 23 (1882), 362-365

> Luna: The study can be used as a historical reference but the limitations must be noted.
> N   3   3

625. MANILA (ARCHDIOCESE). Censo de población de las islas Filipinas perteneciente el año de 1876. Formado por el m. r. arzobispo de Manila. Manila, Estab. tip. del Real colegio de Santo Tomás, 1878. 46p.

> Luna: Includes Christian population only.
> W   5   3

626. _____. Censo de población del Arzobispado de Manila perteneciente al año de 1877. Manila, Estab. tip. de Ramirez y Giraudier, 1878.

> Luna: Historical census materials.
> W   5   3

627. MENDOZA-PASCUAL, ELVIRA. Reinvestigation of birth and death statistics in the Philippines. Phil. Stat. 11, no. 4 (Dec. 1962), 171-189.
    Luna: Descriptive statistical study.
                        S   4   7
    Madigan: Z/S 3   6

628. MORRISON, FRANK S. A study of vital statistics in the Philippines for 1957, and their relation to the annual population increase. Philippines (Republic). Dept. of Health Bulletin 30, no. 2 (Apr./June 1958), 48-52.
    Luna: Descriptive statistical analytical study.
                        N   4   6
    Madigan: S   3   6

629. OÑATE, BURTON T. Enumerated and listed population estimates: PSSH May, 1965. Philippine Economy Bulletin 4, no. 2 (1965), 31-38.
    Luna: Descriptive statistical study.
                        N   4   6
    Madigan: S   5   6

630. PAN, JOSÉ FELIPE DEL. La poblacion de Filipinas. Censo general...Resumen de datos numericos y observaciones escrito para la Exposicion colonial de Amsterdam de 1883. Manila, La Oceania española, 1883. 14p.
    Luna: Historical reference
                        -    3   3

631. PHILIPPINE ISLANDS. CENSUS OFFICE. Census of the Philippine islands taken under the direction of the Philippine Legislature in the year 1918...Compiled and published by the Census office of the Philippine islands. Manila, Bureau of Printing, 1920-1921. 4 vols. in 6.
    Contents: I. Geography, history, and climatology. Appendix. Organization, census acts, and regulations.
           II. Population and mortality.
         III. Agriculture, medicinal plants, forest lands and proper diet.
          IV. Pt. 1. Social and judicial statistics, manufactures, and household industries.
              Pt. 2. Schools, university, commerce and transportation, banks, and insurance.
    Luna: Census materials.
                        W   5   4
    Madigan: This is a poor census from several viewpoints but is the basic statistical source for the period.
                        W   5   5

632. _____. ... Organization of the census of 1918 ... Manila, Bureau of Printing, 1919. 394p. (Bulletin, no. 1)
    Luna: Census materials.
                        W   5   4
    Madigan: This is a poor census from several viewpoints but is the basic statistical source for the period.
                        W   5   5

633. _____. Report. Manila, Bureau of Printing, 1919-1918/19 has title: ... Report of the director of the census to His Excellency the governor-general of the Philippine Islands, covering the operations of the Census office since its organization up to July 31, 1919 ...

```
                    Luna:        W     5     4
                    Madigan:     W     3     4
```

634. _____ (COMMONWEALTH) COMMISSION OF THE CENSUS. ...Census of the Philippines: 1939. Manila, Bureau of Printing, 1940-1943. 5v. in 8.
Contents: I. Reports by province for census of population (in four parts).
           II. Summary for the Philippines and general report for the cen-
suses of population and agriculture.
      III. Reports by provinces for the census of agriculture.
      IV. Report for economic census.
       V. Census atlas of the Philippines.
    Luna: Census materials.
                 W   5   4
    Madigan: Best American-period census of Philippines.
                 W   5   5

635. _____ (REPUBLIC) BUREAU OF THE CENSUS AND STATISTICS. Census of the Philippines, 1948; population classified by province, by city, municipality, and
municipal district, and by barrio. Manila, Bureau of Print., 1951. 258p.
    Luna: Census materials.
                 W   5   6
    Madigan: A census somewhat poor in quality from several viewpoints.
                 But the basic source for the period.
                 W   5   6

636. _____. Census of the population, 1948. Report by province for census of
population. Manila, Bureau of Printing, 1950-1954. 4v. in 7.
    Luna: Census materials.
                 W   5   6
    Madigan: A census somewhat poor in quality from several viewpoints.
                 But the basic source for the period.
                 W   5   6

637. _____. Census of the Philippines, 1960: Population and housing. Manila,
1962-63. 2v. in 56. v.1. Report by province. 55 pts. v.2. Summary report.
    Luna: W   5   6
    Madigan: Census of better quality than 1948 census. Most recent
                 census.
                 W   5   6

638. RAMACHANDRAN, K. V., R. A. ALMENDRALO and M. SIVAMURTHY. Population projections for the Philippines, 1960-1980. Phil. Stat. 12, no. 4 (Dec. 1963),
145-169.
    Luna: Statistical projective study.
                 S & N   4   6
    Madigan: S & N   4   6

639. SALVOSA, LUIS R. The GSIS [Government Service Insurance System] basic mortality table. Phil. Stat. 5, no. 1 (Mar. 1956), 55-65.
    Luna: Statistical study.
                 N   4   6
    Madigan: N   5   6
```

640. SPAIN. INSTITUTO GEOGRÁFICO Y ESTADÍSTICO (1873-1925). Censo de la pobla-
ción de España, según el empadronamiento hecho en 31 de diciembre de 1877
```

por la Dirección general del Instituto geográfico y estadístico. Madrid,
Impr. de la Dirección general del Instituto geográfico y estadístico, 1883-
1884. 2v. Archipiélago Filipino. v.1. 707-744.
    Luna: Census materials.
                 W   5   3

641. _____. Censo de la población de España según el empadronamiento hecho en
31 de diciembre de 1887, por la Dirección general del Instituto geográfico
y estadístico ... Madrid, Impr, de la Dirección general del Instituto geográfico y estadístico, 1891. "Poblacion de las islas de Cuba, Puerto-Rico,
del golfo de Guinea, y del archipiélago Filipino": t. 1, p. [755]-822.
    Luna: Census materials.
                 W   5   3

642. U.S., BUREAU OF THE CENSUS. Census of the Philippine Islands, taken under
the direction of the Philippine Commission in the year 1903, in four volumes
...Comp. and pub. by the U.S. Bureau of the Census. Washington, [Govt.
Print. Off.] 1905. 4v.
    Contents: I.   Geography, history, and population.
                 II. Population.
                III. Mortality, defective classes, education, and families and
                      dwellings.
               IV. Agriculture, social and industrial statistics.
    Luna: Census materials.
                 W   5   4
    Madigan: This Census contains inaccuracies but is the basic sta-
                 tistical source.
                 W   5   4

643. _____. Bulletin 1-3. 1. Population of Philippines by islands, provinces,
municipalities, and barrios in 1903. 1904. 100p. (Prepared in cooperation
with U.S. Census Bureau, Commerce and Labor Dept.) 2. Algué, José. Cli-
mate of Philippines. 1904. 3. Saderra Masó, Miguel. Volcanoes and seis-
mic centers of Philippine Archipelago. 1904. (Census of the Philippine
Islands ... Bulletin 1-3)
    Luna: Census materials.
                 W   5   4
    Madigan: Excellent source for this period.
                 W   5   4

644. VALENZUELA, VICTOR C. Problems in the collection of birth and death statistics in the Philippines. Phil. Stat. 3, no. 1 (Mar. 1954), 60-65.
    Luna: Discusses problems of death and birth data collection.
                 D   4   6
    Madigan: D   3/5   6

645. VIRATA, ENRIQUE T. Philippine death rate computed from census data. Phil.
Stat. 8, no. 4 (Dec. 1959), p.210-217.
    Luna: Statistical analytical study.
                 N   4   6
    Madigan: N   3   6

646. VIVET, ESTEVAN B. Reseña estadística . . . de las Islas Filipinas, en 1845.
Barcelona, 1846. 51p.

Luna: Statistical study; a historical reference.
                 -     4   3

Demography

647. ADAMS, EDITH. New population estimates for the Philippines 1948-1962. Phil. Stat. 7, no. 3 (Sept. 1958), 134-166.
     Luna: Restudies population estimates on the basis of improved methods of projections. Statistical study.
                  S   4   6
     Madigan: Later data has modified usefulness of this work.
                  Z   3   6

648. AROMIN, BASILIO B. Considerations for a Philippine population policy. Phil. Stat. 12, no. 4 (Dec. 1963), 122-144.
     Luna: Descriptive, statistical analytical study.
                  S   4   6
     Madigan: S   3   6

649. _____. Demographic aspects of Philippine economic development. Stat. Rept. 3, no. 4 (Oct. 1959), 11-23.
     Luna: Studies impact of rapid population growth on economic development.
                  S   4   6
     Madigan: S   3   6

650. BANTEGUI, B. C. and BASILIO B. AROMIN. Some aspects of the Philippine population problem. SR 3, no. 8 (Aug. 1962), 10-14, 18.
     Luna: Descriptive, statistical analytical study.
                  N & S 4   6
     Madigan: X & S 3   6

651. BARROWS, DAVID P. Population. I: History of the Population. II: Characteristics of the civilized or Christian tribes. III: Characteristics of the non-Christian tribes. (In: U.S. Bureau of the Census. Census of the Philippine Islands, 1903. v.1. Geography, History and Population. Washington, 1905. p.411-585)
     Luna: Descriptive analysis of the population.
                  G   5   7
     Madigan: Good data for that period.
                  G   4   5

652. BENNETT, DON C. The new official definition of the urban population in the Philippines: a critique. PGJ 9, Nos. 1/2 (Jan./June 1965), 3-10.
     Luna: Descriptive evaluation of the urban-rural definition used in the 1960 census.
                  K   4   6
     Spencer: Useful critique.
                  K   4   6

653. Die Bevölkerung der Philippinen. Mutter Erde 2 (1899), 304-306, 330-333.

Luna: W   3   3

654. BEYER, H. OTLEY. Christian population of the Philippines in 1942. (In: Tangco, Marcelo, The Christian Peoples of the Philippines. NASB 11, no. 1 (Jan./Mar. 1951), 26-28.

    Doherty: E   3   6
    Luna: Descriptive analytical study of the distribution and characteristics of the Christian population.
                  E   4   5
    Madigan: Pioneer work, of mixed quality.
                  E   3   4
    Warren: E   5   5

655. _____. A revised estimate of the population of the Philippine Islands in 1916. Philippine Review Part I. 2, no. 4 (Apr. 1917), 10-70. Part II. 2, no. 5 (May 1917), 56-81.
    Luna: Estimating and re-estimating population at that time was more predictive than projective.
                  E   3   4
    Warren: E   5   4

656. _____. Table I. Population in the Philippines listed according to recognized ethnographic groups. Typescript manuscript. Chicago: Philippine Studies Program, 1942. 4p.
Cited in University of Chicago, Philippine Studies Program. Selected bibliography of the Philippines.
    Luna: Tabulation.
                  E   4   4
    Warren: E   5   5

657. _____. A tabular history of the Philippine population as known at the present time from combined historical, ethnographical and archaeological studies. (In: the Congrès des préhistoriens d'Extrême-Orient. 1st, Hanoi, 1932. [Procèsverbal] p.129-131) Praehistorica Asiae orientalis Hanoi, 1932. v.1.
    Luna: A good attempt at the reconstruction of the Philippine population.
                  E   4   7

658. BLUMENTRITT, FERDINAND. Zur Einwanderungsfrage auf den Philippinen. Oesterreichische Monatsschrift für den Orient 11, no. 1 (Jan. 15, 1885), 16-18.
    Luna: Historical reference for migration studies.
                  N   3   3

659. BUENAFE, MANUEL E. The Philippines and its growing population. Chronicle Yearbook (1961), 18-20.
    Luna: Descriptive informative study.
                  G   4   6

660. _____. Problems of population distribution and urbanization trends in the Philippines. FTY (1961), 168-171.
    Luna: Descriptive analytical study.
                  G   4   6

661. CARO Y MORA, JUAN. The native population of the Philippines. American

I. GENERAL. DEMOGRAPHY. Demography

Monthly Review of Reviews 19 (Mar. 1899), 308-312.
Luna: Descriptive informative essay.
               -       3   3

662. CARROLL, JOHN J. Population increase and geographical distribution in the
Philippines. Phil. Stat. 8, no. 3 (Sept. 1959), 154-175.
Luna: Descriptive analytical study.
               Z   4   7
Madigan: Z.   3   6

663. CHAVES, HIDALGO VELOSO and FRANCISCO VI'SMANOS NAZARET. Population projection of the Philippines, 1960-1975. PSR 11, nos. 1/2 (Jan./Apr. 1963), 76-
91.
Luna: Statistical study.
               N   4   6

664. COLLER, RICHARD W. Population growth and distribution. (In: Hunt, Chester
L. and others. Sociology in the Philippine setting. Rev. ed. Quezon City,
Phoenix Publishing House, 1963. p.304-324)
Luna: Descriptive analytical study.
               Z   4   6
Madigan: Z   3   7

665. CONCEPCION, MERCEDES B. Demographic factors in Philippine development. (In:
Conference on Population, 1st, U.P., 1965. Proceedings ... Quezon City,
1966. p.80-84)

666. _____. The Philippine population crises: fact or fancy? Unitas 39, no. 3
(Sept. 1966), 332-340.
Luna: Descriptive analytical study.
               S   4   6
Madigan: Z   4   6

667. _____. The population of the Philippines. (In: Philippines. Univ. Population
Institute. First Conference on Population, 1965. Quezon City, 1966.
p.185-199)
Luna: Descriptive analytical study.
               S   4   6
Madigan: Splended short summation.
               Z   5   6

668. _____. Under-registration and estimation of births and deaths in a Philip-
pine municipality. PSR 13, no. 4 (Oct. 1965), 227-231.
Luna: Descriptive statistical study.
               S   4   6
Madigan: Z   5   6

669. CONFERENCE ON POPULATION, 1ST, U.P., 1965. Proceedings of the Conference
sponsored by the Population Institute of the U.P. with the support of the
Population Council of New York. Quezon City, U.P. Press, 1966. 519p.

670. DANIELSON, ALBERT L. The effects of interregional migration on the Philippine population. PEB 5, no. 2 (Nov./Dec. 1966), 26-37.
Luna: Descriptive statistical study.
               X   4   7

Madigan: -   3   6

671. DIAZ-TRECHUELO, L. and L. SPINOLA. Manila Española. Notas sobre su evolu-
ción urbana. Estudos Americanos (Seville) 9, no. 44 (May 1955), 447-463.
Cited in Robert Huke, Bibliography of Philippine geography ... 1964, p.53.
    Felix: This is one of the early essays of an excellent historian.
             H   3   2/3

672. DOHERTY, JOHN F. Population growth and fertility control. PS 12, no. 2
(Apr. 1964), 348-351.
    Luna: Descriptive study.
             M/Z   4   6
    Madigan: Z   3   6

673. _____. A sociologist views the population question. Proceedings of the
Summer Institute of Philosophy. Quezon City, Ateneo de Manila Univ., 1964.
Cited in Ateneo de Manila University, Faculty publications as of February,
1967, p.18.
    Luna: Descriptive study.
             M/Z   4   6
    Madigan: Z   3   6

674. [DONOGHUE, JOHN and STELLA PALUSKAS] Demography and settlement. (In: Human
Relations Area Files, Inc. Area handbook on the Philippines. 1956. v.1.
Chapter 7. p.356-412)
    Luna: Historical descriptive study.
             S   4   7
    Madigan: S   3   7

675. DWYER, D. J. The problem of in-migration and squatter settlement in Asian
cities: two case studies, Manila and Victoria-Kowloon. AS 2, no. 2 (Aug.
1964), 145-169.
    Luna: Descriptive analytical study.
             K   3   6

676. FLOR, DIOSDADO. Economic development and population pressure in the Philippines. Unitas 39, no. 3 (Sept. 1966), 357-367.
    Luna: Descriptive analytical study.
             X   3   6

677. GONZALES, LEON MA. Post censal population of the Philippines, 1949-1956.
Institut International de Statistique. Bulletin 36, no. 2 (1958), 272-279.
    Luna: Population projection based on the 1948 census.
             G/O   4   6
    Madigan: G   3   6

678. _____. Thirty years of the rise of Philippine population. FTY (1926/1956.
30th Anniversary no.), 127-129, 169-170.
    Luna: Descriptive informative article.
             G/O   4   7
    Madigan: G   3   7

679. GUERRERO, RENATO MA. Infant mortality in Manila: a comparative study.
Philippine Medical Association. Journal. 39, no. 1 (Jan. 1963), 3-18.

680. GUTIERREZ, JOSE S. Agricultural productivity and population increase: the Philippine case. (In: Philippines. Univ. Population Institute. First Conference on Population, 1965. Quezon City, 1966. p.469-492.
     Luna: Descriptive statistical analytical study.
                      N   4   6
     Madigan: N   3   6

681. HARKAVY, OSCAR and OTHERS. The economic development and population survey mission. Phil. Stat. 11, no. 4 (Dec. 1962), 159-170.
     Luna: Descriptive, statistical graphical analytical study.
                      X   4   6
     Madigan: Z   3   6

682. HAWLEY, AMOS H. Differential population pressure in the Philippines. PSR 2, no. 2 (July 1954), 28-36.
     Madigan: Z   3/5   6

683. _____. Papers in demography and public administration. Revised Ed. Manila, Institute of Public Administration, U.P., 1954. 88p. Publications 6
     Luna: Descriptive analytical study.
                      Z/S   4   6
     Madigan: Z   3/5   6

684. HENARES, ROSARIO A. Some characteristics of the economically active population. Stat. Rept. 1, no. 4 (Oct. 1957), 7-13.
     Luna: Descriptive statistical study.
                      N   4   6
     Madigan: N   3   6

685. HILARIO, ELVIRA A., GRACE S. DAVID and GAUDENCIO VILLANUEVA. Factors guiding the population growth in the Philippines. I: Socio-cultural factors. II: Malaria eradication in the Philippines. III: Tuberculosis control in the Philippines. Unitas 39, no. 3 (Sept. 1966), 341-356.
     Luna: Descriptive article.
                      Y   3   6

686. HUNT, CHESTER L. Changing sex ratio in Philippine cities. SR 4, no. 1 (Jan. 1963), 1-3, 10.
     Luna: Descriptive analytical study.
                      Z   4   6
     Madigan: Z   4   6

687. JUPP, KATHLEEN M. Patterns of population change in the Philippines, 1939 to 1957. Phil. Stat. 9, no. 1 (Mar. 1960), 11-29.
     Luna: Descriptive statistical study.
                      S   4   7
     Madigan: S   4/5   7

688. LENK, SIEGFRIED E. Die Bevölkerung der Philippinen. Eine anthropogeographische Untersuchung ... Leipzig, Doctoral dissertation, Univ. of Leipzig, 1932. 162p.
     Luna: Descriptive analytical study.
                      K   4   7

689. LORIMER, FRANK W. Analysis and projections of the population of the

Philippines. (In: Philippines. Univ. Population Institute. First Conference on Population, 1965. Quezon City, 1966. p.200-314)
    Luna: Statistical projective analysis.
                      Z/S   4   6
    Madigan: Z   4   6(7)

690. _____. Demographic aspects of economic social development. PRBE 2, no. 1 (May 1965), 1-8.

691. LOW, STEPHEN. The effect of colonial rule on population distribution in the Philippines 1898-1941. 1956. Medford, Massachusetts. Thesis (Ph.D.) - Fletcher School of Law and Diplomacy, Tufts Univ.
    Luna: Descriptive analytical study.
                   V   4   7
    Madigan: -   3   4

692. LUNA, TELESFORO W., JR. The geographic distribution of population. Unitas 39, no. 3 (Sept. 1966), 424-439.
    Luna: Descriptive analytical study.
                   K   4   6
    Madigan: K   3/4   6

693. _____. Some geographic techniques used in the study of population distribution. PGJ 6, no. 1 (Jan./Mar. 1958), 33-38.
    Luna: Suggests some geographic techniques for the study of population.
                   K   4   6
    Madigan: K   3   6

694. MCLAUGHLIN, ALLAN J. and VERNON L. ANDREWS. Studies on infant mortality. PJS 5-B, no. 2 (July 1910), 149-160. 5 tables. Discussion on the paper ... 237-243.

695. MADIGAN, FRANCIS C. Some Filipino population characteristics and their relation to economic development. PSR 7, nos. 1/2 (Jan./Apr. 1959), 16-26.
Commentary by Amado A. Castro, pp. 31-33.
Commentary by Basilio Aromin, pp. 27-30.
Reply by Madigan to Aromin. PSR 7, no. 3 (July 1959), 33-39.
    Luna: Descriptive analytical study.
                 M/Z   4   6
    Madigan: One of author's first papers in Philippine demography. Has revised several concepts since.
                 Z   2/3   6

696. _____. Hindsight and foresight: the census of the Philippines, 1948 and 1960. PS 6, no. 1 (Mar. 1958), 87-104.
    Luna: Descriptive analytical study.
                 M/Z   4   6
    Madigan: Evaluates previous critiques on 1948 census and examines quality of 1948 census data.
                 Z   4   6

697. _____. Population and levels of living in the rural Philippines.
Comment by Mercedes B. Concepcion.
(In: Madigan, Francis C., ed. Human factors in Philippine rural development.

Cagayan de Oro City, Xavier University. 1967. Xavier University Studies.
Study no. 1 p.130-153)

698. _____. Population pressures in the Philippines and some ethical aspects of
government planning. Phil. Stat. 11, no. 2 (June 1962), 68-96.
  Luna: Descriptive statistical analytical study.
        M/Z 4   6
  Madigan: Z   4   6

699. _____. Problems of growth--The future population of the Philippines. PS
16, no. 1 (Jan. 1968), 3-31.
  Madigan: An article written for professionals and administrators,
         who are not professional demographers, to acquaint them
         with the essential aspects of the Philippine population
         question. The fruit of twelve years work in this field
         in the Philippines.
         Z 4   6

700. _____. Some recent vital rates and trends in the Philippines: estimates
and evaluation. Demography 2 (1965), 309-316.
  Luna: Descriptive statistical evaluative study.
        M/Z 4   7
  Madigan: Actually covers period 1939.
        Z   4   6

701. _____ and ROSALIA O. AVANCEÑA. Philippine fertility and mortality with spe-
cial reference to the North Mindanao region: a critique of recent estimates.
Part I: The Philippine in general. PSR 12, nos. 1/2 (Jan./Apr. 1964), 35-
42. Part II: The North Mindanao Region. 43-53.
  Luna: Descriptive statistical analytical study.
        M/Z & Z 4   6
  Madigan: Z & Z   4   6

702. MAKANAS, ELPIDIO D. Application of sampling in the 1960 censuses of population and agriculture in the Philippines. Phil. Stat. 8, no. 1 (Mar. 1959),
12-24.
  Luna: Statistical methodological study.
        N   4   6
  Madigan: S   4   6

703. MENDOZA, ELVIRA P. Changes in the structure of the population of the Philip-
pines by provinces, 1903-1948. 1960. 134p. Thesis (M.A.) - U.P.
  Luna: Descriptive statistical study.
        S   4   7
  Madigan: Z/S 3   6

704. MERCADO, NESTOR J. The population of the Philippines: its aspects and prob-
lems. ERJ 11, no. 2 (Sept. 1964), 76-82.
  Luna: Descriptive analytical study.
        X   4   6
  Madigan: -   3   6

705. MEYER, ADOLF B. Die Einwohnerzahl der Philippinischen Inseln in 1871. Petermann's Mitteilungen 20, (1874), 17-19.

Luna: Informative essay.
                   N   3   3

706. _____. The population of the Philippine Islands. Nature 6 (June 27, 1872), 162-163.
              Luna: Informative essay.
                                 N   3   3

707. _____. Ueber die Einwohnerzahl der Philippinischen Inseln. Tijdschrift voor indische taal-, land-en volkenkunde 20, (1873), 434-440.
              Luna: Descriptive informative article.
                                 N   3   3

708. MILLS, VICENTE. The population of the Philippines: its growth and prediction. Phil. Stat. 2, no. 1 (1953), 55-89.
              Luna: Descriptive statistical analytical study.
                                 N   4   7
              Madigan: X   3   6

709. MORRISON, FRANK S. Some comments on birth, death and infant mortality rates in the Philippines, and a suggested device for registration improvement. Phil. Stat. 5, no. 2 (June 1956), 98-105.
              Luna: Evaluative suggestive study.
                                 N   4   6

710. MYRDAL, GUNNAR. The significance of population growth for development planning. Barangay 1, (Aug. 1966), 26-29.
     Index to Periodicals (U.P. Library. Filipiniana Section).
              Luna: Descriptive analytical essay.
                                 X   4   6

711. OÑATE, BURTON T. Estimates of the population and labor force in the Philippines. International rice research institute, Mar. 1965.
     Cited in First Conference on Population, Quezon City, Philippines, 1965. 1966. p.217.
              Luna: Statistical analytical study.
                                 N   4   6
              Madigan: N   5   6

712. _____. Population and food requirements: Philippines. The International Rice Research Institute, Family Planning Workshop, College of Agriculture, U.P., Los Baños, Laguna, Oct. 29, 1965.
     Cited in First Conference on Population, Quezon City, Philippines, 1965. 1966. p.159.
              Integan: Using recommended food allowances as target, a statistician projects food needs up to 1980.
                                 N   5   6
              Luna: Descriptive statistical analytical study with graphical illustrations.
                                 N   4   6
              Madigan: N   5   6

713. PAÑGANIBAN, ANTONIA G. School performance as a factor in Philippine rural-urban migration. 1956. 56p. Thesis (M.A.) - U.P. PSR 4, nos. 2/3 (Apr./July 1956), 2-15.

Coller:	Summary of M.A. thesis-replicates studies done elsewhere and obtains similar results.
	Z 5 6
Luna:	Descriptive analytical study.
	Z 4 6

714. PASCUAL, ELVIRA M. Internal migration in the Philippines. (In: Philippines. Univ. Population Institute. First Conference on Population, 1965. Quezon City, 1966. p.315-353)

Luna:	Descriptive statistical graphical analytical study.
	S 4 6
Madigan:	Basic source of some (sampled) unreleased 1960 census data.
	Z 4/5 6

715. _____. Population redistribution in the Philippines. Unitas 39, no. 3 (Sept. 1966), 453-459.

Luna:	Descriptive analytical study.
	S 4 6
Madigan:	Z 3 6

716. PEREZ, BERNARDINO A. Problems of developing urban and rural definitions for Philippine population statistics. Phil. Stat. 8, no. 3 (Sept. 1959), 185-194.

Luna:	Descriptive evaluative essay.
	N 4 6
Madigan:	Z 5 6

717. The Philippines. Population Index 8, no. 1 (Jan. 1942), 3-9.

Luna:	Descriptive statistical summary.
	W 4 4
Madigan:	W 4 4

718. _____ (REPUBLIC). NATIONAL ECONOMIC COUNCIL. OFFICE OF STATISTICAL COORDINATION AND STANDARDS. The population and other demographic facts of the Philippines. Manila, 1963. 37p. (OSCAS Monograph no. 4)

Luna:	Descriptive statistical analytical study.
	W 4 6
Madigan:	W 3 6

719. POETHIG, RICHARD P. The modern migrant. CC 6, no. 6 (Nov./Dec. 1966), 4-11.

720. Population censuses: prime source of essential labour data. Labor Digest 3, no. 18 (Sept. 15, 1958), 1-13.
Condensed from "The World Programme of Population Censuses: Prime Source of Labour Data," International Labour Review 77, no. 1 (January 1958), 48-68.

| Luna | Descriptive statistical study. |
| | W   4   6 |

721. PRATT, WILLIAM F. Summary of background paper on population projects. (In: Conference on Population, 1st, U.P. 1965. Proceedings ... Quezon City, 1966. p.104-111)

722. RAVENHOLT, ALBERT. Philippine population growth. AUFSR. Southeast Asia

Series 1, no. 1 (Jan. 4, 1953), 8p. (AR-1-'53)

723. RESPICIO, ANNIE P. An analysis of the population data collected in a survey
      of households in selected barrios in the Philippines. 1960. 135p. Thesis
      (M.A.) - U.P.
            Luna: Descriptive statistical analytical study.
                              N   4   6
            Madigan: S   3   6

724. REYES, WILFREDO L. Philippine population growth and health development.
      (In: Philippines. Univ. Population Institute. First Conference on Popula-
      tion, 1965. Quezon City, 1966. p.423-468)
            Luna: Descriptive statistical analytical study.
                              D   4   6
            Madigan: D   3/4   6

725. _____. Summary of background paper: Philippine population growth and
      health development. (In: Philippines. Univ. Population Institute. First
      Conference on Population, 1965. Quezon City, 1966. p.112-115)
            Luna: Descriptive summary.
                              D   4   6
            Madigan: D   3/4   7

726. ROJO, TRINIDAD A. Philippine population problems. PSSHR 11, no. 2 (May
      1939), 134-152.
            Luna: Descriptive analytical study.
                              S   4   4

727. ROSALES, VICENTE J. A. The control of population growth in the Philippines.
      Unitas 39, no. 3 (Sept. 1966), 460-467.
            Madigan: D   3   6

728. ROXAS, SIXTO K. Human resources: key to socio-economic development. SR 5,
      no. 6 (June 1964), 83-87.
            Luna: Underscores maximum utilization and integration of man-
                              power for economic and social development.
                              X   4   6
            Madigan: X   3   6

729. SALCEDO, JUAN. Trends and prospects of population growth. Science Bulletin
      10, no. 2 (Dec. 1965), 4-12.
            Luna: Descriptive analytical article.
                              D   4   6
            Madigan: D   2/3   6

730. SANTOS, ROLANDO A. Philippine population and education. EQ 13, no. 1
      (Aug. 1965), 34-44.
            Luna: Descriptive analytical study.
                              Y   4   6
            Madigan: Y   3   6

731. SANVICTORES, LOURDES L. Is there an economic need for family limitation in
      the Philippines? Unitas 38, no. 3 (Sept. 1965), 439-447.

732. SASTRON, MANUEL D. Colonización de Filipinas. Immigración peninsular . . .

Manila. 1897. 112, [3]p.
 Luna: Historical document on Spanish migration to the Philip-
       pines.
      - 4 3

733. SAUVY, ALFRED. Croissance de la population et de la population active aux
Philippines. Population (Paris) 16, no. 2 (Avril-Juin 1961), 336-340.
 Luna: Descriptive analytical study.
      S 4 6
 Madigan: S 4 6

734. SIMKINS, PAUL D. and FREDERICK L. WERNSTEDT. Growth and internal migrations
of the Philippine population, 1948 to 1960. Journal of Tropical Geography
17, (May 1963), 197-202.
 Luna: Descriptive graphical analytical study.
      K 4 6
 Madigan: Carefully gathered survey data.
      K 5 6
 Spencer: Analytical field study of internal migration based on
      first hand data--good study.
      K 5 6

735. TAEUBER, IRENE B. The bases of a population problem: the Philippines.
Population Index 26, no. 2 (Apr. 1960), 97-114.
 Luna: Descriptive statistical analytical study.
      S 4 4
 Madigan: Uses 1939 Census data but definitely applies to current
      Philippines in various ways.
      S 4 7

736. THOMPSON, WARREN S. The impact of population growth. Chronicle Yearbook
(1961), 22, 24-29.
 Luna: Descriptive analytical study.
      S 4 6
 Madigan: S 4 6

737. _____. Some implications of population changes for national policies.
Stat. Rept. 5, no. 3 (July 1961), 12-17.
 Luna: Descriptive analytical study.
      S 4 6
 Madigan: S 4 6

738. U.N. DEPT. OF ECONOMIC AND SOCIAL AFFAIRS. Population growth and manpower
in the Philippines A joint study by the United Nations and the Government
of the Philippines. National Economic Council of the Philippines. New York,
1960. 66p. (Population Studies, no. 32)
 Luna: Descriptive statistical projective analytical study.
      W 4 7
 Madigan: W 4 6

739. U.S. OPERATIONS MISSION TO THE PHILIPPINES. HEALTH AND SANITATION DIVISION.
A study of vital statistics in the Philippines for 1956 and their relation
to the annual population increase, by Frank S. Morrison, analytical statistician. Manila, 1956. 11p.
 Luna: Descriptive statistical analytical study.

                             W   4   6

Madigan: Companion piece to Morrison's A Study of Vital Statistics
in the Philippines for 1957.

                             W   3   6

740. VILLARAMA, ANTONIO. Maternal mortality in the Philippines. Proceedings of
the First American Congress on Obstetrics and Gynecology, Mumm Print Shop,
Evanston, 1941. p.348-350.
      Luna: Descriptive informative essay.
                      D   4   4
      Madigan: D   3/4   4

741. VIRATA, ENRIQUE T. Population of the Philippine Islands in 1934. NASB 4,
no. 4 (Dec. 1935), 431-436.
      Luna: Statistical projective analytical study.
                      N   4   4
      Madigan: N   3   4

742. VITO DE VERA, FE V. and EFREN MICOR. Internal migration as a temporary solution to the population problems of the Philippines. Unitas 39, no. 3 (Sept.
1966), 440-452.
      Luna: Descriptive statistical article.
                      N   3   6
      Madigan: N   3   6

743. WAGNER, HERMANN und ALEXANDER SUPAN. Die Bevölkerung der Erde. Heft 8,
Areal und Bevölkerung: Philippinen und Sulu-Inseln. Petermanns Geographische
Mitteilungen. Ergänzungsheft No. 101. (1891), 136-138. Die Bevolkerung der
Erde. Heft 9, Ortsstatistik: Philippinen 1887. Petermanns Geographische
Mitteilungen. Ergänzungsheft No. 107. (1893), 87-89.
      Luna: Historical reference.
                      K   3   3
      Spencer: Summaries of data from Spanish sources, and from Spanish
                      census. 1893 item is quite useful.
                      K   4   3

744. YENGOYAN, ARAM A. The initial populating of the Philippines; some problems
and interpretations. (In: Zamora, Mario D., ed. Studies in Philippine anthropology (in honor of H. Otley Beyer). Quezon City, Alemar-Phoenix, 1967.
p.175-185.
      Yengoyan: E   4   1

745. _____. Preliminary notes on a model of the initial populating of the Philippines. Anthropology Tomorrow 6, no. 3 (Apr. 1960), 42-48.
      Luna: Descriptive analytical study.
                      E   3   1
      Madigan: E   3   1

746. ZUMEL-LOPEZ, MARIA LUISA. The aging population in the Philippines: an
economic and social asset or liability? Unitas 39, no. 3 (Sept. 1966),
468-476.
      Madigan: -   3   6

DRINK, DRUGS AND INDULGENCE

747. BACON, RAYMOND F. Some Philippine medicinal plants. Manila Medical Society.
      Bulletin 2, (1910), 53-54.

748. BROWN, WILLIAM H. Official Philippine medicinal plants. (In: Brown,
      William H., ed. Minor products of Philippine forests. Manila, Bureau of
      Printing, 1920-. v.3. 61-75)

749. FELICIANO, R. T. Illicit beverages. PJS 29, no. 4 (Apr. 1926), 465-473.
      2 plates.
          Tiglao: G   3   4

750. GUERRERO, LEÓN MA. Medicinal plants. (In: Census of the Philippine Islands,
      1918. Manila, Bureau of Printing, 1921. v.3. 747-787)
          Tiglao: G   4   4

751. _____. Medicinal uses of Philippine plants. (In: Brown, William H., ed.
      Minor products of Philippine forests. Manila, Bureau of Printing, 1921.
      v.3. 149-246)

752. LEWIS-MINTON, FRANK. Pipe smoking in the Philippines. Philippine Magazine
      34, no. 3 (Mar. 1937), 120-121.
      Reprinted in JEAS 3, no. 1 (Oct. 1953), 101-103.

753. PARDO DE TAVERA, T. H. The medicinal plants of the Philippines. Philadel-
      phia, P. Blakiston's Son & Co., 1901. 269p.

754. QUISUMBING, EDUARDO. Aromatic plants in the Philippines used as ingredients
      or for flavoring. Philippine Pharmaceutical Association Journal 35, (1948),
      49-53.
      Cited by Houston in JEAS, Jan. 1953, p.97.

755. _____. Botanical research of Philippine medicinal plants. Eighth Pacific
      Science Congress of the Pacific Science Association. Proceedings. 1953.
      4:107-112. Quezon City. 1954.

756. _____. Medicinal plants of the Philippines. Manila, Bureau of Printing,
      1951. 1223p. (Philippines (Republic) Dept. of Agriculture and Natural Re-
      sources, Technical Bulletin 16.)

757. ROSARIO, PAZ L. DEL. Tuba intake in eastern Visayas region. Philippine
      Journal of Nutrition 20, no. 4 (Oct./Dec. 1967), 180-192.

758. SULIT, MAMERTO. Possibilities of some Philippine plants for medicinal uses.
      Philippine Pharmaceutical Association. Journal 37, nos. 11/12 (1950), 434-
      448.
      Cited by Houston in JEAS, Jan. 1953, p.101.

759. _____. Some poisonous plants found in the Makiling national park and its
      vicinity. II. Arrow and dog poisons. Philippine Journal of Forestry 1,
      (1938), 211-217.
      Cited by Houston in JEAS, Jan. 1953, p.101.

760. TAYLOR, ARNOLD H. American confrontation with opium traffic in the

Philippines. Pacific Historical Review 36, (Aug. 1967), 307-324.

761. ZARCO, RICARDO M. A short history of narcotic drug addiction in the Philippines, 1521-1959. HB 3, no. 4 (Dec. 1959), 86-100.

ECONOMICS

Economic Development

762. ATABUG, LOURDES C. Sociocultural factors in economic development: the Philippine case. Urbana, 1960. Thesis (Ph.D.) - Univ. of Illinois.

763. ANCHETA, CONSTANCIO M. Economic planning in the Philippines: programs and problems. PEB 5, no. 4 (Mar./Apr. 1967), 22-36.

764. ARENS, RICHARD. Religious rituals and their socio-economic implications in Philippine society. PSR 7, nos. 1/2 (Jan./Apr. 1959), 34-45.

765. BANTEGUI, B. G. Surveys for socio-economic planning and development in the Philippines. Phil. Stat. 8, no. 1 (Mar. 1959), 2-11.
      Legarda: G   3   6

766. BARBER, CLARENCE L. Statistical measures of economic development. Stat. Rept. 4, no. 3 (July 1960), 1-6.
      Legarda: S   3   6

767. BHALLA, A. S. Manpower and economic planning in the Philippines. International Labour Review 94, no. 6 (Dec. 1966), 550-569.

768. BORJA, QUINTIN R. DE, ARMANDO N. GATMAITAN and GREGORIO C. DE CASTRO. Notes on the role of the military in socio-economic development. PJPA 12, no. 3 (July 1968), 266-283.

769. BRAZIL, HAROLD. The conflict of political and economic pressures in Philippine economic development. 1961. Thesis (Ph.D.) - Ohio State Univ. Suggested by Polson.
      Polson: An interesting study of limits on viable planning.
                     X   4   6

770. CORNWELL, WARREN H. Geography and economic development in the Philippines. PGJ 10, nos. 3/4 (July/Dec. 1966), 51-57.

771. CUADERNO, MIGUEL, SR. Problems of economic development. Philippine Economic Review 31, no. 8 (Mar. 1957), 9, 11.
      Source: A bibliography of Mindanao and Sulu. 12p.
      Legarda: G   3   6

772. ENCARNACIÓN, JOSE, JR. Saving and investment in agriculture in relation to national development objective. PEJ 3, no. 2 (second semester 1964), 226-231.
      Legarda: X   4   7

773. ESPIRITU, SOCORRO C. Socio-cultural factors in economic development. Manila. University of the East. College of Liberal Arts and Sciences. Journal 3, no. 1 (1966), 11-19.

774. FOX, ROBERT B. The study of Filipino society and its significance to programs of economic and social development. PSR 7, nos. 1/2 (Jan./Apr. 1959), 2-11.
      Jocano: E   5   7

775. GOLAY, FRANK H. Obstacles to Philippine economic planning. PEJ 4, no. 2 (second semester 1965), 284-309.

776. HARKAVY, OSCAR, DUDLEY KIRK and PHILIP M. HAUSER. The economic development and population survey mission. Phil. Stat. 11, no. 4 (Dec. 1962), 159-170.
      Luna: Descriptive, statistical graphical analytical study.
                        X   4   6
      Madigan: Z   3   6

777. HOUSTON, CHARLES, O., JR. Political and social aspects of Philippine economic development. (In: Espiritu, Socorro C. and Chester L. Hunt., eds. Social Foundations of Community Development: Readings on the Philippines. Manila, Garcia Publishing House, 1964. p.74-84)

778. HUNT, CHESTER L. and THOMAS R. MCHALE. Education and Philippine economic development. Comparative Education Review 9, no. 1 (Feb. 1965), 63-73.

779. _____. Education, attitudinal change and Philippine economic development. PSR 13, no. 3 (July 1965), 127-139.

780. JAMIAS, JUAN F. The verbal culture and the problems of agricultural development in the Philippines. PJP 1, no. 1 (Nov. 1968), 2-6.

781. KRAUSE, WALTER. Planning for economic development: the Philippine case. Phil. Stat. 6, no. 1 (Mar. 1957), 3-22.
      Legarda: X   3   6

782. LORIMER, FRANK. Cultural and demographic aspects of economic development. PSR 13, no. 4 (Oct. 1965), 222-226.

783. _____. Demographic and cultural aspects of economic development. PSR 14, no. 1 (Jan. 1966), 28-30.

784. MCHALE, THOMAS R. A critical history of economic development in the Philippines. 1, The basis for development in the Philippines. JEAS 9, nos. 2/3 (1960), 1-51.
      Legarda: X   4   6

785. _____. An econecological approach to economic development: the Philippines. Cambridge, 1960. Thesis (Ph.D.) - Harvard Univ.

786. _____. Economic development in the Philippines. JEAS 1, no. 3 (Apr. 1952), 1-10.
      Legarda: X   4   6

787. _____. A note: on the need for sociological studies in working out

economic development programs in the Philippines. PSR 5, nos. 3/4 (July/
Oct. 1957), 61-62.

788. _____. The Philippine cultural matrix and economic development. Comment,
no. 2 (first quarter 1957), 21-28.
   Legarda: X   4   6

789. _____. Problems of economic development in the Philippines. Pac. Aff. 25,
no. 2 (June 1952), 160-169.
   Legarda: X   4   6

790. _____. Religion, religious change and economic development in the Philippines. PEJ 1, no. 2 (second semester 1962), 131-146.
With comments by Mary R. Hollnsteiner, 147-154; and Augusto Cesar Espiritu,
155-161.
   Legarda: X   4   7

791. _____. Some notes on the process of economic development. PSR 10, nos.
3/4 (July/Oct. 1962), 164-166.

792. MCPHELIN, MICHAEL. The Filipino first policy and economic growth. PS 8,
no. 2 (Apr. 1960), 271-291.
   Legarda: X   4   6
   Valdepeñas: Fairly brilliant.
          X   3   6

793. _____. Reversing a vicious circle about economic growth with the help of
statistics. Phil. Stat. 10, no. 2 (June 1961), 52-66.
Discussions on Fr. McPhelin's Paper, 67-70.
   Valdepeñas: Fairly perceptive.
          X   4   6

794. MACEDA, MARCELINO N. The human factor in economic development.
Comment by Calvin C. Crawford. (In: Madigan, Francis C., ed. Human factors
in Philippine rural development. Cagayan de Oro City, Xavier University.
1967. Xavier University Studies. Study no. 1. p.60-78)

795. MADIGAN, FRANCIS C. Some Filipino population characteristics and their rela-
tion to economic development. PSR 7, nos. 1/2 (Jan./Apr. 1959), 16-26.
Commentary by Basilio Aromin, p.27-30.
Commentary by Amado A. Castro, p.31-33. Reply by Madigan to Aromin. PSR 7,
no. 3 (July 1959), 33-39.
   Luna: Descriptive analytical study.
          Z   4   6
   Madigan: One of author's first papers in Philippine demography. Has
          revised several concepts since.
          Z 2/3   6

796. MEAD, HUGH S. The economic development of the Philippine Islands during the
American administrations. Chicago, 1941. Thesis (Ph.D.) - Univ. of Chicago.

797. OÑATE, BURTON T. Contributions of statisticians to social and economic development. Phil. Stat. 10, no. 4 (Dec. 1961), 150-163.

798. _____. The role of statisticians in social and economic development. Stat. Rept. 6, no. 1 (Jan. 1962), 21-27.

799. RAVENHOLT, ALBERT. Stretchout in American aid to Philippine development? AUFSR. Southeast Asia Series 1, no. 11 (June 30, 1953), 7p. (AR-12-'53)

800. RIGGS, FRED W. Commentary on 'The study of Filipino society and its significance to programs of economic and social development.' PSR 7, nos. 1/2 (Jan./Apr. 1959), 12-15.
        Jocano: V   4   7

801. ROLA, BIENVENIDO R. Forestry problems and policy implications in the context of economic development. PEB 4, no. 4 (Mar./Apr. 1966), 18-34.

802. ROXAS, SIXTO K. Discovering economic imperatives for national growth. PS 15, no. 2 (Apr./June 1967), 221-240.

803. _____. Lessons from Philippine experience in development planning. PEJ 4, no. 2 (second semester 1965), 355-402.
        Legarda: X   3   6

804. _____. Organizing the next wave of development. PS 15, no. 4 (Oct. 1967), 576-591.

805. SALAS, RAFAEL M. Administrative aspects of Philippine economic development. PJPA 12, no. 1 (Jan. 1968), 31-41.

806. SAMONTE, ABELARDO G. Regional development authorities: role, structure, and feasibility. PJPA 12, no. 2 (Apr. 1968), 110-123.

807. SEMANA, CARIDAD C. Some political aspects of Philippine economic development after independence. Cambridge, 1965. Thesis (Ph.D.) - Harvard Univ.

808. SOBERANO, JOSE D. Economic planning in the Philippines: ecology, politics and administration. Ann Arbor, 1961. 542p. Thesis (Ph.D.) - Univ. of Michigan.

Economics

809. ABELARDE, PEDRO E. American tariff policy towards the Philippines, 1898-1946. New York, King's Crown Press, 1947. 233p.

810. AGPALO, REMIGIO E. Nationalization of retail trade in the Philippines. PJPA 5, no. 2 (Apr. 1961), 129-143.

811. _____. The political process and the nationalization of the retail trade in the Philippines. Quezon City, Office of the Coordinator of Research, U.P., 1962. 344p. (His Ph.D. Thesis - Indiana Univ., 1958)
        Grossholtz: Considerable information on legislative process and polit-
                        ical style.
                V   5   6

> Stauffer: A comprehensive case study of the politics behind the
> passage of a major piece of legislation.
> V   5   6

812. ALDABA-LIM, ESTEFANIA and GLORIA V. JAVILLONAR. Achievement motivation in
Filipino entrepreneurship. International Social Science Journal 20, no. 3
(1968), 397-411.

813. ALVAREZ DE ABREU, ANTONIO. Extracto historial del expediente que pende en
el Consejo Real y Supremo de las Indias, a instancia de la ciudad de Manila
y demás de las Islas Philipinas ... Madrid, J. de Anztia, 1736. 324p.
Excerpts in Blair and Robertson.

814. ARANETA, FRANCISCO. The scope of economics in its relations to morals. PS
3, no. 4 (Dec. 1955), 389-402.
> Valdepeñas: Quite good.
> X   3   6

815. ARANETA, SALVADOR. Economic nationalism and capitalism for all in a directed
economy. Rizal, Philippines. Araneta Univ. Press, 1965. 275p.
> Wickberg: X   3   6

816. ARENDONK, JOEP VAN. Basic relations in theoretical models: a socio-economic
approach. PSR 12, nos. 1/2 (Jan./Apr. 1964), 53-63.
> Legarda: Z   3   7

817. BAUZON, LESLIE E. The Encomienda system as a Spanish colonial institution
in the Philippines, 1571-1604. SJ 14, no. 2 (second quarter, 1967), 197-241.

818. CALALANG, ALFONSO. The near-term prospects for business and the plight of
the Filipino consumer. PRBE 4, no. 1 (Apr. 1967), 18-26.

819. CAÑAMAQUE Y JIMÉNEZ, FRANCISCO DE PAULA. ...Las islas Filipinas; de todo un
poco ... 2. ed. Madrid, F. Fé, Simon y Osler, 1880. 236p.
> Legarda: J   3   3

820. CARROLL, JOHN J. Filipino entrepreneurship in manufacturing. PS 10, no. 1
(Jan. 1962), 100-126.
> Legarda: Z   5   6
> Valdepeñas: Perceptive and well documented.
> Z   5   6

821. _____. The Filipino manufacturing entrepreneur: agent and product of
change. Ithaca, New York. Cornell Univ. Press, 1965. 230p. (His Ph.D.
Thesis - Cornell Univ., 1962)
> Legarda: Z   5   6
> Valdepeñas: A breakthrough in Philippine entrepreneurial analyses.
> Z   5   6

822. _____. The Philippine economy: rising expectations, limited fulfillment.
Solidarity 3, no. 2 (Feb. 1968), 3-25.

823. CASTILLO, ANDRES V. Rural banks and our rural economy. Philippine Economy
Review 4, no. 1 (Aug. 1957), 20-22.
Cited in Index to Philippine Periodicals, v.2, p.93.

Legarda: X   3   6

824.   CASTILLO, GELIA T. Sociological factors in savings and capital accumulation: some research findings. PEJ 3, no. 2 (second semester 1964), 189-197.
     Luna: Descriptive analytical study.
                 Z   4   6
     Sta. Iglesia: Useful observations.
                 Z   3   6

825.   CASTRO, AMADO A. Economics in the public service. PJPA 3, no. 2 (Apr. 1959), 202-207.

826.   _____. An economist looks at social conflict. Comment, no. 4 (third quar-ter 1957), 3-10.
     Legarda: X   4   6

827.   _____. The Philippines: a study in economic dependence. Cambridge, 1954. Thesis (Ph.D.) - Harvard Univ.

828.   COMYN, TOMÁS DE. State of the Philippine Islands. From the Spanish, with notes and a preliminary discourse. By William Walton. London, T. and J. Allman, 1821. 306p.
     Legarda: Has a peculiar introduction and some omissions in transla-tion.
                 X   5   3

829.   CONCEPCION, MERCEDES B. Survey of small establishments: Manila, 1955. Phil. Stat. 5, no. 3 (Sept. 1956), 149-167.
     Legarda: S   5   6

830.   CUTSHALL, ALDEN. Industrialization in the Philippines. PGJ 6, no. 1 (Jan./Mar. 1958), 8-17.
     Spencer: Useful summary--not deep or detailed.
                 K   4   6
     Warren: K   5   6

831.   _____. Trends in economic production in the Philippines. Proceedings. In-ternational Geographical Union. Regional Conference in Japan, 1957. Tokyo, (1959), 600-601.
Suggested by Warren.
     Warren: K   5   6

832.   DALISAY, A. M. Economic research and agricultural extension work: a Phil-ippine experience. (In: Vu, Quoc Thuc and K. F. Walker, eds. Social research and problems of rural development in southeast Asia. Brussels, Unesco, 1963. p.181-188)

833.   EGGAN, FRED. The Philippines and the Bell report. HO 10, no. 1 (Spring 1951), 16-21.

834.   FABELLA, ARMAND V. The socio-economic programme and its imperatives. FTY, (1964), 101-108, 110, 117, 268.
     Legarda: X   4   6

835.   FELIX, ALFONSO, JR. Religion and economics: a lawyer's comments on McHale,

Hollnsteiner and Espiritu. PEJ 2, no. 2 (second semester 1963), 211-223.
   Legarda: -   4   7

836. FLORES, PEDRO V. Economic expectations and results under the Laurel-Langley
   agreement, 1956-1965. SJ 14, no. 1 (first quarter 1967), 55-66.

837. GELLERMAN, SAUL W. Passivity, paranoia, and "pakikisama." [Japan, Philippines, India] Columbia Journal of World Business 2, no. 5 (Sept./Oct.
   1967), 59-66.

838. GOLAY, FRANK H. Economic collaboration: the role of American investment.
   (In: American Assembly. The United States and the Philippines, edited by
   Frank H. Golay. Englewood Cliffs, Prentice-Hall, 1966. p.95-124)

839. _____. Economic consequences of the Philippine Trade Act. Pac. Aff. 28,
   no. 1 (Mar. 1955), 53-70.
      Valdepeñas: Useful and solid analysis.
                   X   4   6

840. _____. The Philippine economy. (In: Guthrie, George M., ed. Six perspectives on the Philippines. Manila, Bookmark, 1968. p.199-279)

841. _____. The Philippines: public policy and national economic development.
   Ithaca, New York. Cornell University Press, 1961. 455p.
      Legarda: X   3   6
      Spencer: Good study.
                   X   4   6
      Valdepenas: The most thorough going professional analysis of postwar
                     Philippine economic development to this date.
                   X   5   6

842. GOODSTEIN, MARVIN E. The pace and pattern of Philippine economic growth:
   1938, 1948 and 1956. Ithaca, N.Y., Southeast Asia Program, Dept. of Asian
   Studies, Cornell University, 1962 [c1961]. 220p.
      Valdepeñas: A very useful statistical comparison.
                   X   4   6

843. GUEVARA, SULPICIO. The legal framework within which business in the Philippines operates. PRBE Part I. 3, no. 1 (May 1966), 30-53. Part II. 3, no. 2
   (Nov. 1966), 21-40.

844. HARDEN, EDWARD W. Report on the financial and industrial condition of the
   Philippine Islands. Washington, Government Printing Office, 1898. 34p.
      Legarda: G   5   3

845. HARTENDORP, A. V. H. History of industry and trade of the Philippines: from
   pre-Spanish times to the end of the Roxas administration. The Quirino administration. Manila, American Chamber of Commerce of the Philippines, 1958.
   743p.
      Legarda: Only very sketchy on the pre-American period.
                   J   3   7
      Valdepeñas: A very useful work.
                   F/H   4   6

846. _____. History of industry and trade of the Philippines; the Magsaysay

89

administration. Manila, Philippine Education Co., 1961. 532p.
>Legarda: J   4   6
>Valdepeñas: As good as the first volume.
>   F/H   4   6

847. HOLLNSTEINER, MARY R. A note to management on traditional Filipino values in business enterprises: the lumber company as a case study. PS 13, no. 2 (Apr. 1965), 350-354.

848. HOOLEY, RICHARD W. Saving in the Philippines, 1951-1960. Quezon City, Institute of Economic Development and Research, U.P., 1963. 109p. (Publications, no. 4)
>Legarda: A pioneering work.
>   X   5   6
>Valdepeñas: An excellent first study.
>   X   5   6

849. HUNT, CHESTER L. Religion and the businessman. DR 1, no. 3 (July 1953), 302-311.
>Hunt: Z   3   7

850. _____. Social aspects of industrialization. (In: Hunt, Chester L. and others. Sociology in the Philippine Setting. Rev. ed. Quezon City, Phoenix Publishing House, 1963. p.238-256)

851. INTERNATIONAL LABOR OFFICE. Report to the government of the Philippines on organization, administration and development of consumer co-operatives. Geneva, 1968. 29p. (ILO/TAP/Philippines/R12)

852. JENKINS, SHIRLEY. Financial and economic planning in the Philippines. Pac. Aff. 21, no. 1 (Mar. 1948), 33-45.

853. KATIGBAK-TAN, PURISIMA. The mass media in business. PRBE 1, no. 2 (Oct. 1964), 40-45.

854. KURIHARA, KENNETH. Economic nationalism in the Philippines. PSSHR 12, no. 2 (May 1940), 147-152.

855. LEDESMA, ANTONIO J. The agrarian problem and the "unrepresented minorities" during the commonwealth. PJPA 11, no. 3 (July 1967), 216-229.

856. LEGARDA, BENITO, JR. American entrepreneurs in the nineteenth-century Philippines. Explorations in entrepreneurial history 9, no. 3 (Feb. 1957), 142-159.
>Onorato: X   5   3
>Valdepeñas: X   4   6

857. _____. Foreign trade, economic change and entrepreneurship in the nineteenth-century Philippines. 1955. 493p. Thesis (Ph.D.) - Harvard Univ.
>Valdepeñas: A good addition to Philippine entrepreneurial studies.
>   X   4   6

858. _____. Philippine economic paradoxes. Phil. Stat. 13, no. 2 (June 1964), 89-112.

859. _____. Two and a half centuries of the galleon trade. PS 3, no. 4 (Dec. 1955), 345-372.

860. _____ and ROBERTO Y. GARCIA. Economic collaboration: the trading relation-ship. (In: American Assembly. The United States and the Philippines, edited by Frank H. Golay. Englewood Cliffs, Prentice-Hall, 1966. p.125-148)

861. LEVY, EMANUEL. Review of economic statistics in the Philippines, interim re-port. Manila, World Bank Resident Mission, 1964. 1v. ("For private circula-tion only")

862. _____. The usefulness of the existing national accounts for the analysis of the Philippine economy. PEJ 5, no. 1 (first semester 1966), 134-145.
     Valdepeñas: A sound evaluation.
                    X   3   **6**

863. MCHALE, THOMAS R. A modern corporation looks at the Philippine economy and society in transition. PSR 14, no. 4 (Oct. 1966), 226-231.

864. MACAPAGAL, DIOSDADO, PRESIDENT. Five-year integrated socio-economic program for the Philippines; address on the state of the nation to the Fifth Congress of the Republic of the Philippines, January 22, 1962. [Manila, 1962] 1v.
     Legarda: G   5   6

865. MADIGAN, FRANCIS C. A new approach to rural development in the Philippines: the local corporation. PSR 16, nos. 1/2 (Jan./Apr. 1968), 74-91.

866. MILLER, HUGO H. Economic conditions in the Philippines, by H. H. Miller, assisted by C. H. Storms. Rev. ed. Boston, Ginn and Co. [c1929] 373p.
     Legarda: F   4   4

867. _____. Principles of economics applied to the Philippines. Boston, Ginn and Co., [1932] 586p.
     Legarda: F   3   4

868. PAL, AGATON P. The Philippines. (In: Lambert, Richard D. and Bert F. Hose-litz, eds. The role of savings and wealth in southern Asia and the West. Paris, Unesco, 1963. p.316-360)

869. PHILIPPINE (REPUBLIC) INDUSTRIAL DEVELOPMENT CENTER. Economic survey report for the province(s). (One volume for each province). Manila, 1961-1962.
     Legarda: W   5   6

870. _____. NATIONAL ECONOMIC COUNCIL. OFFICE OF FOREIGN AID COORDINATION. The impact of foreign aid to the Philippine economy. Stat. Rept. 6, no. 1 (Jan. 1962), 11-20.
     Anderson: Merely a presentation and analysis of the amount and kind
                   of foreign aid to the Philippines rather than (as the title
                   indicates) a study of the impact of this aid upon the larger
                   Philippine economy.
                   W   5   6

871. _____. PROGRAM IMPLEMENTATION AGENCY. The Philippine economic atlas. Manila, 1965. 163p.
     Legarda: W   4   6

872.   QUINTANA, VICENTE U. An economic analysis of straight agricultural loans
       granted by the branches of the development bank of the Philippines in Nueva
       Ecija and Isabela, 1962. Columbus, Ohio, 1964. 155p. Thesis (Ph.D.) -
       Ohio State Univ.
            Sta. Iglesia: Highly useful descriptive and analytical research.
                      Y   5   6

873.   RAMIRO, ROLANDO R. A survey of some attitudes toward current governmental
       policies affecting business and industry. PRBE 2, no. 1 (May 1965), 26-33.

874.   RAVENHOLT, ALBERT. Jeepneys by Sarao; a case study of a self-made young
       Philippine industrialist. AUFSR. Southeast Asia Series 10, no. 10 (Aug.
       1962), 10p. (AR-6-'62)

875.   _____. Shipbuilder for the islands; the role of a new entrepreneur in a
       developing economy. AUFSR. Southeast Asia Series 12, no. 3 (Apr. 1964),
       14p. (AR-3-'64)

876.   RIGGS, FRED W. The Bazaar-canteen model: economic aspects of the prismatic
       society. PSR 6, nos. 3/4 (July/Oct. 1958), 6-59.
            Stauffer: Although this article deals with the Philippine economy,
                            so many implications exist for students of politics as to
                            make it a necessary addition to their working bibliography.
                      V   5   6

877.   RODRIGUEZ, FILEMON C. Status of the Philippine economy. PEB 4, no. 4
       (Mar./Apr. 1966), 5-17.

878.   ROXAS, SIXTO K. Economic ideologies and theories in the current Philippine
       scene. Comment, no. 5 (first quarter 1958), 3-13.

879.   _____. The problems of public administration for economic development. PJPA
       9, no. 1 (Jan. 1965), 3-9.

880.   _____. Trends in economic science in the Philippines. (In Philippines (Re-
       public) National Science Development Board. Inter-Disciplinary Symposia Pro-
       ceedings, National Science and Technology Week, Nov. 20/26, 1961. Theme:
       "State of and Trends in Science and Technology in the Philippines." Area
       VI-Social Sciences. Manila, 1963. 106p. pp. 14-27. Discussion: pp.28-
       33)

881.   SAMSON, ELIZABETH D. The distribution of individual stockholders in the
       Philippines by selected socio-economic characteristics. PRBE 4, no. 2 (Nov.
       1967), 1-22.

882.   SANCIANCO Y GOSON, GREGORIO. El progreso de Filipinas. Estudios económicos,
       administrativos y políticos...Parte económica. Manila, Impr. de la viuda de
       J. M. Perez, 1881. 260p.
            Legarda: O   4   3

883.   SCHURZ, WILLIAM L. The Manila galleon. New York: E. P. Dutton and Co.,
       1939. 453p.
            Coller: Classic, comprehensive socio-political-economic study of
                            a unique maritime venture.
                      H   3   2/3

I. GENERAL. ECONOMICS. Economics

```
        Legarda:      H     4      2/3
        Valdepeñas:   An excellent historical analysis.
                      H     5      2/3
```

884. SICAT, GERARDO P. Analytical aspects of two current economic policies. PEJ 4, no. 1 (1965), 107-119.

885. _____., ed. The Philippine economy in the 1960's. Quezon City, Institute of Economic Development and Research, U.P., 1964. 281p.

886. _____. Some aspects of capital formation in the Philippines. Boston, 1963. Thesis (Ph.D.) - MIT.

887. _____. The structure of Philippine manufacturing: prospects for the 1960's. (In: Sicat, Gerardo P., ed. The Philippine Economy in the 1960's. Institute of Economic Development and Research, U.P., 1964. 188-220)
```
        Legarda:      X     4      6
```

888. _____ and ROSA LINDA P. TIDALGO. Output, capital, labor and population: projections from the supply-side. (In: Philippines. Univ. Population Institute. First Conference on Population, 1965. Quezon City, 1966. p.354-388)
```
        Luna:         Statistical analytical study.
                      X & X  4      6
        Valdepeñas:   Useful.
                      X & X  3      6
        Wernstedt:    X & X  4      6
```

889. SEIDMAN, SAMUEL N. Entrepreneurship and economic change in the Philippines. Exchange News Quarterly 11 (second quarter 1959), 7-9.
```
        Legarda:      X     4      6
```

890. SPENCER, JOSEPH E. Land and people in the Philippines: geographic problems in rural economy. Berkeley, Univ. of California Press, 1952. 282p.
```
        Legarda:      K     4      7
        Spencer:      Summary study of rural problems.
                      K     4/5    7
        Valdepeñas:   A very good first study.
                      K     4      7
```

891. STINE, LEO C. The economic policies of the Commonwealth government of the Philippine Islands. JEAS 10, (Mar. 1966), 1-136. (His Ph.D. Thesis - Univ. of Illinois, 1948.)

892. Symposium: accelerating the rate of Philippine economic growth.
Welcome Address . . . . Francisco Dalupan, p.181.
Introduction . . . . . . Santiago F. de la Cruz, p.182-184.
   Papers:
      View-point of Industry   - Mariano V. del-Rosario, p.185-189.
      View-point of Agriculture - Oscar Ledesma, p. 189-192.
      View-point of Labor   - Norberto Romualdez, Jr., p.192-195.
      View-point of Finance   - Fernando E. V. Sison, p.195-199.
   Discussions:
      Comments on the paper of Mr. Mariano V. del Rosario (Industry) - by
         Angel A. Yoingco, p.200-201.

Comments on the paper of Senator Oscar Ledesma (Agriculture) - by
Lino V. Castillejo, p. 201-203.
Comments on the paper of Secretary Norberto Romualdez, (Labor and
Economic Development) - by Andres V. Castillo. p.203-205.
Comments on the paper of Secretary Fernando E. V. Sison - by Julian
D. Mercado, p. 205-206.
ERJ 8, no. 4 (Mar. 1962), 181-206.

893. TAGUMPAY-CASTILLO, GELIA. Sociological factors in savings and capital accumulation: some research findings. PEJ 3, no. 2 (second semester 1964),
189-197.

894. TORNOW, MAX L. A sketch of the economic condition of the Philippines. U.S.
Senate, 55th Cong., 3d Sess., Senate Document No. 62, Part 2. p.608-626.
Washington, Government Printing Office, 1899.
Legarda: F   5   3

895. TRINIDAD, RUBEN F. The measurement of gross domestic investment in underdeveloped countries with special reference to the Philippines. ERJ 7, no. 1
(June 1960), 37-44.

896. _____ and LETICIA L. SANTOS. Distribution of gross domestic investment by
type of capital goods, industrial use, and purchasers. Stat. Rept. 2, no. 3
(July 1958), 14-18.

897. U.S. ECONOMIC SURVEY MISSION TO THE PHILIPPINES. Report to the President of
the United States. Washington, 1950. 107p. Daniel C. Bell, Chief of Mis-
sion. (Issued also as Publication 4010, Far Eastern series 38, Dept. of
State)
Legarda: W   5   6
Valdepeñas: An extremely useful survey.
                W   5   6

898. VALDEPEÑAS, VICENTE B., JR. The economic challenge in the Philippines. PS
16, no. 2 (Apr. 1968), 278-296.

899. VILLANUEVA, DELANO P. Financial growth and economic development: the Philippines. PRBE 4, no. 1 (Apr. 1967), 1-17.

900. VIRATA, CESAR E. A. Management and industrial engineering in the Philippines.
PRBE 1, no. 2 (Oct. 1964), 71-81.

901. WILLIS, HENRY PARKER. The economic situation in the Philippines. Journal of
Political Economy 13, no. 2 (Mar. 1905), 145-172.
Legarda: X   4   3/4

902. WURFEL, DAVID O. The Bell report and after: a study of the political prob-
lems of social reform stimulated by foreign aid. 1960. Thesis (Ph.D.) -
Cornell Univ.
Grossholtz: Special relations between the U.S. and the Philippines
                and their usefulness as a channel for reform.
                V   4   6

903. ZAFRA, URBANO A. Philippine economic handbook, 1960. Washington, c1960.
304p.

Legarda: G   3   6

EDUCATION

Education

904. AGUILAR, JOSE V. The community schools in the Philippines: an appraisal.
EQ 15, no. 1 (Sept. 1967), 33-40.

905. _____. This is our community school. Manila, Bookman, 1951. 137p.
    Coller: Useful as the expression of policies, aims and methods of
                    a 'founding father' of the community school movement in
                    the Western Visayan area.
                    Y   3   6

906. ALDANA, BENIGNO V. Highlights in the development of the Philippine public
school curriculum. PM 29, no. 8 (Jan. 1933), 351, 381-382.
    Manalang: Summary of the history of curriculum development in pub-
                    lic schools.
                    Y   3   4

907. _____. What the public schools are doing for the cultural minorities. PJE
41, no. 5 (Oct. 1962), 312-314.

908. ALZONA, ENCARNACIÓN. A history of education in the Philippines 1565-1930.
Manila, U.P. Press, 1932. 390p.
Suggested by Manalang.

909. _____. Origins of our educational system. Progress, (1959), 74-77.
    Manalang: The first writer on Philippine educational history.
                    Nationalistic in tone.
                    H   4   6

910. _____. Whither Philippine education? Heritage 1, no. 2 (Oct. 1967), 29-
34.

911. ARANETA, FRANCISCO. Some problems of Philippine education. PS 9, no. 2
(Apr. 1961), 205-219.

912. ARENS, RICHARD. Philippine education in transition. JEAS 7, no. 1 (Jan.
1958), 89-100.

913. BARROWS, DAVID P. What may be expected from Philippine education? Journal
of Race Development 1, no. 2 (Oct. 1910), 156-168.

914. BAZACO, EVERGISTO. History of education in the Philippines. Manila,
Univ. of Santo Tomas Press, 1953. 423p.
    Manalang: A good counterpart to Alzona's work. Clerical bias.
                    Y   3   7

915. BERNARDINO, VITALIANO. The Philippine community school and the well being of

society in rural areas. EQ 4, no. 1 (June 1956), 30-37.

916. _____. Planning education for national development. 1966. **68**p.
"The present report is the result of the author's study at the East-West
Center, Honolulu, Hawaii, from Sept. 1, 1964 to Feb. 28, 1965."

917. _____. Recent developments in Philippine secondary education. UNESCO Regional Office for Education in Asia. Bulletin 2, no. 1 (Sept. 1967), 54-60.

918. CABALFIN, NENITA ADVINCULA. Parental attitudes towards the community school
movement. PSR 4, no. 1 (Jan. 1956), 12-19.
    Coller: Excerpt of research results done for the M.A. degree on
                   this topic.
                   Z   5   6

919. CABREROS LAYA, JUAN. Little democracies (of Bataan). 2d ed. Manila, Inang
Wika Pub. Co., 1951, 241p.
    Coller: The factually-based exhortation which sparked the community school movement on Luzon.
                   Y   4   6
    McMillan: One man's dream or vision that was never quite realized.
                   Y   3   6
    Polson: Description of a school-sponsored community development program.
                   Y   4   6

920. CASTILLO, GELIA. Implications of occupational research on the role of the
                counselor in high school. PSR 13, no. 3 (July 1965), 144-153.
    Manalang: Z   3   6

921. CLEMENTE, URSULA U. Four decades of health education in the Philippine public schools (1900-1940). EQ (Part I) 7, no. 4 (Apr. 1960), 16-22.
                        (Part II) 9, no. 1 (July 1961), 44-69.
    Manalang: Essentially factual account of health education in public schools.
                   Y   4   7

922. CONSTANTINO, E. O. How Philippine education can be improved. Exchange, no. 38
(1967), 16-25.

923. CONSTANTINO, KARINA R. A comparative analysis of the attitudes of students
towards initiations. PSR 15, nos. 3/4 (July/Oct. 1967), 88-94.

924. COLLER, RICHARD W. Role of the Philippine rural high school. PSR 2, no. 2
(July 1954), 42-44.
    Coller: Essay which tries to point out the implications of current
                   trends.
                   Z   3   6

925. CORPUZ, ONOFRE D. Philippine education: problems and prospects. EQ 15,
no. 1 (Sept. 1967), 6-13.

926. _____. Policies on scientific education and "the Brain Drain." SR 8,

no. 8 (Aug. 1967), 46-48.

927. CUYUGAN, RUBEN SANTOS. Education and national purposes. Philippine Educational Forum 15, no. 2 (July 1966), 1-14.

928. ELEVAZO, AURELIO O. Educational research in the Philippines. Unesco Regional Office for Education in Asia. Bulletin 2, no. 2 (Mar. 1968), 174-178.

929. ESLAO, NENA. The learning situation in the home and in the school. CS 2, nos. 2/3 (June/Sept. 1965), 107-115.

930. ESPIRITU, SOCORRO C. A study of the treatment of the Philippines in selected social studies textbooks published in the United States for use in the elementary and secondary schools. Syracuse, 1954. Thesis (Ph.D.) - Syracuse Univ.

931. FLEEGE, URBAN H. First impressions of the community schools. (In: Espiritu, Socorro C. and Chester L. Hunt, eds. Social foundations of community development: readings on the Philippines. Manila, R. M. Garcia, [n.d.] 1964. 577-581)
    Manalang: A useful critique of the Philippine community school.
                 Y   3   6

932. FLORES, PURA M. How the family prepares the child for his formal education. CS 2, nos. 2/3 (June/Sept. 1965), 166-184.

934. FOX, HENRY F. Primary education in the Philippines, 1565-1863. PS 13, no. 2 (April 1965), 207-231.

935. FRESNOZA, FLORENCIO P. Essentials of the Philippine educational system. Rev. ed. Manila, Abiva Pub. House, 1957. 564p.
    Manalang: Basic facts regarding educational system included.
                 Y   3   6

936. HIDALGO, MARIANO O. Social classes in the Philippines and their implications for education. EQ 5, nos. 3/4 (Dec. 1957/Mar. 1958), 258-272.

937. HUNT, CHESTER L. and SEVERINO F. CORPUS. Education in its social setting. (In: Hunt, Chester L. and others. Sociology in the Philippine setting. Rev. ed. Quezon City, Phoenix Publishing House, 1963. p.194-217)

938. _____ and THOMAS R. MCHALE. Education and Philippine economic development. Comparative Education Review 9, no. 1 (Feb. 1965), 63-73.

939. _____. Education, attitudinal change and Philippine economic development. PSR 13, no. 3 (July 1965), 127-139.

940. ISIDRO, ANTONIO. Education in the rural areas. EQ 1, no. 4 (June 1954), 324-331.

941. _____. Philippine education - social reconstruction through the schools. Phi Delta Kappan 39, no. 3 (Dec. 1957), 119-123.
    Manalang: Y   3   7

I. GENERAL. EDUCATION. Education

942. _____ and OTHERS. Compulsory education in the Philippines. (Studies on compulsory education, 9) Paris, UNESCO, 1952. 83p.
   Manalang: Essential facts on subject covered.
                Y   3   6

943. KIM, C. I. EUGENE and CHESTER HUNT. Education and political development: a comparison of Korea and Philippines. Journal of Developing Areas 2, no.3 (Apr. 1968), 407-420.

944. LACUESTA, MANUEL G. Foundations of an American educational system in the Philippines. PSSHR 23, nos. 2/4 (June/Dec. 1958), 115-140.
   Manalang: Y   3   7

945. LANDE, CARL H. The Philippines. (In: Coleman, James S., ed. Education and political development. Princeton, N.J., Princeton Univ. Press, 1956. p.313-349)
   Spencer: Review of educational system and influences by political periods. Good summary.
                V   4   7

946. LAWLESS, ROBERT. Education in democracy versus culture in the Philippines. EQ 15, no. 1 (Sept. 1967), 14-32.

947. MANALANG, PRISCILA S. Philippine education: aims and practices. EQ 14, nos. 2/3 (Oct. 1966/Jan. 1967), 23-42.

948. MASTERSON, WILLIAM F. Production education.
   Comments by Ralph H. Allee and Ernest E. Neal. (In: Madigan, Francis C., ed. Human factors in Philippine rural development. Cagayan de Oro City, Xavier University. 1967. Xavier University Studies. Study no. 1. p.235-248)

949. MIÑOZA, AURORA. Relationship of physical, socio-economic, and attitudinal factors to elementary school training and academic achievement of secondary pupils. 1957. 114p. Thesis (Ph.D.) - Univ. of Michigan.
   Guthrie: P   5   6

950. MORALES, ALFREDO T. Anthropology and education change in the Philippines. GEJ, no. 12 (second semester 1966-1967), 268-295.

951. _____. The concept of culture applied to educational change in the Philippines. EQ 14, no. 4 (Apr. 1967), 13-39.

952. _____. Excellence above democratic and cultural dualisms. SJ 9, no. 3 (July/Sept. 1962), 233-240.

953. _____. Filipino education and technical change. EQ 7, no. 3 (Jan. 1960), 5-16.

954. NIU, PAUL. A study of the curricular problems in Philippine-Chinese schools. 1964. 144p. Thesis (M.A.) - Ateneo de Manila.
   Liao: Y   4   6

955. ORATA, PEDRO T. The philosophy and motivations of barrio high schools.

EQ 14, no. 4 (Apr. 1967), 70-81.

956. _____. Self-supporting public barrio high schools. UNESCO Philippines 5, no. 3 (Mar. 1966), 82-95.

957. Organization of educational planning in the Asian region: Philippines. Unesco Regional Office for Education in Asia. Bulletin 3, no. 1 (Sept. 1968), 165-172.

958. ORTEZA, EVELINA M. Observations on patterns of cultural continuity and schooling in the Philippines. EQ 13, nos. 2/3 (Oct. 1965/Jan. 1966), 16-41.
      Manalang: Y   3   6

959. OSIAS, CAMILO. Education of the non-Christian people. PJE 3, no. 2 (Aug. 1920), 7-13, 16-20.
      Jocano: Y   3   7

960. PAÑGANIBAN, ANTONIA G. School performance as a factor in Philippine rural-urban migration. 1956. 56p. Thesis (M.A.) - U.P. Condensed in PSR 4, nos. 2/3 (Apr./July 1956), 2-15.
      Coller: Replication study - results parallel findings elsewhere on depletion of talented youth from rural areas.
                    Z   5   6
      Luna: Descriptive analytical study.
                    Z   4   6

961. THE PARTICIPANTS IN THE COOPERATIVE LEADERSHIP EDUCATION PROGRAM. Polo-Torres Bugallon: a study of educational leadership. PJPA 1, no. 3 (July 1957), 241-253.
      Manalang: Y   3   6

962. PECSON, GERONIMA T. and MARIA RACELIS, eds. Tales of the American teachers in the Philippines. Manila, Carmelo and Bauermann, 1959. 254p.

963. PHILIPPINE ISLANDS. BOARD OF EDUCATIONAL SURVEY. Survey of the educational system of the Philippine Islands. Manila, Bureau of Printing. 1925. 677p. Paul Monroe, Chairman of the Board.
      Manalang: Evaluation of public school system in the Philippines - American period. Standard reference.
                    Y   4   4

964. QUETCHENBACH, RAYMOND. A socio-psychological theory of administration in a Philippine school setting. PSR 16, nos. 3/4 (July/Oct. 1968), 144-151.

965. RAVENHOLT, ALBERT. Miss Stewart--"our teacher!" AUFSR. Southeast Asia Series 6, no. 6 (Aug. 8, 1958), 10p. (AR-6-'58)

966. _____. The Peace Corps in the Philippines; American volunteer teachers enter Philippine schools. AUFSR. Southeast Asia Series 10, no. 9 (Mar. 1962), 12p. (AR-3-'62)

967. STA. MARIA, FELIXBERTO C. Illiteracy in the rural areas. EQ 15, no. 1 (Sept. 1967), 41-46.

968. SANTOS, ROLANDO A. Education to serve Philippine society. EQ 13, nos. 2/3

(Oct. 1965/Jan. 1966), 132-140.

969. _____. Philippine population and education. EQ 13, no. 1 (Aug. 1965), 34-44.
    Luna: Descriptive analytical study.
                    Y   4   6
    Madigan: Y   3   6

970. SIBLEY, WILLIS E. Culture, education, and national development: tentative observations on the Philippine case. Philippine Educational Forum 14, no. 2 (July 1965), 14-31.
    Manalang: E   3   6

971. SINCO, VICENTE G. Education in Philippine society. Quezon City, U.P., Publications Office, 1959. 186p.
    Manalang: O   3   6

972. [SMITH, GEORGE]. Education. (In: Human Relations Area Files, Inc. Area Handbook on the Philippines. 1956. v.2, Chapter 10, p. 745-995)

973. STAPLETON, ARCHIE C., JR. Modern educational concepts and traditional Philippine culture. SLQ 5, nos. 1/2 (Mar./June 1967), 141-152.

974. UNESCO. CONSULTATIVE EDUCATIONAL MISSION TO THE PHILIPPINES. Report. Paris, 1949. 74p. (UNESCO publication 669)
    Manalang: Standard reference for evaluation teams.
                    Y   4   6

975. _____. PHILIPPINE EDUCATIONAL FOUNDATION. Fifty years of education for freedom, 1901-1951. Manila, National Printing, 1953. 383p.

976. U.S. INTERNATIONAL COOPERATION ADMINISTRATION. A survey of the public schools of the Philippines--1960. Manila, U.S. Operations Mission to the Philippines. 1960. 594p.
Headed by J. Chester Swanson.
    Manalang: Y   3   6

977. YU, LYDIA N. The role of primary education in political socialization: the Japanese and Philippine experiences. PJPA 12, no. 3 (July 1968), 284-299.

Education, Higher

978. ATENEO DE MANILA. Higher education and Philippine culture; a tentative report to the Rector of the Ateneo de Manila by special committees representing the various disciplines to commemorate the centenary of the founding of the Ateneo, 1859-1959. Quezon City, 1960. 196p.

979. BULATAO, JAIME. The graduate students. Philippine Association for Graduate Education Journal 2, no. 2 (1964), 48-56.

980. CARSON, ARTHUR. Higher education in the Philippines. Washington, U.S. Dept.

of Health, Education, and Welfare, Office of Education, [1961] (Bulletin 1961,
no. 29). 251p.
   Manalang: Good summary on facts regarding higher education.
                Y   4   6

981. CORPUZ, ONOFRE D. Institutions of higher learning and research foundations
and their role in the training, development and utilization of scientific and
technological manpower resources. SR 8, no. 4 (Apr. 1967), 7-9.

982. ELEQUIN, ELEANOR T. and SOBERANO, EDITHA M. The U.P. College of Education:
faculty and graduate. EQ 15, no. 2 (Dec. 1967), 32-64.

983. GOODMAN, GRANT K. An experiment in wartime intercultural relations: Philippine students in Japan, 1943-1945. Ithaca, New York, 1962. 34p. (Cornell
Univ. Southeast Asia Program Data paper, no. 46)

984. GUERRERO, AMOR C. The socio-economic composition of the student body in the
U.P. Quezon City, 1955. Thesis (M.A.) - U.P.

985. HALASZ, SARI C. University of California at Los Angeles study of graduate
students from India, Japan, the Philippines and Taiwan: Fall 1959 through
Spring 1965. College and University 43, no. 1 (Fall 1967), 90-107.

986. HARE, A. PAUL and DEAN PEABODY. Attitude content and agreement set in the
autonomy scale for Filipino, American, and African university students. (In:
Bello, Walden F. and Alfonso de Guzman II, eds. Modernization: its impact
in the Philippines, III. Quezon City, Ateneo de Manila Univ. Press, 1968,
p. 105-113)

987. _____ and RACHEL T. HARE. Social correlates of autonomy among university
students in the Philippines, United States, and Africa. (In: Bello, Walden
F. and Alfonso de Guzman II, eds. Modernization: its impact in the Philippines, III. Quezon City, Ateneo de Manila Univ. Press, 1968, p. 92-104)

988. HART, DONN V. The role of universities in the solution of social problems.
CEU.GFS 8 (1957), 28-37.

989. MIÑOZA, AURORA. Studies in education at the U.P. 1918-1962. EQ 10, no. 1
(June 1962), 63-83.
   Manalang: Categorization of studies in education at U.P.
                Good reference.
                Y   3   7

990. MORALES, ALFREDO T. The College of Education, U.P. Unesco Regional Office
for Education in Asia. Bulletin 2, no. 2 (Mar. 1968), 110-114.

991. RAVENHOLT, ALBERT. Cornell at Los Baños; American university participation
in Philippine development. AUFSR. Southeast Asia Series 1, no. 7 (May 16,
1953), 8p. (AR-8-'53)

992. _____. Filipinos who have studied in America: what do they accomplish?
AUFSR. Southeast Asia Series 1, no. 8 (June 3, 1953), 9p. (AR-9-'53)

993. _____. Fulbright research and teaching opportunities in the Philippines.
AUFSR. Southeast Asia Series 1, no. 4 (Feb. 23, 1953), 6p. (AR-4-'53)

994. TRAINING WORKSHOP ON THE EVALUATION OF ASIAN EDUCATIONAL CREDENTIALS, EAST-WEST CENTER, 1965. The evaluation of Asian educational credentials: a workshop report, India, Japan, the Philippines, Taiwan. Edited by Lee Wilcox. New York, National Association for Foreign Student Affairs, 1966. 69p.

995. UMALI, DIOSCORO L. The role of the U.P. in agricultural development. (In: The role of the U.P. in the socio-economic development of the country. Seminar on President Macapagal's Five-Year integrated socio-economic program. Proceedings. U.P., June 27, 1962. p.29-39)
Suggested by Polson.
Polson: Description of the University's present and prospective role.
                 Y   4   6

996. WEIGHTMAN, GEORGE HENRY. A study of prejudice in a personalistic society: an analysis of an attitude survey of college students - U.P. AS 2, no. 1 (Apr. 1964), 87-101.

ETHNIC INFLUENCES

Americans

997. ARANETA, FRANCISCO. American impact on Philippine culture. Solidarity 2, no. 5 (Jan./Feb. 1967), 3-15.

998. BLOUNT, JAMES HENDERSON. The American occupation of the Philippines, 1898-1912. New York and London, Putnam's Sons, 1912, 1913. 664p.
Onorato: G   3   3/4

999. HARTENDORP, A. V. H. The American contribution. FTY, (1952), 104-106, 121.

1000. HUNT, CHESTER L. The Americanization process in the Philippines. India Quarterly 12, no. 2 (Apr./June 1956), 117-130.

1001. LEGARDA, BENITO, JR. American entrepreneurs in the nineteenth-century Philippines. Explorations in entrepreneurial history 9, no. 3 (Feb. 1957), 142-159.
Felix: Excellent; the only work on the subject still worth talking about.
                  X   4   3
Onorato: X   5   3
Valdepeñas: Pretty good.
                  X   4   6

1002. LE ROY, JAMES ALFRED. The Americans in the Philippines; a history of the conquest and first years of occupation. Boston & New York, Houghton Mifflin Company, 1914. 2v.
Onorato: G   3   4

1003. WHEELER, GERALD E. The American minority in the Philippines during the prewar

commonwealth period. AS 4, no. 2 (Aug. 1966), 362-373.
    Onorato: H/Y   4   4

Chinese

1004. AGEO, GABRIEL G. Memorandum on Chinese in Philippines. (In: Philippine
Commission, 1899-1900. Report. 1900. v2. p.432-445)
    Amyot: -   4   3
    Weightman: A conservative, hostile Filipino-oriented summary of
                    Chinese life designed to insure restriction or exclusion
                    of Chinese.
                    X?   3   2/3
    Wickberg: -   3   3

1005. ALIP, EUFRONIO M. Filipinos ponder the Chinese problem. Progress, (1960),
70-74. (Reprinted in: Liao, Shubert S. C., ed. Chinese participation in
Philippine culture and economy. Manila, 1964. p.248-259)
    Liao: H   4   6

1006. _____. Ten centuries of Philippine-Chinese relations; historical, political, social, economic. JH 7, nos. 1/4 (June 1959), 1-188.
    Liao: H   4   6

1007. AMYOT, JACQUES. The Chinese community of Manila: a study of adaptation of
Chinese familism to the Philippine environment. Chicago, Dept. of Anthro-
pology, Univ. of Chicago, 1960. (Chicago Univ. Philippine Studies Program.
Research series, no. 2) Thesis (Ph.D.) - Univ. of Chicago, 1960.
    Amyot: E   5   7
    Liao: E   4   7
    Weightman: One of the few valuable studies in the area. Stress on
                    social not political and economic aspects of Chinese
                    family system.
                    E   5   6
    Wickberg: The title is misleading. This is the best study of
                    Chinese familial system in the Philippines. It is not a
                    study of the community as a whole.
                    E   4   6

1008. _____. The Chinese community of the Philippines. 1957. Thesis (M.A.) -
Univ. of Chicago.
    Amyot: E   3   7
    Liao: E   4   7
    Weightman: Valuable compilation of related data.
                    E   4   7

1009. ANGUS, WILLIAM R. Chinese church life in the Philippines. CC 7, no. 3
(May/June 1967), 19-24.

1010. APPLETON, SHELDON. Communism and the Chinese in the Philippines. Pac. Aff.
32, no. 4 (Dec. 1959), 376-391.
    Coller: Reviews rise of the situation, admits its still-small

dimensions, but recognizes it as tied to a minority-majority group clash.

	V	3	6
Liao:	V	4	6

Weightman: Very good treatment of Sinophobia and anti-communism.

	V	4	6
Wickberg:	V	3	6

1011. BARNETT, MILTON L. Persistence and change in Cantonese-American gambling. PSR 10, nos. 3/4 (July/Oct. 1962), 186-203.

Weightman:	E	3	7

1012. BARNETT, PATRICIA G. The Chinese in Southeastern Asia and the Philippines. American Academy of Political and Social Sciences. Annals. 226 (Mar. 1943), 32-49.

Liao:	V	4	4

Weightman: Dated, but a good summary of pre-war II status.

	V	3	5
Wickberg:	V	3	7

1013. BARRANCO, VICENTE. The Chinese among us. (In: Liao, Shubert S. C., ed. Chinese participation in Philippine culture and economy. Manila, [n.p. 1964.] p.191-194)

Liao:	Q	4	6

1014. BELFORD, SAMUEL W. Our colonial responsibilities; Chinese exclusion from the Philippines. The Arena 23, no. 5 (May 1900), 449-458.

Weightman: Dated, but good. Important background source of exclusion processes.

-	3	3

1015. BEYER, H. OTLEY. Early history of Philippine relations with China. FTY, (1948), 47-49, 60.

Liao:	A	5	1
Weightman:	A	3	1

1016. _____. Early history of Philippine relations with foreign countries, especially China. Manila, National Printing Company, 1948. 17p. "Originally printed as an 'Historical Introduction' to E. Arsenio Manuel's Chinese Elements in the Tagalog Language. 1948."

Amyot:	A	3	1/3
Liao:	A	5	1

Weightman: Details now in some dispute--but reference points for most research in area.

	A	4	1
Wickberg:	A	3	1

1017. BLAKER, JAMES ROLAND. The Chinese newspaper in the Philippines: toward the definition of a tool. AS 3, no. 2 (Aug. 1965), 243-261.

Liao:	J	4	6

Weightman: Of some value.

	V	3	6
Wickberg:	V	3	6

1018. BLUMENTRITT, FERDINAND. Die Chinesen auf den Philippinen. Jahresberichte

der Communal-Oberrealschule von Leitmeritz. 1879. 33p.
Cited in Marcelo Tangco, Anthropology and the Philippines. PSSHR, Aug.
1940, p.209.
    Weightman: Of main interest because of his historic link with Rizal.
              Q   3   2/3
    Wickberg: A standard survey.
              E   4   3

1019. CHAU, JU-KUA. Chau Ju-Kua: his work on the Chinese and Arab trade in the
twelfth and thirteenth centuries, entitled Chu-fan-chi, trans. from the
Chinese and annotated by Friedrich Hirth and W. W. Rockhill, eds. St. Peters-
burg, Printing Office of the Imperial Academy of Sciences, 1911. 288p.
    Wickberg: A/G   5   1

1020. _____. Description of the Philippines. JH 8, no. 1 (Mar. 1960), 72-76.
Reprinted from: Blair & Robertson, v.34, 183-191.
    Liao: H   4   6
    Weightman: Translation of section of classic work of Chao.
              T   5   1
    Wickberg: A unique description of 13th century Chinese sea trade
            probably at a Philippine port.
              A/G   5   1

1021. CHEN, CHIH-MAI. Philippine-Chinese relations: a long view. Philippine
Economy Review 4, (May 1958), 10-12, 39-40.
Cited in Biblio. of Asian Studies, 1958. p.650.
    Liao: G   4   6
    Weightman: Important--only as positional view of Sino ambassador.
              G   2/3   6

1022. CH'EN, CHING-HO. The Chinese community in the sixteenth century Philippines.
Tokyo, Centre for East Asian Cultural Studies, 1968. 176p. (East Asian
Cultural Studies Series, no. 12)

1023. _____. The overseas Chinese in the Philippines during the 16th century.
Hong Kong, Southeast Asia Studies Section, New Asia Research Institute,
1963. (Monograph Series no. 2)
    Liao: Q   4   2
    Weightman: Disappointing--unimaginative reliance on limited sources.
             -    2/3   2

1024. CHEN, SHAO-HSING. The migration of Chinese from Fukien to the Philippines
under the Spanish colonization and to Taiwan under the Dutch colonization:
an analysis of their pattern of development and their correspondences. International Association of Historians of Asia. Second Biennial Conference.
Proceedings. Taipei. (Oct. 6-9, 1962), 459-468.
    Liao: H   4   3
    Wickberg: Z   3   2

1025. CHEN, TA. Chinese migrations, with special reference to labor conditions.
Washington, D.C. U.S. Labor Statistics Bureau. Bulletin 340. July, 1923.
237p. Chapter 6. Chinese in the Philippines, p.97-110.
    Weightman: Data of value; often-quoted reference on subject.
             S   4   4

Wickberg: S   3   7

1026. China. Papers (by Chinese minister) relative to status of Chinese in Phil-
       ippine Islands. Washington, D.C. May 23, 1900. 8p. (S. Doc. 397, 56th
       Cong. 1st sess. In v.35; 3877)
            Weightman: Valuable reference.
                           G   4   5
            Wickberg: G   3   7

1027. China en Filipinas; colección de artículos publicados en el Diario de Manila
       acerca de la immigración asíatica en [!] archipiélago. Manila, Estab. Tip.
       Ramírez y Cia, 1889. 226p.
       Source: U.P. Library. Filipiniana Section. Shelflist.
            Weightman: Rich historic lode.
                           J   5   3
            Wickberg: Anti-Chinese diatribes. Best source for anti-Chinese
                           agitation of the 1880's.
                           V   5   3

1028. CHOW, SHU-KAI. The foundation of Philippine-Chinese amity. (In: Liao,
       Shubert S. C., ed. Chinese participation in Philippine culture and economy.
       Manila, 1964. p.377-380)
            Liao: G   4   6
            Weightman: Chow's position enhances this article in an unusually
                           dreary series.
                           G   3   6

1029. CHUA, ANTONIO ROXAS. Second class Philippine citizenship and nationalism
       of Rizal. (In: Liao, Shubert S. C., ed. Chinese participation in Philip-
       pine culture and economy. Manila, 1964. p.309-313)
            Liao: X   4   6

1030. COBO, FATHER JUAN. Early eyewitness accounts: Father Juan Cobo's account.
       (In: Felix, Alfonso, ed. The Chinese in the Philippines, 1570-1770, vol. 1.
       Manila, Solidaridad Pub. House, 1966. p.133-142)
            Felix: The writer was the second parish priest of Binondo then
                           in the Chinese center in the Philippines.
                           M   5   2
            Wickberg: The author learned Chinese and worked as a missionary
                           among the Manila Chinese.
                           M   5   2

1031. COLLER, RICHARD W. Social-psychological perspective on the Chinese as a
       minority group in the Philippines. PSR 8, nos. 1/2 (Jan./Apr. 1960), 47-
       56.
            Coller: An attempt to apply symbolic interaction theory to the
                           situation.
                           Z   4   7
            Liao: H   4   7
            Weightman: Provocative insights into nature of anti-sinicism.
                           Z   5   6

1032. COMENGE Y DALMAU, RAFAEL. Cuestiones filipinas. 1ª. parte. Los Chinos.
       (Estudio social y político). Manila, Tipolitografía de Chofré y comp.,
       1894. 470p.

> Weightman: One of few Spanish sources, easily available, superior work for a 19th century work.
> H/G   5   3
> Wickberg: Probably the most useful general source on the Chinese in the 19th century Philippines.
> V   5   3

1033. DY, HUANCHAY. Chinese contributions to Philippine progress. FTY, (1953), 139-140.
> Liao: X   4   7

1034. EITZEN, D. STANLEY. Two minorities: the Jews of Poland and the Chinese of the Philippines. Jewish Journal of Sociology 10, no. 2 (Dec. 1968), 221-240.

1035. FELIX, ALFONSO, JR. A bold answer to the Chinese problem. Solidarity 1, no. 1 (Jan./Mar. 1966), 27-31.
> Liao: 0   4   6

1036. _____, ed. The Chinese in the Philippines: 1570-1770. v.1. Manila, Solidaridad Pub. House, 1966). 286p.
> Liao: 0   4   2/3

1037. FLORES, RICARDO V. Chinese influences upon the Filipino way of life. 1949. Thesis (M.A.) - National Univ.
> Liao: Y   4   6

1038. FONACIER, TOMAS S. The Chinese exclusion policy in the Philippines. PSSHR 14, no. 1 (Mar. 1949), 3-28.
> Liao: H   4   7
> Weightman: Summary of research (of his dissertation).
> H   4   4
> Wickberg: H   3   4

1039. _____. The Chinese in the Philippines during the American administration. 1932. 195p. Thesis (Ph.D.) - Stanford Univ.
> Weightman: Surprisingly good; Filipino view of controversies involved. Filipino bias--creates some problems however.
> H   4   5

1040. FOO TAK SUN. The case of the overstaying Chinese visitors in the Philippines. 1960. 169p. Thesis (M.A.) - U.P.
> Liao: H   4   6
> Weightman: Disappointing--because of potentials for imaginative research.
> V   3/4   6

1041. GILL, ROBERT L. Legal aspects of the position of the Chinese in the Philippines. 1942. Thesis (Ph.D.) - Univ. of Michigan.
> Weightman: One of the few detailed reliable dissertations (now dated) on American period.
> H   4   4

1042. GUERRERO, MILAGROS C. The Chinese in the Philippines, 1570-1770. (In: Felix, Alfonso, ed. The Chinese in the Philippines, 1570-1770. Manila,

Solidaridad Pub. House, 1966.p.15-39)
    Felix: The writer teaches history at U.P.
                     H   3   2
    Liao: H   4   2/3

1043. HARTENDORP, A. V. H. The overstaying Chinese problem. (In: Hartendorp, A. V. H. History of industry and trade of the Philippines: the Magsaysay administration. Manila, Philippine Education Co., 1961, p. 201-206)
    Liao: Q   5   6

1044. HORSLEY, MARGARET W. Sangley: the formation of anti-Chinese feeling in the Philippines--a cultural study of the stereotypes of prejudice. 1950. 239p. Thesis (Ph.D.) - Columbia Univ.
    Wickberg: Shows how the Spanish experience with the Moors and Jews in Spain conditioned their attitudes toward the Chinese.
                     E   4   2

1045. HUANG, CHI-LU. Sino-Philippine relations in the last 60 years. (In: Liao, Shubert S. C., ed. Chinese participation in Philippine culture and economy. Manila, [n.p. 1964.] p.116-119)
    Liao: Y   4   3

1046. JANSE, OLOV R. T. Notes on Chinese influences in the Philippines in pre-Spanish times.
Reprinted from Harvard Journal of Asiatic Studies, Vol. 8, no. 1 (Mar. 1944), 34-62. 17 plates.
    Wickberg: Dated but still of use.
                     A   4   1

1047. JENSEN, KHIN MYINT. The Chinese in the Philippines during the American regime: 1898-1946. Madison, 1956. 405p. Thesis (Ph.D.) - Univ. of Wisconsin.
    Weightman: Not too analytical, but an excellent source of material on World War II period of Philippine Chinese.
                     V/H   4/5   4/5
    Wickberg: H   3   4

1048. JIANG, JOSEPH P. L. The Chinese and the Philippine political process. Australian Journal of Politics and History 13, no. 2 (Aug. 1967), 189-203.

1049. JORDANA Y MORERA, RAMÓN. La immigración China en Filipinas. Madrid, Tip. de M. G. Hernandez, 1888. 48p.
    Weightman: Good source material.
                     H   4/5   3
    Wickberg: A standard contemporary account.
                     N   5   3

1050. JU, I-HSIUNG. Chinese contributions to Philippine arts and crafts. CC 7, no. 3 (May/June 1967), 10-18.
    Liao: R   4   7

1051. LAUFER, BERTHOLD. The relations of the Chinese to the Philippine Islands. Smithsonian Miscellaneous Collections 50 (1907), 248-284.
    Weightman: Excellent source--frequently quoted.
                     H/A   5   1-4

Wickberg: Based especially on Chinese accounts.
         A   4   7

1052. LIAO, SHUBERT S. C. How the Chinese lived in the Philippines from 1570 to
1898. Fil-Sino Journal 5, no. 12 (Apr. 1958).
Reprinted (In: Liao, Shubert S. C., ed. Chinese participation in Philippine culture and economy. Manila, [n.p. 1964.] p.19-33)
    Amyot: X   4   7
    Liao: X   4   7

1053. LIU, CHI-TIEN. An approach to the study of early sino-Philippine relations. (In: Felix, Alfonso, ed. The Chinese in the Philippines: 1570-1770. Vol. 1. Manila, Solidaridad Pub. House, 1966. p.252-285)
    Liao: H   4   2/3

1054. LIU, WILLIAM T. Achievement motivation among Chinese youth in Southeast Asia. Asian Survey 5, no. 4 (Apr. 1965), 186-196.

1055. LOCSIN, TEODORO M. Race prejudice--the Chinese question. (In: Liao, Shubert S. C., ed. Chinese participation in Philippine culture and economy. Manila, [n.p. 1964.] p. 260-266)
    Liao: Q   4   6
    Wickberg: J   3   6

1056. MCPHELIN, MICHAEL. The Chinese question. PS 9, no. 2 (Apr. 1961), 333-338.
    Liao: M   4   6
    Wickberg: M   3   6

1057. MACAPAGAL, DIOSDADO P. The role of foreigners here. (In: Liao, Shubert S. C., ed. Chinese participation in Philippine culture and economy. Manila, [n.p. 1964.] p. 358-364)
    Liao: G   4   6
    Wickberg: G   3   6

1058. OCAMPO, ESTEBAN A. DE. Chinese greatest contribution to the Philippines--the birth of Dr. Jose Rizal. (In: Liao, Shubert S. C., ed. Chinese participation in Philippine culture and economy. Manila, [n.p. 1964.] p.89-95)
    Liao: H   5   3

1059. LA OCEANÍA ESPAÑOLA. Los Chinos en Filipinas; males que se experimentan actualmente y peligros de esa creciente inmigración; observaciones, hechos y cifras que se encuentran en artículos que La Oceanía española ... ha dedicado al estudio de este problema social. Manila, Estab. Tip. de "La Oceanía Española," 1886. 130p.
    Weightman: Excellent primary source material.
                   J   5   3
    Wickberg: Typical collection of anti-Chinese arguments from the 1880's.
                   J   5   3

1060. PANGILINAN, MARIE LOU. Comradeship in war. (In: Liao, Shubert S. C., ed. Chinese participation in Philippine culture and economy. Manila, [n.p. 1964.] p.142-143)

Liao: J   4   5

1061. PANLASIGUI, ISIDORO. A comparative study of the lives of Sun Yat-sen and Jose Rizal. FTY (Sept. 1958), 178-182, 195.
Liao: Y   5   7

1062. _____. Dr. Jose Rizal's Chinese ancestry. FTY (1926/1956. 30th anniversary no.), 146-147, 150-151, 186.
Liao: Y   5   3

1063. PHILIPPINE ISLANDS. BUREAU OF CUSTOMS. Chinese and immigration circulars annotated, 1-197, Dec. [26] 1901-Dec. [31] 1907, constructions and decisions. Manila, Bureau of Printing, 1908. 273p.
Wickberg: W   5   4

1064. _____. Chinese and immigration circular 277-293; July 26, 1913-May 20, 1915. [Manila, 1913-15.] various paging. Mimeographed.
Wickberg: W   5   4

1065. _____. Chinese and immigration circular 294-305; Aug. 26, 1915-Sept. 4, 1916. [Manila, 1915-16.] Mimeographed. Discontinued with the Sept. 4, 1916, issue.
Wickberg: W   5   4

1066. _____. BUREAU OF JUSTICE. Opinion of [Ignacio Villamor] attorney general of Philippine Islands, June 8, 1910, on power of governor-general to order expulsion of Chinese persons from Philippine Islands under certain circumstances. Manila, 1910. 34p. (In: Philippine Islands, Justice Bureau. Official opinions of attorney general of Philippine Islands. 1911. v.5. p. 511-551)
Weightman: Biased; inaccurate but an official summary of issue.
             W   5   4
Wickberg: W   5   4

1067. Protest of Chinese government against exclusion of Chinese from Philippines. Washington, D.C. April 18, 1902, 3 p. (H. Doc. 562, 57th Cong. 1st sess. In v.94; 4361)
Weightman: Valuable reference
             G   4   5
Wickberg: G   5   4

1068. PURCELL, VICTOR. The Chinese in Southeast Asia. 2nd ed. London, Oxford Univ. Press, 1965. Part 8. The Chinese in the Philippines. p.493-564.
Amyot: H   3   7
Coller: Classic, most valuable and comprehensive work on the subject.
             H   5   7
Felix: The standard work on Southeast Asia as a whole; sketchy of necessity as regards the Philippines.
             H   4   7
Weightman: 2nd edition completed after his death--grossly inferior to 1st edition. Philippine section--one of worst sections. Misleading and sloppily done.
             G/H   3   7
Wickberg: H   3   7

1069. RAMOS, NARCISO. Mutual accommodation, mutual regard, mutual faith. FTY, (1963), 67-69, 96.
Liao: G   4   6

1070. Relacion verdadera del levantamiento que los Sangleyes o Chinos hizieron en las Filipinas, y de las vitorias que tuuo côntra ellos el Gouernador dõ Sebástiã Hurtado de Corcuera, el año passado de 1640 y 1641. Madrid, Catalina del Barrio y Angulo, 1642. 4p.
Weightman: -   4   2
Wickberg: One of the few accounts of the affair.
                -      5   2

1071. REYES, TEOFILO D., SR. The social and economic adjustments of the Chinese minority in the Philippines. PGJ 3, no. 3 (July/Sept. 1955), 139-142.
Liao: 0   4   6

1072. ROBB, WALTER. I weep for the Chinese. Harper's Magazine 201, no. 1204 (Sept. 1950), 58-63.
Wickberg: J   3   4

1073. ROCES, ALEJANDRO R. For closer Chinese-Filipino cultural relation. (In: Liao, Shubert S. C., ed. Chinese participation in Philippine culture and economy. Manila, [n.p. 1964.] p.49-51)
Liao: Q   4   -

1074. _____. Greater cooperation for greater Philippine progress. (In: Liao, Shubert S. C., ed. Chinese participation in Philippine culture and economy. Manila, [n.p. 1964.] p.366-369)
Liao: Q   4   6

1075. RONQUILLO, BERNARDINO. Philippine Chinese faith in the Nation's future. FTY, (1926-1951), 109, 114.
Liao: J   4   6

1076. RUNES, ILDEFONSO T. China's noble heroes in the Philippines. Manila Guardian 12, (Nov. 30, 1949), 45-48.
Liao: H   4   7

1077. SALAZAR (BISHOP OF THE PHILIPPINES). Early eyewitness account: Bishop Salazar's report to the King. (In: Felix, Alfonso, Jr., ed. The Chinese in the Philippines, 1570-1770. v.1. Manila, Solidaridad Pub. House, 1966. p.119-132)
Felix: The writer was the first bishop and archbishop of Manila. He devoted much time to the conversion of the Chinese and sent the first Spanish missions to that country.
                M   5   2
Liao: M   5   2/3
Wickberg: Standard source. Also available in Retana's Archivo and in Blair and Robertson.
                M   5   2

1078. SALONGA, JOVITO R. China and the Philippines. Solidarity 1, no. 1 (Jan./ Mar. 1966), 37-42.
Liao: 0   4   6

1079. SANTAMARIA, ALBERTO. The Chinese Parian (El Parian De Los Sangleyes). (In: Felix, Alfonso, ed. The Chinese in the Philippines, 1570-1770. Manila, Solidaridad Pub. House, 1966. v.1, no. 9. p.67-118)
    Felix: Excellent research on the subject.
                  H/M   4   2/3
    Liao: M   5   2
    Wickberg: M   3   2

1080. SCHURZ, WILLIAM L. The Chinese in the Philippines. (In: Stephens,Henry M. and Herbert E. Bolton, eds. The Pacific Ocean in history. New York, Macmillan Company, 1917, p.214-222)
    Weightman: H   4   2/3
    Wickberg: H   3   2

1081. _____. The Manila Galleon. New York, E. P. Dutton, 1939. 453p. Chapter 1. The Chinese. p.63-98.
    Suggested by Weightman.
    Weightman: The Manila Galleon is a classic. This article summarizes section on Chinese.
                  H   4   2/3

1082. STORY, RUSSELL M. The problem of the Chinese in the Philippines. American Political Science Review 3, no. 1 (Feb. 1909), 30-48.
    Weightman: Summary view of Sino problem at beginning of American period.
                  V   3/4 3/4
    Wickberg: V   3   7

1083. TACK, TANG. The Chinese in the Philippines. A synthesis. (In: Liao, Shubert S. C., ed. Chinese participation in Philippine culture and economy. Manila, [n.p. 1964.] p.393-405)
    Liao: X   4   6

1084. TAN, ALLEN L. Methods in cross-cultural research: the case of Chinese and Filipinos. GEJ, no. 12 (2nd Semester, 1966-1967), 215-224.

1085. _____. A survey of studies on anti-Sinoism in the Philippines. AS 6, no. 2 (Aug. 1968), 198-207.

1086. TING, SIMON. Common aspirations of Filipinos and Chinese. CC 7, no. 3 (May/June 1967), 5-9.

1087. UY, HENRY CHO-YEE. The Chinese in the Philippines. PM 32, no. 10 (Oct. 1935), 496, 498-499.

1088. _____. The Philippines and Chinese immigration. PM 32, no. 11 (Nov. 1935), 546, 574-575.

1089. VILLAMIN, VICENTE. Filipino-Chinese modus vivendi. (In: Liao, Shubert S. C., ed. Chinese participation in Philippine culture and economy. Manila, [n.p., 1964.] p.412-413)
    Liao: X   4   6

1090. WADA, SEI. The Philippine Islands as known to the Chinese before the Ming period. Tokyo. Toyo Bunko. Research department. Memoirs, no. 4 (1929), 121-166.

121-166.
    Wickberg: Useful information derived from Chinese books of sailing
                    directions and other sources.
                    H   4   1

1091. WANG, TEH-MING. An early mention of the Philippines in Chinese records?
JEAS 1, no. 3 (Apr. 1952), 42-48.
    Weightman: Of some value--but care in reading needed. Lacks disci-
                    pline and too imaginative. Work by Wu Ching-Hong vastly
                    superior. Still one of few good Philippine Chinese his-
                    torians.
                    H   4   1

1092. _____. Historico-critical study of some early Chinese records and their
relations to pre-Spanish Philippine culture. 1954. 173p. Thesis (M.A.) -
U.P.
    Liao: H   4   1/2
    Weightman: H   4   1
    Wickberg: H   3   1

1093. _____. Lim Ah-Hong's affair. JEAS 8, nos. 1/2 (Jan./Apr. 1959), 21-41.
    Liao: H   4   2
    Weightman: H   4   1

1094. WEIGHTMAN, GEORGE H. Anti-sinicism in the Philippines. AS 5, no. 1 (Apr.
1967), 220-231.

1095. _____. The Chinese community in the Philippines. 1952. 222p. Thesis
(M.A.) - U.P.
    Amyot: Z   **5**   7
    Coller: First attempt by a sociologist to study the Manila
                    Chinese in depth. Valuable first-hand data.
                    Z   5   7
    Liao: Z   4   **7**
    Wickberg: Z   3   7

1096. _____. The Philippine Chinese; a cultural history of a marginal trading
community. Ithaca, 1960. 462p. Thesis (Ph.D.) - Cornell Univ.
    Amyot: Z   3   7
    Wickberg: Despite the title there is little history. Description
                    of contemporary organizations is valuable.
                    Z   4   7

1097. _____. The Philippine-Chinese image of the Filipino. Pac. Aff. 40,
nos. 3/4 (Fall/Winter 1967/68), 315-323.

1098. _____. A preliminary ecological description of the Chinese community in
Manila. PSR 3, no. 4 (Nov. 1955), 23-27.
    Coller: Excerpt from his M.A. thesis.
                    Z   5   7

1099. WEST, M. F. A history of the export of ceramics from China during the Ming
Dynasty (1638-1644) to the Philippine Islands and Northern Borneo. 1952.
Thesis (M.A.) - Univ. of Washington.
Cited in Stuart A. Schlegel. Preliminary bibliography of Philippine

culture history. 11p. n.d.
      Weightman: Value to the specialist.
                     A   4   2

1100. WICKBERG, EDGAR B. The Chinese in Philippine economy and society, 1850-
       1898. Berkeley, 1961. 344p. Thesis (Ph.D.) - Univ. of California.
         Felix: Excellent research.
                      H   4   3
         Weightman: An excellent study of both Chinese and Philippine
                      society. One of the best in field.
                      H   5   3
         Wickberg: H   3   7

1101. _____. The Chinese in Philippine life, 1850-1898. New Haven, Yale Univ.
       Press, 1965. 280p. (Yale Southeast Asia Studies, 1)
         Amyot: H   5   3
         Liao: H   5   2/3
         Weightman: Elaboration of (the preceding title). A classic in
                      Filipiniana.
                      H   5   3
         Wickberg: Emphasis on social history, 1850-1898.
                      H   4   7

1102. _____. The Chinese mestizo in Philippine history. JSEAH 5, no. 1 (Mar.
       1964), 62-100.
         Wickberg: Emphasis upon 1750-1898. The only recent analysis of
                      the socio-economic role of the mestizo in this period.
                      H   4   7

1103. WU, CHING-HONG. References to the Chinese in the Philippines during the
       Spanish period found in Blair and Robertson, "The Philippine Islands."
       Nanyang University. Institute of Southeast Asia. Bulletin 1, (1959),
       F1-F90.
       Source: U.P. Library. Filipiniana Section. Shelflist.
         Liao: H   4   7
         Weightman: H   4   2/3

1104. _____. A study of references to the Philippines in Chinese sources from
       earliest times to the Ming Dynasty. PSSHR 24, nos. 1/2 (Jan./June 1959),
       1-181. Thesis (M.A.) - U.P., 1953.
         Felix: Thorough and well done work by a Chinese scholar with a
                      Philippine background.
                      H   4   1/2
         Liao: H   4   7
         Weightman: His M.A. thesis--fascinating, detailed work.
                      H   4   1/2
         Wickberg: Valuable bibliographical tool.
                      H   5   1

1105. _____. Supplements to a study of references to the Philippines in Chinese
       sources from earliest times to the Ming Dynasty (? - 1644). JEAS 7, no. 4
       (Oct. 1958), 307-393.
         Liao: H   4   7
         Weightman: H   4   1/2
         Wickberg: Valuable bibliographical tool.
                      H   5   1

1106. YANG, SE-PENG. Social and economic adjustments of the Chinese minority. ERJ 2, no. 3 (Dec. 1955), 98-101.
        Liao: C   4   6

1107. YAO, SHIONG SHIO. Closer Filipino-Chinese relations. (In: Liao, Shubert S. C., ed. Chinese participation in Philippine culture and economy. Manila, [n.p., 1964.] p.389-392)
        Liao: X   4   6

1108. YAP, SANTIAGO. Chinese influence on the socio-economic life of the Filipinos. Philippine Economic Review 4, (May 1958), 14-15. Index to Periodicals (U.P. Library. Filipiniana Section).
        Liao: X   4   6

1109. YEE, TING FARD. The Chinese in the Philippines. Dept. of Political Science, Univ. of Michigan, June, 1941. 61p. Typescript. Cited in Annotated Bibliography of Philippine Social Sciences. v.3 (part I): Political Science. 1960. p.3.
        Weightman: Extensively quoted although never published--source of much insight into pre-war period.
                    V   3   4

1110. YEH, GEORGE K. A word to our overseas compatriots. FTY, (1958), 18, 20.
        Liao: G   4   7

1111. YOUNG, RUTH C. The role of Chinese women in community welfare in the Philippines. FTY, (1949), 57-58.
        Liao: Y   4   6

1112. YU, KHE THAI. Filipino-Chinese issues can be solved with understanding. (In: Liao, Shubert S., ed. Chinese participation in Philippine culture and economy. Manila, [n.p., 1964.] p.370-372)
        Liao: X   4   6

1113. YUYITUNG, QUENTIN. A Chinese view on Philippine-Chinese tensions. Solidarity 1, no. 1 (Jan./Mar. 1966), 33-36.
        Felix: The writer has personal experience of what he writes. He was persecuted by the Philippine government for his views.
                    J   4/5   7
        Liao: J   4   6
        Weightman: Importance relative to Yu's position as publisher of outspoken Chinese language newspaper.
                    J   3   6
        Wickberg: J   3   6

1114. ZAIDE, GREGORIO F. Changing tides of Sino-Philippine relations. FTY (1949), 25-26, 39-40.
        Liao: H   4   6

1115. _____. Chinese general in the Philippine revolution. FTY, (1955), 155-160.
        Liao: H   5   7
        Wickberg: H   3   3

1116. _____. Chinese have enriched Philippine culture. Pacific Review, (Dec. 1961), 7-11.
Source: Index to Periodicals (U.P. Library. Filipiniana Section).
Liao: H   5   7

1117. _____. Pre-Spanish Chinese contacts with the Philippines. FTY, (1965), 71-74.
Liao: H   4   1

Chinese - Economics

1118. APPLETON, SHELDON. Overseas Chinese and economic nationalization in the Philippines. Journal of Asian Studies 19, no. 2 (Feb. 1960), 151-161.
Amyot: V   4   6
Liao: V   4   6
Weightman: Stresses political and economic insights into de-alienization.
               V   4   6
Wickberg: V   3   6

1119. CASTILLO, ANDRES V. The Chinese role in Philippine economic progress. Central Bank News Digest 13, no. 18 (May 2, 1961), 4-7.
Reprinted (In: Liao, Shubert S. C., ed. Chinese participation in Philippine culture and economy. Manila, [n.p.,1964.] p.172-177)
Liao: X   4   6
Weightman: X   3   6

1120. CHEN, PAUL CHING-SZU. The contribution of the Chinese nationals to the Philippine economy. JEAS 3, no. 4 (July/Oct. 1954), 555-558.
Liao: Y   4   6

1121. CHEN, YEH SHAO. Chinese in Philippine trade. Manila, 1926. 178p. Thesis (M.A.) - U.P.
Cited in T'ai-pei (City) College of Commerce. Bibliography of the Far Eastern Tropics. Taihoku, Taiwan. 1938. p.41.
Weightman: Data of value; dated and superficial analysis.
               X   3   4

1122. CHU, HOI-HORN. Chinese in Philippine economy. 1950. Thesis (M.B.A.) - Manila Central Univ.
Source: Compilation of graduate theses . . . p. 18.
Liao: X   4   6

1123. CASTAÑEDA, CARLOS T. Local Sino industrialists contribute to PI progress. Pacific Review, no. 26 (July 1956), 45-46.
Source: Index to Periodicals (U.P. Library. Filipiniana Section).
Liao: V   4   6

1124. DEE, HOWARD Q. Encouraging active participation of the minority groups in foreign investment. ERJ 2, no. 3 (Dec. 1955), 106-109.
Liao: X   4   6

1125. DIAZ-TRECHUELO, LOURDES. The role of the Chinese in the Philippine domestic economy (1570-1770). (In: Felix, Alfonso, Jr., ed. The Chinese in the Philippines, 1570-1770. vol.1. Manila, Solidaridad Pub. House, 1966. p.175-210)
      Felix: The writer had access to the Archives of the Indies in Seville where she teaches. She has long specialized in Philippine history.
                 H   4   2

1126. LIAO, SHUBERT S. C. Chinese investment in the Philippines. Trade Journal 3, nos. 5/6 (1958).
Cited in Center for East Asian Culture Studies. Research institutes and researchers of Asian studies in the Philippines. 1966. p.10.
      Liao: X   4   6

1127. _____. Chinese participation in Philippine culture and economy. Manila, The Author, 1964. 452p.
      Liao: X   4   7

1128. _____. Contributions of Chinese enterprises in the economic development of the Philippines. ERJ 4, no. 2 (Sept. 1957), 71-79.
      Liao: X   4   6

1129. _____. Investment, employment in Chinese enterprises and the economic development of the Philippines. FTY (1957), 41-44, 141-144, 160, 183.
      Liao: X   5   6
      Wickberg: X   3   6

1130. MARCOS, MARIO P. Foreign investment and the problems of alien minorities. ERJ 2, no. 3 (Dec. 1955), 101-106.
      Liao: X   4   6

1131. MIRAFUENTE, BUENAVENTURA. Chinese contribution to the early economic development of the Philippines. FTY, (1950), 33-34, 38, 40.
      Liao: X   4   3

1132. ONG, SIONG CHO. The Chinese role in the economic and industrial growth of the Philippines. Insurance and Finance 9, no. 8 (Oct. 1961), 16-18.
Cited in Index to Philippine Periodicals, v.7, p.259.
      Liao: X   4   6
      Weightman: X   3   6

1133. PAMINTUAN, CATALINA M. The Chinese in Philippine economy today. 1959. Thesis (M.A.) - National Teachers College.
Source: Compilation of graduate theses...p.185.
      Liao: Y   4   6

1134. QUIASON, SERAFIN D. The early Philippine-China sampan trade. FTY, (1966), 273-277.
      Weightman: Superior to usual FTY articles.
                 H   3   1/2

1135. _____. The Sampan trade, 1570-1770. (In: Felix, Alfonso, ed. The Chinese in the Philippines, 1570-1770. v.1. Manila, Solidaridad Pub. House, 1966. p. 160-174)

Felix: An excellent summary of the trade.
                H   4   2/3
Liao: H   4   2/3
Weightman: H   3   2/3

1136. RAVENHOLT, ALBERT. Chinese in the Philippines--an alien business and middle
class. AUFSR. Southeast Asia Series 3, no. 28 (Dec. 9, 1955), 24p.
(AR-12-'55)
Amyot: J   4   6
Weightman: Summary of present status by a foreign resident journalist.
                J   3   6
Wickberg: J   3   6

1137. _____. The Ling Nam wanton parlor; a Chinese restauranteur in Manila copes
with the problems of success. AUFS-SEA 15, no. 3 (Apr. 1967), 1-15. AUFSR.
Southeast Asia Series 15, no. 3 (Oct. 1967), 15p. (AR-4-'67)

1138. REYNOLDS, HUBERT. Why Chinese traders approached the Philippines late - and
from the South. (In: Zamora, Mario D., ed. Studies in Philippine anthropology (In honor of H. Otley Beyer). Quezon City, Alemar-Phoenix, 1967.
p.463-479)

1139. RUNES, ILDEFONSO T. The Chinese and Philippine economy. Pacific Review 1,
(May 1950), 13-15.
Source: Index to Periodicals (U.P. Library. Filipiniana Section)
Liao: H   4   7
Weightman: Better than one might expect for Pacific Reviews.
                J   3   6

1140. SY, EN. How Chinese nationals can contribute to PI gov't. total economic
mobilization program. Pacific Review, (Dec. 1953), 28-30.
Source: Index to Periodicals (U.P. Library. Filipiniana Section)
Liao: X   4   6

1141. TANG, TACK. The role of the Chinese in the development of Phillippine econ-
omy. Morning Journal, 2nd anniv. sup., (Feb. 1959), 12-13.
Source: Index to Periodicals (U.P. Library. Filipiniana Section)
Liao: X   4   6

1142. WEI, YU-SUN. Chinese contributions to Philippine economy: the record of the
past 32 years. FTY, (1958), 43-44, 47-48.
Liao: G   4   7

1143. WICKBERG, EDGAR B. Early Chinese economic influence in the Philippines,
1850-1898. Pac. Aff. 35, no. 3 (Fall 1962), 275-285.
Felix: A good study for beginners.
                H   3   3
Weightman: Interesting summary of more detailed works in The Chinese
                in Philippine Economy and Society, and The Chinese in
                Philippine Life.
                H   5   3
Wickberg: H   3   3

1144. WU, CHING-HONG. The rise and decline of Chuanchou's international trade and its relation to the Philippine Islands. International Association of Historians of Asia, Second Biennial Conference, Proceedings. Taipei. 1962. p.469-483.

    Liao: H   4   7

    Weightman: Wu is the most reliable and qualified Philippine Chinese working on serious research on Sino-historic contacts.

                      H   4   2/3

1145. ZAIDE, GREGORIO F. Contribution of aliens to Philippine economy. FTY, (1954), 93-96, 133-136, 139.

    Amyot: H   3   7

    Liao: H   4   7

Chinese - Education

1146. BATNAG, JAIME. To close or not to close the sino schools problem? (In: Liao, Shubert S. C., ed. Chinese participation in Philippine culture and economy. Manila, [n.p., 1964.] p.353-356)

    Liao: Q   4   6

1147. CARREON, MANUEL L. Twenty-five years of Chinese schools in the Philippines. FTY, (1926/1951), 119-120.

    Liao: Y   4   6

    Wickberg: Y   3   6

1148. HERNANDEZ, JOSE MA. Chinese schools and communism in the Philippines. (In: Liao, Shubert S. C., ed. Chinese participation in Philippine culture and economy. Manila, [n.p., 1964.] p.338-341)

    Liao: Y   4   6

1149. ISIDRO, ANTONIO. Chinese education in the Philippines. PJE 34, no. 6 (Nov. 1955), 350-351, 402.

    Liao: Y   4   6

1150. NIU, PAUL. A study of the curriculur problems in Philippine-Chinese schools. 1964. v, 144p. Thesis (M.A.) - Ateneo de Manila.

    Liao: Y   4   6

1151. PAO, SHIH TIEN. Chinese schools in the Philippines. FTY, (1961), 185-186.

    Liao: Y   4   6

1152. _____. Should the Chinese schools be abolished? (In: Liao, Shubert S. C., ed. Chinese participation in Philippine culture and economy. Manila, [n.p., 1964.] p.342-352)

    Liao: Y   5   6

1153 _____. What you do not know about the Chinese schools. Examiner - the Asia Newsweekly, Issue No. 292 (Jan. 21, 1968), 7, 27, 31.

    Liao: Y   4   6

1154. PERPIÑAN, JESUS E. New controversy over Chinese schools. (In: Liao,

Shubert S. C., ed. **Chinese** participation in Philippine culture and economy. Manila, [n.p., 1964.] p.331-337)
      Liao: Y   4   6

1155. REYNOLDS, HUBERT. Overseas Chinese college student in the Philippines: a case study. PSR 16, nos. 3/4 (July/Oct. 1968), 132-135.

1156. TANG, TACK. Help solve the school crisis. (In: Liao, Shubert S. C., ed. Chinese participation in Philippine culture and economy. Manila, [n.p., 1964.] p.213-216)
      Liao: X   4   6

1157. WEIGHTMAN, GEORGE H. A study of prejudice in a personalistic society: an analysis of an attitude survey of college students - University of the Philippines. AS 2, no. 1 (Apr. 1964), 87-101.
Suggested by Weightman.

Chinese - Family and Marriage

1158. JUCO, JORGE M. Some legal aspects of Chinese marriages in the Philippines. PSR 14, no. 1 (Jan. 1966), 57-59.
Comment on Harriet Reynolds' Marriage as a focal point in cultural orientation of Chinese adults and children in Ilocos, PSR, v.13, 249-259.
      Liao: S   4   7

1159. MEDINA, BELEN TAN-GATUE. A study in non-European migration: Chinese-Filipino intermarriage. Migration News 7, no. 4 (July/Aug. 1958), 13-15.
      Liao: S   4   6

1160. SU, SING GING. The Chinese family system. PSR 2, no. 3 (Oct. 1954), 17-26.

1161. TAN-GATUE, BELEN. The social background of 30 Chinese-Filipino marriages. PSR 3, no. 3 (July 1955), 3-13.
      Weightman: Summary of item below--small sample, failure to distinguish "ethnic" from "legal" Chinese--still of value since material so limited in field.
                     Z   3/4   6
      Wickberg: Z   3   6

1162. _____. A study of assimilation in Chinese-Filipino families in Manila and suburbs. 1955. 159p. Thesis (M.A.) - U.P.
      Amyot: Z   3   6
      Coller: Empirical **study** providing facts on actual processes in 20 selected families.
                     Z   5   6
      Liao: Z   4   6
      Weightman: Valuable but limited by failure to distinguish "ethnic" vs. "legal" Chinese--very small samples.
                     Z   4   6

1163. WEIGHTMAN, GEORGE H. The Chinese family and sib in the Philippines.
       Lipunan 1, no. 1 (1965), 9-16.

1164. ZARCO, RICARDO M. The Chinese family structure. (In: Felix, Alfonso,
       ed. The Chinese in the Philippines: 1570-1790. Manila, Solidaridad Pub.
       House, 1966. v.1, p.211-222)
           Felix: A good, highly suggestive essay.
                           H/S   3   7
           Liao: Z   4   7

English

1165. JULIAN, ELISA A. British projects and activities in the Philippines, 1795-
       1805. London, 1963. Thesis (Ph.D.) - London School of Oriental and Afri-
       can Studies.

1166. LEEBRICK, KARL C. The English expedition to Manila in 1762, and the
       government of the Philippine Islands by the East India Company. Berkeley,
       1915. Thesis (Ph.D.) - Univ. of California.

1167. LONEY, NICHOLAS. A Britisher in the Philippines or the letters of Nicholas
       Loney. Manila, Bureau of Printing, 1964. 126p.
           Felix: First hand reporting.
                           F/X   5   3

1168. QUIRINO, CARLOS. Aftermath of the British invasion of the Philippines. PS
       16, no. 3 (July 1968), 540-544.

1169. SEED, GEOFFREY. British views of American policy in the Philippines re-
       flected in journals of opinion, 1898-1907. Journal of American Studies 2,
       no. 1 (Apr. 1968), 49-64.

Indians

1170. AIYAR, M. S. RAMASWAMI. Hindu influence in the Philippines. Mythic Society,
       Bangalore, India Quarterly Journal (1934/1935), 103-113.

1171. ASUNCION, DIOSDADO R. Indian elements in Philippine culture. East-West
       Center Review 1, no. 1 (June 1964), 7-12.

1172. FABELLA, GABRIEL, JR. The contemporary Indian community in the Philippines.
       PSSHR 19, no. 1 (Mar. 1954), 15-24.

1173. FRANCISCO, JUAN R. Further notes on Pardo de Tavera's El Sanscrito en la
       Lengua Tagalog. AS 6, no. 2 (Aug. 1968), 223-234.

1174. _____. Indian influences in the Philippines (with special reference to

language and literature). PSSHR 28, nos. 1/3 (Jan./Sept. 1963), 1-310.
Thesis (Ph.D.) - Univ. of Madras.
    Ward: Deals with Sanskrit loan words.
           L   5   1

1175. _____. On the date of the coming of Indian influence in the Philippines.
Philippine Historical Review 1, no. 1 (1965), 136-152.

1176. The Indian community in the Philippines. JEAS 4, no. 1 (Jan. 1955), 41-45.

1177. REGALA-ANGANGCO, OFELIA D. The Indian community in the Philippines. 1956.
169p. Thesis (M.A.) - U.P.
    Coller: First attempt by a sociologist to study these people in
           depth. Very useful data.
           Z   5   7

1178. _____. The Indian community in the Philippines. PSR 6, no. 2 (Apr.
1958), 10-24.
    Coller: Summary and digest of her M.A. thesis.
           Z   5   7

1179. SALAZAR, Z. A. Footnote to Dr. Francisco's "Notes" on Tavera. AS 6, no. 3
(Dec. 1968), 431-444.

1180. SINGH, TEJ PRATAP. Some impressions on Indian and Filipino value system.
PSR 13, no. 4 (Oct. 1965), 210-215.

Japanese

1181. AGONCILLO, TEODORO A. The cultural aspect of the Japanese occupation.
PSSHR 28, no. 4 (Dec. 1963), 351-394.

1182. _____. The fateful years: Japan's adventure in the Philippines, 1941-45.
Quezon City, Garcia, 1965. 2v.

1183. EYRE, JAMES K., JR. Japan and the Philippines under Spanish rule. PSSHR
13, no. 3 (Aug. 1941), 235-244.

1184. GARCIA, MAURO, ed. Documents on the Japanese occupation of the Philippines. Manila, Philippine Historical Association, 1965. 258p. "Separate
from the Philippine Historical Bulletin, v.9, nos. 1/2 (Mar./June 1965)."

1185. GOODMAN, GRANT K. Davao: a case study in Japanese-Philippine relations.
Lawrence, Kansas,Center for East Asian Studies, Univ. of Kansas, 1967.
117p. (International Studies, East Asian Series, Research Publication,
Number One)
Suggested by Goodman.
    Goodman: Highlights all of the factors--economic, political,
           military--which affected contacts between Japan and the
           Philippines during the American colonial period.

H 4 4

1186. _____. An experiment in wartime intercultural relations: Philippine students in Japan, 1943-1945. Ithaca, New York, Southeast Asia Program, Dept. of Asian Studies, Cornell Univ., 1962. 34p. (Cornell Univ., Southeast Asia Program Data paper, no. 46)
Suggested by Goodman.
   Golay: Goodman has approached his research with detachment and objectivity ... penetrating account...
H 4 5

1187. _____. "A flood of immigration" - patterns and problems of Japanese migration to the Philippines during the first four decades of the twentieth century. PHR 1, no. 1 (1965), 170-193.

1188. _____. Four aspects of Philippine-Japanese relations, 1930-1940. New Haven, **Southeast** Asia Studies, Yale Univ., 1967. 237p. (Monograph Series, no. 9)
   Contents:
    Japanese immigration and Philippine politics, p.1-61.
    Philippine-Japanese student exchanges, 1935-1940, p.62-132.
    Japan and Philippine radicalism: the case of Benigno Ramos, p.133-194.
    Manuel L. Quezon's visit to Japan, June-July 10, 1938, p.195-237.
      "A valuable addition ... firm command of important archival material from the Philippines, Japan and America...." **Choice**, May 1968.
H 4 4

1189. _____. General Artemio Ricarte and Japan. JSEAH 7, no. 2 (Sept. 1966), 48-60.

1190. _____. Japanese Pan-Asianism in the Philippines: the 'Hirippin Dai Ajia Kyokai'. Studies on Asia 7, (1966), 133-143.
   Goodman: Examines the Philippine Great Asia Society as one aspect of Japan's "cultural offensive" in the Islands during the 1930's.
H 4 4

1191. _____. Philippine-Japanese professorial exchanges in the 1930's. JSEAH 9, no. 2 (Sept. 1968), 229-240.

1192. _____. The Philippine Society of Japan. Monumenta Nipponica 22, nos. 1/2 (1967), 131-146.
   Goodman: Description in depth of principal vehicle for Philippine-Japanese cultural interchange during the 1930's.
H 4 4

1193. GOSIENGFIAO, VICTOR. The Japanese occupation: "The Cultural Campaign." PS 14, no. 2 (Apr. 1966), 228-242.

1194. GUERRERO, MILAGROS C. A survey of Japanese trade and investments in the Philippines, with special references to Philippine-American reactions 1900-1941. PSSHR 31, no. 1 (March 1966), 1-129.

1195. HARTENDORP, A. V. H. The Japanese occupation of the Philippines. 1st edition. Manila, Bookmark, 1967. 2v.

1196. IRIKURA, JAMES K. Trade and diplomacy between the Philippines and Japan, 1585-1623. New Haven, 1958. Thesis (Ph.D.) - Yale Univ.

1197. IWAO, SEI-ICHI. **Early** Japanese settlers in the Philippines.
    Contemporary Japan
        v.11, no. 1, Jan. 1942, 106-117.
        v.11, no. 2, Feb. 1942, 264-277.
        v.11, no. 3, Mar. 1942, 425-435.
        v.11, no. 4, Apr. 1942, 599-611.

1198. MARQUEZ, ANTONIO. A letter from Davao. Commonwealth Advocate 7, (July 1941), 11-12.
    Source: Index to Periodicals (U.P. Library. **Filipinia**na Section)
        Goodman: Excited journalism but includes interesting documents and some perceptive observations.
        J   3   4

1199. PROVIDO, GENEROSO P. Japanese interests in the Philippines. 1936. Thesis (Ph.D.) - Stanford Univ.
        Goodman: An extremely careful and thoughtful work though based on limited sources.
        G   3   4

1200. SANIEL, JOSEFA M. Four Japanese: their plans for the expansion of Japan to the Philippines. JSEAH 4, no. 2 (Sept. 1963), 1-12. Also published in AS 1, (1963), 52-63.
        Goodman: A unique study though a **bit** heavy with the "plot thesis."
        H   4   3

1201. _____. Japan and the Philippines, 1868-1898. Quezon City, U.P., 1963. 409p. Also published in PSSHR, v.27, nos. 1/4, 1962.
        Goodman: The author's Ph.D. thesis derived in part from research done in Japan.
        H   4   3

1202. SANTIAGO, DOMINGO C. History of Philippine **education** during the Japanese occupation. Quezon City, 1951. 192p. Thesis (M.A.) - U.P.

1203. SCHURZ, WILLIAM L. The Manila **galleon.** New York, E. P. Dutton, 1939. 453p. Chapter 2. The Japanese. p.99-128.
Suggested by Weightman.

1204. SORIANO, RAFAELITA V. H. Japanese occupation of the Philippines, with special reference to Japanese propaganda, 1941-1945. 1948. 438p. Thesis (Ph.D.) - Univ. of **Michigan.**
        Goodman: Particularly valuable for her references to much of the ephemera of propaganda which has now disappeared.
        V   4   5

1205. STEINBERG, DAVID JOEL. Philippine collaboration in World War II. Ann Arbor, Univ. of Michigan Press, 1967. 235p.
Suggested by Goodman.

> Goodman: "...remarkably dispassionate and objective assessment ... Much influenced by the important sociological studies of the Institute of Philippine Culture...." JAS. Nov. 1967, p. 185-6.

1206. SUPREME COMMANDER FOR THE ALLIED POWERS. CIVIL INFORMATION AND EDUCATION SECTION. Foreign Students in Japan, 1896-1947. Tokyo, 1948. 42p. (AR-307-E-E-2)

> Goodman: Somewhat superficial but still the only study in English of the subject. Filipino students are included.
> W   3   4

1207. VELLUT, J. L. Foreign relations of the **second** Republic of the Philippines, 1943-1945. JSEAH 5, (Mar. 1964), 126-142.

Spanish

1208. MACEDA, JOSE. Latin qualities in Brazil and the Philippines. AS 2, no. 2 (Aug. 1964), 223-230.

1209. PHELAN, JOHN LEDDY. The Hispanization of the Philippines: Spanish aims and Filipino responses, 1565-1700. Madison. Univ. of Wisconsin Press, 1959. 218p.

> Felix: A very good work. Unfortunately the author has never been here (Philippines) and it shows.
> H   4   2
> Legarda: Excellent short work in English.
> H   4   2
> Onorato: H   4   2
> Wickberg: Pioneer study.
> H   4   2

1210. ROCES, ALEJANDRO R. Our Spanish cultural heritage. Comment, 5, (First Quarter, 1958), 52-57.

1211. SANTAMARIA, MERCEDES GRAU. Spain's contributions to Filipino culture. Unitas 24, no. 1 (Enero/Marzo 1951), 199-203.

1212. The Spanish community in the present-day Philippines. American Chamber of Commerce of the Philippines. Journal 41, no. 3 (March 1965),101-102, 104.

1213. WHINNOM, KEITH. Spanish in the Philippines. Journal of Oriental Studies 1, no. 1 (Jan. 1954), 129-194.

Other

1214. ABELLA, DOMINGO. A brief introduction to the study of western cultural

penetration in the Philippines. East Asian Cultural Studies 6, nos. 1/4
(Mar. 1967), 176-189.

1215. ALFONSO, OSCAR M. The Portuguese in the Philippines before 1600. **1955.**
144p. Thesis (M.A.) - U.P.
     Felix: The only work I know on the subject.
                      H   3   2

1216. BERNAL, RAFAEL. The Mexican **heritage** in the Philippines. Unitas 37,
no. 2 (June 1964), 292-300.
     Felix: Excellent, besides being the only real work on the sub-
                      ject.
                      H   4   2(3)

1217. _____. México en Filipinas; estudio de uma transculturación. México,
Universidad Nacional Autónoma de México, 1965, 142p. (Instituto de Investi-
gaciones Historicas. Cuadernos, serie histórica, no. 11).

1218. GRIESE, JOHN WILLIAM, JR. The Jewish community in the Philippines. PSSHR
19, no. 1 (Mar. 1954), 12-14.

1219. HARTENDORP, A. V. H. The contributions of the foreign communities to Philippine culture. FTY, (1953), 47-50, 142.

1220. HILL, PERCY A. The Dutch in the Philippines. PM 31, no. 6 (June 1934),
239-240, 248-250, no. 7 (July 1934), 288-291.

EXACT KNOWLEDGE

1221. BANTEGUI, B. G. Perspective of statistical development in the developing
countries of Asia and the Far East. Stat. Rept. 11, no. 4 (Oct./Dec.
1967), 23-32.

1222. COSTA, HORACIO DE LA. The role of the social sciences in public policy.
SR 8, no. 8 (Aug. 1967), 31-34.

1223. FELICIANO, GLORIA D. Limits of western social research methods in rural
Philippines: the need for innovation. Lipunan 1, no. 1 (1965), 114-128.

1224. _____. Sociological factors in the utilization of research findings in
selected regions of the Philippines. (In: Research in the Philippines:
a critical evaluation. A symposium sponsored by Gamma Sigma Delta, Honor
Society of Agriculture, Society for the Advancement of Research in Cooperation with the National Science Development Board. p.71-81)

1225. _____. Some uses of content analysis in social research. PSR 15, nos.
1/2 (Jan./Apr. 1967), 16-21.

1226. HENDERSHOT, GERRY E. Characteristics of the interview situation in a
Manila survey. PSR 16, nos. 3/4 (July/Oct. 1968), 152-161.

I. GENERAL. EXACT KNOWLEDGE

1227. KALAW, MAXIMO M. An introduction to Philippine social science. Manila, U.P. Press, 1933. Manila, Philippine Education Company, 1939. 790p. (Commonwealth Textbook Series)

1228. LANDE, CARL H. Behavioral research in the Philippines. The American Behavioral Scientist 5, no. 10 (June 1962), 41-45.

1229. LYNCH, FRANK and PERLA Q. MAKIL. Sociological surveys in the rural Philippines: some suggestions for interviewers. (In: Bello, Walden F. and Maria Clara Roldan, eds. Modernization: its impact in the Philippines. Quezon City, Institute of Philippine Culture, Ateneo de Manila Univ. Press, 1967. Papers, no. 4. p.106-128)

1230. NATIONAL ACADEMY OF SCIENCES, WASHINGTON, D.C. Scientific explorations of the Philippine Islands. A report by a committee (Board of Scientific Surveys of the Philippine Islands) appointed at the request of the President of the United States. Washington, 1903. 22p. (58th Congress. 3d Session. Senate. Document no. 145)

1231. OÑATE, BURTON T. Development of multi-stage designs for statistical surveys in the Philippines. Stat. Rept. 4, no. 4 (Oct. 1960), 1-48.

1232. RAVENHOLT, ALBERT. Science and the Filipinos. AUFSR. Southeast Asia Series 6, no. 1 (Feb. 12, 1958), 10p. (AR-1-'58)

1233. UICHANCO, LEOPOLDO B. Social responsibility of the present-day scientist. PGJ 11, nos. 1/2 (Jan./June 1967), 13-19.

1234. UMALI, DIOSCORO L. The role of professional and learned societies in the formulation of science policies. SR 8, no. 8 (Aug. 1967), 63-66.

1235. ZAMORA, MARIO D. The role of the CDRC-UP in the Philippine social science research. SR 6, nos. 1/2 (Jan./Feb. 1965), 23-26.

FAMILY AND KINSHIP

1236. ATANGAN, REMEDIOS. What are the values of the Filipino family reflected in education, economics, politics, child rearing social life? PJHE 15, no. 2 (Apr./June 1964), 26-29.

1237. BULATAO, JAIME. The conflict between home values and school values and its effects. CS 2, nos. 2/3 (June/Sept. 1965), 100-106.
　　　Hunt:　　　P　4　-

1238. BUSTRILLOS, NENA R. The family meal and the child in a rural area. Home Economics 1, (Manila) (Oct. 1963), 41-55.
　　　Source: Index to Periodicals (U.P. Library. Filipiniana Section)
　　　　Luna:　　　Descriptive analytical study.
　　　　　　　C　4　6

1239 CARROLL, JOHN J. The family in a time of change. Solidarity 3, (Jan.

1968), 11-17.

1240. _____. The Filipino family. SW 12, no. 3 (July/Sept. 1967), 60-61, 72-73.

1241. CASTILLO, GELIA T., ABRAHAM M. WEISBLAT and FELICIDAD R. VILLAREAL. The concepts of nuclear and extended family: an exploration of empirical referents. International Journal of Comparative Sociology 9, no. 1 (Mar. 1968), 1-40.

1242. CATAPUSAN, BENICIO T. and FLORA E. DIAZ-CATAPUSAN. Displaced migrant families in rural Philippines. Sociology and Social Research 40, no. 3 (Jan./Feb. 1956), 186-189.

1243. _____. Social adjustment of migrant families. PSR 2, no. 3 (Oct. 1954), 11-16.

1244. COLLER, RICHARD W. Changing family patterns in the Philippines and minimizing family tensions. PJHE 11, no. 3 (1960), 10, 23, 68.
Cited in Biblio. of Asian Studies. 1961. p.694.
    Coller: Introduces concept of "secular familism" to describe current trends.
                Z   3   6

1245. CONCEPCION, MERCEDES B. Some socio-economic correlates of completed family size, 1960. PSR 12, nos. 1/2 (Jan./Apr. 1964), 16-26.

1246. CORTEZ, OLIMPIO C., SR. The compadre system. CC 5, no. 6 (Nov./Dec. 1965), 19-22.

1247. COVAR, PROSPERO R. Trends of change in the Filipino family. CC 5, no. 6 (Nov./Dec. 1965), 12-18.

1248. EINSIEDEL, LUZ A. The impact of urbanization resulting from industrialization on Filipino home. Philippine Christian Advance 15, no. 6 (June 1963), 34-37.
    Luna: Descriptive informative essay.
                S   3   6

1249. ESLAO, NENA. The developmental cycle of the Philippine household in an urban setting. PSR 14, no. 4 (Oct. 1966), 199-208.

1250. EUFEMIO, FLORA. Foster mothers: their responses on the parent attitude research instrument [PARI] in relation to their role performance. PSR 15, nos. 3/4 (July/Oct. 1967), 94-105.

1251. FAMILY LIFE WORKSHOP OF THE PHILIPPINES. The Filipino family; selected readings. Quezon City, Alemar-Phoenix Pub. House, 1966. 118p.

1252. FLORES, PURA M. How the family prepares the child for his formal education. CS 2, nos. 2/3 (June/Sept. 1965), 166-184.

1253. _____ and MICHAELA B. GONZALEZ. Thematic responses of father-absent children. PJP 1, no. 1 (Nov. 1968), 7-10.

1254. FOX, ROBERT B. The family and society in the rural Philippines. SR 2, no. 4 (Apr. 1961), 1-5.

1255. _____. The Mestizo (Spanish-Filipino) family in the Philippines. Anthropology Tomorrow 1, no. 1 (1951).

1256. GONZALEZ, PILAR A. Changes in the Filipino family. PSR 3, no. 2 (Apr. 1955), 15-17.

1257. GOROSPE, VITALIANO R. Responsible parenthood in the Philippines today. PS 14, no. 3 (July 1966), 471-481.

1258. GUTHRIE, GEORGE M. Structure of maternal attitudes in two cultures. Journal of Psychology 62, no. 2 (Mar. 1966), 155-165.
         Warren: P   5   6

1259. HOLLNSTEINER, MARY R. Modernization and the challenge to the Filipino family. (In: The Filipino Christian Family in a Changing Society. Manila: Christian Family Movement, 1965. 10-20)

1260. HUNT, CHESTER L. The family. (In: Hunt, Chester L. and others. Sociology in the Philippine Setting. Rev. ed. Quezon City, Phoenix Pub. House, 1963. p.150-172)

1261. KROEBER, A. L. Kinship in the Philippines. American Museum of Natural History. Anthropological Papers 19, pt. 3 (1919), 69-84.
         Warren: E   5   4

1262. LYNCH, FRANK. The conflict between home values and school values. CS 2, nos. 2/3 (June/Sept. 1965), 94-99.

1263. _____. The conjugal bond where the Philippines changes. PSR 8, nos. 3/4 (July/Oct. 1960), 48-51.
         Hunt: Z   4   -

1264. MACARANAS, EDUARDA A. Perceived parental attitudes and scholastic achievement in a group of adolescent boys. PJP 1, no. 1 (Nov. 1968), 11-15.

1265. MENDEZ, PAZ P. The home in the making of the Filipino. CEU.GFS. 19, (1968), 1-10.

1266. MIAO, EMILY. A study of parental attitudes in child and adolescent development. 1965. 140p. Thesis (M.A.) - Ateneo de Manila Univ.
         Guthrie: P   5   6

1267. PACHECO, ANTONIO and TRINIDAD OSTERIA. Some findings on the attitudes toward family size preferences and family limitation. Stat. Rept. 10, no. 3 (July/Sept. 1966), 1-8.

1268. PAL, AGATON P. Aspects of lowland Philippine social structure. PSR 14, no. 1 (Jan. 1966), 31-40.
         Polson: Good descriptive study.
                        Z   4   6
         Hunt: Z   5   6

1269. _____. Social-psychological correlates of family size. PJHE 17, no. 1 (Jan./Mar. 1966), 1-11.

1270. _____ and LINO Q. ARQUIZA. Deviations and adherences in Philippine familism. SJ 4, no. 1 (Jan./Mar. 1957), 1-7.

1271. PALMA, RAFAEL. The Filipino family. Historical Bulletin 11, (June 1967), 132-143.

1272. PEHRSON, ROBERT N. Bilateral kin groupings as a structural type: a preliminary statement. JEAS 3, no. 2 (Jan. 1954), 199-202.
    Polson: A classic and provocative set of descriptive hypotheses.
                E   5   6

1273. PEREZ, BERNARDINO A. Family living surveys. Quezon City, Statistical Center, U.P., 1962. 12p.

1274. PHILIPPINE ASSOCIATION OF UNIVERSITY WOMEN. Talking things over with the growing Filipina; a project of the Philippine Association of University Women. Pura Santillan-Castrence, ed. Manila, Bardavon Book Co., 1951. 192p.
    Almanzor   Q   4   6

1275. RAFEL, S. STEPHEN. Patterns of adjustment in 20 American-Filipina families. PSR 2, no. 3 (Oct. 1954), 3-10.
    Coller: Digest of findings in his M.A. thesis.
                G/S   3   6

1276. REYNOLDS, HARRIET R. The family - a natural agency for community development. Philippine Christian 13, no. 3 (Mar. 1961), 38-40.

1277. _____. The Filipino family and the church. CC 2, no. 4 (July/Aug. 1962), 5-15.
    Hunt: E   4   -

1278. _____. The Filipino family in its cultural setting. Practical Anthropology 9, no. 5 (Sept./Oct. 1962), 223-234)
    Hunt: E   4   -

1279. SANTIAGO, CAYETANO, JR. Welfare functions of the Filipino family. PSR 1, no. 1 (Aug. 1953), 12-15.
    Hunt: Data based on sampling survey of Manila district.
                Z   5   6

1280. SANTOS-CUYUGAN, RUBEN. Socio-cultural change and the Filipino family. SR 2, no. 3 (Mar. 1961), 9-13.

1281. SOENARDI, SOSROOETOYO. Estimating income of low income households in a Philippine city using food expenditures as predictors. Phil. Stat. 12, no. 1 (Mar. 1963), 23-50.

1282. ULGADO, A. The Filipino family in rural development. Social Action (Indian Social Institute) 17, no. 3 (May/June 1967), 194-203.

FINE ARTS

1283   AGUILA, DANI D. Graphic arts. (In: Feliciano, Gloria D. and Crispulo J. Icban, Jr., eds. Philippine mass media in perspective. Quezon City, Capitol Pub. House, 1967. p.37-50)

1284.   ALIP, EUFRONIO M. The development of the native theater in the Philippines. Unitas 10, No. 3 (Sept. 1931), 145-153.
Cited in Helen Butengko, Bibliography of ethnographic titles....JEAS, Oct. 1953.
         Trimillos: R   3   7

1285.   AQUINO, FRANCISCA R. and LUCRECIA R. URTULA. Dances of the Philippines. PQ 2, no. 1 (Oct./Dec. 1961), 29-33.
Cited in Index to Philippine Periodicals, v.7, p. 19.
         Trimillos: R/Y   3   7

1286.   ARGUILLA, LYDIA. Ten years of Tabuena's art. FTY (1960), 231-234, 267.
         Trimillos: Q   3   6

1287.   BRENTON, THADDEUS REAMY. Farming to music in the Philippines. Asia (New York) 34, no. 4 (April 1934), 244-246.
         Trimillos: Only mention of this kind of music.
                         Y   5   4

1288.   BROCKERISHIRE, J. O. A word about native Philippine bands and musicians. Metronome 32, (1916), 17-18.
         Trimillos: Y   5   4

1289.   CASTAÑEDA, DOMINADOR. Trends and influences in fine arts: new traces of westernism have appeared in Philippine art. Progress (1955), 27-34.
Source: Index to Periodicals (U.P. Library. Filipiniana Section)
         Trimillos: Good look at 'Europeanization' of Philippine art.
                         R   5   6

1290.   DENSMORE, FRANCES. Handbook of the collection of musical instruments in the United States National Museum. Smithsonian Institution. U.S. National Museum, Bulletin 136, (1927). 164p.
         Trimillos: Good description. Few organological works on Philippine Islands.
                         E   5   4

1291.   _____. The music of the Filipinos. AA 8, no. 4 (Oct./Dec. 1906), 611-632.
         Trimillos: Description of music making.
                         E   5   4

1292.   The Elusive Filipino Soul:
                 in painting: Jose T. Joya, Jr., 4-7;
                 in theatre: Francisco C. Santos, Jr., 8-10;
                 in music: Eliseo M. Pajaro, 11-13;
                 in dance: Lucrecia M. Urtula, 14-17;
                 in architecture: Leandro V. Locsin, 18-25.
         Exchange, no. 33 (Fourth Quarter 1964)
                 Pfeiffer: R   4   6

1293.   FAUROT, ALBERT L.   The Tailor-made serenade.   SJ 2, no. 1 (Jan. 1955),
        74-81.
       Pfeiffer: R   4   6
       Trimillos: R   3   6

1294.   Forum on Filipino Music:
       The Plight of the Filipino composer, by Dr. Eliseo M. Pajaro, 12-17.
       The Filipino soul through music, by Prof. Felipe Padilla de Leon, 18-23.
       The tempo of Filipino musical life, by Redentor Romero, 24-28.
       Filipino Musical heritage in folk-dances, by Dr. Antonio J. Molina,
          29-35.
       Discussion on the forum on Filipino music, 36-49.
    Comment, no. 19 (Third Quarter 1963).
       Pfeiffer: R   4   6
       Trimillos: The conflict between natural interest and Western
           influence.
           R/Y   3   7

1295.   GAGELONIA, PEDRO A.   Musical instruments of the early Filipinos.   Manila.
        FEUFJ 6, no. 4 (Apr. 1962), 317-327.
    Source: Index to Periodicals (U.P. Library. Filipiniana Section)
       Trimillos: Secondary sources.
           Y   3   7

1296.   GALDON, JOSEPH A.   From Hamlet to Bayanihan.   PS 8, no. 2 (Apr. 1960),
        393-395.
       Trimillos: Documents contemporary cult-scene.
           J   5   6

1297.   GOQUINCO, LEONOR O.   Dance in the Philippines.   Dance Magazine 29, no. 12
        (Dec. 1955), 40-42, 75.
       Trimillos: R   3   6

1298.   _____.   Philippine theatre dance.   Comment, no. 12 (First Quarter 1961),
        56-57.
       Trimillos: R   3   6

1299.   JARA, JOSEFA.   Music of the Philippine Islands.   National Education Asso-
        ciation.   Journal of Proceedings and Addresses (1915), 879-882.
       Trimillos: General.
           Y   3   4

1300.   JUMAWAN, LUCY.   Folk dancing in the Philippine setting.   Horizons Unlimited
        (Dumaguete, Foundation College) 2, no. 3 (Sept. 1963), 26-27.
       Pfeiffer: R   4   6

1301.   KASILAG, LUCRECIA R.   Asian music in education.   University 1, (Feb.
        1966), 4-5+
       Pfeiffer: R   4   6
       Trimillos: Trends in music education.
           Y/R   5   6

1302.   _____.   Evaluating the authenticity of folk songs.   SJ 8, no. 1 (Jan./
        Mar. 1961), 29-33.
       Pfeiffer: R   4   6

Trimillos: Y/R   3   6

1303.   _____ . Philippine music - past and present. Exchange News (Manila), nos.
20/21 (Third/Fourth Quarters 1961), 2-7, 48-53.
Pfeiffer: R   4   6
Trimillos: Good review.
Y/R   4   7

1304.   KATIGBAK, AIDA. The state of music in the Philippines. Unitas 36, no. 3
(Sept. 1963), 373-377.
Trimillos: Criticism of music and life.
J   5   6

1305.   LARDIZABAL, FELISA. Folk music - its place in our public schools. Music
Instructor (Philippine Normal School) 16, no. 1 (June 1933), 39-40.
Cited in Helen Butengko, Bibliography of ethnographic titles. . . JEAS,
Oct. 1953, p.114.
Trimillos: Good historical document.
Y   5   4

1306.   LEDESMA, PURITA (KALAW). Our artists' dilemma. PQ 2, (Oct./Dec. 1961),
34-37.
Source: Index to Periodicals (U.P. Library. Filipiniana Section)
Trimillos: J   3   6

1307.   LOZANO, ALFREDO. Music in the Philippines. FTY (1953), 125-126, 141.
Pfeiffer: V/X   4   6
Trimillos: Kasilag's article is better.
R   4   7

1308.   LUMBERA, BIENVENIDO. The arts in the Philippines: the Tagalog film and
the logic of irony. PS 10, no. 1 (Jan. 1962), 137-144.

1309.   MACEDA, JOSÉ. Means of preservation and diffusion of traditional music:
the Philippine situation. (In: Daniélou, Alain et al., eds. Creating a
wider interest in traditional music: Proceedings of a conference held in
Berlin in cooperation with the International Music Council 12th to the
17th June 1967. Berlin, International Institute for Comparative Studies
and Documentation, 1968?, p.90-93)

1310.   _____ . Music of Southeast Asia: a report of a brief trip. JEAS 5,
no. 3 (July 1956), 297-313.
Pfeiffer: R   4   6
Trimillos: Music trends.
R/E   3   6

1311.   _____ . The place of Asian music in Philippine contemporary society. AS
2, no. 1 (Apr. 1964), 71-75.
Pfeiffer: R   4   6
Trimillos: A Filipino assesses ethnic music.
R/E   5   6

1312.   MADRID, ESTHER SAMONTE. The structure of Philippine music. DR 2, no. 4
(Oct. 1954), 373-383.
Pfeiffer: R   4   6

1313.   _____. What is Philippine folk music? DR 2, no. 2 (Apr. 1954), 114-127.
        Pfeiffer: R   4   6

1314.   MAKILING, JUAN. Music of the Philippines. PQ 1, no. 1 (1951), 52-57.
        Trimillos: General.
                        R   3   7

1315.   MAÑGAHAS, RUBY K. Early Christian church music. DR 6, nos. 2/4 (Apr./
        Dec. 1958), 225-234.
        Pfeiffer: R   4   6

1316.   _____ and JOSÉ MACEDA. The evolution of Philippine music. Barangay
        Forum 1, nos. 3/4 (June/July 1966), 72-77.
        Pfeiffer: R & R   4   6
        Trimillos: R/E & R/E   3   7

1317.   MANUUD, ANTONIO G. Philippine contemporary art: a fait accompli. (In:
        Manuud, Antonio G., ed., Brown Heritage. Quezon City, Ateneo de Manila
        Univ. Press, 1967. p.184-194)

1318.   MAQUISO, ELENA G. Characteristics of indigenous Filipino music. SJ **15,**
        no. 1 (First Quarter 1968), 92-110.

1319.   MOLINA, ANTONIO J. Church music and church musicians in the Philippines.
        CEU.GFS 12, (1961), 1-19.
        Pfeiffer: R   4   6
        Trimillos: Interpretation questionable but primary sources re-
                        liable.
                        R/Y   5   7

1320.   _____. Music of the Philippines. Manila, 1967. 20p. (Aspects of Phil-
        ippine Culture, 3)
        "Third in a series of lectures presented by the National Museum and spon-
        sored by Ambassador and Mrs. William McC. Blair, Jr."

1321.   _____. **Philippine** music and poetry. (In: Manuud, Antonio G., ed.,
        Brown Heritage. Quezon City, Ateneo de Manila Univ. Press, 1967. p.195-
        206)

1322.   _____. A symbol of the struggle for national solidarity (a tribute from
        a musician to a musician). CEU.GFS 9, (1958), 13-19.
        Pfeiffer: R   4   6
        Trimillos: R/Y   3   4

1323.   MONTANO, SEVERINO. Rural theatre in the Philippines. Comment, no. 12
        (First Quarter 1961), 51-55.
        Pfeiffer: Q   3/4   6

1324.   MUNCHOW, JOHN R. Philippine music. Violinist 46, (1930), 159-161.
        Cited in Music Library Association. Notes. 2nd series, v.7, no.1.
        Trimillos: R   3   7

1325.   MUÑOZ, MA. TERESA. Notes on theater: pre-Hispanic Philippines (religion,

myth, religious ritual). (In: Manuud, Antonio G., ed., Brown Heritage.
Quezon City, Ateneo de Manila Univ., 1967. p.648-667)

1326. OCAMPO, GALO B. Contemporary painting of the Philippines. Manila, 1968.
16p. (Aspects of Philippine Culture, 7)
"Seventh in a series of lectures presented by the National Museum and sponsored by Ambassador and Mrs. William McC. Blair, Jr."

1327. _____. The religious element in Philippine art; address at the opening
exercises of the academic year 1965-1966. Manila, Univ. of Santo Tomas.
1966. 130p.
        Doherty: Z   3   7

1328. _____. Three periods of Philippine art. Unitas 31, no. 4 (Oct./Dec.
1958), 740-789. 15 plates.
        Trimillos: R   3   7

1329. PADILLA DE LEON, FELIPE. Music of the Filipinos. JH 4, no. 2 (Jan./Apr.
1956), 24-31.
        Pfeiffer: R   4   6

1330. _____. The music of the Filipinos. FEUFJ 5, (July 1959), 14-21.
        Pfeiffer: R   4   6

1331. PAJARO, ELISEO M. Philippine symphony. 1953. Thesis (Ph.D.) - Univ. of
Rochester.
Cited in Stucki, American Doctoral Dissertations on Asia...p.137.
        Pfeiffer: A significant large musical composition.
                        R   5   6
        Trimillos: Good work on Western music in Philippine Islands.
                        R/Y   4   7

1332. [PALUSKAS, STELLA]. Artistic and intellectual expression. (In: Human Relations Area Files, Inc. Area handbook on the Philippines. 1956. v.3,
Chapter 12. p.1102-1164)
        Trimillos: Good table of instrument distribution.
                        E?   4   7

1333. PARAS-PEREZ, RODOLFO. Commitment and non-commitment in Philippine aesthet-
ics. Solidarity 2, no. 7 (May/June 1967), 22-29.

1334. _____. Philippine modern international cross-currents in art. University College Journal, no. 4 (1962/1963), 51-54.

1335. PHILIPPINES (REPUBLIC) UNESCO NATIONAL COMMISSION. Music in Southeast
Asia; record of proceedings of the first regional music conference of South-
east Asia, held on Aug. 29-31, 1955, at the U.P., Diliman, Quezon City,
Philippines. Manila, 1956. 130p. (Its Publication no. 15).
        Pfeiffer: Unless it has been edited, some reports are in very poor
                        English.
                        W   3   6
        Trimillos: Concern with preserving ethnic identity through music.
                        W   5   6

1336. RAYMUNDO, LUZ J. Classification of folk songs according to grade levels.

SJ 8, no. 1 (Jan./Mar. 1961), 49-54.
    Pfeiffer: R   4   6
    Trimillos: Y   3   6

1337. ROCES, ALFREDO R. Filipino folk art in architecture. Comment, no. 16 (Last Quarter 1962), 153-165.

1338. _____. Philippine art: Spanish period. (In: Manuud, Antonio G., ed., Brown Heritage. Quezon City, Ateneo de Manila Univ. Press, 1967. p.163-183)

1339. ROMERO, REDENTOR. Forum on Filipino music: the tempo of Filipino musical life. Comment, no. 19 (Third Quarter 1963), 24-28.
    Trimillos: R   3   6

1340. ROMUALDEZ, NORBERTO. Musical instruments and airs of long ago. (In: Galang, Zoilo, ed., Encyclopedia of the Philippines. 2nd ed. 1957. v.7, p.64-98)
    Pfeiffer: 0   4   4
    Trimillos: A primary source for instruments, melodies.
                0   5   4

1341. ROSARIO, ALEJANDRO DEL. The collection of folk songs. SJ 8, no. 1 (Jan./ Mar. 1961), 25-28.
    Pfeiffer: R   4   6
    Trimillos: R   3   6

1342. RUBIO, HILARION F. Filipino music in the past three decades. FTY (1926/ 1956. 30th Anniversary no.), 139-140, 157-158, 110A-111I.
    Pfeiffer: R   4   6
    Trimillos: Mostly about composers in western idiom.
                R   4   7

1343. SAMONTE, ESTHER I. A survey of Philippine music - its nature, tendencies, and possibilities for adaptation to Christian worship. New York, 1949. Thesis (M.S.M.) - School of Sacred Music, Union Theological Seminary.
    Pfeiffer: R   4   6

1344. SANTAMARIA, MERCEDES GRAU. Philippine music and dances. Unitas 32, no. 4 (Oct./Dec. 1959), 912-928.
    Trimillos: Secondary source.
                Y/R   3   7

1345. SANTIAGO, FRANCISCO. The development of music in the Philippine islands. Quezon City, U.P. 1957. 22p.
    Pfeiffer: R   4   6
    Trimillos: Good review.
                R   4   7

1346. SCHADENBERG, ALEXANDER. Musik-Instrument der Philippinen-Stamme. Zeit-schrift für Ethnologie. Verhandlungen 18 (1886), 549-551.
    Trimillos: Brief description of use.
                E   5   4

1347. SCHNEIDER, MARIUS. Música Filipina. Anuario Músical (Barcelona) 6

(1951), 91-105.
    Trimillos: Based upon source in Madrid, mostly on mountain group.
           R   4   4/6

1348. TIEMPO, EDITH L. When music sings in the hearts of the people. SJ 8, no. 1 (Jan./Mar. 1961), 20-24.
    Pfeiffer: Q   4   6
    Trimillos: Calls for closer look at lowland song versus literature.
           Q   4   6

1349. TOLENTINO, FRANCISCA (REYES). Philippine national dances. New York, Chicago. Silver Burdett Co., 1946. 371p.
    Trimillos: Standard reference for Philippine dance.
           Y   5   4

1350. TORRES, EMMANUEL. Folk art. Progress (1961), 118-123.

1351. _____. Philippine painting. Exchange News 23 (Second Quarter 1962), 2-3, 22-23.

1352. VILLANUEVA-ARGUILLA, LYDIA. Philippine folk dances. PM 37, no. 7 (July 1940), 267, 276-277.
    Reprinted: JEAS 4, no. 1 (Jan. 1955), 70-72.
        Trimillos: Based largely upon Francisca Tolentino's Philippine National Dances, 1946.
           Y   3   6

1353. WALLS Y MERINO, MANUEL. La música popular de Filipinos. Madrid, F. Fe, 1892. 46p.
    Trimillos: Single reference for this period.
           M   5   3

1354. YOSHIMURA, BIN. The music of the Philippines. Trans. by S. Isobe. Manila: The Department of Information of the Imperial Japanese Forces, Sept. 1942, 9p. in English; 12p. in Japanese.
    Trimillos: V   4   4

1355. ZOBEL, FERNANDO. Filipino artistic expression. PS 1, no. 2 (Sept. 1953), 125-130.

FOLKLORE AND MYTHOLOGY

1356. BUNAG, DANIEL M. Philippine snakelore. JEAS 8, nos. 1/2 (Jan./Apr. 1959), 207-210.

1357. CRAGIN, MICHAEL. A collection of Philippine folklore. Assay; Journal of Anthropology 3 (1968), 72-75.

1358. DEMETRIO, FRANCISCO. Creation myths among the early Filipinos. Asian Folklore Studies 27, pt. 1 (1968), 41-79.

I. GENERAL. FOLKLORE AND MYTHOLOGY

1359. FRANCISCO, JUAN R. Foreign elements in Philippine folk literature. Dialogue (Manila) 4, no. 1 (Dec. 1967), 49-76.

1360. _____. Some Philippine tales compared with parallels in North Borneo. SMJ n.s. 10, nos. 19/20 (July/Dec. 1962), 511-523.

1361. JOCANO, F. LANDA. Philippine mythology and general education. GEJ, no. 12 (Second Semester, 1966-1967), 143-149.

1362. _____. Some aspects of Filipino vernacular literature. (In: Brown Heritage, ed. by Antonio G. Manuud. Quezon City, 1967. p.287-307)

1363. MANUEL, E. ARSENIO. On the study of Philippine folklore. (In: Brown Heritage, ed. by Antonio G. Manuud. Quezon City, 1967. p.253-286)

1364. _____. Philippine folklore bibliography; a preliminary survey. Quezon City, Philippine Folklore Society, 1965. 125p. (Philippine Folklore Society Paper No. 1.)

1365. RAMOS, MAXIMO. Belief in ghouls in contemporary Philippine society. Western Folklore 27, no. 3 (July 1968), 184-190.

1366. _____. Folk beliefs and social control. Solidarity 3, no. 2 (Feb. 1968), 26-35.

1367. STA. MARIA, FELIXBERTO C. Philippine folk songs and ballads: through a changing culture. Southern Folklore Quarterly 24, no. 1 (March 1960), 121-134.

1368. YABES, LEOPOLDO Y. Philippine folk epics. Heritage 1, no. 2 (Oct. 1967), 52-62.

FOOD

1369. ADAMS, WALLACE, HERACLIO R. MONTALBAN and CLARO MARTIN. Cultivation of bangos in the Philippines. PJS 47, no. 1 (Jan. 1932), 1-38. 10 plates.
    Intengan: A detailed account of the cultivation of bangos in fish farms.
                 N   5   4
    Luna: Descriptive analytical study.
                 N   4   4

1370. ADRIANO, F. T. The food value of Philippine mushrooms. PM 28, no. 7 (Dec. 1931), 330-331, 360-362.
    Luna: Descriptive analytical study.
                 N   5   4

1371. AGUILLON, DELFINA B. Nutrition in public health. Nutrition News 15, no. 2 (Apr./June 1962), 32-41.
    Cited in Index to Philippine Periodicals, v.7, p.9.
    Intengan: Briefly highlights the proceedings of the 12th National

138

Nutrition Week Conference.
C   4   6

1372.   ARON, HANS. Diet and nutrition of the Filipino people. PJS 4-B, no. 3
        (June 1909), 195-204.
              Intengan: Although limited in scope, it is one of the earliest docu-
                               ments that recorded the food intake of Filipinos.
                               C   5   4
              Luna: Descriptive analytical study.
                               D   4   4

1373.   BANTEGUI, BERNARDINO G. and JUAN O. SUMAGUI. The food supply situation in
        the Philippines 1963-1964. Stat. Rept. 10, no. 1 (Jan./Mar. 1966), 15-26.
              Intengan: A critical evaluation of the food supply for census years
                               1963 and 1964.
                               N   5   6
              Luna: Descriptive statistical analytical study.
                               N   4   6

1374.   _____. The food supply situation in the Philippines, CY 1965-66. Stat.
        Rept. 11, no. 4 (Oct./Dec. 1967), 11-22.

1375.   BARTOLOME, RAFAEL. The Nation's rice problem: proposals for solution.
        PGJ 7, no. 4 (Oct./Dec. 1963), 206-213.
              Luna: Descriptive statistical prescriptive study.
                               C   4   6
              Spencer: Current status (as of 1963) of recurrent problem.
                               C   4   6

1376.   BAUTISTA, ALICIA P. On Filipino recipes. Philippine Journal of Nutrition
        20, no. 1 (Jan./Mar. 1967), 31-35.

1377.   _____ and OTHERS. Family food plans for Ilocos-Mountain Province, Cagayan
        Valley--Batanes and Southern Tagalog regions. Philippine Journal of Nutri-
        tion 20, no. 2 (Apr./June 1967), 75-82.

1378.   BULATAO-JAYME, JOSEFINA. Nutritional basis in national food planning.
        Philippine Journal of Nutrition 16, no. 2 (Apr./June 1963), 46-51.
              Intengan: A bird's eye view of tools available in the planning
                               and assessment of food situation in the country.
                               C   5   6
              Luna: Descriptive analytical study.
                               C   4   6

1379.   BUSTRILLOS, NENA R. The family meal and the child in a rural area. Home
        Economics 1 (Manila) (Oct. 1963), 41-55.
              Source: Index to Periodicals (U.P. Library. Filipiniana Section).
              Luna: Descriptive analytical study.
                               C   4   6

1380.   CARRASCO, EUFRONIO O. Opportunities for nutrition services from non-
        governmental sectors. SR 5, no. 6 (June 1964), 79-82.
              Intengan: Enumerates various opportunities for nutrition services
                               which can be undertaken to supplement activities of the
                               government.

I. GENERAL. FOOD

<pre>
                          C   5   6
       Luna: Descriptive informative essay read at a conference on
                      nutrition.
                          G   3   6
</pre>

1381. CASSI, PRISCILLA I. and OTHERS. Studies on the minimum calcium requirement of fifteen Filipino adults on controlled intakes. PJS 94, no. 4
(Dec. 1965), 435-448.

1382. _____. Studies on the nutrient requirement of Filipinos: 3. Riboflavin
requirement of some adult Filipinos on controlled intake. PJS 96, no. 3
(Sept. 1967), 273-293.

1383. CASTILLO, GELIA T. Some insights on the human factor in overcoming barriers
to adequate food supply. Philippine Journal of Nutrition 17, no. 2 (Apr./
June 1964), 134-147.
       Intengan: A sociologist **examines** the human factors involved in
                      the problem of increasing agricultural production.
                          Z   4   6
       Luna: Descriptive analytical study.
                          Z   4   6

1384. CONCEPCION, ISABELO. Food composition tables in the Philippines. Nutrition News 13, no. 4 (Oct./Dec. 1960), 14-18.
       Intengan: Briefly summarizes status of food composition table,
                      gives limitations and suggests plans for improvement.
                          C   4   6
       Luna: Statistical analytical study.
                          C   4   6

1385. _____. Food habits of Filipino school children. Acta Medica Philippina
6, no. 2 (Oct./Dec. 1949), 153-167.
       Intengan: An excellent reference in planning food programs for
                      Grades 3-6 school children.
                          C   5   6
       Luna: Descriptive analytical study.
                          C   4   6

1386. _____. The nutritive value and cost of the Philippine constabulary ration.
PJS 62, no. 1 (Jan. 1937), 89-114.
       Intengan: Information is given on nutritional value, cost and types
                      of menus served to soldiers.
                          C   5   4
       Luna: Descriptive statistical analytical study.
                          C   4   6

1387. COOK, HUGH L., DIMAS A. MAULIT and JOSE M. LAWAS. Requirements for **selected**
foods: long-range requirements for selected foods in the Philippines.
Phil. Stat. 7, no. 3 (Sept. 1958), 167-186.
       Luna: Statistical projective study.
                          X   4   6

1388. EJERCITO, MA. JOSEFA (FERRIOLS). Certain factors that affect the food
habits of six nursery school children as observed in the child development

140

laboratory of the U.P., second semester, 1957-1958. 1959. 134p. Thesis (M.H.E.) - U.P.
  Verified in U.P. theses and dissertations index. p.59
      Luna: Descriptive analytical study.
                       C   3   6

1389. Food production forecast, August 1, 1956. PGJ 4, nos. 2/3 (Apr./Sept. 1956), 63-68.
      Intengan: Forecast on palay and corn production by region and by province.
                       C   4   6
      Luna: Statistical estimates of palay and corn production.
                       C   4   6

1390. FRANCISCO, ANACLETO D. and P. J. WESTER. Analysis and food value of some unusual Philippine fruits. PJS 43, no. 4 (Dec. 1930), 655-663. 9 plates.
      Intengan: Chemical analysis of unusual fruits are presented with botanical description and illustrations.
                       C   5   4
      Luna: Descriptive analytical study with tables.
                       N   4   4

1391. GARCIA, PAULINO J. The food and nutrition situation in the Philippines. Nutrition News 13, no. 4 (Oct./Dec. 1960), 42-45.
      Intengan: Underscores the need for an "operating communication network" to close the gap between nutrition researchers and consumers and vice versa.
                       D   4   6
      Luna: Descriptive expository article.
                       G/D   3   6

1392. GARCIA, ROSALINDA M. A socio-anthropological approach to nutrition education. Dietetic Association of the Philippines Bulletin 5, no. 4 (Oct. 1966), 8-10.
  Reprinted: Food and Nutrition Notes and Reviews. (Canberra), vol. 24, nos. 5 and 6 (May & June 1967). p.45-51.
      Intengan: Information given can help define the focus in planning programs in nutrition education.
                       C   4   6

1393. GONZALES, NATIVIDAD A. and JOSEFINA B. JAYME. Study on food preferences. [Part I.] An investigation on the food likes and dislikes of a selected group of adolescent college women in metropolitan Manila. Philippine Journal of Nutrition 18, no. 2 (Apr./June 1965), 114-130.
  [Part II.] An investigation on the food likes and dislikes of a group of adolescent college men in metropolitan Manila. Philippine Journal of Nutrition 20, no. 3 (July/Sept. 1967), 108-119.
      Intengan: Attempts to study reasons and motivations behind food likes and dislikes.
                       C   5   6

1394. GUTHRIE, HELEN A., GEORGE M. GUTHRIE and AMANDA TAYAG. Nutritional status and intellectual performance in a rural Philippine community. PJP 1, no. 1 (Nov. 1968), 28-34.

I. GENERAL. FOOD

1395. GUTIERREZ, PONCIANO C. The fisheries of Paoay Lake. Fisheries Gazette
(Manila, Bureau of Fisheries) 5, no. 5 (May 1961), 13-20.
Suggested by Thomas.
Thomas: The best technical statement on the fisheries biology
            and human use of the largest fishwater lake in Northern
            Luzon.
            C/N   5   6

1396. HERMANO, A. J. and GAVINO SEPULVEDA, JR. The vitamin content of Philippine
foods, III. Vitamin B in various fruits and vegetables. PJS 54, no. 1
(May 1934), 61-73. 1 plate.
Intengan: Thiamine content is qualitatively determined by using
            polyneuritic pigeons.
            N   4   4
Luna: Descriptive analytical study with tables based on
            experiments.
            N   5   4

1397. _____ and P. J. AGUILA. The vitamin contents of Philippine foods, IV.
Vitamins A and B_1 in various fruits and vegetables. PJS 58, no. 4 (Dec.
1935), 425-433.
Intengan: Thiamine and vitamin A contents are determined qualita-
            tively by using experimental animals.
            N   4   4
Luna: Descriptive analytical study with tables based on experi-
            ments.
            N   5   4

1398. HERRE, ALBERT W. C. T. Philippine fisheries and their possibilities. The
Far Eastern Quarterly 4, no. 2 (Feb. 1945), 158-162.
Luna: Describes conditions and extent of fishery resources
            and recommends ways of better development.
            N   3   7
Spencer: Good but thin summary.
            N   4   6

1399. _____ and JOSE MENDOZA. Bangos culture in the Philippine Islands. PJS
38, no. 4 (Apr. 1929), 451-509. 16 plates.
Intengan: The culture of bangos is described as well as other in-
            dustries allied to bangos growing.
            N   5   4
Luna: Historical descriptive analytical study.
            N   3   4
Spencer: Good study, in detail.
            N   4/5   7

1400. HOUSTON, CHARLES O. JR. Nutrition and public health in the Philippines,
1934-1950. JEAS 4, no. 2 (Apr. 1955), 119-136.
Luna: Descriptive informative article.
            S   3   7

1401. INTENGAN, CARMEN LL. Forty-year review of nutrition progress in the Phil-
ippines. Philippine Journal of Nutrition. (Nutrition News) 15, no. 3
(July/Sept. 1962), 14-45.
Intengan: Nutrition work since 1903 is reviewed giving as background

142

information the geographic, agricultural and trade conditions and health statistics.
C   5   7

Luna: Descriptive analytical review of nutrition progress in the Philippines.
C   4   7

1402. _____ and OTHERS. Composition of Philippine foods. I. PJS 82, no. 3 (Sept. 1953), 227-252. II. PJS 83, no. 2 (June 1954), 187-216. III. PJS 84, no. 2 (June 1955), 263-273. IV. PJS 84, no. 3 (Sept. 1955), 343-364. V. PJS 85, no. 2 (June 1956), 203-213.
Intengan: A comprehensive study of the composition of Philippine foods of both animal and vegetable origin.
C   5   6

Luna: Descriptive chemical analysis of Philippine foods with tables.
C   4/5   6

1403. _____. Nutritional evaluation of meals served in government institutions by chemical methods. PJS 83, no. 2 (June 1954), 177-186.
Intengan: Chemical analysis is used in evaluating mostly hospital and children's diets.
C   5   6

Luna: Descriptive analytical study.
C   4   6

1404. JOCANO, F. LANDA. The relevance of anthropology to nutrition research. Philippine Journal of Nutrition 20, no. 4 (Oct./Dec. 1967), 202-210.

1405. LINGAO, ALICIA L. and ALICIA P. BAUTISTA. Survey of food preparation and common cooking practices in Metropolitan Manila, Ilocos-Mt. Province and Cagayan Valley-Batanes Regions. Philippine Journal of Nutrition 18, no. 3 (July/Sept. 1965), 184-203.
Intengan: The cooking practices in 3 out of 10 regions in the Philippines are excellent information material for undertaking future programs.
C   5   6

1406. MANE, ANDRES. Statistics and fisheries conservation. Stat. Rept. 8, no.1 (Jan./Mar. 1964), 8-10.
Intengan: Emphasizes the importance of fishery statistics as a useful tool for the development and conservation of fishery resources.
C   4   6

Luna: Descriptive expository article.
C   3   6

1407. MARTIN, CLARO. The fishing industry--an important food producer. (In: Huke, Robert E., ed. Shadows on the land. Manila, Bookmark, 1963. p.368-393)
Luna: Descriptive analytical study.
C   4   6

1408. [MEDNICK, MELVIN]. Fishing. (In: Human Relations Area Files, Inc. Area Handbook on the Philippines. 1956. v.4, Chapter 17. p.1409-1513)
Luna: Historical descriptive analytical study.

E 4 7

1409. MONTALBAN, HERACLIO and CLARO MARTIN. Two Japanese fishing methods used by Japanese fishermen in Philippine waters. PJS 42, no. 4 (Aug. 1930), 465-480. 8 plates.

Intengan: Detailed description of two Japanese fishing methods used in Philippine waters, types of fishes caught and advantages of each method.
C 4 4

Luna: Descriptive analytical study.
C 4 4

1410. OÑATE, BURTON. Population and food requirements: Philippines. The International Rice Research Institute, Family Planning Workshop, College of Agriculture, U.P., Los Baños, Laguna, Oct. 29, 1965.
Cited in First Conference on Population, Quezon City, Philippines, 1965. 1966. p.159.

Intengan: Using recommended food allowances as target, a statistician projects food needs up to 1980.
N 5 6

Luna: Descriptive statistical analytical study with graphical illustrations.
N 4 6

1411. _____ and ELENA S. QUIOGUE. Variability studies of data from household food consumption surveys: I. Rice and other cereals. Phil. Stat. 15, nos. 1/2 (Mar./June 1966), 1-30.

1412. PAL, AGATON P. Food production program from the viewpoint of a rural sociologist.
Comments by S. C. Hsieh, Thomas R. McHale, Ernesto R. Mondoñedo. (In: Madigan, Francis C., ed. Human factors in Philippine rural development. Cagayan de Oro City, Xavier Univ. 1967. Xavier Univ. Studies. Study no. 1. p. 168-198)

1413. PALAD, JOSE GARCIA and OTHERS. Nutritive value of some foodstuffs processed in the Philippines. PJS 93, no. 3 (Sept. 1964), 355-384.

Intengan: Reports on proximate, mineral, and vitamin contents of 218 processed foods.
C 5 6

Luna: Descriptive chemical analysis of some foodstuffs.
N 4/5 6

1414. PASCUAL, CONRADO R. Maternal and child nutrition problems in a rapidly increasing population. PJPH 9, no. 2 (Apr./June 1964), 21-24.

Intengan: An assessment of nutrition problems of the vulnerable group based on results of clinical and biochemical surveys in six regions of Luzon.
D 4 6

Luna: Descriptive analytical study.
G/D 4 6

1415. _____ and OTHERS. Nutrition survey of 189 households in two regions in the Philippines. Pacific Science Congress. Proceedings. 9th, Bangkok, 1957. Bangkok, 1959. v.15, 75-87.

1416. PHILIPPINES (REPUBLIC) DEPT. OF AGRICULTURE AND NATURAL RESOURCES. BUREAU
OF FISHERIES. Philippine fisheries. Manila, U.P. Press, 1953. 185p. A
compendium of contributions of twenty-two authors.

      Intengan: General reference on fish culture, fish industries and
                            other related topics.
                            W   4   6
      Luna: Statistical materials.
                            W   5   6

1417. _____. INSTITUTE OF NUTRITION. Nutrition survey of 189 households in two
regions in the Philippines, by Conrado R. Pascual and others. Manila, Bureau
Print., 1958. 68p.

      Intengan: The first extension nutrition survey attempted on a re-
                            gional scale.
                            W   5   6
      Luna: Data collection and analysis.
                            W   5   6

1418. _____. Latest results of the Philippines Statistical Survey of Households.
Stat. Rept. 2, no. 3 (July 1958), 37-41.

      Intengan: Tabulated data of status of labor force is presented.
                            W   5   6
      Luna: Compilation of statistical materials.
                            W   4   6

1419. _____ NATIONAL ECONOMIC COUNCIL. OFFICE OF STATISTICAL COORDINATION AND
STANDARDS. The food balance sheets of the Philippines for 1953 to 1962.
Stat. Rept. 7, no. 4 (Oct./Dec. 1963), 1-47.

      Intengan: A revised report based on 1960 population census and on
                            a standardized procedure.
                            W   5   6
      Luna: Statistical estimates of food supply available for food
                            consumption.
                            W   4   6

1420. _____. The food balance sheets of the Philippines for 1958, 1959, and
1960. Stat. Rept. 5, no. 4 (Oct. 1961), 1-21.

      Intengan: The first food balance sheet prepared by the Office of
                            Statistical Coordination and Standards (OSCAS), National
                          Economic Council. Discusses details of its preparation.
                            W   5   6
      Luna: Statistical estimates of food supply available for con-
                            sumption.
                            W   4   6

1421. _____. The food balance sheet of the Philippines for 1961. Stat. Rept.
6, no. 4 (Oct./Dec. 1962), 1-9.

      Intengan: Unlike previous food balance sheets, data on non-farm
                            production are introduced.
                            W   5   6
      Luna: Statistical estimates of food supply available for con-
                            sumption.
                            W   4   6

1422. _____. The food balance sheet of the Philippines for CY 1966. Stat. Rept.
11, no. 4 (Oct./Dec. 1967), 1-10.

1423. QUIOGUE, ELENA S. Food consumption and supply in the Philippines. Philippine Journal of Nutrition 9 (July/Sept. 1966), 173-193.

1424. _____ and OTHERS. Dietary patterns and food habits. Nutrition News 13, no. 4 (Oct./Dec. 1960), 19-27.
        Intengan: Basis of the report is the nutrition survey of Ilocos-Mt. Province.
                        C   4   6
        Luna: Descriptive analytical study.
                        C   4/5   6

1425. QUISUMBING, EDUARDO. Philippine plants used for arrow and fish poisons. PJS 77, no. 2 (June 1947), 127-177.
        Intengan: Complete description of plant, scientific and local names and the poisonous principle are presented.
                        N   5   6
        Luna: Descriptive analytical study.
                        N   4   7

1426. _____. Vegetable poisons of the Philippines. Philippine Journal of Forestry 5, nos. 2/4 (Fourth Quarter 1947), 145-171.
        Intengan: A tabulated presentation of plants poisonous to man, animals and fish.
                        N   5   6
        Luna: Descriptive analytical study.
                        N   4   7

1427. _____. Wild species for foodstuffs and their domestication in the Philippines. (In: Symposium on the impact of man on humid tropics vegetation, Goroka, Territory of Papua and New Guinea, Sept. 1960...Canberra, A.J. Arthur, Commonwealth Govt. printer, 1962. p.90-93)

1428. ROLLA-BUSTRILLOS, NENA. Food management practices of homemakers in the rural areas. (In: Espiritu, Socorro C. and Chester L. Hunt, eds. Social foundations of community development; readings on the Philippines. Manila, R.M. Garcia [n.d.] p.54-61)
        Luna: Descriptive analytical study.
                        C   4/5   6

1429. SACAY, FRANCISCO M. The food supply and population of the Philippines. PA 33, no. 3 (Jan./Mar. 1950), 203-217.
        Luna: Descriptive analytical study.
                        C   4   7

1430. _____. Some factors affecting engagement in farming of agricultural-school graduates. PA 36, no. 5 (Oct. 1952), 259-262.
        Luna: Descriptive analytical study.
                        C   4   6

1431. SALCEDO, JUAN, JR. Better nutrition for a greater Philippines. Philippine Journal of Nursing 15, no. 3 (July/Sept. 1962), 11-13.
Cited in Index to Philippine Periodicals. v.7, p. 352.
        Intengan: A keynote address delivered at the First Food and Nutrition Exposition enjoining proper nutrition for a healthy nation.
                        D   4   6

Luna: Descriptive informative essay.

G/D   3   6

1432. _____. Considerations in the assessment of the nutritional needs of children at the early stages of national development. Science Bulletin 10, no. 3 (Mar. 1966), 4-10.

Intengan: A top nutrition scientist discusses factors of utmost consideration in the assessment of nutritional status and food needs of children.

D   4   6

Luna: Descriptive prescriptive article.

G/D   3   6

1433. _____. A cross-sectoral approach in nutrition program planning. SR 6, nos. 9/11 (Sept./Nov. 1965), 17-20.

Intengan: The promotion of nutrition among related agencies as they exist in the Philippines.

D   4   6

Luna: Descriptive prescriptive article.

G/D   3   6

1434. SAMSON, PABLO JR. Food consumption demonstration survey. Stat. Rept. 8, no. 4 (Oct./Dec. 1964), 7-13.

Intengan: A statistician reports on the planning and field operation of a survey conducted as a part of the course of the Food and Agricultural Organization Training Center on Food Consumption Survey for Asia and the Far East.

N   5   6

Luna: Statistical prescriptive methodology.

N   4   6

1435. SANTOS, F. O. and S. J. ASCALON. Amount of nutrients in Philippine food materials. PA 20, no. 6 (Nov. 1931), 402-409.

Intengan: Reports on caloric and proximate composition of foods by unit of measure.

N   4   4

Luna: Descriptive statistical analytical study.

N   4   4

1436. TABLANTE, NATHANIEL B. Food and population problems in the Philippines. AS 4, no. 2 (Aug. 1966), 374-380.

1437. UMALI, AGUSTIN F. Guide to the classification of fishing gear in the Philippines. Washington: Government Printing Office. 1950. 165p. (Dept. of the Interior, Fish and Wildlife Service. Research Report 17)

Intengan: A detailed guide to the classification of indigenous fishing gear with descriptions and illustrations.

N   5   6

Luna: Descriptive analytical study.

N   4   4

1438. _____. The Japanese bean trawl used in Philippine waters. PJS 48, no. 3 (July 1932), 389-410. 5 plates.

Intengan: A detailed description of the Japanese bean trawler used in the Philippines, the adoption of which the author recommended to Filipino fishermen.

N   4   4

Luna: Descriptive analytical study.
        N 4 4

1439. VALENCIA, ELPIDIO. Nutrition and public health. Nutrition News 12, no. 4 (Oct./Dec. 1959), 19-20, 26, 31.
    Luna: Descriptive informative address.
         D 3 6

1440. VALENZUELA, ABELARDO. Composition and nutritive value of Philippine food fishes. PJS 36, no. 2 (June 1928), 235-242.
    Luna: Descriptive analytical study with plates.
         N 5 4

1441. _____ and P. J. WESTER. Composition of some Philippine fruits, vegetables, and forage plants. PJS 41, no. 1 (Jan. 1930), 85-102. 22 plates.
    Intengan: The proximate composition of forty-nine items are presented, properly described and illustrated.
         C 5 4
    Luna: Descriptive analytical study with plates.
         N 5 4

1442. VARONA, A. P. and J. V. CASTILLO. Consumption of basic food items in the Philippines. PGJ 6, no. 2 (Apr./June 1958), 67-74.
    Intengan: Increased consumption of rice and corn as a result of population growth is presented for a twelve year period, 1946-1957.
         C 4 6
    Luna: Descriptive statistical graphical study.
         X/C 4 6

1443. VEGA-YAP, GLORIA and REMEDIOS O. ALCANTARA. Purchasing patterns, consumption habits and preferences for rice and corn. PA 45, nos. 1/2 (June/July 1961), 1-28.
    Luna: Descriptive analytical study.
         C 4/5 6

1444. WESTER, PETER J. The food plants of the Philippines. 3d rev. ed. Manila, Bureau of Printing, 1924. (Philippine Islands. Bureau of Agriculture Bulletin no. 39) First and second editions are in the Philippine Agricultural Review, v.9, 1916; v.14, 1921.
    Suggested by McHale.

GEOGRAPHY

1445. BALDORIA, PEDRO L. Political geography of the Philippines. PGJ 1, no. 1 (First Quarter 1953), 15-23.
    Luna: Analyzes the impact on geographic location to political development.
         V 4 6
    Spencer: Fair summary.
         V 3 7

1446. BROWN, WILLIAM H. Useful plants of the Philippines. Manila, Bureau of Print., 1941-1946. 3v. (Philippines (Commonwealth) Dept. of Agriculture and Commerce. Technical Bulletin 10) v.1: Reprinted in 1951. v.2: Reprinted in 1954.

1447. BURKILL, ISSAC HENRY. A dictionary of the economic products of the Malay Peninsula. London, Published on behalf of the governments of the Straits Settlement and Federated Malay States by the Crown agents for the Colonies. 1935. 2v.
Suggested by McHale.

1448. BURLEY, T. M. A land use inventory for the Philippines? A suggested technique from Australia. PGJ 9, nos. 1/2 (Jan./June 1965), 11-25.
        Luna: Underscores the need for land inventory and suggests a procedure based on an Australian system.
                    K   4   6
        Spencer: C   4   6

1449. CASTRILLO, ZOILO. Land use and land resources. ERJ 7, no. 2 (Sept. 1960), 82-88.
        Luna: Descriptive analytical study.
                   G/O   4   6

1450. CHAMBERLAIN, ALEXANDER F. Notes on the Philippines from the American Antiquarian. Philippine Studies: I. Place-Names. JEAS 8, nos. 3/4 (July/Oct. 1959), 33-57.
        Luna: Relates significance of place names to ethnic characteristics.
                   Z   3   7

1451. CRESSEY, PAUL F. The development of Philippine cities. SJ 5, no. 4 (Oct./Dec. 1958), 349-361.
        Grossholtz: Indicates diverse characteristics of Philippine cities and difficulty of defining "urbanism."
                   V   4   7

1452. _____. Urbanization in the Philippines. Sociology and Social Research 44, no. 6 (July/Aug. 1960), 402-409.
        Luna: Descriptive analytical study.
                   Z   4   6
        Spencer: Z   3   7
        Wernstedt: Z   3   7

1453. CRUZ, SANTIAGO R. and TEOFILO M. MENDOZA. Agricultural meteorology: Philippine rainfalls. PGJ 3, no. 2 (Apr./June 1955), 80-91. 11 plates.
        Luna: Statistical analytical study with maps indicating agroclimatic regions.
                   C   4   7
        Spencer: Basic data, good interpretation.
                   C   4   7
        Wernstedt: Excellent source for climatic (rainfall) data and analyses.
                   C   4   7

1454. DICKERSON, ROY ERNEST and OTHERS. Distribution of life in the Philippines.

Manila, Bureau of Printing, 1928. 322p. (Philippine Islands. Bureau of
Science. Monograph 21) 42 plates.
> Luna: Descriptive analytical study of historical value showing
> progress on this type of work.
> N   4   4
> Spencer: Excellent basic study, now somewhat dated.
> N   4/5   7

1455. DOERR, ARTHUR H. A land inventory for the Philippines? PGJ 7, no. 1 (Jan./
Mar. 1963), 52-55.
> Luna: Discusses the importance of land inventory and suggests
> a system based on the Puerto Rican scheme.
> K   4   6
> Wernstedt: K   3   6

1456. [DONOGHUE, JOHN, ROBERT B. FOX and WILLIS SIBLEY]. The land. (In: Human Relations Area Files, Inc. Area Handbook on the Philippines. 1956. vol. I,
Chapter 2, p.11-50)
> Luna: Historical descriptive study.
> Z   4   7
> Warren: E   5   6

1457. DUPREE, LOUIS B. A survey of the geography and geology of the Philippines,
with emphasis on the Pleistocene. JEAS 3, no. 2 (Jan. 1954), 183-198.
> Luna: Critical evaluation of the geographic and geologic aspects
> of the Philippines and the need for further work along
> such lines.
> N   4   7

1458. EINSIEDEL, LUZ A. The impact of urbanization resulting from industrialization on Filipino home. Philippine Christian Advance 15, no. 6 (June 1963),
34-37+.
> Luna: S   3   6

1459. GUTIERREZ, JOSE S. Agricultural land utilization for the last two census
years. PGJ 3, no. 4 (Oct./Dec. 1955), 189-203.
> Luna: N   4   7
> Spencer: N   4   7

1460. HERRE, ALBERT W. C. T. Check list of Philippine fishes. Washington, U.S.
Govt. Printing Office. 1953. 977p. (U.S. Fish and Wildlife Service.
Research Report 20)

1461. HOWE, FREDERIC C. Philippine homestead settlement plans. PM 35, no. 2
(Feb. 1938), 82-83.
> Luna: Descriptive informative article.
> -   3   4

1462. HUKE, ROBERT E. Shadows on the land; an economic geography of the Philippines. Manila, Bookmark, 1963. 428p.
> Spencer: K   5   7
> Wernstedt: K   5   7

1463. JORDANA Y MORERA, RAMÓN. Bosquejo geográfico é histórico-natural del archipiélago Filipino. Madrid, Impr. de Moreno y Rojas, 1885. 461p.

Luna: Descriptive analytical study.
                  N   4   7

1464. JURIKA, STEPHEN. The political geography of the Philippines. Stanford,
       1962. 206p. Thesis (Ph.D.) - Stanford Univ.
             Luna: Descriptive analytical study.
                               K   4   7

1465. KOLB, ALBERT. Die Philippinen. Leipzig, K. F. Koehler, 1942. 503p.
       Suggested by Luna.
             Luna: Descriptive analytical study; quite extensive in treat-
                               ment specially with regard to pre-WW II conditions.
                               K   4   7

1466. LAFOND DE LURCY, GABRIEL. Les Philippines. Société de Géographie Bulle-
       tin. Ser. 3, v. 6 (1846), 151-177.
             Luna: Descriptive analytical study.
                               K   4   3

1467. LEE, GEO. S. The Philippines: our far-off possessions. Geographical So-
       ciety of Philadelphia Bulletin 18, (1920), 1-25. pl.
             Luna: Descriptive analytical study.
                               K   4   7
             Spencer: Early, secondary source seminar paper. Fair for date
                               published. Now only useful for comparative sense.
                               K   2/3   7

1468. LESACA, REYNALDO M. Rural water supplies in the Philippines, 1963. SR 4,
       no. 12 (Dec. 1963), 16-20.
             Luna: Descriptive informative article.
                               C   3   6

1469. LUNA, TELESFORO W., JR. The land and natural resources of the Philippines.
       (In: Philippines. Univ. Population Institute. First Conference on Popu-
       lation, 1965. Quezon City, 1966. p.161-184)
             Luna: Descriptive analytical study.
                               K   4   6
             Spencer: Good summary study.
                               K   4   7
             Wernstedt: K   3/4   7

1470. _____. Physical aspects and natural resources of the Philippines. PRBE
       2, no. 2 (Dec. 1965), 28-53.

1471. MAMISAO, JESUS P. Soil conservation trends in the Philippines. PGJ 7,
       no. 1 (Jan./Mar. 1963), 56-64.
             Luna: Descriptive analytical study with tabular and graphic
                               presentations.
                               N   4   6
             Spencer: Good statistical summary of land resources.
                               N   3   6
             Wernstedt: N   3   7

1472. MANALO, EUGENIO B. The distribution of rainfall in the Philippines. PGJ
       4, no. 4 (Oct./Nov. 1956), 104-167.

Luna: Descriptive analytical study with maps, graphs and tables.
                     N   4   7

Spencer: The best study of rainfall available. Statistical and
                     cartographic.
                     N   4   7

Wernstedt: Excellent precipitation data source and analysis.
                     N   4   7

1473. MERRILL, ELMER D. An enumeration of Philippine flowering plants. Bureau of Printing. 4 vols. 1923-1926. (Philippine Islands. Bureau of Science. Publication no. 18)
Suggested by McHale.

1474. _____. A flora of Manila. Manila, Bureau of Printing, 1912. 490p. (Philippine Islands. Publication no. 5)

1475. _____. Plant life of the Pacific world. New York, Macmillan Co., 1945. 295p.
Suggested by McHale.

1476. NAZARET, FRANCISCO V. and FELISA R. BARRETTO. Concepts and definition of urban-rural areas in the Philippines. Phil. Stat. 12, nos. 2/3 (June/Sept. 1963), 89-108.
Luna: Descriptive evaluative study.
                     N   4   6
Spencer: Discussion of criteria for Philippine urbanism.
                     G   5   6
Wernstedt: First attempts to classify urban centers and populations.
                     N   4   7

1477. NEGADO, SUSANO R. The development of waterworks and sewerage systems in the Philippines and its relation to the socio-economic life of the people. Manila, 1959. 217p. Thesis (M.S.) - Mapua Institute of Technology.
Cited in Compilation of graduate theses...p.344.
Luna: Descriptive statistical study.
                     G/C   4   7

1478. PARSON, RUBEN L. Geography and resource management. PGJ 8, nos. 1/2 (Jan./June 1964), 3-11.
Luna: Descriptive analytical study with broad applications.
                     K   4   7

1479. PELZER, KARL J. Pioneer settlement in the Asiatic tropics; studies in land utilization and agricultural colonization in Southeastern Asia. American Geographical Society. 1945. (Special Publication no. 29) Chapter 4. Landless Filipinos, p. [81]-114.
Luna: Descriptive analytical study with maps and tables.
                     K   4   4
Spencer: Excellent study of settlement activities in Mindanao.
                     K   5   7
Wernstedt: Survey of resettlement programs in Philippines and Indonesia.
                     K   5   4/5

1480. PEREZ, BERNARDINO A. Notes on classifying urban-rural areas. Stat. Rept. 7,

no. 3 (July/Sept. 1963), 14-16.
    Luna: Descriptive evaluative essay.
                N   4   6

1481. QUISUMBING, EDUARDO. Recent ethnobotanical studies in the Philippines. (In: Symposium on the impact of man on humid tropics vegetation, Goroka, Territory of Papua and New Guinea, Sept. 1960...Canberra, A. J. Arthur, Commonwealth Govt. Printer, 1962. p.330-331)

1482. _____. The vanishing species of plants in the Philippines. (In: Symposium on the impact of man on humid tropics vegetation, Goroka, Territory of Papua and New Guinea, Sept. 1960...Canberra, A. J. Arthur, Commonwealth Govt. Printer, 1962. p.344-349)

1483. READE, CHARLES C. Town planning in the Philippines. Preliminary report to the Chief Secretary to Government by the Government Town Planner, Federated Malay States, in regard to Town Planning in the Philippine Islands, and the City of Baguio, with special reference to Cameron's Highlands. Kuala Lumpur, Town Planning Department, Federated Malay States, 1928. 30p.
    Luna: C   4   4

1484. REED, ROBERT RONALD. Hispanic urbanism in the Philippines: a study of the impact of Church and State. JEAS 11, (Mar. 1967), 1-222. Maps, illus. (His M.A. Thesis - Univ. of California, Berkeley, 1966)
    Luna: Historical descriptive analytical study.
                K   4   7
    Spencer: Good as a thesis, has useful secondary summary.
                K   4   7

1485. ROSELL, DOMINADOR Z. Knowledge of geography vital to developing nation. SR 6, nos. 9/11 (Sept./Nov. 1965), 6-7.
    Luna: Descriptive article.
                C/K   3   7
    Spencer: C   3   6

1486. _____. Research and development of water resources of the Philippines. PGJ 11, nos. 1/2 (Jan./June 1967), 4-12.

1487. SANTOS, AURORA. Land distribution. Philippines Today 2, no. 2 (Oct. 1954), 27-30.
    Luna: Descriptive informative article.
                -    3   6

1488. SICAT, GERARDO P. and ROSA LINDA P. TIDALGO. Output, capital, labor and population: projections from the supply-side. (In: Philippines. Univ. Population Institute. First Conference on Population, 1965. Quezon City, 1966. p.354-388.
    Luna: X   4   6
    Valdepenas: Useful.
                X   3   6
    Wernstedt: X   4   6

1489. SPENCER, JOSEPH E. The cities of the Philippines. Journal of Geography 57, no. 6 (Sept. 1958), 288-294.

Luna: Descriptive analytical study.
                  K   4   6
Grossholtz: A useful description of city growth.
                  K   4   6
Spencer: Attempt to clarify issue of political vs. urbanized area
                  of Philippine Island cities.
                  K   4   6
Wernstedt: Attempts to define an urban population of each chartered
                  city.
                  K   4   6

1490. _____. Land use in the upland Philippines. (In: Institute of Pacific Re-
       lations. International Secretariat. The development of upland areas in the
       Far East. New York, 1949. v. 1, p.26-57.
       Spencer: K   4   7

1491. _____. The Philippine Islands. (In: Freeman, Otis W., ed. Geography of
       the Pacific. New York, Wiley, 1951. p.298-327)
       Luna: Descriptive analytical study.
                         K   4   7
       Spencer: Summary chapter on historical and cultural geography.
                         K   4   7
       Wernstedt: Overview of Philippine geography.
                         K   4   7

1492. _____. Philippine soil, water, and wood are worth money now. PGJ 5, no. 3
       (July/Sept. 1957), 57-69.
       Luna: Descriptive evaluative article.
                         K   3   7
       Spencer: Urging Philippine conservation of resources.
                         K   3   7
       Wernstedt: K   3   7

1493. _____. The Philippines: an island borderland. (In: Spencer, Joseph E.
       Asia, East by South; a cultural geography. New York, Wiley, 1954. p.284-
       299)
       Luna: Historical descriptive analytical study with maps.
                         K   4   7
       Spencer: Summary chapter on historical and cultural geography.
                         K   4   7
       Wernstedt: Textbook treatment of Philippine geography with emphasis
                         on historical evolution.
                         K   4   7

1494. SUCGANG, ROBERTO R. Social planning for housing and community participation.
       PSR 12, nos. 3/4 (July/Oct. 1964), 178-184.
       Luna: Descriptive analytical study.
                         S   4   6

1495. TIKHONOV, D. I. (Dwellings and various types of rural settlements in the
       Philippines; in Russian.) Sbornik Muzeya Antropologii i Etnografii, Akademiya
       Nauk SSSR, Moscow 23, (1966), 222-233.
       Cited in Index to current periodicals...Royal Anthropological Institute.
       Oct./Dec. 1966, p. 352.
       Luna: Descriptive analytical study.

                              E   4   7

1496. ULLMAN, EDWARD L. Trade centers and tributary areas of the Philippines.
       Geographical Review 50, no. 2 (Apr. 1960), 203-218.
           Anderson: Five levels of trade centers are identified with the main
                            indicator being differential densities in traffic flow.
                            The report concludes with some notes on the geographic
                            centrality of the trade points and the modification of
                            the hierarchy as the economy continues to modernize.
                            Maps.
                            K   5   6
           Luna: Descriptive statistical analytical study with maps.
                            K   4   6
           Spencer: Clear discussion of regional focus of regional trade.
                            K   4   6
           Wernstedt: Categories of urban centers in trade hierarchy.
                            K   4   6

1497. U.S. CONGRESS. SENATE. The Philippine islands, a brief compilation of the
       latest information and statistics obtainable on the numbers, areas, popula-
       tion, races and tribes, mineral resources, agriculture, exports and imports,
       forests, and harbors of the Philippine islands. Feb. 15, 1900. (56th Con-
       gress, 1st Session. Senate Document no. 171) 29p.
           Luna: Descriptive statistical analytical study.
                            W   4   7
           Spencer: Compilation. Useful only as bare thin summary at end of
                            Spanish era.
                            W   3   3
           Wernstedt: Excellent resume of Philippine geography after Spanish-
                            American War.
                            W   4   3

1498. WERNSTEDT, FREDERICK L. and JOSEPH E. SPENCER. The Philippine island world:
       a physical, cultural, and regional geography. Berkeley and Los Angeles,
       Univ. of California Press, 1967. 742p.
           Luna: Encyclopedic treatment on a topical and regional basis.
                            K   4   7
           Polson: A well-organized and comprehensive study.
                            K   5   7
           Thomas: Most complete geographical account (albeit very traditional
                            geography) ever written about the Philippines. Covers both
                            physical and cultural elements and regions.
                            K   4   7

1499. ZAIDI, IQTIDAR HUSAIN. A sample of land use survey on the campus of the
       University of the Philippines Diliman, Quezon City, Philippines.
       PGJ 3, no. 4 (Oct./Dec. 1955), 177-188.
           Luna: Micro-geographic field study.
                            K   4   6
           Spencer: Sample survey of a local area--useful as a guide.
                            K   5   6

1500. ZINGG, ROBERT M. American plants in Philippine ethnobotany. PJS 54, no. 2
       (June 1934), 221-274.

HEALTH AND SICKNESS

1501. ALOMIA, A. Role of the public health nurses in the prevention of communicable diseases. PJN 29, no. 2 (Mar./Apr. 1960), 65-67.
      Tiglao: D   3   6

1502. AYCARDO, MANUEL MA. How good was our health in 1954? Phil. Stat. 4, no. 4 (Dec. 1955), 157-172.
      Tiglao: One of the few social studies made in relation to a specific disease on a comprehensive basis.
                  D   4   6

1503. BULATAO, JAIME. New psychological concepts and their application to nursing. Proceedings of the First Convocation on Nursing and the Behavioral Sciences, (Quezon City: U.P., 1960).
Cited in Ateneo de Manila Univ., Faculty publications as of February, 1967. p.18.
      Bulatao: P   3   6
      Guthrie: P   3   6

1504. CALDERON, FERNANDO. Some data concerning the medical geography of the Philippines. PJS 9-B, no. 3 (June 1914), 199-218.
      Tiglao: D   5   4

1505. CALUAG, JOSE L. Problems in health administration. Philippines (Republic) Bureau of Health. Bulletin. 24 (July/Aug. 1948), 263-268.
Source: Index to Periodicals (U.P. Library. Filipiniana Section)
      Tiglao: D   3   6

1506. CAÑOS, RODOLFO T. The **nation's** health: 1964. FTY (1964), 233-238, 240.
      Tiglao: G/D   3   6

1507. COLLER, RICHARD W. Health innovations in rural areas. PSR 10, nos. 1/2 (Jan./Apr. 1962), 59-68.

1508. _____. Philippine public health **programs** in a transitional society. PSR 9, nos. 1/2 (Jan./Apr. 1961), 47-58.
      Doherty: Analysis of various reports and attempt at explaining the patterns shown.
                  Z   3   6

1509. CUYUGAN, RUBEN SANTOS. Social sciences in the health care of society. PJN 29, no. 2 (Mar./Apr. 1960) 72-75, 78.
      Tiglao: A good exposé of the role of social science in health care.
                  Z   3   6

1510. DALTON, J. ALBERT. Trends in Philippine mental health promotion: clinical pastoral training. SLQ 5, nos. 1/2 (Mar./June 1967), 89-98.

1511. DEUTSCHMAN, ZYGMUNT. Public health and medical services in the Philippines. Far Eastern Quarterly 4, no. 2 (Feb. 1945), 148-157.

1512. DUQUE, FRANCISCO Q. A challenge to nurses in the nation's new frontier. PJN 31, no. 3 (May/June 1962), 148-150, 179.

I. GENERAL. HEALTH AND SICKNESS

      Tiglao: Succinct expression of health problems and social factors
                  related to them.
                  G/D   4   6

1513.   _____. Evaluation of the public health program and proposals to improve it.
PMAJ 33, no. 10 (Oct. 1957), 763-766.
      Tiglao: Good use of data and interpretation for evaluative pur-
                  pose.
                  D   4   6

1514.   FOX, ROBERT B. Sociological aspects of medical care in rural Filipino society. PJPH 4, no. 4 (Oct./Dec. 1959), 138-142.
      Tiglao: A good analysis of the sociological aspects of medical
                  care in the Philippine society.
                  E   4   6

1515.   GARCIA, CARLOS P. In the field of social amelioration. (Speech delivered
during the closing day of the National Health Conference at the Manila Hotel
on July 24, 1959). Philippine Health Digest 1, no. 2 (Aug. 1959), 20-23,
33.
Cited in Index to Philippine Periodicals, v.4, p.115.
      Tiglao: G   3   6

1516.   GARCIA, PAULINO J. Designs in public health. PMAJ 34, no. 5 (May 1958),
323-325.
      Tiglao: G   3   6

1517.   _____. Health hopes in the Philippines. EQ 2, no. 1 (Aug. 1954), 132-138.
      Tiglao: G   3   6

1518.   HARVEY, PHILIP. Native medical practice in the Philippines, with introductory observations. New York Medical Journal 74 (Aug. 3, 1901), 203-212.

1519.   HEALEY, L. Hyperuricemia in Filipinos: interaction of heredity and environment. [by] L. A. Healey, Maurice D. Skeith, John L. Decker, and Pelagia S.
Bayani-Sioson. (In the American Journal of Human Genetics. New York, 1967.
vol. 19, (no.2), Mar. 1967, p. 81-85. map, tables)

1520.   HEISER, VICTOR G. An American doctor's odyssey: adventures in forty-five
countries. New York, W. W. Norton & Co., 1936. 544p.
      Coller: First-hand account of pioneer health efforts in Philip-
                  pines and elsewhere. A classic.
                  D   5   4

1521.   _____. Sanitation in the Philippines with special reference to its effect
upon other tropical countries. Journal of Race Development 3, no. 2 (Oct.
1912), 121-134.

1522.   _____. Unsolved health problems peculiar to the Philippines. PJS 5-B,
no. 2 (July 1910), 171-178.

1523.   HOUSTON, CHARLES O., JR. Nutrition and public health in the Philippines,
1934-1950. JEAS 4, no. 2 (Apr. 1955), 119-136.
      Luna: Descriptive informative article.
                  H   3   7

1524. ICASIANO, MARIANO C. Legal aspects of the school health services in the
       Philippines. Philippine Health Journal 8, no. 4 (Dec. 1961), 11-12, 24.
           Tiglao: Good for historical studies.
                            G   4   6

1525. _____. Mental health in public health. Philippine Health Journal 9, no. 2
       (July 1962), 12-13.

1526. _____. The practice of medicine and the practice of public health. PMAJ
       36, no. 4 (Apr. 1960), 281-283.
           Tiglao: G   3   6

1527. _____. Public and professional relationship in public health work. Philip-
       pine Health Journal 7, no. 2 (May 1960), 23-24.
           Tiglao: A brief description of the relationship of public health
                            work and community organization.
                            G   3   6

1528. JACINTO, CARMELO P. The nation's health. Progress (1954), 40-42.
       Source: Index to Periodicals (U.P. Library. Filipiniana Section)
           Tiglao: D   3   6

1529. JIMENEZ, TERESITA T. A study of health practices in the slum of barrio Boni-
       facio. PSR 3, no. 3 (July 1955), 28-31.
           Coller: Report based on original field work for the M.A. degree,
                            basic data for recent studies.
                            Z   5   6

1530. JOCANO, F. LANDA. Cultural context of folk medicine: some Philippine
       cases. PSR 14, no. 1 (Jan. 1966), 40-48.
           Tiglao: E   4   6

1531. LIEBAN, RICHARD W. The dangerous Ingkantos: illness and social control in
       a Philippine community. AA 64, no. 2 (Apr. 1962), 306-312.

1532. MANALO, FERNANDO D. Evaluation of the public health program and proposals
       to improve it. PMAJ 34, no. 6 (June 1958), 394-397.
           Tiglao: An excellent diagnosis of the political factors that serve
                            as deterrents in the implementation of an efficient public
                            health program and recommendations for solving these.
                            D   3   6

1533. MAYUGA, PEDRO N. The government and private medical practice in the Philip-
       pines. Philippine Federation of Private Medical Practitioners Journal 14,
       nos. 6/7 (June/July 1965), 324-327.
           Tiglao: D   3   6

1534. _____. Role of the hospital in the Philippine public health system. Phil-
       ippine Medical Association. Journal 39, no. 11 (Nov. 1963), 870-874.
           Tiglao: D   3   6

1535. NAVARRO, JOSE S. The science of managing people. PJPH 1, nos. 4/5 (June
       1956), 10-13.
           Tiglao: D   3   6

1536. NOLASCO, J. A. and JACINTO J. DIZON. A study of the distribution of the health personnel in the rural areas. PJPH 1, nos. 4/5 (June 1956), 15-22.
    Tiglao: D   3   6

1537. PERSONS, R. C. Report on **sanitary** relations of Philippine Islands to the naval fleet. Surgeon-General of the Navy. Report. Washington (1909), 200-208.

1538. RAMOS, PAZ G. Historical background of health education in the **Philippines**. EQ 14, no. 1 (July 1966), 4-13.
    Tiglao: Y   4   7

1539. ROSARIO, FANNY C. DEL. Utilization of a rural health center and implications for social casework. 1959. 149p. Thesis (M.A.) - U.P.
    Coller: Basic data gathered in a field study near Manila.
                    S   5   6

1540. SALCEDO, JUAN, JR. The health of the nation. Philippine Yearbook (1950/1951), 43-44, 51.
    Tiglao: Good reference for historical developments in public health.
                    D/Y   3   6

1541. _____. Philippine public health today. FTY (1953), 65-66.
    Tiglao: D/Y   3   6

1542. _____. Recent developments in the Philippine public health program. Philippine Health Journal 7, no. 3 (Aug. 1960), 24-28.
    Tiglao: D/Y   3   6

1543. _____. Voluntary organizations and the health programme. SR 6, nos. 9/11 (Sept./Nov. 1965), 2-5.
    Tiglao: Excellent exposé showing relation of health and disease and socio-economic milieu in which they exist.
                    D/Y   4   6

1544. SAMSON, JOSE A. Schizophrenia among Filipino children. Unitas 38, no. 2 (June 1965), 298-310.
    Guthrie: P   4   6

1545. SISON, A. G. and OTHERS. The **influence** of American occupation on the life span of the Filipino and on the incidence of degerative disease. Acta Medica Philippina 5, no. 3 (Jan. 1959), 1-8.

1546. STAUFFER, ROBERT B. The development of an interest group: the Philippine Medical Association. Quezon City, U.P. Press, 1966. 192p.
    Coller: Reports on original research of this organization. A Pioneering study.
                    V   5   6
    Grossholtz: V   3   6

1547. TAN, ANTONIO G. A study of health, hygienic, and sanitary conditions obtaining among rural homes. Quezon City, Philippines. U.P. Community Development Research Council. 1960. 59p. (Study Series, no. 10)

I. GENERAL. HEALTH AND SICKNESS

Coller: Basic data based on an extensive field survey.
                              -     5   6

1548. _____. The U.P. and rural health problems. EQ 5, no. 1 (June 1957), 65-74.

1549. TIGLAO, TEODORA V. Health practices in a Philippine rural community. [Quezon City] Community Development Research Council, U.P., 1964. 232p. (Study Series, no. 23)
      Coller: One of the best reports yet on actual, detailed behavior in this area of life. Very careful work, bringing forth original and essential data.
                 S   5   6
      Villanueva: Interpretation of health data over a time for empirical purposes.
                 S   4   6

1550. _____. A reevaluation of health practices in a Philippine rural community. 1963. Thesis (Ph.D.) - Columbia (Teachers College)

1551. VALDEZ, BASILIO. The public health movement. Philippine Health Journal 9, no. 1 (Mar. 1962), 2-4.
      Tiglao: Brief but good analysis of the social factors that defer public health movement in the Philippines.
                 D   3   6

1552. VERGARA-VALENZUELA, AMANDA and RICHARD LIEBAN. A study of medical practices in the Philippines. Acta Medica Philippina 16, no. 1 (July/Sept. 1959), 31-39.
      Tiglao: A very concise but clear interpretation of some of the cultural determinants in the acceptance of modern medical services.
                 D & E 4   6

1553. VICTORIANO, NICANOR. Possibility of integrating nutrition clinic service into the rural health unit program. Nutrition News 15, no. 4 (Oct./Dec. 1956), 28-33.
Cited in Index to Philippine Periodicals, v.2, p.649.
      Tiglao: An 'exposé' of functions of the RHU and some cultural factors in nutrition work.
                 D/G   3   6

1554. VILLEGAS, A. Primitive medicine in the Philippines. Annals of Medical History 5 (Sept. 1923), 229-241.

1555. WASHBURN, WILLIAM S. Health conditions in the Philippines. PJS 3-B, no. 4 (Sept. 1908), 269-284.

1556. WISE, J. C. Notes on the health and sanitary condition of Hawaii and the Philippines. Surgeon-General of the Navy. Report. Washington (1899), 152-155.

1557. WORLD HEALTH ORGANIZATION. Methodology of health protection for local areas. Abstracts of Report on the Philippines. 6p. Geneva. May 1952.
Cited in United Nations Documents Index, 1952, p. 246.

1558. YOUDE, SHERYL R. A sociological analysis of the acceptance and rejection

of modern medical practice in a Philippine barrio. 1960. 156p. Thesis (M.A.)
- U.P.
Cited in U.P. theses and dissertations index, p.230.
   Coller: Analysis of who accepted clinic treatment and why in a small
          village.
          Z   5   6
   Tiglao: A very concise but clear interpretation of some of the cul-
          tural determinants in the acceptance of modern medical ser-
          vices.
          Z   4   6

HEAVY AND LIGHT INDUSTRIES

1559. ARIAS, MAGDALENA. The influence of cottage industries on the socio-economic
status of the Philippine rural areas. CEU.GFS 6 (1955), 236-258.

1560. CHANGSIRIVATHANATHAMRONG, BOONKUL. The Philippine rubber industry. PRBE 3,
no. 1 (May 1966), 1-16.

1561. CROWE, CLIFFORD H. Philippine pottery. American Ceramics Society. Transaction 14 (1912), 723-730.

1562. FOSTER, GEORGE M. Resin-coated pottery in the Philippines. AA 58, no. 4
(Aug. 1956), 732-733.

1563. GALVANTE, JESUS R., PACIENTE B. UDAN, and GREGORIO D. SALVADOR. Philippine
arts and crafts. Manila, Bookman, 1958. 147p.
   Spencer: Fairly complete discussion.
          -   3   7

1564. LUNA, TELESFORO W., JR. Manufacturing in the Philippines. PGJ 7, no. 1
(Jan./Mar. 1963), 6-17.
   Spencer: Good study.
          K   4   6

1565. OPIANA, GIL O. and I. OLAYAO. The economic importance of Philippine clays
and other local ceramic materials. Philippine Geologist 6, no. 1 (Dec.
1951), 5-14.
   Spencer: Study of clay resources for economic application.
          C & G 5   7

1566. PHILIPPINES (REPUBLIC) NATIONAL ECONOMIC COUNCIL. The survey on the social
implications of small-scale industries in the Philippines: 1959. Manila,
1960. 92p. (Statistical Survey, C.P. 60106)

1567. RAVENHOLT, ALBERT. Hydroelectric power and Philippine industrialization.
AUFSR. Southeast Asia Series 1, no. 12 (July 10, 1953), 8p. (AR-13-'53)

1568. [SIBLEY, WILLIS E. and CHARLES CALLENDER]. Industry. (In: Human Relations
Area Files, Inc. Area handbook on the Philippines. 1956. vol.4, Chapter 20,

p.1593-1645)
    Warren: E   5   6

1569. SICAT, GERARDO P. and AURORA S. MAMINTA. Structure of manufacturing indus-tries in terms of their ranks. PRBE 3, no. 2 (Nov. 1966), 1-20.

1570. [SMITH, GEORGE]. Mining. (In: Human Relations Area Files, Inc. Area hand-book on the Philippines. 1956. vol.4, Chapter 18, p.1514-1576)

1571. VELASCO, EMMANUEL T. Consumption of electricity in the greater Manila area. PRBE 1, no. 2 (Oct. 1964), 46-61.

HISTORY AND CULTURE CHANGE

1572. ADUARTE, DIEGO and BALTASAR DE SANTA CRUZ. Historia de la provincia del Santo Rosario de la Orden de Predicadores en Philippinas, Japon, y China. Manila, 1640. v.1, Reprinted in 1693, issued with v.2. v.2 by Baltasar de Santa Cruz. 1693.
Synopsis in Blair and Robertson. v.30-32.
    Felix: Excellent account by a second generation missionary.
                M   5   2
    Legarda: M   5   2
    Phelan: M   5   2
    Wickberg: M   5   2

1573. AGONCILLO, TEODORO A. Philippine history and institutions in the general education program. University College Journal, no. 1 (First Semester 1961), 93-101.

1574. _____ and OSCAR M. ALFONSO. A short history of the Filipino people. Que-zon City, U.P. 1961. 629p.

1575. ALCANTARA, ADELAIDA and OTHERS. The barrio council of Tulayan; a prelimi-nary investigation of directed cultural change. For Anthropology 201, Dept. of Anthropology, U.P. Quezon City, 1957. 53p.
Source: Filipiniana, 1968, p.613.
    Villanueva: Good study on contemporary political process.
                  Z   5   6

1576. ALCÁZAR, JOSÉ DE. Historia de los dominios españoles en Oceania; Filipinas. Manila, Impr. de D. J. Atayde y comp. 1895. 207p.
    Phelan: H   2/3   3

1577. ALFONSO, OSCAR M. Taft's views on "The Philippines for the Filipinos". AS 6, no. 3 (Dec. 1968), 237-247.

1578. ARTIGAS Y CUERVA, MANUEL. Historia de Filipinas. Manila, La Pilarica, 1916. 687p.

Felix: Fair general history with plenty of data not subsequently
                published.
                H   3   7
Phelan: H   3   7

1579.   BEST, ELSDON. Pre-historic civilisation in the Philippines. Polynesian So-
        ciety Journal 1, no. 1 (Apr. 15, 1892), 118-125, 195-201.

1580.   BEYER, H. OTLEY. Philippine pre-historic contacts with foreigners. From
        the "Historical Introduction" by Dr. H. Otley Beyer, of "Chinese Elements in
        the Tagalog Language" by E. Arsenio Manuel (1948), 9-25.
                Wickberg: A   3   1

1581.   _____. Pre-historic Philippines. (In: Galang, Zoilo M., ed. Encyclope-
        dia of the Philippines. v.15 (1958), 1-37. 9 plates.

1582.   _____ and JAIME C. DE VEYRA. Philippine saga: a pictorial history of the
        archipelago since time began. Manila, Capitol Publishing, 1952. 152p.
                Legarda: Atrocious paper and format, but interesting content and
                                pictures.
                                E   3   7
                Wickberg: A   3   7

1583.   BLAIR, EMMA H. and JAMES A. ROBERTSON. The Philippine Islands,1493-1898.
        Cleveland, Ohio, Arthur H. Clark Co. 1903-1909. 55v.
                Felix: Insufficient from 1750-1898.
                                H   5   1-3
                LeRoy: Invaluable and monumental collection of source material
                                for the history of the Philippines before and during the
                                Spanish regime. American Historical Review, Oct. 1903,
                                p.149.
                Onorato: G/H/Y   5   1-3

1584.   BOURNE, EDWARD GAYLORD. Discovery, conquest, and early history of the Phil-
        ippine Islands...Being a separate issue of the historical introduction to
        Blair & Robertson's "The Philippine islands: 1493-1898". Cleveland, Ohio,
        The Arthur H. Clark Company, 1907. v.1, p.19-87.
                Legarda: Excellent introduction to Philippine history.
                                H   4   1-2
                Phelan: H   4   1-2
                Wickberg: H   3   2

1585.   BRUMAN, HENRY J. The Asiatic origin of the Huichol still. Geographical Re-
        view 34, no. 3 (July 1944), 418-427.
                Spencer: Marginal for Philippines.
                                K   4   1

1586.   BYRNES, FRANCIS C. Some missing variables in diffusion research and inno-
        vation. PSR 14, no. 4 (Oct. 1966), 242-256.
                Polson: An exposition on the importance of technical and human
                                relations skills in change agents.
                                S   4   6

1587.   CALDERON, AURELIO B. An analysis of Steinberg's use of walang hiya to ex-
        plain Filipino elite collaboration in World War II. PSR 15, nos. 3/4 (July/

Oct. 1967), 141-150.

1588. CARROLL, JOHN J. Changing patterns of social structure in the Philippines 1896-1963. Quezon City, Ateneo de Manila Univ. Press, 1968. 236p.

1589. _____. Contemporary Philippine historians and Philippine history. JSEAH 2, no. 3 (Oct. 1961), 23-35.

1590. COMYN, TOMÁS DE. Estado de las islas Filipinas en 1810, brevemente descrito por Tomás de Comyn. Madrid, Impr. de Repullés, 1820. 190p.
Suggested by Wickberg.
Legarda: X   5   3

1591. _____. State of the Philippines in 1810, being an historical, statistical, and descriptive account of the interesting portion of the Indian archipelago. London, 1821.
Reprint of translation in A. Craig, Former Philippines through foreign eyes. 1917, p. 357-458.
Translated from the Spanish with notes and a preliminary discourse by William Walton; and Philippine progress prior to 1898, by Conrado Benitez. Manila, Filipiniana Book Guild, 1969. 248p. illus.
Reprint of the 1821 translation of Comyn's Estado de las Islas Filipinas, published in 1820.

1592. CORPUZ, ONOFRE D. The Philippines. Englewood Cliffs, New Jersey, Prentice-Hall, Inc., 1965. 149p. (Modern Nations in Historical Perspective. A Spectrum Book, S-616)

1593. _____. Western colonisation and the Filipino response. JSEAH 3, no. 1 (Mar. 1962), 1-23.
Legarda: V   4   7

1594. COSTA, HORACIO DE LA. Philippine historical and social science source materials repositories abroad. SR 5, nos. 9/10 (Sept./Oct. 1964), 7-12.

1595. _____. Readings in Philippine history; selected historical texts presented with a commentary. Manila, Bookmark, 1965. 351p.

1596. CRAIG, AUSTIN, ed. The former Philippines thru foreign eyes. Manila: Philippine Education Co., 1916. 552p. (Also published by D. Appleton and Co., 1917)
Legarda: An interesting collection marred by spotty editing.
                  H   3   7
Wickberg: Convenient compilation of scattered source material.
                  Y   5   7

1597. _____ and CONRADO BENITEZ, eds. Philippine progress prior to 1898. Manila, Philippine Education Co., Inc., 1916. 136p.
Legarda: Much of the material later turned up in Benitez History.
                  H   3   7

1598. CUSHNER, NICHOLAS P. British consular dispatches and the Philippine independence movement, 1872-1901. PS 16, no. 3 (July 1968), 501-534.

1599. CUYUGAN, RUBEN SANTOS. Some theoretical considerations in the cultural transformation of a modernizing society: the Philippine case. Comment 18 (Second Quarter 1963), 52-60.

1600. DELGADO, JUAN JOSE. Historia general sacro-profana, política y natural de las islas del Poniente llamadas Filipinas. Manila, Imp. de el Eco de Filipinas de D. Juan Atayde, 1892. 1009p. (Biblioteca historica filipina v.1)
   Legarda: M 5   7
   Phelan: M/H 4/5 2/3
   Wickberg: M 3   7

1601. DOUGLAS, LOUIS H. Modernization in a transitional setting: a Philippines case study. Civilisations (Brussels) 18, no. 2 (1968), 204-231.

1602. EGGAN, FRED. Cultural drift and social change. Current Anthropology 4, no. 4 (Oct. 1963), 347-355.
   Polson: A significant paper on possible directions of cultural change through analysis of kinship terminology.
         E 4   6
   Warren: E 5   6

1603. ELKINS, RICHARD E. Culture change in a Philippine folk society. PSR 14, no. 3 (July 1966), 160-166.

1604. FORBES, WILLIAM CAMERON. The Philippine Islands. Boston and New York, Houghton Mifflin Company, 1928. 2v.
   Grossholtz: Sections on political parties and civil service based on personal experience as Governor General.
         G 5   4
   Legarda: Not unbiased, but at least outspoken.
         G 5   7
   Onorato: G 4/5 7
   Phelan: G/H 3   4
   Wickberg: G 5   7

1605. FORES-GANZON, GUADALUPE. The status of historical research in our country. In Philippines (Republic) National Science Development Board. Inter-disciplinary Symposia Proceedings, National Science and Technology Week, November 20-26, 1961. Theme: "State of and Trends in Science and Technology in the Philippines". Area VI-Social Sciences. Manila, [1963] 106p. Mimeographed. p.35-40. Discussion: p.41-51.

1606. [FOX, ROBERT]. Culture history. (In: Human Relations Area Files, Inc. Area Handbook on the Philippines, 1956. v.I. Chapter 4, p.250-320)
   Phelan: E 4   7
   Warren: E 5   7
   Wickberg: E 4   7

1607. _____. The Philippines in prehistoric times. SR 3, no. 9 (Sept. 1962), 1-16. Reprinted: (In: Alip, Eufronio M., ed. The Philippines of yesteryears. Manila, Alip, 1964. p.283-317. 2 plates)
   Peterson: A 3   1

1608. FRIEND, THEODORE. Between two empires; the ordeal of the Philippines, 1929-1946. New Haven, Yale Univ. Press, 1965. 312p. (Yale historical publications. Studies, 22)

1609. GASPAR DE SAN AGUSTIN. Conquistas de las Islas Philipinas: la temporal,
       por las armas del Señor Don Phelipe segundo el prudente; y la espiritual,
       por los religiosos del Orden de nuestro padre San Augustin: fundación y
       progressos de su provincia del santíssimo nombre de Jesus. Parte primera.
       Madrid, 1698. 2v. (In: Blair and Robertson. v.40. p.183-295)
       Legarda: M   5   2
       Phelan: H   5   2
       Wickberg: M   5   2

1610. GRUNDER, GAREL A. and WILLIAM E. LIVEZEY. The Philippines and the United
       States. Norman, Univ. of Oklahoma Press, 1951. 315p.
       Grossholtz: Concentrates on negotiations and agreements in the 1940's
                      with particular emphasis on economic problems.
       V   3   7

1611. HANKE, LEWIS. Cuerpo de documentos del siglo XVI, sobre los derechos de
       España en las Indias y las Filipinas; descubiertos y anotados por Lewis
       Hanke...editados por Agustín Millares Carlo.   Mexico, D. F. Fondo de cul-
       tura economica, 1943. 364p.
       Phelan: H   5   2
       Wickberg: H   3   2

1612. HANNAFORD, EBENEZER. History and description of the picturesque Philippines
       with entertaining accounts of the people and their modes of living, customs,
       industries, climate and present conditions. Springfield, Ohio, Crowell and
       Kirkpatrick Co., 1900. 138p.
       Legarda: Notable for numerous illustrations.
       G   3   3/4

1613. HASSELL, ELIZABETH L. The Sri-Vijayan and Majapahit empires and the theory
       of their political association with the Philippine Islands. 1952. Thesis
       (M.A.) - U.P. Published in PSSHR 18, no. 1 (1953), 3-86.
       Wickberg: H   3   1

1614. [HESTER, EVETT D.]. History and character of the economy. (In: Human Rela-
       tions Area Files, Inc. Area Handbook on the Philippines. Chicago, Univer-
       sity of Chicago for the Human Relations Area Files, Inc., 1956. v.3. Chap-
       ter 15, p.1243-1299)
       Phelan: X   4   4-6
       Wickberg: X   3   7

1615. _____, FRANK LYNCH and WILLIS SIBLEY . Modern history. (In: Human Rela-
       tions Area Files, Inc. Area Handbook on the Philippines. 1956. v.1.
       Chapter 3, p.51-249)
       Phelan: X   4   4-6

1616. HOLLNSTEINER, MARY R. Some principles of culture change and their relation
       to the Philippines. PSR 6, no. 1 (Jan. 1958), 1-7.

1617. HOUSTON, CHARLES O., JR. The Philippines, commonwealth to republic: an
       experiment in applied politics. Pt. I: The economic bases. New York,
       1952. 710p. Thesis (Ph.D.) - Columbia Univ.

1618. HUNT, CHESTER L. Changing social patterns in the Philippines. SJ 9, no. 1
       (Jan./Mar. 1962), 32-43.

I. GENERAL. HISTORY AND CULTURE CHANGE

1619. JOCANO, F. LANDA. The beginnings of Filipino society and culture. PS 15, no. 1 (Jan. 1967), 9-40.

1620. _____. The Philippines at Spanish contact: an essay in ethnohistory. (In: Manuud, Antonio G., ed. Brown heritage. Quezon City, Ateneo de Manila Univ. Press, 1967. p.49-89)

1621. JUAN DE LA CONCEPCIÓN. Historia general de Philipinas. Manila, de la Rosa y Balagtas, 1788-1792. 14v.
       Legarda: M   5   2
       Phelan: H   4/5   2/3
       Wickberg: M   5   2/3

1622. KEESING, FELIX M. Cultural trends in the Philippines. Far Eastern Quarterly 4, no. 2 (Feb. 1945), 102-108.
       Phelan: E   4   7

1623. _____. The Philippines: a nation in the making...Issued under the auspices of the Univ. of Hawaii and the American Council, Institute of Pacific Relations. (Shanghai, Hong Kong, Kelly and Walsh, limited, 1937. 137p.)
       Onorato: E   4/5   4
       Wickberg: E   3   4

1624. LEONARDO Y ARGENSOLA, BARTOLOMÉ JUAN. Conquista de las islas Malucas. Madrid, A. Martin, 1609. 407p. (In: Blair and Robertson. v.16: 217-317)
       Legarda: M   5   2
       Phelan: H   5   2
       Wickberg: M   5   2

1625. MCHALE, THOMAS R. American colonial policy towards the Philippines. JSEAH 3, no. 1 (Mar. 1962), 24-43.

1626. _____. A modern corporation looks at the Philippine economy and society in transition. PSR 14, no. 4 (Oct. 1966), 226-231.
       Polson: An argument for the contribution of social science in business development.
                     X   4   6

1627. _____. The Philippine society in transition. (In: American Assembly. The United States and the Philippines, edited by Frank H. Golay. Englewood Cliffs, Prentice-Hall, 1966. p.32-49)

1628. _____. The Philippines in relationship to the main currents of Far Eastern history. JEAS 3, no. 3 (Apr. 1954), 339-341.
       Wickberg: X   3   7

1629. _____. The Philippines in transition. Journal of Asian Studies 20, no. 3 (May 1961), 331-341.
       Wickberg: X   3   6

1630. MAJUL, CESAR ADIB. Mabini and the revolution. DR 5, nos. 1/4 (Jan./Dec. 1957), 1-470.
       Legarda: V   4   3

167

1631. _____. The role of **Islam** in the history of the Filipino people. AS 4, no. 2 (Aug. 1966), 303-315.

1632. MANIS, JEROME G. Philippine culture in transition. SJ 7, no. 2 (Apr./ June 1960), 105-133.

1633. MARTÍNEZ DE ZÚÑIGA, JOAQUÍN. Historia de las islas Philipinas,...Sampaloc, Impreso por Fr. Pedro Arguelles de la Concepción, 1803. 687p.

Felix:	An excellent summary.		
	M	4	2/3
Legarda:	M	4	2/3
Phelan	H	3	3/3
Wickberg:	M	5	2/3

1634. _____. An historical view of the Philippine Islands exhibiting their discovery, population, language, government, manners, customs, productions and commerce. Translated by John Maver. London, T. Davison, 1814. 2v. Reprinted in 1966, Manila, Filipiniana Book Guild, Publications 10.

Legarda:	The parts omitted in translation almost make it Hamlet minus Prince of Denmark.		
	M	3	2/3
Phelan:	H	3	2/3
Wickberg:	M	5	7

1635. MEDINA, JUAN DE. Historia de los sucesos de la Orden de n. gran p. S. Agustin de estas islas Filipinas,...Manila, Chofré y comp., 1893. 279p. (Biblioteca histórica filipina, v.4) (In: Blair and Robertson. v.23: 121-297, v.24: 29-179)

Phelan:	H	5	2/3
Wickberg:	M	5	7

1636. MONTERO Y VIDAL, JOSÉ. El Archipiélago Filipino y las Islas Marianas, Carolinas y Palaos: su Historia, Geografía y Estadística. Madrid, Imprenta y fundación de M. Tello, 1886. 511p.
Suggested by Geoghegan.

Geoghegan:	Good collection of secondary material. Many population statistics, and some economic data of 19th Cent. Geographical and population description of most major areas.		
	H	4	7

1637. _____. Historia general de Filipinas desde el descubrimiento de dichas islas hasta nuestros dias. Madrid, M. Tello, 1887-95. 3v.

Legarda:	Useful despite errors.		
	J	3	7
Phelan:	H	4	7
Wickberg:	G	3	7

1638. MORGA, ANTONIO DE. The Philippine islands, Moluccas, Siam, Cambodia, Japan, and China, at the close of the sixteenth century. Tr. by Henry E. J. Stanley. London, printed for the Hakluyt Society, 1868. 431p.

Felix:	The author suppresses very much. Such as his own share in the Chinese revolt of 1603.		
	G	5	2
Legarda:	G	5	2

I. GENERAL. HISTORY AND CULTURE CHANGE

        Onorato: M   4/5   1/2
        Phelan: G/H   5   1/2
        Wickberg: Leading source for Philippine society on eve of Spanish
                       conquest and early years of Spanish period.
                       G   5   7

1639.   _____. Sucesos de las islas Filipinas; nueva edición enriquecida con los escritos inéditos del mismo autor, ilustrada con numerosas notas que amplían el texto y prologada extensamente por W. E. Retana, Madrid, V. Suárez, 1909. 591p.

1640.   ONORATO, MICHAEL P. A brief review of American interest in Philippine development and other essays. Berkeley, Calif., McCutchan Pub. Corp., 1968. 137p.

1641.   _____. Leonard Wood: His first year as Governor General, 1921-1922. AS 4, no. 2 (Aug. 1966), 353-361.

1642.   PALMA, ANDRES DE LEON. Economic history of the Philippines. Berkeley, 1931. Thesis (Ph.D.) - Univ. of California.

1643.   PASTELLS, PABLO. Historia general de las Islas Filipinas. (In: Spain. Archivo general de Indias, Seville. Catalogo de los documentos relativos a las Islas Filipinas...Tom: 1-6, 1925-1930)
        Legarda: M   4   7
        Phelan: M/H   5   2
        Wickberg: Extensive quotations from archival sources.
                       M   5   2

1644.   PHELAN, JOHN LEDDY. The Hispanization of the Philippines: Spanish aims and Filipino responses, 1565-1700. Madison, Univ. of Wisconsin Press, 1959. 218p.
        Felix: A very good work. Unfortunately the author has never been here and it shows.
                       H   4   2
        Legarda: Excellent and short work in English.
                       H   4   2
        Onorato: H   4   1/2
        Wickberg: Pioneer study.
                       H   4   2

1645.   _____. Some ideological aspects of the conquest of the Philippines. The Americas; a quarterly review of Inter-American cultural history 13, no. 3 (Jan. 1957), 221-239.
        Wickberg: H   3   2

1646.   PHILIPPINE PERSPECTIVE. Philippine perspective; lectures on the pre-history and history of the Philippines. Quezon City, Ateneo de Manila, 1964. Mimeographed.
        Contents: Part I. The First Filipinos, by F. Landa Jocano; The New Stone Age, by F. Landa Jocano; Intimations of Iron, by Alfredo E. Evangelista; Sri Vijaya and Madjapahit, by Lourdes Rausa-Gomez; Islam, by Thomas J. O'Shaughnessy; Origins of the Philippine Languages, by Cecilio Lopez; Resume, by Frank Lynch.
             Part II. Outpost of Empire, 1521-1600, by Horacio de la Costa;

Alarms and Excursions, 1600-1660, by Horacio de la Costa; The Service
of Both Majesties, 1660-1760, by Domingo Abella; The Formative Century,
1760-1870, by Horacio de la Costa; Of Books and Schools, by Miguel A.
Bernad; The Colonial Economy, by Benito F. Legarda; Propaganda and Revolution, 1870-1899, by Carlos Quirino.
Legarda: Uneven quality.
-      3   7

1647. PHILIPPINES (REPUBLIC) BUREAU OF PUBLIC LIBRARIES. Outline of Philippine
local history and folklore, by Severino I. Velasco. Manila, Produced by
National Media Production Center, Dept. of General Services, 1963. [26p.]
"This manual was prepared in 1938 by Atty. Severino I. Velasco..."

1648. _____. BUREAU OF PUBLIC SCHOOLS. Collection and compilation of historical
and cultural materials regarding barrios, towns or cities, and provinces.
Memorandum, no. 48 (June 15, 1963), 2p., 4p.

1649. _____. UNESCO NATIONAL COMMISSION. The Philippines in pre-historic times;
a handbook for the first National Exhibition of Filipino Pre-history and
culture, by Robert B. Fox. Manila, 1959. 40p. 20 plates. "Sponsored by
the UNESCO National Commission of the Philippines with the cooperation of
the National Museum."
Solheim: A popular summary of Philippine prehistory.
A/E   4   1/2

1650. POLSON, ROBERT A. The impact of change on the villagers of the Philippines.
Indian Sociological Bulletin 3, no. 3 (Apr. 1966), 191-199.

1651. _____. Social science and social change. PSR 13, no. 2 (Apr. 1965), 70-
78.
Polson: The role of behavioral science in development programs.
Z   4   6

1652. POMERLEAU, RAYMOND. The Lagulo Spring Development Project: community participation in planned social change. PJPA 11, no. 1 (Jan. 1967), 72-82.

1653. QADIR, SYED A. Adoption of technological change in the rural Philippines:
an analysis of compositional effects. Ithaca, N.Y., 1967. Thesis (Ph.D.) -
Cornell Univ.

1654. QUEZON, MANUEL L. The good fight. New York, Appleton-Century Co., 1946.
335p.
Suggested by Grossholtz.
Grossholtz: Quezon's autobiography.
V   5   7

1655. RETANA Y GAMBOA, WENCESLAO EMILIO. Mando del general Weyler en Filipinas, 5
junio, 1888-17 noviembre 1891;---apuntes y documentos para la historia polí-
tica, administrativa y militar de dichas islas. Madrid, M. Minueso de los
Rios, 1896. 437p.
Legarda: G   3   3
Wickberg: G   5   3

1656. REYES, PEDRITO and OTHERS. Pictorial history of the Philippines. Manila,
Capitol Publishing House, Inc., 1953. 512p.

Legarda: See [Philippine Saga, by H. O. Beyer], of which this is
                  a later version.
                  J   3   7

Polson: Popular presentation of historical highlights.
                  J   3   7

1657.   REYES Y FLORENTINO, ISABELO DE LOS.   Historia de Filipinas.   tomo 1. Manila,
        Impr. de D.E. Balbas, 1889.   101p.   (Biblioteca de la Revista Católica de
        Filipinas)
                  Wickberg: Q   3   7

1658.   RIBADENEIRA, MARCELO DE.   Historia de las islas del archipiélago Filipino y
        reinos de la Gran China, Tartaria, Cochinchina, Malaca, Siam, Cambodge y
        Jappon.   Ed., prólogo y notas por Juan R.de Legísima.   Madrid, La Editorial
        Católica, 1947.   652p.   "[De la obra]que figura en nuestra Biblioteca Naci-
        onal con la signatura R. 6664, edición de 1601, transcribimos la presente
        edición."
                  Felix: Excellent primary data.
                                  M   5   2
                  Legarda: M   5   2
                  Phelan: M/H   5   2

1659.   [RIOS CORONEL, HERNANDO DE LOS].   Memorial, y relacion para sv magestad, del
        procvrador general de las Filipinas, de lo que conuiene remediar, y de la
        riqueza que ay en ellas, y en las islas del Maluco.   Madrid, por la viuda
        de F. Correa, 1621. 87p.   French translation in M. Thevenot, Relations de
        divers voyages curieux, Paris, 1696.   (In: Blair and Robertson. v.19:183-
        300)
                  Legarda: G   5   2
                  Phelan: G   5   2
                  Wickberg: G   5   2

1660.   ROXAS-LIM, AURORA.   Chinese pottery as a basis for the study of Philippine
        proto-history.   (In: Felix, Alfonso, ed. The Chinese in the Philippines,
        1570-1770.   vol.I. Manila, Solidaridad Pub. House, 1966, p.223-245)
                  Felix: Excellent study on a little researched subject.
                                  Y   4   1
                  Wickberg: Y   3   1

1661.   RŌYAMA, MASAMICHI, and TATSUJI TAKEUCHI.   The Philippine polity: a Japanese
        view.   Edited by Theodore Friend.   New Haven, Southeast Asia Studies, Yale
        Univ.,1967.   293p.   (Monograph Series 12)
        Suggested by Grossholtz.
                  Grossholtz: Summary of the findings of the Japanese Research Commis-
                                  sion for the civil advisor to the Japanese Military Ad-
                                  ministration during World War II.
                                  V   4   7

1662.   SALAMANCA, BONIFACIO.   Filipino reaction to American Rule, 1901-1913.   Ham-
        den, Conn., Shoe String Press, 1968.   310p.   (His Ph.D. Thesis - Yale Univ.,
        1965)
        Suggested by Grossholtz and Onorato.
                  Grossholtz: Filipino politicians positions and negotiations on key
                                  economic and political issues of period based on American
                                  sources.

```
                    V      4      4
         Onorato:   H      4      4
```

1663. SALAZAR, VICENTE DE. Historia de la provincia de el Santissimo Rosario de Philipinas, China, y Tonking. Manila, Collegio y universidad de Santo Tomas, 1742. (In: Blair and Robertson. v.43: 25-93.
```
         Phelan:    M      5      2
         Wickberg:  M      5      2
```

1664. SAPAULA, CRISPINA C. The peopling of the Philippines. Indiana Academy of Science. Proceedings, 72 (1962), 82-85.

1665. SCHLEGEL, STUART A. The Upi Espiritistas: a case study in cultural adaptation. Journal for the Scientific Study of Religion 3/4, no. 2 (Apr. 1965), 198-212.
```
         Warren:        E      5      6
```

1666. SCOTT, WILLIAM HENRY. Prehispanic source materials for the study of Philippine history. Manila, University of Santo Tomas Press, 1968. 156p.

1667. SIBLEY, WILLIS E. Social structure and planned change: a case study from the Philippines. HO 19, no. 4 (Winter 1960/1961), 209-211.

1668. Sobre una "Reseña" histórica de Filipinas; colección de artículos . . . en el diario Catolico Libertas, en refutacion de . . . errores que . . . T. H. Pardo de Tavera ha escrito . . . en su "Reseña" histórica. Manila, Sto. Thomas, 1906. 206p.
```
         Wickberg:      Critique of Pardo de Tavera's interpretations of Philip-
                        pine history.
                        M      5      7
```

1669. Social change. (In: Hunt, Chester L. and others. Sociology in the Philippine setting. Rev. ed. Quezon City, Phoenix Publishing House, 1963. p.341-355)

1670. SONNICHSEN, ALBERT. Ten months a captive among Filipinos; being a narrative of adventure and observation during imprisonment on the island of Luzon, P.I. New York, Charles Scribner's Sons, 1901. 388p.
```
         Legarda:       G      5      3/4
```

1671. SPAIN.MINISTERIO DE FOMENTO. Cartas de Indias. Publícalas por primera vez el Ministerio de fomento. Madrid, Imprenta de Manuel G. Fernandez, 1877. 877p.
```
         Phelan:        H      5      2/3
```

1672. SPECTOR, ROBERT M. W. Cameron Forbes in the Philippines: a study in proconsular power. JSEAH 7, no. 2 (Sept. 1966), 74-92.

1673. STEINBERG, DAVID JOEL. Philippine collaboration in World War II. Ann Arbor, Univ. of Michigan Press, 1967. 235p.
Based on his Ph.D. thesis, The Philippines during world war two: a study in political collaboration. Harvard Univ., 1964.
```
         Goodman:       "...remarkably dispassionate and objective assessment....
                        Much influenced by the important sociological studies of
```

the Institute of Philippine Culture at the Ateneo de Manila..." Journal of Asian Studies. November 1967, p.185-186.

```
                    H       4       5
Onorato:            H       4       4/5
```

1674.   TANGCO, MARCELO. Cultural traits in connection with the crises of life in pre-Spanish Philippines. PSSHR 4, no. 1 (Jan. 1932), 12-16.

1675.   WANG, TEH-MING. Historico-critical study of some early Chinese records and their relations to pre-Spanish Philippine culture. 1954. 173p. Thesis (M.A.) - U.P.

```
    Liao:           H       4       1
    Weightman:      Of some value--but care in reading needed. Lacks description
                    and too imaginative. Work by Wu Ching-hong vastly superior.
                    Still one of few good Philippine Chinese historians.
                    H       4       1
    Wickberg:       H       3       1
```

1676.   WILLIAMS, DANIEL RODERICK. The United States and the Philippines. Garden City, N.Y., Doubleday, Page & Company, 1924. 335p.

```
    Onorato:        G/O     3       4
    Wickberg:       V       3       4
```

1677.   WORCESTER, DEAN CONANT. The Philippines past and present. New ed. in one volume, with biographical sketch and four additional chapters by Ralston Hayden. New York, Macmillan Co., 1930. 862p.

```
    Felix:          Highly critical but not unduly so.
                    G       3       4
    Legarda:        G       3       7
    Onorato:        G       4       7
    Phelan:         G       4       7
    Wickberg:       G       5       4
```

1678.   WURFEL, DAVID. Trade union development and labor relations policy in the Philippines. Industrial and Trade Relations Review 12, no. 4 (July 1959), 582-608.

1679.   ZAIDE, GREGORIO F. Philippine political and cultural history. Manila, Philippine Education Co., [1949] 2v.

```
    Phelan:         H       3       7
    Wickberg:       H       3       7
```

1680.   _____. The Philippines since pre-Spanish times. Manila, R. P. Garcia, 1949. 486p.

```
    Onorato:        H       3       1
```

INFANCY AND CHILDHOOD

1681.   BANTEGUI, B. G. Status of statistics on children and youth in the Philippines. Stat. Rept. 11, no. 3 (July/Sept. 1967), 1-10.

1682. BERNARDINO, VITALIANO. The child study program in the Philippines. PJE 39, no. 9 (Feb. 1961), 568-569, 621.
Guthrie: Y 3 6

1683. DOMINGO, MARIA FE. Child-rearing practices in barrio Cruz-na-Ligas. 1961. 210p. Thesis (M.A.) - U.P.
(Verified in U.P. Theses and dissertations index... p.56)

1684. FLORES, PURA M. Immanent justice in Filipino children and youth. PSR 12, nos. 3/4 (July/Oct. 1964), 151-159.
Guthrie: P 5 6

1685. _____ and ILUMINADA GOMEZ. Maternal attitudes toward child rearing. Philippine Educational Forum 13, no. 3 (Nov. 1964), 27-40.
Guthrie: P 5 6

1686. GUTHRIE, GEORGE M. The Filipino child and Philippine society; research reports and essays. Manila, Philippine Normal College Press, 1961. 142p. (Philippine Normal College monograph series, no. 1)
Guthrie: P 5 6
Polson: A later report on the project described in the following title.
  P 5 6

1687. _____ and PEPITA J. JACOBS. Child rearing and personality development in the Philippines. Univ. Park, Pennsylvania State Univ. Press, 1966. 223p.
Guthrie: P 5 6
Nurge: Limited to Manila and surrounding suburbs.
  P 3 6
Polson: A rich study on child-rearing attitudes and some suggestive hypotheses on the relation of child rearing to personality development.
  P 5 6

1688. GUTHRIE, HELEN A. Infant feeding practices in the Philippines. Tropical and Geographical Medicine 14, no. 2 (June 1962), 164-170.
Guthrie: N 5 6
Nurge: N 5 6

1689. HARE, RACHEL T. Cultural differences in the use of guilt and shame in child rearing: a review of research on the Philippines and other non-Western societies. (In: Guthrie, George M. and others, eds. Modernization: its impact in the Philippines II. Quezon City, Institute of Philippine Culture, Ateneo de Manila Univ. Press, 1967. Papers, no. 5. p.35-76)

1690. HOFILEÑA, FERNANDO P. The child in the Fil-American setting. Unitas 38, no. 4 (Dec. 1965), 505-510.

1691. MIAO, EMILY. A study of parental attitudes in child and adolescent development. 1965. 140p. Thesis (M.A.) - Ateneo de Manila Univ.
Guthrie: P 5 6

1692. MIÑOZA, AURORA A. Problems in the study of Filipino children. EQ 15, no. 1 (Sept. 1967), 58-67.

1693. _____. Studies on the Filipino child. EQ 6, nos. 1/2 (June/Sept. 1958),
67-70.
Guthrie: P   4   6

1694. NURGE, ETHEL. Economic functions of the child in the rural Philippines.
PSR 4, no. 1 (Jan. 1956), 7-11.
Guthrie: E   5   6
Nurge: E   5   6

1695. PECSON, GERONIMA T. Our Filipino children. Manila, National Media Production Center, 1962.
Guthrie: Y   3   6

1696. PHILIPPINE ISLANDS. PUBLIC WELFARE BOARD...A report on child welfare work in
the Philippine Islands submitted by Dr. Jose Fabella, Secretary, Public Welfare Board, and Director, Bureau of Dependent Children. (English and Spanish)
Manila, Bureau of Printing, 1920. 39p.

1697. PHILIPPINES (REPUBLIC) SOCIAL WELFARE ADMINISTRATION. National report of the
Philippines on the theme "The Child in the Family."
Presented to the Second International Study Conference on Child Welfare,
Japan, 1958. Mimeo.
Guthrie: Y   5   6

1698. PRUDENCIO, CARMEN. A preliminary survey of the child guidance clinics in
certain Philippine public schools. 1941. 348p. Thesis (M.A.) - U.P.

1699. SOLIS, MIGUELA M. Adequate understanding of our children. EQ 8, no. 3
(Jan. 1961), 44-56.

1700. _____. Living and learning develop children.
Philippine Educator
        Part I.   12, no. 9 (Feb. 1958), 6-9.
        Part II.   12, no. 10 (Mar. 1958), 10-13.
        Part III. 13, no. 1 (June 1958), 41-44.
        Part IV.   13, no. 2 (July 1958), 103-106.
        Part V.   13, no. 4 (Sept. 1958), 227-234.
Cited in Index to Philippine Periodicals, v.3, p.399.
Guthrie: Y   3   6

1701. _____. Understanding the Filipino child. Manila, R. S. Bartolome, 1957.
215p.
Guthrie: Y   3   6

1702. TAYAG, AMANDA HENSON. Filipino children's moral judgments. Philippine Educational Forum 13, no. 3 (Nov. 1964), 45-52.
Guthrie: P   5   6

1703. TEMPORAL, ALMA M. Some Filipino child-rearing practices and personality development. SJ 14, no. 3 (1968), 385-398.

1704. AGONCILLO, TEODORO A. The Filipino intellectuals and the revolution. PSSHR 18, no. 2 (June 1953), 125-140.

1705. ALZONA, ENCARNACION. Ideals of the Filipinos. (In: Batacan, Delfin Fl. Looking at ourselves. Manila, Philaw Publishing, 1956? p.262-283)

1706. BULATAO, JAIME C. Personalism versus efficiency in business. CC 7, no. 1 (Jan./Feb. 1967), 12-16.

1707. CASIÑO, ERIC S. Philippine culture and the Filipino intellectuals. UNESCO Philippines 4, no. 12 (Dec. 1965), 389-395.

1708. COLLER, RICHARD W. Collective behavior. (In: Hunt, Chester L. and others. Sociology in the Philippine setting. Rev. ed. Quezon City, Phoenix Publishing House, 1963. p.72-91)

1709. ESPIRITU, SOCORRO C. Nature and role of group behavior. (In: Hunt, Chester L. and others. Sociology in the Philippine setting. Rev. ed. Quezon City, Phoenix Publishing House, 1963. p.11-24)

1710. HUNT, CHESTER L. Comments on "Patterns of social relationships in the Philippines". PSSHR 19, no. 1 (Mar. 1954), 9-11.

1711. JOCANO, F. LANDA. Rethinking "smooth interpersonal relations". PSR 14, no. 4 (Oct. 1966), 282-291.

1712. KAUT, CHARLES. Utang na loob: a system of contractual obligation among Tagalogs. Southwestern Journal of Anthropology 17, no. 3 (Autumn 1961), 256-272.

    Coller: The basic and initial statement on this key system and its values.
                     E   5   6
    Polson: A good analysis of reciprocity and the development of an utang-na-loob relationship.
                     E   4   6
    Warren: E   5   6

1713. KROEF, JUSTUS M. VAN DER. Patterns of cultural conflict in Philippine life. Pac. Aff. 39, nos. 3/4 (Fall/Winter 1966-67), 326-338.

1714. LAWLESS, ROBERT. A comparative analysis of two studies on utang na loob. PSR 14, no. 3 (July 1966), 168-172.

1715. LYNCH, FRANK. The man in the middle. PJPA 11, no. 3 (July 1967), 206-209.

1716. _____. A note on the meaning of the term "intellectual elite" in the Philippines. East-West Center Review 3, no. 1 (June 1966), 1-6.

1717. PHILIPPINES. UNIVERSITY. GRADUATE COLLEGE OF EDUCATION. COMMITTEE ON HUMAN DEVELOPMENT RESEARCH. Friendship choices among U.P. students. EQ 12, no. 2 (Oct. 1964), 17-32.

1718. SCHLEGEL, STUART A. Personal alliances in lowland Philippine social structure. Anthropology Tomorrow 10, no. 1 (1964), 50-65.

I. GENERAL. INTERPERSONAL RELATIONS

1719. STEINBERG, DAVID JOEL. The web of Filipino allegiance. Solidarity 2, no. 6 (Mar./Apr. 1967), 23-34.

1720. YABES, LEOPOLDO Y. The Filipino scholar. University College Journal 5, (First Semester 1963/1964), 86-105.

1721. _____. Two intellectual traditions. AS 1, (1963), 84-104.

LABOR

1722. BANTEGUI, B. G., and B. A. PEREZ. Measuring labor force participation in a transitional economy. Bulletin de l'Institut International de Statistique 38, no. 21 (1960), 245-258.

1723. BEARDSLEY, J. W. Labor conditions in Philippine Islands. Engineering News 54, no. 21 (Nov. 23, 1905), 538-544.

1724. BELTRAN, ANITA K. G. Occupational origins and variations in patterns of occupational succession; the case of Filipino university students. 1963. Thesis (Ph.D.) - Univ. of Chicago.

1725. CALDERON, CICERO D. From compulsory arbitration to collective bargaining in the Philippines. International Labour Review 81, no. 1 (Jan. 1960), 1-24.

1726. CARROLL, JOHN J. Philippine labor unions. PS 9, no. 2 (Apr. 1961), 220-254.

1727. CARTER, E. C. Sanitary conditions as affecting contracts for works in the Philippine Islands. Engineering News 54, no. 21 (Nov. 23, 1905), 544-545.

1728. CASTILLO, GELIA T. Occupation evaluation in the Philippines. PSR 10, nos. 3/4 (July/Oct. 1962), 147-157.

1729. _____. Occupational sex roles as perceived by Filipino adolescents. PSR 9, nos. 1/2 (Jan./Apr. 1961), 2-11.

1730. _____. A study of occupational evaluation in the Philippines. Ithaca, 1960. 148p. Thesis (Ph.D.) - Cornell Univ.

1731. _____. A study of occupational evaluation in the Philippines. PSSHR 26, no. 2 (June 1961), 129-165. Adapted from her thesis.

1732. CLARK, VICTOR S. Labor conditions in the Philippines. U.S. Bureau of Labor. Bulletin no. 58 (May 1905), 721-905.

1733. CUSHNER, NICHOLAS P. Shipyard labor in the colonial Philippines. Second Biennial Conference. Proceedings. International Association of Historians of Asia. Taipei. 1962. p.603-611.

1734. DAVID, RANDOLF S. Human relations on the waterfront: the cabo system.

I. GENERAL. LABOR

PSR 15, nos. 3/4 (July/Oct. 1967), 135-140.

1735. DOHERTY, JOHN F. Criteria for occupational evaluation. PSR 13, no. 2 (Apr. 1965), 78-84.

1736. ESPINA, LUZ R. An economic study of collective bargaining contracts in the Philippines. Published under the title "An Economic Study of Collective Bargaining Contracts in the Philippines." In PL as follows:
        Part I.   1, no. 5 (Sept. 1962), 6-14.
        Part II.   1, no. 7 (Nov. 1962), 13-19.
        Part III. 2, no. 1 (Jan. 1963), 17-23.
        Part IV.   2, no. 2 (Feb. 1963), 16-20.

1737. FERNANDEZ, PERFECTO V. The roots of our present labor policies. Heritage 1, no. 2 (Oct. 1967), 39-52.

1738. HUNT, CHESTER L. Female occupational roles and urban sex ratios in the United States, Japan, and the Philippines. Social Forces 43, no. 3 (Mar. 1965), 407-417.

1739. INTERNATIONAL LABOUR ORGANIZATION. Report. Employment of women and minors in the Philippines. Labor Review 1, (Apr. 1965), 33-50.
        Source: Index to Periodicals. (U.P. Library. Filipiniana Section)
        Almanzor: W   4   6

1740. KUNDE, THELMA A. and RENE V. DAWIS. Comparative study of occupational prestige in three western cultures. Personnel and Guidance Journal 37, no. 5 (Jan. 1959), 350-352.

1741. KURIHARA, KENNETH K. Labor in the Philippine economy. Palo Alto, Stanford Univ. Press, 1945. 97p.

1742. LASKER, BRUNO. Foreword. (In: Kurihara, Kenneth K. Labor in the Philippine Economy.) Stanford Univ. Press, 1945. 97p.

1743. OÑATE, BURTON T. Estimates of the population and labor force in the Philippines. International Rice Research Institute, Mar. 1965.

1744. PEREZ, PRESENTACION T. Problems of employed women in certain professional groups in the Philippines and their educational implications. 1954. 288p. Thesis (Ph.D.) - Univ. of Minnesota.
        Almanzor: Y   5   6

1745. PHELAN, JOHN LEDDY. Free versus compulsory labor: Mexico and the Philippines, 1540 to 1648. Comparative Studies in Society and History 1, no. 2 (Jan. 1959), 189-201.

1746. POETHIG, RICHARD P. Occupational mobility among Philippine Protestant seminary graduates. SLQ 5, nos. 1/2 (Mar./June 1967), 117-140.

1747. _____ and JOHN J. CARROLL. Two views: the religious approach to a national purpose for Philippine labor. Solidarity 1, no. 3 (July/Sept. 1966), 75-92.

1748. RAVENHOLT, ALBERT. Social yeast in the sugar industry; Jesuits organize the plantation workers. AUFSR. Southeast Asia Series 7, no. 4 (April 23,

178

1959), 12p. (AR-3-'59)

1749. SALAZAR, MELITON. Philippine labor unions: an appraisal. Pac. Aff. 26,
no. 2 (June 1953), 146-155.

1750. SERQUIÑA, CONRADO A. A sociological analysis of labor unionism in the Phil-
ippines. 1952. 213p. Thesis (M.A.) - U.P.
Cited in Theses abstracts. I, p.52.
   Coller: Social history approach, has copious documentation useful
          to scholars.
        Z   3   7

1751. SMITH, ROBERT J., CHARLES E. RAMSEY, and GELIA CASTILLO. Parental authority
and job choice: sex differences in three cultures. American Journal of
Sociology 69, (Sept. 1963), 143-149.

1752. TIRYAKIAN, EDWARD A. The evaluation of occupations in an underdeveloped
country: the Philippines. Cambridge, Mass., 1956. 171p. Thesis (Ph.D.) -
Harvard Univ.

1753. _____. Occupational satisfaction and aspiration in an underdeveloped coun-
try: the Philippines. Economic Development and Cultural Change 7, no. 4
(July 1959), 431-444.
   Guthrie: Z   5   6
   Polson: A suggestive paper on a thinly studied topic.
         Z   5   6

1754. _____. The prestige evaluation of occupations in an underdeveloped country:
the Philippines. American Journal of Sociology 63, no. 4 (Jan. 1958), 390-
399.

1755. U.S. DEPT. OF LABOR. LABOR STATISTICS BUREAU. Foreign labor information:
labor in the Philippines; by Alice W. Shurcliff. Dec. 1956. 23p.

1756. _____. PHILIPPINE COMMISSION. Compilation of notes and reports on the
labor conditions in Philippine Islands. [From Report of the Philippine Commission, 1902. Part 1] (In: Philippine Commission. 8th report, 1907
[with reports of departments, bureau officers, 1907, etc.]. 1908. [pt. 2]
appendix, p.965-1023)

1757. WURFEL, DAVID. Some notes on the political role of labor movements: a
Philippine case study. Labor Review (U.P.) 1, no. 4 (Apr. 1965), 11-32.

LAND TENURE AND LAND REFORM

1758. ALLEN, JAMES S. Agrarian tendencies in the Philippines. Pac. Aff. 11,
no. 1 (Mar. 1938), 52-65.
Rejoinders:
   Compañia General de Tabacos de Filipinas
     Pac. Aff. 11, no. 4 (Dec. 1938), 493-495.
     Pac. Aff. 12, no. 3 (Sept. 1939), 304-309.

Anderson: A brief historical survey of types of land tenure followed by a statistical analysis of prevalent types at the
present and the prevalent problems in the 1930's.
J   4   7

1759. AQUINO, BENIGNO, JR. A critique of the land reform program. Solidarity 1,
no. 2 (Apr./June 1966), 72-77.
Anderson: A criticism of the Land Reform Code of 1963 especially
regarding financing. A report of the farmer's opinions
of the bill.
G   4   6

1760. _____. Looking ahead: a proposal for cooperative ownership. Solidarity 2,
no. 8 (July/Aug. 1967), 39-46.

1761. ARNALDO, MARCELO V. The agrarian problems of the Philippines and their solutions. SJ 2, no. 1 (Jan. 1955), 31-50.
Anderson: A brief historical survey followed by ten basic problem
areas for the agrarian population and an extensive treatment of each one and how the 1954 legislation dealt with
them. Finally, presentation of solutions.
X   3   7
Sta. Iglesia: X(G)   3   7

1762. BERNAL, ENRIQUETA A. The role of landlords in Philippine agricultural devel-
opment. 1967. 221p. Thesis (M.S.) - U.P. College of Agriculture.
Sta. Iglesia: Highly useful descriptive research.
Y   5   6

1763. BULL, FRATE. Land reform in the Philippines, 1950-1958. International Co-
operation Administration. n.d. 10p.
Suggested by Polson.
Polson: A compilation of advances in land reform.
C   4   6

1764. CUNNINGHAM, CHARLES H. Origin of the friar lands question in the Philippines.
American Political Science Review 10, no. 3 (Aug. 1916), 465-480.
Anderson: A general historical review of the question of friar land
and the conflict between the Orders and the Spanish-
Philippine colonial government.
H   3   2/3

1765. CUTSHALL, ALDEN. Problems of land ownership in the Philippine Islands. Economic Geography 28, no. 1 (Jan. 1952), 31-36.
Anderson: Generalizing essay on the entirety of the Philippines.
Describes the land-holding patterns, social, political
and economic factors affecting it and suggests some future
trends.
K   3   6

1766. DALISAY, AMANDO M. The effects of land reform on income distribution. ERJ
2, no. 2 (Sept. 1955), 61-67.
Anderson: A brief article demonstrating short-run ill effects of
land reforms on agricultural incomes but showing the long-
run positive effects. Need for rural development along

with land reform.
X   3   6/7
Sta. Iglesia: Useful economic analysis.
X(Y/G) 4   6

1767.   ENTENBERG, BARBARA.   Agrarian reform and the Hukbalahap. Far Eastern Survey
15, no. 16 (Aug. 1946), 245-248.
Anderson: A brief plea for better understanding of the Huks and
their goals. Author states they were allies of the U.S.
in World War II and have been the victim of biased propaganda.
J   3   5/6

1768.   ESTRELLA, CONRADO F.   The Philippine land reform program: its nature, me-
chanics, accomplishments and problems. Solidarity 2, no. 8 (July/Aug. 1967),
30-38.

1769.   FERRER, CORNELIO M.   Landlordism a world issue. PSR 2, no. 2 (July 1954),
37-41.
McMillan: Highlights perceptively an issue which has troubled the
Philippine for centuries.
M   4   7

1770.   FERRY, DON M.   Land tax reform and Philippine agricultural development. New
Haven, 1962. Thesis (Ph.D.) - Yale Univ.

1771.   FRAKE, CHARLES O.   Malayo-Polynesian land tenure. AA 58, no. 1 (Feb. 1956),
170-173.
Anderson: A brief but insightful note on the adaptive nature of land
tenure systems in the southwest Pacific. (response to
article by W. Goodenough)
E   4   7

1772.   GOLAY, FRANK H.   Economic aspects of Philippine agrarian reform. PSR 4,
no. 1 (Jan. 1956), 20-32.
Anderson: Credit and financial problems engendered by reform measures, viewed from a framework of general economically
relevant concepts.
X   4   6/7
Sta. Iglesia: X(Y)   3   6

1773.   GOZON, BENJAMIN M.   The land reform program. Solidarity 1, no. 2 (Apr./June
1966), 62-65.
Sta. Iglesia: G   3   6

1774.   GUEVARA, SULPICIO.   A second look at the Agricultural Land Reform Code of
1963. PRBE 1, no. 1 (Feb. 1964), 31-55.

1775.   GUTIERREZ, JOSE SEBASTIAN.   Basic cultural attitudes toward land ownership
and land taxation in the Philippines. ERJ 5, no. 4 (Mar. 1959), 394-405.
Anderson: A short history of the tenure systems imposed by different
governments combined with tables to show present attitudes
of tenants towards tenure systems.
X   3   7

1776. HARTENDORP, A. V. H. The proposed land reform act. The American Chamber of the Philippines. Journal 39, (Apr. 1963), 164-184.
> Anderson: Extensive commentary on the major provisions of this bill. Criticism of disregard of landowner's rights, powerful agencies and element of compulsion to sell land cheaply to the government. Useful "property" sector. Criticism of a "Utopian" bill.
> J   4   6

1777. HERNANDEZ, TERESITA J. An analysis of the social and legal aspects of farm tenancy in the Philippines. 1954. 199p. Thesis (Master of Laws) - U.P. Source: U.P. Library. Filipiniana Section. Shelflist.
> Anderson: Description of tenancy systems, their problems, governmental efforts and reports which have attempted to remedy the situation.
> O/S   3   7
> Sta. Iglesia: Highly useful analysis.
> Y   4   6

1778. HESTER, EVETT D., PABLO MABBUN, et al. Some economic and social aspects of Philippine rice tenancies. PA 12, no. 9 (Feb. 1924), 367-444.
> Anderson: Remains the outstanding research survey on Philippine land tenure written during the American period. Required reading for every student of the subject.
> X(F/G) 4   4
> McMillan: A penetrating, coldly objective analysis - one of the best!
> X   4   7
> Sta. Iglesia: Highly useful descriptive research.
> X(Y)   5   4

1779. LANSANG, JOSE A. The political answer to land reform. Solidarity 1, no. 2 (Apr./June 1966), 66-71.
> Anderson: Interesting approach to land reform. Land reform is difficult because of people's varying perceptions of what it should be. Their analysis of reform to produce a surplus for industrialization.
> J   3   7

1780. LEDESMA, ANTONIO J. The Encomienda system and the ambivalence of Spain's colonial policy in the Philippines. PJPA 11, no. 4 (Oct. 1967), 273-285.

1781. MCMILLAN, ROBERT T. Land tenure in the Philippines. Rural Sociology 20, no. 1 (Mar. 1955), 25-33.
> Anderson: A useful survey of issues and suggested action regarding land tenure by the co-author of Rivera-McMillan surveys of rural Philippines.
> Z   4   4/6
> Sta. Iglesia: Valuable description and analysis.
> Z   5   6

1782. MACASPAC, ISIDRO S. Land reform aspects of the agricultural development program. ERJ 8, no. 3 (Dec. 1961), 149-156.
> Anderson: A review of land reform policy and programs in relation to their role in the attainment of the long range economic and social objectives of agricultural development.

I.   GENERAL. LAND TENURE AND LAND REFORM

```
                      G/Y   4     6
       Sta. Iglesia:  G     3     6
```

1783. MANAHAN, MANUEL P. The prospects for land reform. Solidarity 2, no. 8 (July/Aug. 1967), 12-16.

1784. MONTEMAYOR, JEREMIAS U. Progress and problems of land reform in the Philippines. (In: Brown, James R. and Sein Lin, eds. International Seminar on Land Taxation, Land Tenure, and Land Reform in Developing Countries, Tai-pei, 1967. Land reform in developing countries. West Hartford, Conn., Univ. of Hartford, c1968. p.199-218. Discussion...p.219-222)

1785. _____. The role of farmers' organization in land reform. Comment, no. 15 (Third Quarter 1962), 9-18.
       Anderson: An articulate appeal for the inclusion of tenants in execution of land reform programs. Consideration of positive experience of peasant participation in the Federation of Free Farmers.
```
                      Y/O   4     6
       Sta. Iglesia:  Y/O   3     6
```

1786. MORROW, ROBERT. The economics of Philippine land reform - a foreign observer's views. Comment; The Filipino Journal of Ideas, Discussion and the Arts. no. 15 (Third Quarter 1962), 19-30.
       Anderson: Suggestive overview of pertinent land reform issues as of 1962.
```
                      C     4     -
       Sta. Iglesia:  C     3     6
```

1787. PHILIPPINES (REPUBLIC) NATIONAL LAND REFORM COUNCIL. PLANS AND PROGRAMS OFFICE. Historical background and social implications of the Agricultural Land Reform Code. Quezon City. 1964? 53p.

1788. _____. OFFICE OF ECONOMIC CO-ORDINATION. Report and recommendations of the advisory committee on large estates. Manila, Apr. 1951.
       Cited in A. P. Pal, Rural sociology in the Philippines, Current Sociology 8, no. 1, 1959.
       Sta. Iglesia: High level office report.
```
                      W     4     9
```

1789. RAHMANN, RUDOLF. Shifting cultivation and notions on landed property. PSR 11, nos. 1/2 (Jan./Apr. 1963), 38-44.
       Anderson: Additional confirmation of the general relationships between swidden types of land use and land tenure.
```
                      E     4     6
```

1790. RAVENHOLT, ALBERT. Philippine land reform. AUFSR. Southeast Asia Series 1, no. 3 (Feb. 4, 1953), 8p. (AR-3-'53)

1791. _____. The United States pushes Philippine land reform and gets nowhere. AUFSR. Southeast Asia Series 1, no. 9 (June 17, 1953), 6p. (AR-10-'53)

1792. ROOSEVELT, THEODORE. Land problems in Puerto Rico and the Philippine Islands. Geographical Review 24, (1934), 182-204.

I. GENERAL. LAND TENURE AND LAND REFORM

1793. RUIZ, LEOPOLDO T. Farm tenancy and cooperatives in the Philippines. Far Eastern Quarterly 4, no. 2 (Feb. 1945), 163-169.
Anderson: Brief survey of the pre-World War II conditions of farm tenancy problems.
Z 3 7

1794. SACAY, ORLANDO J. The Philippine land reform program. PEJ 2, no. 2 (Second Semester 1963), 169-183.
Sta. Iglesia: Y/X 3 6

1795. SALAMANCA, BONIFACIO S. Was the Philippine encomienda a land grant? Historical Bulletin (Philippine Historical Ass.) 7, no. 1 (Mar. 1963), 34-51.
Anderson: Through detailed documentation this study points out the lack of reference to land in encomiendere titles and concludes that they were not land grants and thus not the precursors of the hacienda system.
H 5 2

1796. SANTOS, GUILLERMO S. Agricultural tenancy reforms: an appraisal of major policies and their implementation. Comment, no. 15 (Third Quarter 1962), 31-39.
Sta. Iglesia: O 3 6

1797. _____. The role of land reform in rural development. ERJ 2, no. 3 (Dec. 1955), 149-154.
Anderson: Review of government attempts to cope with tenancy problems from 1952. Uses survey data to establish the problems and finally discusses Agricultural Tenancy Commission.
G 4 6
Sta. Iglesia: O 3 6

1798. STA. IGLESIA, JESUS. [Farm tenancy in the Philippines]. (In Philippines (Republic) National Science Development Board. Inter-Disciplinary Symposia Proceedings, National Science and Technology Week, Nov. 20-26, 1961. Theme: "State of and Trends in Science and Technology in the Philippines". Area I-Agriculture. [Manila, 1963]. Mimeographed. p.54-58)
Anderson: A survey of state of research into problems of farm tenancy by a leading investigator in agricultural economics.
X 4 6

1799. SORONGON, ARTURO P. A special study of landed estates in the Philippines; analysis and findings. Manila, Philippines. United States Operations Mission to the Philippines. 1955. 39p.

1800. SPENCER, JOSEPH E. Land and people in the Philippines; geographic problems in rural economy. Berkeley, Univ. of California Press, 1952. 282p.
Suggested by Luna.
Luna: Descriptive analytical study.
E 4 7

1801. TAI, HUNG-CHAO. The political process of land reform: a comparative study. Civilisations 18, no. 1 (1968), 61-79.

1802. TAKIGAWA, TSUTOMU. Landownership and land reform problems of the Philippines. Developing Economies 2, no. 1 (Mar. 1964), 58-77.

184

1803. U.S. MUTUAL SECURITY AGENCY. SPECIAL TECHNICAL AND ECONOMIC COMMISSION TO
THE PHILIPPINES. Philippine land tenure reform; analysis and recommendations. Prepared by Robert S. Hardie. Manila, 1952. 42p. 239p. of appen-
dices.

    Anderson: Famous report creating cause célèbre in relations between
                United States Embassy and Philippine government. Fore-
                sighted in many respects.
                X   3   6/7
    McMillan: A classic document never accepted by Philippine govern-
                ment.
                X   5   7
    Sta. Iglesia: Very useful report on land tenure situation.
                W   4   7

1804. VELMONTE, JOSÉ E. Farm tenancy problems in the Philippines with particular
reference to tenancies in rice-producing regions. PA 27, no. 7 (Dec. 1938),
515-529.

    Intengan: Factors responsible for growth of tenancy in the Philip-
                pines are given based on tenancy surveys of the last 15
                years. Cites possible solutions to problem.
                C   4   4
    Luna: Descriptive analytical study.
                X   4   4

1805. VIRATA, ENRIQUE T. Agrarian reform; a bibliography. Quezon City, Community
Development Research Council, U.P. 1965. 239p.

    Anderson: An excellent annotated bibliography exhaustively covering
                the literature on governmental efforts towards agrarian
                reform.
                Y   4   7
    Sta. Iglesia: Highly helpful guide to literature.
                Y   4   7

1806. WURFEL, DAVID. Philippine agrarian reform under Magsaysay. Far Eastern
Survey. Part I. 27, no. 1 (Jan. 1958), 7-16.
          Part II. 27, no. 2 (Feb. 1958), 23-30.
    Luna: Descriptive analytical article.
                V   3   6

LANGUAGE AND LITERATURE

1807. ABELLA, DOMINGO. Some notes on the historical background of Philippine Literature. (In: Manuud, Antonio G., ed. Brown Heritage. Quezon City,
Ateneo de Manila Univ. Press, 1967. p.34-48)

1808. AGUILAR, JOSE V. The significance of bilingualism in Philippine education.
PJE 30, (Jan. 1952), 391-392.
    Ward: -   3   5

1809. _____. Vernaculars and English as tools of value structure. PJE 33,
(Jan. 1955), 438-440.

I. GENERAL. LANGUAGE AND LITERATURE

Ward: -   3   5

1810. ALEJANDRO, RUFINO. Meeting the national language problem. FEU Faculty
Journal 9, (Second Quarter 1964/1965), 50-58.
      Ward: Many aspects of structure and sociolinguistics are pre-
sented.
L   3   6

1811. ALIP, EUFRONIO M. On the Philippine language question. Unitas 9, no. 8
(Nov. 1930), 443-459.

1812. BERNAL, RAFAEL. Mexican influence in Filipino language. Unitas 36, no. 2
(June 1963), 312-315.

1813. BIERMANN, B. Chinesische Sprachstudien in Manila. Neue Zeitschrift für Missionswissenschaft (1951), 18-23.
Cited in C. R. Boxer, Some aspects of Spanish historical writing on the Philippines, Historians of Southeast Asia, G. E. Hall, ed. 1961. p.209.

1814. BLAKE, FRANK R. Philippine literature. AA 13, no. 3 (July/Sept. 1911),
449-457.

1815. BLUMENTRITT, FERDINAND. Lenguas y razas de Filipinas. Revista de Geografía
Comercial. no. 48 (Oct. 31, 1887), 552-557.

1816. BUENAVENTURA, AMPARO S. Socio-cultural aspect of language. PSR 13, no. 4
(Oct. 1965), 219-222.
      Ward: A sociolinguistic/ethnolinguistic article of general prin-
ciples with only marginal application to the Philippines.
L   3   6

1817. _____. Some problems related to Philippine multilingualism. PSR 11, nos.
1/2 (Jan./Apr. 1963), 142-147.

1818. BUTTE, GEORGE C. F. Shall the Philippines have a common language? Unitas
10, no. 3 (1931), 113-122.

1819. CASPER, LEONARD. Cultural resurgence in Philippine literature. I: In English. Literature East and West 9, no. 1 (Mar. 1965), 7-15.

1820. _____. The great accommodation: Filipino-English. South Atlantic Quarterly 59, no. 2 (Spring 1960), 184-191.

1821. _____, ed. Modern Philippine short stories. Albuquerque, Univ. of New Mexico Press, 1962. 235p.

1822. _____. New writing from the Philippines; a critique and anthology. Syracuse, N.Y. Syracuse Univ. Press, 1966. 411p.

1823. CHRÉTIEN, DOUGLAS. A classification of twenty-one Philippine languages. PJS
91, no. 4 (Dec. 1962), 485-506.
      Llamzon: Uses lexico-statistical method of classification. Results
are tentative.
L   4   7
      Ward: Historical-comparative study but without sound

correspondence sets being established.
L   5   6

1824. CONANT, CARLOS EVERETT. The language problem in the Philippines. Lake Mohonk Conference on the Indian and other Dependent Peoples. Report of the 33rd Annual [Conference] (1915), 98-102.

1825. _____. The names of Philippine languages. Anthropos 4, (1909), 1069-1074.
    Ward: An early attempt to specify an inventory of Philippine languages.
            L   3   4

1826. _____. The Pepet law in Philippine languages. Anthropos 7, (Nov./Dec. 1912), 920-947.
    Llamzon: Purely linguistic article. Treats of sound laws and reflexes. Phonological.
            L   5   7
    Ward: Historical changes of vowels from Proto-Malayo-Polynesian. Many Philippine languages are exemplified.
            L   4   4

1827. _____. The RGH law in Philippine languages. American Oriental Society. Journal 31, part 1 (Dec. 1910), 70-85.
    Llamzon: Likewise, purely linguistic article. Sound laws.
            L   5   7
    Ward: Historical changes of vowels from Proto-Malayo-Polynesian. Many Philippine languages are exemplified.
            L   4   4

1828. CONKLIN, HAROLD C. Lexicographical treatment of folk taxonomies. (In: Householder, Fred W. and Sol Saporta, eds. Problems in lexicography; a report. (Publication 21 of the Indiana Univ. Research Center in Anthropology, Folklore, and Linguistics. p.119-141), Bloomington, 1962.)
    Llamzon: Generally theoretical; useful even for information on Philippine Islands.
            L   3   7
    Ward: Ethno-linguistics aspects of dictionary making. Use of Hanunoo data.
            E   5   7

1829. _____. Outline gazetteer of native Philippine ethnic and linguistic groups. Chicago, Philippine Studies Program, Univ. of Chicago, 1952. 13p. Mimeo.
    Jocano: An excellent and informative material, though brief.
            E   5   6

1830. _____. Philippine languages. 4p. (In: Section 6. A survey of personnel, materials and programs for the teaching of Southeast Asian languages, determination of needs, and recommendations for an appropriate program of research. Report of a conference at the American Council of Learned Societies, December 11-18, 1959. New York, American Council of Learned Societies, 1960)

1831. CONSTANTINO, ERNESTO, CONSUELO J. PAZ and MARIETTA N. POSONCUY. The personal pronouns of Tagalog, Ilukano, Isinai and Kapampangan. (In: Zamora, Mario D., ed. Studies in Philippine anthropology (in honor of H. Otley Beyer). Quezon City, Alemar-Phoenix, 1967. p.567-591)

1832. COSTENOBLE, HERMANN. Philippine language notes. PM 33, no. 10 (Oct. 1936), 495, 510.
> Ward: General discussion of language relationships but without any data.
>
> L   3   6

1833. DORN, LOUIS. Philippine language trends. Practical Anthropology 14, no. 4 (July/Aug. 1967), 174-185.

1834. DOTY, EDITH A. A glossary of "Filipinisimos" in the Spanish language found in Philippine publications of the period 1890-1920. Ann Arbor, 1958. 361p. Thesis (Ph.D.) - Univ. of Michigan.

1835. [FOX, ROBERT B. and GEORGE SMITH]. Chapter 6. "Language". (In: Human Relations Area Files Inc., Area handbook on the Philippines. 1956. v.1, p.321-355) Sub-contractor's Monograph HRAF-16.
> Llamzon: Excellent source material for general evaluation of language situation in Philippine Islands.
>
> E   5   7
>
> Ward: Classification of Philippine peoples mainly by language spoken. Distribution/location of speech communities.
>
> A   4   6

1836. FRANCISCO, JUAN R. Indian influences in the Philippines; with special reference to language and literature. 1960. Thesis (Ph.D.) - Univ. of Madras. Published in PSSHR 28, nos. 1/3 (Jan./Sept. 1963), 1-310.
> Ward: Deals with Sanskrit loan words.
>
> L   5   1

1837. _____. The new function of ancient Philippine scripts. PSSHR 28, no. 4 (Dec. 1963), 416-423. 2 plates.
> Ward: Cultural innovations in use of traditional writing system.
>
> L   3   6

1838. _____. Notes on Philippine palaeography. HB 8, no. 1 (Mar. 1964), 37-44.
> Ward: Evaluation of some works dealing with the subject of the old pre-Spanish writing system.
>
> L   3   7

1839. _____. Palaeographic studies in the Philippines. SMJ 13, no. 27 (Nov. 1966), Special Monograph no. 1. 417-426.
> Ward: Evaluation of some works dealing with the subject of the old pre-Spanish writing system.
>
> L   3   7

1840. FREI, ERNEST J. The historical development of the Philippine national language. PSSHR 14, no. 4 (Dec. 1949), 367-400.
>   15, no. 1 (Mar. 1950), 45-79.
>   15, no. 2 (June 1950), 163-194.
> Ward: Very useful work summarizing the events and social factors in the national language question, linguistic studies of Tagalog and bibliographical notes.
>
> L   4   4-6

1841. GARDNER, FLETCHER. Philippine Indic studies. San Antonio, Texas, Witte

Memorial Museum 8, (1943), 105p.
  Ward: Has much primary data on comparative writing systems. But
       it is really not excellent.
       A/L 5   6

1842. HARTENDORP, A. V. H. Philippine languages. American Chamber of Commerce of
the Philippines. Journal 30, no. 3 (1954), 92-93, 91, 108.
  Ward: Socio-linguistic information on location, size, importance
       of Philippine languages.
       X 3   6

1843. HEALEY, ALAN. Three-letter abbreviations of Malayo-Polynesian (Austronesian)
language names. Te Reo 5 (1962), 36-40.

1844. HEMPHILL, RODERICK J. The Philippine language scene. PSR 10, nos. 1/2 (Jan./
Apr. 1962), 26-33.
  Ward: Information on the competition between Tagalog, Spanish
       and English for the role of national language.
       L 4   6

1845. HOSILLOS, LUCILA V. The emergence of Filipino literature toward national
identity. AS 4, no. 3 (Dec. 1966), 430-444.

1846.   . Philippine-American literary relations, 1898-1941. Bloomington,
1964. 200p. Thesis (Ph.D.) - Indiana Univ.

1847. HUNT, CHESTER L. Language choice in a multilingual society. Sociological
Inquiry 36, no. 2 (Spring 1966), 240-253.
  Ward: Very good but not as much detail or systemization as would
       be liked.
       Z 5   6

1848. JOAQUIN, NICK. Popcorn and gaslight. PQ 2, no. 2 (Sept. 1953), 30-36.
  Pfeiffer: J/R 4   6

1849. JOCANO, F. LANDA. Linguistic elements in socialization progress. Philippine
Educational Forum 13, no. 3 (Nov. 1964), 3-9.
  Ward: Kinship terms are the subject and data.
       E 5   6

1850. JUAN, E. SAN, JR. Cultural resurgence in Philippine literature. II: In
Tagalog. Literature East and West 9, no. 1 (Mar. 1965), 16-26.

1851. KNOWLTON, EDGAR C., JR. Philippine and other exotic loan words in Paterno's
Ninay, by Edgar C. Knowlton, Jr. Pacific Science Congress. 9th, Bangkok,
1957. Proceedings. Bangkok, 1963. 3, 99-102.

1852. LARSON, DONALD N. The Philippine language scene. PSR 11, nos. 1/2 (Jan./
Apr. 1963), 4-12.
  Ward: Socio-linguistic: applied linguistics in national lan-
       guage planning.
       L 3   6

1853. LLAMZON, TEODORO A. On Tagalog as dominant language. PS 16, no. 4 (Oct.
1968), 729-749.

1854. _____. Recent trends in language teaching. PS 8, no. 2 (Apr. 1960), 320-333.
      Llamzon: Not informative on Philippine language situation. Summarizes method of language teaching.
                    L   3   6
      Ward: Treats general linguistic principles with only slight application being made to Philippine languages.
                    L   4   6

1855. _____. The subgrouping of Philippine languages. PSR 14, no. 3 (July 1966), 145-150.
      Llamzon: Reports and summarizes latest classifications of Philippine Islands languages.
                    L   4   7

1856. LOPEZ, CECILIO. Classifiers in Philippine languages. PJS 96, no. 1 (Mar. 1967), 1-7.

1857. _____. A contribution to our language problem. Philippine Social Science Review 3, no. 2 (Nov. 1930), 107-117.
            3, no. 3 (May 1931), 273-283.
      Ward: National language planning interest.
                    L   4   4

1858. _____. General features of Philippine languages. Philippine Social Science Review 9, no. 3 (Sept. 1937), 201-207.
      Ward: Comparative Tagalog, Iloko Bisayan.
                    L   5   6

1859. _____. The language situation in the Philippine Islands. Prepared for the Institute of Pacific Relations. Manila, 1931. 47p.
      Llamzon: Excellent summary and evaluation of language situation in Philippine Islands.
                    L   4   7
      Ward: Good general orientation.
                    L   3   7

1860. _____. A manual of the Philippine national language. 3rd ed. Manila, Bureau of Printing, 1941. 327p.
      Llamzon: Purely linguistic. Grammatical features of Tagalog only.
                    L   3   7
      Ward: Grammar handbook.
                    L   5   7

1861. _____. Origins of Philippine languages. (In: Philippine Perspective; lectures on the prehistory and history of the Philippines. Manila, Ateneo de Manila, 1964. 37p. Mimeographed)
Revised version published in PS 15, no. 1 (Jan. 1967), 130-166.
      Ward: Comparative work on some thirty languages.
                    L   5   -

1862. _____. Our language problem. PSSHR 4, no. 2 (Apr. 1932), 93-100.

1863. LUMBERA, BIENVENIDO. Philippine literature and the Filipino personality. (In: Manuud, Antonio G., ed. Brown Heritage. Quezon City, Ateneo de

Manila Univ. Press, 1967. p. 1-15)

1864. _____. Tradition and influences in the development of Tagalog poetry
(1570-1898). Bloomington, 1967. 375p. Thesis (Ph.D.) - Indiana Univ.

1865. MCCARRON, JOHN. Some notes on language in culture. (In: Manuud, Antonio
G., ed. Brown Heritage. Quezon City, Ateneo de Manila Univ. Press, 1967.
p.207-224)

1866. MANUEL, E. ARSENIO. Chinese elements in the Tagalog language, with an historical introduction by H. Otley Beyer. Manila, Filipiniana Publications,
1948. 25, 139p.
        Llamzon: Purely linguistic treatment of Chinese loan words in
                        Tagalog.
                        L   3   7
        Ward: A good deal of detail. Controversial conclusions.
                        L   4   7

1867. _____. An outline of the origin and development of Philippine languages
and their relation with the Chinese language. FTY (1953), 103-108, 113-118,
123-124.
        Ward: Comparative method.
                        L   4   7

1868. _____. Pre-proto-Philippinesian: the structural elements of stems and
words in some Philippine languages. Philippine Educational Forum 15, no. 1
(Mar. 1966), 1-26.
        Ward: A good deal of detail.
                        L   4   7

1869. MANUUD, ANTONIO G., ed. Brown heritage: essays on Philippine cultural tradition and literature. Quezon City, Ateneo de Manila Univ. Press, 1967.
885p.

1870. MARCILLA Y MARTIN, CIPRIANO. Estudios de los antiguos alfabetos filipinos.
Malabón, Tipo-lit. del Asilo de huerfanos, 1895. 107p.

1871. MORALES, ALFREDO T. The national language in the contemporary scene.
(Problems in cultural change in southeast Asia.) SJ 6, no. 1 (Jan./Mar.
1959), 28-41.
        Ward: Sociology of the education scene, editorial in nature.
                        Y   2/3   6

1872. O'CONNOR, LILLIAN. The "Mother tongue" and socialization. PSR 3, no. 2
(Apr. 1955), 7-10.
        Coller: Notes a few of the obstacles in shifting from English to
                        Philippine languages and vice versa.
                        L   3   6
        Ward: Theoretically oriented and only very general character-
                        ization of Philippine language sound systems.
                        L   3   6

1873. PANGANIBAN, CONSUELO TORRES. Spanish elements in the Tagalog language.
Unitas 24, num. 3 (Julio/Sept. 1951), 600-673.
           24, num. 4 (Oct./Dec. 1951), 846-877.

25, num. 1 (1952), 86-118.
Ward: Word borrowings.
L   5   2/3

1874. PANGANIBAN, JOSE VILLA. A Filipino national language is not impossible.
Unitas 30, num. 4 (Oct./Dec. 1957), 855-862.
Ward: Editorial, in part sociolinguistic description of Tagalog
English controversy.
L   3   6

1875. _____. Language and nationalism. Comment, no. 11 (Second Quarter 1960),
18-32.
Ward: Editorial.
L   3   6

1876. _____. The national language becomes national. Panorama 13, (Mar. 1961),
74-83.
Ward: Historical background, comparisons made to English and
other Philippine languages.
L   3   -

1877. _____. Pilipino and the Filipino. Progress (1961), 184-189.
Ward: Word borrowings, common vocabulary shared with other Phil-
ippine languages.
L   3   6

1878. _____. The present situation of "Pilipino". Unitas 39, no. 2 (June 1966),
301-306.

1879. _____. Studies in word relationships among Philippine languages, Malay and
Bahasa Indonesia. Unitas 36, no. 1 (Mar. 1963), 131-143.
Ward: Comparative word formation.
L   3   -

1880. PANIZO, ALFREDO. The linguistic problem in the Philippines. Unitas 34,
no. 3 (1961), 30-38.
Ward: National language planning, some language universals
given.
L?   3   -

1881. PANLASIGUI, ISIDORO. On language, nationalism and culture. DR 1, no. 1
(Jan. 1953), 95-103.

1882. PARDO DE TAVERA, TRINIDAD H. Les Anciennes alphabets de Philippines.
Annales de l'Extrême Orient 7, (Julliet 1884/Juin 1885), 204-210, 232-239.
Ward: L   3   1/2

1883. _____. Contribución para el estudio de los antiguos alfabetos Filipinos.
Losana, Jaunin Hermanos, 1884. 30p.
Llamzon: Excellent information source on alphabets of Philippine
Islands languages.
L   5   1
Ward: L   3   1/2

1884. PASCASIO, EMY M. Language: an aid to cross-cultural understanding. PSR

192

12, nos. 1/2 (Jan./Apr. 1964), 84-88.
> Ward: Ethno-linguistic study of term systems of Tagalog, Iloko, English.
> L   3   6

1885. _____. Language in relation to social change. PSR 15, nos. 1/2 (Jan./Apr. 1967), 6-15.

1886. _____. The language situation in the Philippines from the Spanish era to the present. (In: Manuud, Antonio G., ed. Brown Heritage. Quezon City, Ateneo de Manila Univ. Press, 1967. p.225-252)

1887. _____. The role of language in culture in the teaching of literature. Philippine Journal for Language Teaching 3, nos. 1/2 (Oct. 1964), 19-26.
> Ward: Ethnolinguistic study.
> L   3   6

1888. PHELAN, JOHN LEDDY. Philippine linguistics and Spanish missionaries, 1565-1700. Mid-America 37, no. 3 (July 1955), 153-170.
> Llamzon: Copious, dependable source on language situation and linguistic publications in Philippine Islands.
> H   5   2
> Ward: Bibliographical coverage.
> H   3   2/3

1889. PIKE, KENNETH L. A syntactic paradigm. Language 39, no. 2 (part 1) (Apr./June 1963), 216-230.

1890. PITTMAN, RICHARD SAUNDERS. Notes on the dialect geography of the Philippines. [2d ed. Grand Forks] Summer Institute of Linguistics, Univ. of North Dakota, 1952. 112p.
> Llamzon: Tentative attempt to locate the chief dialect areas in Philippine Islands.
> L   5   7
> Ward: Areal diversity of speech.
> L   5   6

1891. PRATOR, CLIFFORD H. Language teaching in the Philippines. A Report to the U.S. Educational Foundation in the Philippines. Manila, June 28, 1950. 96p.
> Llamzon: Continues C. Lopez's The Language Situation in the Philippines (1931). Evaluation and description of language situation in Philippine Islands.
> L   5   6
> Ward: Good initial presentation but now dated.
> L   4   6

1892. RAMOS, MAXIMO. The sociological bearings of our language problems. EQ 5, nos. 3/4 (Dec. 1957/Mar. 1958), 219-231.
> Ward: Y   3   6

1893. RAVENHOLT, ALBERT. Filipino language dilemma. AUFSR. Southeast Asia Series 4, no. 6 (May 22, 1956), 11p. (AR-5-56)

1894. RETANA Y GAMBOA, WENCESLAO EMILIO. Los antiguos alfabetos de Filipinas. Madrid, Vda. de M. Minuesa de los Rios. 1895. 12p.

I. GENERAL. LANGUAGE AND LITERATURE

Ward: H   3   1-3

1895. ROJO, TRINIDAD A. The language problem in the Philippines. (Research Monograph No. 1, The Philippine Research Bureau) New York - Manila, 1937. 64p.
> Llamzon: General survey of situation from educator's point of view.
>   -   3   6
> Ward: Sociolinguistic background in promoting Tagalog as the national language.
>   -   3   6

1896. SCHEERER, OTTO. Outline of the history of exploration of the Philippine languages and their relations in east and west. Philippine Review 3, nos. 1/2 (Jan./Feb. 1918), 59-67.
> Ward: Largely a comparative study.
>   L   3   -

1897. _____. The problem of a national language for the Philippine Islands in the light of the history of languages. Philippine Review 5, no. 7 (July 1920).
> Cited by Charles O. Houston, JEAS, Jan. 1953, p.100.
> Ward: A theoretical discussion of the implications of historical relatedness to the question of national language.
>   L   3   4

1898. SCOTT, WILLIAM HENRY. Prehispanic source materials for the study of Philippine history. Manila, Univ. of Santo Tomas Press, 1968. 156p.

1899. SECHREST, LEE, LUIS FLORES, and LOURDES ARELLANO. Language and social interaction in a bilingual culture. Journal of Social Psychology 76, Second Half (Dec. 1968), 155-161.

1900. THOMAS, DAVID and ALAN HEALY. Some Philippine language subgroupings: a lexicostatistical study. Anthropological Linguistics 4, no. 9 (Dec. 1962), 21-33.

1901. THOMPSON, RICHARD N. Survey study of the languages of the Philippine Islands: their number, type, importances and location together with the approximate number of speakers of the principal Christian, Pagan and Mohamedan languages. Community Press, Pampango, Province, 1953. 111p.
> Ward: Somewhat nontechnical work but one which does bring together a fair amount of sociolinguistic data.
>   -   3   4/6

1902. TUCKER, G. RICHARD. Judging personality from language usage: a Filipino example. PSR 16, nos. 1/2 (Jan./Apr. 1968), 30-39.

1903. VERSTRAELEN, EUGENE. Soundshifts in some dialects of the Philippines. Anthropos 57, fasc. 3/6 (1962), 826-856.

1904. WARES, ALAN C., comp. Bibliography of the Summer Institute of Linguistics: 1935-1968. Santa Ana, California, Summer Institute of Linguistics, 1968. 124p. Philippines: 47-52, 100-104.

1905. ZAMORA, BENIGNO. The role of the Filipino language in the development of our national culture. Symposium on Filipino Culture. Manila, Cultural

Foundation of the Philippines. 1961. 9p.
   Ward: Sociolinguistic history.
        L   3   4/5

LAW AND JUSTICE

1906. [ARELLANO, C. S. and F. TORRES.] The judiciary. (In: Census of the Philippine Islands, 1903. Washington, U.S. Bureau of the Census, 1905. v.1, 389-410)
    Stone: Baseline reference on Philippine judiciary.
        H/G   4   7

1907. BAJA, EMANUEL A. Law and order organizations in the Philippines.
    PM 28, no. 1 (June 1931), 21-22, 46.
        28, no. 2 (July 1931), 76-77.
    Stone: -   4   4

1908. BATUNGBACAL, JOSE. A comparative study of the ancient laws of the Filipinos. JH 8, no. 4 (Dec. 1960), 365-372.
    Stone: Interesting diachronic approach to legal systems in Philippines.
       -     4   7

1909. BEYER, H. OTLEY. Philippine customary law. A collection of source material brought together, 1912-1931, first as a part of a general Philippine ethnographic study and later (in more specific form) as a contribution to the European, American, and Philippine committees engaged in the collecting and study of the customary law of Indonesia. Manila, 1931-1932. 11v. Original and microfilm in the Library of Congress.
    Stone: Invaluable but almost inaccessible data.
       E   5   7

1910. BULATAO, JAIME C. The Baranggay and the rule of law. Rotary Balita. Issue no. 1275 (Nov. 17, 1966), 1-4.
    Stone: Interesting use of generalizations based on colleagues data.
       P   4   7

1911. BUNYE, ALFREDO M. The Philippine penal system and its contribution to rural cultural development. FTY (1955), 163, 165-167, 179.
    Stone: G   4   7

1912. _____. The Philippine prison system.
    Unitas. Part I. 25, no. 2 (Apr./June 1952), 219-269.
             Part II. 25, no. 3 (July/Sept. 1952), 489-526.
             Part III. 25, no. 4 (Oct./Dec. 1952), 730-767.
             Part IV. 26, no. 1 (Jan./Mar. 1953), 111-128.
             Part V. 26, no. 3 (July/Sept. 1953), 595-625.
             Part VI. 26, no. 4 (Oct./Dec. 1953), 734-772.
             Part VII. 31, no. 1 (Jan./Mar. 1958), 121-169.
             Part VIII. 31, no. 2 (Apr./June 1958), 248-279.

I. GENERAL. LAW AND JUSTICE

         Stone: G   4   7

1913. CAMUS, MANUEL. The status of aliens in the Philippines. The legal status
of aliens in Pacific countries. (In: Mackenzie, Norman A., ed. The legal
status of aliens in Pacific countries. London, New York, Oxford Univ. Press,
1937. p.288-301.
         Stone: -   4   4

1914. Code of Calantiao (Kalantiaw code). Filipiniana reference shelf 1, no. 2
(Jan. 1941), 43, 36. (Date of code - 1433.)
Cited in Charles O. Houston, A preliminary bibliography of Philippine anthro-
pology. JEAS, Jan. 1953.
         Scott: "... no present evidence that any Filipino ruler by the
                         name of Kalantiaw ever existed or that the Kalantiaw penal
                         code is any older than 1914." Prehispanic source mate-
                         rials for the study of Philippine history. 1968, p. 136.

1915. CONGRESO PENAL Y PENITENCIARIO HISPANO-LUSO-AMERICANO Y FILIPINO. 2D, SAO
PAULO. 1955. Estudio juridico penal y penitenciario del indio; trabajos
preparatorios, poencias, debates y acuerdos del II Congreso Penal y Penitenciario Hispano-Luso-Americano y Filipino, Sao Paulo, Brasil, 19-25 de ...
Madrid, Ediciones Cultura hispanica, 1956. 253p.
         Stone: W   4   7

1916. FERNANDO, ENRIQUE M. Brief survey of the legal status of aliens in the
Philippines. Civilisations (International Institute of Differing Civilizations) 9, no. 2 (1959), 173-183.
         Stone: Excellent discussion by one of country's foremost juris-
                         prudents.
                  O/Y   5   6

1917. FLORES, PURA M. Immanent justice in Filipino children and youth. PSR 12,
nos. 3/4 (July/Oct. 1964), 151-159.
         Guthrie: P   5   6

1918. PHILIPPINES (REPUBLIC) PENAL COLONY, IWAHIG. Souvenir program: golden jubilee 50th anniversary of the Iwahig Penal Colony, Palawan, Nov. 16, 1954.
Manila, Calsam Printers, 1954. 87p.
         Stone: W   5   7

1919. ROBERTSON, JAMES A. The social structure of, and ideas of law among, early
Philippine peoples; and a recently-discovered pre-Hispanic criminal code of
the Philippine Islands. (In: Stephens, Henry M. and Robert E. Bolton, eds.
The Pacific ocean in history. New York, Macmillan Company, 1917. p.160-
191)
         Stone: H   4   7

1920. SHAW, BRUNO. Prison without bars. Colliers 137, (May 11, 1956), 56-57.
         Stone: Popular account by free-lance journalist.
                  J   3   4

1921. SORIANO, LEODEGARIO V. The formalistic aspects of contemporary Philippine
penal administration. PJPA 9, no. 4 (Oct. 1965), 314-323.
         Stone: Model-building by a political scientist.
                  V   5   6

MARRIAGE

1922. ALIP, EUFRONIO M. Marriage customs and ceremonies in the pre-Spanish Philippines. Unitas 10, no. 8 (Feb. 1932), 440-446.

1923. ANGELES, NOLI DE LOS. Marriage and fertility patterns in the Philippines. PSR 13, no. 4 (Oct. 1965), 232-248.

1924. BIELOUSS, EVA GABRIELLE. The marriage ceremonies of the Philippine peoples. Primitive Man 11, nos. 3/4 (July/Oct. 1938), 37-58.

1925. CALHOUN, JOHN W. American-Filipino marriages: a descriptive study of interracial problem marriages involving United States military personnel and Filipinos. 1955. 153p. Thesis (M.A.) - U.P.
Coller: Case studies by a personnel officer at a large American military base.
G   5   6

1926. COLLER, RICHARD and ASSOCIATES. A sample of courtship and marriage attitudes held by U.P. students. PSR 2, no. 3 (Oct. 1954), 31-45.
Coller: Results of small survey done by students, and edited and revised by instructor.
Z   3   6

1927. GUTIERREZ-GONZALEZ, ELIZABETH. Duration of marriage and perceptual behavior of spouses. PJP 1, no. 1 (Nov. 1968), 53-61.

1928. HUNT, CHESTER L. and RICHARD W. COLLER. Intermarriage and cultural change; a study of Philippine-American marriages. Social Forces 35/36, no. 3 (Mar. 1957), 223-230.
Coller: Revised and expanded analysis of data found in Rafel's Intermarriage (1954, Thesis (M.A.) - U.P.) by two sociologists.
Z   4   6

1929. JUCO, JORGE M. Fault, consent and breakdown - the sociology of divorce legislation in the Philippines. PSR 14, no. 2 (Apr. 1966), 67-76.

1930. LE GENTIL, M. Some of the usages and customs of the natives of the Philippines and their marriages, from "Voyage dans le Mer des Indes". (Translated from the original French by the Hon. Fred C. Fisher.) PM 26, no. 2 (July 1929), 82-83, 103-104.

1931. LIQUETE, L. GONZALEZ. Old marriage customs in the Philippines.
PM 28, no. 1 (June 1931), 17-18, 48-51.
   28, no. 2 (July 1931), 83-84, 92-93.
   28, no. 5 (Oct. 1931), 227-229, 232-234.
   28, no. 8 (Jan. 1932), 402-404, 429-430.

1932. LOBINGIER, CHARLES SUMNER. The primitive Malay marriage law. AA 12, no. 2 (Apr./June 1910), 250-256.

1933. NURGE, ETHEL. Factors operative in mate selection in a Philippine village. Eugenics Quarterly 5, no. 3 (Sept. 1958), 162-168.
Coller: Part of data collected during ethnological study of a Leyte village.
E   5   6

I. GENERAL. MARRIAGE

1934. RAFEL, S. STEPHEN. Intermarriage: a critical evaluation of twenty post world war II intermarriages between Filipinas and Americans on the island of Luzon. 1954. 189p. Thesis (M.A.) - U.P.
        Coller: Case studies by an officer of adjustment patterns in or near a large American military base.
        G/S   5   6

1935. REYNOLDS, HARRIET R. Evaluation and expectations toward mate selection and marriage of Filipino college students. PSR 14, no. 4 (Oct. 1966), 212-226.

1936. SARREAL, ROBERTO A. Patterns of age at marriage in Manila, 1952. PSR 2, no. 3 (Oct. 1954), 27-30.
        Coller: Original compilation from marriage license records. Done by a graduate student.
        S   5   6

1937. SMITH, PETER C. Age at marriage: recent trends and prospects. PSR 16, nos. 1/2 (Jan./Apr. 1968), 1-16.

MOBILITY AND SOCIAL STRATIFICATION

1938. CATAPUSAN, BENICIO T. Ethnic and racial distance. PSSHR 30, no. 1 (Mar. 1965), 87-108.

1939. _____. Patterns of social relationships in the Philippines. PSSHR 19, no. 1 (Mar. 1954), 5-8.
        Hunt: One of few sources of data on this topic.
        Z   3   6

1940. _____. Social distance in the Philippines. Sociology and Social Research 38, no. 5 (May/June 1954), 309-312.
        Hunt: Same data as above.
        Z   3   6

1941. HARRIS, EDWARD E. Prestige and functional importance correlates in the Philippines. PSR 15, nos. 3/4 (July/Oct. 1967), 105-108.

1942. HIDALGO, MARIANO O. Social classes in the Philippines and their implications for education. EQ 5, nos. 3/4 (Dec. 1957/Mar. 1958), 258-272.

1943. HOLLNSTEINER, MARY, E.P. PATANÑE and RICHARD P. POETHIG. Tensions of the rising Filipino middle class. CC 7, no. 1 (Jan./Feb. 1967), 17-21.

1944. HUNT, CHESTER L. Caste and class. (In: Hunt, Chester L. and others. Sociology in the Philippine Setting. Rev. ed. Quezon City, Phoenix Publishing House, 1963. p.94-117)

1945. _____. Relationship of ethnic groups. (In: Hunt, Chester L. and others. Sociology in the Philippine Setting. Rev. ed. Quezon City, Phoenix Publishing House, 1963. p.118-146)

I. GENERAL. MOBILITY AND SOCIAL STRATIFICATION

1946. _____. Social distance in the Philippines. Sociology and Social Research 40, no. 4 (Mar./Apr. 1956), 253-260.

1947. JENKS, ALBERT E. Assimilation in the Philippines, as interpreted in terms of assimilation in America. American Journal of Sociology 19, no. 6 (May 1914), 773-791.

1948. LASKER, BRUNO. The shadow of unfreedom. Far Eastern Quarterly 4, no. 2 (Feb. 1945), 127-134.

1949. LYNCH, FRANK. Continuities in Philippine social class. HB 6, no. 1 (Mar. 1962), 40-51.

1950. _____. Trends report of studies in social stratification and social mobility in the Philippines. East Asian Cultural Studies 4, nos. 1/4 (Mar. 1965), 163-191.

1951. MECHTRAUD, SISTER, S. Whither social changes. PSR 12, nos. 1/2 (Jan./Apr. 1964), 88-95.

1952. The peasant war in the Philippines; a study of the causes of social unrest in the Philippines- an analysis of Philippine political economy. PSSHR 23, nos. 2/4 (June/Dec. 1958), 373-436.
      Grossholtz: An insider's account of the HUK movement. Extremely useful.
           -     5   6
      Stauffer: Historical essay on the underlying causes of the Philippine peasant revolution, presented as an unsigned "document." Militant anti-Establishment point of view.
           -     4   7

1953. PHILIPPINE ISLANDS. DEPT. OF THE INTERIOR. ... Slavery and peonage in the Philippine Islands, by Dean C. Worcester, Secretary of the Interior. Manila, Bureau of Printing, 1913. 120p.

1954. _____. LEGISLATURE. PHILIPPINE ASSEMBLY. COMMITTEE ON SLAVERY AND PEONAGE. ... Informe sobre la esclavitud y peonaje en Filipinas. Compilado en vista de los informes parciales y exhibitos presentados por el comité especial investigador de la Asamblea filipina al honorable presidente de la misma. Manila, Bureau of Printing, 1914. 334p.

1955. SAPAULA, CRISPINA C. The prestige variable in sociocultural change in the Philippines: 1565-1898. Bloomington, 1966. 151p. Thesis (Ph.D.) - Indiana Univ.

1956. SCAFF, ALVIN H. Class stratification in the EDCOR communities. PSR 2, no. 2 (July 1954), 4-11.
      Polson: An interesting study based on survey material of integration in Economic Development Corps communities.
           Z   5   6

1957. _____. Social stratification and the rehabilitation of ex-Huks in the Philippines. Washington (State) State University. Pullman. Research Studies 23, no. 2 (June 1955), 83-91.
      Polson: An interesting study based on survey material of

I. GENERAL. MOBILITY AND SOCIAL STRATIFICATION

integration in EDCOR communities.
Z   4   6

NATIONALISM

1958. AGONCILLO, TEODORO A. The development of Filipino nationalism. Progressive Review, no. 7 (1965), 1-54.
Onorato: H   3   7

1959. ALZONA, ENCARNACION. Cultural nationalism in the Philippines. DR 9, no. 4
(Oct. 1961), 433-448.

1960. FAUNDO, BERARDO D. A sociological study of the nationalization youth movement of the Philippines. 1961. 226p. Thesis (M.A.) - U.P.
Coller: Participant-observation plus questionnaire data on a
post-war political and vociferous youth group.
Z   5   6

1961. FIGURACION, MELANIO S. Background and development of Philippine nationalism,
1872-1899. Pittsburgh, 1958. 395p. Thesis (Ph.D.) - Univ. of Pittsburgh.

1962. HARRISSON, TOM. Background to Philippine nationalism: the complex impacts
of past influences from Brunei Bay and elsewhere. Brunei Museum Journal,
vol. 2, no. 1 (1970), 209-237.

1963. MCCORMICK, J. SCOTT. Philippine nationalism as revealed by a study of the
content of newspapers. Philippine Social Science Review 3, no. 2 (Nov.
1930), 149-176.

1964. MILNE, R. S. The uniqueness of Philippine nationalism. JSEAH 4, no. 1
(Mar. 1963), 82-96.

1965. OCAMPO, ESTABAN [i.e. ESTEBAN] A. DE. Dr. Jose Rizal, father of Filipino
nationalism. JSEAH 3, no. 1 (Mar. 1962), 44-55.

1966. QUINTOS, ROLANDO N. On true nationalism. Solidarity 2, no. 7 (May/June
1967), 30-37.

1967. STARNER, FRANCES A. The problems of Philippine nationalism. PSSHR 22,
no. 3 (Sept. 1957), 259-298.

THE PEOPLE: CULTURAL-LINGUISTIC GROUPS (GENERAL WORKS)

1968. [AMYOT, JACQUES and OTHERS.] Chapter 5 - The People. Human Relations Area
Files Inc. The Philippines. v.1, p.265-320. Sub-contractor's Monograph
HRAF-16.
Jocano: Still the best material on Philippine society and culture.

I. GENERAL. THE PEOPLE: CULTURAL-LINGUISTIC GROUPS (GENERAL WORKS)

E   5   7

1969. BEAN, ROBERT BENNETT. Notes on the hairy men of the Philippine islands and elsewhere. AA 15, no. 3 (July/Sept. 1913), 415-424. 9 plates.

1970. _____. Philippine types. AA n.s. 12, (July/Sept. 1910), 377-389. 9 plates.
          Warren: D   5   4

1971. _____. The racial anatomy of the Philippine Islanders. Philadelphia and London, J. B. Lippincott Company, 1910. 236p.
          Jocano: D   3   4

1972. BEST, ELSDON. The races of the Philippines. Polynesian Society. Journal 1, no. 1 (Apr. 15, 1892), 7-19.
          Jocano: H   3   4

1973. BEYER, H. OTLEY. The non-Christian people of the Philippines. (In: Census of the Philippine Islands 1918. v.2. (1921), 907-957. Manila: Bureau of Printing)
          Jocano: Still a good reference on population estimate.
          E   4   4

1974. _____. The Philippine people of pre-Spanish times. PM 32, no. 10 (Oct. 1935), 482, 515-517.
          Jocano: A popular article on Philippine,prehistory.
          E   5   1

1975. BLUMENTRITT, FERDINAND. List of the native tribes of the Philippines and of the languages spoken by them. Smithsonian Institution Annual Report (June 1899), 527-547. 10 plates.
Translated with introduction and notes by O. T. Mason from Zeitschrift der Gesellschaft für Erdkunde zu Berlin 25 (1890), 127-146.
          Jocano: Most of his works were based on secondary sources; not often reliable.
          A   3   3

1976. _____. Die Mestizen der Philippinen Inseln. Revue Coloniale Internationale 1, no. 4 (1885), 253-262.
          Jocano: A   3   3

1977. _____. Race questions in the Philippine Islands. Popular Science Monthly 55, no. 4 (Aug. 1899), 472-479.
          Jocano: A   3   3

1978. _____. Las razas del archipiélago filipino. I. Vademecum etnográfico de Filipinas. II. Las razas indígenas de Filipinas. Madrid, Estab. tip. de Fortanet, 1890. 70p. "Publicado en el Boletin de la Sociedad geográfica de Madrid."
          Jocano: A   3   3

1979. _____. Las Razas indígenas de Filipinas. Suplemento al artículo publicado bajo el mismo título ... SGMB 35, no. 135 (1893), 213-217.
          Jocano: A   3   3

1980. _____. Die Seelenzahl der einzelnen eingebornen Stämme der Philippinen. Bijdragen tot de taal - land - en volkenkunde van Nederlandsch-Indiè 39, (1890), 121-123.
        Jocano: A   3   3

1981. _____. Ueber die staaten der Philippinischen eingebornen in den zeiten der conquista. Wien, E. Hölzel, 1885. 34p. Separat-abdruck aus den "Mittheilungen der kais. Königl. geographischen gesellschaft in Wien," 28 (1885), 49-82.
        Jocano: A   3   3

1982. _____. Vademecum etnográfico de Filipinas. SGMB 27 (1889), 246-271.
        Jocano: A   3   3

1983. _____. Versuch einer ethnographie der Philippinen. Gotha, J. Perthes, 1882. 69p. (In: Petermanns Mittheilungen. Gotha, 1882. Ergänzungsband 15, ergänzungsheft no. 67)
        Jocano: A   3   3

1984. _____. Views of Dr. Rizal, the Filipino scholar, upon race difference. Translated by Robert L. Packard of portions of an article in Internationales archiv für ethnographie 10, no. 2, 88-92. Popular Science Monthly 61, (July 1902), 222-229.
        Jocano: A   5   3

1985. BRINTON, DANIEL G. The peoples of the Philippines. AA 11, no. 10 (Oct. 1898), 293-307. 1 plate.

1986. _____. The races of the Philippine archipelago. Scientific American Supplement 1198, (Dec. 17, 1898), 19210-19212.

1987. CAMPA, BUENAVENTURA. Etnografía Filipina. Los Mayóyaos y la raza Ifugao. (Apuntes para un estudio.) Madrid, Viuda de M. Minuesa de los Rios, 1894. 165p.
Reprinted in La Politica de España en Filipinas, v. 4 and 5, 1894-95.
        Jocano: M   5   3

1988. CHIRINO, PEDRO. Relación de las islas Filipinas y de lo que en ellas han trabajado los padres de la Compañia de Jesus ... 2 ed. Manila, Balbás, 1890. 275p. (In: Blair and Robertson. v.12: 169-321 and v.13: 27-217)
        Jocano: An excellent account of the contact period.
        M   5   2

1989. COLE, FAY-COOPER. The peoples of Malaysia. New York, D. Van Nostrand, 1945. Chapter 7, The Philippines, p.126-197.

1990. _____. Peoples of the Philippines. Natural History 34, no. 6 (Oct. 1934), 507-522.
        Jocano: Still an excellent reference material.
                  E   5   4
        Warren: E   5   7

1991. COLIN, FRANCISCO. Native races and their customs. From his Labor Evangélica, Chapters 4, 13-16 of Book I. Madrid, 1663. (In: Blair and Robertson. v.40: 37-98)

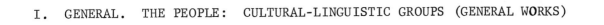

Jocano: M   5   2

1992. CONKLIN, HAROLD C. Outline gazetteer of native Philippine ethnic and lin-
       guistic groups. Chicago, Philippine Studies Program, Univ. of Chicago, 1952.
       13p. Mimeographed.
          Jocano: An excellent and informative material, though brief.
          E   5   6

1993. EVANGELISTA, ALFREDO. Indigenous cultural minorities of the Philippines.
       Hemisphere 9, no. 5 (May 1965), 30-35.

1994. FOLKMAR, DANIEL. Album of Philippine types (found in Bilibid prison in
       1903), representing 37 provinces and islands. Manila, Bureau of Public
       Printing, 1904. 5p. 80 plates.
          Coller: Study in physical anthropology, well-illustrated with
                           photographs of various head types.
                           D   5   4
          Jocano: Not very conclusive in that the basis are prisoners'
                           measurement.
                           D   3   4

1995. FOX, ROBERT B. Pre-Historic foundations of contemporary Filipino culture
       and society. Comment, no. 5 (First Quarter 1958), 39-51.
          Jocano: A good summary of Philippine prehistory.
          E   5   1

1996. _____. Pre-Spanish influences in Filipino culture. Philippine Educator
       12, no. 10 (Mar. 1958), 14-20, 22.
          Jocano: A good summary of Philippine prehistory.
          E   5   1

1997. GALANG, RICARDO. Ancient culture of Filipinos. Commonwealth Advocate 5,
       (Nov. 1939), 17-
       Source: Index to Periodicals (U.P. Library. Filipiniana Section)
          Jocano: E   4   1

1998. GONZALEZ, MARY A. The religious minorities in the Philippines. Unitas 36,
       no. 3 (Sept. 1963), 366-372.

1999. HARTENDORP, A. V. H. The progressive stone age men of the Philippines.
       PM 29, no. 2 (July 1932), 57-58.
          Jocano: J   4   1

2000. JENKS, ALBERT ERNEST. The splayed or so-called "Casco foot" in the Filipino.
       AA 7, no. 3 (July/Sept. 1905), 509-513.

2001. JOCANO, F. LANDA. The first Filipinos. (In: Philippine perspective; lec-
       tures on the prehistory and history of the Philippines. Manila, Ateneo de
       Manila, 1964. 25p.) Mimeo.
       Revised version published in PS,The beginnings of Filipino society and cul-
       ture 15, no. 1 (Jan. 1967), 9-40.
          Jocano: E   4   1

2001a. _____. Our changing minorities. Progress (1959), 99-105.
          Jocano: E   4   6

2002.   KRIEGER, HERBERT W.   ...Peoples of the Philippines...Washington, Smithsonian
        Institution, 1942. iv. 86p. 24 plates. maps (part fold.)   (...War
        background studies. no.4) (Publ. 3694)
               Jocano: A good reference on early documents on the Philippines.
                         E   4   7

2003.   _____. Races and peoples in the Philippines. Far Eastern Quarterly 4,
        no. 2 (Feb. 1945), 94-101.
               Jocano: E   4   7

2004.   _____. ...Peoples of the Philippines. 2nd and rev. ed. New York, 1928.
        245p. (American Museum of Natural History. Handbook Series, no. 8)
               Jocano: E   4   7

2005.   LAFOND DE LURCY, GABRIEL. Description des habitants primitifs des Philip-
        pines, ou des noirs de l'intérieur appartenant à quelques-unes des îles de
        ce groupe. Société de Géographie Bulletin. 2e sér, 4 (1835), 308-341.
        Cited in Griffin, Bibliography of the Philippine Islands, p.38.

2006.   LAMBRECHT, FRANCIS. Land and landownership pertaining to Philippine cultur-
        al minorities. (Report) SLQ 5, nos. 1/2 (Mar./June 1967), 198-202.

2007.   MALLARI, CARMEN B. The early Filipinos. Home, School and Community (pub-
        lished by Philippine Book Company) 9, no. 4 (Feb. 1962), p. 14-15.
               Jocano: Y   3   7

2008.   MEYER, ADOLPH B. Album von Philippinen-Typen[I]. Dresden, Wilhelm Hoffmann,
        1885. 10p. 32 plates [including photographs taken in 1872]
               Jocano: E   3   7

2009.   _____ and ALEXANDER SCHADENBERG. Album von Philippinen-Typen[II]. Nord
        Luzon. Negritos, Tingianen, Bánaos, Ginaanen, Silípanen, Calingas, Apoyáos,
        Kianganen, Igorroten und Ilocanen. Dresden, Stengel and Markert ("German
        and Spanish letter press"); Manila and Cebu: Otto Koch; London, Kegan Paul,
        Trench, Trübner and Co., 1891. 19p. 50 plates [including Schadenberg's
        1886-1889 photographs]
               Jocano: E   3   7

2010.   _____. Die Philippinen. I. Nord-Luzon: Tingianen, Bánaos, Ginaanen,
        Silípanen, Apoyáos, Kianganen, Igorroten, Irayas und Ilocanen. Dresden,
        Stengel and Markert, 1890. 26p. 23 plates [including Schadenberg's 1886-
        1889 photographs] (Publicationen aus den Königlichen Ethnographischen Mu-
        seum zu Dresden, VIII)
               Jocano: E   3   7

2011.   MILLER, MERTON L. Philippine researches. AA 9, no. 1 (Jan./Mar. 1907),
        234-236.

2012.   MILLER, OLIVER C. The semi-civilized tribes of the Philippine Islands.
        American Academy of Political and Social Science. Annals 18 Part 1 (July
        1901), 43-63.

2013.   MONTANO, J. Sur les races des Philippines. Société d'anthropologie de
        Paris. Bulletins 7, no. 1, Series 3 (Jan./Mar. 1884), 51-58.

2014. NORBECK, EDWARD. David P. Barrows' notes on Philippine ethnology. JEAS 5, no. 3 (July 1956), 229-254.
      Jocano: E   4   7

2015. OSIAS, CAMILO. Education of the non-Christian people. PJE 3, no. 2 (Aug. 1920), 7-13, 16-20.
      Jocano: Y   3   7

2016. PARDO DE TAVERA, T. H. Etimología de los Nombres de Razas de Filipinas. Manila, 1901. 20p.
      Jocano: D   4   7

2017. PASCUAL, NERI DIAZ. A report on the socio-economic present status of the cultural minorities of the Philippines. Unitas 40, no. 1 (Mar. 1967), 207-234.
      Jocano: D   5   7

2018. PATANÑE, E. P. The aborigines of the Philippines. Hemisphere 8, (May 1964), 30-33.
      Jocano: E   5   7

2019. PHILIPPINE ISLANDS. BUREAU OF NON-CHRISTIAN TRIBES. Report of the Bureau of non-Christian tribes of the Philippine Islands---1st (1901/1902) - Report year ends August 31. (Also in Philippine Commission 3rd annual report, 1902 pt. 1. 1903) For other annual reports, see Philippine Commission, 1900-1916, Annual reports.
      Frake: G   4   3/4
      Jocano: Still excellent reference material.
                   W   5   7

2020. PHILIPPINES (REPUBLIC) SENATE. COMMITTEE ON NATIONAL MINORITIES. Report on the problems of Philippine cultural minorities. Manila, Congress of the Philippines, Senate, 1963. 36p.
      Jocano: W   5   6

2021. RAHMANN, RUDOLF. Our responsibilities toward the cultural minorities. SR 6, nos. 7/8 (July/Aug. 1965), 5-12, 18.
Reprinted in American Chamber of Commerce of the Philippines. Journal 41, no. 7 (July 1965), 322, 324-325, 328.
      Jocano: M   3   6

2022. _____ . Our responsibilities toward the cultural minorities. (In: Zamora, Mario D., ed. Studies in Philippine anthropology (In honor of H. Otley Beyer). Quezon City, Alemar-Phoenix, 1967. p.443-462)

2023. RICH, JOHN. Conferences on the cultural minorities. PS 15, no. 1 (Jan. 1967), 177-182.

2024. _____ . The Sagada and Ayala conferences on the cultural minorities. (Report) SLQ 5, nos. 1/2 (Mar./June 1967), 194-196.

2025. SALEEBY, NAJEEB M. Origin of the Malayan Filipinos. Manila, Philippine Academy, 1912. 37p. (Papers of the Philippine Academy, v.1, pt. 1)
      Jocano: E   3   7

2026. SAN ANTONIO, JUAN FRANCISCO DE. The native peoples and their customs. From his Chroncias de la apostolica provincia. . . Manila, 1738-1744 3v. (In: Blair and Robertson, v.40: 296-373)
Jocano: A good early account.
         M   5   7

2027. SCHURMAN, JACOB GOULD. The native peoples of the Philippines. (In: U.S. Philippine Commission, 1899-1900. Report. Jan. 31, 1900. Washington, Govt. Print. Off., 1900-1901, p.11-16) (56th Congress, 1st Session. Senate. Document no. 138)
Jocano: A good appraisal of Philippine problems.
         Y   3   7

2028. _____. The Philippine Islands and their people; an address by John [sic]G. Schurman. American Geographical Society. Bulletin 32, no. 2 (1900), 133-150.
Jocano: A good appraisal of Philippine problems.
         Y   3   7

2029. SKINNER, GEORGE A. "Casco foot" in the Filipino. AA 6, no. 2 (Apr./June 1904), 299-302.

2030. SULLIVAN, LOUIS R. Racial types in the Philippine Islands. New York, American Museum of Natural History. Anthropological Papers 23, pt. 1 (1918), 61p.
Jocano: Good reference on early physical anthropology in Philippine Islands.
         E   3   7

2031. TAFT, WILLIAM H. The people of the Philippine Islands. Independent 54 (May 8, 1902), 1099-1104.
Jocano: G   3   7

2032. TANGCO, MARCELO. The Christian peoples of the Philippines. NASB 11, no. 1 (Jan./Mar., 1951), 1-115.
Jocano: E   4   7

2033. _____. Racial and cultural history of the Filipinos. PSSHR 10, no. 2 (May 1938), 110-126.

2034. VIRCHOW, RUDOLF. Die Bevölkerung der Philippinen. Akademie der Wissenschaften zu Berlin. Sitzungsberichte. (1897), 279-289.
Jocano: Based on secondary materials.
         E   3   7

2035. _____. The peopling of the Philippines. Translated with notes by O. T. Mason. Smithsonian Institution. Annual Report, (1899), 509-526. 3 plates.
Jocano: E   3   7

2036. WHITE, WILLIAM LAWRENCE. The challenge of the national minorities. SJ 15, no. 1 (First Quarter 1968), 87-91.

2037. _____. The Philippine national minorities and PANAMIN. SR 9 (Jan. 1968), 20-22.

2038. WORCESTER, DEAN CONANT. The non-Christian peoples of the Philippine Islands.
Separates of articles in the National Geographic Magazine: Field sports
among the wild men of Northern Luzon, 22, no. 3 (Mar. 1911), 215-267, 54
illus. Taal volcano and its recent destructive eruption, 23, no. 4 (Apr.
1912), 313-367, 45 illus. Head-hunters of northern Luzon, 23, no. 9 (Sept.
1912), 833-930, 103 illus. The non-Christian peoples of the Philippine
Islands, 24, no. 11 (Nov. 1913), 1157-1256, 89 colored and b/w illus. Fur-
nished with collective binder's title. Available at the Library of Congress.
    Jocano: So far the best of all early works.
              E   5   7

2039. ZÚÑIGA, JOAQUIN MARTÍNEZ DE. The people of the Philippines. (In: Blair
and Robertson, v.43: 113-127)

POLITICAL SCIENCE

Local Government and Territorial Organization

2040. ALCANTARA, ADELAIDA and OTHERS. The barrio council of Tulayan; a preliminary investigation of directed cultural change. For Anthropology 201, Dept.
of Anthropology, U.P. Quezon City, 1957. 53p.
Source: Filipiniana 1968, p. 613.
    Villanueva: Good study on contemporary political process.
              Z   5   6

2041. ALLRED, WELLS M. An evaluation and a demonstration of the implementation of
the barrio charter of the Philippines.   Quezon City, Community Development Research Council, U.P., 1962. 122p. (Studies Series, no. 13)
    Polson: A good study of attitudes towards barrio government. V 5 6
    Stauffer: Survey of impact of new barrio charter in selected sites;
               also a report of participant-observer success in foster-
               ing change.
              V   4   6
    Villanueva: Good study of contemporary political process.
              X   5   6

2042. BERNABE, DAISY G. Philippine city charters--a formal comparison. PJPA 10,
nos. 2/3 (Apr./July 1966), 136-153.
    Grossholtz: V   3   7
    Stauffer: Formal, descriptive comparison of legal provisions of
               existing city charters.
              V   3   6

2043. COLLER, RICHARD W. The urban community. (In: Hunt, Chester L. and others.
Sociology in the Philippine Setting. Rev. ed. Quezon City, Phoenix Publishing House, 1963. p.284-303)
    Grossholtz: A general description based on limited data and some as
               yet uninvestigated assumptions.
              Z   3   6

2044.   CORPUS, MANUEL T.   Indices for local personnel development in the Philippines.   PJPA 12, no. 4 (Oct. 1968), 429-436.

2045.   CRESSEY, PAUL F.   The development of Philippine cities.   SJ 5, no. 4 (Oct./Dec. 1958), 349-361.
        Grossholtz: Indicates diverse characteristics of Philippine cities and difficulty of defining "urbanism."
                        V   4   7

2046.   The establishments of local governments. PSSHR 4   (Oct. 1932), 299-302.
        Grossholtz: Describes legal and administrative basis of local government under Americans and extent to which Spanish system adapted.
                        -          4   4

2047.   FELICIANO, GLORIA C.   The press and local government.   PJPA 12, no. 3 (July 1968), 256-265.

2048.   FRANCISCO, GREGORIO A., JR.   Wanted: "municipal managers" for the Philippines.   PJPA 1, no. 2 (Apr. 1957), 131-143.
        Stauffer: An exposition of the municipal manager as an instrument to strengthen local government. The idea has never gained support.
                        V   3   6
        Villanueva: Good interpretation of possibilities of manager system in Philippine local government.
                        V   4   6

2049.   GORVINE, ALBERT and GONZALES REYNALDO.   A management attitude towards the decentralization issue in the Philippines.   PJPA 11, no. 3 (July 1967), 200-205.

2050.   GUZMAN, RAUL P. DE.   Local autonomy as partnership for socio-economic development.   Comment no. 21 (1964), 21-24.
        Stauffer: Analysis of alternative options for decentralization in the Philippines.
                        V   4   6

2051.   _____. Philippine local government issues, problems and trends. PJPA 10, nos. 2/3 (Apr./July 1966), 231-241.
        Stauffer: Useful review article.
                        V   5   6
        Villanueva: An excellent definition of current issues and presentation of some views.
                        V   4   6

2052.   _____. Research and policy-making: the UP-GSPA local government research project. PSR 14, no. 4 (Oct. 1966), 209-212.

2053.   _____. Special issue on local government and development: an introductory note. PJPA 10, nos. 2/3 (Apr./July 1966), 105-107.
        Villanueva: An excellent definition of current issues and presentation of some views.
                        V   4   6

2054. HOLLNSTEINER, MARY R. The development of political parties on the local level: a social anthropological case study of Hulo municipality, Bulacan. PJPA 4, no. 2 (Apr. 1960), 111-131.
        Grossholtz: A careful investigation of relationship between local factions and national political parties.
                Z   5   6
        Stauffer: Historical reconstruction of factional groups in a Philippine municipality on which political party alignments rest.
                Z   5   7

2055. _____. The dynamics of power in a Philippine Municipality. Quezon City, Community Development Research Council, U.P., 1963. 227p. (Study series no. 7)
        Grossholtz: The classic study of the socio-cultural roots of politics at the local level.
                Z   5   6
        Stauffer: Very important case study. Adds a great deal to our knowledge of local politics as well as to cross-cultural research methodology.
                Z   5   6
        Villanueva: An excellent case study of political processes in a barrio.
                Z/E   5   6

2056. _____. The lowland Philippine alliance system in municipal politics. PSR 10, nos. 3/4 (July/Oct. 1962), 167-171.
        Grossholtz: An explicit statement of inter-elite ties derived from above.
                Z   5   6
        Stauffer: Exposition of alliances as basis of Philippine politics, derived from empirical work in municipality near Manila.
                Z   5   6

2057. _____. A lowland Philippine municipality in transition. Practical Anthropology 8, no. 2 (Mar./Apr. 1961), 54-62.
        Stauffer: Excellent summary of her work on the power structure of Hulo.
                Z   5   7

2058. LAQUIAN, APRODICIO A. The city in nation-building; politics and administration in metropolitan Manila. Manila, School of Public Administration. U.P. 1966. 219p. (Studies in Public Administration, no. 8)

2059. LAUREL, JOSÉ P. Local government in the Philippine Islands. With an introduction by Máximo M. Kalaw. Manila, 1926. La Pilarica Press. 539 [1]p.
        Grossholtz: Legalistic description of formal institutions and administration.
                V   5   7

2060. LEWIS, A. B. Local self-government: a key to national economic advancement and political stability. PJPA 2, no. 1 (Jan. 1958), 54-57.
        Villanueva: A good view of the role of local government in development.
                X   4   6

2061. LUTZ, EDWARD A. The public service state and local self-rule. PJPA 3, no. 1 (Jan. 1959), 75-85.
        Villanueva: Excellent presentation of the role of local government in overall development.
                    V/X   4   6

2062. LUYKX, NICOLAAS G. M. Some comparative aspects of rural public institutions in Thailand, the Philippines and Vietnam. 1962. 893p. Thesis (Ph.D.) - Cornell Univ.

2063. MCMILLAN, ROBERT T. Local government in the Philippines. PSR 2, no. 2 (July 1954), 18-27.
        McMillan: Description of a highly centralized government with little delegated power to local government.
                    Z   4   7
        Stauffer: Z   4   6

2064. MANGLAPUS, RAUL S. Decentralization for democracy. FTY (1964), 199-201, 220.
        Stauffer: Arguments for decentralization, and analysis of the bill he sponsored in the Senate in 1964.
                    G   3   6

2065. _____. Local autonomy: key to economic progress. PJPA 3, no. 1 (Jan. 1959), 58-60.
        Grossholtz: Statement of arguments for local autonomy by the leading political proponent.
                    V   5   6

2066. _____. The need for local autonomy. Comment no. 21 (1964), 16-20.
        Grossholtz: Statement of arguments for local autonomy by the leading political proponent.
                    V   5   6
        Stauffer: Explanation of a proposed decentralization bill and arguments in its support.
                    G   3   6

2067. MARIANO, LEONARDO C. Congress and local autonomy. PJPA 1, no. 4 (Oct. 1957), 363-378.
        Polson: An analysis of the fate of the 1957 local autonomy bill.
                    V   4   6
        Stauffer: An interesting case study of the politics of congressional action on a local autonomy bill; somewhat marred by inclusion of extraneous material.
                    V   3   6
        Villanueva: V   4   6

2068. _____. Financing local government. PJPA 9, no. 1 (Jan. 1965), 50-59.
        Stauffer: Summary of problems faced in financing local government.
                    V   3   6
        Villanueva: V   4   6

2069. _____. The president and local autonomy. PJPA 3, no. 1 (Jan. 1959), 39-45.
        Polson: Good analysis of the limits on the President's power over

210

                         local governments.
                         V   4   6
            Villanueva: V   4   6

2070. MARTINEZ, ANTONIO M. and OTHERS. Handbook for barrio councils. 1st. ed.
       Manila, Insular Pub. Co., 1961. 171p.
            Villanueva: A good handbook for laymen.
                          G   3   6

2071. OLIVAR, JOSE D. Administration and management of barrio finance. Quezon
       City, Community Development Research Council, U.P., 1966. 123p.
            Polson: An excellent study, though based on a small sample, of
                          the operationalization of the barrio finance laws.
                          V   5   6
            Stauffer: A valuable empirical study that brings earlier work up-
                          to-date.
                          V   5   6
            Villanueva: An excellent analysis of financing status of barrio
                          councils.
                          G   5   6

2072. A Philippine middletown. PM 36, no. 6 (June 1939), 245-247.
            Grossholtz: A brief description of the economic conditions of a munic-
                          ipality indicating among other things the character of
                          landlord-tenant relations.
                          -    5   4

2073. PHILIPPINES. UNIVERSITY. INSTITUTE OF PUBLIC ADMINISTRATION. Research
       findings on problems of local government. PJPA 3, (Jan. 1959), 11-15.
            Stauffer: Summary of main findings from various sources to the date
                          of publication.
                          W   3   6

2074. _____ (REPUBLIC) PRESIDENTIAL ASSISTANT ON COMMUNITY DEVELOPMENT. What
       municipal mayors say about local autonomy and community development. (Semi-
       nar on Local Autonomy and Community Development, Los Baños, Laguna, April 3-
       5, 1959) Manila, 1959. 64p.
            Polson: Report on a conference organized to generate pressure for
                          greater municipal powers.
                          W   3   6

2075. RAVENHOLT, ALBERT. Village democracy--will it be given a chance? AUFSR.
       Southeast Asia Series 4, no. 1 (Jan. 21, 1956), 10p. (AR-1-'56)

2076. _____. Why Cardona wants electricity; a case study of a town at grips with
       economic crisis and political reality. AUFSR. Southeast Asia Series 9,
       no. 3 (July 1961), 12p. (AR-5-'61)

2077. RIGGS, FRED W. Economic development and local administration: a study in
       circular causation. PJPA 3, no. 1 (Jan. 1959), 86-146.
            Polson: A suggestive article on dependence and decentralization.
                          V   4   6
            Stauffer: Philippine data are used to build an important segment of
                          his larger model of the prismatic society.
                          V   5   6
            Villanueva: Insight into sociological and political backdrops of local

government problems and promise.
V   5   6

2078. RIVERA, JUAN FAÑGON. The legislative process of local governments. Quezon
City, U.P. Press, 1956. 392p.
      Villanueva: 0   4   7

2079. ROMANI, JOHN H. and M. LADD THOMAS. A survey of local government in the
Philippines. Manila, Institute of Public Administration, U.P., 1954. 136p.
      Grossholtz: A useful reference for the early post war structure of
               local government.
               V   4   6
      Stauffer: Good overview of various levels of local government based
               on interviews, augmented by secondary material.
               V   4   7
      Villanueva: Excellent interpretation, after a broad survey, of contem-
               porary problems of local government.
               V/C   5   6

2080. SADY, EMIL J. Central agencies and institutions for the improvement of local
government. PJPA 10, nos. 2/3 (Apr./July 1966), 242-255.
      Villanueva: Excellent view of ways to improve local government systems.
               V/E   4   6

2081. SAMONTE, ABELARDO G. Decentralization and development: some basic issues.
PJPA 11, no. 2 (Apr. 1967), 129-137.

2082. SANTOS, BIENVENIDO N. Politics in the barrio. PM 31, no. 6 (June 1934),
226, 257-258.
      Grossholtz: Semi-fictionalized account of politicians campaigning.
               Q   5   4

2083. SHORT, LLOYD M. The relationship of local and national government in the
Philippines. Manila, Institute of Public Administration, U.P., 1955. 72p.
(Publications of the Institute of Public Administration, no. 16)
      Grossholtz: Covers formal relationship only and is now out of date.
               V   3   6
      Villanueva: Excellent interpretation, after a broad survey, of con-
               temporary problems of local government.
               V   4   6

2084. SIBLEY, WILLIS E. Leadership in a Philippine barrio. PJPA 1, no. 2 (Apr.
1957), 154-159.
      Polson: A brief analysis of the social correlates of local leader-
               ship.
               E   4   6
      Stauffer: A modified community power structure study applied to a
               Philippine barrio.
               E   5   6
      Villanueva: Excellent analysis of political processes in barrio.
               E   5   6

2085. SPENCER, JOSEPH E. The cities of the Philippines. Journal of Geography 57,
no. 6 (Sept. 1958), 288-294.
      Grossholtz: A useful description of city growth.

                    K   4   6

Luna: Descriptive analytical study.

                    K   4   6

Spencer: Attempt to clarify issue of political vs. urbanized area of Philippine Island cities.

                    K   4   6

Wernstedt: Attempts to define an urban population of each chartered city.

                    K   4   6

2086. THOMAS, M. LADD. Historical origins of Philippine centralism. JSEAH 4, no. 2 (Sept. 1963), 73-90.

       Coller: Careful work on the centralized nature of Philippine government from a public administration perspective.

                    V   4   7

2087. VILLANEUVA, ALFREDO B. Concepts of local autonomy in the Philippines. Minneapolis, 1961. Thesis (Ph.D.) - Univ. of Minnesota. 319p.

       Polson: An excellent study on the evolution of an idea.

                    V   4   6

2088. _____. Social forces responsible for local autonomy in the Philippines. JSEAH 9, no. 1 (Mar. 1968), 147-160.

2089. VILLANUEVA, BUENAVENTURA M. The barrio and self-government; a critical study of the competence of barrio citizens to conduct self-government. Quezon City, Community Development Research Council, U.P., 1968. 262p. (Study Series no. 1)

2090. _____. Some unsettling questions in Philippine local government. PJPA 5, no. 3 (July 1961), 210-225.

       Stauffer: Analysis of major forces for change at the barrio level and of research needed as a result.

                    V   4   6

       Villanueva: V   4   6

2091. _____. A study of the competence of barrio citizens to conduct barrio government. Quezon City, Community Development Research Council, U.P., 1959. 223p. (Study Series no. 1)

       Polson: Excellent study of political attitudes and behavior.

                    V   5   6

       Stauffer: Baseline monograph drawing on survey data from a national sample of barrio residents. Behavioral and attitude variables probed.

                    V   5   6

       Villanueva: A good evidence of barrio peoples' capability for political development.

                    V   5   6

2092. _____ and OTHERS. Government and administration of a municipality. Quezon City, Community Development Research Council, U.P., 1966. 136p.

       Polson: A sophisticated application of American urban political study categories with results that are uneven but in places highly suggestive.

                    V   5   6

I. GENERAL. POLITICAL SCIENCE. Local Government and Territorial . . .

        Stauffer: A major empirical study of politics in a provincial mu-
                       nicipality near Manila.
                       V   5   6
        Villanueva: Excellent case study of dynamics of local government
                       politics and administration.
                       V & Z   5   6

2093. XAVIER UNIVERSITY. RESEARCH INSTITUTE FOR MINDANAO CULTURE. STAFF. Politics
and rural development programs in the Philippines.
Comments by Nick Joaquin and Salvador A. Parco. (In: Madigan, Francis C.,
ed. Human factors in Philippine rural development. Cagayan de Oro City,
Xavier University, 1967. Xavier University Studies. Study no. 1. p.88-
103)

2094. ZAMORA, MARIO D. Political history, autonomy and change: The case of the
Barrio Charter. AS 5, no. 1 (Apr. 1967), 79-100.

Political Behavior and Organization

2095. ABAYA, HERNANDO J. Betrayal in the Philippines. New York, A. A. Wyn, Inc.,
1946. 272p.
Suggested by Grossholtz.
     Grossholtz: A discussion of the treatment of those who collaborated
                     with Japan during World War II by a reporter with strong
                     opinions.
                     J   3   7

2096. ABELLO, AMELIA B. Pattern of Philippine public expenditure, 1951-1960.
PRBE 1, no. 1 (Feb. 1964), 65-83.

2097. ABRENICA, CESAR B. The political and social framework of development strategy in the underdeveloped countries. I. The political framework of development strategy. ERJ 14, no. 1 (June 1967), 16-24.

2098. ABUEVA, JOSE V. Bridging the gap between the elite and the people in the
Philippines. PJPA 8, no. 4 (Oct. 1964), 325-347.
     Grossholtz: V   3   6
     Stauffer: Important study of elite-mass relations and the progress
                     developed by Magsaysay to bridge the gap between classes.
                     V   5   6

2099. _____. Social backgrounds and recruitment of legislators and administrators in the Philippines. PJPA 9, no. 1 (Jan. 1965), 10-29.
     Grossholtz: Emphasis on social backgrounds.
                     V   5   6
     Stauffer: Excellent empirical study.
                     V   5   6

2100. AGBAYANI, AMEFIL. Indices of change: the Philippine senate. Honolulu,
1966. 113p. Thesis (M.A.) - Univ. of Hawaii. Condensed in PJPA 11, no. 1
(Jan. 1967), 13-23.

214

I. GENERAL. POLITICAL SCIENCE. Political Behavior and Organization

> Grossholtz: Orientation of senate as measured by content analysis
> of senate debates. Weak on political context, strong
> on statistical analysis.
> V   3   6
> Stauffer: Application of Parsonian and legislative role theory to
> Philippine Senate data.
> V   5   6

2101. AGONCILLO, TEODORO A. Filipino response to American political and cultural institutions. Heritage 1, no. 2 (Oct. 1967), 7-28.

2102. AGPALO, REMIGIO E. The political process and the nationalization of the retail trade in the Philippines. Quezon City, Office of the Coordinator, U.P., 1962. 344p. (His Ph.D. Thesis - Indiana Univ.,1958)
> Grossholtz: Considerable information on legislative process and political style.
> V   5   6
> Stauffer: A comprehensive case study of the politics behind the passage of a major piece of legislation.
> V   5   6

2103. ALLISON, WILLIAM W. Decision making in a bi-cultural community: an essay in the political process of transitional societies. SR 7, no. 9 (Sept. 1966), 3-11.
> Stauffer: Creative application of structural-functional theory in a case study of political change.
> V   5   6

2104. ARCELLANA, EMERENCIANA Y. The status of political science research. In Philippines (Republic) National Science Development Board. Inter-Disciplinary Symposia Proceedings, National Science and Technology Week, November 20-26, 1961. Theme: "State of and Trends in Science and Technology in the Philippines". Area VI-Social Sciences. Manila, [1963?] 106p. Mimeographed. p.69-77. Discussion: p.78-85.

2105. COLLER, RICHARD W. The administrator's role in the Philippines and technical assistance programs. PJPA 6, no. 2 (Apr. 1962), 118-121.
> Coller: Uses case-study approach to discuss informal patterns and their meanings in Philippine society.
> Z   4   6
> Stauffer: Brief exploration of how some general sociological laws might be applied to explain certain behavior patterns of Philippine administrators.
> Z   4   6

2106. CONCEPCION, MERCEDES B. Mitigated bureaucracy. PSR 8, nos. 3/4 (July/Oct. 1960), 22-25.
> Coller: Points out the personal element that alters Philippine bureaucracy - an historical view.
> Z   4   7

2107. BARROWS, DAVID P. A decade of American government in the Philippines, 1903-1913. Yonkers-on-Hudson, N. Y. World Book Co., 1914.
> Grossholtz: First hand account of political scientist who spent nine years in the country, six as Director of Education.

215

V   5   4

2108. BUENO, IONE D. The formal and informal organization of a civic agency.
(Condensed by Ofelia Regala-Angangco) PSR 8, nos. 3/4 (July/Oct. 1960),
33-47.
      Coller: Based on her M.A. thesis - abstract and theoretical
                      discussion of findings.
                      Z   3   6

2109. CASAMBRE, NAPOLEON J. Manuel L. Quezon and the Jones bill. PSSHR 23
(June/Dec. 1958), 265-282.
Suggested by Grossholtz.
      Grossholtz: Based largely on Quezon's public pronouncements during
                      Congressional hearings on the bill.
                      H   3   4

2110. COLLANTES, AUGURIO L. A bibliography on taxation in the Philippines.
Manila, Joint Legislative-Executive Tax Commission, 1968. 38p.

2111. CORPUZ, ONOFRE D. The bureaucracy in the Philippines. Manila, Institute
of Public Administration, U.P., 1957. 268p. (Studies in public administration, no. 4) His Ph.D. Thesis - Harvard Univ., 1955.
      Grossholtz: The baseline study of Philippine bureaucracy from a
                      historical perspective.
                      V   4   7
      Polson: A good study which focuses on the bureaucracy as a so-
                      cial institution.
                      V   4   7
      Stauffer: Standard work on the growth of the Philippine bureau-
                      cracy.
                      V   5   7
      Villanueva: An excellent historical interpretation of development
                      of Philippine bureaucracy.
                      V   4   7

2112. _____. The cultural foundations of Filipino politics. PJPA 4, no. 4
(Oct. 1960), 297-310.
      Grossholtz: An essay utilizing cultural variables as an explanation
                      of Philippine politics.
                      V   3   6
      Polson: An argument, largely descriptive, of cultural discon-
                      tinuity between elite and mass.
                      V   3   7
      Stauffer: An integration of the findings in the social science
                      literature on Philippine culture as it affects politics.
                      V   5   7

2113. _____. The Philippines. Englewood Cliffs, N. J., Prentice-Hall, Inc.,
1965. 149p. (The modern nations in historical perspectives, S-616)
      Stauffer: Best single general historical study of the development
                      of the Philippine political system by a political scien-
                      tist.
                      V   5   7

2114. _____. The presidency and the bureaucracy: trends and prospects.

Solidarity 3, no. 7 (July 1968), 3-8.

2115. _____. Realities of Philippine foreign policy. (In: American Assembly. The United States and the Philippines, edited by Frank H. Golay. Englewood Cliffs, Prentice-Hall, 1966. p.50-66)

2116. CORTES, IRENE R. The Philippine presidency: a study of executive power. Quezon City, Univ. of the Philippines Law Center, 1966. 327p.
Suggested by Stauffer.
    Stauffer: A review, largely formal and legalistic, of the powers of the Philippine president.
        Y   4   7

2117. CUADERNO, MIGUEL. The framing of the Constitution of the Philippines. Manila, Philippine Education Co., 1937. 183p.
Suggested by Grossholtz.
    Grossholtz: Useful description of the arguments and decisions of the 1934 Constitutional Convention.
        V   3   4

2118. CUNNINGHAM, CHARLES HENRY. The residencia in the Spanish colonies. Southwestern Historical Quarterly 21 (Jan. 1918), 253-278.
    Grossholtz: H   4   3

2119. DIA, MANUEL A. Filipino farmers' image of government: a neglected area in developmental change. PJPA 9, no. 2 (Apr. 1965), 153-166.
    Luna: Descriptive analytical study.
        S   4   6
    Stauffer: Report based on field survey materials; summaries of earlier studies included.
        Z   4   6

2120. DIAZ-PASCUAL, NERY. The Philippine government and the cultural minorities. (Report) SLQ 5, nos. 1/2 (Mar./June 1967), 196-198.

2121. EDRALIN, JOSEFA S. Bibliographic notes on fiscal administration in the Philippines. PJPA 8, no. 3 (July 1964), 246-251.
    Stauffer: Useful review of the literature on Philippine fiscal administration.
        Y   4   6

2122. ELLIOTT, CHARLES B. The Philippines to the end of the Commission Government: a study in tropical democracy. Indianapolis, Bobbs-Merrill, 1917. 541p.
Suggested by Grossholtz.
    Grossholtz: Extremely useful on the pattern of decision making among the American officials by a member of the Commission.
        G   5   4

2123. _____. The Philippines to the end of the military regime; America overseas. Indianapolis, Bobbs-Merrill, 1917. 541p.
Suggested by Grossholtz.
    Grossholtz: Especially useful on the establishment of civil government and disputes between American military and civilian officials.

                                G   3   4

2124.   ENCARNACION, VICENTE, JR. The citizens party--a study in contemporary so-
        cial movements. Quezon City, 1954. 144p. Thesis (M.A.) - U.P.
            Grossholtz: Shows characteristics of intellectual reformers in
                           Philippine politics.
                           V   5   6

2125.   FELIZMEÑA, REMEDIOS C. Civil service examinations and appointments revis-
        ited. PJPA 8, no. 1 (Jan. 1964), 32-45.
            Stauffer: Descriptive overview of the processes described in the
                           title.
                           Y   3   6

2126.   FLORES, TOMAS W., EUGENIA BELENO, and ROMUALDO B. TADENA. The salary net-
        work in the executive branch of the Philippine government. PJPA 5, no. 2
        (Apr. 1961), 144-158.
            Stauffer: Largely a review of the groups that gained exemption
                           from the comprehensive wage and position classification
                           system.
                           P   3   6

2127.   FORBES, WILLIAM CAMERON. The Philippine islands. Boston and New York,
        Houghton Mifflin Company, 1928. 2v.
            Grossholtz: Sections on political parties and civil service based
                           on personal experience as Governor General.
                           G   5   4
            Legarda: Not unbiased, but at least outspoken.
                           G   5   7
            Onorato: G   4/5   7
            Phelan: G   3   4
            Wickberg: G   5   4

2128.   FRANCISCO, GREGORIO A., JR. Career development of Filipino higher civil
        servants. PJPA 4, no. 1 (Jan. 1960), 1-18.
            Stauffer: V   4   6

2129.   _____. Higher civil servants in the Philippines (a study of the back-
        grounds, career patterns, and attitudes of Filipino higher officials).
        Minneapolis, 1960. Thesis (Ph.D.) - Univ. of Minnesota.

2130.   _____ and RAUL P. DE GUZMAN. The "50-50 agreement": a political admin-
        istrative case. PJPA 4, no. 4 (Oct. 1960), 328-347.
            Grossholtz: The classic study of Congressional bargaining over the
                           pork barrel budget.
                           V   5   6
            Stauffer: Important case study in the politics of staffing the
                           Philippine civil service.
                           V   5   6

2131.   GAMBOA, MA. ELENA and RAUL P. DE GUZMAN. The redistricting bill of 1961.
        PJPA 7, no. 1 (Jan. 1963), 11-26.
        Suggested by Grossholtz.
            Grossholtz: Case study of Congressional politics and pattern of
                           representation.

V   4   7

2132. GROSSHOLTZ, (THELMA) JEAN. The bargaining process and democratic development; a study of Philippine politics. 1961. Thesis (Ph.D.) - M.I.T.
      Polson: An application of the Almond model that is of uneven
                    value.
                    V   4   6

2133. _____. The Philippines: midterm doldrums for Marcos. Asian Survey 8,
no. 1 (Jan. 1968), 52-57.

2134. _____. Politics in the Philippines, a country study. Boston, Little,
Brown and Co., 1964. 293p. (The Little, Brown Series in Comparative
Politics)
Suggested by Stauffer.
      Stauffer: Very popular application of the structural-functional
                    paradigm to the Philippines. Adapted from her doctoral
                    dissertation.
                    V   5   7

2135. GUZMAN, RAFAEL V. DE. Administrative reform in the Philippines: an overview. PJPA 12, no. 4 (Oct. 1968), 395-412.

2136. GUZMAN, RAUL P. DE. Patterns in decision-making; case studies in Phillippine public administration. Manila, Graduate School of Public Administration, U.P.; distributed by the East-West Center Press, Honolulu, 1963.
569p.
      Grossholtz: Uneven but some excellent case studies based on docu-
                    ments, interviews and some analysis.
                    V   3   6
      Stauffer: Excellent collection of case studies; they provide one
                    of the best views available of the politics of admin-
                    istration in a developing nation.
                    V   5   6
      Villanueva: Excellent classroom materials, with highly useful in-
                    sights into Philippine administration.
                    V   5   6

2137. HAYDEN, JOSEPH RALSTON. The Philippines; a study in national development.
New York, Macmillan Co., 1942. 984p.
Suggested by Grossholtz.
      Grossholtz: The basic study of political development during the
                    American period and government and politics of the Com-
                    monwealth.
                    V/G   4   4
      Onorato: V/G   4   4
      Polson: The best descriptive and analytical work on the Ameri-
                    can period.
                    V   5   4

2138. HEADY, FERREL. The Philippine administrative system-a fusion of east and
west. (In: Siffin, William J., ed. Toward the comparative study of public administration. Bloomington, Indiana, Indiana University. Dept. of
Government, [c1957] 1959. p.253-277)

Stauffer: An important analysis of Philippine administrative prac-
                tices. Data are organized within an ecological categori-
                zation system.
                V   5   6
Villanueva: Excellent analysis and prognosis.
                V/C   4   6

2139. [HESTER, EVETT D. and CHARLES KAUT]. Political structure. (In: Human Rela-
      tions Area Files, Inc., Area handbook on the Philippines. 1956. vol.3,
      Chapter 13, p.1167-1219)
          Stauffer: A rather formal overview of Philippine government. Greatest
                          emphasis is given to the "leftist movement" from the
                          1930s through the early Magsaysay era.
                          E   3   7

2140. HOLLNSTEINER, MARY R. Power and politics: passion and pastime in the Phil-
      ippines. Solidarity 2, no. 6 (Mar./Apr. 1967), 3-13.

2141. KALAW, MÁXIMO M. Development of Philippine politics (1872-1920)...Manila,
      P.I., Oriental Commercial Company, Inc., 1927. 491p.
          Grossholtz: A key work on the development of parties and institutions
                          by a political scientist who was involved in the events
                          described.
                          V   5   4

2142. LANDE, CARL H. The Philippines. (In: Coleman, James S., ed. Education and
      political development. Princeton, N. J., Princeton Univ. Press, 1965. p.313-
      349)
          Spencer: Review of educational system and influences by political
                          periods. Good summary.
                          V   4   7

2143. _____. Political attitudes and behavior in the Philippines. PJPA 3, no.3
      (July 1959), 341-365.
          Grossholtz: Based on electoral analysis.
                          V   3   6
          Polson: Good analysis of the national political process.
                          V   4   6
          Stauffer: Important base-line survey of Philippine political atti-
                          tudes.
                          V   5   6

2144. LAQUIAN, APRODICIO A. Isla de Kokomo: politics among urban slum dwellers.
      PJPA 8, no. 2 (Apr. 1964), 112-122.
          Polson: An excellent case study of an urban slum and the problem
                          of value system breakdown.
                          V   5   6
          Stauffer: Report on a survey of slum dwellers in Manila that un-
                          covers important processes relevant to political develop-
                          ment.
                          V   5   6

2145. LEGARDA, TRINIDAD F. Philippine women and the vote. PM 28, no. 4 (Sept.
      1931), 163-165, 196-200.
          Almanzor: Q   3   4

2146. LOPEZ, SALVADOR P. The colonial relationship. (In: American Assembly. The United States and the Philippines, edited by Frank H. Golay. Englewood Cliffs, Prentice-Hall, 1966. p.7-31)

2147. LYNCH, FRANK. The less entangled civil servant. PJPA 5, no. 3 (July 1961), 201-209.
        Stauffer: Review of his well known "SIR" concept as a major factor affecting bureaucracy. Ends with a proposal for escaping the impact of these values.
               E   5   6
        Villanueva: Useful insights into the sociology of Philippine public administration.
               E   5   6

2148. MAJUL, CESAR ADIB. Mabini and the Philippine revolution. Quezon City, U.P. Press, 1960. 477p. (Philippine Studies Series, 4)
        Suggested by Stauffer.
        Stauffer: Very important component in the literature on Mabini's political philosophy and his role in the revolution.
               Q   4   7

2149. _____. The political and constitutional ideas of the Philippine revolution of 1896-1898. Quezon City, U.P., 1957. (Based on the author's thesis, Cornell Univ., 1957. 304p.)
        Grossholtz: An analysis of the differences and similarities in the ideas of revolutionary reformers, ilustrados and katipuneros.
               V   4   3

2150. MALCOLM, GEORGE A. First Malayan republic: the story of the Philippines. Boston, Christopher Publishing House, 1951. 460p.
        Grossholtz: Emphasizes American rather than Filipino participation. Unblemished praise for American rule by a Justice of the Philippine Supreme Court.
               G   5   4

2151. _____ and MÁXIMO M. KALAW. Philippine government; development, organization and functions. Manila, P.I., The Associated Publishers; New York City, D. C. Heath & Company, c1923. 373p.
        Grossholtz: Textbook describing organization of formal government under the Jones Law.
               G   3   4

2152. MANGLAPUS, RAUL S. Faith in the Filipino: the ripening revolution. Manila, Regal Publishing Co., 1961. 204p.
        Grossholtz: The political philosophy of the leading political reform candidate.
               V   3   6
        Stauffer: V   3   6

2153. [MAS Y SANS, SINIBALDO DE]. A nineteenth century Spanish diplomat's view of Philippine colonial policy. [English translation of a passage from vol. 3, Informe sobre el estado de las Islas Filipinas en 1842] PA 26, no. 3 (Aug. 1937), 225-228.
        Grossholtz: A Spanish observer's view of the need for reform and the

revolutionary movement he sensed impending.
G   5   3

2154. MAYO, KATHERINE. The isles of fear; the truth about the Philippines. New
York: Harcourt, Brace and Company, 1925. 372p.
    Grossholtz: A muckracking reportorial view of inequality and the po-
        litical oligarchy in the Philippines.
        J   3   4

2155. MILNE, R. S. The co-ordination and control of government corporations in
the Philippines. PJPA 5, no. 4 (Oct. 1961), 293-320.
    Stauffer: Survey of the activities performed by the Office of Eco-
        nomic Coordination.
        V   3   6

2156. ONORATO, MICHAEL P. The Jones Act and Filipino participation in government.
Solidarity 2, no. 8 (July/Aug. 1967), 86-93.

2157. _____. The tragedy of the Philippine-American experience. Solidarity 3,
(Jan. 1968), 3-10.

2158. PAL, AGATON P. The sociology of politics. (In: Hunt, Chester L. and others.
Sociology in the Philippine Setting. Rev. ed. Quezon City, Phoenix Publishing House, 1963. p.218-237)
    Stauffer: Fine summary of the Philippine political process as seen
        by a sociologist.
        Z   5   6

2159. PALMA, RAFAEL. Our campaign for independence from Taft to Harrison (1901-
1921). Manila, Bureau of Printing, 1923. 47p.
Suggested by Grossholtz.
    Grossholtz: Annotated by Teodoro Kalaw. The views of purposes and
        achievements by an important Nacionalista leader.
        V   5   7

2160. PECK, CORNELIUS J. Nationalism, 'race' and developments in the Philippine
law of citizenship. Journal of Asian and African Studies 2, nos. 1/2
(Jan./Apr. 1967), 125-145.

2161. PHILIPPINE ISLANDS. GOVERNOR. Report...to the Secretary of War.... [20
annual reports covering the years 1916 to 1935] 20v. Washington: Government Printing Office, 1917-1937.
    Grossholtz: Invaluable source of American activities, legislation,
        election statistics, economy, civil service, etc.
        W   5   4
    Stauffer: Extensive annual compilations of statistics and summaries
        of work done by various units of the colonial government.
        W   4   4

2162. PHILIPPINES (COMMONWEALTH). PRESIDENT. Annual report. 1st-4th. 1935/36-
1939. Report of the President (of the Commonwealth) of the Philippines to
the President of the United States. (Four annual reports covering the period
Nov. 15, 1935 to June 30, 1939.) 4 vols. Washington, Government Printing
Office, 1937 to 1940.
    Grossholtz: Invaluable source of American activities, legislation,
        election statistics, economy, civil service, etc.

                                W   5   4
            Stauffer: Brief reports paralleling those of the High Commissioner.
                                W   3   4

2163. _____ (REPUBLIC). PRESIDENT. Messages of the President. v.1- 1935-
Manila, Bureau of Printing. Previously issued by: Philippines (Common-
wealth) President.
Suggested by Grossholtz.
      Grossholtz: W   5   7

2164. PLEHN, CARL C. Taxation in the Philippines. Philippine Social Science Review 13, no. 1 (Feb. 1941), 79-117.
Reprinted in Journal of History (Philippine National Historical Society) 10,
no. 2 (June 1962), 135-192.
Suggested by Grossholtz.
      Grossholtz: Description of the types of taxation imposed by the
                     Spanish and changes over time and under the American re-
                     gime.
                     C   4   7

2165. RAMSAY, ANSIL. Ramon Magsaysay and the Philippine peasantry. PSSHR 30,
no. 1 (Mar. 1965), 65-86.

2166. RAVENHOLT, ALBERT. The peso price of politics. AUFSR. Southeast Asia
Series 6, no. 4 (May 17, 1958), 10p. (AR-4-'58)

2167. _____. The president [Magsaysay] will hear of this. AUFSR. Southeast
Asia Series 3, no. 8 (Apr. 30, 1955), 8p. (AR-4-'55)

2168. _____. Ramon Magsaysay is nominated; the public shares in Philippine politics. AUFSR. Southeast Asia Series 1, no. 6 (Apr. 18, 1953), 8p. (AR-7-
'53)

2169. _____. Tony Diaz runs for Congress; profile of a young politician against
the pattern of Filipino politics. AUFSR. Southeast Asia Series 9, no. 5
(Nov. 1961), 24p. (AR-6-'61)

2170. RIGGS, FRED W. The bazaar-canteen model: economic aspects of the prismatic
society. PSR 6, nos. 3/4 (July/Oct. 1958), 6-59.
      Stauffer: Although this article deals with the Philippine economy,
                    so many implications exist for students of politics as to
                    make it a necessary addition to their working bibliog-
                    raphy.
                    V   5   6

2171. _____. A model for the study of Philippine social structure. PSR 7,
no. 3 (July 1959), 1-32.
      Jocano: V   4   7

2172. _____. Political interference: theory and practice. PJPA 4, no. 4 (Oct.
1960), 311-327.
      Stauffer: Philippine data used as a basis for building a theory of
                    the causes and consequences of political interference in
                    the administrative process. Valuable for understanding
                    Philippine administrative problems.

V   5   6

2173.   _____. The "Sala" model: an ecological approach to the study of comparative administration. PJPA 6, no. 1 (Jan. 1962), 3-16.
        Stauffer: Important theoretical model based on Philippine data.
V   5   6

2174.   _____. The social sciences and public administration. PJPA 3, no. 2
(Apr. 1959), 219-250.

2175.   ROMANI, JOHN H. The Philippine pattern of centralization and decentralization. PSSHR 20, no. 1 (Mar. 1955), 87-103.
        Stauffer: Good review of a continuing debate on a subject of con-
                siderable interest in Philippine politics.
V   4   7

2176.   _____. The Philippine presidency. Manila, Institute of Public Administra-
tion, U.P., 1956. 237p.
        Grossholtz: The basic descriptive study of the presidential office,
                its legal and political powers and functions.
V   4   6
        Stauffer: Although somewhat dated both as to data and methodology,
                this is still a very useful base on which to begin a
                study of the Philippine presidency.
V   5   7

2177.   ROTH, DAVID F. Towards a theory of the role of the Philippine presidency in
the politics of modernization. Claremont, 1968. 319p. Thesis (Ph.D.) -
Claremont Graduate School.

2178.   ROWE, L. S. The establishment of civil government in the Philippines.
American Academy of Political and Social Science. Annals 20 (1902), 313-
327.
Suggested by Grossholtz.
        Grossholtz: V   4   4

2179.   SAMONTE, ABELARDO G. The role of public enterprise in Philippine national
development. International Review of Administrative Sciences 33, no. 2
(1967), 139-144.

2180.   SEMAÑA, CARIDAD C. Philippine politics and economic development. PJPA 11,
no. 1 (Jan. 1967), 24-40.

2181.   SIMBULAN, DANTE C. A study of the socio-economic elite in Philippine poli-
tics and government, 1946-1963. Canberra, 1965. 464p. Thesis (Ph.D.) -
Australian National Univ.
        Grossholtz: Detailed study of the economic oligarchy in the Philip-
                pines and its political dominance.
V   4   7
        Stauffer: Most complete study of its kind available on the Philip-
                pines. Deserves wide use.
V   5   6

2182.   SOBERANO, JOSÉ D. Tax structure and administration: the Philippine situation. PJPA 11, no. 2 (Apr. 1967), 98-118.

2183. STARNER, FRANCES L. Magsaysay and the Philippine peasantry; the agrarian impact on Philippine politics, 1953-1956. Berkeley, Univ. of California Press, 1961. 294p. (Univ. of California publications in political science, v.10)
      Grossholtz: Political, administrative and sociological reasons for the failures of land reform in the Philippines.
                    V   4   6
      Polson: An excellent study of the limits on rural political mobilization.
                    V   5   6
      Stauffer: A balanced, scholarly evaluation of a vital era in Philippine political development.
                    V   5   6

2184. STAUFFER, ROBERT B. A legislative model of political development. PJPA 11, no. 1 (Jan. 1967), 3-12.

2185. _____. Philippine legislators and their changing universe. Journal of Politics 28, no. 3 (Aug. 1966), 556-597.
      Grossholtz: Utilizes aggregate election statistics.
                    V   3   6
      Polson: An analysis of continuities and changes in legislative recruitment patterns.
                    V   5   6

2186. THOMAS, M. LADD. Centralism in the Philippines: past and present causes. Social Research 30, no. 2 (Summer 1963), 203-219.
      Stauffer: A review of forces working to sustain a high degree of central control of local government in the Philippines.
                    V   3   7

2187. TORRES, RAMON. Toward social justice in the Philippines. Pan-Pacific 2, (Jan./Mar. 1938), 31-37.
      Grossholtz: Description of the Quezon program by the Secretary of Labor who was a leading spokesman for reform.
                    V   5   4

2188. TURNBULL, WILFRID. Bringing a wild tribe under government control. PM
      Part I. 26, no. 12 (May 1930), 782-783, 794, 796, 798.
      Part II. 27, no. 1 (June 1930), 31-32, 36, 38, 40, 42.
      Part III. 27, no. 2 (July 1930), 90-91, 116-118, 120.

2189. U.S. CONGRESS. SENATE. SPECIAL COMMITTEE ON CONDITIONS IN THE PHILIPPINES. Investigation of conditions in the Philippines. Report[s] of ... member[s] of the Special Committee appointed June 16, 1934, to investigate conditions in the Philippines ... by Senator Tydings and others. Washington, U.S. G.P.O., 1935. Part I. 22p. Part II. 13p. (74th Cong. 1st Sess. Senate. Doc. 57)
      Grossholtz: Compiled by Senator Tydings and others on tour to ascertain effect of economic provisions of Tydings-McDuffie Act.
                    W   5   4

2190. _____. HIGH COMMISSIONER TO THE PHILIPPINE ISLANDS. Report of the U.S. High

Commissioner to the Philippine Islands to the President and Congress of the
United States. [Seven annual reports covering the periods Nov. 15, 1935
to June 30, 1942, and Sept. 14, 1945 to July 4, 1946.] 7v. Washington,
G.P.O., 1937 to 1947.
        Grossholtz: W   5   4
        Stauffer: A great deal of raw data, largely economic, that could
                be of some use in aggregate analysis.
            W   4   4

2191. _____. PHILIPPINE COMMISSION, 1900-1916. Report of the Philippine Commission to the Secretary of War...(Annual reports nos. 1 to 16 covering the years 1900 to 1915.) 32 vols. Washington, G.P.O., 1901 to 1916.
     Grossholtz: Excellent source material.
     W   5   4
     Stauffer: Some of the annual reports are quite extensive, others so compressed as to lose much utility. Probably of some interest to historians.
     W   4   4

2192. _____. SPECIAL MISSION ON INVESTIGATION TO THE PHILIPPINE ISLANDS. Condition in Philippine Islands. Report of the Special mission to the Philippine Islands to the Secretary of War. Washington, G.P.O., 1922. 58p. Leonard Wood, Chairman. (67th Cong., 2d Sess. House, Dec. 325)
   Grossholtz: Wood-Forbes mission. Unsympathetic description of operation of Jones Law and Filipinization under Harrison.
   W 5 4
   Onorato: W 5 4
   Stauffer: Possibly more valuable for its contribution to the study of American politics than of the Philippines.
   W 3 4

2193. VAN DER KROEF, JUSTUS M. Patterns of cultural conflict in Philippine life. Pac. Aff. 39, nos. 3/4 (Fall/Winter 1966-67), 326-338.

2194. VILLANUEVA, BUENAVENTURA M. To govern or not to govern: a case study. PJPA 3, no. 1 (Jan. 1959), 24-38.
   Stauffer: Case study of the political pressures for and against passage of the "Omnibus Local Autonomy Bill of 1957".
   V 4 6
   Villanueva: V 5 6

2195. VILORIA, LEANDRO A. Reorganization in the Philippine national government prior to 1954. PJPA 5, no. 1 (Jan. 1961), 31-51.
   Stauffer: Useful history of various reorganizations of the Philippine bureaucracy, 1898-1954.
   V 3 6

2196. WENGERT, EGBERT S. Some thoughts on executive development in the Philippine government. PJPA 2, no. 4 (Oct. 1958), 348-362.
   Stauffer: While limited to interviews with two bureau directors, valuable insights emerge on the interaction of bureaucrats and politicians.
   V 3 6

2197. WILLIAMS, DANIEL R. The odyssey of the Philippine Commission. Chicago,
A. C. McClurg & Co., 1913. 264p.
Suggested by Grossholtz.
   Grossholtz: A critical view of the devolution of authority to Fili-
                  pinos by an American official.
                  G   3   4

2198. WURFEL, DAVID O. The Bell report and after: a study of the political prob-
lems of social reform stimulated by foreign aid. 1960. Thesis (Ph.D.) -
Cornell Univ.
   Grossholtz: Special relations between United States and Philippines
                  and usefulness as channel for reform.
                  V   4   6

2199. _____. Foreign aid and social reform in political development: a Philippine case study. American Political Science Review 53, no. 2 (June 1959),
456-482.
   Stauffer: One of the best case studies available dealing with the
                 use of foreign aid to force political change on one of the
                 new nations.
                 V   5   6

2200. _____. Individuals and groups in the policy process. PJPA 9, no. 1 (Jan.
1965), 30-42.
   Stauffer: A comprehensive evaluation of the major interest groups
                 operating within the Philippines, viewed against a tradi-
                 tion of personal power.
                 V   5   6

2201. _____. The Philippines (In: Kahin, George McTurnan, ed. Governments and
politics of southeast Asia. 2d ed. Ithaca, New York, Cornell Univ. Press,
1964. p.679-769)
   Grossholtz: Fundamental description of system.
                  V   3   7
   Stauffer: Best general treatment available by an American of the
                 Philippine political system.
                 V   5   7

2202. _____. Problems of decolonization. (In: American Assembly. The United
States and the Philippines, edited by Frank H. Golay. Englewood Cliffs,
Prentice-Hall, 1966. p.149-173)

2203. YABES, LEOPOLDO Y. The American administration in the Philippines. Solidarity 2, no. 5 (Jan./Feb. 1967), 16-26.

2204. YAMANE, FELIPA C. The political and social framework of development strategy
in the underdeveloped countries. II. The social framework of development
strategy. ERJ 14, no. 1 (June 1967), 25-31.

Political Movements

2205. ALDABA-LIM, ESTEFANIA and OTHERS. A cursory study of the Lapiang Malaya-- its membership, organization and implications to present Philippine society. PSR 15, nos. 3/4 (July/Oct. 1967), 151-162.

2206. ARANETA, A. S. The origins of the Communist Party of the Philippines and the Comintern, 1919-1930. Oxford, 1966. Thesis (D. Phil.) - Oxford Univ.

2207. CATER, SONYA DIANE. The Philippine Federation of Free Farmers; a case study in mass agrarian organization. Ithaca, N. Y. 1959. Southeast Asia Program, Dept. of Far Eastern Studies, Cornell Univ., 1959. 147p. (Data Paper no. 35)

    Grossholtz: Based on documents, interviews and observation.
                V   4   6

    Polson: An excellent study of the national FFF.
                V   4   6

    Spencer: Good study in political science, revision of M.A. thesis.
                V   4   6

    Stauffer: A balanced analysis of problems facing those attempting to organize peasants. Data drawn from early years of FFF.
                V   4   6

2208. CLIFFORD, MARY DORITA. Aglipayanism as a political movement. St. Louis, 1960. 585p. Thesis (Ph.D.) - St. Louis Univ.
Suggested by Grossholtz.

    Grossholtz: A careful, well-documented account of the origins and controversy over the movement by an unsympathetic scholar.
                V   4   4

2209. FIFIELD, RUSSELL H. The Hukbalahap today. Far Eastern Survey 20, no. 2 (Jan. 1951), 13-18.

    Grossholtz: V   3   6

    Stauffer: Survey of the Huk position at that date. Of some topical value.
                V   4   6

2210. GUERRERO, MILAGROS C. The Colorum uprisings, 1924-1931. AS 5, no. 1 (Apr. 1967), 65-78.

2211. HOEKSEMA, RENZE L. Communism in the Philippines; a historical and analytical study of communism and the Communist Party in the Philippines and its relations to communist movements abroad. Cambridge, Mass., 1956. Thesis (Ph.D.) - Harvard Univ.
Suggested by Grossholtz.

    Grossholtz: The basic study of the development of the Philippine Communist Party and its links with other Communist Parties.
                V   5   7

2212. KROEF, JUSTUS M. VAN DER. Communist fronts today in the Philippines. Problems of Communism 16, no. 2 (Mar./Apr. 1967), 65-75.

2213. LAVA, JOSE. Milestones in the history of the Philippine Communist Party, by

I. GENERAL. POLITICAL SCIENCE. Political Movements

"Gregorio Santayana" (pseud.). Manila? 1950. 54p.
Suggested by Grossholtz.
    Grossholtz: Written by a politburo leader shortly before his arrest,
                apparently for internal party use.
                V   5   7

2214. LOPEZ, OSCAR J. A history of the communist movement in the Philippines.
n.p., 195? 46p. Photocopy of typewritten manuscript.
Suggested by Grossholtz.
    Grossholtz: A short history based mainly on secondary sources written
                as an MA thesis.
                V   3   7

2215. MCPHELIN, MICHAEL and OTHERS. Political transmission 15. PS 8, no. 1
(Jan. 1960), 3-50.
    Grossholtz: An analysis and refutation of the Communist Party docu-
                ment by leading Jesuit scholars.
                X   4   6
    Stauffer: Comments by four editors on a current Communist Party
                document. Analysis varies from careful refutation to
                routine, pat anti-communist argument.
                X   3   6

2216. The peasant war in the Philippines; a study of the causes of social unrest
in the Philippines - an analysis of Philippine political economy. PSSHR
23, nos. 2/4 (June/Dec. 1958), 373-436.
    Grossholtz: An insider's account of the HUK movement. Extremely
                useful.
                -     5   6
    Stauffer: Historical essay on the underlying causes of the Phil-
                ippine peasant revolution, presented as an unsigned
                "document". Militant anti-Establishment point of view.
                -     4   7

2217. PHILIPPINES (REPUBLIC) HOUSE OF REPRESENTATIVES. Report on: 1. The il-
legality of the Communist Party of the Philippines. 2. The functions of
the Special Committee on Un-Filipino Activities. Published by the Special
Committee on Un-Filipino Activities. Manila, Bureau of Printing, 1951. 168p.
(HR. 2nd Congress. 2nd Session. Rept. no. 2)

2218. _____ SENATE. COMMITTEE ON NATIONAL DEFENSE AND SECURITY. Committee report no. 1123 on the security problem posed by the Huk movement and on the
government's performance in central Luzon. Manuel P. Manahan, Chairman.
Manila, 1967. 42p.

2219. POMEROY, WILLIAM J. The forest, a personal record of the Huk guerrilla
struggle in the Philippines. New York, International Publishers, 1963.
224p.
Suggested by Grossholtz.
    Grossholtz: An inside view of the Communist guerrilla movement by
                an American Communist who participated.
                V   5   7

2220. _____. Political struggles in the Philippines. New Times no. 50 (Dec.
18, 1968), 13-14.

2221. RAVENHOLT, ALBERT. Philippine rural reconstruction movement--a worker tells his story. AUFSR. Southeast Asia Series 3, no. 10 (May 7, 1955), 8p. (AR-5-'55)

2222. _____. The Philippine rural reconstruction movement--barrio folk awaken. AUFSR. Southeast Asia Series 3, no. 6 (Apr. 5, 1955), 8p. (AR-2-'55)

2223. _____. Rural reconstruction with co-operatives; a case study of the Philippine Rural Reconstruction movement. AUFSR. Southeast Asia Series 15, no. 1 (June 1967), 17p. (AR-2-'67)

2224. SCAFF, ALVIN H. The Huk revolt in the Philippines. Pacific Spectator 5, no. 3 (Summer 1951), 335-341.
        Stauffer: Summary of causes of the revolt followed by policy re-
                       commendations for United States.
                       Z   3   6

2225. _____. The Philippine answer to communism. Stanford, Stanford Univ. Press, 1955. 165p.
        Grossholtz: Description of resettlement programs and the results
                       with respect to the Huk insurgency.
                       V   4   6
        Polson: A good study of the Huk rebellion with emphasis on the
                       Government's socio-economic counter-measures.
                       Z   5   6
        Stauffer: Sociological study of the resettlement program designed
                       to "win the hearts" of the Huks.
                       Z   3   6

2226. STURTEVANT, DAVID R. Guardia de Honor: revitalization within the revolu- tion. AS 4, no. 2 (Aug. 1966), 342-352.

2227. _____. No uprising fails - each one is a step in the right direction. Solidarity 1, no. 4 (Oct./Dec. 1966), 11-21.

2228. _____. Philippine social structure and its relation to agrarian unrest. 1958. 259p. Thesis (Ph.D.) -Stanford Univ.

2229. _____. Sakdalism and Philippine radicalism. Journal of Asian Studies 21, no. 2 (Feb. 1962), 199-213.
        Grossholtz: H   4   7
        Polson: Some interesting material.
                       H   3   4
        Stauffer: Excellent background material for perspective on agra-
                       rian problem as it affects Philippine politics.
                       H   5   4

2230. _____. Sakdalism and Philippine radicalism. Dialogue 4, no. 1 (Dec. 1967), 3-26.

2231. TARUC, LUIS. Born of the people. New York, International Publishers, 1953. 286p.
        Suggested by Grossholtz.
        Grossholtz: Huk leader's account of development and purpose of the

movement.
V   5   7

2232. _____. He who rides a tiger; the story of Asian guerrilla leader. New
York, F. A. Praeger, 1967. 188p.
Suggested by Grossholtz.
    Grossholtz: Huk leader's apologia after 13 years in prison.
                    V   3   7

2233. YEN, Y. C. JAMES. Philippine rural reconstruction movement. Philippine
Economy Review 4, no. 10 (May 1958), 30-35, 38.
    Polson: A statement of the philosophy underlying the PRRM by
                    its articulator.
                    Y   4   6

Political Parties, Pressure Groups and Elections

2234. AGABIN, PACIFICO A. Money and elections: the myth of one-man one-vote.
Heritage 1, no. 2 (Oct. 1967), 35-39.

2235. AGPALO, REMIGIO E. Interest groups and their role in the Philippine political system. PJPA 9, no. 2 (Apr. 1965), 87-106.
    Stauffer: An analytic typology of political systems and interest
                    group types is applied to Philippine data. An important
                    contribution.
                    V   5   7
    Villanueva: Excellent case study on decision making and political
                    processes.
                    V   5   6

2236. ANDO, HIROFUMI. The altar and the ballot-box: the Iglesia Ni Kristo in
the 1965 Philippine elections. PJPA 10, no. 4 (Oct. 1966), 359-366.
    Grossholtz: Description weakened by failure to document actual
                    strength of Iglesia.
                    V   3   6
    Stauffer: A valuable case study of the role of religion in a Phil-
                    ippine presidential election.
                    V   4   6

2237. BATERINA, VIRGINIA F. A study of money in elections in the Philippines.
PSSHR 20, no. 1 (Mar. 1955), 39-86.
        20, no. 2 (June 1955), 137-212.
(Her M.A. thesis, A study of money in elections in the Philippines with em-
phasis on the financing of political parties. U.P., 1953. 201p.)
Suggested by Grossholtz and Stauffer.
    Grossholtz: Utilizes Commission of Election reports and interviews.
                    V   5   6
    Stauffer: Important pioneering study of an aspect of political
                    behavior in the Philippines.
                    V   4   7

2238. CONCEPCION, RODOLFO F. Operation quick count. PS 10, no. 1 (Jan. 1962), 145-150.
        Grossholtz: Describes machinery set up by Manila press and others to channel election results to Manila quickly.
                     -     3   6

2239. COQUIA, JORGE R. The Philippine presidential election of 1953. Manila, Univ. Pub. Co., 1955. 392p.
Suggested by Grossholtz.
        Grossholtz: Case study of the Magsaysay election.
                     V   3   6

2240. CORPUZ, ONOFRE D. Filipino political parties and politics. PSSHR 23, nos. 2/4 (June/Dec. 1958), 141-157.
        Grossholtz: Cultural variables as explanation of parties and their role in system.
                     V   3   6
        Stauffer: A broad view of Philippine political parties utilizing the Duverger theoretical framework.
                     V   5   7

2241. FRANTZICH, STEVE. Party switching in the Philippine context. PS 16, no. 4 (Oct. 1968), 750-768.

2242. HEALY, GERALD W. The modern voter and morality. PS 1, no. 2 (Sept. 1953), 131-143.
        Grossholtz: Useful insight into political perceptions of Philippine intellectuals.
                     Q   3   6

2243. LANDE, CARL H. Leaders, factions, and parties; the structure of Philippines politics. New Haven, Southeast Asia Studies, Yale Univ., 1965. 148p. (Monograph series, no. 6)
Revision of a doctoral dissertation, Politics in the Philippines, Harvard Univ., 1958.
        Grossholtz: Organization and function of political parties utilizing aggregate voting data over a time period.
                     V   5   6
        Polson: Good analysis of the national political process.
                     V   4   6
        Stauffer: Standard work on the subject. Essential reading for anyone working on Philippine politics.
                     V   5   7

2244. _____. Parties and politics in the Philippines. Asian Survey 8, no. 9 (Sept. 1968), 725-747.

2245. _____. Party politics in the Philippines. (In: Guthrie, George M., ed. Six perspectives on the Philippines. Manila, Bookmark, 1968. p.85-131)

2246. _____. The Philippine political party system. JSEAH 8, no. 1 (Mar. 1967), 19-39.

2247. LIANG, DAPEN. The development of Philippine political parties. Hongkong, Printed by South China Morning Post, 1939. 286p. (His Ph.D. Thesis - New York Univ., 1937)

> Grossholtz: The base study of the role of the political parties in
> securing self-government and independence.
> V   4   4
>
> Stauffer: The only major work on Philippine political parties dur-
> ing the American occupation. Historical, formal. Ends
> with beginning of Commonwealth era.
> V   4   4

2248. MEADOWS, MARTIN. Implications of the 1965 Philippine election: a view
from America. AS 4, no. 2 (Aug. 1966), 381-391.

2249. MILNE, R. S. The party system and democracy in the Philippines. Political
Science 13, no. 2 (Sept. 1961), 31-44.
> Stauffer: A good review of party developments during the first de-
> cade of Philippine independence.
> V   4   6

2250. RAVENHOLT, ALBERT. Politics and business; Nacionalista Party convention becomes an arena for contending Philippine pressure groups. AUFSR. Southeast
Asia Series 9, no. 2 (June 1961), 10p. (AR-4-'61)

2251. REGALA, ROBERTO. The development of representation in the Philippines.
Philippine Law Journal 11, no. 3 (Sept. 1931), 63-88 and 11, no. 4 (Oct.
1931), 111-1939.
Suggested by Grossholtz.
> Grossholtz: 0   4   7

2252. STAUFFER, ROBERT B. The development of an interest group: the Philippine
medical association. Quezon City, U.P. Press, 1966. 192p.
> Coller: Reports on original research of this organization. A
> pioneering study.
> V   5   6
> Grossholtz: V   3   6

2253. _____. Interest group theory: variations in a developing country. PJPA
8, no. 4 (Oct. 1964), 271-287.

2254. _____. Philippine interest groups: an index of political development.
AS 3, no. 2 (Aug. 1965), 193-220.

2255. STYSKAL, RICHARD A. Strategies of influence among members of three voluntary associations in the Philippines. Eugene, 1967. 209p. Thesis (Ph.D.) -
Univ. of Oregon.

2256. TAFT, WILLIAM H. Political parties in the Philippines. American Academy
of Political and Social Science. Annals 20 (1902), 307-312.
Suggested by Grossholtz.
> Grossholtz: The Civil Governor's view of the Federal Party.
> G   5   4

2257. VILLANUEVA, BUENAVENTURA M. and GELIA CASTILLO. The party struggle and the
people's mandate. Comment, no. 14 (1962), 11-23.
> Stauffer: Report of a public opinion survey before the 1961 elec-
> tions. Useful for attitudes of voters on parties and
> candidates.

                        V   4   6
        Villanueva: V/Z   5   6

2258.   WURFEL, DAVID O. Comparative studies in political finance: the Philippines.
        Journal of Politics 25, no. 4 (Nov. 1963), 757-773.
                Stauffer: V   5   6

2259.   _____. The Philippine elections: support for democracy. Asian Survey 2,
        no. 3 (May 1962), 25-37.
                Grossholtz: V   3   6
                Stauffer: Thorough coverage of the 1961 presidential elections; in-
                                cludes an analysis of political trends in the Philippines
                                since independence.
                                V   5   6

                        PROPERTY AND EXCHANGE

2260.   ABRAHAM, WILLIAM I. The national income of the Philippines and its distribu-
        tion; report and recommendations of the National Income Adviser under the
        United Nations Technical Assistance Program. Manila, 1953. 54p.
                Anderson: X   5   6
                Legarda: The pioneering work on the subject.
                                X   5   6
                Valdepeñas: A most useful breakthrough in Philippine social accounts.
                                X   5   6

2261.   _____. Problems of national income measurement in underdeveloped countries,
        with special reference to the Philippines. New York, 1954. 132p. Thesis
        (Ph.D.) - Columbia Univ.

2262.   ALIP, EUFRONIO M. Laws, customs, and practices of inheritance of the Pre-
        Spanish Philippines. PSSHR 4, no. 1 (Jan. 1932), 76-80.
                Anderson: Use of historical data made but specific references are
                                not given.
                                H   3   1

2263.   BANTEGUI, BERNARDINO G. Composition and growth of national income in the
        Philippines. ERJ 6, no. 4 (Mar. 1960), 235-242.
                Anderson: The history of income estimation in the Philippines, con-
                                cepts involved and general findings in the period of
                                1948-60. It indicates the growth of national output and
                                input.
                                X   5   6

2264.   _____. Questions and observations on the article "On the Accuracy of Phil-
        ippine National Income Accounts" by Gerardo P. Sicat. PRBE 2, no. 1 (May
        1965), 46-52.
        Sicat, Gerardo P. ---Reply. 53-55.

2265.   BARBER, CLARENCE L. National income estimates in the Philippines. PEJ 4,

no. 1 (First Semester 1965), 64-96.
    Legarda: S   4   6
    Valdepeñas: Good reference.
                     X   3   6

2266.   _____. Some notes on income distribution in the Philippines. Phil. Stat. 9, no. 2 (June 1960), 46-59.
    Legarda: S   4   6
    Valdepeñas: X   3   6

2267.   BOWDITCH, NATHANIEL. Early American-Philippine trade: the journal of Nathaniel Bowditch in Manila, 1796. Edited and with an introd. by Thomas R. McHale and Mary C. McHale. New Haven, Yale University, Southeast Asia Studies, 1962. 65p. (Southeast Asia Studies. Monograph series, no. 2)
    Anderson: Provides colorful description of Manila and excellent details on commerce in a critical period of change. Excellent analysis and contextualization of the journal by McHale.
                     X/H   4/5   3
    Legarda: X   5   3

2268.   BULATAO, JAIME. Value orientation of the Filipino consumer. Marketing Horizons 3, no. 1 (Jan. 1964), 66-69.

2269.   Central bank household survey of consumer expenditures. Stat. Rept. 3, no. 4 (Oct. 1959), 24-27.
    Anderson: Survey (through interviews) of 1000 households in Manila metropolitan area including household income and expenditures.
                     W   5   6
    Legarda: W   4   6

2270.   CENTRAL BANK OF THE PHILIPPINES. DEPT. OF ECONOMIC RESEARCH. History of national income estimation in the Philippines. Stat. Rept. 2, no. 2 (Apr. 1958), 1-4.
    Legarda: W   4   6

2271.   FLORENTINO, PEDRO F. The use of economic census results and other census sample survey data in national income estimation in the Philippines. Stat. Rept. 8, no. 2 (Apr./June 1964), 38-48.
    Anderson: Describes the estimation procedure and points to the potential uses of the 1948 and 1960 censuses.
                     X   3   6

2272.   GUERRERO, MILAGROS C. A survey of Japanese trade and investments in the Philippines, with special reference to Philippine-American reactions 1900-1941. PSSHR 31, no. 1 (Mar. 1966), i-xv, 1-129.

2273.   HEALY, GERALD W. Usury in the Philippines today. PS 3, no. 2 (June 1955), 136-156.
    Anderson: Defines and analyzes usury in the Philippines and outlines the conflict between legal and conventional rates and between the creditor's versus the debtor's self-interest.
                     -      3   6

I. GENERAL. PROPERTY AND EXCHANGE

2274. HICKS, GEORGE L. Philippine foreign trade, 1950-1965. Basic data and major characteristics. Washington, D.C. Center for Development Planning, National Planning Association, 1966. 69p. (Field Work Report no. 10)

2275. _____. Philippine foreign trade statistics: supplementary data and interpretations, 1954-1966. Washington, D.C. Center for Development Planning, National Planning Association, 1967. 45p. (Field Work Report, no. 20)

2276. INDOLOS, MAXIMO. Private property and ideology. Solidarity 2, no. 7 (May/June 1967), 38-45.

2277. MCPHELIN, MICHAEL. Philippines: international trade and problems of modernization. PS 14, no. 4 (Oct. 1966), 553-569.

2278. MAULIT, DIMAS A. Income ratio between rural and urban workers in the Philippines. ERJ 6, no. 2 (Sept. 1959), 83-95.
    Anderson: Based on a nation-wide census: comparison of income by type of specific activities and suggestions of some causes for the income discrepancy between rural and urban areas.
                X   5   6

2279. ORDINARIO, CANDIDO. Income distribution and expenditure patterns among families in the Philippines. Stat. Rept. 3, no. 4 (Oct. 1959), 1-10.
    Anderson: Uses data obtained in 1957 by the Philippines Survey of Households to investigate living standards of rural and urban families and to indicate the causes of the income distribution and varieties of expenditures.
                G   5   6

2280. ORDOÑO, EUSTAQUIO O. The pattern of post-war income distribution in the Philippines. ERJ 11, no. 3 (Dec. 1964), 132-148.
    Anderson: Different post-war income distribution surveys are reviewed and compared and the 'present' level of income and prices are presented and analyzed. Tables.
                X   5   6

2281. PHILIPPINE STATISTICAL ASSOCIATION. TASK COMMITTEE "A" OF THE RESEARCH COMMITTEE. An inquiry into the statistics of the national income of the Philippines. Phil. Stat. 6, no. 3 (Sept. 1957), 129-158.
    Legarda: S   5   6

2282. PHILIPPINES (REPUBLIC) NATIONAL ECONOMIC COUNCIL. OFFICE OF STATISTICAL COORDINATION AND STANDARDS. An analysis of the national income accounts of the Philippines for the years 1956 and 1957 [including supporting tables and technical notes]. Stat. Rept. 2, no. 2 (Apr. 1958), 11-27.
    Anderson: Presentation and analysis of primary data of the disposition of national output and the amount, composition and distribution of the national income.
                W   5   6
    Legarda: W   5   6

2283. _____. An analysis of the national income accounts of the Philippines for the years 1957 and 1958 [including supporting tables and technical notes]. Stat. Rept. 3, no. 2 (Apr. 1959), 1-22.

I. GENERAL. PROPERTY AND EXCHANGE

        Anderson: For annotation, see no. 2282.
                    W   5   6
        Legarda: W   5   6

2284. _____. An analysis of the national income accounts of the Philippines for the years 1958 and 1959 [including supporting tables and technical notes]. Stat. Rept. 4, no. 2 (Apr. 1960), 1-27.
        Anderson: For annotation, see no. 2282.
                    W   5   6
        Legarda: W   5   6

2285. _____. Analysis of the national income of the Philippines for CY 1958-1960 [including supporting tables and technical notes]. Stat. Rept. 5, no. 2 (Apr. 1961), 1-35.
        Anderson: For annotation, see no. 2282.
                    W   5   6
        Legarda: W   5   6

2286. _____. Analysis of the national income of the Philippines for CY 1959-1961 [including supporting tables and technical notes]. Stat. Rept. 6, no. 2 (Apr. 1962), 1-30.
        Anderson: For annotation, see no. 2282.
                    W   5   6
        Legarda: W   5   6

2287. _____. Analysis of the national income of the Philippines for CY 1960-1962 [including supporting tables and technical notes]. Stat. Rept. 7, no. 2 (Apr./June 1963), 1-23.
        Anderson: For annotation, see no. 2282.
                    W   5   6
        Legarda: W   5   6

2288. _____. Analysis of the national income of the Philippines for CY 1961-1963 [including supporting tables and technical notes]. Stat. Rept. 8, no. 2 (Apr./June 1964), 1-37.
        Anderson: For annotation, see no. 2282.
                    W   5   6
        Legarda: W   5   6

2289. _____. The national income of the Philippines for CY 1962-1964 [including supporting tables and technical notes]. Stat. Rept. 9, no. 2 (Apr./June 1965), 1-29.
        Legarda: W   5   6

2290. _____. The national income of the Philippines CY 1964-1965 [including supporting tables and technical notes]. Stat. Rept. 10, no. 2 (Apr./June 1966), 1-20.
        Legarda: W   5   6

2291. _____. The national income of the Philippines CY 1964-1966. [including technical notes]. Stat. Rept. 11, no. 2 (Apr./June 1967), 1-36.
        Legarda: W   5   6

2292. QUIASON, SERAFIN D. English country trade with the Philippines, 1644-1765. Quezon City, U.P. Press, 1966. 230p.

2293. _____. A synopsis of early English country trade with the Philippines. University College Journal 5, (First Semester 1963/1964), 26-34.

2294. [SIBLEY, WILLIS E]. Chapter 22 "Overseas Trade." (In: Human Relations Area Files, Inc. Area handbook on the Philippines. 1956. v.4, p.1676-1693)

    Anderson: Brief survey of external trade, emphasizing U.S.-Philippine trade relations, historically and current (to 1955).

                    E   3   7

2295. SICAT, GERARDO P. On the accuracy of Philippine national income accounts. PRBE 1, no. 2 (Oct. 1964), 21-39.

2296. TRINIDAD, RUBEN F. Basic concepts in the measurement of the nation's output. Stat. Rept. 2, no. 2 (Apr. 1958), 5-10.

    Anderson: Discusses concepts relevant to the measurement of the nation's output and some aspects of the Philippine situation which necessitate modification of methods and categories from those applicable to industrial countries.

                    X   3   6

    Legarda: X   4   6

2297. _____. National income accounting with special reference to the Philippines. ERJ 8, no. 1 (June 1961), 39-45.

    Anderson: See above.

                    X   3   6

    Legarda: X   4   6

2298. ULLMAN, EDWARD L. Trade centers and tributary areas of the Philippines. Geographical Review 50, no. 2 (Apr. 1960), 203-218.

    Anderson: Five levels of trade centers are identified with the main indicator being differential densities in traffic flow. The report concludes with some notes on the geographic centrality of the trade points and the modification of the hierarchy as the economy continues to modernize.

                    K   5   6

    Luna: Descriptive statistical analytical study with maps.

                    K   4   6

    Spencer: Clear discussion of regional focus of regional trade.

                    K   4   6

    Wernstedt: Categories of urban centers in trade hierarchy.

                    K   4   6

2299. WERNSTEDT, FREDERICK L. Philippine interisland shipping and trade. PGJ 4, no. 1 (Jan./Mar. 1956), 17-21.

    Anderson: Traces the development of inter-island trade and analyzes its present day character in terms of goods moved, companies involved, and types of parts functioning.

                    K   4   6

    Spencer: Excerpt out of Wernstedt's The role and importance of Philippine interisland shipping and trade. 1957.

                    K   5   6

2300. _____. The role and importance of Philippine interisland shipping and trade. Ithaca, Southeast Asia Program, Dept. of Far Eastern Studies, Cornell University, 1957. 132p.

    Anderson: A careful study moving from an expansion of the geographic base, historical development and present-day inter-island shipping pattern in general to a study of individual major ports.

          K   4   7

    Coller: Basic field study data-baseline study in its field.

          K   5   7

    Luna: Historical descriptive analytical study.

          K   4   7

    Spencer: First hand field study excellent.

          K   5   7

2301. WHEATLEY, PAUL. Geographical notes on some commodities involved in Sung Maritime Trade. Royal Asiatic Society. Malayan Branch. Journal 32, (pt. 2), no. 186 (June 1959), 5-139.

    Anderson: Useful discussion of Chinese trade in Southeast Asia during the Sung period. Outlines principal commodities exchanged.

          K   4   5

RELIGION

Ecclesiastical Organization

2302. ACHÚTEGUI, PEDRO S. DE and MIGUEL A. BERNARD. The Aglipayan churches and the census of 1960. PS 12, no. 3 (July 1964), 446-459.

    Gowing: Analyses the numerical decline of Aglipayanism.

          Q and Q 4   6

2303. _____. Religious revolution in the Philippines; the life and church of Gregorio Aglipay, 1860-1960. Manila, Ateneo de Manila, 1960-1966.

v.1. From Aglipay's birth to his death: 1860-1940.

v.2. Iglesia Filipina Independiente.

    Doherty: Misuse of sources, excessively polemical, only extant history on Aglipay.

          Q and Q 3   4

    Gowing: Excellent factual study of PIC and its founder, but hostile in its interpretation.

          Q and Q 4   7

2304. ADUARTE, DIEGO. Historia de la provincia del Santo Rosario de la Orden de Predicadores en Philippinas, Japon, y China. Manila, 1640.

v.1, Reprinted in 1693, issued with v.2.

v.2, by Baltasar de Santa Cruz. 1693.

Synopsis in Blair and Robertson. v.30-32.

    Felix: Excellent account by a second generation missionary.

          M   5   2

    Legarda: M   5   2

Phelan: M   5   2
Wickberg: M   5   2

2305.   AGUILA, NORMA ALAMPAY. Fiestas and hospitality. CC 5, no. 6 (Nov./Dec. 1965), 23-26.

2306.   ARENS, RICHARD. Social scientists point the way to religious acculturation and accommodation. PSR 6, no. 1 (Jan. 1958), 14-18.

2307.   BAZACO, EVERGISTO. The church in the Philippines. Manila, Univ. of Sto. Tomas Press, 1938. 464p.
        Gowing: Useful in part but generally biographical.
                       M   3   7

2308.   BINGLE, ERNEST J. and KENNETH G. GRUBB. Statistics of Protestant missions: educational and medical work (based on information collected for World Christian Handbook 1952). Mimeo. London, World Dominion Press, 1953. 56p.
        Doherty: -   3   7

2309.   _____. World Christian handbook. Second edition. London, World Dominion Press, 1952. 389p.
        Cited in Univ. of Chicago. Philippine Studies Program. Selected Bibliography of the Philippines. p.59.
        Doherty: -   3   7

2310.   BULATAO, JAIME. A social-psychological view of the Philippine Church. CS 2, no. 1 (Mar. 1965), 3-18.
        Doherty: Author develops some challenging hypothesis.
                       P   4   7

2311.   Catholic Directory of the Philippines 1953? Manila, Catholic Trade School. Annual. 1955 pub. in 1954. 475p.
        Doherty: Published yearly. Good source of Catholic statistical
                       data. Not sure of its accuracy but only such source.
                       W   4   6
        Gowing: Published yearly, invaluable for statistical data on the
                       Roman Catholic Church in Philippines.
                       W   5   6

2312.   CHIRINO, PEDRO. Relation of the Filipinas Islands and of what has there been accomplished by the Fathers of the Society of Jesus. 1604. (In: Blair and Robertson. v.12:169-321; v.13:9-217)

2313.   COLIN, FRANCISCO. Labor evangélica, ministerios apostolicos de los obreros de la Compañia de fundación y progressos de su provincia en las islas Filipinas. Madrid, 1663. 2nd ed. by Pablo Pastells. Barcelona, Impr. y litografia de Henrich y compañia, 1900-02. 3v.

2314.   COQUIA, JORGE R. Legal status of the church in the Philippines. Washington, Catholic Univ. of America Press, 1950. 224p. (His Ph.D. Thesis - Catholic Univ., 1950)
        Gowing: Basic study of the subject.
                       O   4   6

2315.   CORNISH, LOUIS C. The Philippines calling. Philadelphia, Dorrance, 1942.

I. GENERAL. RELIGION. Ecclesiastical Organization

313p.
    Gowing: Useful description of pre-war Aglipayanism.
                M   4   4

2316. COSTA, HORACIO DE LA. The development of native clergy in the Philippines. Theological Studies (Woodstock, Maryland, Woodstock College) 8 (1947), 219-250.
Cited in Univ. of Chicago, Philippine Studies Program, Selected bibliography of the Philippines. p.60.
    Doherty: Excellent study of development of native clergy.
                H   4   7
    Gowing: Classic study of the subject.
                H   4   3

2317. _____. The Jesuits in the Philippines: 1581-1959. PS 7, no. 1 (Jan. 1959), 68-97.
    Doherty: Based on data collected for work below.
                H   4   7

2318. _____. The Jesuits in the Philippines, 1581-1768. Cambridge, Harvard Univ. Press, 1961. 702p.
    Doherty: A first class historical study.
                H   4   7
    Gowing: Classic study of the subject.
                H   4   2

2319. _____. Philippines. Catholic Encyclopaedia. New York, The Gilmary Society, Supplement 2 (1950), 8p.
    Doherty: Excellent article.
                H   4   7

2320. _____. The role of the laity in the development of the Catholic church in the Philippines. The Filipino Christian Family in a Changing Society. Manila: Christian Family Movement, (Dec. 3/5,1965), p.1-9.
    Doherty: Excellent insights.
                H   4   7

2321. COVAR, PROSPERO R. Congregation as a social process in the Watawat ng Lahi. PSR 8, nos. 3/4 (July/Oct. 1960), 1-16.
    Coller: Based on his M.A. thesis in part.
                Z   5   6
    Doherty: As far as I know Cover's are the only studies of this group.
                Z   3   7

2322. _____. The Iglesia Watawat ng Lahi: a sociological study of a social movement. 1961. Thesis (M.A.) - U.P.
    Coller: Unique religious cult focused on Rizal, studied by participant observation.
                Z   5   6
    Doherty: Z   3   7

2323. CUERQUIS, FLORENCIO R. The baptismal rites in Protestant churches in the Philippines. PS 16, no. 1 (Jan. 1968), 169-177.

241

2324. CUSHNER, NICHOLAS P. A note on Jesuits, linguistics and the Philippine missions. Neue Zeitschrift für Missionswissenschaft 19, no. 2 (1963), 116-121.
  Doherty: Excellent.
        Z 4   7

2325. DOHERTY, JOHN F. The image of the priest: a study in stereotyping. PSR 12, nos. 1/2 (Jan./Apr. 1964), 70-76.
  Doherty: Sample limited in scope. Interpretation of data well received.
        Z 4   6
  Gowing: Pioneering study, revealing.
        Z 5   6

2326. EVANGELISTA, OSCAR L. Religious problems in the Philippines and the American Catholic Church, 1898-1907. AS 6, no. 3 (Dec. 1968), 248-262.

2327. FERNANDEZ, PERFECTO V. The legal status of the churches in the Philippines. DR 8, nos. 1/3 (Jan./Sept.1960), 23-120.

2328. GASPAR DE SAN AGUSTÍN. Conquistas de las islas Philipinas: 1a temporal, por las armas del señor don Phelipe Segundo el Prudente; y 1a espiritval, por los religiosos del orden de nuestro padre San Augustin...Madrid, En la imprenta de m. Rviz de Mvrga, 1698; Valadolid, L.N. de Gaviria, 1890. 2v. (In: Blair and Robertson. v.40:183-295)
The second volume, compiled by Casimiro Diaz from the manuscript left by Gaspar de San Agustin. . .
   Legarda: M 5   2
   Phelan: H 5   2
   Wickberg: M 5   2

2329. GOWING, PETER G. Christianity in the Philippines, yesterday and today. SJ 12, no. 2 (Apr./June 1965), 109-151.

2330. _____. Islands under the cross; the story of the Church in the Philippines. Manila, National Council of Churches in the Philippines, 1967. 286p.

2331. HISTORICAL CONSERVATION SOCIETY. The christianization of the Philippines. Published by the Historical Conservation Society and the University of San Agustin. Translated by Rafael Lopez and Alfonso Felix, Jr., Manila, 1965. 428p. Text in Spanish and English. (Its News Bulletin, 6)
  Gowing: Useful translation of old Spanish documents related to the subject.
      M 4/5   2

2332. HUNT, CHESTER L. Moslem and Christian in the Philippines. Pac. Aff. 28, no. 4 (Dec. 1955), 331-349.
  Doherty: Z 3   7

2333. ITURRALDE, JULIA. The development of Filipino anticlericalism during the Spanish regime: an analytical study of social change. 1955. Thesis (M.A.) - Ateneo de Manila.
  Doherty: Z 3   7

I. GENERAL. RELIGION. Ecclesiastical Organization

2334. JUAN DE LA CONCEPCIÓN. Historia general de Philipinas. Manila, A de la
Rosa y Balagtas, 1788-1792. 14v.
    Legarda: M   5   2
    Phelan: H   4/5   2/3
    Wickberg: Valuable for factual reference.
                  M   5   2/3

2335. KAVANAGH, JOSEPH J. The"Iglesia ni Cristo". PS 3, no. 1 (Mar. 1955), 19-42.
    Doherty: Careful account.
              Z   4   7

2336. LAUBACH, FRANK C. Islam in the Philippines. Moslem World 13, no. 1 (Jan. 1923), 57-66.

2337. _____. The people of the Philippines; their religious progress and preparation for spiritual leadership in the Far East. New York, George H. Doran Company, 1925. 515p.
    Gowing: Often cited, but tends to be homiletical rather than factual.
              M   3   7

2338. [LYNCH, FRANK]. Aglipayanism. (In: Human Relations Area Files, Inc. Area handbook on the Philippines. Chicago: Univ. of Chicago for the Human Relations Area Files, Inc., 1956. v.2. p.687-717)
    Doherty: Very comprehensive and objective history.
              E   4   7

2339. [_____]. Catholicism. (In: Human Relations Area Files, Inc. Area handbook on the Philippines. Chicago: Univ. of Chicago for the Human Relations Area Files, Inc., 1956. v.2. p.476-686)
    Doherty: Excellent summary account.
              E   4   7

2340. [_____]. Iglesia ni Kristo. (In: Human Relations Area Files, Inc. Area handbook on the Philippines. Chicago: Univ. of Chicago for the Human Relations Area Files, Inc., 1956. v.2. p.718-729)
    Doherty: Excellent.
              E   4   7

2341. _____. Town fiesta: an anthropologist's view. Philippines International 6, no. 6 (May 1962), 4-11, 26-27. (Also published in Human Relations Area Files, Inc. Area handbook on the Philippines. Chicago: Univ. of Chicago for the Human Relations Area Files, Inc., 1956. v.2. p.621-645, 674-681)
    Doherty: Good, popular presentation.
              Z   3   7

2342. [_____ and JACQUES AMYOT]. Chapter 9. Organized religion. (In: Human Relations Area Files, Inc. Area handbook on the Philippines. Chicago: Univ. of Chicago for the Human Relations Area Files, Inc., 1956. v.2. p.471-744)
    Doherty: Excellent.
              E   4   7

2343. MARTIRES, MYRNA. Folk festivals of the Philippines. Manila, 1968. 16p.

I. GENERAL. RELIGION. Ecclesiastical Organization

(Aspects of Philippine Culture, 6)
"Sixth in a series of lectures presented by the National Museum and sponsored
by Ambassador and Mrs. William McC. Blair, Jr."

2344. MEDINA, JUAN DE. Historia de los sucesos de la Orden de n. gran P.
S. Agustin de estas islas Filipina-----Manila, Chofré y comp., 1893. 279p.
(Biblioteca histórica Filipina [v.4]) (In: Blair and Robertson. v.23:121-
297 and v.24:29-179)
    Phelan: H   5   2/3
    Wickberg: M   5   7

2345. MURILLO VELARDE, PEDRO. Historia de la provinica de Philipinas de la Compañia de Jesus: segunda parte, que comprehende los progresos de esta provincia desde el año de 1616 hasta el de 1716. Manila, 1749.

2346. O'SHAUGHNESSY, THOMAS J. Philippine Islam and the Society of Jesus. PS 4,
no. 2 (Ignatian No., 1956), 215-245.
    Doherty: Scholarly and objective.
         Q   4   7

2347. PÉREZ, ANGEL, Comp. Relaciones Agustinianas de las razas del norte de Luzon,
coleccionadas por el Rdo.P. fray Angel Pérez. Manila, Bureau of Public Printing, 1904. 411p. (Department of the Interior. Ethnological survey. Publications. v.3. Spanish edition)

2348. PHILIPPINES CHRISTIAN YEAR BOOK 1962-1963. Benjamin I. Guansing, ed. Manila,
Union Theological Seminary, 1962. 161p.
    Doherty: Valuable source.
         M   3   6
    Gowing: A useful compendium marred by careless editing.
         M   3   6

2349. PHILIPPINES HISTORICAL COMMITTEE. The beginnings of Christianity in the Philippines. Papers read at the historical symposium held at the National Library Auditorium from April 10-11, 1965. Manila, 1965. 254p.
    Doherty: Useful but uneven.
         W   4   2
    Gowing: A symposium of essays of uneven scholarship and quality,
         but generally good.
         W   3/4   2

2350. PILAR, MARCELO HILARIO DEL. La Soberanía monacal en Filipinas. Apuntes sobre la funesta preponderancia del fraile en las islas, asi en lo politico, como e
lo económico y religioso. Barcelona, Imprenta de F. Fossas, 1888. 76p.
    Gowing: Reflected popular animosity towards friars.
         J   3   3

2351. POETHIG, RICHARD P. The Philippine Independent Church: the agony of Philippine nationalism. SJ 14, no. 1 (First Quarter, 1967), 27-54.

2352. _____. Philippine social issues from a Christian perspective. Manila,
United Church of Christ in the Philippines, 1963. 222p.
Cited in Biblio. of Asian Studies, 1964. p.152.
    Doherty: Valuable.
         M   3   6

    Gowing: A symposium of essays.
                     M   3/4   6

2353. _____. Summary of a study on background of Protestant seminarians. PSR 13,
    no. 2 (Apr. 1965), 85-90.
         Gowing: A Protestant counterpart to Doherty's The Image of the
                          Priest.
                     M   5   6

2354. RIBADENEIRA, MARCELO DE, O.F.M. Historia de las islas del Archipiélago Fili-
    pino y reinos de la Gran China, Tartaria, Cochinchina, Malaca, Siam, Cambodge
    y Japón. Madrid, La Editorial Católica 1947. 652p. (Colección España misi-
    onera, 3)

2355. RIVERA, JUAN A. The Aglípayan movement. PSSHR 9, no. 4 (Dec. 1937), 301-
    328; 10, no. 1 (Feb. 1938), 9-34.
         Gowing: The earliest extensive study of the PIC, done by an Agli-
                          payan.
                     G   4   4

2356. ROBERTSON, JAMES A. The Aglipay schism in the Philippines. Catholic Histori-
    cal Review 4, no. 3 (Oct. 1918), 315-344.

2357. ROTZ, HENRY W. A study of the recruitment, training, support and performance
    of church leaders in three Protestant denominations in the Philippine Federa-
    tion of Christian Churches. Ithaca, 1956. 442p. Thesis (Ph.D.) - Cornell
    Univ.
         Gowing: A reliable, pioneering study.
                     -     4/5   6

2358. SAN ANTONIO, JUAN FRANCISCO DE. Chronicas de la apostolica Provincia de S.
    Gregorio de religiosos descalzos de n.s.p. S. Francisco en las Islas Phil-
    ipinas, China, Japon, etc. 2v. Manila, 1738-1744. 3v.

2359. SCOTT, WILLIAM HENRY. The Philippine Independent Church in history. SJ 10,
    no. 3 (July/Sept. 1963), 298-310.
         Doherty: Scholarly and objective.
                     E   4   7
         Gowing: A highly readable interpretation.
                     E   4   7

2360. SITOY, T. VALENTINO, JR. The coming of Protestant missions to the Philip-
    pines. SJ 14, no. 1 (First Quarter 1967), 1-26.

2361. _____. The search for unity among non-Roman Christians in the Philippines.
    SJ 12, no. 2 (Apr./June 1965), 196-210.
         Gowing: A useful summary and interpretation.
                     Y   3   7

2362. STA. ROMANA, JULITA REYES. The Iglesia ni Kristo: a study. JEAS 4, no. 3
    (July 1955), 329-437. (His M.A. thesis - Univ. of Manila, 1955)
         Gowing: -   4   7

2363. _____. Membership and the norm of discipline in the Iglesia ni Kristo.

PSR 3, no. 1 (Jan. 1955), 4-14.
>   Gowing: Based on the author's fine M.A. thesis on the I.N.K.
>   -   4   7

2364. WISE, FRANCIS H. The history of the Philippine Independent Church (Iglesia
Filipina Independiente). 1955. 273p. Thesis (M.A.) - U.P.
Cited in Compilation of graduate theses . . . p.289.
>   Gowing: M   3   7

Religious Beliefs and Practices

2365. ARENS, RICHARD. Religious rituals and their socio-economic implications in
Philippine society. PSR 7, nos. 1/2 (Jan./Apr. 1959), 34-45.
Commentary by Timoteo Oracion, p.46-50.
>   Doherty: E   3   7
>   Hunt: E   5   6

2366. BUENAVENTURA, TEODOSIO. Tendencies in religion among our youth. PSSHR 5,
no. 2 (Apr. 1933), 137-140.
>   Doherty: Interesting data, well presented.
>   Z   3   6

2367. BULATAO, JAIME. Case study of a Quezon City poltergeist. PS 16, no. 1
(Jan. 1968), 178-188.

2368. _____. Religion and healing. Medical Forum 4, no. 3 (1961), 141-143.
Cited in Ateneo de Manila Univ., Faculty publications as of Feb., 1967.
p.18.
>   Doherty: Good, interesting data.
>   P   3   7

2369. _____. Two views of creation and two views of creatures. Conference Bulletin of the Archdiocese of New York 29, no. 2 (1952), 82-89.
Cited in Ateneo de Manila Univ., Faculty publications as of Feb., 1967.
p.18.
>   Doherty: Interesting data.
>   P   3   6

2370. CONCEPCION, MERCEDES B. Ritual mourning: a cross-cultural comparison. PSR
10, nos. 3/4 (July/Oct. 1962), 182-186.
>   Doherty   Z   3   7

2371. _____. Ritual mourning: culturally specified crowd behavior. AQ 35,
no. 1 (Jan. 1962), 1-9.
>   Doherty: Z   3   7

2372. DEATS, RICHARD L. Nationalism and Christianity in the Philippines. Dallas,
Southern Methodist Univ. Press, 1968. 207p.
Suggested by Gowing.

2373. DEMETRIO, FRANCISCO. Death: its origin and related beliefs among the early

Filipinos. PS 14, no. 3 (July 1966), 355-395.
    Doherty: Useful but one-sided.
          Z   3   7

2374.   _____. The Engkanto belief: an essay in interpretation. PSR 16, nos.
3/4 (July/Oct. 1968), 136-143.

2375. DOHERTY, JOHN F. The role of women in the church. Proceedings of Student
Catholic Action Seminar. Baguio City, Mar. 1965.
Cited in Ateneo de Manila Univ., Faculty publications as of Feb. 1967. p.38.
    Almanzor   Z   4   6

2376. _____. Sociology and religion: religious maturity. PS 12, no. 4 (Oct.
1964), 681-698.
    Doherty: Valuable insights into Philippine religion.
        Z   3   7

2377. _____. Sociology and the study of religion. PS 12, no. 3 (July 1964),
473-493.
    Doherty: Valuable insights into Philippine religion.
        Z   3   7

2378. DONAHUE, ELIZABETH ANN. A study of the psychological characteristics of
three sub-groups in a religious congregation of women as revealed by a battery of standardized tests. 1963. 177p. Thesis (M.A.) - Ateneo de Manila
Univ.
    Doherty: Very interesting study.
        Z   3   7

2379. FELIX, ALFONSO, JR. Religion and economics: a lawyer's comments on McHale,
Hollnsteiner and Espiritu. PEJ 2, no. 2 (Second Semester 1963), 211-223.
    Legarda: O   4   7

2380. FOX, ROBERT B. The function of religion in society. Practical Anthropology
6, no. 5 (Sept./Oct. 1959), 212-218.
    Doherty: Good, but assumes functional as only valid scientific ap-
            proach.
        E   3   7

2381. FRANCISCO, JUAN R. Notes on the Indo-Philippine images. (In: Zamora,
Mario D., ed. Studies in Philippine anthropology (In honor of H. Otley
Beyer). Quezon City, Alemar-Phoenix, 1967. p.117-127)

2382. GONZALES, ENRIQUE. The baptismal rites in Filipino Christian churches. PS
16, no. 1 (Jan. 1968), 160-168.

2383. GONZALEZ, MARY A. The religious minorities in the Philippines. Unitas 36,
no. 3 (Sept. 1963), 366-372.

2384. HART, DONN V. The Filipino villager and his spirits. Solidarity 1, no. 4
(Oct./Dec. 1966), 65-71.
    Doherty: Good.
        E   3   7

2385. HOUSTON, CHARLES O., JR. An introduction to a discussion on religious

acculturation. PSR 6, no. 1 (Jan. 1958), 8-13.
    Doherty: Good.
              H   3   7

2386. HUNT, CHESTER L. Religion and society. (In: Hunt, Chester L. and others. Sociology in the Philippine setting. Rev. ed. Quezon City, Phoenix Publishing House, 1963. p.173-193)

2387. _____. Religion and the businessman. DR 1, no. 3 (July 1953), 302-311.
    Hunt: Z   3   7

2388. JOCANO, F. LANDA. Filipino Catholicism: a case study in religious change. AS 5, no. 1 (Apr. 1967), 42-64.

2389. _____. Filipino folk Catholicism. Philippine Educational Forum 15, no. 3 (Nov. 1966), 41-60.

2390. _____. Notes on Philippine divinities. AS 6, no. 2 (Aug. 1968), 169-182.

2391. KROEBER, ALFRED L. ...The history of Philippine civilization as reflected in religious nomenclature. American Museum of Natural History. Anthropological Papers 19, pt. 2 (1918), 35-67.
    Doherty: Excellent.
              E   4   7

2392. LARSON, DONALD N. Church, plaza, and marketplace. Practical Anthropology 10, no. 4 (July/Aug. 1963), 167-174.

2393. MINTON, FRANK LEWIS. The Asuang. PM 26, no. 1 (June 1929), 23, 38-39.

2394. OCAMPO, GALO B. The religious element in Philippine art; address at the opening exercises of the academic year 1965-1966. Manila, Univ. of Santo Tomas. 1966. 130p.
    Doherty: Z   3   7

2395. OOSTERWAL, GOTTFRIED. Messianic movements. PSR 16, nos. 1/2 (Jan./Apr. 1968), 40-50.

2396. ORACION, TIMOTEO. Commentary on "religious rituals and their socio-economic implications in Philippine society". PSR 7, nos. 1/2 (Jan./Apr. 1959), 46-50.

2397. PHELAN, JOHN LEDDY. Pre-baptismal instruction and the administration of baptism in the Philippines during the sixteenth century. Americas 12, no. 3 (July 1955), 3-23.

2398. QUIRINO, CARLOS and MAURO GARCIA. The manners, customs, and beliefs of the Philippine inhabitants of long ago; being chapters of "a late 16th century Manila manuscript", transcribed, translated and annotated. PJS 87, no. 4 (Dec. 1958), 325-453. 16 plates.

2399. RAMOS, MAXIMO. Necromancy in the barrio. PM 30, no. 5 (Oct. 1933), 188-189. Reprinted: JEAS 4, no. 2 (Apr. 1955), 288-291.

2400. _____. Secrets in the barrio funeral. Philippine Magazine 34, no. 11 (Nov. 1937), 498, 502, 504.

2401. _____. Some other-world inhabitants of the Philippine countryside. PM
Part I. 33, no. 7 (July 1936), **347**, 359-362.
Part II. 33, no. 10 (Oct. 1936), 506-508.

2402. RAVENHOLT, ALBERT. Religion enters Philippine schools and politics. AUFSR.
Southeast Asia Series 3, no. 25 (Sept. 22, 1955), 14p. (AR-11-'55)

2403. REYNOLDS, HARRIET R. The Filipino **family** and the church. CC 2, no. 4
(July/Aug. 1962), 5-15.
  Hunt: E 4   -

2404. RIZAL Y ALONSO, JOSE. The indolence of the Filipino...Manila, 1913. 66p.
Pub. in La Solidaridad, no. 35059, July 15-Sept. 15, 1890. This ed. tr. by
Charles Derbyshire and ed. by Austin Craig.
Cited in Doris Welsh, Catalogue of printed materials relating to the Philippine Islands...p.108.
  Doherty: A work of importance by the national hero.
       Z 5 7

2405. SCHUMACHER, JOHN N. The depth of Christianization in early seventeenth-century
Philippines. PS 16, no. 3 (July 1968), 535-539.

2406. _____. Some historical considerations on the evangelization of the Philippines. CS 2, no. 4 (Dec. 1965), 222-237.
  Doherty: Excellent article by a very competent historian.
       H 4 1

2407. ZOBEL DE AYALA, FERNANDO. Philippine religious imagery. Quezon City, Ateneo
de Manila, 1963. 154p.
  Doherty: Excellent.
       R 4 7
  Gowing: Now a standard reference; illustrated.
       R 4 7

SEX AND REPRODUCTION

2408. ALCONIS, MARIA S. An analytical study of the social problem of illegitimacy
in the Philippines. 1960. Thesis (M.A.) - Univ. of Sto. Tomas.
Cited in Compilation of Graduate Theses...p.420.
  Luna: Descriptive analytical study.
       S 3 6

2409. CONCEPCION, MERCEDES B. Fertility differences among married women in the
Philippines. 1963. Thesis (Ph.D.) - Univ. of Chicago.
  Luna: Descriptive statistical analytical study.
       S 4 7
  Madigan: Excellent monograph on fertility in Philippines, based on

I. GENERAL. SEX AND REPRODUCTION

1956 & 1958 PSSH data.
S   4   6

2410. _____. On fertility and family planning in the Philippines. ERJ 14, no. 1 (June 1967), 41-52.

2411. _____ and WILHELM FLIEGER. Studies of fertility and fertility planning in the Philippines. Demography 5, no. 2 (1968), 714-731.

2412. DOMANTAY, JUANITA P. The socio-economic problems of unwed mothers. SW 6, no. 3 (Mar. 1961), 551, 556.
  Luna: Descriptive analytical study with broad application.
      S   4   6

2413. HAWLEY, AMOS H. Fertility in an urban population in the Philippines. Phil. Stat. 2 (Dec. 1953), 270-288.
  Reprinted in U.P. Institute of Public Administration. Papers in demography and public administration. Manila, 1954. p.27-45.
  Luna: Descriptive statistical analytical study.
      Z/S   4   6
  Madigan: Z/S   3/5   6

2414. JUPP, KATHLEEN M. Urban-rural differentials in the fertility of married women in the Philippines in 1956. Phil. Stat. 9, no. 2 (June 1960), 60-71.
  Luna: Descriptive statistical analytical study.
      S   4   6
  Madigan: S   3   6

2415. MANALILI, ALFREDO LUIS CURA. The family planning movement and the Protestant's view. Unitas 39, no. 3 (Sept. 1966), 383-399.

2416. NAZARET, FRANCISCO V., A. DIAZ and K. V. RAMACHANDRAN. Differential fertility by occupational groups in the Philippines. Phil. Stat. 11, no. 1 (Mar. 1962), 2-19.
  Luna: Descriptive statistical analytical study.
      N   4   6
  Madigan: S   3   6

2417. _____ and HIDALGO V. CHAVES. Fertility survey of 1963 in the Philippines. PSR 12, nos. 1/2 (Jan./Apr. 1964), 5-16.
  Luna: Descriptive statistical study.
      N   4   6
  Madigan: S   3   6

2418. PADUA, REGINO G. A study of the incidence of illegitimate births among Filipinos. Philippine Islands Medical Ass. Journal 21, (1932), 430-439.
  Cited in Charles O. Houston, A preliminary bibliography of Philippine anthropology....JEAS, Jan. 1953)
  Luna: Descriptive analytical study.
      D   4   4

2419. SOMERS, SISTER MARIE ELISE. The fertility problems as viewed by three leading Dutch theologians. Unitas 39, no. 3 (Sept. 1966), 368-382.
  Luna: Analytical review of the writings of three Dutch theologians.

250

I. GENERAL. SEX AND REPRODUCTION

```
                    M/N    4      6
      Madigan:       M    2/3     6
```

SOCIAL PROBLEMS

2420. ALDABA-LIM, ESTEFANIA J. Girls juvenile delinquency in the Philippines.
1938. 296p. Thesis (M.A.) - U.P.
```
      Almanzor:       P     5      4
```

2421. ANGELES, SIXTO DE LOS. Estudios sobre antropología criminal en las Islas
Filipinas....Manila, Bureau of Printing, 1919. 163p.

2422. _____. El problema de la prostitución en Filipinas. Revista Filipina de
Medicina y Farmacia 12, no. 4 (Abril 1921), 97-103.

2423. AQUINO, BELINDA A. and APRODICIO A. LAQUIAN. Squatter economics and public
policy. PJPA 11, no. 4 (Oct. 1967), 286-297.

2424. ASHBURN, FRANKLIN G. Some police problems and paradoxes in Manila. Lipunan
1, no. 1 (1965), 17-23.

2425. BOGARDUS, EMORY S. Social problems in the Philippines. Sociology and Social
Research 21, (July/Aug. 1937), 565-570.

2426. CARROLL, JOHN J. and SALVADOR. A. PARCO. Social organization in a crisis situation: the Taal disaster, a research report submitted to the Asia Foundation. Manila, Philippine Sociological Society, 1966. 59p. (PSS Special
papers, no. 1)
```
      Bulatao:       A very scholarly gathering of data and analysis.
                      Z     5      6
      Guthrie:        Z     4      6
```

2427. DOHERTY, JOHN. Crime: a symptom of change. PSR 13, no. 1 (Jan. 1965), 14-
18.
```
      Almanzor:       Z     4      6
```

2428. FIERRO, VITO N. DEL. The solution to the country's social ills. EQ 5,
no. 1 (June 1957), 75-78.
```
      Almanzor:       -     3      6
```

2429. GOMEZ, C. M. FR. ANTONIO VENCES. Study and analysis of criminality among
Filipino youth. 1948. Thesis (Ph.D.) - Univ. of Santo Tomas.
Cited in Compilation of graduate theses...p.428.
```
      Almanzor:       -     5      6
```

2430. LAQUIAN, APRODICIO A. The meaning of Tondo. Solidarity 3, (Jan. 1968), 56-
69.

2431. MACARAIG, SERAFIN E. Social problems. Manila, Educational Supply Co., 1929.
431p.
```
      Almanzor:       Z     5      4
```

251

I. GENERAL. SOCIAL PROBLEMS

        Coller: Social problems book by first Filipino Ph.D. in sociology.
                       Takes controversial stands in the E. A. Ross tradition.
                       Z   4   7

2432. MATELA, ARCADIO G. The rural areas - two views: I. Rural social problems.
       Barrio Courier 1, no. 6 (Apr. 1956), 4, 24.
       Cited in Index to Philippine Periodicals, v.1, p.241.
            Almanzor: Y   3   6

2433. _____. Rural social problems. PJE 36, no. 5 (Oct. 1957), 290-291, 329.
       Cited in Index to Philippine Periodicals, v.3, p.247.
            Almanzor: Y   3   6

2434. OPPENFELD, HORST VON. Some internal causes of rural poverty in the Philip-
       pines. Malayan Economic Review 4, no. 1 (Apr. 1959), 42-53.

2435. PHILIPPINE ISLANDS. OFFICE OF PUBLIC WELFARE COMMISSIONER. The government
       orphanage. Manila, Bureau of Printing, 1921. 19p.
            Almanzor: W   3   4

2436. _____. PUBLIC WELFARE BOARD. A report on child welfare work in the Philip-
       pine Islands submitted by Dr. Jose Fabella, Secretary, Public Welfare Board,
       and Director, Bureau of Dependent Children. (English and Spanish) Manila,
       Bureau of Print., 1920. 39p.
            Almanzor: D   4   4

2437. PHILIPPINE MENTAL HEALTH ASSOCIATION, INC. A study for the prevention of
       juvenile delinquency in the Philippines. 1958. Quezon City, Philippine
       Mental Health Association. Booklet, 30p.
       Source: Ateneo de Manila. Institute of Philippine Culture. Author/title
       cards to the Research Data Files.
            Almanzor: W   3   6

2438. [PHILIPPINES (REPUBLIC) OFFICE OF THE PRESIDENT]. SPECIAL COMMITTEE REPORT.
       Squatting and slum dwelling in metropolitan Manila. PSR 16, nos. 1/2 (Jan./
       Apr. 1968), 92-105.

2439. STONE, RICHARD L. and JOY MARSELLA. Mahirap: a squatter community in a
       Manila suburb. (In: Bello, Walden F. and Alfonso de Guzman II, eds.
       Modernization: its impact in the Philippines, III. Quezon City, Ateneo de
       Manila Univ. Press, 1968. p.64-91) (IPC Papers no. 6.)

2440. U.N. DEPT. OF SOCIAL AFFAIRS. Comparative study on juvenile delinquency:
       Part IV. Asia and the Far East, New York: 1953. 123p. (U.N. Document ST/
       SOA/SD/1, add. 3)
            Almanzor: W   4   6

2441. VIBAR, ELISEO A. Understanding the Filipino character and the prevention of
       crimes. Unitas 38, no. 4 (Dec. 1965), 559-569.
            Almanzor: 0   3   6

2442. ZABALLERO, FRINE' C. Juvenile delinquency in the Philippines. FTY (1961),
       242-246.
            Almanzor: 0   4   6

SOCIAL WORK

2443. ALMANZOR, ANGELINA C. Philippine experiences in the development of indige-
nous teaching materials for social work. SW 9, (Nov./Dec. 1964), 98-99.
Source: Index to Periodicals (U.P. Library. Filipiniana Section)
Almanzor: S 5 6

2444. _____ and OTHERS. The social work concepts of self-determination and con-
fidentiality viewed within Philippine value orientation. Manila, Philippine
School of Social Work, 1965.
Cited in International Social Work 12, no. 1 (1969), p.80.

2445. BENETUA, NESTORA L. A historical survey of social work in the Philippines
from the Spanish era to the present, 1954. CEU.GFS 6 (1955), 259-274.
Almanzor: S 4 6

2446. CROOKES, SPENCER H. A private talk to and about our social work profession
in the Philippines. SW 9, (Sept./Oct. 1964), 82-83.
Source: Index to Periodicals (U.P. Library. Filipiniana Section)
Almanzor: C 3 6

2447. DEATS, RICHARD L. Christian responsibility for social welfare. CC 5, no. 2
(Mar./Apr. 1965), 4-9.

2448. EINSIEDEL, LUZ A. Social work principles and Filipino culture. CC 5, no. 2
(Mar./Apr. 1965), 16-19.

2449. GUZMAN, LEONORA DE. Social planning and social work. SW 9, nos. 9/10
(Sept./Oct. 1964), 76-77, 90.
Almanzor: S 4 6

2450. HUNT, CHESTER L. Social work. (In: Hunt, Chester L. and others. Sociol-
ogy in the Philippine Setting. Rev. ed. Quezon City, Phoenix Publishing
House, 1963. p.326-340)
Almanzor: Z 3 6

2451. JOYA, PETRA R. DE. The role of social welfare in the overall national devel-
opment program. Philippine Economy Bulletin 3, (Nov./Dec. 1964), 39-47.
Source: Index to Periodicals (U.P. Library. Filipiniana Section)
Almanzor: S 4 6

2452. KATZ, ARTHUR. The social worker's role in social policy. SW 7, (Mar. 1962),
810-811.
Source: Index to Periodicals (U.P. Library. Filipiniana Section)
Almanzor: S 4 6

2453. LEGARDA, BENITO JR. The challenge to social work in developing countries.
Central Bank News Digest 17, (Dec. 7, 1965), 2-5.
Source: Index to Periodicals (U.P. Library. Filipiniana Section)
Almanzor: X 4 6

2454. LOZANO, OLIMPIA U. The role of the social worker in government child caring
institutions. SW 2, (May/June 1957), 44-45.
Source: Index to Periodicals (U.P. Library. Filipiniana Section)
Almanzor: S 4 6

2455. MITCHELL, THOMAS A. Social work practice in institutions for children. SW 6, no. 10 (Nov. 1961), 728-731.
Cited in Index to Philippine Periodicals, v.7, p.239.
Almanzor: S   4   6

2456. NATIONAL CONFERENCE OF SOCIAL WORKERS. Proceedings of the first. Published by the Philippine Association of Social Workers in SW 2, (Apr./July 1957), 35-80. (Reviewed in PS, (Dec. 1957), 489-491, by Charles R. McKenney)
Almanzor: W   5   6

2457. OCAMPO, FELICISIMO. Social security and old-age insurance in the Philippines. Philippine Labor 1, no. 7 (Nov. 1962), 7-8.
Almanzor: G   3   6

2458. PARAISO, VIRGINIA A. Social welfare in the Philippines. Survey 88, no. 4 (Apr. 1952), 172-176.
Almanzor: S   5   6

2459. PELAYO, JOSE O. One year of social work. FTY (1965), 263-264, 266, 272.
Almanzor: D   3   6

2460. PHILIPPINES (REPUBLIC) PRESIDENT'S ACTION COMMITTEE ON SOCIAL AMELIORATION. Philippine social trends; basic documents pertinent to long-range social welfare planning in the Philippines, assisted by United Nations consultants. Manila, Bureau of Printing, 1950. 54p.
Verified in Filipiniana 1968, Part I, p.663.
Almanzor: W   5   6

2461. _____. Social amelioration and you; report to the people of the Philippines [prepared by Amado A. Lansang]. Manila, Bureau of Printing, 1949. 41p.
Verified in Filipiniana 1968, Part I, p.663.
Almanzor: W   5   6

2462. The place of religion in social work practice. SW 2, (Dec. 1957), 107-108.
Source: Index to Periodicals (U.P. Library. Filipiniana Section)
Almanzor: W   3   6

2463. QUINTOS, JOSE MA. The decentralization of welfareville institutions. SW 10, nos. 3/4 (Mar./Apr. 1965), 142-143, 159.
Cited in Index to Philippine Periodicals, v.10, p. 206.
Almanzor: G   4   6

2464. STANDER, GOLDA G. Social work and social action in the Philippines. Philippine Educational Forum 3, no. 3 (Third Quarter 1952), 15-20.
Almanzor: C   3   6

2465. SUCGANG, ROBERTO R. Social work in the Philippines. CC 5, no. 2 (Mar./Apr. 1965), 10-15.

2466. U.N. DEPT. OF SOCIAL AFFAIRS. Social welfare information series on current literature and national conferences, vol.4, no. 10. Philippines, Jan./Dec. 1949. 8p. ST/SOA/SER.F/4:10.
Cited in U.N. documents index, 1951. no. 1636.
Almanzor: W   5   6

SOCIOLOGY

2467. BENITEZ, CONRADO, RAMONA S. TIRONA and LEON GATMAYTAN. Philippine social life and progress. Ed. by Hugo H. Miller. Boston, Ginn and Co. 1937. 551p.
    Coller: High school text, well written and fairly objective - factual.
                Y   3   4

2468. CATAPUSAN, BENICIO T. Development of sociology in the Philippines. PSR 5, nos. 3/4 (July/Oct. 1957), 53-57.
    Coller: Z   3   9

2469. _____ and FLORA E. DIAZ-CATAPUSAN. Sociology. 2nd ed. Manila, 1953. 567p.
    Coller: Introductory college text, social problems orientation.
                Z   4   7

2470. COLLER, RICHARD. Notes on applied sociology. PSR 3, no. 2 (Apr. 1955), 11-14.
    Coller: Discussion of problems met while doing field study in a Leyte Village.
                Z   3   6

2471. CORDERO, FELICIDAD V. and ISABEL S. PANOPIO. General sociology focus on the Philippines. Manila, College Professors Publishing Corporation, 1967. 465p.

2472. CUYUGAN, RUBEN SANTOS. Research in sociology: trends, problems, and possibilities. (In Philippines (Republic) National Science Development Board. Inter-Disciplinary Symposia Proceedings, National Science and Technology Week, Nov. 20-26, 1961. Theme: "State of and Trends in Science and Technology in the Philippines". Area VI-Social Sciences. 1963?. 106p. Mimeo. pp.53-63) Discussion: pp.64-67.
    Coller: Attempts to analyse the difficulties impeding sociological development in the Philippines.
                Z   4   7

2473. ESPIRITU, SOCORRO C. and OTHERS. Sociology and social living. Manila, R. P. Garcia Publishing, 1956. 260p.
Source: U.P. Library. Filipiniana Section. Shelflist.
    Coller: High school text - objective, factual, good general overview.
                S   3   7

2474. HOUSTON, CHARLES O. Some views of sociology, social sciences, and scientific objectives: being a selected compilation and discussion of methods, objectives, and ends of human attitudes. PSR 5, nos. 3/4 (July/Oct. 1957), 9-52.
    Coller: Actually an analysis of sociology itself - brings in the philosophy of the social sciences.
                H   4   7

2475. HUNT, CHESTER L. Sociology and national integration. SJ 8, no. 3 (July/ Sept. 1961), 189-197.

2476.   _____ and SEVERINO F. CORPUS. The role and scope of sociology. (In: Hunt, Chester L. and others. Sociology in the Philippine Setting. Rev. ed. Quezon City, Phoenix Publishing House, 1963. p.1-10)
        Coller: College text presentation - useful mention of how soci-
                        ology developed in the Philippines.
                        Z   3   7

2477.   _____ and OTHERS. Sociology in the Philippine setting. Rev. ed. Quezon City, P.I., Phoenix Publishing House, 1963. 373p.
        Coller: College text - some original data - fairly useful analy-
                        sis throughout.
                        Z   3   7

2478.   MACARAIG, SERAFIN E. Community problems; an elementary study of Philippine social conditions. Manila, The Educational Supply, 1933. 212p.
        Coller: Social problems book by first Filipino Ph.D. in Sociology.
                        Takes controversial stands in the E. A. Ross tradition.
                        Z   4   7

2479.   _____. Introduction to sociology. Manila, Educational Supply, 1938. 456p.
        Coller: First general sociology text by a Filipino Ph.D. in soci-
                        ology. Uses E. A. Ross approach.
                        Z   4   7

2480.   _____. Social problems. Manila, P.I., Educational Supply Company, 1929. 431p.
        Almanzor: Z   5   4
        Coller: Social problems book by first Filipino Ph.D. in sociology.
                        Takes controversial stands in the E. A. Ross tradition.
                        Z   4   7

2481.   MECHTRAUD, SISTER M. The scope and field of sociology. PSR 5, nos. 3/4 (July/Oct. 1957), 3-5.
        Coller: Defining the field in terms of its pattern of develop-
                        ment.
                        Z   3   7

2482.   Metasociology: an editorial foreword. PSR 5, nos. 3/4 (July/Oct. 1957), 1-2.
        Coller: Z   3   7

2483.   ONG, GENARO V. On the scope and field of sociology. PSR 5, nos. 3/4 (July/Oct. 1957), 6-7.
        Coller: Further considerations of meta-sociology.
                        Z   3   7

2484.   STOODLEY, BARTLETT H. Sociological theory in the Philippine setting. PSR 3, no. 1 (Jan. 1955), 15-24.
        Coller: Original thinking on the question - stimulating reading
                        for all new to the topic.
                        Z   4   7

2485.   WARRINER, CHARLES K. The prospects for a Philippine sociology. PSR 9, nos. 1/2 (Jan./Apr. 1961), 12-18.
        Coller: Takes a stand on the topic which touched off a strong
                        debate.
                        Z   4   7

STANDARD OF LIVING AND RECREATION

2486. AGCAOILI, T. D. Movies. (In: Feliciano, Gloria D. and Crispulo J. Icban, Jr., eds. Philippine mass media in perspective. Quezon City, Capitol Publishing House, 1967. p.133-161)

2487. ARTIGAS Y CUERVA, MANUEL. Origin and early history of cockfighting in the Philippines. PA 27, no. 1 (June 1938), 1-2.

2488. BARTOLOME, CANDIDO C. Philippine recreational games. Manila, U.P. 1936. 95p.

2489. BERNARDO, GABRIEL A. Sungka-Philippine variant of a widely distributed game. PSSHR 9, no. 1 (Mar. 1937), 1-36.

2490. CULIN, STEWART. Philippine games. AA 2, no. 4 (Oct./Dec. 1900), 643-656.

2491. JENKS, ALBERT E. Tang-ga, a Philippine Pa-Ma-To game. AA 8, no. 1 (Jan./ Mar. 1906), 82-87. 1 plate.

2492. RUNES, I. T. General standards of living and wages of workers in the Philippine sugar industry. Report in the international series of the Institute of Pacific Relations. Manila, Philippine Council, Institute of Pacific Relations, 1939. 42p. (International research series)

TOTAL CULTURE

2493. ALDABA-LIM, ESTEFANIA J. The emotional maturity of a nation. Philippines International 9, (May 1965), 18-22.
Source: Index to Periodicals (U.P. Library. Filipiniana Section)
Jocano: P   3   7

2494. ALZONA, ENCARNACION. Our cultural heritage. FTY (1952), 99-100, 110.
Jocano: Y   3   7

2495. ARANETA, FRANCISCO. The problem of cultural diversity. PS 12, no. 2 (Apr. 1964), 232-243.
Jocano: -   3   7

2496. BANTUG, JOSE P. The composite character of our culture. Unitas 23, no. 3 (Julio/Sept. 1950), 612-618.
Jocano: D   3   7

2497. BARROWS, DAVID P. David P. Barrows' notes on Philippine ethnology, edited by Edward Norbeck. David Prescott Barrows: Bibliography of writing in the Philippine Islands, p.254. JEAS 5, no. 3 (July 1956), 229-254.
Jocano: Excellent reference material.
                E   5   7

2498. _____. A friendly estimate of the Filipinos. Asia 21, (1921), 944-949.

2499. BATACAN, DELFIN F. Looking at ourselves; a study of our peculiar traits as a people. Manila, Philaw Pub., 1956. 301p.
      Jocano: A good humorous essay from layman's point of view.
               Y   3   7

2500. BERREMAN, JOEL V. Filipino stereotypes of racial and national minorities. Pacific Sociological Review 1, no. 1 (Spring 1958), 7-12.
      Jocano: E   3   7

2501. _____. Philippine attitudes toward racial and national minorities. Washington (State) State University, Pullman. Research Studies 25, no. 2 (June 1957), 186-194.
      Jocano: E   3   7

2502. BEYER, H. OTLEY. Philippine ethnography; a collection of original sources relating to the Islands as a whole, or to regions comprehending more than one ethnographic group...Manila, 1918-   .
      Jocano: An excellent source for published and unpublished materials.
               E   5   7

2503. BLUMENTRITT, FERDINAND. Breve diccionario etnográfico de Filipinas. Publicado en "La España Oriental". Manila, Imp. de Sta. Cruz, 1889. 16p.
      Jocano: A   3   7

2504. _____. Diccionario etnográfico de Filipinas. La Política de España en Filipinas 7, (April 15, 1897), 162-167, (April 30, 1897), 207-213, (May 15, 1897), 237-242.
      Jocano: A   3   7

2505. BRIONES, MANUEL. Philippine culture and the new order. Philippine Review 1, (Apr. 1943), 12-15.
      Source: Index to Periodicals (U.P. Library. Filipiniana Section)
      Jocano: G   3   7

2506. CARROLL, JOHN J. Changing patterns of social structure in the Philippines, 1896-1963. Quezon City, Ateneo de Manila Univ. Press, 1968. 236p.

2507. _____. Philippine social organization and national development. PS 14, no. 4 (Oct. 1966), 575-590.
      Jocano: Z   5   7

2508. CASTRENCE, PURA SANTILLAN. State and culture. Comment, no. 5 (First Quarter 1958), 76-86.
      Jocano: G   3   7

2509. CONSTANTINO, JOSEFINA D. The Filipino mental make-up and science. PSR 14, no. 1 (Jan. 1966), 18-28.

2510. _____. Rejuvenating the Filipino mentality. Pillars 1, (June 1944), 27-30.
      Source: Index to Periodicals (U.P. Library. Filipiniana Section)
      Jocano: J   3   7

2511. CONSTANTINO, RENATO. The Filipinos in the Philippines and other essays.

I. GENERAL. TOTAL CULTURE

Quezon City, Filipino Signatures, 1966. 152p.
Jocano: Q   3   7

2512. COSTA, HORACIO DE LA. History and Philippine culture. PS 9, no. 2 (Apr. 1961), 346-354.
Jocano: A brief but informative view on need for rewriting Philippine history.
H   4   7

2513. CRUZ, AMELITA REYSIO. What makes the Filipino mind? Far Eastern Free Masons 44, (Dec. 1963), 37-38.
Source: Index to Periodicals (U.P. Library. Filipiniana Section)
Jocano: J   3   7

2514. CUYUGAN, RUBEN SANTOS. Technical assistance and Philippine society: a sociological view. PJPA 5, no. 3 (July 1961), 194-200.
Jocano: A good essay on Philippine social organization.
Z   4   7

2515. DAROY, PETRONILO BN. The teaching of Pilipino and imagination of culture. UP Research Digest 2, no. 1 (Jan. 1963), 15-18.
Jocano: Q   3   7

2516. DE YOUNG, JOHN E. The nature of culture. (In: Hunt, Chester L. and others. Sociology in the Philippine Setting. Rev. ed. Quezon City, Phoenix Publishing House, 1963. p.25-37)
Jocano: Z   3   7

2517. EGGAN, FRED. Philippine social structure. (In: Guthrie, George M., ed. Six perspectives on the Philippines. Manila, Bookmark, 1968. p.1-48)

2518. [FOX, ROBERT B]. Chapter 1 - General character of the society. (In: Human Relations Area Files, Inc. Area handbook on the Philippines. 1956. v.1, p.1-10) Subcontractor's monograph HRAF - 16.
Jocano: A good generalization on Philippine society.
E   5   7
Warren: E   5   7

2519. _____. The study of Filipino society and its significance to programs of economic and social development. PSR 7, nos. 1/2 (Jan./Apr. 1959), 2-11.
Jocano: E   5   7

2520. [_____ and RICHARD POPE]. Chapter 8. Social organization. (In: Human Relations Area Files, Inc. Area handbook on the Philippines. 1956. v.1, p.413-470) Subcontractor's monograph HRAF - 16.
Jocano   E   5   7

2521. GAFFUD, MIGUEL B. Cultural and spiritual values and nationalism. (In: Abella, Pedro F., ed. Glimpses of Philippine Culture. Published by the Unesco National Commission of the Philippines. Manila, 1964. p.5-14)
Jocano: Y   3   7

2522. GUIANG, HONESTA F. A comparison of expressed values of prospective teachers in American and Philippine cultures. Syracuse, 1964. 153p. Thesis (Ph.D.) - Syracuse Univ.

2523. GUTHRIE, GEORGE M. Conflicts of culture and the military advisor. Institute for Defense Analyses. Nov. 1966. 60p. (Research Paper P-300)
Jocano: P   3   7

2524. _____. Cultural preparation for the Philippines. (In Textor, Robert B., editor: Cultural frontiers of the Peace Corps. Cambridge, Mass. and London, Eng., M.I.T. Press, 1966. p.15-34)

2525. HAMM, DAVID L. Western culture and Philippine life. International Review of Missions 47, no. 188 (Oct. 1958), 386-400.

2526. HERRE, ALBERT W. Some sources of Philippine culture. Mid-Pacific Magazine 49, no. 1 (Jan./Mar. 1936), 39-45.
Jocano: N   3   7

2527. HOLLNSTEINER, MARY R. Regionalism and color as divisive elements in Philippine society. Solidarity 2, no. 9 (Sept./Oct. 1967), 1-4.

2528. JOCANO, F. LANDA. Rethinking Filipino cultural heritage. Lipunan 1, no.1 (1965), 53-72.
Jocano: E   4   7

2529. KALAW, TEODORO M. Cinco reglas de nuestra moral antigua; una interpretación. 2 ed. rev., 1947. 158p. 6 plates. (Philippines (Republic) Bureau of Public Libraries. Manuales de Información, no. 5)
Jocano: H   4   7

2530. LE ROY, JAMES A. Race prejudice in the Philippines. Atlantic Monthly 90, (July 1902), 100-112.

2531. MACARAIG, SERAFIN E. Social attitudes of Filipinos toward foreigners in the Philippines. PSSHR 11, no. 1 (Feb. 1939), 26-33.
Jocano: Z   3   7

2532. MALLARI, ISMAEL V. Footnote to Philippine culture. University of the East. College of Liberal Arts and Sciences Journal 1, no. 1 (1964), 10-22.
Jocano: Y   3   7

2533. _____. Pliant like the bamboo. Philippine Prose & Poetry 4, 179-183.
Jocano: Q   3   7

2534. MANGLAPUS, RAUL S. Philippine culture and modernization. (In: Bellah, Robert N., ed. Religion and progress in modern Asia. New York, Free Press, 1965. p.30-42)
Jocano: G   4   7

2535. MOLINA, ANTONIO M. Filipino culture. Unitas 36, no. 3 (Sept. 1963), 346-351.
Jocano: H   3   7

2536. MORALES, ALFREDO T. The creative Filipino mentality. EQ 10, no. 1 (June 1962), 56-62.
Jocano: Y   3   7

2537. _____. Filipino resurgence through cultural encounter. DR 3, no. 2

(Apr. 1955), 109-122.
Jocano: Y   3   7

2538. _____. For an oriental synthesis. Progress, (1958), 26-29, 31-33.
Jocano: Y   3   7

2539. _____. Philippine-American cultural interaction - an Asian perspective.
Solidarity 2, no. 5 (Jan./Feb. 1967), 27-40.

2540. _____. Westernization and social outlook in the Philippines. PJE 33,
no. 5 (Nov. 1954), 298-300, 349.
Jocano: Y   3   7

2541. MUNARRIZ, NATIVIDAD. Acceptance of American culture among students from
the Philippines, New York, 1960. Thesis (Ph.D.) - Columbia Univ. (Teachers
College)

2542. NABONG, JUAN. Colonial mentality. Philippine Christian 11, no. 3 (Mar.
1959), 8-10.
Source: Index to Periodicals (U.P. Library. Filipiniana Section)
Jocano: Y   3   7

2543. NAKPIL, CARMEN G. The hybrid character of contemporary Filipino culture.
Comment, no. 5 (First Quarter 1958), p.58-63.
Jocano: A short, highly critical essay.
J   3   7

2544. ORR, KENNETH G. The sources on characteristics of the people of the Philippine Islands. Eugene, Dept. of Anthropology, Univ. of Oregon, 1956.
35p.

2545. OSIAS, CAMILO. Filipino traits. National Forum 1, (Aug. 1922), 34-49.
Source: Index to Periodicals (U.P. Library. Filipiniana Section)
Jocano: Y   3   7

2546. PAL, AGATON P. Aspects of lowland Philippine social structure. PSR 14,
no. 1 (Jan. 1966), 31-40.

2547. _____. The people's conception of the world.   (In: Espiritu, Socorro C.
and Chester L. Hunt, eds. Social Foundations of Community Development:
Readings on the Philippines. Manila, Garcia Publishing House, 1964.
p.390-398)
Jocano: Z   4   7

2548. PARDO DE TAVERA, T. H. The new Filipino mentality. National Forum 1,
no. 4 (Oct. 1922), 24-44.
Source: Index to Periodicals (U.P. Library. Filipiniana Section)
Jocano: D   4   4

2549. PASCUAL, RICARDO ROQUE. The social and cultural development of the Philippines and its international consequences. Manila, Philippine Council, Institute of Pacific Relations. [n.d.] 84p.

2550. PATANÑE, E. P. The Filipino image. Solidarity 1, no. 1 (Jan./Mar. 1966),
11-14.

I. GENERAL. TOTAL CULTURE

        Jocano: J   3   7

2551. PÉREZ, ANGEL, comp. Relaciones Agustinianas de las razas del norte de Lu-
zon, coleccionadas por el Rdo. P. fray Angel Pérez. Manila, Bureau of
Public Printing, 1904. 411p. (Philippine Islands. Ethnological survey.
Publications. v.III. Spanish ed.)
        Jocano: M   4   4

2552. PHILIPPINE (REPUBLIC) NATIONAL MUSEUM OF THE PHILIPPINES. Guide book. The
hall of indigenous Filipino cultures. Herran, Manila, Dept. of Education
[1968] 20p. illus.

2553. RAVENHOLT, ALBERT. Filipinos on a bus ride; observations on the contrast
between rural attitudes and Manila's "nationalism". AUFSR. Southeast Asia
Series 7, no. 1 (Mar. 5, 1959), 12p. (AR-2-'59)

2554. RECTO, CLARO M. The resurgence of Filipino culture. Philippine Review 1,
(Mar. 1943), 1-7.
Source: Index to Periodicals (U.P. Library. Filipiniana Section)
        Jocano: G   4   7

2555. RIGGS, FRED W. Commentary on [Robert B. Fox's] 'The study of Filipino society
and its significance to programs of economic and social development'. PSR 7,
nos. 1/2 (Jan./Apr. 1959), 12-15.
        Jocano: V   4   7

2556. _____ . A model for the study of Philippine social structure. PSR 7, no. 3
July 1959), 1-32.
        Jocano: V   4   7

2557. ROCES, ALEJANDRO R. Enhancement of national culture. Philippine Journal
of Govt. Accountants 4, (Oct./Dec. 1962), 29-30+.
Source: Index to Periodicals (U.P. Library. Filipiniana Section)
        Jocano: G   3   7

2558. RODRIGUEZ, E. S. The culture of our forefathers. Phil-China Cultural Journal 1, (Sept. 1947), 1-7.
Source: Index to Periodicals (U.P. Library. Filipiniana Section)
        Jocano: J   3   7

2559. ROMULO, CARLOS P. Our national identity. University College Journal (U.P.)
no. 5 (First Semester 1963/1964), 3-12.
        Jocano: Y   3   7

2560. STURTEVANT, DAVID R. Philippine social structure and its relation to agrarian unrest. 1958. 259p. Thesis (Ph.D.) - Stanford Univ.

2561. SZANTON, DAVID L. Cultural confrontation in the Philippines. (In Textor,
Robert B., ed. Cultural frontiers of the Peace Corps. Cambridge, Mass.
and London, Eng., M.I.T. Press, 1966. p.35-61)
        Jocano: An excellent view of foreigner's experience in another
                   culture.
                   E   5   7

2562. WARRINER, CHARLES K. Myth and reality in the social structure of the

Philippines. PSR 8, nos. 3/4 (July/Oct. 1960), 26-32.

2563. WEIGHTMAN, GEORGE HENRY. A study of prejudice in a personalistic society:
an analysis of an attitude survey of college students-University of the
Philippines. AS 2, no. 1 (Apr. 1964), 87-101.

2564. YABES, LEOPOLDO Y. Mutual appreciation of Eastern and Western cultural
values. DR 8, (Oct. 1960), 567-585.
      Jocano: Y   3   7

2565. ZAMORA, MARIO D. The peasant cultures of India and the Philippines. Ithaca, N.Y., Cornell Univ. 1959.
Cited by Zamora in General Education Journal (U.P.), no. 12 (Second Semester
1966/67), p.188.

TRANSPORTATION

2566. [FOX, ROBERT B.].Chapter 21. Domestic transportation. (In: Human Relations
Area Files, Inc., Area handbook on the Philippines. 1956. v.4. p.1646-
1675)
Sub-contractor's Monograph HRAF-16.
      Luna: Historical descriptive analytical study.
                        E   4   7
      Wernstedt: E   3   7

2567. GALANG, RICARDO E. Types of watercraft in the Philippines. PJS 75, no. 3
(July 1941), 291-306. 13 plates.
      Luna: Descriptive analytical pictorial study.
                        S   5   4

2568. STANFORD RESEARCH INSTITUTE. An economic analysis of Philippine domestic
transportation, final report, by Robert O. Shreve and others. Prepared for
the National Economic Council of the Republic of the Philippines. Menlo Park,
Calif., 1957. 7v. (SRI Project no. IU-1554)
      Luna: Analyzes transportation problems and recommends remedial
                        measures.
                        X/K   4   6
      Wernstedt: Excellent survey of transportation demands and facilities.
                        X/K   5   6

2569. VILLANUEVA, PATROCINIO S. The value of rural roads. Quezon City, Community
Development Research Council, U.P., 1959. 74p.
      Coller: Provides documentation of outcomes that were too often
                        taken for granted.
                        S   5   6
      Luna: Descriptive semi-technical statistical analytical study.
                        S   4/5   6
      Polson: A good study on a topic about which there is little hard
                        data.
                        V   5   6
      Villanueva: V   5   6

2570. WERNSTEDT, FREDERICK L. The role and importance of Philippine inter-island shipping and trade. Ithaca, Southeast Asia Program, Dept. of Far Eastern Studies, Cornell Univ., 1957. 132p. (Data paper no. 26)

        Anderson: A careful study moving from an expansion of the geographic base, historical development, and present-day inter-island shipping pattern in general, to a study of individual major ports. Maps, tables.
                          K   4   5/6

        Coller: Basic field study data - baseline study in its field.
                          K   5   6

        Luna: Historical descriptive analytical study.
                          K   4   7

        Spencer: First hand field study excellent.
                          K   5   7

WOMEN

2571. ABAYA, CONSUELO. The Filipino woman is sitting pretty. Philippine Yearbook, (1950/1951), 68-71.
        Almanzor: Q   3   6

2572. AGUILA, CONCEPCION A. Women in a challenging world. CEU.GFS 7, (1956), 1-6.
        Almanzor: Y   4   6

2573. ALZONA, ENCARNACION. The Filipino woman: a backward glance: 1925-1950. FTY, (1926/1951), 95-96.
        Almanzor: Y   4   4

2574. _____. The Filipino woman; her social, economic, and political status 1565-1933. Manila, U.P. Press, 1934. 94p.
        Almanzor: Y   4   2

2575. _____. Rizal's legacy to the Filipino woman. FTY, (1954), 103-104, 125-130.
        Almanzor: Y   4   6

2576. _____. Rizal's legacy to the Filipino woman. 2d ed., 1956 rev. Pasay City, 1956. 20p.
        Almanzor: Y   4   6

2577. _____. The role of Filipino women in the Republic. FTY, (1953), 99-100, 121-122, 141.
        Almanzor: Y   4   6

2578. _____. The social and economic status of Filipino women, 1565-1932. Manila, U.P. Press, 1933. 33p. (Institute of Pacific Relations. 5th Biennial Conference, Banff, 1933. Data papers)
        Almanzor: Y   4   7

2579. _____. What of the Filipino woman? Philippine Review 1, no. 1 (Mar. 1943),

33-38.
Source: Index to Periodicals. (U.P. Library. Filipiniana Section)
    Almanzor: Y   4   5

2580. ARCEO-ORTEGA, ANGELINA. A career-housewife in the Philippines. (In: Ward,
    Barbara E., ed. Women in the new Asia. Paris, UNESCO, 1963. p.365-373)
    Almanzor: Q   4   6

2581. BASS, FLORA (GARDNER). Philippine women and dolls. Laguna Beach, Calif.,
    Mermaid Books, 1955. 111p.
    Almanzor: J   3   9

2582. BENAVIDES, ENRIQUETA R. The Filipino woman's role. FTY, (1961), 239-241,
    260.
    Almanzor: Y   4   6

2583. DOHERTY, JOHN F. The role of women in the church. Proceedings of student
    Catholic Action Seminar, Baguio City, March 1965.
    Cited in Ateneo de Manila Univ., Faculty publications as of Feb. 1967. p.38.
    Almanzor: Z   4   6

2584. ENRILE-GUTIERREZ, BELEN. The role of women . . . in the economic development
    of the Philippines. U.P. Economic Bulletin, (1960/1961), 2-22.
    Almanzor: Y   4   6

2585. FLORES, PURA M. Career women and motherhood in a changing society. Philip-
    pine Educational Forum 14, no. 1 (Mar. 1965), 50-56.
    Almanzor: Y   4   6

2586. FOX, ROBERT. Men and women in the Philippines. (In: Ward, Barbara E., ed.
    Women in the New Asia. Paris, UNESCO. 1963. p.342-364)
    Almanzor: E   5   6

2587. GAMBOA, MELQUIADES J. The Filipino woman and the law. PSSHR 6, no. 4 (Oct.
    1934), 299-305.
    Almanzor: D   3   4

2588. INTERNATIONAL LABOUR ORGANIZATION. Report. Employment of women and minors
    in the Philippines. Labor Review 1, (Apr. 1965), 33-50.
    Source: Index to Periodicals (U.P. Library. Filipiniana Section)
    Almanzor: W   4   6

2589. KALAW, PURA (VILLANUEVA). Filipino women - the challenge they meet. Manila,
    Crown Print., 1951. 15p.
    Source: U.P. Library. Filipiniana Section. Shelflist.
    Almanzor: Q   3   6

2590. LEGARDA, TRINIDAD F. Philippine women and the vote. PM 28, no. 4 (Sept.
    1931), 163-165, 196-200.
    Almanzor: Q   3   4

2591. _____. The role of the Filipino woman in nation building. FTY, (1962),
    239-240.
    Almanzor: Q   3   6

I. GENERAL. WOMEN

2592. MAGSAYSAY, RAMON. Women in the Philippines. PJHE 6, no. 4 (Apr./June 1955), 3-4.
        Almanzor: G   3   6

2593. MENDOZA-GUAZÓN, MARIA PAZ. The development and progress of the Filipino women. 2nd ed. Manila, Kiko Printing Press, 1951. 72p.
        Almanzor: H   4   6

2594. _____. My ideal Filipino girl. n.p., 1931. 189p.
    Source: U.P. Library. Filipiniana Section. Shelflist.
        Almanzor: H   4   6

2595. _____. Woman's status under independence: a discerning glimpse into the future of fair sex. Philippine Yearbook 1, (1933/1934), 17, 24.
        Almanzor: H   4   4

2596. NAKPIL, CARMEN GUERRERO. The Filipino woman. Philippines Quarterly 1, no. 4 (Mar. 1952), 8-10, 16-17.
        Almanzor: Q   4   6

2597. _____. Woman enough and other essays. Quezon City, Vibal Pub. Co., 1963. 149p.
    Cited in Bibliography of Asian Studies, 1963, p.151.
        Almanzor: Q   4   6

2598. OROSA, SEVERINA (LUNA). Rizal and the Filipino woman. Rizal's liga Filipina. Manila, 1961. 47p.
        Almanzor: D   3   6

2599. OSMEÑA, SERGIO. The moral and spiritual influence of Filipino women. Manila, Bureau of Printing, 1941. 11p.
    Source: U.P. Library. Filipiniana Section. Shelflist.
        Almanzor: G   4   5

2600. PALMA, RAFAEL. In defense of the modern Filipino woman. (In: Philippines (Republic) Bureau of Public Schools. Philippine prose and poetry, v.2. Manila, 1951. p.79-80)
        Almanzor: Y   4   7

2601. PECSON, GERONIMA T. Fifty years of feminist movement in the Philippines. FTY, (1955), 42-44, 79-80.
        Almanzor: Y   4   6

2602. _____. The Philippines. (In: International Institute of Differing Civilizations. 31st Session, Brussels, 1958: Women's role in the development of tropical and sub-tropical countries; report of the XXXIth meeting, held in Brussels on 17th, 18th, 19th and 20th September 1958. Brussels, 1959. p.344-354)

2603. PEREZ, PRESENTACION T. The Filipino woman and her education before the twentieth century. Home Economics (Manila) 1, (Oct. 1963), 2-23.
    Source: Index to Periodicals (U.P. Library. Filipiniana Section)
        Almanzor: Y   3   6

2604. _____. Problems of employed women in certain professional groups in the

Philippines and their educational implications. 1955. 288p. Thesis (Ph.D.)
- Univ. of Minnesota.
Almanzor: Y   5   6

2605. PHILIPPINE ASSOCIATION OF UNIVERSITY WOMEN. Talking things over with the
growing Filipina; a project of the Philippine University Women. Pura Santillan-Castrence, ed. Manila, Bardavon Book Co., 1951. 192p.
Almanzor: Q   4   6

2606. PHILIPPINES. UNIVERSITY. COLLEGE OF EDUCATION. DEPT. OF HOME ECONOMICS.
Towards an educated Filipino womanhood. EQ 6, nos. 1/2 (June 1958/Sept.
1958), 71-79.
Almanzor: W   3   6

2607. POLICARPIO, PAZ T. Filipino women in history. 1924. 126p. Thesis (B.S.)
- U.P.
Almanzor: Y   4   4

2608. RAMOS, MAXIMO. Secrets of the barrio housewife. PM 35, no. 9 (Sept. 1938),
426, 430, 432.
Almanzor: Y   3   4

2609. RODRIGUEZ, FILEMON C. Women and the socio-economic development. Power and
Industry 10, no. 4 (Apr. 1963), 8-10, 12, 26.
Cited in Index to Philippine Periodicals, v.8, p.423.
Almanzor: G   4   6

2610. SAN ANDRES-ZIGA, TECLA. The role of the Filipino woman in the community.
PJN 33, no. 4 (July/Aug. 1964), 194-196, 198.
Almanzor: G   4   6

2611. SAN DIEGO, LOURDES P. Today's Filipina and morality. FTY, (1965), 227,
244.
Almanzor: O   4   6

2612. SUBIDO, TRINIDAD (TARROSA). The feminist movement in the Philippines, 1905-
1955. A golden book to commemorate the golden jubilee of the feminist movement in the Philippines. Manila, National Federation of Women's Clubs,
1955. 76p.
Almanzor: -   4   6

2613. TAGUMPAY-CASTILLO, GELIA and SYLVIA HILOMEN-GUERRERO. The Filipino woman:
a study in multiple roles. Journal of Asian and African Studies 4, no. 1
(1969), 18-29.

2614. TIRONA, RAMONA S. Whither art thou going, woman? Philippine Educational
Forum 11, no. 1 (Mar. 1962), 22-29.
Cited in Bibliography of Asian Studies, 1962, p. 120.
Almanzor: R   4   6

2615. U.S. DEPT. OF LABOR. WOMEN'S BUREAU. Filipino women, their role in prog-
ress of their nation by Felina Reyes. 1951. 9p. (L13.2:F47)
Cited in U.S. Monthly Catalog, 1951.
Almanzor: W   4   6

2616. VEYRA, SOFIA R. DE. The Filipino woman in war and in peace. (In: Philippine Prose and Poetry (Philippines (Commonwealth) Bureau of Education.
v.I, p.122-126)
        Almanzor: Q   4   9

PART II

LUZON

A - BY SUBJECT

GENERAL

2617. AQUINO, SIMEON. Life in Payeo. JEAS 3, no. 4 (July/Oct. 1954), 561-611.

2618. BARROWS, DAVID P. The head-hunters of Northern Luzon. Independent (New York) 55, no. 2841 (May 14, 1903), 1140-1146.
        Maher   G   5   4

2619. _____. A preliminary report of explorations among the tribes of the Cord-
        illera Central of northern Luzon. 1903. 19p. (In: Beyer Collection of
        Filipiniana. v.14/14. paper 98) Microfilm copy at Yale Univ.
        Cited in Harold Conklin, Ifugao bibliography, 1968. p.7.
            Bello: A good pioneer survey but lacks detailed ethnographic
                             studies. One of the few available reports on the region.
                             E   3   4
            Maher: G   5   4

2620. BEYER, H. OTLEY. Headhunters and others of Northern Luzon. The Cablenews-
        American Yearly Review Number, (Aug. 28, 1911), 96, 118.
        Cited in Harold Conklin, Ifugao bibliography, 1968. p.12-13.
        Maher: E   5   4

2621. COLE, FAY COOPER. Distribution of the non-Christian tribes of Northwest-
        ern Luzon. AA n.s. 11, no. 3 (July/Sept. 1909), 329-347. 6 plates.
            Maher: E   5   7
            Scheans: An early article that shaped much thought on the "tribes"
                             of Northern Luzon.
                             E   4/5   7

2622. DOZIER, EDWARD P. Land use and social organization among the non-Christian
        tribes of northwestern Luzon. Symposium: Patterns of land utilization and
        other peoples. American Ethnological Society. Proceedings. 1961. p.2-6.
        Suggested by Bello.
            Bello: An excellent study of Mountain Province cultural ecology.
                             E   5   7

2623. DUFF, ROGER. An ethnographic excursion to the Mountain Province of Luzon,
        Philippines. Polynesian Society. Journal 63, nos. 3/4 (Sept./Dec. 1954),
        234-242. 5 plates.
            Maher: E   5   4

2624. EGGAN, FRED. Some social institutions in the Mountain Province and their
        significance for historical and comparative studies. JEAS 3, no. 3 (Apr.
        1954), 329-335.
            Bello: An excellent discussion of cultural change in the area;
                             presents original view as regards historical reconstruc-
                             tion of Mountain Province institutions.

```
                         E      5       7
        Maher:           E      5       4
        Scheans:         E      4/5     7
```

2625. GALVEY, GUILLERMO. [Diary of expedition to Benguet in 1829]   (In: Scheerer, The Nabaloi dialect, p.173-8) Manila, Bureau of Printing, 1905. p.85-199. (Philippine Islands. Ethnological Survey. Publications. v.II, pt. II-III)

2626. GONZÁLES, JULIO. The Batanes Islands. Manila, Univ. of Santo Tomas Press, 1966. 112p.

2627. GRISHAM, GLEN. Trinidad valley. PM 28, no. 1 (June 1931), 30-31, 44-45.

2628. KEESING, FELIX M. The ethnohistory of Northern Luzon. Stanford, California, Stanford Univ. Press, 1962. 362p. (Stanford anthropological series, no. 4)

        Bello: An excellent attempt at historical reconstruction in the area topping historical and ethnographic materials not previously utilized.
                    E   5   7
        Maher: An important effort to reconstruct the cultural history of Northern Luzon from early records.
                    E   4   7
        Scheans: Standard secondary source.
                    E   4   7
        Thomas: A regional history of indigenous life and culture contact as reconstructed from Spanish published sources. Did not use archival materials in Spain.
                    E   4   7

2629. MADDELA, INOCENCIO B. The Tirong, ancient people of the Babuyan Islands. JEAS 3, no. 1 (Oct. 1953), 97-100.

2630. MALUMBRES, JULIAN. Breves noticias sobre las tribus salvages del norte de Luzon. 1903. 10p. (In: Beyer Collection of Filipiniana. v.14/9. Paper 15) Microfilm copy at Yale Univ.
        Cited in Harold Conklin, Ifugao bibliography, 1968. p.48.
        Maher: M   5   3

2631. _____. Letter to the Provincial from Diadi, January 6, 1887. El Correo Sino-Annamita 21, (1887), 173-192.
        Cited in William Henry Scott, Cordillera bibliography. p.40.
        Maher: M   5   3

2632. _____. Letter to the Provincial from Maguleng. 30 Aug. 1890. El Correo Sino-Annamita 24, (1890), 486-494.
        Cited in William Henry Scott, Cordillera bibliography. p.40.
        Maher: M   5   3

2633. _____. Letter to the Provincial from Quiangan, March 23, 1889. El Correo Sino-Annamita 23, (1889), 417-463.
        Cited in William Henry Scott, Cordillera bibliography. p.40.
        Maher: M   5   3

2634. _____. Letter to the Provincial from Quiangan, June 12, 1889. El Correo
Sino-Annamita 23, (1889), 473-485.
Cited in William Henry Scott, Cordillera bibliography. p.40.
Maher: M   5   3

2635. MANAWIS, MARIANO D. The life of the Nueva Ecija peasant. PM 31, no. 1
(Jan. 1934), 12, 42.

2636. _____. Social relations in the Cagayan. PM 35, no. 5 (May 1938), 235,
245-246.

2637. MILLÁN Y VILLANUEVA, CAMILO. Ilocos Norte, descripción general de dicha
provincia. Manila, Imprenta de "El Eco de Filipinas", 1891. 221p.
Thomas: Almanac and "data-book"--a description of Province near
                 end of Spanish period.
                 G   3   3

2638. NYDEGGER, WILLIAM F. Tarong: a Philippine barrio. Ithaca, 1960. 415p.
Thesis (Ph.D.) - Cornell Univ.
Scheans: Somewhat weak on social organization.
                 E   5   6

2639. PÉREZ, ANGEL. Apuntes para un diccionario etnográfico del norte de Luzon.
(In: Pérez, Angel, ed.:   Relaciones agustinianas de las razas del norte
de Luzon. Manila, Bureau of Printing, 1904. p.345-380) (Philippine Is-
lands. Ethnological Survey. Publications. v.3)
Bello: A good source document for Northern Luzon ethnography.
                 M   4   1-3 (7)
Maher: M   5   3

2640. _____. Relaciones Agustinianas de las razas del Norte de Luzon. Manila,
Bureau of Printing, 1904. 411p. (Philippine Islands. Ethnological Survey.
Publications. v.3)
Eggan: M   3-5   3
Maher: M   5   5

2641. RIVERA CASTILLET, EDVIGIO DE. Cagayan province and her people. Manila,
Community Publishers, 1960. 510p.
Thomas: Compilation of data in style of a country almanac. Pro-
                 fusely illustrated with pictures of places and people.
                 Numerous biographies. Excellent for a cross-section of a
                 northern province.
                 J   3   7

2642. SCHADENBERG, ALEXANDER. Beiträge zur ethnographie von Nord-Luzon (Filipi-
nen). Anthropologischen Gesellschaft in Wien. Mittheilungen 18 (1888),
265-271.
Maher: E   5   3

2643. SCOTT, WILLIAM HENRY. On the Cordillera: a look at the peoples and cultures
of the Mountain Province. Manila, MCS Enterprises, Inc., 1966. 352p.
Bello: An excellent collection of original studies on the Moun-
                 tain Province, particularly on the southern, central and
                 western parts of the area.
                 H/E   4   7

Maher: A collection of previously published articles by a mis-
                sionary-scholar closely familiar with the area.
                M   4/5   7
Scheans: A compilation of Scott's articles, scientific and liter-
                ary.
                M   5   7

2644.   _____. Some calendars of Northern Luzon. AA 60, no. 3 (June 1958), 563-
570.
Bello: One of the very few descriptions of this aspect of Moun-
                tain Province culture.
                H/E   5   7
Maher: M   5   7
Scheans: Excellent survey.
                M   5   7

2645.   _____. Staunton of Sagada: Christian civilizer. Historical Magazine of
the Protestant Episcopal Church 31, no. 4 (Dec. 1962), 306-339.
Scheans: Study of a remarkable missionary.
                M   4/5   7

2645a.   STEWART, KILTON R. The old man of the mountains in Luzon. PM 31, no. 2
(Feb. 1934), 55-56, 85-86.
Maher: E   3   4

2645b.   VILLAVERDE, JUAN FERNANDEZ. [Letter from Aritao] 5 July 1889, El Correo
Sino-Annamita 23, (1889), 486-488.
Maher: M   5   3

2646.   _____. Letter to the Provincial from Ibung. 28 March 1885, El Correo
Sino-Annamita 20, (1886), 7-18.
Cited in William Henry Scott, Cordillera bibliography. p.60.
Maher: M   5   3

2647.   _____. Letter to the Provincial from Ibung. 11 July 1886. El Correo
Sino-Annamita 20, (1886), 19-25.
Cited in William Henry Scott, Cordillera bibliography. p.60. For other
letters by Villaverde, consult this bibliography.
Maher: M   5   3

2648.   _____. Letter to the Provincial from Solano 13 March 1889. El Correo
Sino-Annamita 23, (1889), 411-416.
Cited in William Henry Scott, Cordillera bibliography. p.61.
Maher: M   5   3

2649.   _____. Letter to the Provincial from Solano. 17 October 1889. El Correo
Sino-Annamita 24, (1890), 455-457.
Cited in William Henry Scott, Cordillera bibliography. p.61.
Maher: M   5   3

2650.   _____. Letter to the Provincial from Solano. 28 October 1889. El Correo
Sino-Annamita 24, (1890), 458-460.
Cited in William Henry Scott, Cordillera bibliography. p.61.
Maher: M   5   3

2651. _____. Letter to the Provincial from Solano. 27 Nov. 1889. El Correo Sino-
Annamita (1890), 461-462.
Cited in William Henry Scott, Cordillera bibliography. p.61.
    Maher: M   5   3

2652. WILLCOX, CORNÉLIS DE WITT. The head hunters of Northern Luzon. From Ifugao
to Kalinga, a ride through the mountains of Northern Luzon with an appendix
on the independence of the Philippines. Kansas City, Mo., Franklin Hudson
Pub. Co., 1912. 304p.
    Maher: T/H   3   4

2653. WILSON, LAURENCE L. The skyland of the Philippines. Baguio, Baguio Printing & Pub. Co., Inc., 1953. 184p.
    Bello: A good introduction to life and culture in the Mountain
                Province. Presents some original data on Benguet culture
                and administration of the Mountain Province.
                B/J   4   7
    Scheans: A wonderful potpourri on the Mountain Province.
                F   4/5   7

2654. _____. Some notes on the mountain peoples of North Luzon. JEAS Part I
1, no. 3 (Apr. 1952), 54-62. Part II 2, no. 2 (Jan. 1953), 29-36.
5 figs. Part III 3, no. 3 (Apr. 1954), 309-320.
(Originally printed in the Baguio Midland Courier.)
    Maher: F   5   7
    Scheans: Solid information by a gifted "Amateur".
                F   5   7

2655. WORCESTER, DEAN C. Head-hunters of Northern Luzon. [Covers Negritos, Ilongots, Kalingas and Ifugaos] National Geographic Magazine 23, no. 9 (Sept.
1912), 833-930. 102 photos.
    Maher: G   3   4

2656. _____. The non-Christian tribes of Northern Luzon. PJS 1, no. 8 (Oct.
1906), 791-875. 67 plates.
    Maher: G   3   4

Agriculture and Food

2657. ASUNCION, DANIEL F. A study of marketing rice in Nueva Ecija. PA 21, no. 3
(Aug. 1932), 177-193.
    Intengan: A detailed study of methods and cost of marketing rice in
                Nueva Ecija, the rice granary of Luzon.
                C   3   4

2658. BAGUILAT, TEODORO B. Palay marketing on the farm level in Nueva Ecija, Cagayan and Iloilo, 1955-1956. PA 42, no. 1 (June 1958), 18-35.
    Intengan: A detailed account and appraisal of Palay marketing on
                the farm level in three provinces.
                C   4   6
    Sta. Iglesia: Highly useful descriptive research.

Y(G)   5   6

2659.   _____. Some aspects of marketing vegetables in La Trinidad, Mountain Province. PA 39, no. 7 (Dec. 1955), 428-437.
            Sta. Iglesia: Highly useful descriptive research.
                        Y(G)   5   6

2660.   BEYER, H. OTLEY. The origin and history of the Philippines rice terraces. Philippine International 8, no. 2 (June/July 1964), 18-27.
            Maher: E   4/5   7

2661.   BRATTON, C. A. and L. S. ROBERTSON. Farming methods and returns on 126 rice farms in Roxas, Isabela, in 1952. PA 37, no. 9 (Feb. 1954), 534-542.
            Intengan: An economic study among families on owner-operated and tenant-operated farms.
                        C   4   6
            Sta. Iglesia: Highly useful descriptive research.
                        Y   5   6

2662.   CHRISTIE, EMERSON B. Notes on irrigation and cooperative irrigation societies in Ilocos Norte. PJS 9-D, no. 2 (Apr. 1914), 99-115. 1 plate.
            Intengan: Information is given on early attempts to construct irrigation works in Ilocos Norte.
                        G   4   4
            Scheans: Still the only published source on this topic.
                        G   5   7
            Thomas: Only details published to date on first-hand study of important Ilocano institution--the cooperative irrigation society.
                        E   5   4

2663.   DALISAY, AMANDO M. Factors related to income and cost of production of rice on tenant holdings in Cabiao, Nueva Ecija. PA 26, no. 9 (Feb. 1938), 730-756.
            Intengan: An excellent reference on factors that affect income and cost of production of rice tenant holders in Nueva Ecija.
                        C   4   4
            Sta. Iglesia: Highly useful descriptive research.
                        Y(G)   5   4

2664.   DAYYO, SILVERIO C. The rural credit situation and credit experiences of farmers in Bauguen, Ilocos Sur. PA 40, no. 9 (Feb. 1957), 486-497.
            Intengan: The study showed none of the farmers made use of credit facilities set up for them by ACCFA and the rural banks.
                        C   4   6
            Sta. Iglesia: Highly useful descriptive research.
                        G   5   6

2665.   DOZIER, EDWARD P. Land use and social organization among the non-Christian tribes of northwestern Luzon. Symposium: patterns of land utilization and other peoples. American Ethnological Society. Proceedings. 1961. p.2-6.
            Bello: An excellent study of Mountain Province cultural ecology.
                        E   5   7

2666.   GARCIA, NATIVIDAD V. A study of the socio-economic adjustments of two

Ilocano villages to Virginia tobacco production. Quezon City: Community
Development Research Council, U.P., 1962. (Abstract series no. 15)
Cited in Wernstedt and Spencer, The Philippine Island World...1967.

> Thomas: First hand-data on Ilocano (Ilocos Sur and La Union)
> adaptation to Virginia tobacco introduction.
> Z   5   6

2667. MABBUN, PABLO N. Farm credit in Aparri, Cagayan. PA 25, no. 6 (Nov. 1936),
493-506.

> Intengan: Discusses farm credit facilities extended by PNB branch
> in Aparri, Cagayan.
> C   4   4
> Sta. Iglesia: Highly useful descriptive research.
> G   5   4

2668. MANAWIS, MARIANO D. The Cagayan hunter. PM 34, no. 7 (July 1937), 309,
319.

2669. _____. The Cagayan valley peasant as a farmer. PM 34, no. 5 (May 1937),
214, 222, 224.

2670. _____. Tobacco culture in the Cagayan valley. PM 34, no. 12 (Dec. 1937),
548, 550.

2671. _____. The tobacco dealers and the Cagayan valley peasant. PM 35, no. 1
(Jan. 1938), 30, 40, 42.

2672. MERCADO, G. C. Sidelights of the nutrition survey, Ilocos - Mountain Province region, April-June 1960. Philippine Health Journal 8, no. 1 (Mar.
1961), 4-8.

> Intengan: Narrates actual experiences and observations of a nutri-
> tionist in one of its regional surveys.
> C   3   6

2673. MONTILLA, JOSE. The Ipon fisheries of northern Luzon. PJS 45, no. 1 (May
1931), 61-75. 6 plates.

> Intengan: Describes methods of catching the fry of various species
> of gobies that spawn in the sea. Its economic importance
> and conservation are discussed.
> C   5   4

2674. PEREDO, BENJAMIN D., E.J. ECHON and P. C. KUHONTA. Rice mills and cost of
milling palay in Nueva Ecija. PA 41, nos. 1/2 (June/July 1957), 85-106.

> Intengan: A survey which studied milling facilities and factors af-
> fecting cost of milling. Recommendations for improvement
> are given.
> C   4   6
> Sta. Iglesia: Highly useful descriptive and analytical research.
> Y(G)   5   6

2675. PHILIPPINES (REPUBLIC) FOOD AND NUTRITION RESEARCH CENTER. Nutrition survey
of Ilocos-Mountain Province region.
By E. S. Quiogue and others. Manila, NSDB Printing Press, 1963. 88p.
Suggested by Intengan.

> Intengan: A comprehensive assessment of the nutritional status

conducted on a regional scale.
C   5   6

2676.   _____. Nutrition survey of the Cagayan Valley-Batanes region.
By E. S. Quiogue and others. Manila, NSDB Printing Press, 1963. 89p.
    Intengan: A comprehensive assessment of the nutritional status con-
                   ducted on a regional scale.
                   C   5   6

2677.   QUINTANA, VICENTE U. Palay marketing practices of farmers in Gapan and San
Antonio, Nueva Ecija, 1955-1956. PA 41, no. 6 (Nov. 1957), 327-343.
    Intengan: Factors are cited which influence palay marketing prac-
                   tices of farmers in two towns of Nueva Ecija.
                   C   3   6
    Sta. Iglesia: Highly useful descriptive research.
                   Y   5   6

2678.   ROMANO, FELINO B. Warehouses and rice mills in some towns of Nueva Ecija.
PA 38, nos. 2/3 (July/Aug. 1954), 211-224.
    Intengan: Gives information and recommendation for improvement of
                   existing milling and storage facilities in 13 towns in
                   Nueva Ecija.
                   C   5   6
    Sta. Iglesia: Highly useful descriptive research.
                   Y   5   6

2679.   SACAY, FRANCISCO M., QUIRINO T. TAGORDA and GREGORIO B. FERNANDEZ. An economic and social study of tobacco farming in Isabela. PA 33, no. 2 (Oct./
Dec. 1949), 88-96.

2680.   _____ and OTHERS. The economic and social status of rice farmers in the
Ilocos region. PA 40, no. 1 (June 1956), 649-658.
    Intengan: The poor economic status and low living standards of the
                   farm families studied are attributed to small farm size
                   and poor farming methods employed.
                   C   3   6
    Sta. Iglesia: Highly useful descriptive research.
                   Y(G) 5   6

2681.   SCOTT, WILLIAM HENRY. Growing rice in Sagada. PEJ 2, no. 1 (First Semester
1963), 85-96.
    Scheans: M   5   7

2682.   _____. A preliminary report on upland rice in northern Luzon. SWJA 14,
no. 1 (Spring 1958), 87-105.
    Maher: M   5   7
    Scheans: Broke new ground on this topic.
                   M   5   7

2683.   SUTER, CAROL B. Strengthening cooperation and coordination in community nutrition work in Isabela. Philippine Journal of Nutrition 20, no. 2 (Apr./
June 1967), 66-74.

2684.   SUTER, DWAYNE. Technological problems of the Cagayan valley and their possible solution. SJ 11, nos. 1/2 (Mar./June 1964), 76-83.

Intengan: An analysis of the technological problems of the region
                and approaches to the solution of some of them.
                C   3   6

ARCHAEOLOGY

2685. BARTLETT, HARLEY H. Jar burials in the Babuyan group, Philippine Islands.
Michigan Academy of Science, Arts and Letters. Papers 23, (1937), 1-20.
5 plates.
        Solheim: Report on fieldwork in the Babuyan Islands, just north
                        of Luzon.
                        N   5   1/2

2686. KOENIGSWALD, G. H. R. VON. Preliminary report on a newly-discovered stone
age culture from Northern Luzon, Philippine Islands. AP 2, no. 2 (Winter
1958), 69-70. 1 plate.
        Maher: D   5   1
        Scheans: Brief note on an important find.
                        D   5   1
        Solheim: First and only report on palaeolithic tools found in the
                        Cagayan valley by the author.
                        D   5   1

2687. SOLHEIM, WILHELM G., II. Jar burial in the Babuyan and Batanes Islands and
in Central Philippines, and its relationship to jar burial elsewhere in the
Far East. PJS 89, no. 1 (Mar. 1960), 115-148. 10 plates.
        Maher: A   5   1
        Scheans: Beyerian diffusionist study.
                        A   4/5   1
        Solheim: New data and reinterpretation of jar burials found in the
                        Philippines and elsewhere in Asia.
                        A   4/5   1

2688. _____ and TERRY SHULER. Further notes on Philippine pottery manufacture:
Mountain Province and Panay. JEAS 8, nos. 1/2 (Jan./Apr. 1959), 1-10.
        Hart: A   5   7
        Maher: A   5   7
        Sibley: A   5   7

2689. VANOVERBERGH, MORICE and ROBERT HEINE-GELDERN. Der Megalithkomplex auf der
Philippinen-Insel Luzon. Anthropos 24 (Jan./Apr. 1929), 317-321.
        Maher: E   4/5   7
        Solheim: E/A   4?   1

BEHAVIOR PROCESS AND PERSONALITY

2690. LYNCH, FRANK. Philippine values: social acceptance. PS 10, no. 1 (Jan.

1962), 82-99.
Reprinted: Lynch, Frank, compiler, Four readings on Philippine values.
Quezon City, Ateneo de Manila Univ. Press, 1964. 2nd ed. 1964. (IPC Papers, no. 2), p.1-21.
    Bello: An excellent study of Philippine values--one of the first attempts to use value approach to modern Philippine society; presents some useful guidelines for further research.
                E   4   7

BUILDINGS, TOOLS AND EQUIPMENT

2691. LEGARDA Y FERNANDEZ, BENITO. Colonial churches in Ilocos. PS 8, no. 1 (Jan. 1960), 121-158.

2692. SCOTT, WILLIAM HENRY. Cordillera architecture of Northern Luzon. Folklore Studies (Society of the Divine World. Tokyo, Japan) 21 (1962), 186-220.
    Maher: M   5   7
    Scheans: Excellent data.
                M   5   7

CLOTHING, ADORNMENT AND MATERIALS

2693. VANOVERBERGH, MORICE. Dress and adornment in the mountain province of Luzon, Philippine Islands. Catholic anthropological conference. Publications. (Washington, D.C.) 1, no. 5 (Nov. 1929), 181-244.
    Maher: M   5   4
    Scheans: Standard source emphasizing similarities rather than differences.
                M   5   7

COMMUNITY AND COMMUNITY DEVELOPMENT

2694. SACAY, FRANCISCO M. and FLORENDO R. NAANEP. A study of farm, home, and community conditions in a farm village of Ilocos Norte as a basis for formulating a program of rural education. PA 29, no. 7 (Dec. 1940), 555-570.

DRINKS, DRUGS AND INDULGENCE

2695. BEYER, H. OTLEY. Report on the use of a fermented rice drink in Northern
Luzon. (In: The Alcohol industry of the Philippine Islands, Part III, PJS
7-A, no. 2 (Apr. 1912), 97-119)
Maher: E   5   4

ECONOMICS

2696. DAVIS, WILLIAM G. Economic limitations and social relationships in a Philippine marketplace: capital accumulation in a peasant economy. (In: Van
Niel, Robert, ed. Economic factors in Southeast Asian social change. Honolulu, Asian Studies Program, Univ. of Hawaii, 1968. p.1-28) (Asian studies
at Hawaii, no. 2)

2697. GUY, GEORGE SY-CHUAN. A descriptive and comparative study of the economic
life of the mountain tribes of northern Luzon, Philippines. Cebu, 1957.
209p. Thesis (M.S.) - Univ. of San Carlos.
Maher: A useful summary of already published data.
               E   4   7

2698. _____. The economic life of the mountain tribes of northern Luzon, Philippines. JEAS 7, no. 1 (1958), 1-88.
Maher: E   4   7

2699. IRVING, EARL M. and JOSE C. QUEMA. Reconnaissance geology of the Burgos-
Pasuquin area, Ilocos Norte, Philippines. Philippine Geologist 2, no. 3
(June 1948), 1-17. Suggested by Thomas.
Thomas: The only field geologic study of Ilocos Norte (part there-
               of), which puts the sparcity of mineral resources into
               proper perspective.
               N   5   6

2700. PHILIPPINES (REPUBLIC) INDUSTRIAL DEVELOPMENT CENTER. Economic survey of
Ilocos Norte. Manila, 1962? 41p.? Mimeographed.
Suggested by Thomas.
Thomas: A compilation of "Facts" including much data known only
               in government offices in Laoag, the provincial capital.
               G/X   3   6

EDUCATION

2701. DEPRE, ALBERT A. A follow-up study of the graduates of three Catholic high
schools of the mountain province. Manila, 1957. 80p. Thesis (M.A.) -
Ateneo de Manila Univ.
Sals: High standard of scholarship.
               M   5   6

2702. SACAY, FRANCISCO M. Educational and occupational pursuits of former students in the Batangas and Ilocos Norte high schools. PA 32, no. 2 (Oct./Dec. 1948), 114-123.

2703. TADAOAN, PIO M. A critical study of the educational problems of the non-Christian tribes of the mountain province. 1953. 229p. Theses (M.A.) - U.P. Cited in Theses abstracts. I. p.70.
    Sals: Y   4   7

2704. _____. Education in the Mountain Province. Sagada Social Studies (Sagada, Mt. Province), no. 4 (June 1955), 1-61.
Suggested by Warren.
Cited in William H. Scott, Cordillera bibliography. 1970. p.55.
    Warren: Y   5   6

ETHNIC INFLUENCES

2705. REYNOLDS, HARRIET R. Background and distribution of Chinese families in the Ilocos provinces, Philippines. 1959. Thesis (M.A.) - Hartford Seminary.
    Scheans: The sources on the Chinese of the Ilocos.
                   M   5   7
    Thomas: Data principally for Vigan, Ilocos Sur.
                   M/Z   5   6
    Weightman: A valuable contribution to research on Chinese in Philippines but superceded by item no. 2707.
                   E   5   6

2706. _____. Continuity and change as shown by attitudes of two generations of Chinese in the Ilocos Provinces, Philippines. SJ 13, no. 1 (Jan./Mar. 1966), 12-21.
    Weightman: Brief summary of part of findings in Continuity and change in the Chinese family...
                   E   4   6
    Wickberg: E   4   7

2707. _____. Continuity and change in the Chinese family in the Ilocos Provinces, Philippines. 1964. 381p. Thesis (Ph.D.) - Hartford Seminary.
    Weightman: A classic - should be published in modified form.
                   E   5   6
    Wickberg: E   4   7

2708. _____. Marriage as a focal point in cultural orientation of Chinese adults and children in Ilocos. PSR 13, no. 4 (Oct. 1965), 249-259.
    Weightman: Published portion of Ph.D.
                   E   5   6

2709. _____. Reply to Professor Juco's article (January 1966 issue of the PSR) on "Legal aspects of Chinese marriages in the Philippines". PSR 14, no. 3 (July 1966), 167-168.
    Weightman: Brief classification of legalistic points.
                   E   5   6

2710. REYNOLDS, IRA HUBERT. Chinese acculturation in Ilocos: economic, political, religious. 1964. 475p. Thesis (Ph.D.) - Hartford Seminary.
    Weightman: Good treatment of evasion techniques used to affect na-
                  tionalization laws.
                  E   5   6
    Wickberg: E   4   6

2711. _____. Economic acculturation of the Chinese in Ilocos. 1959. Thesis (M.A.) - Hartford Seminary.
    Scheans: M   5   7
    Thomas: Data principally for Vigan, Ilocos Sur.
                  M/S   5   6
    Weightman: M.A. thesis - elaborated later in Ph.D.
                  E   5   6

FAMILY AND KINSHIP

2712. EGGAN, FRED. Some aspects of bilateral social systems in the Northern Philippines. (In: Zamora, Mario D., ed. Studies in Philippine anthropology (In honor of H. Otley Beyer). Quezon City, Alemar-Phoenix, 1967. p.186-203)

2713. NYDEGGER, WILLIAM F. and CORINNE NYDEGGER. The mothers of Tarong, Philippines. (In: Minturn, Leigh and William W. Lambert, eds. Mothers of six cultures; antecedents of child rearing. New York, Wiley, 1964. p.209-221)
    Scheans: Emphasis on child rearing.
                  E   5   6

2714. SCHLEGEL, STUART A. Personal alliances in lowland Philippine social structure. Anthropology Tomorrow 10, no. 1 (1964), 50-65.

2715. TADAOAN, PIO M. The peace pact as a means of social control in the Mountain Province. PSSHR 19, no. 1 (Mar. 1954), 87-103.

FINE ARTS

2716. GRISHAM, GLEN. Benguet cañaos. PM 27, no. 12 (May 1931), 724, 748-749.

2717. JACINTO, VISITACION E. Folk music from the Iloko region and its educational possibilities. 1961. 414p. Thesis (M.A.) - U.P.
    Cited in U.P. theses and dissertations index. p.93.
    Trimillos: Y   3   6

2718. MACEDA, JOSÉ. Chants from Sagada Mountain Province. Philippines. Ethnomusicology. Part I. 2, no. 2 (May 1958), 45-55. Part II. 2, no. 3 (Sept. 1958), 96-107.
    Pfeiffer: R   5   6

Trimillos: One of the first systematic studies for a music.
                  E/R   5   6

FOLKLORE AND MYTHOLOGY

2719. ALARCÓN, RUPERTO. A description of the customs of the peoples of Kiangan,
Bunhian and Mayoyao, 1857. Translated by William Henry Scott. Indiana.
University. Folklore Institute. Journal 2, no. 1 (June 1965), 78-100.
      Maher: M   5   3

2720. BEYER, WILLIAM. Mountain folk art. Manila, 1968. 16p. (Aspects of Philippine Culture, 5) "Fifth in a series of lectures presented by the National
Museum and sponsored by Ambassador and Mrs. William McC. Blair, Jr."

2721. FREI, ERNEST J. Laurence Lee Wilson: recorder of Mountain Province folk-
lore. SLQ 5, nos. 1/2 (Mar./June 1967), 41-66.
Appendix I- The Wilson Collection of Folklore. p.51-60.
Appendix II- Publications of Larry Wilson. p. 61-62.
Appendix III- Aeta Material Collected by Damian Amazona. p. 63-64.

2722. RIGUERA, FLORENCIO. "Sumang": a folk rite in Ilocos. PSR 16, nos. 1/2
(Jan./Apr. 1968), 66-73.

2723. SCHEANS, DANIEL J. A Remontado legend from Ilocos Norte. PS 15, no. 3
(July 1967), 496-497.

GEOGRAPHY AND DEMOGRAPHY

2724. CRUZ, CORNELIO CASTOR. The Mountain Province: a geographic study of its
assets, possibilities and handicaps. NASB 1, no. 4 (Nov. 1931), 343-378.
9 plates.

2725. HERNANDO, MANUEL M. The Batanes islands. PM 31, no. 10 (Oct. 1934), 422-
423.

2726. JAUG, JOSE O. This town called Dolores. PGJ 4, no. 1 (Jan./Mar. 1956),
30-35.
      Spencer: Useful summary on a local town.
                    K   4   7

2727. LUNA, TELESFORO W., JR. Land utilization in Ilocos Norte. PGJ 7, no. 3
(July/Sept. 1963), 133-142.
      Spencer: Land use--agricultural survey, some primary data.
                    K   4/5   6
      Thomas: Summary of physical geography and land use of his native
                    province by the geography professor at the Univ. of the
                    Philippines.

K   4   6

2728. PHILIPPINES (REPUBLIC) BUREAU OF THE CENSUS AND STATISTICS. A social census of Vigan, Ilocos Sur and Lipa, Batangas; a study of postwar human resources of the Philippines based on data secured from the population of two communities, Dec. 1947, conducted jointly as an inter-government project, with the assistance of three consultants of social welfare from United Nations, Lake Success. Manila, 1948. 167p.
Suggested by Scheans.

2729. SALAMANCA, BONIFACIO S. Man's role in changing the surface of Luzon: a skeletal survey. HB 6, no. 4 (Dec. 1962), 337-365.
      Thomas: Publication of a paper first prepared for a graduate seminar in geography of southeast Asia while author was a graduate student at Yale University.
      H   3   7

HEALTH AND SICKNESS

2730. CHENG, CHARLES L. Problems encountered in highland medical practice. PSR 13, no. 2 (Apr. 1965), 90-96.

2731. GRISHAM, GLEN. Pagan priests of Benguet. PM 29, no. 9 (Feb. 1933), 399-400, 420-422.

2732. MANAWIS, MARIANO D. Cagayan peasant health measures. PM 34, no. 10 (Oct. 1937), 451, 456, 458.

2733. WILLETS, DAVID G. General conditions affecting the public health and diseases prevalent in the Batanes Islands, P.I. PJS 8B, no. 1 (Feb. 1913), 49-57.

HISTORY AND CULTURE CHANGE

2734. [ALENCON, FERDINAND PHILIPPE MARIE D'ORLEANS, DUC D'] Lucon en Mindanao. Extraits d'un journal de voyage dans l'Extrême Orient. Avec une carte de l'archipel des Philippines...Paris, Michel Lévy frères, 1870. 222p.

2735. EGGAN, FRED. Comments on assimilation in the Mountain Province. PSSHR 19, no. 1 (Mar. 1954), 104-106.
      Maher: E   5   7

2736. _____. Cultural drift and social change. Current Anthropology 4, no. 4 (Oct. 1963), 347-355.

2737. _____. Some aspects of culture change in the northern Philippines. AA n.s. 43, no. 1 (Jan./Mar. 1941), 11-18.

             Maher: E   5   7
             Scheans: Highly influential article.
                       E   4/5   7

2738. _____. Some social institutions in the Mountain Province and their significa
for historical and comparative studies. JEAS 3, no. 3 (Apr. 1954), 329-
335.
             Maher: E   5   4
             Scheans: Elaborates on the preceding article.
                       E   4/5   7

2739. KEESING, FELIX M. and MARIE KEESING. Taming Philippine headhunters; a
study of government and of cultural change in northern Luzon. Stanford,
Stanford Univ. Press, 1934. 288p.
             Bello: A standard sourcebook for all who want to understand so-
                            cial and political developments in the Mountain Prov-
                            ince. Should be a good reference book for students of
                            Philippine public administration.
                       E   5   7
             Maher: An overview of the Mountain Province during the American
                            period.
                       E   4/5   4
             Scheans: Standard source.
                       E   4/5   7
             Thomas: The standard reference (a classic) on directed cultural
                            change (applied anthropology) on the pagan tribes of
                            Mountain Province.
                       E   4   4

2740. MALUMBRES, JULIAN. Historia de Cagayan. Manila, Tip. Linotype de Santo
Tomas, 1918. 463p.
             Maher: M   4/5   7

2741. _____. Historia de la Isabela. Manila, Tip. Linotype de Santo Tomas,
1918. 676p.
             Maher: M   4/5   7

2742. _____. Historia de Nueva Vizcaya y provincia Montañosa. Manila, Tip.
Linotype de Santo Tomas, 1919. 428p.
             Maher: A useful source on Spanish contacts in the Mountain
                            Province.
                       M   4/5   7

2743. VARGAS, BENITO. The Camiguin No. 2 island; its history and resources. Acta
Manilana 4, no. 2 Series A (Dec. 1968), 110-119.

2744. WILSON, LAURENCE L. A brief history of the Mountain Province, Luzon. JEAS
2, no. 3 (Apr. 1953), 29-38.
             Maher: F   4   7

2745. _____. Mt. Province trends. JEAS 4, no. 1 (Jan. 1955), 51-53.

2746. _____. Occupational acculturation in the Mountain Province. JEAS 3, no. 1
(Oct. 1953), 87-96.
             Maher: F   4/5   7

INDUSTRIES

2747.   CHRISTIE, EMERSON B.   Notes on the pottery industry in San Nicolas, Ilocos
        Norte. PJS 9D, no. 2 (Apr. 1914), 117-121. 3 plates.
              Thomas: First scientific account of techniques used in backyard
                                 "cottage industry" for which poblacion of San Nicolas is
                                 best known.
                                 E   5   4

2748.   _____. Notes on the wood-working industry of San Vincente, Ilokos Sur.
        PJS 7D, no. 4 (Aug. 1912) 231-240. 4 plates.

2749.   _____. The stone industry at San Esteban, Ilokos Sur. PJS 7D, no. 4
        (Aug. 1912), 213-231. 5 plates.

2750.   SCHEANS, DANIEL J.   The pottery industry of San Nicolas, Ilocos Norte.
        JEAS 9, no. 1 (Jan. 1960), 1-38. 26 photos.
              Thomas: A more detailed and up-to-date article, but a companion
                                 piece to Christie's 1914 classic. ("Notes on the pot-
                                 tery industry in San Nicolas, Ilocos Norte.")
                                 E   5   6

2751.   SOLHEIM, WILHELM G., II and TERRY SHULER.   Further notes on Philippine pot-
        tery manufacture: Mountain Province and Panay. JEAS 8, nos. 1/2 (Jan./
        Apr. 1959), 1-10.
              Hart: A   5   7
              Maher: A   5   7
              Sibley: A   5   7

INFANCY AND CHILDHOOD

2752.   MANAWIS, MARIANO D.   Childhood in the Cagayan valley. PM 33, no. 8 (Aug.
        1936), 396, 414.

2753.   NYDEGGER, WILLIAM F.   Tarong; an Ilocos barrio in the Philippines. (In:
        Whiting, Beatrice, ed. Six cultures, studies in child rearing. New York,
        Wiley, 1963. p. 693-867)
        Separately published: Tarong: an Ilocos barrio in the Philippines. New
        York, John Wiley, 1966. 180p. (Six cultures series, v.6)
              Bello: An excellent study of an Iloko village--one of the few
                                 undertaken so far--presents some good ethnography on
                                 Iloko. But contains certain errors on native terms,
                                 particularly on kinship.
                                 E   5   6
              Maher: E   5   6
              Scheans: Abridgement of Tarong: a Philippine barrio. Ph.D. The-
                                 sis - Cornell Univ. 1960.
                                 E   5   6
              Thomas: The most detailed study in existence of an Ilocano bar-
                                 rio, based upon Ph.D. dissertation in anthropology.
                                 Done in northern Ilocos Sur; emphasis in birth-childhood-
                                 adolescence.

E   5   6

2754.   SCOTT, WILLIAM HENRY. Boyhood in Sagada. Anthropological Quarterly 31,
        no. 3 (July 1958), 61-72.
            Maher: M   5   7
            Scheans: A unique study.
                            M   5   7

INTERPERSONAL RELATIONS

2755.   HOLLNSTEINER, MARY R. Reciprocity in the lowland Philippines. PS 9, no. 3
        (July 1961), 387-413.
            Polson: A good discussion of the various categories of this pat-
                            tern.
                            E   4   6

LABOR

2756.   WILSON, LAURENCE L. Occupational acculturation in the Mountain Province.
        JEAS 3, no. 1 (Oct. 1953), 87-96.
            Maher: F   4/5   7

LANGUAGE AND LITERATURE

2757.   FOX, ROBERT B., WILLIS E. SIBLEY and FRED EGGAN. A preliminary glottochro-
        nology for Northern Luzon. AS 3, no. 1 (Apr. 1965), 103-113.
            Maher: E   4/5   7
            Scheans: Implications have never been explored.
                            E   4/5   7
            Ward: Historical study on language separation.
                            A/E   5   6

2758.   SCHEERER, OTTO. Linguistic travelling notes from Cagayan (Luzon). Anthro-
        pos 4 (1909), 801-804.
            Ward: Kalinga vocabulary.
                            L   3   4

2759.   VANOVERBERGH, MORICE. Some undescribed languages of Luzon. Nijmegen, Dek-
        ker & van de Vegt N. V., 1937. 200p. (Publications de la Commission d'
        Enquête Linguistique . . . III)
            Llamzon: Purely lexical lists of the various Negrito and Aeta
                            languages of Luzon.
                            E   4   7
                Maher: M   5   4

288

Ward: Primary data on Casiguran Negrito language.
           M/L   5   4

MARRIAGE

2760. MANAWIS, MARIANO D. Courtship and marriage among the peasants of Cagayan.
      PM 32, no. 3 (Mar. 1935), 146-147, 150-151.

THE PEOPLE: CULTURAL-LINGUISTIC GROUPS (GENERAL WORKS)

2761. MEYER, ADOLPH B. Album von Philippinen-Typen[I] Dresden, Wilhelm Hoffmann,
      1885. 10p. 32 plates [including photographs taken in 1872].
         Jocano: E   3   7

2762. _____ and ALEXANDER SCHADENBERG. Album von Philippinen-Typen [II] Nord
      Luzon. Negritos, Tingianen, Bánaos, Ginaanen, Silípanen, Calingas, Apoyáos,
      Kianganen, Igorroten und Ilocanen. Dresden, Stengel and Markert ("German
      and Spanish letter press"); Manila and Cebu: Otto Koch; London, Kegan Paul,
      Trench, Trübner and Co., 1891. 19p. 50 plates [including Schadenberg's
      1886-1889 photographs]
         Jocano   E   3   7

2763. _____. Die Philippinen. I. Nord-Luzon: Tingianen, Bánaos, Ginaanen, Silí-
      panen, Apoyáos, Kianganen, Igorroten, Irayas und Ilocanen. Dresden, Stengel
      and Markert, 1890. 26p. 23 plates [including Schadenberg's 1886-1889 pho-
      tographs] (Publicationen aus den Königlichen Ethnographischen Museum zu
      Dresden, VIII)
         Jocano: E   3   7

2764. SCHEERER, OTTO. Zur ethnologie der Inselkette zwischen Luzon und Formosa.
      Deutschen Gesellschaft für Natur-und Völkerkunde Ostasiens 11, no. 1 (1906),
      1-31.

2765. WORCESTER, DEAN CONANT. The non-Christian peoples of the Philippine Islands.
      National Geographic Magazine 24, no. 11 (Nov. 1913), 1157-1256. 89 colored
      and b/w illus.

POLITICAL ORGANIZATION AND BEHAVIOR

2766. CASTILLO, GELIA T. and OTHERS. Leaders and leadership patterns in four se-
      lected barrios of Los Baños, Laguna. Laguna, College of Agriculture, U.P.
      1962. 161p. Abstract in PSR 11, nos. 1/2 (Jan./Apr. 1963), 44-51.

2767. KEESING, FELIX M. and MARIE KEESING. Taming Philippine headhunters; a study
of government and of cultural change in northern Luzon. Stanford, Stanford
Univ. Press, 1934. 288p.
    Bello: A standard sourcebook for all who want to understand so-
cial and political developments in the Mountain Province.
Should be a good reference book for students of Philippine public administration.
                E   5   7
    Maher: An overview of the Mountain Province during the American
period.
                E   4/5   4
    Scheans: Standard source.
                E   4/5   7
    Thomas: The standard reference (a classic) on directed cultural
change (applied anthropology) on the pagan tribes of
Mountain Province.
                E   4   4

2768. WILSON, LAURENCE L. Sapao: Walter Franklin Hale. In Memoriam. JEAS 5,
no. 2 (Apr. 1956), 1-38.
    Maher: Biography of an American civil servant whose career
spanned much of the American experience in the Mountain
Province.
                E   4/5   7

PROPERTY AND EXCHANGE

2769. DOZIER, EDWARD P. Land use and social organization among the non-Christian
tribes of Northwestern Luzon. American Ethnological Society. Annual Spring
Meeting. 1961: Proceedings. 1961. p.2-6.

RELIGIOUS BELIEFS AND PRACTICES

2770. ALVAREZ, MANUEL FRANCISCO. Mision de San Agustin de Banna; costumbres y pro-
piedades de los infieles. (In Pérez, Angel, comp.: Relaciones agustinianas
de las razas del norte de Luzon. p.207-218, tab.) (In Philippine Islands.
Bureau of Science. Division of Ethnology. Publications. v.3. Manila, 1904.
"Spanish edition."

2771. BARTLETT, HARLEY H. Jar burials in the Babuyan group, Philippine Islands,
especially those of Dalupiri Island. Michigan Academy of Science, Arts and
Letters. Papers 23 (1937), 1-20. 5 plates.
    Anderson: Description of finds and speculation of possible Chinese
influence in the region.
                C   5   4

2772. BELLO, MOISES C. Some observations on beliefs and rituals of the Bakun-

Kankanay. (In: Zamora, Mario D., ed. Studies in Philippine anthropology (In honor of H. Otley Beyer). Quezon City, Alemar-Phoenix, 1967. p.324-342)

2773. DERAEDT, JULES. Religious representations in Northern Luzon. SLQ 2, no. 3 (1964), 245-348.
      Sals: Highly scholarly work.
                   E   5   7

2774. FLATTERY, PHYLLIS. Aspects of divination in the Northern Philippines. Chicago, Philippine Studies Program, Dept. of Anthropology, Univ. of Chicago, 1968. 108p. (Research series, no. 6)
      Warren: E   5   7

2775. GEEROMS, HENRY. Former Spanish missions in the Cordillera (N. Luzon). SLQ Part I. 3, no. 1 (Mar. 1965), 17-56; Part II. 3, no. 3 (Sept. 1965), 437-480; Part III. 4, no. 3 (Sept. 1966), 373-436.
      Sals: L   5   7

2776. GRISHAM, GLEN. Pagan priests of Benguet. PM 29, no. 9 (Feb. 1933), 399-400, 420-422.

2777. LEGARDA Y FERNANDEZ, BENITO. Colonial Churches of Ilocos. PS 8, no. 1 (Jan. 1960), 121-158. 16 plates.

2778. MANAWIS, MARIANO D. Death in the Cagayan valley. PM 33, no. 12 (Dec. 1936), 600-601.

2779. _____. The farmer's life in the Cagayan valley. PM 29, no. 9 (Feb. 1933), 394-395.

2780. _____. Minannamay. PM 36, no. 3 (Mar. 1939), 122-123.

2781. MILLER, MERTON L. The burial mounds of Camiguin island. PJS 6D, no. 1 (Feb. 1911), 1-5. 5 plates.

2782. PÉREZ, ANGEL. comp. Relaciones Agustinianas de las razas del Norte de Luzon. Manila, Bureau of Printing, 1904. 411p. (Philippine Islands. Ethnological Survey. Publications. v.3)
      Eggan: M   3-5   3
      Maher: M   5   5

2783. SCOTT, WILLIAM HENRY. The Apo-Dios concept in Northern Luzon. Practical Anthropology 8, no. 5 (Sept./Oct. 1961), 207-216.
      Maher: M   5   7
      Sals: E   5   7

2784. SOLHEIM, WILHELM G.,II. Notes on burial customs in and near Sagada Mountain Province. PJS 88, no. 1 (Mar. 1959), 123-133. 1 plate.
      Maher: A   5   7

SEX AND REPRODUCTION

2785. REGUDO, ADRIANA C. Fertility patterns of ever-married women in the Ilocos, Central Luzon and Bicol regions. 1960. 100p. Thesis (M.A.) - U.P.
    Madigan: Analyzes sample of otherwise unreleased 1960 Census data.
            Z   4/5   6

STANDARD OF LIVING AND RECREATION

2786. LAVA, HORACIO C. Levels of living in the Ilocos region. Prepared for the Philippine Council, Institute of Pacific Relations. Manila, Carmelo and Bauermann, 1938. 94p. (College of Business Administration, U.P. Study no. 1) Thesis (Ph.D.) - Stanford Univ., 1938/39.

2787. WORCESTER, DEAN C. Field sports among the wild men of northern Luzon. National Geographic Magazine 22, no. 3 (Mar. 1911), 215-267. 54 illus.

GENERAL

2788. BEAN, ROBERT B. and FEDERICO S. PLANTA. The men of Cainta. PJS 6D, no. 1 (Feb. 1911), 7-15. 1 plate.
    Anderson: A description of the physical (racial) characteristics of the people of Cainta with supportive tables and plates.
    D   5   4

2789. LE GENTIL, M. Some of the usages and customs of the natives of the Philippines and their marriages, from "Voyage dans le Nordes Indes." Manners, customs and usages of Manila one hundred sixty years ago. Translated from the original French by Fred C. Fisher.
    PM Part I: 26, no. 2 (July 1929), 82-83, 103-104.
        Part II: 26, no. 4 (Sept. 1929), 205-207, 240-244.
        Part III: 26, no. 6 (Nov. 1929), 339-340, 366, 368, 370, 372, 374.
        Part IV: 26, no. 10 (Mar. 1930), 639-641, 650.
        Part V: 26, no. 11 (Apr. 1930), 716-717, 726, 728.
    Anderson: Of special value because of rarity of foreign observer's descriptions in the latter half of the 18th century. Broad description of conditions and customs of the times.
    T   5   3

2790. HILL, PERCY A. Romance and adventure in old Manila. Manila, Philippine Education Co., Inc., 1928. 315p. Manila, Filipiniana Book Guild, 1964. 259p. (Filipiniana Book Guild, 7)
    Anderson: A series of stories or tales (unrelated) which are skillfully put into a variety of specific historical settings and which at times round out documented events.
    F   3   2

2791. HOLLNSTEINER, MARY R. Comment on an inventory of sociological and anthropological research in progress, Luzon-based institutions/individuals, June 1963. PSR 11, nos. 1/2 (Jan./Apr. 1963), 116-124.
    Bello: A good survey for institutions backed survey, but not complete for individual researches, e.g., the work of some missionaries in Mountain Province are not included.
    Z   4   7

2792. _____. Inventory of sociological and anthropological research in progress, Luzon-based institutions/individuals, June 1963. PSR 11, nos. 1/2 (Jan./Apr. 1963), 107-116.
    Scheans: Useful survey of kinds of research being done.
    E   5   7

2793. MACMICKING, ROBERT. Recollections of Manila and the Philippines, during 1848, 1849, and 1850. Edited and annotated by Morton J. Netzorg. Manila, Filipiniana Book Guild, 1967. 296p. (Publications of the Filipiniana Book Guild, 11)
    Anderson: An excellent personal account of religions and social customs and the state of manufacture, agriculture, and trade in and surrounding Manila during the years 1848-50.
    X   5   3
    Felix: An excellent report on Manila since 1850.
    F/X   5   3

2794. THOMPSON, ROBERT WALLACE. A 17th century gazetteer of Manila. SJ 6, no. 3 (July/Sept. 1959), 179-189.
    Anderson: Consists of extensive quotes out of the 1629 completed Compendio y Descripción de las Indias Occidentales by Antonio Vázquez de Espinosa. Interspersed comments by the 'editor' appear and topics include: friars, Chinese, life in Manila, the Audiencia, ecclesiastical matters, and Islam.
         L   4   2

2795. TUBANGUI, HELEN R. Manila area study. Philippine Historical Review 1, no. 1 (1965), 334-364.

2796. WILKES, CHARLES. Manila in 1842. (In: Craig, Austin, ed. The Former Philippines Thru Foreign Eyes. New York, Appleton, 1916. p.459-493)
    Anderson: T   5   3

2797. _____. Narrative of the United States exploring expedition. During the years 1838, 1839, 1840, 1841, 1842. Philadelphia, Lea and Blanchard, 1845. v.5. Chapter 8. Manila (1842), p.275-319.
    Anderson: A short but succinct characterization of the physical outlay of particularly Manila and the Sulu archipelago as well as a description of the social, political and economic life of their respective inhabitants as observed by the author during the _few_ days of his stay.
         T   5   3
    Arce: T   3   2
    Nimmo: E   3   2

AGRICULTURE AND FOOD

2798. ALDABA, VICENTE C. Fishing methods in Manila Bay. PJS 47, no. 3 (Mar. 1932), 405-423. 5 plates.
    Anderson: Exhaustive descriptive survey with illustrations.
         -      5   4

2799. ARAGONES, SANTOS G. Tenancy, land-use, and farm management practices in Macalong, Asingan, Pangasinan. PA 40, no. 4 (Sept. 1956), 147-162.
    Anderson: A survey of types of farmers and relation between farmers net income and years of schooling, crop yields, and area of cropland in a barrio.
         C   5   6
    Sta. Iglesia: Highly useful descriptive research.
         Y   5   6

2800. ARON, HANS. Medical survey of the town of Taytay. Part VI. The food of the people of Taytay from a physiological standpoint. PJS 4B, no. 4 (Aug. 1909), 225-231. 22 plates.
    Anderson: Investigation through interviews of 25 families of the dietary and nutritional intake as it relates to their health.

D   3   4

2801. BAUTISTA, DANILO T. and ROGELIO P. MEGINO. Perceptions of some Laguna rice farmers about the Masagana rice culture. PSR 14, no. 3 (July 1966), 155-159.

2802. CABRERA, DOMINGO R. A study of farm ownership in five typical farming towns in Pangasinan. PA 19, no. 3 (Aug. 1930), 179-191.
    Anderson: Sample includes 389 farms presumably controlled by owner-operators. It surveys the farm size, made of acquisition of the farms, size of income and surplus savings of individual farms.
    C   5   4

2803. FELICIANO, GLORIA D. Sociological considerations in communicating change to Filipino farmers in five barrios of the land reform pilot area in Bulacan Province. PSR 14, no. 4 (Oct. 1966), 257-265.
    Sta. Iglesia: Highly useful description.
    Y   4   6

2804. GUTIERREZ, MARCIANO and F. O. SANTOS. The diet of low income families in Tondo district, Manila. Acta Medica Philippina 1, no. 2 (Oct./Dec. 1939), 171-193.
    Anderson: One day survey of 210 low income families concentrating on their caloric intake, the protein, mineral and vitamin composition of their diets and food costs vis-a-vis income per household provided.
    D   5   4

2805. _____. The food consumption of one hundred four families in Paco district, Manila. PJS 66, no. 4 (Aug. 1938), 397-416.
    Anderson: Investigation of dietary habits of persons who are free to choose their food according to their custom. Addendum: specific study over a period of two months.
    D   5   4

2806. GUZMAN, LEOPOLDO P. DE. An economic analysis of agricultural loans granted by rural banks in Luzon. PA 39, no. 10 (Mar. 1956), 611-619.
    Sta. Iglesia: Highly useful descriptive and analytical research.
    Y   5   6

2807. HAKIM, RUSLI. A comparison of lending policies of Facomas and rural banks in Polo and Baliwag, Bulacan. PA 44, no. 1 (June 1960), 30-44.
    Anderson: Investigation of the amount of loans, the security offered, interest and repayment rates and an analysis of foreclosure.
    C   5   6
    Sta. Iglesia: Highly useful descriptive and analytical research.
    G   5   6

2808. MARTIN, CLARO. Methods of smoking fish around Manila Bay. PJS 55, no. 1 (Sept. 1934), 79-89. 2 plates.
    Anderson: Detailed description and illustrations.
    C   5   6

2809. PASCUAL, CONRADO R. and OTHERS. Nutrition survey of 189 households in two regions in the Philippines. Stat. Rept. 2, no. 1 (Jan. 1958), 6-18.
    Anderson: Survey in Bicol and Central Luzon; sample 189 households. Dietary, clinical and biochemical study employing the 3-day method.
                        W   5   6

2810. PHILIPPINES (REPUBLIC) FOOD AND NUTRITION RESEARCH CENTER. Nutrition survey of metropolitan Manila. By E. S. Quiogue and others. Manila, NSDB Printing Press, 1962. 79p.
Suggested by Intengan.
    Intengan: A comprehensive assessment of the nutritional status conducted on a regional scale.
                        C   5   6

2811. _____. Nutrition re-survey of metropolitan Manila. Stat. Rept. 6, no. 3 (July 1962), 1-19.
    Anderson: Compares a 1958 with a 1959 dietary, clinical and biological survey to determine personal variations in food intake and to see whether 5-day surveys are better than 3-day ones.
                        W   5   6
    Sta. Iglesia: Highly useful description.
                        W   4   6

2812. PIRON, JORGE. Land tenure and level of living in Central Luzon. PS 4, no. 3 (Sept. 1956), 391-410.
    Anderson: Provinces involved: Cavite, Rizal, Pampanga, Nueva Ecija and Tarlac. Indicates the slow movement of owner-operators into tenancy.
                        -     5   6

2813. SANDOVAL, P. R., S. C. HSIEH and B. V. GAON. Productivity status of lowland rice farms: a case study of pre-land reform conditions. PA 51, no. 1 (June 1967), 1-19.

2814. TABLANTE, NATHANIEL B. and MELCHOR F. CONSTANTINO. The marketing of duck eggs in Morong, Pasig, and Pateros, Rizal. PA 36, no. 6 (Nov. 1952), 303-309.
    Anderson: Examination of the relation between sized flock quantity of eggs marketed, problems in marketing, methods of selling, price fluctuations on hand of 181 duck raisers.
                        C   5   6
    Sta. Iglesia: Highly useful descriptive research.
                        Y(X) 5   6

ARCHAEOLOGY

2815. BEYER, H. OTLEY. Catalogue of the hacienda Ramona archaeological collection, from Porac, Pampanga Province. Manila: 1936-1939. Typescript. 30p. Not completed.

Cited by Manuel in Zamora, Studies in Philippine anthropology. 1967. p.43.
   Solheim: A   5?   1/2

2816. _____. Manila ware, a study of the Manila ware kilns at San Pedro, Makati, Rizal province and surviving example from other sites. About 30 typewritten pages, 30 plates. (1946-1947).
Cited by Manuel in Zamora, Studies in Philippine anthropology. 1967. p.44.
   Solheim: A   5?   2/3

2817. _____. Notes on a collecting trip in the province of Pangasinan, during Aug.-Sept. 1913, with a list of the museum specimens collected. Philippine Ethnographic Series. Pangasinan set, v. 2. (1913), paper 41.
Cited by Manuel in Zamora, Studies in Philippine anthropology. 1967. p.32.
   Solheim: Primarily of historical interest.
              A   5   1-3

2818. _____. Tektites in Luzon. Manila, Nov. 25, 1928. 21p. Mimeographed edition.
Cited in Charles O. Houston, A preliminary bibliography of Philippine anthropology...JEAS, Jan. 1953.
   Bello: Excellent primary data by a specialist on the subject.
         A   5   1

2819. _____ and WALTER ROBB. New data on Chinese and Siamese ceramic wares of the 14th and 15th centuries. PM 27, no. 3 (Aug. 1930), 150-153, 200-204; PM 27, no. 4 (Sept. 1930), 220-223, 250, 252, 254. 33 figures.
   Peterson: An early comment on porcelains in the Philippines.
         A   5   1
   Solheim: Valuable source material.
         A   5   1-3

2820. BUSICK, RALPH. Rizalites--Philippine tektites--with a description of the Pugad Babuy site. Michigan Academy of Science, Arts and Letters. Papers 23, (1937), 21-27.
   Solheim: F/X   5?   1

2821. LYNCH, FRANK. Prehistoric novaliches. Woodstock Letters 78, no. 4 (Nov. 1949), 336-338.
   Solheim: A/E   4?   1

2822. _____. A typological study of the neolithic stone implements of the Rizal-Bulakan region of Luzon, in comparison with those from other parts of the Philippines and neighboring areas. 1949. 195p. 23 figures. Thesis (M.A.) - U.P.
   Solheim: The most detailed typological study of stone tools from the Philippines that is available.
         A/E 4/5   1

2823. MACEDA, GENEROSO S. Late eighteenth-century kiln-reject jars excavated at the San Juan de Dios hospital foundation. PJS 59, no. 4 (Apr. 1936), 573-577. 2 plates.
   Solheim: A   5?   3

2824. RAHMANN, RUDOLF. The fourth Far-Eastern prehistory congress. Quezon City and Manila, November 16-28, 1953. Anthropos 49, nos. 3/4 (1954), 687-688.

Solheim: E   3   6

BEHAVIOR PROCESS AND PERSONALITY

2825. BULATAO, JAIME. The Manileno's mainsprings. (In: Lynch, Frank, comp. Four readings on Philippine values. Quezon City, Ateneo de Manila Univ. Press, 1964. p.50-86) (IPC papers, no. 2)

BUILDINGS, TOOLS AND EQUIPMENT

2826. AGLIBUT, ANDRES P. and A. V. LIPIO. A study of rural housing conditions of one hundred families in Añgono, Rizal. PA 33, no. 2 (Oct./Dec. 1949), 103-110.

2827. CONCEPCION, MERCEDES B. Survey of life in Manila: a report on housing conditions. Phil. Stat. 4, no. 4 (Dec. 1955), 178-192.

2828. MALLARI, I. V. Architects and architecture in the Philippines. PM 27, no. 3 (Aug. 1930), 156-157, 186, 188, 190, 192-194; PM 27, no. 5 (Oct. 1930), 296-297, 314, 316, 319, 321-322.

CLOTHING, ADORNMENT AND MATERIALS

2829. GALANG, RICARDO E. Mat weaving in Apalit and vicinity, Province of Pampanga, Luzon. Folklore Studies 12, (1953), 113-114.

2830. GOZUM, PATRICIO C. Mat industry in Apalit, Province of Pampanga, Luzon. Folklore Studies 12, (1953), 111-113.

COMMUNITY DEVELOPMENT AND TERRITORIAL ORGANIZATION

2831. ANDERSON, JAMES N. Some aspects of land and society in a Pangasinan community. PSR 10, nos.1/2 (Jan./Apr. 1962), 41-58.
    Polson: An excellent analysis of bilateral kinship and its relation to economic interaction.
    E   5   6

2832. ARCINAS, FE RODRIGUEZ. An exploratory study of the socio-economic structure of the Diliman community. PSR 3, no. 4 (Nov. 1955), 28-39.

2833. EVANGELISTA, ALFREDO. The Nipa community of Bubog Paobong, Bulacan, Phil-
lippines. 1959. 56p. Thesis (M.A.) - Univ. of Chicago.

2834. KRAUSS, WILMA R. Differentiation of associations in Manila, 1929-1964.
PJPA 10, no. 4 (Oct. 1966), 343-358.

2835. LAQUIAN, APRODICIO A. Manila's urban renewal program. PJPA 10, nos. 2/3
(Apr./July 1966), 176-183.

2836. RIVERA, GENEROSO F. and ROBERT T. MCMILLAN. An economic and social survey
of rural households in central Luzon. Manila: Philippine Council for
United States Aid and the United States Operations Mission to the Philippines, 1954. 179p.

2837. TURLEY, ROY. Community organization in Tondo. CC 6, no. 6 (Nov./Dec.
1966), 19-25.

2838. UMALI, D. L. and G. D. FELICIANO. A socio-economic study of selected barrios in the land reform area, Bulacan. UP College of Agriculture, College,
Laguna, Philippines, 1963-1964.

2839. VELMONTE, JOSÉ E. and OTHERS. Living conditions in farm homes in Mendez
Nuñez and Amadeo, Cavite; Mangatarem, Pangasinan; and Camiling, Tarlac.
PA 22, no. 10 (Mar. 1934), 745-776.

ECONOMICS

2840. BOXER, CHARLES R. The Manila Galleon: 1565-1815. History Today 8, no. 8
(Aug. 1958), 538-547.

2841. CASTRO, AMADO A., JAMES A. STORER and A. CESAR CORVERA. An economic survey
of the Limay, Bataan area. Quezon City, Institute of Economic Development
and Research, U.P., 1960. 93p.

2842. MCINTYRE, WALLACE E. The retail pattern of Manila. Geographical Review
45, (Jan. 1955), 66-80.
          Spencer: Summary survey.
                       K   4   7

EDUCATION

2843. DULATRE-PADILLA, LUZ. The status of Chinese secondary schools in the city
of Manila. 1954. 89p. Thesis (M.A.) - U.P.
Cited in Compilation of graduate theses ..., p. 67.

Weightman: Good data - little analysis. Rapid changes make this a still picture of 1954 pattern.
Y   4   6

ETHNIC INFLUENCES

2844. AMYOT, JACQUES. The Chinese community of Manila: a study of adaptation of Chinese familism to the Philippine environment. Chicago, Dept. of Anthropology, Univ. of Chicago, 1960. (Chicago. University. Philippine Studies Program. Research series, no. 2) Thesis (Ph.D.) - Univ. of Chicago. 1960.
Amyot   E   5   4-7
Liao: E   4   7
Weightman: One of the few valuable studies in the area. Stress on social not political and economic aspects of Chinese family system.
E   5   6
Wickberg: The title is misleading. This is the best study of Chinese familial system in the Philippines. It is not a study of the community as a whole.
E   4   6

2845. BELTRAN, ANITA G. Cultural retention and religious affiliation of Chinese secondary students in Manila. 1957. 277p. Thesis (M.A.) - U.P.
Amyot: Z   3   6
Coller: Carefully-done work on assimilation from the empirical viewpoint.
Z   5   6
Weightman: Excellent--one of few scientific discussions of Chinese schools in Philippine Islands.
Z   5   6

2846. BERNAL, RAFAEL. The Chinese colony in Manila, 1570-1770. (In: Felix, Alfonso, ed. The Chinese in the Philippines, 1570-1770. Manila, Solidaridad Pub. House, 1966. p.40-66)
Phelan: H   4   2/3

2847. BLUMENTRITT, FERDINAND. Die Chinesen Manilas. Nach dem Spanischen des Don Isabelo de los Reyes. Globus 57, no. 7 (1890), 97-100.
Weightman: Over-rated; over quoted arm-chair research of a friend of Rizal.
Q   3   3
Wickberg: Q   5   3

2848. DULATRE-PADILLA, LUZ. The status of Chinese secondary schools in the city of Manila. 1954. 89p. Thesis (M.A.) - U.P.
Cited in Compilation of graduate theses ..., p. 67.
Weightman: Good data--little analysis. Rapid changes make this a still picture of 1954 pattern.
Y   4   6

2849. GRIESE, JOHN W., JR. The Jewish community in Manila. 1955. 105p. Thesis
(M.A.) - U.P.
Cited in Thesis abstracts II. p.96.
    Coller: Social history - based on interviews, library research,
          and field observations.
          Z   5   7

2850. SYCIP, FELICIDAD (CHAN). Chinese Buddhism: a study of the social structure of the Seng Guan Temple. 1957. 228p. Thesis (M.A.) - U.P.
Cited in U.P. theses and dissertations index. p.200.
    Amyot: Z   3   6
    Coller: Only study of its kind - fieldwork done by a person who
          had unusually good access to resources.
          Z   5   6
    Weightman: Interesting data - to be read with care. Nonsense clas-
          sification of "pure" vs. "impure" Buddhist temples.
          Z   4   6

2851. TAN-GATUE, BELEN. A study of assimilation in Chinese-Filipino families in
Manila and suburbs. 1955. 159p. 62 tables. Thesis (M.A.) - U.P.
Cited in Compilation of graduate theses ..., p. 427.
    Amyot: Z   3   6
    Coller: Empirical study providing facts on actual processes in
          20 selected families.
          Z   5   6
    Liao: S   4   6
    Weightman: Valuable but limited by failure to distinguish "ethnic"
          vs. "legal" Chinese - very small samples.
          Z   4   6

2852. WEIGHTMAN, GEORGE HENRY. Community organization of Chinese living in Manila. PSSHR 19, no. 1 (Mar. 1954), 25-39.
    Amyot: Z   5   6

FAMILY AND KINSHIP

2853. ANDERSON, JAMES N. Kinship and property in a Pangasinan barrio. Los Angeles, 1963. 394p. Thesis (Ph.D.) - UCLA.
    Anderson: Useful study of Pangasinan kinship, social and economic
          organization. Much tabular data to support analysis.
          Barrio-town study set in central Pangasinan.
          E   4/5   7
    Polson: The fuller thesis version of "Some aspects of land and
          society in a Pangasinan community".
          E   5   7
    Spencer: Good study - discussion.
          E   4/5   7

2854. CASTILLO, GELIA TAGUMPAY and JUANITA F. PUA. Research notes on the contemporary Filipino family: findings in a Tagalog area. PJHE 14, no. 3 (July/
Sept. 1963), 4-35.

Polson: An excellent study of the relationships of family characteristics to social and economic status.
Z   5   6

2855. CONCEPCION, MERCEDES B. and WILHELM FLIEGER. Family building patterns of young Manila couples. PSR 16, nos. 3/4 (July/Oct. 1968), 162-183.

2856. DOMINGO, MARIA FE. Child-rearing practices in barrio Cruz-na-Ligas. 1961. 210p. Thesis (M.A.) - U.P.

2857. PRATT, WILLIAM F. Family size and expectations in Manila. SLQ 5, nos. 1/2 (Mar./June 1967), 153-184.

GEOGRAPHY AND DEMOGRAPHY

2858. CLEMENTS, PAUL. Medical survey of the town of Taytay. VIII. Vital statistics. PJS 4B, no. 4 (Aug. 1909), 241-246.

2859. HERNANDO, EUGENIO. Life tables for the native resident population of the city of Manila for the year 1920. PJS 34, no. 2 (Oct. 1927), 161-185.

2860. MCINTYRE, WALLACE E. The retail pattern of Manila. Geographical Review 45, (Jan. 1955), 66-80.
Spencer: Summary survey.
K   4   7

2861. SAMONTE, QUIRICO S. A descriptive analysis of contemporary land value patterns of the city of Manila. 1954. 49p. Thesis (M.A.) - U.P.
Cited in Theses abstracts II, p. 13.
Coller: Statistical analysis of trends - brief - empirical.
Z   5   6

2862. _____. Land value patterns in Manila. PSR 3, no. 1 (Jan. 1955), 25-34.

HEALTH AND SICKNESS

2863. JIMENEZ, TERESITA T. A study of the health practices in the slum of barrio Andres Bonifacio. 1955. 181p. Thesis (M.A.) - U.P.
Coller: Participant-observation and interviews to gather first-hand data on values, attitudes, and actual practices - a landmark when done.
Z   5   6
Tiglao: Y   3   6

2864. LARA, ALMA F. Health needs of the rural area of Quezon City and their educational implications. 1954. 127p. Thesis (M.A.) - U.P.
Tiglao: Y   4   6

2865. STRONG, RICHARD P. Medical survey of the town of Taytay. XV. Summary and conclusions. PJS 4B, no. 4 (Aug. 1909), 289-301. 20 plates.

2866. TIGLAO, TEODORA V. Health practices in a rural community. Diliman Q.C., Community Development Research Council, U.P., 1964. 232p. Study series,no.23.

HISTORY AND CULTURE CHANGE

2867. DOUGLAS, LOUIS H. Modernization in a transitional setting: a Philippines case study. Civilisations (Brussels) 18, no. 2 (1968), 204-231.

2868. FELICIANO, GLORIA D. Sociological considerations in communicating change to Filipino farmers in five barrios of the land reform pilot area in Bulacan Province. PSR 14, no. 4 (Oct. 1966), 257-265.
        Sta. Iglesia: Highly useful description.
                Y   4   6

2869. LE GENTIL, M. Manila from the 16th to the 18th century. Translated from the original French by Fred C. Fisher. PM 36, no. 8 (Aug. 1939), 328-329, 337.

2870. _____. Manila one hundred sixty years ago. PM 26, no. 4 (Sept. 1929), 205-207, 240-244.

2871. HOLLNSTEINER, MARY R. A lowland Philippine municipality in transition. Practical Anthropology 8, no. 2 (Mar./Apr. 1961), 54-62.

2872. LARKIN, JOHN A. The place of local history in Philippine historiography. JSEAH 8, no. 2 (Sept. 1967), 306-317.

2873. REED, ROBERT R. The colonial origins of Manila and Batavia: desultory notes on nascent metropolitan primacy and urban systems in Southeast Asia. AS 5, no. 3 (Dec. 1967), 543-562.

INDUSTRIES

2874. LUNA, TELESFORO W., JR. Manufacturing in greater Manila. PGJ 8, nos. 3/4 (July/Dec. 1964), 55-86.

2875. WITT, J. C. Methods of burning pottery in the vicinity of Manila and their influence on the quality of the product. PJS 13A, no. 2 (Mar. 1918), 59-63. 2 plates.

LAND TENURE AND LAND REFORM

2876. DIOKNO, JOSE W. Legal aspects of land reform: the Central Luzon experience. Solidarity 2, no. 8 (July/Aug. 1967), 4-11.

2877. FELICIANO, GLORIA D. Sociological considerations in communicating change to Filipino farmers in five barrios of the land reform pilot area in Bulacan Province. PSR 14, no. 4 (Oct. 1966), 257-265.

MOBILITY AND SOCIAL STRATIFICATION

2878. ARCINAS, FE RODRIGUEZ. An exploratory study of the socio-economic structure of the Diliman community. PSR 3, no. 4 (Nov. 1955), 28-39.

2879. KRAUSS, WILMA R. Differentiation of associations in Manila, 1929-1964. PJPA 10, no. 4 (Oct. 1966), 343-358.

POLITICAL ORGANIZATION AND BEHAVIOR

2880. CUNNINGHAM, CHARLES HENRY. The audiencia in the Spanish colonies as illustrated by the audiencia of Manila (1583-1800). Berkeley, 1919. 479p. Thesis (Ph.D.) - Univ. of California. (Univ. of California publications in history. v.9)

2881. HOLLNSTEINER, MARY R. The dynamics of power in a Philippine municipality. Quezon City, Community Development Research Council, U.P., 1963. 227p. (Study Series no. 7)
    Grossholtz: The classic study of the socio-cultural roots of politics at the local level.
                   Z   5   6
    Stauffer: Very important case study. Adds a great deal to our knowledge of local politics as well as to cross-cultural research methodology.
                   Z   5   6
    Villanueva: An excellent case study of political processes in a barrio.
                   Z/E 5   6

2882. LAQUIAN, APRODICIO A. The city in nation-building; politics and administration in metropolitan Manila. Manila, School of Public Administration, U.P., 1966. 220p. (Studies in Public Administration, no. 8)
    Grossholtz: V   3   6

2883. _____. Politics in metropolitan Manila. PJPA 9, no. 4 (Oct. 1965), 331-342.
    Grossholtz: V   3   6

2884. WENGERT, EGBERT S. and PRIMITIVO R. DE LEON. A case study of decision-making in city government: The Aviles-Legarda-Mendiola traffic experiment

in Manila. PJPA 1, no. 2 (Apr. 1957), 108-126.
    Grossholtz: Excellent case study of administrative politics.
                   V   5   6

PROPERTY AND EXCHANGE

2885. ANDERSON, JAMES N. Kinship and property in Pangasinan barrio. Los Angeles,
       1963. 394p. Thesis (Ph.D.) - U.C.L.A.
           Anderson: Useful study of Pangasinan and Ilokano kinship, social
                           and economic organization. Much tabular data to support
                           analysis. Barrio-town study set in central Pangasinan.
                           E   4/5   7
           Polson: The fuller thesis version of "Some aspects of land and
                           society in a Pangasinan community". PSR, 1962.
                           E   5   6
           Spencer: Good study - discussion.
                           E   4/5   7

2886. PIRON, JORGE. Land tenure and level of living in central Luzon. PS 4, no.
       3 (Sept. 1956), 391-410.
           Anderson: Provinces involved: Cavite, Rizal, Pampanga, Nueva
                           Ecija and Tarlac. Indicates the slow movement of owner-
                           operators into tenancy.
                           -       5   6

RELIGIOUS BELIEFS AND PRACTICES

2887. AHLBORN, RICHARD. The Spanish churches of Central Luzon (I). PS 8, no. 4
       (Oct. 1960), 802-813.

2888. ALONZO, MANUEL P., JR. The diocese and cathedral of Manila. HB 7, no. 2
       (June 1963), 116-131.
           Anderson: Well documented commentary on the development of the
                           Catholic administration framework and missionary activi-
                           ties during the early Spanish period.
                           M   4   2

2889. AUGUSTIN, DEMETRIO R. Ceremonies in connection with the dead in Malolos,
       Bulacan. PSR 4, nos. 2/3 (Apr./July 1956), 32-39.
           Anderson: General description of ceremonies surrounding death with
                           emphasis on specific games played during wake.
                           -       3   6

2890. DICHOSO, FERMIN. Some superstitious beliefs and practices in Laguna, Phil-
       ippines. Anthropos 62, fasc. 1/2 (1967), 61-67.

2891. GANNETT, LUCY M. J. A parish feast at Manila. Independent (New York) 50, no. 2589 (July 14, 1898), 105-107.

Anderson: Popular description of the patron's day fiesta of Paco.
Q   3   3

2892. SYCIP, FELICIDAD (CHAN). Chinese Buddhism: a study of the social structure of the Seng Guan temple. 1957. 228p. Thesis (M.A.) - U.P. Cited in U.P. theses and dissertations index. p.200.
Amyot: Z   3   6
Coller: Only study of its kind - fieldwork done by a person who had unusually good access to resources.
Z   5   6
Weightman: Interesting data - to be read with care. Nonsense classification of "pure" vs. "impure" Buddhist temples.
Z   4   6

SEX AND REPRODUCTION

2893. HAWLEY, AMOS H. Rural fertility in Central Luzon. American Sociological Review 20, no. 1 (Feb. 1955), 21-27.

2894. REGUDO, ADRIANA C. Fertility patterns of ever-married women in the Ilocos, Central Luzon and Bicol regions. 1960. 100p. Thesis (M.A.) - U.P.
Madigan: Analyzes sample of otherwise unreleased 1960 census data.
Z   4/5   6

SOCIAL PROBLEMS

2895. ALDABA-BALUYUT, DIWATA. Social group work in Manila city jail. SW 6, no. 4 (Apr. 1961), 570-571, 581, 586.
Stone: Z   3   6

2896. ARCINAS, FE RODRIGUEZ. A socio-economic study of Manila squatters. PSR 3, no. 1 (Jan. 1955), 35-41.
Stone: First study of squatter community in Manila. Useful as foundation reading.
Z   5   6

2897. ASHBURN, FRANKLIN G. The recent inquiries into the structure-function of conflict gangs in the Manila city jail. AS 3, no. 1 (Apr. 1965), 126-144.
Stone: Excellent discussion of Philippine pathological behavior.
Z   5   6

2898. CATUNCAN, MILAGROS M. The etiology of suicide in Manila and suburbs. PSR 7, no. 4 (Oct. 1959), 26-33.
Stone: Demographic approach to causes of suicide.
Z   4   6

2899. _____. A sociological study of suicide patterns in Manila and its suburbs. 1956. 100p. Thesis (M.A.) - U.P.
      Stone: Demographic approach to causes of suicide.
           Z   4   6

2900. DOHERTY, JOHN F. Crime, a symptom of change. PSR 13, no. 1 (Jan. 1965), 14-18.

2901. HOLLNSTEINER, MARY R. Inner Tondo as a way of life. SLQ 5, nos. 1/2 (Mar./June 1967), 13-26.

2902. KATIGBAK, MARIA KALAW. A survey of four major Catholic social welfare agencies in Manila and suburbs. 1953. 175p. Thesis (M.A.) - U.P.
Cited in Theses abstracts. I. p.79.
      Stone: G   4   6

2903. LANSANG, FLORA C. A profile of a Manila slum. 1951. 56p. Thesis (M.A.) - Philippine Women's Univ.
Cited in Compilation of graduate theses ... p.419.
      Stone: Descriptive account of slum in Manila.
          Z   5   6

2904. MABUNAY, LETICIA D. A study of juvenile delinquency during vacation months in the city of Manila from 1946 to 1952. Unitas 26, no. 4 (Oct./Dec. 1953), 773-853.
      Stone: Demographic data.
          Z   4   6

2905. RAMOS, CARLOS P. Manila's metropolitan problem. PJPA 5, no. 2 (Apr. 1961), 89-117.
      Stone: Public administration approach to Manila's growth problem.
      V/Y/G 5   6

STANDARD OF LIVING AND RECREATION

2906. AGBANLOG, ANSELMO. A study of the standard of living in the towns of Balungao and San Carlos, Pangasinan. PA 18, no. 10 (Mar. 1930), 581-603.

2907. SANTIAGO, ALICIA A. Leisure-time activities of high school students in Central Luzon. EQ 1, no. 2 (Dec. 1953), 144-154.

TOTAL CULTURE

2908. KAUT, CHARLES. Process and social structure in a Philippine lowland settlement. (In: Studies on Asia, 1960. ed. by Robert K. Sakai. Lincoln, Univ. of Nebraska Press, 1960. p.35-50)

GENERAL

2909. JAGOR, [FEDOR]. On the natives of Naga, in Luzon. Philippine Islands.
Ethnological Society of London 2, no. 2 (July 1870), 170-175.

2910. LYNCH, FRANK. Some notes on a brief field survey of the hill people of
Mt. Iriga, Camarines Sur, Philippines. Primitive Man 21, nos. 3/4
(July/Oct. 1948), 65-73.

2911. MARASIGAN, PETRONILA C. Social activities in Cuenca, Batangas. PSR 4,
nos. 2/3 (Apr./July 1956), 47-53.

2912. MILLER, MERTON L. The non-Christian people of Ambos, Camarines. PJS 6D,
no. 6 (Dec. 1911), 321-325. 4 plates.

2913. PHELAN, JOHN L. Spanish penetration into the southern Philippines (1578-
1662). (In: Papers read at the Mindanao Conference. May 1955. Chicago,
Philippine Studies Program, Univ. of Chicago. 4p. Dittoed)

2914. ZINGG, ROBERT M. Batangas Province. PM 25, no. 9 (Feb. 1929), 512-513,
530-532.

AGRICULTURE AND FOOD

2915. AKHTAR, MUHAMMAD I. The effect of innovation on farm income in two selected
barrios of Laguna, Philippines, 1958-1962. 1963. 104p. Thesis (M.S.) -
U.P.
Cited in U.P. theses and dissertations index. p. 6.
   Sta. Iglesia: Highly useful descriptive and analytical research.
      S   5   6

2916. ALDABA, VICENTE C. The Dalag fishery of Laguna de Bay. PJS 45, no. 1
(May 1931), 41-59. 2 plates.
      Intengan: Culture of dalag in Laguna de Bay is studied and measures
                     for its protection.
      C   5   4

2917. _____. Fishing methods in Laguna de Bay. PJS 45, no. 1 (May 1931), 1-
28. 12 plates.
      Intengan: Describes methods of catching fish by species.
      C   5   4

2918. _____. Fishing methods in Manila Bay. PJS 47, no. 3 (Mar. 1932), 405-
423. 5 plates.
      Intengan: Describes specialized methods for catching different
                     kinds of fish.
      C   5   4

2919. _____. The Kanduli fishery of Laguna de Bay. PJS 45, no. 1 (May 1931),
29-39.
      Intengan: Fish culture of the most important fish in Laguna de Bay

is described, giving regulatory measures for its continued propagation.
C   5   4

2920. ATIENZA, JOSÉ C. Studies on the consumption of sugar for one year by fifty
Filipino families in Calauan, Laguna. PA 22, no. 4 (Sept. 1933), 274-284.
     Intengan: Reported sugar consumption is 14.4 kilogram per capita,
                     a value higher than previous reports.
                     C   3   4

2921. BAUTISTA, DANILO and ROGELIO P. MEGINO. Perceptions of some Laguna rice
farmers about the Masagana rice culture. PSR 14, no. 3 (July 1966), 155-
159.
     Sta. Iglesia: Highly useful descriptive research.
                     Y   5   6

2922. CRUZ, DALMACIO A. Organization and operation of duck farms in Mayondon and
Bayog, Los Baños, Laguna. PA 40, no. 8 (Jan. 1957), 399-412.
     Intengan: The operation of duck farms is analyzed and recommenda-
                     tions for improving the business are given.
                     C   3   6
     Sta. Iglesia: Highly useful description and analytical research.
                     Y   5   6

2923. DEOMAMPO, N. R. Comparative economic analysis of experimental data on the
use of tractor and carabao in lowland rice farming. PA 52, nos. 7/8 (Dec.
1968/Jan. 1969), 535-546.

2924. DIAZ, RALPH C. and HORST and JUDITH VON OPPENFELD. Case studies of farm
families, Laguna province, Philippines. [College] Laguna, Dept. of Agricultural Economics, College of Agriculture, U.P. 1961. 92p.
     Arce: X   5   6
     Sta. Iglesia: Highly useful descriptive research.
                     Y   5   6

2925. HOSILLOS, LILIA V. The retailing of fresh fruits and vegetables in the
public market of Calamba, Laguna. PA 36, no. 3 (Aug. 1952), 158-170.
     Intengan: Describes the retailing of fresh fruits and vegetables
                     in a Philippine town.
                     C   3   6
     Sta. Iglesia: Highly useful descriptive and analytical research.
                     G   5   6

2926. KEARL, C. D., C. D. VILLANUEVA, and A. N. PAGADUAN. Marketing palay in
Hanggan, Bay, and Lecheria and Banlic, Calamba, Laguna. PA 40, no. 2
(July 1956), 90-97.
     Intengan: Specific information on marketing system employed by
                     rice farmers is given to serve as basis for improving
                     the same.
                     C   3   6
     Sta. Iglesia: Highly useful descriptive and analytical research.
                     Y   5   6

2927. MABBUN, PABLO N. Marketing coconut products in Tayabas and Laguna. PA
19, no. 5 (Oct. 1930), 283-298.

Intengan: An analytical study of the methods of financing, produc-
               tion and marketing used in the coconut and copra trade
               of two provinces.
               C   3   4
Sta. Iglesia: Highly useful descriptive research.
               Y(G)   5   4

2928.   _____. A study of the marketing of copra in Lucena, Tayabas. PA 18, no.
10 (Mar. 1930), 621-633.
         Intengan: Gives recommendation on copra marketing in the capital
                        of a large coconut producing region.
                        C   3   4
         Sta. Iglesia: Highly useful descriptive research.
                        Y(G)   5   4

2929. MARIANO, LEONARDO, JR. and RAOUL R. URSUA. The changing attitude of farmers in pump irrigated areas in the Bicol provinces. PGJ 5, nos. 1/2 (Jan./
June 1957), 26-36.
         Intengan: Benefits brought to farmers by irrigation system may
                        pave the way for adoption of improved farm techniques.
                        C   5   6
         Sta. Iglesia: G   3   6

2930. MERCADO, C. M., M. E. PABALE and C. C. AGREDA. Some effects of mass media
on farmers under two situations in three Laguna barrios: an analysis. PA
50, no. 9 (Feb. 1967), 871-887.

2931. NASOL, R. L. and M. S. SAMSON. Farm management study of abaca farms in Albay. PA 51, no. 1 (June 1967), 20-31.

2932. PHILIPPINES (REPUBLIC) FOOD AND NUTRITION RESEARCH CENTER. Nutrition sur-
vey of southern Tagalog region. By E. S. Quiogue and others. Manila, NSDB
Printing Press, 1965. 88p.
Suggested by Intengan.
         Intengan: A comprehensive assessment of the nutritional status
                        conducted on a regional scale.
                        C   5   6

2933. RAYMUNDO, DOMICIANO E. Retailing of farm products in the public market of
San Pablo City. PA 37, nos. 1/2 (June/July 1953), 16-22.
         Sta. Iglesia: Highly useful descriptive research.
                        Y(G)   5   6

2934. ROBERTSON, L. S. and C. A. BRATTON. Investment and income of 107 tenant
farmers in San Pablo City in 1952. PA 38, nos. 4/5 (Sept./Oct. 1954), 398-
404.
         Intengan: Survey was done on coconut farms. Information on income,
                        its variation and causes; operating procedures and prac-
                        tices, privileges; characteristics of tenants, etc.
                        C   3   6
         Sta. Iglesia: Highly useful descriptive and analytical research.
                        Y   5   6

2935.   _____ and N. B. TABLANTE. Investment and income on 132 coconut farms in
Indang, Cavite, in 1952. PA 38, no. 1 (June 1954), 48-56.

        Intengan: Characteristics of coconut farms, labor and its use, farm
                         practices, income and earnings are reported.
                         C   3   6
        Sta. Iglesia: Highly useful descriptive and analytical research.
                         Y   5   6

2936. RIVERA, LOLITA C. The expenditure of incomes of rural families in Dayap, Ca-
      lauan, Laguna. PA 39, no. 5 (Oct. 1955), 237-248.
        Sta. Iglesia: Highly useful descriptive research.
                       G   5   6

2937. SACAY, FRANCISCO M. and E. P. AGUSTIN. Equity of the share lease used among
      rice farmers in Calamba, Laguna. PA 35, no. 3 (Aug. 1951), 109-114.
        Intengan: Contains useful information on returns to tenants and
                         landlord on a 50-50, 55-45 and 70-30 share lease.
                         C   3   6
        Sta. Iglesia: Highly useful descriptive and analytical research.
                         Y   5   6

2938. _____ and FABIANA E. ALVIAR. A survey of farm, home, and community condi-
      tions of rice farmers in the barrios of Cabuyao, Laguna, as basis for formu-
      lating a program of rural improvement. PA 35, no. 7 (Dec. 1951), 368-374.
        Intengan: Information gathered can be used for improvement of ru-
                         ral improvement programs.
                         C   3   6
        Sta. Iglesia: Highly useful descriptive research.
                         Y   5   6

2939. _____ and MARTIN V. JARMIN. A study of economic and social conditions in a
      farm village of Laguna. PA 31, no. 1 (July/Aug./Sept. 1947), 44-51.
        Intengan: A study of the conditions, problems and needs of a farm
                         village to serve as basis in the formulation of an ef-
                         fective rural improvement program.
                         C   3   4
        Sta. Iglesia: Highly useful descriptive research.
                         Y   5   6

2940. SACAY, ORLANDO J. Farm investment and income of rice farmers in the Maahas-
      Maitim area, Laguna, 1952-1953. PA 38, nos. 4/5 (Sept./Oct. 1954), 306-
      319.
        Intengan: Information given can be useful to credit institutions,
                         for establishing economic levels and for general operat-
                         ing procedures.
                         C   3   6
        Sta. Iglesia: Highly useful descriptive research.
                         Y   5   6

2941. SANTELICES, JULIAN V. Social and economic conditions of coconut farmers in
      Calolbon, Catanduanes. PA 42, no. 6 (Nov. 1958), 222-230.
        Intengan: Reports on economic and social conditions of farmers in a
                         Filipino town.
                         C   3   6
        Sta. Iglesia: Highly useful descriptive research.
                         Y   5   6

2942. SANTOS, F. O. Studies on the plane of nutrition of families of laborers in Calabanga, Camarines Sur. PA 27, no. 9 (Feb. 1939), 755-764.
    Intengan: Reports on food consumed by families using inventory method. Data is expressed in man units per family.
        C   3   4

2943. TABLANTE, NATHANIEL B. and ISABELO A. AMURAO. Marketing coffee produced in the province of Batangas. PA 36, no. 9 (Feb. 1953), 430-438.
    Intengan: Gives information on methods and channels used in marketing coffee; and recommendations for improving the system.
        C   3   6
    Sta. Iglesia: Highly useful descriptive research.
        Y   5   6

2944. _____ and MARCOS M. NUESTRO. Marketing coconuts and copra in the upland towns of Cavite. PA 36, no. 10 (Mar. 1953), 492-502.
    Intengan: The principal coconut-producing towns of Cavite were surveyed. Problems discussed.
        C   3   6
    Sta. Iglesia: Highly useful descriptive research.
        Y   5   6

2945. _____ and DOMINADOR M. TOMBO, JR. The marketing of mandarins, citrus nobilis lour., produced in 1951 in the province of Batangas. PA 35, no. 8 (Jan. 1952), 415-427.
    Intengan: Problems of recommendations are given on the system of marketing of citrus.
        C   3   6
    Sta. Iglesia: Highly useful descriptive research.
        Y   5   6

2946. TALAVERA, FLORENCIO. The fisheries of Lake Sampaloc, San Pablo, Laguna province, Luzon. PJS 48, no. 3 (July 1932), 411-427. 4 plates.
    Intengan: Gives reasons for decrease in fish supply in Lake Sampaloc as well as suggested remedies.
        C   4   4

2947. VEJERANO, TOMAS M. Marketing pineapples from Indang and Amadeo, Cavite, in 1954. PA 39, no. 8 (Jan. 1956), 496-503.
    Sta. Iglesia: Highly useful descriptive research.
        S   5   6

2948. VELMONTE, JOSE E. and ALFONSO B. CASTRO. An economic and social survey of sugar cane tenancies on the Calamba sugar estate, Laguna. PA 30, no. 4 (Sept. 1941), 314-338.
    Intengan: A study on sugar tenancy typical in this area.
        C   3   5
    Sta. Iglesia: Highly useful descriptive research.
        Y(G)   5   5

2949. VILLADOLID, DEOGRACIAS V. Methods and gear used in fishing in Lake Taal and the Pansipit River. PA 20, no. 9 (Feb. 1932), 571-575. 4 plates.
    Intengan: Report on the fishing gear and fishing methods of the region.
        C   3   4

2950.   _____ and MAMERTO D. SULIT. A list of plants used in connection with fishing activities in the Laguna de Bay regions and in Batangas Province, Luzon. PA 21, no. 1 (June 1932), 25-35.
     Intengan: Lists of Philippine plants grouped according to usage in fishing activities of the region.
     C   4   4

ARCHAEOLOGY

2951. BEYER, H. OTLEY. Catalogue and accession book of the Roth-Beyer collection of late neolithic material from Batangas. vol. II. pts. 4-7. 1933-1935. 495p. (Beyer Batangas archaeological series: set 25. Two Volumes. Typescripts. Manila)
     Solheim: Primarily of historical interest.
     A   5   1

2952. _____. Special catalogue of Rizal province tektites (including all except those from Sta. Mesa and Kubao sites). 1 vol. (as yet incomplete). Manila: 1941-1947. In Philippine Tektites Series, Suppl. Set.
Cited by Manuel in Zamora, Studies in Philippine anthropology. p.44.
     Solheim: A   5?   1

2953. EVANGELISTA, ALFREDO and JAIME CABRERA. Shell cultural materials from a Marinduque cave. Philippine International 7, no. 10 (1964), 6-7.
     Solheim: A   5?   1

2954. FOX, ROBERT B. The Calatagan excavations; two 15th century burial sites in Batangas, Philippines. PS 7, no. 3 (Aug. 1959), 321-390. 165 plates.
     Solheim: The major work on Asian porcelains and Philippine pottery for this period.
     A/E   5   1/2

2955. _____ and ALFREDO EVANGELISTA. The Bato caves, Sorsogon Province, Philippines; a preliminary report of a jar burial-stone tool assemblage. JEAS 6, no. 1 (Jan. 1957), 49-55. Also published in National Research Council of the Philippines Bulletin no. 42 (June 1958), 116-125, with 4 photos, as: The Bato Caves, Sorsogon Province; a preliminary site report.
     Solheim: Important data on Philippine pottery and the late Neolithic.
     A/E and A   5   1

2956. _____. The cave archaeology of Cagraray Island, Albay province, Philippines. JEAS 6, no. 1 (Jan. 1957), 57-68.
     Solheim: Reports on sites.
     A/E and A   5   1

2957. LEGASPI, AVELINO. A brief report on Verde Island, Batangas, Philippines. The Research Foundation in Philippine Anthropology and Archaeology, Inc. 1966. Mimeographed.
Cited in Robert Fox, The archaeological record of Chinese influence in the Philippines. Philippine Studies, 1967, p.62.

Solheim: A   3   1/2

2958. [PHILIPPINES (REPUBLIC)]JOSE RIZAL NATIONAL CENTENNIAL COMMISSION. The National Museum special exhibition of the Calatagan excavations. Manila, Bureau of Printing, 1961. 36p.

2959. SOLHEIM, WILHELM G.,II. Jar burial in the Babuyan and Batanes Islands and in Central Philippines, and its relationship to jar burial elsewhere in the Far East. PJS 89, no. 1 (Mar. 1960), 115-148. 10 plates.

2960. _____. Preliminary report on archaeological field work in San Narciso, Tayabas, P. I. JEAS 1, no. 1 (Oct. 1951), 70-76. 8 plates.
      Solheim: Report on jar burial sites of Early Iron Age time.
      A   5   1

COMMUNITY DEVELOPMENT AND TERRITORIAL ORGANIZATION

2961. EINSIEDEL, LUZ A. Success and failure in selected community development projects in Batangas. Quezon City, 1960. 125p. (Community Development Research Council, U.P. Study Series no. 3)

2962. PARCO, SALVADOR A. Regional development planning: the Bicol experiment. PJPA 9, no. 3 (July 1965), 265-274.

2963. VELMONTE, JOSÉ E., JUAN O. JUMAGUI and PEDRO H. VIRAY. Living conditions in farm homes in Mendez Nuñez and Amadeo, Cavite; Mangatarem, Pangasinan; and Camiling, Tarlac. PA 22, no. 10 (Mar. 1934), 745-776.

ECONOMICS

2964. CRUZ, DALMACIO A. Management and operation of rice retail stores in Laguna, 1958. PA 43, no. 10 (Mar. 1960), 637-655.
      Sta. Iglesia: Highly useful descriptive research.
      Y   5   6

2965. QUINTANA, VICENTE U. An economic study of retail stores in Los Baños and Calamba, Laguna, and San Pablo City, 1957. PA 43, no. 9 (Feb. 1960), 577-582.
      Sta. Iglesia: Highly useful descriptive research.
      Y   5   6

EDUCATION

2966. SACAY, FRANCISCO M., NICOLAS C. CAMELLO, and LUCIANO E. LACTAO. A prewar study of the availability of public-school education to children in the barrios of Bay and Calauan, Laguna. PA 32, no. 4 (Apr./June 1949), 312-317.

2967. _____, GIL F. SAGUIGUIT, and FAUSTINO BRUAL. Educational and occupational pursuits of former students in the Batangas and Ilocos Norte high schools. PA 32, no. 2 (Oct./Nov./Dec. 1948), 114-123.

FAMILY AND KINSHIP

2968. CASTILLO, GELIA T., FELICIDAD V. CORDERO, and MANUEL R. TANCO. A scale to measure family level of living in four barrios of Los Baños, Laguna. PSR 15, nos. 3/4 (July/Oct. 1967), 67-87.

2969. GUERRERO, SYLVIA H. An analysis of husband-wife roles among Filipino professionals at U.P. Los Baños campus. PSR 13, no. 4 (Oct. 1965), 275-281.

GEOGRAPHY AND DEMOGRAPHY

2970. ALCACHUPAS, RAMON C. Land tenure in Los Baños, Laguna. PA 39, no. 2 (July 1955), 74-80.
           Sta. Iglesia: Highly useful descriptive research.
                           G   5   6

2971. EUBINAG, AURORA F. The economic geography of the city of San Pablo. PGJ 3, no. 2 (Apr./June 1955), 101-103.
           Spencer: Student paper listing occupations etc. of a town.
                           K   4/5   6

2972. PHILIPPINES (REPUBLIC) BUREAU OF THE CENSUS AND STATISTICS. A social census of Vigan, Ilocos Sur and Lipa, Batangas; a study of postwar human resources of the Philippines based on data secured from the population of two communities, Dec. 1947, conducted jointly as an intergovernment project, with the assistance of three consultants on social welfare from United Nations, Lake Success. Manila, 1948. 167p.
Suggested by Scheans.

2973. ROMERO, ISIDORO A. Notes on Isla Verde. PGJ 4, nos. 2/3 (Apr./Sept. 1956), 86-88.
           Spencer: Summary notes and map of island.
                           C   4   6

2974. SALAZAR, FRANCISCO G. Geography of Sorsogon province with particular emphasis on soils and crops. PGJ 4, no. 1 (Jan./Mar. 1956), 22-29.
           Spencer: Summary of soils and crops.

                       C   4   6

2975. ZARATE, EDNA C. The economic geography of Biñan. PGJ 3, no. 2 (Apr./June 1955), 104-109.
         Spencer: Student paper listing occupations.
               K   4/5   6

HEALTH AND SICKNESS

2976. CEDEÑO, JUAN P. The problems in the relationships of private medical practitioners and municipal health officers. Philippine Medical Association Journal 38, no. 5 (May 1962), 346-352.
         Tiglao: D   3   6

2977. PASION, HONORIO D. Albay central school community pilot project in health - its organization and administration. Philippine Health Journal 7, no. 4 (Nov. 1960), 13-15, 27.
         Tiglao: Y   3   6

HISTORY AND CULTURE CHANGE

2978. POMERLEAU, RAYMOND. The function of legitimation in the social change process: the Lagulo project. PJPA 11, no. 4 (Oct. 1967), 305-315.

2979. _____. The Lagulo spring development project: community participation in planned social change. PJPA 11, no. 1 (Jan. 1967), 72-82.

2980. QUIRINO, CARLOS and MAURO GARCIA. "Narrative of Mr. Juan Masolong, first Christian of Lilio, Laguna, and the founding of the town in 1572;"an 18th century manuscript, translated and annotated with a complete transcription of the original Tagalog text. Buletin ng Kapisanang Pangkasaysayan ng Pilipinas (Bulletin of the Philippine Historical Association), no. 4 (June 1958), 13-49.

MOBILITY AND STRATIFICATION

2981. LYNCH, FRANK. Social class in a Bikol town. Chicago, Philippine Studies Program, Dept. of Anthropology, Univ. of Chicago, 1959. 175p. (Research series, no. 1) His Ph.D. thesis - Univ. of Chicago. 1959.
         Arce: E   5   7

POLITICAL ORGANIZATION AND BEHAVIOR

2982. CASTILLO, GELIA T., PATROCINIO S. VILLANUEVA, and FELICIDAD V. CORDERO. Leaders and leadership patterns in four selected barrios of Los Baños, Laguna. Laguna, U.P. College of Agriculture, 1962. 161p. Draft copy: for limited distribution. Abstracted in PSR 11, nos. 1/2 (Jan./Apr. 1963), 44-51.
      Arce: Z   5   6
      Grossholtz: Generates some data but difficult to interpret.
                   Z/S   5   6

RELIGIOUS BELIEFS AND PRACTICES

2983. ABELLA, DOMINGO. Bikol annals; a collection of vignettes of Philippine history. [1st ed.] Manila, privately published, 1954. v.1. The See of Nueva Caceres.

2984. CALLEJA-REYES, JOSÉ. Ibalón: an ancient Bicol epic. PS 16, no. 2 (Apr. 1968), 318-347.

2985. LYNCH, FRANK. An Mga Asuwang: a Bicol belief. PSSHR 14, **no.** 4 (Dec. 1949), 401-427.

SEX AND REPRODUCTION

2986. REGUDO, ADRIANA C. Fertility patterns of ever-married women in the Ilocos, Central Luzon and Bicol regions. 1960. 100p. Thesis (M.A.) - U.P.
      Madigan: Analyzes sample of otherwise unreleased 1960 census data.
              Z   4/5   6

STANDARD OF LIVING AND RECREATION

2987. CASTILLO, GELIA T., FELICIDAD V. CORDERO, and MANUEL R. TANCO. A scale to measure family level of living in four barrios of Los Baños, Laguna. PSR 15, nos. 3/4 (July/Oct. 1967), 67-87.

2988. ROBERTSON, L. S. and O. J. SACAY. The living conditions of 101 men students in the U.P. College of Agriculture, 1953-54. PA 38, nos. 2/3 (July/Aug. 1954), 160-167.

2989. _____ and N. B. TABLANTE. Expenditures of 117 men students in the U.P. College of Agriculture, 1952-53. PA 39, no. 2 (July 1955), 68-73.

B. BY CULTURAL-LINGUISTIC GROUP

APAYAO - GENERAL

2990. SCHEANS, DANIEL J. The Apayao of Ilocos Norte. Ethnohistory 11, no. 4
(Fall 1964), 394-398.
      Scheans: Corrects data in Keesing's The Ethnohistory of Northern
                Luzon, (1962) on Ilocos Norte.
                E   5   7

2991. VANOVERBERGH, MORICE. The Isneg. Washington, D.C. 1932. 80p. (Catholic
Anthropological Conference. Publications 3, no. 1)
      Scheans: Standard source.
                M   5   7

2992. _____. The Isneg life cycle.
      I. Birth, education, and daily routine. Catholic Anthropological Con-
ference. Publications 3, no. 2 (Mar. 1936), 81-186.
      II. Marriage, death and burial. Catholic Anthropological Conference.
Publications 3, no. 3 (Dec. 1938), 187-280.
      Scheans: Standard source.
                M   5   7

2993. WILSON, LAURENCE L. Apayao life and legends. Baguio, P.I., 1947. 195p.
Quezon City, Bookman, 1967. 267p.
      Scheans: Popular account by a long time resident of Mt. Province.
                F   5   7

APAYAO - AGRICULTURE AND FOOD

2994. KEESING, FELIX M. The Isneg: shifting cultivators of the Northern Philippines. SWJA 18, no. 1 (Spring 1962), 1-19.
      Scheans: Excellent summary account based on field work in the
                1930's. A survey of the literature.
                E   5   7

2995. VANOVERBERGH, MORICE. Isneg domestic economy. Annali Lateranensi 18,
(1954), 119-256.
      Scheans: M   5   7

2996. _____. The Isneg farmer. Catholic Anthropological Conference. Publications 3, no. 4 (Aug. 1941), 281-386.
      Scheans: M   5   7

APAYAO - BUILDINGS, TOOLS AND EQUIPMENT

2997. VANOVERBERGH, MORICE. Isneg buildings. PJS 82, no. 1 (Mar. 1953), 77-108.
4 plates.

Scheans: M   5   7

APAYAO - CLOTHING, ADORNMENT AND MATERIALS

2998. VANOVERBERGH, MORICE. Isneg domestic economy. Annali Lateranensi 18 (1954), 119-256.
Scheans: M   5   7

APAYAO - EDUCATION

2999. VANOVERBERGH, MORICE. The Isneg life cycle. I. Birth, education, and daily routine. Catholic Anthropological Conference. Publications 3, no. 2 (Mar. 1936), 81-186.
Scheans: Standard source.
M   5   7

APAYAO - FINE ARTS

3000. VANOVERBERGH, MORICE. Isneg songs. Anthropos 55, fasc. 3/4 (1960), 463-504. Anthropos 55, fasc. 5/6 (1960), 778-824.

APAYAO - HEALTH AND SICKNESS

3001. VANOVERBERGH, MORICE. The Isneg body and its ailments. Annali Lateranensi 14, (1950), 193-293.

APAYAO - LANGUAGE AND LITERATURE

3002. SCHEERER, OTTO. Isneg texts with notes. PJS 36, no. 4 (Aug. 1928), 409-447.

APAYAO - MARRIAGE

3003. BATIL, AMOR. Courtship and marriage in Apayao. PM Part I. 32, no. 5 (May 1935), 241, 252. Part II. 32, no. 6 (June 1935), 285, 306. Reprinted in JEAS 8, nos. 1/2 (Jan./Apr. 1959), 202-206.
        Scheans: Popular accounts.
                   -      3   7

3004. FACULO, A. Wedding and other rites in Apayao. PM 32, no. 6 (June 1935), 285, 302, 304, 306.
        Scheans: -   3   7

3005. REYNOLDS, HARRIET R. Modern marriage and courtship among the Isneg, Apayao (abstract). PSR 16, nos. 3/4 (July/Oct. 1968), 191-192.

3006. VANOVERBERGH, MORICE. The Isneg life cycle: II. Marriage, death and burial. Catholic Anthropological Conference. Publications 3, no. 3 (Dec. 1938), 187-280.
        Scheans: M   5   7

APAYAO - RELIGIOUS BELIEFS AND PRACTICES

3007. BATIL, AMOR. Meeting in Apayao. PM 31, no. 4 (Apr. 1934), 148-149, 166-167.
        Scheans: -   3   4

3008. CARRILLO, MANUEL. Breve relación de las missiones de las quatro naciones llamadas Igorrotes, Tinguianes, Apayaos y Adanes ... Madrid, Impr. del Consejo de Indias, 1756. 37p. (In: Retana. Archivo del bibliófilo filipino. v.1)
        Eggan: Report on Spanish missions in Northern Luzon.
                   M   3   3

3009. FACULO, A. Wedding and other rites in Apayao. PM 32, no. 6 (June 1935), 285, 302, 304, 306.
        Scheans: -   3   7

3010. VANOVERBERGH, MORICE. The Isneg life cycle: II. Marriage, death and burial. Catholic Anthropological Conference. Publications 3, no. 3 (Dec. 1938), 187-280.
        Scheans: M   5   7

3011. _____. Religion and magic among the Isneg.
        Anthropos 48, nos. 1/2 (1953), 71-104.   Part I.   The spirits.
                   48, nos. 3/4 (1953), 557-568.   II.   The Shaman.
                   49, nos. 1/2 (1954), 233-275.   III. Public sacrifices.
                   49, nos. 5/6 (1954), 1004-1012.   IV.   Other observances.
                   50, nos. 1/3 (1955), 212-240.   V.   Samples of Pakkaw.

3012. WILSON, LAURENCE L. Apayao life and legends. Baguio, Philippines, 1947. 195p. Quezon City, Bookman, 1967. 267p.

> Scheans: Popular account by a long time resident of Mt. Province.
> F   5   7

BIKOL

3013. LYNCH, FRANK. Social class in a Bikol town. Chicago, Philippine Studies
Program, Dept. of Anthropology, Univ. of Chicago, 1959. 175p. (Research
series, no. 1) His Ph.D. Thesis - Univ. of Chicago. 1959.
Arce: E   5   7

3014. NAVARRO, MAXIMINA. Tribal marriage customs among the Bicols. The College
Folio (Manila, Univ. of the Philippines, College of Philosophy, Science and
Letters and College of Engineering) 1, no. 2 (Dec. 1910), 65-68.

DUMAGAT (CASIGURAN, FAMY)

3015. FOX, ROBERT B. Notes on the orchids and people of Northeast Polillo Island,
Quezon Province. Philippine Orchid Review 3, no. 1 (Feb. 1950), 16-21.
10 plates.

3016. HEADLAND, THOMAS N. and ELMER P. WOLFENDEN. The vowels of Casiguran Duma-
gat. (In: Zamora, Mario D., ed., Studies in Philippine anthropology (in
honor of H. Otley Beyer). Quezon City, Philippines, 1967. p.592-596.)

3017. MACEDA, GENEROSO S. The Dumagats of Famy. 1932. Thesis (M.A.) - U.P.

3018. _____. The Dumagats of Famy. PJS 57, no. 2 (June 1935), 235-251.
5 plates.

3019. TURNBULL, WILFRID. Bringing a wild tribe under government control.
PM Part I. 26, no. 12 (May 1930), 782-783, 794, 796, 798.
            II. 27, no. 1 (June 1930), 31-32, 36, 38, 40, 42.
            III. 27, no. 2 (July 1930), 90-91, 116-118, 120.

3020. _____. The "Dumagats" of North-East Luzon.
PM 26, no. 3 (Aug. 1929), 131-133, 175-178.
        no. 4 (Sept. 1929), 208-209, 237-240.

3021. _____. Early days in the constabulary.
PM 29, no. 2 (July 1932), 75-76, 85-86.
    29, no. 4 (Sept. 1932), 168-169.
    29, no. 5 (Oct. 1932), 211, 214-215.
    29, no. 6 (Nov. 1932), 256-259, 262-263.
    29, no. 7 (Dec. 1932), 309, 320-321.
    29, no. 9 (Feb. 1933), 407-408, 413-414.
    29, no. 10 (Mar. 1933), 452, 465.
    29, no. 11 (Apr. 1933), 499, 508.

29, no. 12 (May 1933), 537, 543-544, 546.
30, no. 1 (June 1933), 23-24, 36.
30, no. 2 (July 1933), 64-65, 71-72.
30, no. 3 (Aug. 1933), 104, 110, 112, 114-115.
30, no. 4 (Sept. 1933), 153-154, 159-160.
30, no. 5 (Oct. 1933), 197, 205-208.

3022. VANOVERBERGH, MORICE. Some undescribed languages of Luzon. Nijmegen, Dekker and van de Vegt, N. V., 1937. 200p. (Publications de la Commission d'Enquete Linguistique ... III)

Llamzon: Purely lexical lists of the various Negrito and Aeta languages of Luzon.
              E   4   7
Maher: M   5   4
Ward: Primary data on Casiguran Negrito language.
              M/L   5   4

GADDANG

3023. CAMPA, JOSÉ DE LA. Gaddanen, Ilongoten, Ibilaos, und Negritos des valle de Cagayan (Luzon). Translation from the Spanish by Ferdinand Blumentritt. Anthropologischen Gesellschaft in Wien. Verhandlungen. 14 (1884), 52-54.
Wallace: Useful historical document.
              -      4   3

3024. GALANG, RICARDO E. Ethnographic study of the Yogads of Isabela. PJS 56, no. 1 (Jan. 1935), 81-91. 3 plates.

3025. GAMBOA, ENRIQUETA T. The educational implications of the folkways, mores, and religious beliefs of the Gadangs. Quezon City, 1960. 241p. Thesis (M.Ed.) - U.P.

3026. LAMBRECHT, GODFREY. Anitu rites among the Gaddang. PS 8, no. 3 (July 1960), 584-602.

3027. _____. The customs of the Christian Gadang people; (an ethnological study of the survivals of the Gadan animistic religion as a cultural proof of their Indonesian origin). 1948. Thesis (M.A.) - Univ. of Sto. Tomas. Cited in Compilation of graduate theses ... p.286.
Wallace: Standard baseline reference on Christian Gaddang.
              M   3   6

3028. _____. The Gadang of Isabela and Nueva Vizcaya: survivals of a primitive animistic religion. PS 7, no. 2 (Apr. 1959), 194-218.

3029. TROYER, LESTER O. Gaddang affirmatives and negatives. AS 6, no. 1 (Apr. 1968), 99-101.

3030. _____. Linguistics as a window into man's mind: Gaddang time segmentation. GEJ, no. 12 (Second Semester, 1966/1967), 109-118.

3031. WALLACE, BEN J. Gaddang agriculture: the focus of ecological and cultural change. 1967. Thesis (Ph.D.) - Univ. of Wisconsin.
    Wallace: Primary data on swidden and plow agriculture on the Pagan Gaddang communities.
    E   5   6

3032. _____. Gaddang rice cultivation: a ligature between man and nature. PSR 15, nos. 3/4 (July/Oct. 1967), 114-122.
    Wallace: Shallow but objective and reliable source on the Pagan Gaddang.
    E   3   6

3033. _____. Pagan Gaddang spouse exchange. Ethnology 8, no. 2 (Apr. 1969), 183-188.

IBALOY

3034. BALLARD, D. LEE, JR. Inibaloi onomatopoeia. Philippine Journal for Language Teaching 4, nos. 1/2 (May 1966), 72-74.

3035. BARNETT, MILTON L. Subsistence and transition of agricultural development among the Ibaloi. (In: Zamora, Mario D., ed. Studies in Philippine anthropology (In honor of H. Otley Beyer). Quezon City, Alemar-Phoenix, 1967. p.299-323)

3036. CAMPA, JOSÉ DE LA. Gaddanen, Ilongoten, Ibilaos, und Negritos des valle de Cagayan (Luzon). Translation from the Spanish by Ferdinand Blumentritt. Anthropologischen Gesellschaft in Wien. Verhandlungen. 14 (1884), 52-54.
    Wallace: Useful historical document.
    -    4   3

3037. CLAERHOUDT, ALFONSO. The songs of a people: Igorot customs in eastern Benguet. Saint Louis Quarterly 4, no. 2 (June 1966), 163-278.
    Eggan: Beautifully written and accurate.
    M   5   4

3038. _____. Why the crow has black feathers: an Ibaloi tale. Primitive Man 3, nos. 3/4 (July/Oct. 1930), 75-77.

3039. GALVEY, G. The Ibaloi Igorot seventy-five years ago; account of a Spanish expedition to Benguet in the year 1829. (In: Scheerer, Otto, The Nabaloi dialect. p.173-178) Manila, Bureau of Printing, 1905. p.85-199. (Philippine Islands. Ethnological Survey. Publications. v.II, pt. II-III)

3040. LEAÑO, ISABEL. The Ibaloy sing for the dead. PSR 13, no. 3 (July 1965), 154-189.

3041. _____. The Ibaloys of Takdian--their social, economic and religious life. 1958. 408p. Thesis (M.A.) - Philippine Women's Univ.

3042. MOSS, CLAUDE R. Nabaloi law and ritual. Berkeley, Univ. of California

Press, 1920. (Univ. of California. Publications in American archaeology and ethnology. v.15, no. 3)

3043. _____. Nabaloi tales. Berkeley, Univ. of California Press, 1924. (Univ. of California. Publications in American archaeology and ethnology. v.17, no. 5). p.227-353.

3044. _____ and A. L. KROEBER. Nabaloi songs. Berkeley, Univ. of California Press. 1919. (Univ. of California. Publications in American archaeology and ethnology. 15, no. 2, 187-206)

3045. SCHEERER, OTTO. The Nabaloi dialect; by Otto Scheerer. The Bataks of Palawan, by Edward Y. Miller. Manila, Bureau of public printing, 1905. p.85-199. Illus. (Music), pl. LXIII-XCI, tables. (Department of the Interior. Ethnological survey. Publications. vol. II, pts. II-III) (Philippine islands. Ethnological survey. Publications. vol. II, pts. II-III)

3046. WILSON, LAURENCE L. Nabaloi shamanism and sympathetic magic. PSSHR 18, no. 2 (June 1953), 187-193.

IBANAG

3047. SOLHEIM, WILHELM G.,II. Ibanag pottery manufacture in Isabela, Philippines. JEAS 3, no. 3 (Apr. 1954), 305-307.

IFUGAO - GENERAL

3048. BARROWS, DAVID P. The head-hunters of Northern Luzon. Independent (New York) 55, no. 2841 (May 14, 1903), 1140-1146.
   Maher: G   3   4

3049. _____. Memorandum upon the district of Quiangan. 1903. 5p. (In: Beyer collection of Filipiniana. v.14/9, paper 12) Microfilm copy at Yale Univ. Cited in Harold Conklin, Ifugao bibliography. 1968. p.7.
   Maher: G   5   4

3050. _____. A preliminary report of explorations among the tribes of the Cordillera Central of Northern Luzon. 1903. 19p. (In: Beyer collection of Filipiniana. v.14/14, paper 98) Microfilm copy at Yale Univ. Cited in Harold Conklin, Ifugao bibliography. 1968. p.7.
   Maher: Contains material on conditions at the beginning of American control.
   G   5   4

3051. BARTON, ROY FRANKLIN. Autobiographies of three pagans in the Philippines. New Hyde Park, New York, Univ. Books, 1963. 271p. First published in London in 1938 under title: Philippine pagans.

            Maher: A classic in the life history approach to the study of
                             culture.
                             E   5   4
            Sals: E   3   4

3052. _____. The half-way sun; life among the head-hunters of the Philippines.
New York, Brewer and Warren, 1930. 315p.
            Maher: The basic general account of Ifugao culture.
                             E   5   4
            Sals: E   4   4

3053. _____. Numputol--the self-beheaded. PM 37, no. 10 (Oct. 1940), 384-386,
394-396.
            Maher: Like other articles Barton did for journals such as
                             Philippine Magazine or Asia, this is popularly written
                             but contains primary data.
                             E   5   4

3054. _____. Paths of vengeance in Luzon. Travel 55, no. 6 (Oct. 1930), 24-
29, 53.
            Maher: E   5   4
            Sals: E   4   4

3055. _____. Philippine pagans; the autobiographies of three Ifugaos...London,
George Routledge & Sons. 1938. 271p.
            Maher: E   5   4

3056. BEYER, H. OTLEY. Anthropometrical measurements of 50 Ifugao men and women,
taken in the subprovince of Ifugao in July and August, 1910. 7p. (In:
Beyer Collection of Filipiniana. v.14/16, paper 164) Microfilm copy at
Yale Univ.
Cited in Harold Conklin, Ifugao bibliography. 1968. p.12.
            Maher: E   5   4

3057. _____. A brief study of the material culture of the Ifugao tribe of the
island of Luzon. 1909. 17p. (In: Beyer collection of Filipiniana.
v.14/15, paper 125) Microfilm copy at Yale Univ.
Cited in Harold Conklin, Ifugao bibliography. 1968. p.12.
            Maher: E   5   4

3058. _____. The history and ethnography of the Ifugao people; being a complete
collection of all known printed and manuscript information relating to the
history and ethnography of the Ifugao people of northern Luzon, Philippine
Islands, uniformly edited, annotated, and translated into English under the
general supervision of H. Otley Beyer and Roy Franklin Barton with the cooperation of...Prof. R. B. Dixon [and others]..Manila, 1912-   . v. illus.,
ports., plan, tables, (His: [Beyer collection of Filipiniana. sect. A,
set 14a])
Cited in Harvard Univ. Peabody Museum...Library. Catalogue: Author. v.3,
p.105. Microfilm copy at Yale Univ.
            Maher: A valuable compilation of reports on Ifugao. Many sub-
                             jects and many authors.
                             E   5   7

3059. _____. The Igorotes. Philippine Education 4, no. 4 (1907), 14-18.

Eggan: Beyer's first paper - on the Ifugao primarily.
                G/E   5   4

3060. _____ and TUGINAI PAIT. List of specimens in the ethnological collection from the Ifugao, Igorot, and Bontok peoples of northern Luzon, collected for the Peabody Museum of Ethnology, by H. Otley Beyer and Tuginai Pait. October, 1908. Cambridge, Mass. Typed copy. 7p. (In: Beyer collection of Filipiniana. v.14/16, Paper 141) Microfilm copy at Yale Univ. Cited in Harold Conklin, Ifugao bibliography, 1968. p.12.
      Maher: E   5   5

3061. BLUMENTRITT, FERDINAND. Die Kianganen (Luzon). Aus dem Missionsberichte des Domini Kaners P. Villaverde auszugsweise übersetzt und mit Anmerkungen versehen.
      Ausland Part I. 64, no. 6 (Feb. 9, 1891), 118-120.
               Part II. 64, no. 7 (Feb. 16, 1891), 129-132.
      Maher   E   3   3

3062. _____. The Quianganes of Luzon. Popular Science Monthly 39 (July 1891), 388-393. "Translated...from Das Ausland."
      Maher   E   3   3

3063. CAMPA, BUENAVENTURA. Los Mayóyaos y la raza: Apuntes para un estudio.
      El Correo Sino-Annamita 26 (1892), 169-208.
                          27 (1893), 279-321.
      Published as: Etnografía filipina. Los Mayóyaos y la raza Ifugao (Apuntes para un estudio). Madrid, Viuda de M. Minuesa de los Rios, 1894. 165p.
      Maher: M   5   3

3064. COLE, FAY-COOPER. The Ifugao. (In: Cole, Fay-Cooper, The peoples of Malaysia. New York, D. Van Nostrand Co., Inc., 1945. p.130-139)
          Maher: A useful but brief description of Ifugao culture.
                    E   4   4

3065. CONKLIN, HAROLD C. Ifugao bibliography. New Haven, Conn., 1968. 75p. (Yale Univ., New Haven. Southeast Asia Studies. Bibliography series, no. 11)

3066. CRESPILLO, ALBERTO. Ifugao love potions and charms. PM 34, no. 7 (July 1937), 308, 318.
        Sals: H   3   5

3067. DAIT, JUAN B. Ifugao symbol of royalty. Sunday Times Magazine 18, (Mar. 24, 1963), 36-37.
        Sals: Q   4   9

3068. DULAWAN, LOURDES S. The Ifugaos. Unitas 40, no. 1 (Mar. 1967), 4-52.

3069. JOSE, F. SIONIL. A Bontoc visit. Comment 23, (1967), 58-72.

3070. KANE, SAMUEL E. Life or death in Luzon; thirty years of adventure with the Philippine highlanders. Indianapolis, Bobbs-Merrill Co., 1933. 331p. English edition: Thirty years with the Philippine head-hunters. London, Jarrolds, 1934. 288p.
      Eggan: Kane was a government official--much of data from

Jenks, etc.
G   3   4
Maher: Contains some interesting personal experiences of the
early days of American administration.
G   3   4

3071. LAMBRECHT, FRANCIS. The Mayawyaw ritual.
Part I.   Rice culture and rice ritual. Catholic Anthropological Conference. Publications.
4, no. 1 (Dec. 1932), 1-167.
II.   Marriage and marriage ritual. Catholic Anthropological Confer-
ence. Publications.
4, no. 2 (Mar. 1935), 169-325.
III.   Death and death ritual. Catholic Anthropological Conference.
Publications.
4, no. 3 (Mar. 1938), 327-493.
IV.   Property and property ritual. Catholic Anthropological Confer-
ence. Publications.
4, no. 4 (Oct. 1939), 495-711.
V.   Go-betweens and priests. Catholic Anthropological Conference.
Publications.
4, no. 5 (Dec. 1941), 713-754.
VI.   Illness and its ritual. JEAS 4, no. 4 (Oct. 1955), 1-155.
VII. Hunting and its ritual. JEAS 6, no. 1 (1957), 1-28.
Maher: A thorough and detailed description.
E/M   5   4
Sals: E   5   3/4

3072. LEÓN OF KUTUG. Extract from the "Munhúdhúd"...obtained from León of Kutug,
an Ifugao from Kiángan... With a preface by H. Otley Beyer. 1902. 2, 8p.
(In: Beyer collection of Filipiniana. v.14/9, paper 19) Microfilm copy
at Yale Univ.
Cited in Harold Conklin, Ifugao bibliography. 1968. p.46.
Maher: I   5   7

3073. LOOFS, HELMUT H. A dying megalithic culture - urgent ethnological research
among the Ifugao, Luzon, Philippines. International Committee on Urgent
Anthropological and Ethnological Research. Bulletin no. 7 (1965), 29-32.
Maher: E   3   6

3074. _____. Urgent ethnological research among the Ifugao, Luzon, Philippines.
International Committee on Urgent Anthropological and Ethnological Research.
Bulletin no. 8 (1966), 77-82.

3075. LOWIE, ROBERT H. Ifugao. (In: Lowie, Robert H. Primitive society. New
York, Liveright Publishing Co., 1920. p.409-412)
Maher: E   4   4

3076. MEAD, MARGARET. Interpretative statement (Ifugao). (In: Mead, Margaret,
ed. Cooperation and competition among primitive peoples. New York and London, McGraw-Hill Book Co., 1937. p.499-500)
Maher: E   4   4

3077. MERRILL, ELMER D. Quiangan, a brief description written in 1903. 3p.

(In: Beyer collection of Filipiniana. v.14/9, paper 13) Microfilm copy
at Yale Univ.
Cited in Harold Conklin, Ifugao bibliography. 1968. p.51.
    Maher: N   5   4

3078. ROGINSKY, J. J. and R. F. BARTON. Ifugao somatology. PJS 74, no. 4 (Apr.
1941), 349-365.
    Maher: E   5   4

3079. SCOTT, WILLIAM HENRY. The Ifugaos a hundred years ago. Unitas 40, no. 1
(Mar. 1967), 53-65.

3080. STARR, JUNE. Leadership and cognatic residence groups in Ifugao, Bontok,
and Kalinga. 1961. 77p. Thesis (M.A.) - Columbia Univ.
    Eggan: E   4   4
    Maher: E   4   7

3081. STEWART, KILTON R. The old man of the mountains in Luzon. PM 31, no. 2
(Feb. 1934), 55-56, 85-86.
    Maher: E   3   4

3082. TAYLOR, CARL N. Walking through Ifugao. PM 26, no. 12 (May 1930), 778-
779, 798, 800, 802.

3083. VILLAVERDE, JUAN. The Ifugaos of Quiangan and vicinity. Translated, edited
and illustrated by Dean C. Worcester. With notes and addendum by L. E. Case.
PJS 4A, no. 4 (July 1909), 237-262. 15 plates.
    Maher: Significant observations by a 19th century Spaniard.
                M   5   3

3084. WILLCOX, CORNÉLIS DE WITT. The head hunters of Northern Luzon. From Ifugao
to Kalinga, a ride through the mountains of Northern Luzon, with an appendix
on the independence of the Philippines. Kansas City, Mo., Franklin Hudson
Pub. Co., 1912. 304p.
    Maher: T/H   3   4

3085. WILSON, LAURENCE L. The Ifugao calendar. 4 typescript p. Baguio, 1955.
Cited in Harold Conklin, Ifugao bibliography. 1968. p.74.
    Maher: F   5   7

3086. WORCESTER, DEAN C. Head-hunters of northern Luzon. National Geographic
Magazine 23, no. 9 (Sept. 1912), 833-930. 102 photos and maps.
    Maher: G   3   4

3087. _____. The non-Christian peoples of the Philippine Islands. National Geographic Magazine 24, no. 11 (Nov. 1913), 1157-1256. 32 colored photos and
41 black and white photos.
    Maher: G   3   4

3088. _____. Notes on some primitive Philippine tribes. National Geographic Magazine 9, no. 6 (June 1898), 284-301.
    Maher: G   3   4

IFUGAO - AGRICULTURE AND FOOD

3089. BEYER, H. OTLEY. The origin and history of the Philippine rice terraces. Eight Pacific Science Congress. Proceedings. 1 (1955), 387-398. 6 plates.
      Maher: Interesting speculations on Ifugao prehistory by an experienced specialist.
               E   4/5   7

3090. _____ and ELMER D. MERRILL. Ifugao economic plants, 1911. 29p. (In: Beyer collection of Filipiniana. v.14/9, paper 23) Microfilm copy at Yale Univ. Cited in Harold Conklin, Ifugao bibliography. 1968. p.15.
      Maher: An early effort at ethnobotany which has provided comparative date for Conklin's more recent work.
               E/N   5   4

3091. BOSTON, W. S. The Banaue rice terraces. PM 37, no. 4 (Apr. 1940), 138-139.

3092. CONKLIN, HAROLD C. Ifugao ethnobotany 1905-1965: the 1911 Beyer-Merrill report in perspective. Economic Botany 21, no. 3 (July/Sept. 1967), 243-272. (Also in Zamora, Mario D., ed. Studies in Philippine anthropology. Quezon City, Alemar-Phoenix Publishing House, 1967. p.204-262.)
      Maher: A study in Ifugao ethnobotany including Conklin's recent work and previously unpublished data gathered at the beginning of the century by Beyer and Merrill.
               E   5   7

3093. _____. Some aspects of ethnographic research in Ifugao. New York Academy of Sciences. Transactions. Series II, 30, no. 1 (Nov. 1967), 99-121.
      Maher: A report on recent research using new methods and fresh concepts.
               E   5   6

3094. LAMBRECHT, FRANCIS. The Mayawyaw ritual: 1. Rice culture and rice ritual. Catholic Anthropological Conference. Publications 4, no. 1 (Dec. 1932), 1-167.
      Maher: E/M   5   4
      Sals: E   5   4

3095. _____. The Mayawyaw ritual: 7. Hunting and its ritual. JEAS 6, no. 1 (Jan. 1957), 1-28.
      Maher: A systematic continuation of the author's earlier efforts toward a detailed description of the ritual of the Mayawyaw Ifugao.
               E/M   5   4
      Sals: E   5   4

3096. WRIGHT, HAMILTON. Savage irrigation in Luzon; the wonderful rice terraces of the headhunting Ifugaos. Scientific American 106, (1912), 108, 116-117.

IFUGAO - ARCHAEOLOGY

3097. LOOFS, HELMUT H. A dying megalithic culture - urgent ethnological research among the Ifugao, Luzon, Philippines. International Committee on Urgent Anthropological and Ethnological Research. Bulletin 7 (1965), 29-32.
      Maher: E   3   6

3098. _____. Some remarks on "Philippine Megaliths". AS 3, no. 3 (Dec. 1965), 393-402.
      Maher: E   3   6

3099. SOLHEIM, WILHELM G., II and TERRY SHULER. Further notes on Philippine pottery manufacture: Mountain Province and Panay. JEAS 8, nos. 1/2 (Jan./Apr. 1959), 1-10.
      Hart: A   5   7
      Maher: A   5   7
      Sibley: A   5   7

IFUGAO - BEHAVIOR PROCESS AND PERSONALITY

3100. GUINID, MARTIN. A psychological study of the customs, mores, taboos of the Ifugao people. 1941. 265p. Thesis (M.A.) - U.P.
Cited in Compilation of graduate theses... p.412.
      Sals: Y   3   7

IFUGAO - BUILDINGS, TOOLS AND EQUIPMENT

3101. LAMBRECHT, FRANCIS. Ifugaw villages and houses. Catholic Anthropological Conference. Publications 1, no. 3 (Aprl 1929), 117-141.
      Maher: Detailed description of Ifugao houses and house construction, with some village maps.
                       E/M   5   4
      Sals: E   5   3/4

IFUGAO - CLOTHING, ADORNMENT AND MATERIALS

3102. LAMBRECHT, FRANCIS. Ifugaw weaving. Folklore Studies (Society of the Divine World. Tokyo, Japan) 17 (1958), 1-53. 22 plates.
      Maher: E/M   5   4
      Sals: E   5   3/4

IFUGAO - DRINK, DRUGS AND INDULGENCE

3103. BEYER, H. OTLEY. Report on the use of a fermented rice drink in Northern
Luzon. (In: The alcohol industry of the Philippine Islands. Part III.
By H. D. Gibbs and F. Agcaoili. PJS 7-A, no. 2 (Apr. 1912), 103-106)
    Maher: E   5   4
    Sals: A   4   4

IFUGAO - ECONOMICS

3104. BARTON, ROY FRANKLIN. Ifugao economics. Berkeley, Univ. of California
Press, 1922. (Univ. of California publications in American archaeology and
ethnography. v.15, no. 5) 385-446, plates 38-45.
    Maher: A detailed account of the economic institutions of a
                    preliterate society.
                    E   5   4
    Sals: E   3   -

3105. GOLDMAN, IRVING. The Ifugao of the Philippine Islands. (In: Mead, Margaret, ed. Cooperation and competition among primitive peoples. ..New York
and London, McGraw-Hill Book Co., 1937. p.153-179)
    Maher: A useful but selective summary.
                    E   4   4

3106. UYAN, VENANCIO T. A proposed program of the high school for the improvement of Ifugao economy. 1958. 242p. Thesis (M.Ed.) - U.P.
Cited in U.P. theses and dissertations index. p.214.
    Sals: Y   3   7

IFUGAO - EDUCATION

3107. LORICA, LORETO Q. Teaching in an Ifugao community. Philippine Educator 10,
no. 2 (July 1955), 32-33.
    Maher: Y   3   6

3108. SALS, FLORENT JOSEPH. Primitive education among the Ifugaos: physical,
mental and vocational. PS 2, no. 3 (Sept. 1954), 266-285.
    Maher: M/Y   4   7
    Sals: Y   4   7

3109. _____. Primitive education among the Ifugaos: religious and moral. PS 3,
no. 1 (Mar. 1955), 70-89.
    Maher: M/Y   4   7
    Sals: Y   4   7

3110. _____. A study of primitive education among the Ifugaos. 1952. Thesis
(M.A.) - Ateneo de Manila.

Cited in Compilation of graduate theses ... p. 208.
        Maher: M/Y   4   7
        Sals: Y   4   7

IFUGAO - FAMILY AND KINSHIP

3111.   BARTON, ROY FRANKLIN. Reflections in two kinship terms of the transition to
        endogamy. AA n.s. 43, no. 4, pt. 1 (Oct./Dec. 1941), 540-549.
            Maher: E   5   4

3112.   LAMBRECHT, FRANCIS. Genealogical tree of Kiangan. JEAS 3, no. 4 (July/
        Oct. 1954), 366-369.
            Maher: A striking example of the extent of Ifugao genealogical
                            memory.
                            E/M   5   7
            Sals: E   5   7
3113.   _____. Genealogical trees of Mayawyaw. JEAS 2, no. 3 (Apr. 1953), 21-27.
            Maher: E/M   5   7
            Sals: E   5   7

3114.   _____. Ifugao genealogies. Social Justice Review 41, (Jan. 1949), 296-
        301.
            Maher: E/M   5   7
            Sals: E   5   7

IFUGAO - GEOGRAPHY AND DEMOGRAPHY

3115.   CONKLIN, HAROLD C. Some aspects of ethnographic research in Ifugao. New
        York Academy of Sciences. Transactions. Series II, 30, no. 1 (Nov. 1967),
        99-121.

3116.   VELÁSQUEZ, JOAQUIN. Census of the Ifugao clan district of Damag, Province
        of Isabela. 1903. 4p. (In: Beyer Collection of Filipiniana. v.14/16,
        paper 145) Microfilm copy at Yale Univ.
        Cited in Harold Conklin, Ifugao bibliography. 1968. p.66.
            Maher: G   5   3

IFUGAO - HEALTH AND SICKNESS

3117.   GUTHRIE, GEORGE M. Impressions of Ifugao health and social activities.
        Univ. Park, Pa., Dept. of Psychology, Pennsylvania State Univ., 1964. 68p.
        (Research Bulletin, no. 42)

3118. LAMBRECHT, FRANCIS. The Mayawyaw ritual: VI. Illness and its ritual.
       JEAS 4, no. 4 (Oct. 1955), 1-155.
             Maher: E/M   5   4
             Sals: E   5   7

IFUGAO - HISTORY AND CULTURE CHANGE

3119. MEIMBAN, MAXIMO (Compiler). Historical documents from the subprovince of
       Ifugao, P.I. 1911. 185p. (In: Beyer Collection of Filipiniana. v.14/13,
       paper 89) Microfilm copy at Yale Univ.
       Cited in Harold Conklin, Ifugao bibliography. 1968. p.51.
             Maher: G   4   7

IFUGAO - INDUSTRIES

3120. HARTENDORP, A. V. H. Ifugao wood carving. Philippines Quarterly 1, no. 2
       (Sept. 1951), 17-28.

IFUGAO - LANGUAGE AND LITERATURE

3121. NEWELL, LEONARD E. A Batad Ifugao vocabulary. New Haven, Conn., Human Re-
       lations Area Files, Inc., 1968. 230p. (HRAFlex Book OA19-001)

3122. _____. An Ifugao text. Oceania Linguistic Monographs 3, (1958), 73-76.
             Maher: L   5   6

IFUGAO - MARRIAGE

3123. BARTON, ROY FRANKLIN. How marriage-prohibitions arose. PM 35, no. 8 (Aug.
       1938), 380-381, 394.
             Maher: E   4   7

3124. LAMBRECHT, FRANCIS. The Mayawyaw ritual: 2. Marriage and marriage ritual.
       Publications 4, no. 2 (Mar. 1935), 169-325.
             Maher: E/M   5   4
             Sals: E   5   7

IFUGAO - MOBILITY AND SOCIAL STRATIFICATION

3125. BAGUILAT, RAYMUNDO. The Ifugao Hagabi. PM 37, no. 2 (Feb. 1940), 65.
        Reprinted in JEAS 4, no. 1 (Jan. 1955), 108-109.
              Maher: -   4   4
              Sals: 0   3   7

3126. LAMBRECHT, FRANCIS. Genealogical tree of Kiangan. JEAS 3, no. 4 (July/
        Oct. 1954), 366-369.
              Maher: A striking example of the extent of Ifugao genealogical
                          memory.
                          E/M   5   7
              Sals: E   5   7

IFUGAO - POLITICAL ORGANIZATION AND BEHAVIOR

3127. BARTON, ROY FRANKLIN. ... Ifugao law. California. Univ. Publications in
        American Archaeology and Ethnology 15, no. 1 (Feb. 15, 1919), 1-186. 33
        plates.
              Maher: A classic study of primitive law.
                          E   5   4

3128. _____. Lawsuit and good custom à la Ifugao. Asia (New York) 29, no. 8
        (Aug. 1929), 599-607, 660-664.
              Maher: E   5   4

3129. _____. Philippine pagans; the autobiographies of three Ifugaos...London,
        George Routledge and Sons, Ltd., 1938. 271p. 24 plates.
              Maher: E   5   4

3130. _____. White man's law among Filipino tribesmen; U.S. versus Wild Rasp-
        berry, Limitit, Of-a-Soundness, Too-Little, and Father-of-Landslides. Asia
        (New York) 30, no. 6 (June 1930), 410-416, 445-448.
              Maher: E   5   4

3131. HOEBEL, E. ADAMSON. The Ifugao, private law in northern Luzon. (In:
        Hoebel, Edward A., ed. The law of primitive man; a study in comparative
        legal dynamics. Cambridge, Harvard Univ. Press, [1954]. 1964. p.101-126)
              Maher: Important for the interpretive and theoretical view it
                          brings to the Ifugao data.
                          E   4   4

3132. LAMBRECHT, FRANCIS. Ifugao custom and the moral law. PS 10, no. 2 (Apr.
        1962), 275-303.
              Maher: E/M   4/5   4
              Sals: E   5   7

3133. _____. The Ifugao law of customs in the light of natural moral law and
        primitive revelation. Sower, Part I. 2, no. 4 (Dec. 1960), 191-204;
        Part II. 3, (Second Quarter 1961), 94-112.

Maher: An interesting examination of Ifugao law from the per-
         spective of Catholic theology.
         E/M 5/4 4
Sals: E 5 7

3134. LEON, RAYMUNDO DE. Law and politics with the Ifugaos. Philippine International 6, no. 3 (Feb. 1962), 18-21, 25, 27.
    Sals: Y 3 7

IFUGAO - PROPERTY AND EXCHANGE

3135. GALLMAN, JEFF D. Slave-dealing in Ifugao. 1912. 17p. (In: Beyer Collection of Filipiniana. v.14/16, paper 144) Microfilm copy at Yale Univ.
   Cited in Harold Conklin, Ifugao bibliography. 1968. p.34.
    Maher: G 5 7

3136. LAMBRECHT, FRANCIS. The Mayawyaw ritual: 4. Property and property ritual.
   Catholic Anthropological Conference. Pub. 4, no. 4 (Oct. 1939), 495-711.
    Maher: E/M 5 4
    Sals: E 5 7

3137. _____. Property laws of custom among the Ifugaos. SJ 11, nos. 1/2 (Mar./
   June 1964), 57-70.
    Maher: E/M 5 4
    Sals: E 5 7

3138. _____. Private property laws of custom among the Ifugaos. Saint Louis
   Quarterly 2, no. 2 (June 1964), 129-146.
    Maher: E/M 5 4
    Sals: E 5 7

3139. RADIN, PAUL. Systematized property law: the Ifugao. (In: Radin, Paul, ed.
   Social Anthropology. New York and London, McGraw-Hill Book Co., 1932. p.113-
   123)
    Maher: E 4 4

IFUGAO - RELIGIOUS BELIEFS AND PRACTICES

3140. ALARCÓN, FRAY RUPERTO. A description of the customs of the peoples of Ki-
   angan, Bunhian and Mayoyao, 1857.
   Translated by William Henry Scott. Indiana. Univ. Folklore Institute.
   Journal 2, no. 1 (June 1965), 78-100.
    Maher: A very early report.
         M 5 3

3141. BARTON, ROY FRANKLIN. The funeral of Aliguyen. (In: Willcox, Cornelius
   De Witt. The head hunters of northern Luzon, from Ifugao to Kalinga.

Kansas City, Franklin Hudson Publishing, 1912. p.126-138)
    Maher: E   5   4

3142. _____. The half-way sun; life among the headhunters of the Philippines.
New York, Brewer and Warren, Inc., 1930. 315p.
    Maher: The basic general account of Ifugao culture.
                    E   5   4
    Sals: E   4   4

3143. _____. The harvest feast of the Kiangan Ifugao. PJS 6D, no. 2 (Apr.
1911), 81-105. 8 plates.
    Maher: Basic descriptive material on one of the most important
                    of Ifugao ceremonies.
                    E   5   4

3144. _____. Hunting soul-stuff; the motive behind headtaking as practised by
Ifugaos of the Philippines. Asia (New York) 30, no. 3 (Mar. 1930), 188-
195, 225-226.
    Maher: E   5   4

3145. _____. Ispolsovanie mifov kak magii u gornikh chasti Filippin. Sovetaka-
ia Etnografiia, no. 3 (1935), 77-95. ("The use of myths as magic among the
mountain tribes of the Philippines. English translation from the Russian,
by Joshua Kunitz, for the Human Relations Area Files, duplicated for the
files." Conklin, Ifugao bibliography. 1968. p.9.

3146. _____. My Ifugao brother's gods. Asia (New York) 29, no. 10 (Oct. 1929),
806-814, 822-824.
    Maher: E   5   4

3147. _____. The mythology of the Ifugaos. Philadelphia, American Folklore Society, 1955. 244p. (American Folklore Society. Memoirs. v.46.)
    Maher: Most extensive source on eastern Ifugao mythology.
                    E   5   4

3148. _____. Myths and their magic use in Ifugao. PM 37, no. 9 (Sept. 1940),
348, 351.
Reprinted: JEAS 3, no. 4 (1954), 477-479.
    Maher: E   5   4

3149. _____. The religion of the Ifugaos. Menasha, Wisconsin, American Anthropological Association, 1946. 219p. (Memoir series of the American Anthropological Association, no. 65)
    Maher: A basic source on religion in eastern Ifugao.
                    E   5   4
    Sals: E   5   7

3150. _____. The religion of the Kiangan Ifugao with an appendix by H. Otley
Beyer, containing an introduction, notes, and cross references to this manuscript. 1910-1911. 328 typescript. (In: Beyer Collection of Filipiniana. v.14/2) Microfilm copy at Yale Univ.
Cited in Harold Conklin, Ifugao bibliography. 1968. p.8.
    Maher: E   5   4
    Sals: E   5   7

3151. BEYER, H. OTLEY. Appendix to Roy Franklin Barton's The Religion of the Kiangan Ifugaos. 1911. p.264-328. (In: Beyer Collection of Filipiniana.
v.14/2. Microfilm copy at Yale Univ.)
Cited in Harold Conklin, Ifugao bibliography. 1968. p.8.
    Maher: E   5   4
    Sals: A   4   7

3152. _____. Origin myths among the mountain peoples of the Philippines. PJS
8D, no. 2 (Apr. 1913), 85-117. 4 plates.
    Maher: E   5   4
    Sals: A   4   7

3153. _____ and ROY FRANKLIN BARTON. An Ifugao burial ceremony. PJS 6D, no. 5
(Nov. 1911), 227-252. 10 plates.
    Maher: E   5   4
    Sals: A   4   4

3154. CASE, L. E. Why the Ifugaos take the heads of their enemies. PJS 4A, no. 4
(July 1909), 255-260.
    Maher: G   5   4

3155. DUFF, ROGER S. An ethnographic excursion to the mountain province of Luzon,
Philippines. Mourning rites for an Ifugao mountaineer. Polynesian Society
Journal 63, nos. 3/4 (Sept./Dec. 1954), 234-242. 5 plates.
    Maher: Description of a post-war Himong ceremony for a man who
              died by violence in central Ifugao.
             E   5   6

3156. GUINID, MARTIN. A psychological study of the customs, mores, taboos of the
Ifugao people. 1941. 265p. Thesis (M.A.) - U.P.
Cited in Compilation of graduate theses ... p.412.
    Sals: Y   3   7

3157. IMATUNG, PABLO. Ifugao religious ceremonies, 1910. 31p. (In: Beyer Collection of Filipiniana. v.14/9, paper 18) Microfilm copy at Yale Univ.
Cited in Harold Conklin, Ifugao bibliography. 1968. p.38.
    Maher: I   5   7

3158. KANE, SAMUEL E. Baguio, gateway to wonderland. Describing 20 trips in the
mountain province with interesting customs of the mountain people. Manila,
Sugar News Press, 1931. 148p.
    Maher: G   3   4

3159. KOENIGSWALD, GUSTAV H. R. VON. Bemerkungen zum Skelettkult: Beobachtungen
auf Java und den Philippinen. Anthropologischer Anzeiger 23/24, nos. 2/3
(1960), 168-177.
    Maher: D   5   7

3160. LAMBRECHT, FRANCIS. Adoption of Ifugao local customs in christianity.
Saint Louis Quarterly 1, no. 1 (Mar. 1963), 5-30.
Reprinted: PSR 11, (Jan./Apr. 1963), 12-28.
    Maher: E/M   5   7
    Sals: E   5   7

3161. _____. Ancestors' knowledge among the Ifugaos and its importance in the

religious and social life of the tribe. JEAS 3, no. 4 (July/Oct. 1954), 359-365.
    Maher: E/M   5   7
    Sals: E   4   7

3162. _____. R. F. Barton's book on the religion of the Ifugaos. Anthropos 51, nos. 1/ 2 (1956), 311-319.
    Maher: A critical review of Barton by a fellow specialist in Ifugao religion.
                E/M 4/5   4
    Sals: E   5   7

3163. _____. The Hudhúd of Dinulawan and Bugan at Gonhadan. SLQ 5, nos. 3/4 (Sept./Dec. 1967), 267-713.

3164. _____. Ifugao custom and the moral law. PS 10, no. 2 (Apr. 1962), 275-303.
    Maher: E/M 5/4   4
    Sals: E   5   7

3165. _____. The Ifugao law of custom in the light of natural moral law and primitive revelation. Sower 2, no. 4 (Dec. 1960), 191-204; 3, (Second Quarter 1961), 94-112.
    Maher: An interesting examination of Ifugao law from the perspective of Catholic theology.
                E/M 4/5   4
    Sals: E   5   7

3166. _____. Ifugaw hudhud literature. (In: Brown heritage, ed. by Antonio G. Manuud. Quezon City, 1967. p.816-837)

3167. _____. The Mayawyaw ritual: 3. Death and death ritual. Catholic Anthropological Conference. Publications 4, no. 3 (Mar. 1938), 327-493.
    Maher: E/M   5   4
    Sals: E   5   7

3168. _____. The Mayawyaw ritual: 5. Go-betweens and priests. Catholic Anthropological Conference. Publications 4, no. 5 (Dec. 1941), 713-754.
    Maher: E/M   5   4
    Sals: E   5   7

3169. _____. The missionary as anthropologist: religious belief among the Ifugao. PS 5, no. 3 (Sept. 1957), 271-286.
    Maher: E/M   5   4
    Sals: E   5   7

3170. _____. The religion of the Ifugao. PSR 10, nos. 1/2 (Jan./Apr. 1962), 33-40.
    Maher: E/M   5   4
    Sals: E   5   7

3171. LI, YIH-YUAN. The structure of the Ifugao religion. Academia Sinica, Taipei. Institute of Ethnology. Bulletin no. 9 (Spring 1960), 387-409. English text: 387-398. Chinese text: 399-409.

3172. MALUMBRES, JULIAN, ed. The religious beliefs of the Kiangan Ifugaos. By Juan
Fernandez Villaverde; with an introd. and notes by J. Malumbres; translated
into English from the original Spanish text by H. Otley Beyer, with the assistance of John M. Garvan and Emerson B. Christie. In Ifugao People, v.3,
paper 3. TS 167p. (1912-15). For first publication, see no. 3175.
Cited by Manuel in Zamora. Studies in Philippine Anthropology. p.33.
Maher: M   5   3

3173. REID, LAWRENCE. Comment on "The acceptance of Ifugao customs into Christianity". PSR 11, nos. 1/2 (Jan./Apr. 1963), 28-31.

3174. SALS, FLORENT JOSEPH. Primitive education among the Ifugaos: religious
and moral. PS 3, no. 1 (Mar. 1955), 70-89.
Maher: M/Y   4   7
Sals: Y   4   7

3175. VILLAVERDE, JUAN FERNANDEZ. Supersticiones de los Igorrotes Ifugaos. Ed.,
with introd. and notes by Fr. Julian Malumbres. El Correo Sino-Annamita 38
(1912), 281-455. (In: Beyer Collection of Filipiniana. v.14/12, paper 71)
Microfilm copy at Yale Univ.
Cited in Harold Conklin, Ifugao bibliography. 1968. p.72.
Maher: First hand reports of 19th century customs and myths by
                a Spanish priest.
                M   5   3

IFUGAO - STANDARD OF LIVING AND RECREATION

3176. BAGUILAT, RAYMUNDO. The Ifugao Hagabi. PM 37, no. 2 (Feb. 1940), 65.
Reprinted in: JEAS 4, no. 1 (Jan. 1955), 108-109.
Maher: -   4   4
Sals: 0   3   7

3177. WORCESTER, DEAN C. Field sports among the wild men of northern Luzon. National Geographic Magazine 22, **no.** 3 (Mar. 1911), 215-267.
Maher: G   3   4

IFUGAO - TOTAL CULTURE

3178. CONKLIN, HAROLD C. Some aspects of ethnographic research in Ifugao. New
York Academy of Sciences. Transaction. Series II. 30, no. 1 (Nov. 1967),
99-121.
Maher: A report on recent research using new methods and fresh
                concepts.
                E   5   6

3179. GOLDMAN, IRVING. The Ifugao of the Philippine Islands. (In: Mead, Margaret, ed. Cooperation and competition among primitive peoples...New York

and London, McGraw-Hill Book Co., 1937. p.153-179)
   Maher: E   4   4

                    IGOROT-BONTOC   -   GENERAL

3180. BARTON, ROY FRANKLIN. The Igorots today. Asia (New York) 41, no. 6 (June
       1941), 307-310.
          Eggan: Brief account of modern adjustment of Igorots of Sagada.
                          E   5   4

3181. BEAN, ROBERT BENNETT. The Benguet Igorots. A somatologic study of the
       live folk of Benguet and Lepanto-Bontoc. PJS 3A, no. 6 (Dec. 1908), 413-
       472. 8 plates.
          Eggan: Primarily observations on physical types in Benguet.
                          D   3-5   4

3182. BEYER, H. OTLEY. Correspondence and records concerning the Igorot mummy
       (Ano). Philippine Ethnographic Series, Igorot Set, v.6 (1915-1920), papers
       47 and 48.
       Cited by Manuel in Zamora, Studies in Philippine Anthropology. 1967. p.34.
          Eggan: E   4   4

3183. _____. The history and ethnography of the Bontok people; being a complete
       collection of all known printed and manuscript information relating to the
       history and ethnography of the Bontok people of northern Luzon, Philippine
       Islands uniformly edited, annotated, and translated into English. 5 vols.
       Cited in Harvard Univ. Peabody Museum...Library. Catalogue: Authors.
       v.3, p.105.
          Eggan: A basic source collection of manuscripts and documents.
                          E   3-5   3/4

3184. _____. The Igorotes. Philippine Education 4, no. 4 (1907), 14-18.

3185. _____ and TUGINAI PAIT. List of specimens in the ethnological collection
       from the Ifugao, Igorot, and Bontok peoples of northern Luzon, collected
       for the Peabody Museum of Ethnology, by H. Otley Beyer and Tuginai Pait.
       Oct. 1908. Cambridge, Mass. Typed copy. 7p. (In: Beyer Collection of
       Filipiniana. v.14/16, paper 141) Microfilm copy at Yale Univ.
       Cited in Harold Conklin, Ifugao bibliography. 1968. p.12.
          Maher: E   5   5

3186. BLUMENTRITT, FERDINAND. Igorroten und andere wilde Stämme der Philippinen.
       Zeitschrift für Ethnologie. Verhandlungen 16 (1884), 56-57.
          Eggan: Derived from secondary sources--mainly Spanish.
                          E   3   3

3187. _____. Die Igorroten von Pangasinan. Nach den Mittheilungen des Mission-
       ärs P. Fr. Mariano Rodriguez. Kaiserlich Konigliche Geographischen Gesell-
       schaft in Wien. Mitteilungen. 43, nos. 3/4 (1900), 87-100.
          Anderson: Short ethnographic note by Fr. Mariano Rodrigues. trans-
                          lated by Blumentritt. It mentions the racial features

of the Igorrots, their house and village forms, their agricultural practices and religious representations. Furthermore, their manufacture, forms of usury, marriage practices as well as some of their games, diseases and household items are outlined.

N   5   3

Eggan: Derived from secondary sources--mainly Spanish.

E   3   3

3188. _____. Mittheilungen über die negritos und die Kopfjägerstämme des nördlichen Luzon. Globus 45, no. 5 (1884), 74-78.

Eggan: Derived from secondary sources--mainly Spanish.

E   3   3

Warren: N   3   3

3189. CORDERO, NARCISO. Note on the measurements of height and weight of Igorots. Philippine Islands Medical Association Journal 10, no. 4 (Apr. 1930), 159-161.

Eggan: Primarily relevant to physical anthropology.

D   4?   4

3190. DINWIDDIE, WILLIAM. The Igorrote's endurance. Current literature; a magazine of contemporary record 29, no. 3 (Sept. 1900), 328-329.

Eggan: William Dinwiddie was Governor of Mountain Province. Brief.

G   5   4

3191. EGGAN, FRED and WILLIAM HENRY SCOTT. Ritual life of the Igorots of Sagada: from birth to adolescence. Ethnology 2, no. 1 (Jan. 1963), 40-54.

Eggan: Detailed account.

E and M/E   5   4

3192. _____. Ritual life of the Igorots of Sagada: courtship and marriage. Ethnology 4, no. 1 (Jan. 1965), 77-111.

Eggan: Detailed survey.

E and M/E   5   4

3193. JENKS, ALBERT ERNEST. Ba-long-long, the Igorot boy. Illustrated by Marian Deborah Seiders. Chicago, Row, Peterson & Co. [1907] 183p.

Eggan: Written for boys but based on field research.

E   5   4

3194. _____. The Bontoc Igorot. Manila, Bureau of Public Printing, 1905. 226p. (Philippine islands. Ethnological survey. Publications. v.1)

Eggan: Standard reference. Excellent on material culture.

E   5   4

3195. KANE, SAMUEL E. Life or death in Luzon; thirty years of adventure with the Philippine highlanders. Indianapolis, Bobbs-Merrill Co., 1933. 331p. (English edition: Thirty years with the Philippine head-hunters. London, Jarrolds, 1934. 288p.)

Eggan: Kane was a government official--much of data from Jenks, etc.

G   3   4

Maher: Contains some interesting personal experiences of the early days of American administration.
G   3   4

3196. KROEBER, ALFRED L. Measurements of Igorotes. AA n.s. 8, no. 1 (Jan./Mar. 1906), 194.
Eggan: Measurements of Igorots at St. Louis Exposition. 1904.
E   4   4

3197. MEYER, HANS. Die Igorroten. (In: Eine Weltreise: Plauderein über eine zweijährige Erdumseglung. Leipzig und Wien. Verlag des Bibliographischen Instituts, 1885. p.505-543)
Cited in William H. Scott, Cordillera bibliography. 1970. p.42.
Eggan: Excellent German account of Igorots.
K/E   5   3

3198. _____. Die Igorrotes von Luzon (Philippinen). Zeitschrift für Ethnologie. Verhandlungen 15 (1883), 377-390.
Eggan: Excellent German account of Igorots.
K/E   5   3

3199. OAKES, CHRISTOPHER. Bontoc the year around. Baguio Midland Courier (June 22, 1947), 8-16.
Cited in William H. Scott, Cordillera bibliography. 1970. p.44.
Eggan: Account for newspaper.
J?   5?   4

3200. ORENDAIN, JUAN CLARO. Philippine wonderland. Baguio, Philippines. 1940. 334p.
Eggan: Travel account.
J   5   4

3201. PACYAYA, ALFREDO G. Life in a Sagada dap-ay. Gold Ore 4, no. 17 (May 2, 1951); 4, no. 18 (May 9, 1951).
Cited in William H. Scott, Cordillera bibliography. 1970. p.45.
Eggan: Pacyaya is a native of Sagada and a government official.
I/E   5   4

3202. _____. The Sagada ebgan. Gold Ore 5, no. 1 (July 27, 1951), 2-4.
Cited in William H. Scott, Cordillera bibliography. 1970. p.45.
Eggan: I/E   5   4

3203. PASSMORE, FRED. Our changing mountain-men. PM 36, no. 4 (Apr. 1939), 158-160.
Eggan: -   3   4

3204. PÉREZ, ANGEL. Igorrotes, estudio geográfico y etnográfico sobre algúnos distritos del norte de Luzon. Manila, Imprenta de "El Mercantil", 1903. 419p.
Eggan: An excellent but brief survey of Igorot municipalities.
M   3/5   3

3205. _____. Memoria descriptive de Benguet y sus misiones arreglada por el P. Fr. Angel Pérez. (In: Pérez, Angel, ed.: Relaciones agustinianas de las razas del norte de Luzon. p.163-206) pl. VI-VII. Manila, Bureau of

Printing, 1904. p.163-206. (Philippine Islands. Ethnological survey.
Publications. v.3)
    Eggan: M   3-5   3
    Maher: M   5   3

3206. RODRÍQUEZ, MARIANO. Etnografía filipina: Igorrotes y Salvajes de la Cordillera Nordeste de Pangasinan. El Correo Sino-Annamita. 28 (1894), 261-
321; 29 (1895), 313-379.
Reprinted in La Política de España en Filipinas.
              5, no. 106 (Feb. 26, 1895), 55-56.
                  no. 107 (Mar. 12, 1895), 67-71.
                  no. 109 (Apr. 9, 1895), 92-94.
                  no. 110 (Apr. 23, 1895), 105-107.
                  no. 111 (May 7, 1895), 125-127.
                  no. 112 (May 21, 1895), 142-144.
                  no. 113 (June 4, 1895), 148-151.
    Eggan: Annual letters.
             M   5   3

3207. SCHADENBERG, ALEXANDER. Beiträge zur Kenntnis der im Innern Nordluzons le-
benden Stämme. Zeitschrift für ethnologie. Verhandlungen   20 (1888), 34-
42; 21 (1889), 674-700.
    Eggan: Schadenberg was an excellent observer.
            J/K   5   3

3208. SCHEIDNAGEL, MANUEL. Filipinas. Igorrotes. SGMB 12, (Feb. 1882), 148-152.
    Eggan: Brief reference.
            -      3   3

3209. SCHIER, S. S. Ken-say of the sky world. Asia (New York) 41, no. 2 (Feb.
1941), **75-78**.
    Eggan: Amateur ethnologist and collector of folklore.
            E(?) 3-5   4

3210. SCOTT, WILLIAM HENRY. The word Igorot. PS 10, no. 2 (Apr. 1962), 234-
248.
    Eggan: Excellent knowledge of Mountain Province.
            M/E   5   4

3211. STARR, JUNE. Leadership and cognatic residence groups in Ifugao, Bontok,
and Kalinga. 1961. 77p. Thesis (M.A.) - Columbia Univ.
    Eggan: E   4   4
    Maher: E   4   7

3212. VILLAVERDE, JUAN F. Plan de misiones para reducir á los Igorrotes de **Nueva**
Vizcaya, Isabela y Cagayan. Manila, Est. Tip. del Colegio de Sto. Tomás.,
1880. 28p.
    Eggan: Villaverde was an outstanding missionary.
            M   5   3

3213. VIVAR, PEDRO DE. Relación del establecimiento y estado de las nuevas misiones [en la nación de Igorrotes, 1755-56, y cartas de varios padres misi-
oneros] (In: Pérez, Angel, comp.: Relaciones agustinianas de las razas
del norte de Luzon. p.131-162) (Philippine Islands. Ethnological survey.
Publications. v.3)

Eggan: M   3   3

3214. WHITMARSH, PHELPS. Among the wild Igorrotes. Outlook 65, no. 4 (May 26, 1900), 213-218.
      Eggan: Popular account of United States administrator.
      G   5   4

3215. _____. The land of the Igorrotes. Outlook 64, no. 17 (April 28, 1900), 960-966.
      Eggan: Popular account of United States administrator.
      G   5   4

3216. ZINGG, ROBERT M. The Bontocs - a primitive Malay of the Philippines. Inter-Ocean 11, (1930), 227-232.
Cited in Robert B. Fox, A selected bibliography of the peoples of Mt. Province, Northern Luzon, Philippines. Chicago, Univ. of Chicago.
      Eggan: Brief account by teacher who later became ethnologist.
      E   5   4

IGOROT-BONTOC - AGRICULTURE AND FOOD

3217. ACLOP, LEONARD. Home life in Tetep-an. Some notes on family and food in a Western Bontoc village of Northern Luzon in the Philippines. Folklore Studies (Society of the Divine World. Tokyo, Japan) 20, (1961), 275-290.
      Eggan: Aclop is a native of this community. Excellent account.
      I   5   4

3218. BIRKET-SMITH, KAJ. The rice cultivation and rice-harvest feast of the Bontoc Igorot. Det Kongelige Danske Videnskabernes Selskab, Historisk-Filologiske Meddelelser 32, nr. 8 (1952), 24p. 16 plates.
      Eggan: Brief account but good data.
      E   5   4

IGOROT-BONTOC - ARCHAEOLOGY

3219. VIRCHOW, R. Schädel der Igorroten. Zeitschrift fur Ethnologie. Verhandlungen 15 (1883), 390-400.
      Eggan: Study of Igorot skulls.
      D   4   3

3220. _____. Ueber Negrito-und Igorrotenschädel von den Philippinen. Zeitschrift für Ethnologie. Verhandlungen 4 (1872), 204-209.
      Eggan: Study of Igorot skulls.
      D   4   3
      Warren: D   5   3

IGOROT-BONTOC - CLOTHING, ADORNMENT AND MATERIALS

3221. GRISHAM, GLEN. The native dress of the Igorot people. PM 28, no. 7 (Dec. 1931), 339, 352, 354-356.

3222. JENKS, ALBERT E. Bontoc Igorot clothing. AA n.s. 6, no. 5 (Oct./Dec. 1904), 695-704. 5 plates.
   Eggan: Based on field research.
          E 5   4

IGOROT-BONTOC - COMMUNITY DEVELOPMENT AND TERRITORIAL ORGANIZATION

3223. BASCO, CARMEN VIBAR. Two Bago villages: a study. JEAS 5, no. 2 (Apr. 1956), 125-212.
   Bello: Presents original materials on Bago culture--the only village study undertaken so far in that area.
          Y 5   4
   Eggan: Study of "New Christian" Igorot Communities.
          S? 5   4

IGOROT-BONTOC - ECONOMICS

3224. JENKS, ALBERT ERNEST. The Bontoc Igorot. Manila, Bureau of Public Printing, 1905. 226p. (Philippine Islands. Ethnological survey. Publications. v.1)
   Eggan: Standard reference. Excellent on material culture.
          E 5   4

IGOROT-BONTOC - EDUCATION

3225. BAUTISTA, MARCELINO. In the Igorot country - A PPSTA [Philippine Public School Teachers Assn.] chapter convention. Philippine Educator 11, no. 10 (Apr. 1957), 26-31.
   Eggan: Y 3   4

3226. SCOTT, WILLIAM HENRY. Educational work with a cultural minority. SJ 11, nos. 1/2 (Mar./June 1964), 39-48.
   Eggan: Education among the Igorots.
          M/E 5   4

3227. STEEN, REV. JOHN P. VAN DE. Critical issues in Bontoc education. 1956. 102p. Thesis (M.A.) - Ateneo de Manila Univ.
   Eggan: M.A. thesis.
          Y 5   4

II. LUZON. B. CULTURAL-LINGUISTIC GROUP. IGOROT-BONTOC - FAMILY AND ....

IGOROT-BONTOC - FAMILY AND KINSHIP

3228. ACLOP, LEONARD. Home life in Tetep-An. Some notes on family and food in a Western Bontoc village of Northern Luzon in the Philippines. Folklore Studies (Society of the Divine World. Tokyo, Japan) 20, (1961), 275-290.
Eggan: Aclop is a native of this community. Excellent account.
              I   5   4

3229. EGGAN, FRED. The Sagada Igorots of northern Luzon. (In: Murdock, George Peter, ed. Social structure in Southeast Asia. 1960. p.24-50) (In:Wenner-Gren Foundation for Anthropological Research, Inc. Viking Fund Publications in anthropology, no. 29)
Eggan: Social structure of Sagada Igorots.
              E   5   4

3230. HIMES, RONALD S. The Bontok kinship system. PSR 12, nos. 3/4 (July/Oct. 1964), 159-172.
Eggan: Good account.
              S   5   4

3231. KEESING, FELIX M. Some notes on Bontok social organization, Northern Philippines. AA 51, no. 4, pt. 1 (Oct./Dec. 1949), 578-601.
Eggan: Excellent account.
              E   5   4

IGOROT-BONTOC - FINE ARTS

3232. CLAERHOUDT, ALFONSO. The songs of a people: Igorot customs in Eastern Benguet. SLQ 4, no. 2 (June 1966), 163-278.

3233. GARCÍA, MOTOS M. and M. SCHNEIDER. Catálogo de los instrumentos musicales "igorrotes" conservados en el Museo Etnológico de Madrid. Antropología y Etnología (Madrid), 4 (1951), 9-19.
Eggan: Musical instruments.
              -        4   3

3234. REID, LAWRENCE. Dancing and music. PSR 9, nos. 3/4 (July/Oct. 1961), 55-82.
Eggan: Excellent.
              M/L   5   4

3235. VANOVERBERGH, MORICE. Dadáy-and Lakúgey-songs in Lepanto Igorot as it is spoken at Bauko. Anthropos 41, nos. 1/3 (1946/1949), 177-184.
Eggan: Excellent.
              M/E   5   4

3236. _____. Songs in Lepanto-Igorot as it is spoken at Bauko. Vienna-Mödling, St. Gabriel's Mission Press, 1954. 141p. (Studia Instituti Anthropos, v.7)
Eggan: Excellent.
              M/E   5   4

IGOROT-BONTOC - HISTORY AND CULTURE CHANGE

3237. GRISHAM, GLEN. Transition. PM 31, no. 3 (Mar. 1934), 118, 122-125.

3238. PACYAYA, ALFREDO G. Acculturation and culture change in Sagada. SJ 11, nos. 1/2 (Mar./June 1964), 14-25.
Eggan: Good study of own village.
               I/Y   5   4

3239. _____. A study of the effects of acculturation on the life and culture of the Sagada natives of western Bontoc. 1961. Thesis (M.A.) - Baguio Colleges. Cited in SJ, (Mar./June 1964),p. 14.
Eggan: M.A. thesis.
               I/Y   5   4

3240. SCOTT, WILLIAM HENRY. Cultural change among Igorots in mining companies. CC 7, no. 1 (Jan./Feb. 1967), 22-27.
Eggan: Brief account.
               M/E   5   4

IGOROT-BONTOC - LANGUAGE AND LITERATURE

3241. REID, LAWRENCE A. Phonology of Central Bontoc. Polynesian Society. Journal. 72, no. 1 (Mar. 1963), 21-26.

3242. SCHEERER, OTTO. The Igorrotes of Benguet (North Luzon). (In: Philippine Commission, 1900. Reports 1901. About 25 photos (56th Congress. Senate. 2d Session. Doc. no. 112. p. 149-161)
Eggan: Good.
               L/E   5   4

3243. SEIDENADEL, CARL W. The first grammar of the language spoken by the Bontoc Igorot. Chicago, The Open Court Publishing Company, 1909. 592p. Suggested by Coller.

3244. SHETLER, JO. Balangao non-verbal nuclei. AS 6, no. 2 (Aug. 1968), 208-222.

IGOROT-BONTOC - INDUSTRIES

3245. WILSON, LAURENCE L. Igorot mining methods. Baguio, Catholic School Press, 1932. 32p.
Eggan: J/E   5   4

3246. _____. Primitive mining in the Philippines; gold and copper mining methods of the Igorot on the island of Luzon and an account of some of the religious beliefs by which their work is influenced. Far Eastern Review 29, no. 12

(Dec. 1933), 555-558.
    Eggan: J/E   5   4

IGOROT-BONTOC - MARRIAGE

3247. EGGAN, FRED, and WILLIAM HENRY SCOTT. Ritual life of the Igorots of Sagada:
courtship and marriage. Ethnology 4, no. 1 (Jan. 1965), 77-111.
    Eggan: Detailed survey.
                E and M/E   5   4

3248. MALIAMAN, DALMACIO. Bontoc courtship. PM 35, no. 1 (Jan. 1938), 28-29.
    Eggan: Brief but good.
                I   5   4

3249. PACYAYA, ALFREDO G. Changing customs of marriage, death and burial among
the Sagada. Practical Anthropology 8, no. 3 (May/June 1961), 125-133.
    Eggan: Native writer.
                I/Y   5   4

3250. REID, LAWRENCE. A Guinaang wedding ceremony. PSR 9, nos. 3/4 (July/Oct.
1961), 1-53.
    Eggan: Excellent.
                M/L   5   4

IGOROT-BONTOC - POLITICAL ORGANIZATION AND BEHAVIOR

3251. WILSON, LAURENCE L. The nationalization of the Igorots, some notes on political acculturation. JEAS 4, no. 2 (Apr. 1955), 245-249.
    Eggan: Long time resident.
                J/E   5   4

IGOROT-BONTOC - RELIGIOUS BELIEFS AND PRACTICES

3252. BACDAYAN, ALBERT S. Religious conversion and social reintegration in a
Western Bontoc village complex. SLQ 5, nos. 1/2 (Mar./June 1967), 27-40.

3253. BEURMS, CHARLES J. Sacrifices among the Bago-Igorot. Primitive Man 2, nos.
1/2 (Jan./Apr. 1929), 27-32.
    Eggan: Good account.
                M/E   5   4

3254. CARRILLO, MANUEL. Breve relación de las missiones de las quatro naciones
llamadas Igorrotes, Tinguianes, Apayaos y Adanes . . . Madrid, Impr. del

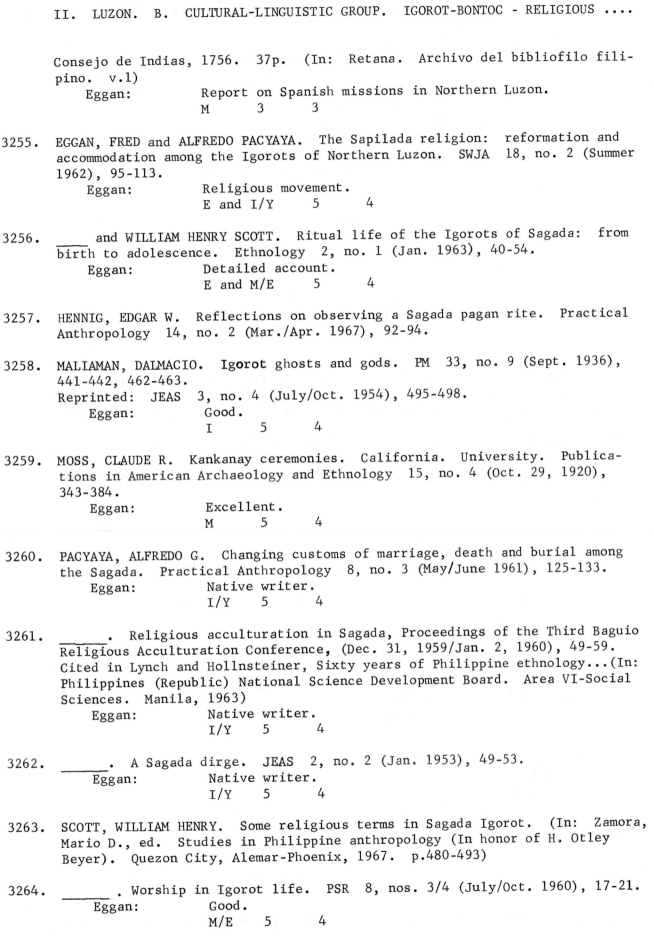

Consejo de Indias, 1756. 37p. (In: Retana. Archivo del bibliofilo filipino. v.1)
>Eggan: Report on Spanish missions in Northern Luzon.
>   M   3   3

3255. EGGAN, FRED and ALFREDO PACYAYA. The Sapilada religion: reformation and
accommodation among the Igorots of Northern Luzon. SWJA 18, no. 2 (Summer
1962), 95-113.
>Eggan: Religious movement.
>   E and I/Y   5   4

3256. ____ and WILLIAM HENRY SCOTT. Ritual life of the Igorots of Sagada: from
birth to adolescence. Ethnology 2, no. 1 (Jan. 1963), 40-54.
>Eggan: Detailed account.
>   E and M/E   5   4

3257. HENNIG, EDGAR W. Reflections on observing a Sagada pagan rite. Practical
Anthropology 14, no. 2 (Mar./Apr. 1967), 92-94.

3258. MALIAMAN, DALMACIO. **Igorot** ghosts and gods. PM 33, no. 9 (Sept. 1936),
441-442, 462-463.
Reprinted: JEAS 3, no. 4 (July/Oct. 1954), 495-498.
>Eggan: Good.
>   I   5   4

3259. MOSS, CLAUDE R. Kankanay ceremonies. California. University. Publications in American Archaeology and Ethnology 15, no. 4 (Oct. 29, 1920),
343-384.
>Eggan: Excellent.
>   M   5   4

3260. PACYAYA, ALFREDO G. Changing customs of marriage, death and burial among
the Sagada. Practical Anthropology 8, no. 3 (May/June 1961), 125-133.
>Eggan: Native writer.
>   I/Y   5   4

3261. _____. Religious acculturation in Sagada, Proceedings of the Third Baguio
Religious Acculturation Conference, (Dec. 31, 1959/Jan. 2, 1960), 49-59.
Cited in Lynch and Hollnsteiner, Sixty years of Philippine ethnology...(In:
Philippines (Republic) National Science Development Board. Area VI-Social
Sciences. Manila, 1963)
>Eggan: Native writer.
>   I/Y   5   4

3262. _____. A Sagada dirge. JEAS 2, no. 2 (Jan. 1953), 49-53.
>Eggan: Native writer.
>   I/Y   5   4

3263. SCOTT, WILLIAM HENRY. Some religious terms in Sagada Igorot. (In: Zamora,
Mario D., ed. Studies in Philippine anthropology (In honor of H. Otley
Beyer). Quezon City, Alemar-Phoenix, 1967. p.480-493)

3264. _____. Worship in Igorot life. PSR 8, nos. 3/4 (July/Oct. 1960), 17-21.
>Eggan: Good.
>   M/E   5   4

3265. VANOVERBERGH, MORICE. Prayers in Lepanto-Igorot or Kankanay as it is spoken at Bauco.
JEAS [Part I] 2, no. 2 (Jan. 1953), 1-28.
      [Part II] 2, no. 3 (Apr. 1953), 69-107.
      [Part III] 2, no. 4 (July 1953), 39-105.
Bello: Excellent original material gathered by one who lived in the region and knows the language.
              M/E   5   1/2
Eggan: Excellent.
              M/E   5   4

3266. _____. Tales in Lepanto-Igorot as it is spoken at Bauco.
JEAS [Part I] 1, no. 1 (Oct. 1951), 1-42.
      [Part II] 1, no. 2 (Jan. 1952), 61-118.
      [Part III] 1, no. 3 (Apr. 1952), 67-130.
      [Part IV] 1, no. 4 (July 1952), 31-85.
      [Part V] 2, no. 1 (Oct. 1952), 83-102.
Eggan: Excellent.
              M/E   5   4

3267. VILLAVERDE, JUAN FERNANDEZ. Supersticiones de los Igorrotes Ifugaos. Edited, with an introduction and notes, by Julian Malumbres. El Correo Sino-Annamita 38 (1912), 281-455. (In: Beyer collection of Filipiniana. 14/12. paper 71)
Cited in Harold Conklin, Ifugao bibliography. 1968. p.72.
Eggan: Missionary reports and letters.
              M   3   3

IGOROT-BONTOC - STANDARD OF LIVING AND RECREATION

3268. DINWIDDIE, WILLIAM. An Igorrote feast. Harper's Weekly 45, no. 2338 (Oct. 12, 1901), 1028-1029.
Eggan: Brief.
              G   5   4

3269. MALIAMAN, DALMACIO. Boc-boc-nit, the Bontoc rock-fight. PM 34, no. 3 (Mar. 1937), 125, 133, 135.
Eggan: Excellent.
              I   5   4

3270. SIMMS, S. C. Bontoc Igorot games. AA n.s. 10, no. 4 (Oct./Dec. 1908), 563-567.
Eggan: E   3   4

IGOROT-BONTOC - TOTAL CULTURE

3271. CAWED-OTEYZA, CARMENCITA. The culture of the Bontoc Igorots. Unitas 38, no. 3 (Sept. 1965), 317-377. 19 plates.

3272. DAOAS, JOHN K. S. The Bontoc-Igorot: a survey. 1957. Thesis (M.A.) -
Lyceum of the Philippines.
Cited in Compilation of graduate theses . . .Suppl. 9.
        Eggan: I   5   4

3273. EGGAN, FRED. The Sagada Igorots of northern Luzon. (In: Murdock, George
Peter, ed. Social structure in Southeast Asia. New York, 1960. p.24-50)
(Wenner-Gren Foundation for Anthropological Research, Inc., Viking Fund Pub-
lications in anthropology, no. 29)
        Eggan: Social structure of Sagada Igorots.
                        E   5   4

3274. KEESING, FELIX M. Some notes on Bontok social organization, Northern Philippines. AA 51, no. 4, pt. 1 (Oct./Dec. 1949), 578-601.
        Eggan: Excellent account.
                        E   5   4

3275. OTEYZA, CARMENCITA CAWED. The culture of the Bontoc Igorots. Unitas 38,
no. 3 (Sept. 1965), 317-377.
        Eggan: I   5 ?   4

3276. ROBERTSON, JAMES A. The Igorots of Lepanto. PJS 9-D, no. 6 (Nov. 1914),
465-529. 9 plates.
        Eggan: Compilation of municipal reports etc.
                        H   3   3/4

ILOKANO - GENERAL

3277. APOSTOL, JOSE P. The Ilocanos in Zambales. JH 4, no. 2 (Jan./Apr. 1956),
3-15.

3278. BELLO, MOISES. Chapter 23. The Ilokano. (In: Human Relations Area Files,
Inc. Area handbook on the Philippines. 1956. v.4, p.1695-1728) Sub-
Contractor's monograph HRAF-16.
        Bello: A combination of original and secondary data with inter-
                        pretations by a native who has lived in the region.
                        E   4   7
        Scheans: Basic introductory source.
                        E   4   7
        Thomas: Best article-length summary of total culture of Ilocanos.
                        Unfortunately, never published in a book or journal that
                        received wide distribution.
                        E   4   7

3279. BEYER, H. OTLEY. Chronological catalogue of Iloko works in the B.C.F. n.p.,
[192-] 16 numb. leaves. (His: Partial list of books in the Beyer collection
of Filipiniana...[pt. 1])
Cited in Harvard Univ. Peabody Museum...Library. Catalogue: Author. v.3,
p.104.

Scheans:	A/E	3	7
Thomas:	A	3	7

3280. _____. Ethnography of the Iloko people...Manila, 1918-20. 5v. (His: [Beyer collection of Filipiniana. sect. A, set 7a])
Cited in Harvard Univ., Peabody Museum...Library. Catalogue: Author. v.3, p.104.

Scheans:	A/E	3	4
Thomas:	Based upon first-hand accounts written by Ilocano students in Beyer's classes. Not critically evaluated, however; not theoretically oriented. Useful for "facts" and "attitudes" of the period 1910-1920.		
	A	3	4

3281. COLE, FAY-COOPER. The Ilocano. (In: The Peoples of Malaysia. New York, Van Nostrand Company, 1945. p.173-182)
Suggested by Thomas.

Thomas:	Cole's only summary statement about the Ilocano was the best in existence until superseded by Bello, Ilokano. (In: HRAF, Area handbook on the Philippines. v.4, p.1695-1728)		
	E	4	7

3282. EGGAN, FRED. Some social institutions in the Mountain Province and their significance for historical and comparative studies. JEAS 3, no. 3 (Apr. 1954), 329-335.

Bello:	An excellent discussion of cultural change in the area; presents original view as regards historical reconstruction of Mountain Province institutions.		
	E	5	7
Maher:	E	5	4
Scheans:	E	4/5	7

3283. KEESING, FELIX M. The ethnohistory of northern Luzon. Stanford, California, Stanford Univ. Press, 1962. 362p. (Stanford Anthropological series, no. 4)

Bello:	An excellent attempt at historical reconstruction in the area topping historical and ethnographic materials not previously utilized.		
	E	5	7
Maher:	An important effort to reconstruct the cultural history of Northern Luzon from early records.		
	E	4	7
Scheans:	Standard secondary source.		
	E	4	7
Thomas:	A regional history of indigenous life and culture contact as reconstructed from Spanish published sources. Did not use archival materials in Spain.		
	E	4	7

3284. MILLÁN Y VILLANUEVA, CAMILO. Ilocos Norte, descripción general de dicha provincia. Manila, Imprenta de "El Eco de Filipinas", 1891. 221p.

Thomas:	Almanac and "data-book"--a description of Province near end of Spanish period.		
	G	3	3

3285. NYDEGGER, WILLIAM F. Tarong: a Philippine barrio. Ithaca, 1960. 415p.
Thesis (Ph.D.) - Cornell Univ.
    Scheans: Somewhat weak on social organization.
                     E   5   6

3286. WI, WILFREDO A. Political, social and economic development of Santo Domingo,
Ilocos Sur. 1956. 157p. Thesis (M.A.) - Univ. of Manila.
Suggested by Scheans.

3287. YABES, LEOPOLDO Y. The Adam and Eve of the Ilocanos. JEAS 7, no. 2 (Apr.
1958), 216-220.
    Scheans: Q   3   7
    Thomas: Q   3   7

ILOKANO - AGRICULTURE AND FOOD

3288. CHRISTIE, EMERSON B. Notes on irrigation and cooperative irrigation societies in Ilocos Norte. PJS 9D,   no. 2 (Apr. 1914), 99-115. 1 plate.
    Intengan: Information is given on early attempts to construct irri-
                     gation works in Ilocos Norte.
                     G   4   4
    Scheans: Still the only published source on this topic.
                     G   5   4
    Thomas: Only details published to date on first-hand study of
                     important Ilocano institution--the cooperative irrigation
                     society.
                     E   5   4

3289. DAYYO, SILVERIO C. The rural credit situation and credit experiences of
farmers in Bauguen, Ilocos Sur. PA 40, no. 9 (Feb. 1957), 486-497.
    Intengan: The study showed none of the farmers made use of credit
                     facilities set up for them by ACCFA and the rural banks.
                     C   4   6
    Sta. Iglesia: Highly useful descriptive research.
                     G   5   6

3290. GARCIA, NATIVIDAD V. A study of the socio-economic adjustments of two Ilocano villages to Virginia tobacco production. Quezon City: Community Development Research Council, U.P., 1962. (Abstract Series no. 15)
Suggested by Thomas.

3291. LEWIS, HENRY T. Socioeconomic variability in two Ilocano barrios of northern
Luzon, Philippines. Berkeley, 1967. 292p. Thesis (Ph.D.) - Univ. of California.

3292. MERCADO, G. C. Sidelights of the nutrition survey, Ilocos - Mountain Province
region, April-June 1960. Philippine Health Journal 8, no. 1 (Mar. 1961), 4-
8.
    Intengan: Narrates actual experiences and observations of a nutri-
                     tionist in one of its regional surveys.
                     C   3   6

3293. MONTILLA, JOSE. The Ipon fisheries of northern Luzon. PJS 45, no. 1 (May 1931), 61-75. 6 plates.
   Intengan: C   5   4

3294. RODRIGUEZ, HERMINIA SOLLER. Tobacco marketing practices of farmers in Cabugao, Ilocos Sur. PA 43, no. 8 (Jan. 1960), 521-532.
Suggested by Scheans.

3295. SACAY, FRANCISCO M. and OTHERS. The economic and social status of rice farmers in the Ilocos region. PA 40, no. 1 (June 1956), 649-658.
   Intengan: The poor economic status and low living standards of the farm families studied are attributed to small farm size and poor farming methods employed.
           C   3   6
   Sta. Iglesia: Highly useful descriptive research.
           Y(G) 5   6

3296. VANOVERBERGH, MORICE. Iloko hunting and fishing basketry and netting. Primitive Man 21, nos. 3/4 (July/Oct. 1948), 39-64.
   Scheans: M   5   7
   Thomas: M   5   4

3297. VAN WINKLE, HAROLD. Salt from sand in Ilocos. PM 30, no. 2 (July 1933), 52, 76-77.
Suggested by Scheans.

ILOKANO - BUILDINGS, TOOLS AND EQUIPMENT

3298. VANOVERBERGH, MORICE. Iloko constructions. PJS 62, no. 1 (Jan. 1937), 67-88. 8 plates.
   Scheans: Detailed contributions by one of the best missionary-ethnographers.
           M   5   7
   Thomas: One of more than a dozen articles by Catholic missionary-scientist, emphasizing material culture and language study.
           M   5   4

3299. _____. Iloko furniture and implements. PJS 64, no. 4 (Dec. 1937), 413-433. 2 plates.
   Scheans: Detailed contributions by one of the best missionary-ethnographers.
           M   5   7
   Thomas: M   5   4

3300. _____. The Iloko kitchen. PJS 60, no. 1 (May 1936), 1-10.
   Scheans: Detailed contributions by one of the best missionary-ethnographers.
           M   5   7
   Thomas: M   5   4

ILOKANO - CLOTHING, ADORNMENT AND MATERIALS

3301. VANOVERBERGH, MORICE. Iloko hunting and fishing, basketry and netting. Primitive Man 21, nos. 3/4 (July/Oct. 1948), 39-64.
    Scheans: M   5   7
    Thomas: One of more than a dozen articles by Catholic missionary-scientist, emphasizing material culture and language study.
                  M   5   4

3302. _____. Iloko weaving dictionary. Annali Lateranensi 5 (1941), 221-252.
    Scheans: M   5   7
    Thomas: M   5   4

ILOKANO - COMMUNITY DEVELOPMENT AND TERRITORIAL ORGANIZATION

3303. RASAY, DANIEL. The Vigan community center. CC 3, no. 1 (Jan./Feb. 1963), 20-24.
Suggested by Scheans.

3304. SACAY, FRANCISCO M. and FLORENDO R. NAANEP. A study of farm, home and community conditions in a farm village of Ilocos Norte as a basis for formulating a program of rural education. PA 29, no. 7 (Dec. 1940), 555-570.
Suggested by Scheans.

ILOKANO - ECONOMICS

3305. LEWIS, HENRY T. Socioeconomic variability in two Ilocano barrios of Northern Luzon, Philippines. 1967. 292p. Thesis (Ph.D.) - Univ. of California, Berkeley.

ILOKANO - EDUCATION

3306. CADAY, CAROLINA T. A comparison of the pre-war and post-war status of public elementary classroom teachers in Ilocos Norte. (1939-40 and 1953-54), 1955. 106p. Thesis (M. Ed.) - U.P.
Suggested by Scheans.

3307. JACINTO, VISITACION E. Folk music from the Iloko region and its educational possibilities. Quezon City, 1961. 414p. Thesis (M.A.) - U.P.

3308. SACAY, FRANCISCO M. and FLORENDO R. NAANEP. A study of farm, home, and community conditions in a farm village of Ilocos Norte as a basis for

formulating a program of rural education. PA 29, no. 7 (Dec. 1940), 555-570.
Suggested by Scheans.

3309. _____ and OTHERS. Educational and occupational pursuits of former students in the Batangas and Ilocos Norte high schools. PA 32, no. 2 (Oct./Nov./Dec. 1948), 114-123.
Suggested by Scheans.

ILOKANO - ETHNIC INFLUENCES

3310. REYNOLDS, HARRIET. Background and distribution of Chinese families in the Ilocos provinces, Philippines. 1959. Thesis (M.A.) - Hartford Seminary Foundation.

Scheans:	The sources on the Chinese of the Ilocos.
	M 5 7
Thomas:	Data principally for Vigan, Ilocos Sur.
	M/Z 5 6
Weightman:	A valuable contribution to research on Chinese in Philippines but superceded by Continuity and change in the Chinese family in the Ilocos Provinces, Philippines.
	E 5 6

3311. _____. Continuity and change as shown by attitudes of two generations of Chinese in the Ilocos Provinces, Philippines. SJ 13, no. 1 (Jan./Mar. 1966), 12-21.

Weightman:	Brief summary of part of findings in Continuity and change in the Chinese family. . . .
	E 4 6
Wickberg:	E 4 7

3312. _____. Continuity and change in the Chinese family in the Ilocos Provinces, Philippines. 1964. 381p. Thesis (Ph.D.) - Hartford Seminary Foundation.

Weightman:	A classic - should be published in modified form.
	E 5 6
Wickberg:	E 4 7

3313. _____. Marriage as a focal point in cultural orientation of Chinese adults and children in Ilocos. PSR 13, no. 4 (Oct. 1965), 249-259.

Weightman:	Published portion of Ph.D.
	E 5 6

3314. _____. Reply to Professor Juco's article (January, 1966 issue of the PSR) on "Legal Aspects of Chinese Marriages in the Philippines." PSR 14, no. 3 (July 1966), 167-168.

Weightman:	Brief classification of legalistic points.
	E 5 6

3315. REYNOLDS, IRA HUBERT. Chinese acculturation in Ilocos: economic, political, religious. 1964. 475p. Thesis (Ph.D.) - Hartford Seminary Foundation.

Weightman:	Good treatment of evasion techniques used to affect

                        nationalization laws.
                        E   5   6
            Wickberg: E   4   6

3316. _____. Economic acculturation of the Chinese in Ilocos. 1959. Thesis
(M.A.) - Hartford Seminary Foundation.
            Scheans: M   5   7
            Thomas: Data principally for Vigan, Ilocos Sur.
                        M/S   5   6
            Weightman: MA thesis - elaborated later in Ph.D.
                        E   5   6

                        ILOKANO - FAMILY AND KINSHIP

3317. NYDEGGER, WILLIAM F. and CORINNE NYDEGGER. The mothers of Tarong, Philip-
       pines. (In: Minturn, Leigh and William W. Lambert, eds. Mothers of six
       cultures; antecedents of child rearing. New York, Wiley, 1964. p.209-221)
            Scheans: Emphasis on child rearing.
                        E   5   6

3318. SCHEANS, DANIEL J. Anak ti digos Ilokano name changing and ritual kinship.
       PSR 14, no. 2 (Apr. 1966), 82-85.
            Bello: Original data gathered by a trained observer.
                        E   5   7
            Scheans: Of interest in the study of forms of ceremonial kinship.
                        E   5   7
            Thomas: E   5   6

3319. _____. Kith-centered action groups in an Ilokano barrio. Ethnology 3,
       no. 4 (Oct. 1964), 364-368.
            Thomas: Data based upon barrio Suban, on north shore of Lake
                        Paoay, Ilocos Norte.
                        E   5   6

3320. _____. The Suban Ilocano kinship configuration: an application of innova-
       tion theory to the study of kinship. Eugene, 1962. 122p. Thesis (Ph.D.) -
       Univ. of Oregon.
            Scheans: Substantive data was printed as "Suban Society" (PSR,
                        1963, 216-235).
            Thomas: Based upon field research and residence in barrio Suban,
                        situated along north shore of Lake Paoay, province of
                        Ilocos Norte.
                        E   5   6

3321. _____. Suban society. PSR 11, nos. 3/4 (July/Oct. 1963), 216-235.
            Scheans: Kinship study of an Ilocos Norte barrio.
                        E   5   7
            Thomas: E   5   6

ILOKANO - FINE ARTS

3322. ZOBEL DE AYALA, FERNANDO. Silver ex-votos in Ilocos. PS 5, no. 3 (Sept. 1957), 261-267.
       Scheans: R   5   7

ILOKANO - GEOGRAPHY AND DEMOGRAPHY

3323. FONACIER, TOMAS S. The Ilokano movement: a new frontier on Philippine history. DR 1, no. 1 (Jan. 1953), 89-94.
       Bello: A good summary by an Ilokano historian of the expansion of Iloko people to various places in the Philippines-- lacks detail but gives some useful clues to historical reconstruction.
                       H   4   2-4
       Thomas: Best summary statement, though brief, about Ilocano migration, by long-time Dean of Arts and Sciences at the University of Philippines (and himself an Ilocano).
                       S   4   7

3324. LUNA, TELESFORO W., JR. Land utilization in Ilocos Norte. PGJ 7, no. 3 (July/Sept. 1963), 133-142.
       Spencer: Land use--agricultural survey, some primary data.
                       K   4/5   6
       Thomas: Summary of physical geography and land use of his native Province by the geography professor at the University of the Philippines.
                       K   4   6

3325. ROBB, WALTER. The Ilokano: why he migrates; where he goes. American Chamber of Commerce of the Philippines. Journal 7, no. 5 (May 1927), 6-7.
       Thomas: J/Q   3   4

ILOKANO - HEALTH AND SICKNESS

3326. ALBANO, VIRGINIA G. A study of the health practices of the students of the Ilocos Norte Normal School. 1959. 339p. Thesis (M.A.) - Arellano Univ. Suggested by Scheans.

ILOKANO - HISTORY AND CULTURE CHANGE

3327. CHRISTIE, E. B. Notes on Iloko ethnography and history. (In: Beyer Collection on Philippine Folklore. Social Customs and Beliefs, 1914. v.10,

paper 392)
Cited by Felix M. Keesing, Ethnohistory of Northern Luzon. 1962.
    Scheans: E   3   7
    Thomas: E   3   7

3328. EGGAN, FRED. Some aspects of culture change in the northern Philippines.
AA n.s. 43, no. 1 (Jan./Mar. 1941), 11-18.
    Maher: E   5   7
    Scheans: Highly influential article.
                    E   4/5   7

3329. _____. Some social institutions in the Mountain and their significance for
historical and comparative studies. JEAS 3, no. 3 (Apr. 1954), 329-335.
    Maher: E   5   4
    Scheans: Elaborates on the preceding article .
                    E   4/5   7

3330. ORR, KENNETH G. The Christianized Ilocanos and the pagan Tinguian; a study
of acculturation in the Philippine Islands. Falls Church? Va., 1956. 48p.
    Eggan: E   3   4
    Scheans: Reworking of the literature with interview data from an
                    informant from Ilocos Sur.
                    E   3   7

3331. REYES Y FLORENTINO, ISABELO DE LOS. ...Historia de Ilocos. Manila, Establecimiento tipografico la Opinion, 1890. 2v. First published as articles
in Diario de Manila, El Comercio, España Oriental, etc. v.1, Pre-Spanish,
v.2, Spanish period.
Suggested by Scheans.

ILOKANO - INDUSTRIES

3332. CHRISTIE, EMERSON B. Notes on the pottery industry in San Nicolas, Ilocos
Norte. PJS 9D, no. 2 (Apr. 1914), 117-121. 3 plates.
    Thomas: First scientific account of techniques used in backyard
                    "cottage industry" for which poblacion of San Nicolas is
                    best known.
                    E   5   4

3333. _____. Notes on the wood-working industry of San Vincente, Ilokos Sur.
PJS 7D, no. 4 (Aug. 1912), 231-240.
Suggested by Scheans.

3334. _____. The stone industry at San Esteban, Ilokos Sur. PJS 7, no. 4 (Aug.
1912), 213-231.
Suggested by Scheans.

3335. CRISOSTOMO, NOE RA. The Ilocos pot industry. PM 34, no. 4 (Apr. 1937),
168, 183.
Suggested by Scheans.

3336. REYNO, RODOLFO U. The bathrobe- and towel-weaving industry of Paoay. PM 30, no. 7 (Dec. 1933), 287, 297.
Suggested by Scheans.

3337. SCHEANS, DANIEL J. The pottery industry of San Nicolas, Ilocos Norte. JEAS 9, no. 1 (Jan. 1960), 1-38. 26 photos.
    Thomas: A more detailed and up-to-date article, but a companion piece to Christie's 1914 classic. ("Notes on the pottery industry in San Nicolas, Ilocos Norte.")
                E   5   6

ILOKANO - INFANCY AND CHILDHOOD

3338. NYDEGGER, WILLIAM F. Tarong; an Ilocos barrio in the Philippines. (In: Whiting, Beatrice, ed. Six cultures, studies in child rearing. New York, Wiley, 1963. p.693-867)
Separately published: Tarong: an Ilocos barrio in the Philippines. New York, John Wiley, 1966. 180p. (Six cultures series, v.6)
    Bello: An excellent study of an Iloko village--one of the few undertaken so far-presents some good ethnography on Iloko. But contains certain errors on native terms, particularly on kinship.
                E   5   6
    Maher: E   5   6
    Scheans: Abridgement of Tarong: a Philippine barrio. Ph.D. Thesis - Cornell University. 1960.
                E   5   6
    Thomas: The most detailed study in existence of an Ilocano barrio, based upon Ph.D. dissertation in anthropology. Done in northern Ilocos Sur; emphasis in birth-childhood-adolescence.
                E   5   6

ILOKANO - LANGUAGE AND COMMUNICATION

3339. CALIP, JOSE RESURRECCION. Ilocano colloquialisms. PM 36, no. 2 (Feb. 1939), 70-71.
Reprinted: JEAS 4, no. 1 (Jan. 1955), 59-61.
    Scheans: Q   5   7

3340. VANOVERBERGH, MORICE. Notes on Iloko. Anthropos 23, nos. 5/6 (Sept./Dec. 1928), 1029-1050.
    Thomas: One of more than a dozen articles by Catholic missionary-scientist, emphasizing material culture and language study.
                M   5   4

3341. YABES, LEOPOLDO Y. A brief survey of Iloko literature, from the beginning to its present development, with a bibliography of work pertaining to the Iloko people and their language. Manila, The Author, 1936. 155p. Suggested by Thomas.

Thomas: There is little "literature" or even written materials in Ilocono language. Useful for bibliography.

B/Q   3   7

ILOKANO - MARRIAGE

3342. DUMLAO, ALEJANDRO. Ancient marriage customs among the Ilocanos. The College Folio (U.P. College of Philosophy and Letters and College of Engineering) 1, no. 3 (Feb. 1911), 135-141.

3343. MAGBAG, CRESENCIO S. The topak in the Ilocano wedding. PM 32, no. 1 (Jan. 1935), 33.

Scheans: Short popular account.

-        5   7

3344. REYNO, RODOLFO U. Customary wedding among the Ilocanos. PM 35, no. 7 (July 1938), 336, 346, 348.

3345. SCHEANS, DANIEL J. The Ilocano: marriage and the land. PSR 13, no. 1 (Jan. 1965), 57-62.

Bello: A good documentation of Iloko practice by a trained observer.

E   5   6

Scheans: Functional interpretation of the role of marriage lano (sabong) in an Ilocos norte barrio.

E   5   7

Thomas: Based upon field research and residence in barrio Suban, situated along north shore of Lake Paoay, province of Ilocos Norte.

E   5   6

3346. _____. Patterns of kin-term usage among young Ilocanos and a method for determining them. PSR 16, nos. 1/2 (Jan./Apr. 1968), 17-29.

ILOKANO - MOBILITY AND SOCIAL STRATIFICATION

3347. VANOVERBERGH, MORICE. Animal names in Iloko. American Oriental Society. Journal 48, no. 1 (Mar. 1928), 1-33.

Scheans: M   5   7

Thomas: One of more than a dozen articles by Catholic missionary-scientist, emphasizing material culture and language study.

M   5   4

3348. _____. Plant names in Iloko. American Oriental Society. Journal 47, no. 2 (June 1927), 133-173.
        Scheans: M   5   7
        Thomas: M   5   4

ILOKANO - RELIGIOUS BELIEFS AND PRACTICES

3349. ACHUTEGUI, PEDRO S. DE and MIGUEL A. BERNAD. Religious revolution in the Philippines; the life and church of Gregorio Aglipay, 1860-1960. Manila, Ateneo de Manila, 1960-1966.
v.1. From Aglipay's birth to his death: 1860-1940.
v.2. Iglesia Filipina Independiente.
    Doherty: Misuse of sources, excessively polemical, only extant history on Aglipay.
                      Z   3   4
    Gowing: Excellent factual study of PIC and its founder, but hostile in its interpretation.
                      Y   4   7

3350. BLUMENTRITT, FERDINAND. Festbräuche der Ilocanen (Luzon). Nach der "Oceania Espanole." Ausland 58, no. 15 (Apr. 13, 1885), 284-285.
Cited in Philippine Islands. Legislature. 1914. Philippine Assembly. Vida y obras de Ferdinand Blumentritt. p.55.
    Thomas: N   3   3

3351. _____. Sitten und Bräuche der Ilocanen (Luzon). Nach J. de los Reyes, Ando und Javier (Folk-lore Ilocano).
Globus 48, no. 12 (1885), 183-186.
        48, no. 13 (1885), 200-202.
        51, no. 23 (1887), 359-361.
        51, no. 24 (1887), 376-377.
    Thomas: N   3   3

3352. POBRE-YÑIGO, VIRGILIO D. Mourning customs in Paoay. PM 33, no. 5 (May 1936), 257-258.
Reprinted in JEAS 8, nos. 1/2 (1959), 215-217.
Suggested by Scheans.

3353. REYES Y FLORENTINO, ISABELO DE LOS. Die religiösen Anschauungen der Ilocanen (Luzon). Kaiserlich-Konigliche Geographische Gesellschaft in Wien 31 (1888), 552-575.
    Thomas: An interesting statement--a forerunner to the formation (a decade later) of the Aglipayan movement (Philippine Independent Church).
                      J/Q   5   3

3354. RIGUERA, FLORENCIO. "Sumang": a folk rite in Ilocos. PSR 16, nos. 1/2 (Jan./Apr. 1968), 66-73.

3355. ROLA, CEFERINO. A note on Iloko death and burial customs and beliefs. Primitive Man 10, no. 2 (Apr. 1937), 30-31.
    Thomas: -   3   4

3356. YABES, LEOPOLDO Y. The Ilocano epic: a critical study of "The Life of Lam-
ang." PSSHR 23, nos. 2/4 (June/Dec. 1958), 283-337.
Suggested by Thomas.
   Thomas: Folklore, in extenso, placed into cultural perspective.
                   B/Q   3   7

3357. _____. The Ilocos' black Christ. PM 29, no. 12 (May 1933), 525-526, 551.
Suggested by Scheans.

3358. ZÓBEL DE AYALA, FERNANDO. Silver ex-votos in Ilocos. PS 5, no. 3 (Sept.
1957), 261-267.
   Scheans: R   5   7

ILOKANO - STANDARD OF LIVING AND RECREATION

3359. BLUMENTRITT, FERDINAND. Festbräuche der Ilocanen (Luzon).   Nach der
"Oceanía Española." Ausland 58, no. 15 (Apr. 13, 1885), 284-285.
Cited in Philippine Islands. Legislature. 1914. Philippine Assembly.
Vida y obras de Ferdinand Blumentritt. p.55.
   Thomas: N   3   3

3360. LAVA, HORACIO. Levels of living in the Ilocos region. Prepared for the
Philippine Council, Institute of Pacific Relations. Study no. 1. Manila,
Carmelo and Bauermann, 1938. 94p. (College of Business Administration,
U.P. Study no. 1) Thesis (Ph.D.) - Stanford Univ. 1938/39.

3361. VANOVERBERGH, MORICE. Iloko games. Anthropos 22, nos. 1/2 (Jan./Apr.
1927), 216-243.
   Scheans: M   5   4
   Thomas: One of more than a dozen articles by Catholic missionary-
                   scientist, emphasizing material culture and language
                   study.
                   M   5   4

ILOKANO - TOTAL CULTURE

3362. LEWIS, HENRY T. Socioeconomic variability in two Ilocano barrios of northern Luzon, Philippines. Berkeley, 1967. 282p. Thesis (Ph.D.) - Univ. of
California.

ILONGOT

3363   BARROWS, DAVID PRESCOTT. The Ilongot or Ibilao of Luzon. Popular Science
Monthly 7, no. 6 (Dec. 1910), 521-537.

3364.   BEAN, ROBERT BENNETT. Filipino ears: IV. Ilongot and Mañgyan. PJS 8D,
no. 5 (Oct. 1913), 357-368. 20 plates.

3365.   CAMPA, BUENAVENTURA. Una visita á las rancherías de Ilongotes. El Correo
Sino-Annamita 25 (1891), 563-646.

3366.   CAMPA, JOSÉ DE LA. Gaddanen, Ilongoten, Ibilaos, und Negritos des valle de
Cagayan (Luzon). Translation from the Spanish by Ferdinand Blumentritt.
Anthropologischen Gesellschaft in Wien. Verhandlungen 14 (1884), 52-54.
        Wallace: Useful historical document.
                        -     4   3

3367.   SCHEERER, OTTO. On a quinary notation among the Ilongots of Northern Luzon.
PJS 6D, no. 1 (Feb. 1911), 47-49.

3368.   TUGBY, DONALD J. The Ilongot of North-east Luzon. Acta Anthropologického
Kongresu, Brno, 1965. Moravské Museum, Brno, 1967, 253-255.

3369.   _____. A model of the social organization of the Ilongot of Northeast Luzon. Journal of Asian and African Studies 1, no. 4 (Oct. 1966), 253-260.

3370.   TURNBULL, WILFRID. Among the Ilongots twenty years ago.
PM Part I. 26, no. 5 (Oct. 1929), 262-263, 307-310.
        Part II. 26, no. 6 (Nov. 1929), 337-338, 374, 376, 378-379.
        Part III. 26, no. 7 (Dec. 1929), 416-417, 460, 462, 464, 466, 468-470.

3371.   WILSON, LAURENCE L. Ilongot life and legends. Baguio, P.I., 1947. 109p.
Quezon City, Bookman, 1967. 148p.

ISINAI

3372.   GALANG, RICARDO E. Ethnographic notes on the Isinais of Nueva Vizcaya.
PJS 58, no. 4 (Dec. 1935), 503-511. 3 plates.

3373.   PAZ, CONSUELO J. Ad in Isinai. AS 3, no. 1 (Apr. 1965), 114-125.

IVATAN

3374.   ALFONSO, JULIO G. The Batanes Islands. Acta Manilana, no. 2 (June 1966),
3-112. 11p. of photos.

3375.   GONZÁLES, JULIO. The Batanes Islands. Manila, Univ. of Santo Tomas Press,

1966. 112p.

3376. MANUEL, E. ARSENIO. Informe sobre las Islás Batanes (1775-1780). PSSHR 18, no. 2 (June 1953), 99-123.

Anderson: Document to the Spanish King from the Governor of the Philippines in 1780--ordered to gather all available data on Batanes Island. By four Dominicans: Mathias Suarez, Juan Fernandez, Don Pedro Yriarte (former mayor of Cagayan) and Don Joaquin Melgarejo (merchant and trader in Batanes for five months). Melgarejo's **narrative** is most informative on ethnography-clothing, jewelry, marriage, house-type, and burial customs. Supplements Dampier's account. In Spanish.

G/M/T   3   3

3377. REID, LAWRENCE A. An Ivatan syntax. Honolulu, 1966. 160p. (Oceanic linguistics. Special publications, no. 2) The author's Ph.D. thesis - Univ. of Hawaii, 1966.

3378. SCHEERER, OTTO. ... The Batan dialect as a member of the Philippine group of languages. Manila: Bureau of Printing, 1908. 141p. (Philippine Islands. Ethnological Survey. Publications. v.5, pt. I-II)

3379. YAMADA, YUKIHIRO. Fishing economy of the Itbayat, Batanes, Philippines with special reference to its vocabulary. AS 5, no. 1 (Apr. 1967), 137-219.

3380. _____. Phonology of Itbayaten. PJS 94, no. 3 (Sept. 1965), 373-394.

KALINGA - GENERAL

3381. BARTON, R[oy] F[ranklin]. The Kalingas, their institutions and custom law. Chicago, Univ. of Chicago Press, 1949. 275p. (Univ. of Chicago. Publications in anthropology. Social anthropological series)

3382. BEYER, H. OTLEY, comp. The history and ethnography of the Itneg-Kalinga peoples; being a complete collection of all known printed and manuscript information relating to the history and ethnography of the Itneg-Kalinga peoples of northern Luzon, Philippine Islands, uniformly edited, annotated and translated into English...Manila, sect. A, set 16a.

Cited in Harvard Univ., Peabody Museum...Library. Catalogue: Author. v.3, p.105.

3383. BILLIET, FRANCIS. Kalingga riddles. Primitive Man 3, nos. 3/4 (July/Oct. 1930), 71-74.

3384. DOZIER, EDWARD P. The Kalinga of northern Luzon, Philippines. New York, Holt, Rinehart & Winston, 1967. 102p. (Case studies in cultural anthropology)

Thomas: A paperback which is a condensation of Mountain Arbiters.

E   5   6

3385. _____. Mountain arbiters; the changing life of a Philippine hill people.

Tuscon, Arizona, Univ. of Arizona Press, 1966. 299p.
    Polson: A good study of assimilation.
                E   5   6

3386. LINDEMANS, LEON. A Kalinga story. La Dulli 'yaw kan kiwa' da - Dulliyaw
and Kiwada. Folklore Studies 14, (1955), 197-201.

3387. SCOTT, WILLIAM HENRY. Economic and material culture of the Kalingas of Madukayan. SWJA 14, no. 3 (Autumn 1958), 318-337.

3388. STARR, JUNE. Leadership and cognatic residence groups in Ifugao, Bontok,
and Kalinga. 1961. 77p. Thesis (M.A.) - Columbia Univ.
      Eggan: E   4   4
      Maher: E   4   7

3389. SUGGUIYAO, MIGUEL and ROSARIO SUGGUIYAO. Kalinga primitive culture.
SLQ Part I. 1, no. 3 (Sept. 1963), 289-304
       Part II. 2, no. 2 (June 1964), 181-200.

KALINGA - BEHAVIOR PROCESS AND PERSONALITY

3390. DOZIER, MARIANNE F. North Kalinga personality configurations and child-
rearing patterns. International Congress of Anthropological and Ethnological Sciences. 6th, Paris, 1960: Compte-rendu. 1963. tome II. Ethnologie, 1er vol., p.[49]-52.

KALINGA - ECONOMICS

3391. SCOTT, WILLIAM HENRY. Economic and material culture of the Kalingas of Madukayan. SWJA 14, no. 3 (Autumn 1958), 318-337.

KALINGA - MARRIAGE

3392. BILLIET, FRANCIS. Kalingga marriage prohibitions. Primitive Man 8, no. 3
(July 1935), 71-72.

KALINGA - MOBILITY AND SOCIAL STRATIFICATION

3393. DOZIER, EDWARD P. The Kalinga of northern Luzon, Philippines. New York,

Holt, Rinehart & Winston, 1967. 102p. (Case studies in cultural anthropology)
> Thomas: A paperback which is a condensation of Mountain Arbiters.
> E   5   6

3394. _____. Mountain arbiters; the changing life of a Philippine hill people. Tuscon, Arizona, Univ. of Arizona Press, 1966. 299p.
> Polson: A good study of assimilation.
> E   5   6

KALINGA - POLITICAL ORGANIZATION AND BEHAVIOR

3395. BARTON, R[oy] F[ranklin]. The Kalingas; their institutions and custom law. Chicago, Ill., Univ. of Chicago. 1949. 275p. (Univ. of Chicago. Publications in anthropology. Social anthropological series)

3396. _____. Primitive Kalinga peace treaty-system.
PM Part I. 38, no. 5 (May 1941), 190-191.
Part II. 38, no. 6 (June 1941), 235-237.

KALINGA - RELIGIOUS BELIEFS AND PRACTICES

3397. SCHEERER, OTTO. Kalinga texts from the Balbalásang-Gináang group. PJS 19, no. 2 (Aug. 1921), 175-207.

3398. SCOTT, WILLIAM HENRY. Social and religious culture of the Kalingas of Madukayan. SWJA 16, no. 2 (Summer 1960), 174-190.

KANKANAY

3399. BELLO, MOISES C. Methods of field research in a Benguet village. GEJ, no. 12 (Second Semester 1966/1967), 43-65.

3400. _____. Some notes on house styles in a Kankanai village. AS 3, no. 1 (Apr. 1965), 41-54. 4 plates.
> Bello: Original materials with source comparative notes. Ethnographic study.
> E   4   7
> Eggan: Based on field research.
> E   5   4

3401. ENCARNACION, VICENTE, JR. Leadership in a Benguet village. PS 9, no. 4

(Oct. 1961), 571-583.
    Bello: It presents original data on Kankanai leadership pat-
terns, but lacks depth. A good case study for public
administration students.
               Z   4   6

3402. _____. Types of authority in a Benguet village. PJPA 1, no. 4 (Oct.
1957), 379-391.
    Bello: A good study, descriptive and theoretical, of local
authority in a southern Kankanai village.
               Z   5   6

3403. KEESING, FELIX M. Population and land utilization among the Lepanto, Northern Philippines. Congrès International de Géographie 2, (1938), Travaux
de la Section III C, 458-464.
    Eggan: Excellent
               E   5   4

3404. LILLO DE GRACIA, MAXIMINO. Filipinas, distrito de Lepanto: descripcíon
general acompañada de itinerario y croquis del territorio...Manila, Impr.
del Colegio de Sto. Tomas, 1877. 88p.
    Eggan: G?   3   3

3405. MALIAMAN, DALMACIO. Holy wedlock in Lepanto. PM 36, no. 12 (Dec. 1939),
499, 501-502.
    Eggan: Good, brief account.
               I   5   4

3406. MOSS, CLAUDE R. Kankanay ceremonies. California. University. Publications in American Archaeology and Ethnology 15, no. 4 (Oct. 29, 1920),
343-384.
    Eggan: Excellent.
               M   5   4

3407. VANOVERBERGH, MORICE. Prayers in Lepanto-Igorot or Kankanay as it is spoken
at Bauco.
JEAS Part 1. 2, no. 2 (Jan. 1953), 1-28.
      Part II. 2, no. 3 (Apr. 1953), 69-107.
      Part III. 2, no. 4 (July 1953), 39-105.
    Bello: Excellent original material gathered by one who lived in
the region and knows the language.
             M/E   5   7
    Eggan: Excellent.
              M/E   5   4

3408. _____. Songs in Lepanto-Igorot as it is spoken at Bauko. Vienna-Mödling,
St. Gabriel's Mission Press.1954.141p.(Studia Instituti Anthropos, v.7)
    Eggan: Excellent
              M/E   5   4

3409. _____. Tales in Lepanto-Igorot as it is spoken at Bauco.
JEAS Part I. 1, no. 1 (Oct. 1951), 1-42.
      Part II. 1, no. 2 (Jan. 1952), 61-118.
      Part III. 1, no. 3 (Apr. 1952), 67-130.
      Part IV. 1, no. 4 (July 1952), 31-85.

Part V. 2, no. 1 (Oct. 1952), 83-102.
Eggan: Excellent.
                M/E   5   4

KAPAMPANGAN - GENERAL

3410.   BEYER, H. OTLEY. Ethnography of the Pampangan people; a comprehensive col-
        lectional of original sources. . .Manila, 1918-   . (His: [Beyer collec-
        tion of Filipiniana. section A, set 5a])
        Cited in Harvard Univ., Peabody Museum. . .Library. Catalogue: Author.
        v.3, p.104.

3411.   _____. Pampangan literature series, B.C.F. n.p., [192-] 2 numb.p.His:
        Partial list of books in the Beyer collection of Filipiniana...[pt. 8])
        Typewritten - carbon-copy.
        Cited in Harvard Univ. Peabody Museum. . .Library. Catalogue: Author.
        v.3, p.106.

3412.   GALANG, RICARDO C. Ethnographic study of the Pampangans. Ms. Chicago,
        Philippine Studies Program, Univ. of Chicago. 1940. 130p.
        Cited in Area Handbook on the Philippines, v.2, p.683.

3413.   HENSON, MARIANO A. The province of Pampanga and its towns (A. D. 1300-1955)
        with the genealogy of the rulers of central Luzon. 3d, rev. ed. [Pampanga,
        1963] 217p. San Fernando, 1955. 169p.
            Anderson: A compendium including statistics on the province, an out-
                            line of its history, description of its present-day indus-
                            try, education, religion and politics and the presentation
                            of other largely unrelated items of information.
                            Q   3   7

3414.   JUAN DE PLASENCIA. Customs of the Pampangas in their lawsuits. (In: Blair
        and Robertson. v.16: 321-329).

3415.   PEREZ, ALEJANDRINO Q. The Pampango folklore; proverbs, riddles, folksongs.
        Unitas 41, no. 1 (Mar. 1968), 67-123.

3416.   SANGALANG, LUZ E. Survey of the communities of Pampanga as a basis for the
        evaluation of subject matter content in general science. Quezon City, 1956.
        136p. Thesis (M.A.) - U.P.

3417.   TAYAG, RENATO D. The Angeles story. Manila, Benipayo Press. 1956. 56p.
            Anderson: An expose of United States-Philippine relations in Angeles
                            and social criticism of politics, values and Filipino
                            foibles.
                            J   3   6

KAPAMPANGAN - FAMILY AND KINSHIP

3418. GALANG, RICARDO C. Kinship usages among the Pampangos. PM 33, no. 9
(Sept. 1936), 452, 454-455.
Reprinted in JEAS 4, no. 1 (Jan. 1955), 115-117.
Anderson: A listing of Pampanga kin terms with short notes indicat-
ing their usage.
-      3   4

KAPAMPANGAN - HISTORY AND CULTURE CHANGE

3419. LARKIN, JOHN A. The evolution of Pampangan society: a case study of social
and economic change in the rural Philippines. 1966. 189p. Thesis (Ph.D.)
- New York Univ.

3420. _____. The place of local history in Philippine historiography. JSEAH 8,
no. 2 (Sept. 1967), 306-317.

KAPAMPANGAN - LANGUAGE AND LITERATURE

3421. AGUAS, JUAN S. Juan Crisostomo Soto and Pampangan drama. DR 10, no. 3
(July 1962), 1-138.

3422. BERGAÑO, DIEGO. Arte de la langua Pampanga. Manila, Imprenta de la Com-
pañia de Jesus, por S. L. Sabino, 1729. 11p. 363 (i.e. 362), 14p.
Reprinted ed. Manila, Tip. del Colegio de Santo Tomás, 1916. 231p. (in
double columns)
Ward: Latin framework for Pampango grammar.
L   3   2/3

3423. PANIZO, ALFREDO and RODOLFO V. CORTEZ. Introduction to the Pampango theatre. Unitas 41, no.1(Mar. 1968), 124-137.

NEGRITO - GENERAL

3424. ARBUES, LILIA R. The Negritos as a minority group in the Philippines. PSR
8, nos. 1/2 (Jan./Apr. 1960), 39-46.

3425. BARROWS, DAVID P. The Negrito and allied types in the Philippines. (1873)
AA n.s. 12, no. 3 (July/Sept. 1910), 358-376.
Warren: G   3   4

3426. BEAN, R. BENNETT. Filipino ears: III. Negrito. PJS 6D, no. 2 (Apr. 1911),

107-125. 18 plates.
      Warren: D   5   4

3427.   _____. Human types. Quarterly Review of Biology 1, no. 3 (July 1926), 360-392.
      Warren: D   5   4

3428.   _____. Types among the inland tribes of Luzon and Mindanao. PJS 8D, no. 6 (Dec. 1913), 455-462. 9 plates.
      Warren: D   5   4

3429.   _____. Types of Negritos in the Philippine Islands. AA n.s. 12, no. 2 (Apr./June 1910), 220-236.
      Warren: D   5   4

3430.   BEYER, H. OTLEY. Ethnography of the Negrito-Aeta peoples; a collection of original sources. Manila, 1918 (His: Beyer Collection ---. Sect. A. Set 17a) Cited in Harvard Univ. Peabody Museum...Library. Catalogue: Subjects. v.18, p. 41.
      Warren: E   3   4

3431.   BLUMENTRITT, FERDINAND. Die Baluga-Negritos der provinz Pampanga (Luzon). Globus 41, no. 15 (1882), 238-239.
      Warren: N   3   3

3432.   _____. Beiträge zur kenntnis der Negritos. Aus spanischen Missionsberichten zusammengestellt. Zeitschrift der Gesellschaft für Erdkunde zu Berlin 27 (1892), 63-68.
      Warren: N   3   3

3433.   _____. Mittheilungen über die Negritos und die Kopfjägerstämme des nördlichen Luzon. Globus 45, no. 5 (1884), 74-78.
      Eggan: Derived from secondary sources--mainly Spanish.
                        E   3   3
      Warren: N   3   3

3434.   _____. Die Negritos am Oberlaufe des Rio Grande de Cagayan. Nach den missionsberichten des P- Fray Buenaventura Campa. Königliche Geographische Gesellschaft in Wien. Mitteilungen 36 (1893), 329-331.
      Warren: N   3   3

3435.   _____. Die Negritos der Philippinen. Globus 48, no. 1 (1885), 7-9.
      Warren: N   3   3

3436.   _____. Die Negritos von Baler. Königliche Geographische Gesellschaft in Wien. Mitteilungen 27 (1884), 317-321.
      Warren: N   3   3

3437.   _____. Die Philippinischen Negritos in den Zeiten der Conquista. Deutsche Rundschau für Geographie und Statistik 15, no. 6 (Mar. 1893), 274-275.
      Warren: N   3   3

3438.   _____. Mittheilungen über die Negritos und die Kopfjägerstämme des nördlichen Luzon. Globus 45, no. 5 (1884), 74-78.

Eggan: Derived from secondary sources--mainly Spanish
               E   3   3
Warren: N   3   3

3439. BORNEMANN, FRITZ. J. M. Garvans Materialien über die Negrito der Philip-
      pinen und P. W. Schmidts Notizen dazu. Anthropos 50 (1955), 899-930.
      Warren: -   5   4

3440. CAMPA, JOSÉ DE LA. Gaddanen, Ilongoten, Ibilaos, und Negritos des valle de
      Cagayan (Luzon). Translation from the Spanish by Ferdinand Blumentritt.
      Anthropologischen Gesellschaft in Wien. Verhandlungen 14 (1884), 52-54.
      Wallace: Useful historical document.
                     -     4   3

3441. CHAMBERLAIN, ALEX F. Etymology of the name Aëta (Eta, Ita). AA n.s. 2,
      no. 4 (Oct./Dec. 1900), 773-774.

3442. COOPER, JOHN M. Andamanese-Semang-Eta cultural relations. Primitive Man
      13, no. 2 (Apr. 1940), 29-47.

3443. DAMIAN, AMAZONA. Some customs of the Aetas of the Baler area, Philippines.
      Primitive Man 24, no. 2 (Apr. 1951), 21-34.

3444. EICKSTEDT, E. VON. Die Negritos und das Negritoproblem. Anthropologischer
      Anzeiger 4, no. 4 (1927), 275-293.
      Warren: D   4   4

3445. EMBREE, JOHN F. Tribal atlas of Malaysia. Dept. of Anthropology, Univ. of
      Chicago.
      Cited in Charles P. Warren, Negrito groups in the Philippines: preliminary
      bibliography. Chicago, Univ. of Chicago.
      Warren: E   5   4

3446. ESTEL, LEO A. Racial types on Mindoro. JEAS 1, no. 4 (July 1952), 21-29.
      Warren: D   5   6

3447. FOX, ROBERT B. Orchids and Negritos. Philippine Orchid Review 3, no. 3
      (Nov. 1950), 3-7.
      Warren: E   5   6

3448. _____. The Pinatubo Negritos: their useful plants and material culture.
      PJS 81, nos. 3/4 (Sept./Dec. 1952), 173-391. 18 plates.
      Warren: E   5   6

3449. GARVAN, JOHN M. The Negritos of the Philippines. Edited by Hermann Hocheg-
      ger. Horn-Wien, Verlag Ferdinand Berger, 1963. 288p. (Wiener Beiträge zur
      Kulturgeschichte und Linguistik, Band XIV)
      Warren: G/Y   5   4

3450. _____. Our Philippine pygmies--their gentle and genial ways. PM 31, no. 9
      (Sept. 1934), 378-379, 398-399; 31, no. 11 (Nov. 1934), 479-480, 507-509.
      Warren: G/Y   5   4

3451. _____. The Pygmies of the Philippines; together with the private notes of
      Wilhelm Schmidt on the above. Posieux(Freiburg), Anthropos-Institut, 1954.

1232p. microfilm. 35 mm. (Micro-Bibliotheca Anthropos, v.19)
Warren: G/Y   5   4

3452. GENET-VARCIN E. Les négritos de l'Ile de Lucon (Philippines). Ouvrage pub-
lié sous les auspices de la Société d'Anthropologie de Paris. Edite avec le
concours du Centre National de la Recherche Scientifique. Paris, Masson,
1951. 259p.
Warren: D   5   6

3453. _____. Les négritos de Lucon (Philippines): étude ostéometrique comparai-
son entre les différentes races pygmées. L'Anthropologie 53, (Avril 1949),
33-67.
Warren: D   5   6

3454. GLORIA, MANUEL. A visit to the Negritos of Central Panay, Philippine Islands.
Primitive Man 12, no. 4 (Oct. 1939), 94-102.

3455. KNEELAND, SAMUEL. The negritos of Luzon. Science 1 (Feb./June 1883), 415-
417.

3456. MACEDA, GENEROSO S. The Remontados of Rizal province. PJS 64, no. 3 (Nov.
1937), 313-321. 4 plates.

3457. MARCHE, ALFRED. Rapport général sur une mission à la presqu' île Malacca et
aux îles Philippines. Archives des Missions Scientifiques et littéraires.
ser. 3, 10, (1883), 331-372.
Warren: T   5   3

3458. MEYER, ADOLF B. Album of Filipine-types. III. Negritos, Manguianes, Bago-
bos. About 190 figures on 37 plates in heliotype. Dresden, Stengel, 1904.
German and translation.
Warren: N   5   3

3459. _____. The distribution of the Negritos in the Philippine Islands and elsewhere. Dresden, Stengel, 1899. 92p. A revised translation by Miss C. S.
Fox of two chapters from a larger work on the Negritos, in v. 9 of the Publications
of the Royal Ethnographical Museum of Dresden.
Warren: N   5   3

3460. _____. Los Negritos de las Filipinas. SGMB 3, (1877), 71-73.
Warren: N   5   3

3461. _____. Die Negritos der Philippinen. Petermann's Mitteilungen 20, (1874),
19-22.
Warren: N   5   3

3462. _____. Die Philippinen. Dresden, Stengel and Markert, 1893. v.II. Negritos. (Publicationen aus dem Königlichen ethnographischen museum zu Dresden
9)
Warren: N   5   3

3463. _____. Die Philippinen. II. Negritos. Notice of. Anthropological Institute. Journal 25, (1896), 172-176.
Warren: N   5   3

3464.   _____. Ueber die Beziehungen zwischen Negritos und Papuas. ZE. Verhandlungen. 7, (1875), 47-48.
           Warren: N   5   3

3465.   _____. Ueber die Negritos der Aetas der Philippinen. Dresden. 1878.
Cited in Marcelo Tangco, Anthropology and the Philippines. PSSHR, Aug.
1940.
           Warren: N   5   3

3466.   _____. Ueber die Negritos der Philippinen. Natuurkundig Tijdschrift voor
Nederlandsch-Indië 33, (1873), 32-40.
Cited in Charles P. Warren, Negrito groups in the Philippines: preliminary
bibliography. Chicago, Univ. of Chicago. 1959. p.9.
           Warren: N   5   3

3467. MEYER, HANS. Reisen im nördlichen Luzon. Globus 43, no. 10 (1883), 169-
172.

3468. NEWTON, PHILIP P. Observations on the negritos of the Philippine Islands.
American Journal of Physical Anthropology 3/4, no. 1 (Jan./Mar. 1920), 1-24.
           Warren: D   3   4

3469. PANIZO, ALFREDO   The Negritos or Aetas. Unitas 40, no. 1 (Mar. 1967),
66-101.

3470. PARKER, LUTHER. Report on work among the negritos of Pampanga during the
period from April 5th to May 31st, 1908. AS 2, no. 1 (Apr. 1964), 105-130.

3471. PATERNO, PEDRO ALEJANDRO. Los itas. Madrid, Impr. de los sucesores de Cuesta, 1890. 439p.

3472. QUATREFAGES DE BRÉAU, ARMAND DE. Les Négritos. Société de Geographie. Bulletin   Ser. 6, 3 (1872), 306-310.
           Warren: -   5   3

3473.   _____. The Pygmies. London. (Translation of Les Pygmées, by Frederick
Starr. 1887). New York, D. Appleton, 1895. 255p. Chapter 5. Aetas of
Luzon, and Mamanuas of Mindanao.
           Maceda: A small part of the work treats about the Negritos.
                          E   4   7
           Warren: -   5   3

3474. RAHMANN, RUDOLF. Field work among the Aetas. Carolinian (Cebu City, Univ.
of San Carlos) 19, (1955).
Cited in Centre for East Asian Culture Studies.Research institutes and researchers of Asian studies in the Philippines. 1966. p. 69.
           Warren: M   5   6

3475.   _____. The Negritos of the Philippines and the early Spanish missionaries.
(In: Festschrift Paul Schebesta zum 75. Wien-Mödling, St. Gabriel - Verlag,
1963. Studia Instituti Anthropos, v.18, p.137-157)
           Warren: M   5   7

3476.   _____. Vor 25000 Jahren kamen die Negritos. Werler Anzeiger aus Stadt und
Land, 14, (1956).

Cited in Research institutes and researchers of Asian studies in the Philippines. 1966. p.69.
    Warren: M   5   6

3477. _____ and MARCELINO N. MACEDA. Notes on the Negritos of Northern Negros.
Anthropos 50, (1955), 810-836. 3 plates.
    Warren: M & E 5   6

3478. REED, WILLIAM A. The Negritos of the Philippines. Southern Workman 23
(1904), 273-279.
    Warren: G   3   4

3479. _____. Negritos of Zambales. Manila, Bureau of public printing, 1904.
90p. (Philippine islands Ethnological Survey Publications, vol. II, pt. 1)
    Warren: G   5   4

3480. SCHADENBERG, ALEXANDER. Ueber die Negritos der Philippinen. ZE 12 (1880),
133-174.
    Warren: N   5   3

3481. SCHEBESTA, PAUL. Die Negrito Asiens. Wien-Mödling, St.-Gabriel-Verlag,
1952-1957. (His Die Pygmäenvölker der Erde, Reine 2)
    Band I. **Geschichte**, Geographie, Umwelt, Demographie und Anthropologie
        der Negrito. 1952. 496p. 16 plates.
    Band II. Ethnographie der Negrito.
        1. Halbband. Wirtschaft und Soziologie. 1954. 340p. 42 plates.
        2. Halbband. Religion und Mythologie. 1957. 336p. 8 plates.
    (Studia Instituti Anthropos. vols. 6, 12, 13)
    Warren: E   5   6

3482. SULLIVAN, LOUIS R. The pygmy races of man. Natural History 19, no. 6
(Dec. 1919), 687-695.

3483. VANOVERBERGH, MORICE. Additional notes on Negritos of Northern Luzon. Anthropos 31, nos. 5/6 (Sept./Dec. 1936), 948-954.
    Warren: M   5   4

3484. _____. A few short visits to Negritos of northern Luzon. (In: Koppers,
Wilhelm, ed. Festschrift publication d'hommage offerte au P. W. Schmidt.
Wien, 1928. p.760-763)
    Warren: M   5   4

3485. _____. Negritos of eastern Luzon.
Anthropos 32, (Sept./Dec. 1937), 905-928. 4 plates.
           33, (1938), 119-164. 1 plate.
    Warren: M   5   4

3486. _____. Negritos of northern Luzon.
Anthropos 20, nos. 1/2 (Jan./Apr. 1925), 148-199. 2 plates.
           20, nos. 3/4 (May/Aug. 1925), 399-443. 10 plates.
    Warren: M   5   4

3487. _____. Negritos of northern Luzon again.
Anthropos 24, nos. 1/2 (Jan./Apr. 1929), 3-75.
           25, nos. 1/2 (Jan./Apr. 1930), 25-71.
           25, nos. 3/4 (May/Aug. 1930), 527-565.

              Warren: M   5   4

3488.   _____. Philippine negrito culture: independent or borrowed? Primitive Man 6, no. 2 (Apr. 1933), 25-35.
              Warren: M   5   4

3489. WARREN, CHARLES P. Negrito groups in the Philippines: preliminary bibli-ography. Chicago, Philippine Studies Program, Dept. of Anthropology, Univ. of Chicago, 1959. 16p. Mimeo.
              Warren: E   3   7

NEGRITO - ARCHAEOLOGY

3490. CAMPBELL, JOHN MARTIN. Neolithic implements as magical objects among the Negritos of Pampanga, Luzon. (In: Solheim, William G., ed. Anthropology at the Eighth Pacific Science Congress Far-Eastern Prehistory Congress, Quezon City, Philippines, 1953. Honolulu, Social Science Research Inst., Univ. of Hawaii, 1968. p.1-6. illus.) (In Asian and Pacific archaeology series, no. 2)

3491. EICKSTEDT, EGON VON. **Untersuchungen** an Philippinischen Negrito skeletten. Ein Beitrag zum Pygmäenproblem und zur osteomorphologischen Methodik. Zeit-schrift für Morphologie und Anthropologie 29, (1931), 307-464.
              Warren: D   5   4

3492. VIRCHOW, RUDOLF. Schädel und Skelette von den Philippinen, namentlich von Negritos. ZE Verhandlungen 11, (1879), 426-428.
              Warren: D   5   3

3493. _____. Üeber Negrito-und Igorrotenschädel von den Philippinen. ZE. Verhandlungen 4 , (1872), 204-209.
          Eggan: Study of Igorot skulls.
                      D   4   3
              Warren: D   5   3

3494. _____. Ueber den Schädelbau der Bewohner der Philippinen,... insbesondere der Negritos. ZE. Verhandlungen 3, (1871), 33-42.
              Warren: D   5   3

3495. WASTL, JOSEF. Beitrag zur Anthropologie der Negrito von Ost-Luzon. Anthropos 52, nos. 5/6 (1957), 769-812. 2 plates.

NEGRITO - BEHAVIOR PROCESS AND PERSONALITY

3496. GARVAN, JOHN M. Pygmy personality. Anthropos 50, (1955), 769-796.
              Warren: G/Y   5   6

3497. STEWART, KILTON R. Children of the forest. PM 31, no. 3 (Mar. 1934), 105-106, 125.
Reprinted: JEAS 4, no. 2 (Apr. 1955), 293-296.

3498. _____. Pygmies and dream giants. New York, W. W. Norton and Co., Inc., 1954. 295p.

NEGRITO - ECONOMICS

3499. SANTOS, SALVADOR A. Economic advancement among the Negritos of Pampanga. College Folio (U.P. College of Philosophy, Science and Letters and College of Engineering) 3, no. 3 (Nov. 1912), 118-121.

3500. SCHEBESTA, PAUL. Die Negrito Asiens. Band II. Ethnographie der Negrito. 1. Halbband. Wirtschaft und Soziologie. Studia Instituti Anthropos 12. (1954), 340p. 42 plates.
Warren: E   5   6

NEGRITO - GEOGRAPHY AND DEMOGRAPHY

3501. BARTLETT, HARLEY HARRIS. The problem of Negrito and "Vedda" elements in the population of Sumatra. Fifth Pacific Science Congress, Proceedings. Victoria and Vancouver, B. C., Canada, 1933. (1934), 2851-2862.

3502. BEYER, H. OTLEY. Distribution of Negritos according to the records of the bureau of non-Christian tribes. Unpublished typescript manuscript, Museum and Institute of Archaeology and Ethnology. U.P., Manila. n.d.
Cited in Charles P. Warren, Negrito groups in the Philippines: preliminary bibliography. 1959.
Warren: E   5   4

3503. HADDON, ALFRED C. The races of man and their distribution. Rev. ed. Cambridge [Eng.] The Univ. Press, 1929. 184p.
Warren: D   4   4

3504. LAPICQUE, LOUIS. La race négrito,et sa distribution géographique. Annales de Geographie de Paris 5, (1895/1896), 407-424.

NEGRITO - HISTORY AND CULTURE CHANGE

3505. BEST, ELSDON. Prehistoric civilisation in the Philippines. Polynesian Society Journal 1, no. 1 (Apr. 15, 1892), 118-125, 195-201.

NEGRITO - LANGUAGE AND LITERATURE

3506. CHRETIEN, DOUGLAS. The dialect of the Sierra de Mariveles Negritos. Berkeley, Univ. of California Press, 1951. (Univ. of California publications in linguistics, v.4, no. 2, 61-110)
Warren: L   5   6

3507. KERN, H. Over de taal der Philippijnsche Negritos. Bijdragen tot de taal-, land- en Volkenkunde van Nederlandsch- Indië 30, (1882), 243-261.

3508. MEYER, ADOLF B. Die Negrito-Sprache. ZE. Verhandlungen 6, (1874), 255-257.

NEGRITO - RELIGIOUS BELIEFS AND PRACTICES

3509. ORACION, TIMOTEO S. The Bais forest preserve Negritos: some notes on their rituals and ceremonials. SR 6, nos. 7/8 (July/Aug. 1965), 23-30.
Warren: E   5   6

3510. RAHMANN, RUDOLF. Burial in a standing or sitting position among Philippine Negritos. Anthropos 51, nos. 3/4 (1956), 741-742.

3511. SCHEBESTA, PAUL. Die Negrito Asiens. Band II. Ethnographie der Negrito. 2. Halbband. Religion und Mythologie. Studia Instituti Anthropos 13 (1957), 336p. 8 plates.
Warren: E   5   6

NEGRITO - STANDARD OF LIVING AND RECREATION

3512. GARVAN, JOHN M. How our Philippine pygmies fill the passing hour. PM 31, no. 8 (Aug. 1934), 323-325, 353-356.
Warren: G/Y   5   4

NEGRITO - TOTAL CULTURE

3513. LYNCH, FRANK. Some notes on a brief field study survey of the Hill people of Mt. Iriga, Camarines Sur, Philippines. Primitive Man 21, nos. 3/4 (July/Oct. 1948), 65-73.
Warren: E   5   5

PANGASINAN

3514. ANDERSON, JAMES N. Kinship and property in Pangasinan barrio. Los Angeles, 1963. 394p. Thesis (Ph.D.) - UCLA.
        Anderson: Useful study of Pangasinian kinship, social and economic organization. Much tabular data to support analysis. Barrio-town study set in central Pangasinan.
                      E   4/5   7
        Polson: The fuller thesis version of "Some aspects of land and society in a Pangasinan Community ".
                      E   5   7
        Spencer: Good study-discussion.
                      E   4/5   7

3515. _____. Some aspects of land and society in a Pangasinan community. PSR 10, nos. 1/2 (Jan./Apr. 1962), 41-58.
        Polson: An excellent analysis of bilateral kinship and its relation to economic interaction.
                      E   5   6

3516. BLUMENTRITT, FERDINAND. Die Igorotten von Pangasinan, Nach den Mittheilungen des Missionärs P. Fr. Mariano Rodriguez. Kaiserlich-Königliche Geographische Gesellschaft in Wien. Mitteilungen. 43, nos. 3/4 (1900), 87-100.
        Anderson: Short ethnographic note by P. Fr. Mariano Rodrigues. Translated by Blumentritt. It mentions the racial features of the Igorrots, their house and village forms, their agricultural practices and religious representations. Furthermore, their manufacture, forms of usury, marriage practices as well as some of their games, diseases and household items are outlined.
                      M   5   3
        Eggan: Derived from secondary sources--mainly Spanish.
                      E   3   3

3517. FLORMATA, GREGORIO. Memoria sobre la provincia de Pangasinan. Manila, Imp. La Democracia, 1901. 52p.

3518. RODRÍGUEZ, MARIANO. Etnografía filipina: Igorrotes y Salvajes de la Cordillera Nordeste de Pangasinan. El Correo Sino-Annamita. 28 (1894), 261-321, 29 (1895), 313-379.
Reprinted in La Politica de Espana en Filipinas.
        5, no. 106 (Feb. 26, 1895), 55-56.
           no. 107 (Mar. 12, 1895), 67-71.
           no. 109 (Apr. 9, 1895), 92-94.
           no. 110 (Apr. 23, 1895), 105-107.
           no. 111 (May 7, 1895), 125-127.
           no. 112 (May 21, 1895), 142-144.
           no. 113 (June 4, 1895), 148-151.
         Eggan: One of annual letters.
                      M   5   3

3519. SCHACHTER, PAUL MORRIS. A contrastive analysis of English and Pangasinan. Berkeley, 1960? 159p. Thesis (Ph.D.) - Univ. of California.

TAGALOG - GENERAL

3520. FRANCISCO, JUAN R. Tagalogs at the Spanish contact. (In: Philippines Historical Committee. The beginnings of Christianity in the Philippines. Manila, 1965. p.176-200)

3521. JUAN DE PLASENCIA. Customs of the Tagalogs. (In: Blair and Robertson 7: 173-196.

3522. KNEELAND, SAMUEL. The Tagals of Luzon. Science 1,(Feb./June 1883), 297-298.

3523. PATERNO, PEDRO ALEJANDRO. El Cristianismo en la antigua civilización tagálog; contestacion al M.R.P.Fr.R.Martínez Vigil de la Orden de predicadores, obispo de Oviedo. Madrid, Imprenta moderna, 1892. 88p.

3524. _____. La familia tagálog en la historia universal? con un apéndice: contestación al M.R.P.Fr.R.Martínez Vigil dé la Orden de predicadores, obispo de Oviedo. Madrid, Imprenta de los sucesores de Cuesta, 1892. 152p.

3525. _____. El individuo Tagálog y su arte, en la exposición historico-americana. Madrid, Impr. de los Sucesores de Cuesta, 1893. 102p.

3526. PIERCE, CHARLES C. The races of the Philippines - the Tagals. American Academy of Political and Social Science. Annals. 18, part 1 (July 1901), 21-42.

TAGALOG - BEHAVIOR PROCESS AND PERSONALITY

3527. HIMES, RONALD S. Cognitive mapping in the Tagalog area (II). (In: Modernization: its impact in the Philippines II. Guthrie, George M. and others, eds. Quezon City, Ateneo de Manila Univ. Press, 1967. IPC Papers, no. 5. p.125-168)

3528. KAUT, CHARLES. The principle of contingency in Tagalog society. AS 3, no. 1 (Apr. 1965), 1-15.

3529. _____. Utang na loob: a system of contractual obligation among Tagalogs. SWJA 17, no. 3 (Autumn 1961), 256-272.
   Coller: Analysis of social relations based on fieldwork - a classic work already.

E   5   6
3530. LYNCH, FRANK and RONALD S. HIMES. Cognitive mapping in the Tagalog area. [Part I] (In: Bello, Walden F. and Maria Clara Roldan, eds. Modernization: its impact in the Philippines. Quezon City, Institute of Philippine Culture, Ateneo de Manila Univ. Press, 1967. IPC Papers, no. 4. p.9-52) For Part II, see Himes, Ronald S.

TAGALOG - FAMILY AND KINSHIP

3531. CASTILLO, GELIA TAGUMPAY and JUANITA F. PUA. Research notes on the contemporary Filipino family: findings in a Tagalog area. PJHE 14, no. 3 (July/Sept. 1963), 4-35.
       Polson: An excellent study of the relationships of family characteristics to social and economic status.
       Z   5   6

3532. GARCIA, MAURO. Tagalog kinship terms and usages. PM 34, no. 1 (Jan. 1937), 32, 34.

3533. STOODLEY, BARTLETT H. Some aspects of Tagalog family structure. AA 59, no. 2 (Apr. 1957), 236-249.
       Coller: Discussion of family roles, especially husband and wife, in context of societal change.
       Z   4   6

TAGALOG - LANGUAGE AND LITERATURE

3534. FREI, ERNEST J. Tagalog as the Philippine national language; the inception and development of the idea of a national language, final choice of Tagalog, and the history and character of its grammatical treatment and promotion. Hartford, Conn., 1947. 430p. Thesis (Ph.D.) - Hartford Seminary Foundation.

3535. GARCIA, MAURO. Secret dialects in Tagalog. PM 31, no. 1 (Jan. 1934), 28, 30.
Reprinted in JEAS 4, no. 2 (Apr. 1955), 299-300.

3536. LLAMZON, TEODORO. A note on predication in Tagalog. PSR 14, no. 3 (July 1966), 150-154.
       Llamzon: Purely linguistic article: concerned with syntactic construction in Tagalog.
       L   3   7

3537. _____. Tagalog phonology. Anthropological Linguistics 8, no. 1 (Jan. 1966), 30-39.

3538. _____. Tagalog reflexes of PMP. Anthropological Linguistics 8, no. 3, part II (Mar. 1966),13-23.

3539. LOPEZ, CECILIO. Foreign influences in Tagalog. Philippine Review 2, no. 2 (Apr. 1944), 43-49.

3540. _____. The Tagalog language (an outline of its psycho-morphological analysis). Publications of the Institute of National Language. Bulletin no. 5,

Aug. 1940. Manila, Bureau of Printing. 23p.

3541. _____. Tagalog words adopted from Spanish. Philippine Social Science Review 8, no. 3 (Sept. 1936), 223-246.
    Llamzon: Purely linguistic article. However the influence of Spanish over Tagalog which is reflected by borrowing might be of interest to ethnologists.
    L   3   7

3542. MANUEL, E. ARSENIO. The Origin of the Tagalog language and the Chinese contributions to its growth. FTY (1949), 33-36, 93-96.

3543. ORDOÑEZ, E. A. Notes on the Tagalog revival. Comment, no. 11 (Second Quarter 1960), 33-38.

3544. PANGANIBAN, CONSUELO TORRES. Spanish elements in the Tagalog language. Unitas 24, no. 3 (Julio/Sept. 1951), 600-673;
          24, no. 4 (Oct./Dec. 1951), 846-877;
          25, no. 1 (Enero/Marzo 1952), 86-118.
    Ward: Word borrowings.
          L   5   2/3

3545. SANTOS, LOPE K. Sources and means for further enrichment of Tagalog as our national language. Philippine Social Science Review
          9, no. 2 (June 1937), 101-124;
          9, no. 4 (Dec. 1937), 329-354;
          10, no. 1 (Feb. 1938), 43-56.

TAGALOG - RELIGIOUS BELIEFS AND PRACTICES

3546. GARDNER, FLETCHER. Philippine (Tagalog) superstitions. Journal of American Folklore 19, no. 74 (July/Sept. 1906), 191-204.

3547. JAVIER, BENEDICTO M. Tagalog belief in thunder and lightning. College Folio. U.P., College of Philosophy, Science and Letters and College of Engineering. 3, no. 2 (Oct. 1912), 83-85.

3548. RAÑOLA, ANDRES. Tagalog superstitions and beliefs. College Folio. U.P., College of Philosophy, Science and Letters and College of Engineering. 1, no. 4 (Apr. 1911), 161-181.

TAGALOG - TOTAL CULTURE

3549. HOLLNSTEINER, MARY R. Tagalog social organization. (In: Manuud, Antonio G., ed., Brown heritage: essays on Philippine cultural tradition and literature. Quezon City, Ateneo de Manila Univ. Press, 1967. p.134-148)

3550. KAUT, CHARLES R. Banság and Apelyido: problems of comparison in changing
Tagalog social organizations. (In: Zamora, Mario D., ed., Studies in
Philippine anthropology (In honor of H. Otley Beyer). Quezon City, Alemar-
Phoenix, 1967. p.397-418)

TINGUIAN - GENERAL

3551. BLUMENTRITT, FERDINAND. Begleitworte zur Karte der Tinguianen - Wohnsitze.
Kaiserlich Königliche Geographische Gesellschaft in Wien. Mittheilungen 30
(1887), 14-17.
    Eggan: Compilation.
                E   3   3

3552. COLE, FAY-COOPER. The Philippine forge group. Chicago, Field museum of
natural history, 1922. 3p. (Field museum of natural history [Anthropology
leaflet, no. 2])
    Eggan: Museum exhibit.
                E   5   4

3553. _____. Tinggian. PJS 3-A, no. 4 (Sept. 1908), 197-213. 9 plates.
    Eggan: Brief preliminary account.
                E   5   4

3554. _____. The Tinguian; social, religious, and economic life of a Philippine
tribe...with a chapter on music by Albert Gale. The R. F. Cummings Philippine expedition. Chicago, 1922. (Field museum of natural history. Publication 209. Anthropological series, vol. XIV, no. 2) p.231-493. 83 plates
and 26 text figures.
    Eggan: Basic study of Tinguian.
                E   5   4

3555. COLE, MABEL (COOK). Savage gentlemen. New York, D. Van Nostrand Company,
Inc., c1929. 249p.
    Eggan: Wife of Fay-Cooper Cole. Popular account.
                B   5   4

3556. HIGDON, ELMER K. Among the Tinguians. Philippine Presbyterian, (Mar./May
1935).
Cited in A. B. Espina, Music of the Philippines, and the development of sacred music there. N.Y. Union Theological Seminary, 1961, p.308.
    Eggan: M   5   4

3557. REYES Y FLORENTINO, ISABELO DE LOS. Die Tinguianen (Luzon). Translated
from the Spanish by Ferdinand Blumentritt. Kaiserlich-Königliche Geographische Gesellschaft in Wien. Mittheilungen. 30 (1887), 5-14, 69-77, 138-
154.
    Eggan: Compilation and observation.
                I   3   3

TINGUIAN - EDUCATION

3558. TERRENAL, REGINA C. A socio-economic and educational study of the Tinguians of central Abra, 1964. 186p. Thesis (M.Ed.) - Univ. of San Carlos.
    Eggan: Missionary teacher.
                 I/Y   5   4

TINGUIAN - FINE ARTS

3559. GALE, ALBERT. Music. (In: The Tinguian; social, religious, and economic life of a Philippine tribe, by Fay-Cooper Cole. Chicago, Field Museum of Natural History, Anthropological series. Chicago, 1922. v.14, no. 2. p.443-485)
    Eggan: Analysis of music of Tinguian.
               Q   4   4

TINGUIAN - HISTORY AND CULTURE CHANGE

3560. EGGAN, FREDERICK. Culture change among the Tinguian of Luzon; [by] Dr. Frederick Eggan; discussed by W. Lloyd Warner. (In: Chicago. Univ. seminar on racial and cultural contacts. Proceedings, 1935/1936. [Chicago, 1936] p. 34-41)
    Eggan: Note: Later published in American Anthropologist. 43, no. 1 (Jan./Mar. 1941), 11-18: "Some Aspects of Culture Change in the Northern Philippines ".
               E   5   4

3561. ORR, KENNETH G. The Christianized Ilocanos and the pagan Tinguian; a study of acculturation in the Philippine Islands. Falls Church? Va, 1956. 48p.
    Eggan: E   3   4
    Scheans: Reworking of the literature with interview data from an informant from Ilocos Sur.
               E   3   7

TINGUIAN - RELIGIOUS BELIEFS AND PRACTICES

3562. CARRILLO, MANUEL. Breve relación de las missiones de las quatro naciones llamadas **Igorrotes**, Tinguianes, Apayaos y Adanes . . . Madrid, Impr. del Consejo de Indias, 1756. 37p. (In: Retana. Archivo del bibliófilo filipino, v.1)
    Eggan: Report on Spanish missions in Northern Luzon.
               M   3   3

3563. COLE, FAY-COOPER. A study of Tinguian folk-lore. New York, 1915. 55p. Thesis (Ph.D.) - Columbia Univ.
      Eggan: Folklore.
                   E   5   4

3564. _____. ...Traditions of the Tinguian; a study in Philippine folk-lore. Chicago, 1915. 226p. (Field museum of natural history. Publication 180. Anthropological series. v. XIV, no. 1)
      Eggan: Essentially same as A Study of Tinguian Folk-lore. (His doctoral dissertation)
                   E   5   4

3565. EGGAN, FRED. Ritual myths among the Tinguian. Journal of American Folklore 69, no. 274 (Oct./Dec. 1956), 331-339.
      Eggan: E   5   4

3566. MILLARE, FLORENCIO D. The Tinguians and their old form of worship. PS 3, no. 4 (Dec. 1955), 403-414.
      Eggan: M   5   4

PART   III

THE   BISAYAN

AND

PALAWAN   ISLANDS

A. BY SUBJECT

GENERAL

3567. ARANETA, FRANCISCO and MIGUEL A. BERNAD. "Bisayans" of Borneo and the "Tagalogs" and "Visayans" of the Philippines. SMJ 9, nos. 15/16 (July/Dec. 1960), 542-564.

Hart:	M&Q	3	7
Llamzon:	Popular, journalistic description of situation.		
	E	3	7
Ward:	Comparative study with a fair amount of words presented.		
	M&Q	3	7

3568. BEYER, H. OTLEY, comp. Ethnography of the Bisaya peoples; a comprehensive collection of original sources...Manila, 1918-   . (His: Beyer collection of Filipiniana. Section A, set 1a)
Cited in Harvard Univ. Peabody Museum ... Library. Catalogue: Subjects. v.18, p.42.

Nurge:	E	3	4
Sibley:	Many of these are students' papers, of uneven quality.		
	E	3	4

3569. _____. Ethnography of the Mindoro-Palawan peoples; a collection of original sources...Manila, 1918-   . (His: Beyer collection of Filipiniana. Section 4, set 12a, 1918)
Cited in Harvard Univ. Peabody Museum ... Library. Catalogue: Subjects. v.18, p.40.

Nurge:	E	3	4
Sibley:	Many of these are students' papers, of uneven quality.		
	E	3	4

3570. BLUMENTRITT, FERDINAND. Die Bergstämme der Insel Negros (Philippinen). Kaiserlich-Königliche Geographische Gesellschaft in Wien. Mittheilungen 32, (1889), 508-515.

Hart:	Based on published data, author never visited Philippine Islands.		
	A	3	3

3571. _____. Die Eingebornen der Insel Palawan. Bemerkungen zu des D. Francisco Javier de Moya "Las Islas Filipinas. Estudios historicos." Deutsche Rundschau für Geographie und Statistik 6, no. 4 (Jan. 1884), 161-167.

Hart:	A	3	3

3572. CARROLL, JOHN B. Notes on the Bisaya in the Philippines and Borneo. JEAS 8, nos. 1/2 (Jan./Apr. 1959), 42-72.

3573. _____. The word Bisaya in the Philippines and Borneo. SMJ 9, nos. 15/16 (July/Dec. 1960), 499-541.

3574. CRUZ, BEATO DE LA. Blessing on this house. PM 37, no. 2 (Feb. 1940), 60, 66, 67.

Hart:	-	3/5	4

3575. EALDAMA, EUGENIO. The Monteses of Panay. PM 35, no. 1 (Jan. 1938), 24-25, 50-52.

35, no. 2 (Feb. 1938), 95-97, 107.
35, no. 3 (Mar. 1938), 138, 149-150.
35, no. 5 (May 1938), 236, 242, 244-245.
35, no. 6 (June 1938), 286-287.
35, no. 9 (Sept. 1938), 424-425.
35, no. 10 (Oct. 1938), 468-469, 487-490.
Hart: X   4   4

3576. ECHAÚZ, ROBUSTIANO. ... Apuntes de la isla de Negros. Manila, Tipo-lit. de Chofré y comp.ª 894. 191p.
        Hart: Author lived in Negros Occidental--most of book on Occidental province.
                         X   5   3

3577. ELLINGER, TAGE U. H. Explorations in the interior of southwest Palawan. PSSHR 17, no. 3 (Sept. 1952), 215-245. 3 plates.

3578. FOX, ENRIQUETA (Translator). Bisayan accounts of early Bornean Settlements in the Philippines recorded by Father Santarén. Chicago, Philippine Studies Program, Department of Anthropology, Univ. of Chicago, 1954. 24p. (Univ. of Chicago. Philippine Studies Program. Transcript no. 4)
        Sibley: I/M   3   1

3579. FRANCISCO, JUAN R. Palawan Journal. U.P. Anthropology Bulletin 3, no. 1 (First semester 1967/1968), 13-15, 18-27.

3580. HARRISSON, TOM. "Bisaya": Borneo - Philippine impacts of Islam. SMJ 7, no. 7 (June 1956), 43-47.
        Hart: E   3   7

3581. _____. "Bisaya" in North Borneo and elsewhere. Sabah Society Journal, no. 2 (Mar. 1962), 6-13.
        Hart: E   3   7

3582. HART, DONN V. A personal narrative of a Samaran Filipina. AS 3, no. 1 (Apr. 1965), 55-70.

3583. _____. "Tambal para sa uhaw": The ethnography of the buri palm in barrio Caticugan, Negros, Philippines. PJS 94, no. 3 (Sept. 1965), 339-372.

3584. LOARCA, MIGUEL DE. Relation of the Filipinas Islands. [1582]. (In: Blair and Robertson. v.5: 34-187.

3585. MADIGAN, FRANCIS C. Research in the Visayas-Mindanao area. PSR 11, nos. 1/2 (Jan./Apr. 1963), 125-130.
        Hart: Sociologist-priest with long residence in Mindanao.
                         M/Z   4   7

3586. MARCHE, ALFRED. Lucon et Palaouan; six années de voyages aux Philippines. Paris, Librairie Hachette, 1887. 406p.

3587. NURGE, ETHEL. Life in a Leyte village. Seattle, Univ. of Washington Press, 1965. 157p. (American Ethnological Society. Monograph no. 40)
        Hart: Anthropologist-trained in Whiting tradition--best on specific data dyad relationship.

```
                        E      5      6
        Nurge:          E      5      6
        Sibley:         One of few published accounts of Central Philippine Is-
                        land village life.
                        E      5      6
```

3588. PAL, AGATON P. A Philippine barrio: a study of social organizations in
relation to planned cultural change. Ithaca, New York, 1956. 400p.
Thesis (Ph.D.) - Cornell Univ. Part II (Chapters 4-11) "A case study of a
Philippine barrio," published in JEAS 5, no. 4 (Oct. 1956), 333-486.
```
        Coller:         Careful and comprehensive field study of a village in
                        Southern Leyte.  Economics and communications are par-
                        ticularly well-covered.
                        Z      5      6
        McMillan:       A careful analysis of rural social organization.
                        Z      4      6
        Polson:         The most comprehensive description of a Visayan barrio.
                        Z      5      6
```

3589. POVEDANO, DIEGO LOPE. The Robertson text and translation of the Povedano
manuscript of 1572, edited by E. D. Hester, with notes on Kabunian by Fred
Eggan and on the Bisayan syllabary by Robert Fox. Chicago, 1954   Philippine Studies Program, Dept. of Anthropology, Univ. of Chicago, 1954. 63p.
(Philippine Studies Program. Transcript no. 2)
```
        Scott:          "... appear to be deliberate fabrications with no his-
                        toric validity."  Prehispanic source materials for the
                        study of Philippine history.  1968.  p.136.
        Sibley:         Some question exists concerning the authenticity of this
                        manuscript.
```

3590. _____. The Povedano manuscript of 1578. The ancient legends and stories
of the Indios Jarayas, Jiguesinas, and Igneines which contain their beliefs
and diverse superstitions. Translated and annotated by Rebecca P. Ignacio.
1954. 72p. (Transcript no. 3, Philippine Studies Program, Univ. of Chicago)
```
        Scott:          "... appear to be deliberate fabrications with no historic
                        validity."  Prehispanic source materials for the study of
                        Philippine history.  1968.  p.136.
```

3591. PUTONG, CECILIO. Bohol and its people. Manila, 1965. 164p.
```
        Hart:           Y      3      7
```

3592. RAHMANN, RUDOLF. Research possibilities in the Visayas. Philippine Association for Graduate Education. 1st regional seminar, June 1964, 30-37.
```
        Hart:           Chancellor of San Carlos University - done   Philippine
                        Island research on Negritos.
                        E/M    4      6
```

3593. REYES Y FLORENTINO, ISABELO DE LOS. ... Las islas Visayas en la época de la
conquista. 2 ed. Manila, Tipo-litografía de Chofré y ca., 1889. 114p.
(Biblioteca de "La España oriental)
```
        Hart:           M/Q    5      7
```

3594. SANTARÉN, TOMAS. Bisayan accounts of early Bornean settlements in the Philippines. Introductory note by Fred Eggan and note on texts by E. D. Hester.
SMJ 7, no. 7 (June 1956), [22]-42.

3595. AQUINO, MARCELO V. Some aspects of agricultural loans granted by five rural banks in the Visayas and Mindanao, 1953. PA 39, no. 9 (Feb. 1956), 510-515.

    Intengan: An interesting account of the ritual in the planting of sweet potato.

                      C   5   6

    Sta. Iglesia: Highly useful descriptive research.

                      G   5   6

3596. ARENS, RICHARD. Animism in the rice ritual of Leyte and Samar. PSR 4, no. 1 (Jan. 1956), 2-6.

    Hart: The seven articles by Arens are based on interviewing informants and extensive travel in Leyte and Samar when the author was associated with St. Paul College in Tacloban.

                      M/E   5   6

    Sibley: M   5   6

3597. _____. Animistic fishing ritual in Leyte and Samar. PSR 4, no. 4 (Oct. 1956), 24-28.

    Hart: M/E   5   6

    Sibley: M   5   6

3598. _____. Camote ritual in Leyte and Samar. East and West (Instituto Italiano Per Il Medio Ed Estremo Oriente) 7, (July 1956), 173-176.

    Hart: M/E   5   6

    Nurge: M   5   6

    Sibley: M   5   6

3599. _____. The corn ritual in Leyte and Samar. PSR 4, nos. 2/3 (Apr./July 1956), 29-31.

    Hart: M/E   5   6

    Nurge: M   5   6

    Sibley: M   5   6

3600. _____. The fishing industry of San Jose, Tacloban City, Leyte. JEAS 5, no. 1 (Jan. 1956), 1-34.

    Hart: M/E   5   6

    Sibley: M   5   6

3601. _____. Notes on camote rituals in Leyte and Samar Islands, Philippines. PJS 85, no. 3 (Sept. 1956), 343-347. 2 plates.

    Hart: M/E   5   6

    Nurge: M   5   6

    Sibley: M   5   6

3602. _____. The rice ritual in the East Visayan Islands, Philippines. Folklore Studies (Society of the Divine World. Tokyo, Japan) 16, (1957), 268-290. 12 photos.

    Hart: M/E   5   6

    Sibley: M   5   6

3603. ARNALDO, MARCELO V. A summary of the situation of the agricultural credit co-operative associations in the island of Panay. PA 19, no. 8 (Jan. 1931), 531-539.

        Intengan: An evaluation of the operation of agricultural credit co-
operative associations in Panay with recommendations.
C   3   4

3604. BAGUILAT, TEODORO B. Palay marketing on the farm level in Nueva Ecija, Cagayan and Iloilo, 1955-1956. PA 42, no. 1 (June 1958), 18-35.
        Sta. Iglesia: Highly useful descriptive research.
        Y(G)   5   6

3605. BANOGON, RODOLFO C. A study of lowland rice farming (Farm management study
of Negros Oriental). SJ 6, no. 4 (Oct./Dec. 1959), 334-354.
        Sta. Iglesia: Highly useful descriptive research.
        Y   5   6

3606. BARRERA, ALFREDO. Palawan's edible bird's nest. PGJ 6, no. 2 (Apr./June
1958), 62-66.
        Intengan: Bird's nest industry in Palawan is described. This is
popularly served as "nido" soup.
C   3   6
        Spencer: C   4   6
        Wernstedt: C   3   6

3607. BAWAGAN, MARGARITA P. Marketing of farm products produced in Bantayan, Cebu.
PA 37, nos. 1/2 (June/July 1953), 76-83.
        Intengan: This study revealed that marketing was haphazard and crude,
storage and/or warehousing facilities are not used, credit
facilities not adequate and farm products are sold un-
graded.
C   3   6
        Sta. Iglesia: Highly useful descriptive research.
        Y   5   6

3608. BOKINGO, BENJAMIN A. Diversified crop farming (Farm management study of
Negros Oriental). SJ 6, no. 4 (Oct./Dec. 1959), 355-374.
        Intengan: A study of the problems of diversified crop farming in
Negros Oriental; presented some lines of action designed
to improve their standard of living.
C   4   6
        Sta. Iglesia: Highly useful descriptive research.
        Y   5   6

3609. CAGAMPANG, FELIPE V. An economic study of sugar cane farms in Negros Oriental. SJ 5, no. 2 (Apr./June 1958), 119-139.
        Intengan: A study of the general situation prevailing in 31 small
sugar cane farms in a district in Negros Oriental.
C   3   6
        Sta. Iglesia: Highly useful descriptive research.
        Y   5   6

3610. _____ and BENJAMIN A. BOKINGO. Socio-economic conditions of laborers in
sugar cane plantations in Negros Oriental. SJ 6, no. 2 (Apr./June 1959),
109-121.
        Intengan: An analysis of the prevailing management practices of
sugar cane plantations in Negros Oriental and of labor
problems.

```
                              C     4     6
          Sta. Iglesia:  Highly useful descriptive research.
                              Y     5     6
```

3611. _____ and H. B. RAMACHO. How coconut farmers make a living (Farm management study of Negros Oriental). SJ 6, no. 4 (Oct./Dec. 1959), 312-333.
    Intengan: A survey to study the general condition of the average coconut farmers in Negros Oriental upon which recommendations for improving farm practices shall be based.
```
                              C     4     6
          Sta. Iglesia:  Highly useful descriptive research.
                              Y     5     6
```

3612. CAINTIC, CRISOGONO, U., J. C. STA. IGLESIA, and H. VON OPPENFELD. Management practices, costs and returns of sugar cane farms in the Victorias milling district College, Laguna, College of Agriculture, Univ. of the Philippines, 1962. 67p. (Technical Bulletin 10)
          Sta. Iglesia: Highly useful descriptive and analytical research.
```
                              Y     5     6
```

3613. CAMPOS, AMADO C. Commercial-scale poultry production in Cebu. PA 37, nos. 1/2 (June/July 1953), 9-15.
    Intengan: Survey revealed problems of poultry trade in Cebu. Remedial measures are suggested.
```
                              C     4     6
```

3614. COROCOTO, SIMON P. and MOISES L. SARDIDO. The economic and social conditions of rice farmers in Palapag, Samar. Researcher 1, no. 1 (Feb. 1965), 35-49.

3615. GERVACIO, EMMANUEL T. Livelihood of corn farmers (Farm management study of Negros Oriental). SJ 6, no. 4 (Oct./Dec. 1959), 283-311.
    Intengan: A study of management practices of corn farmers designed to provide materials for use in agricultural extension and community development work.
```
                              C     4     6
          Sta. Iglesia:  Highly useful descriptive research.
                              Y     5     6
```

3616. GUTHRIE, HELEN A. Nutrition in a fishing community. (In: Bello, Walden F. and Alfonso de Guzman II, eds. Modernization: its impact in the Philippines, III. Quezon City, Ateneo de Manila Univ. Press, 1968, p.129-148. IPC Papers no. 6)

3617. HART, DONN V. Hunting and food gathering activities in a Bisayan barrio. JEAS 4, no. 1 (Jan. 1955), 1-13.
    Hart: Based on author's research in South Negros, 1950-51.
```
                              E     5     6
```
    Sibley: Excellent detailed data on Southeast Negros settlement area.
```
                              E     5     6
```

3618. _____. Securing aquatic products in Siaton municipality, Negros Oriental province, Philippines. Manila, Bureau of Printing, 1956. 84p. (Institute of Science and Technology. Monograph 4)

Hart:	Based on author's research in South Negros, 1950-51.
	E 5 6
Intengan:	A survey report of fishing methods and associated practices employed in the region.
	E 4 6
Sibley:	Excellent detailed data on Southeast Negros settlement area.
	E 5 6
Wernstedt:	E 4 7

3619. _____. "Tambal para sa uhaw"; the ethnography of the buri palm in barrio Caticugan Negros, Philippines. PJS 94, no. 3 (Sept. 1965), 339-370. 2 plates.

3620. HESTER, EVETT D. and GERÓNIMO M. MIÑANO. Tenancy on coconut holdings in the municipality of Looc, Province of Romblon. PA 10, no. 4 (Nov. 1921), 145-168.

3621. ILAG, LEODEGARIO M. Economic implications of technological change on the Philippine sugar industry: a case study of some farms in the Victorias Mill district. PRBE 2, no. 1 (May 1965), 9-25.

3622. _____. Farm management analysis of some sugar-cane farms in the Victorias Mill district, Philippines, 1961-1962. 1964. 145p. Thesis (M.S.) - U.P. Cited in U.P. theses and dissertations index, p. 91.
     Sta. Iglesia: Highly useful descriptive and analytical research.
          Y   5   6

3623. JOCANO, F. LANDA. Agricultural rituals in a Philippine barrio. PSR 15, nos. 1/2 (Jan./Apr. 1967), 48-56.

3624. KALAW, MOISES M. A report of two month's extension work in the Visayan Islands. PA 18, no. 1 (June 1929), 65-77.
     Intengan: A report of the activities of an agricultural extension worker setting up copra driers in several localities.
          C   3   4

3625. MANULAT, MARIO V. The rural credit system in Naghalin, Kanangga, Leyte. PA 38, nos. 6/7 (Nov./Dec. 1954), 471-483.
     Intengan: A survey of the rural credit system prevailing in a particular Leyte barrio at the time.
          C   3   6
     Sta. Iglesia: Highly useful descriptive research.
          Y   5   6

3626. MERRILL, ELMER DREW. The ascent of Mount Halcon, Mindoro. PJS 2A, no. 3 (June 1907), 179-205. 1 plate.
     Frake: N   5   4

3627. MILLER, E. Y. The tugda, or rice planter, of the Coyunos, Philippine Islands. Smithsonian Institution. Miscellaneous Collections 47, (1905), 375-376. 2 plates.

3628. MONTALBAN, HERACLIO R. Investigations on fish preservation at Estancia, Panay, Philippine Islands. PJS 42, no. 2 (June 1930), 309-335. 5 plates.

Intengan: Describes existing methods of fish preservation and im-
              provements made.
              C   4   4

3629. NURGE, ETHEL. Problems of food preservation in a Philippine village. Rip
      Van Winkle Clinic. Proceedings 2 (Winter 1960), 13-17.
      Cited in Medical Anthropology Newsletter. Sept. 1970, p. 23.

3630. POLSON, ROBERT A. and AGATON P. PAL. Food supply and food habits in the
      Dumaguete city trade area. SJ 4, no. 2 (Apr./June 1957), 107-113.
              Hart: Z&Z   5   6
              Sibley: Z&Z   5   6
              Sta. Iglesia: Highly useful descriptive research.
                           Z&Z   5   6
              Wernstedt: Good detailed pioneer study.
                           Z&Z   4   6

3631. QUINTANA, EMILIO U. Costs and returns of palay production in Iloilo, 1952-
      53. PA 39, no. 3 (Aug. 1955), 147-150.
              Intengan: A study on palay production on irrigated and non-irrigated
                           lowland in Iloilo.
                           C   3   6
              Sta. Iglesia: Highly useful descriptive research.
                           Y   5   6

3632. _____. The economic and social conditions of abaca farmers in Baybay,
      Leyte. PA 35, no. 9 (Feb. 1952), 451-470.
              Intengan: Many findings among abaca farmers are presented. Factors
                           that contribute to low income and sub-standard of living
                           are discussed.
                           C   3   6
              Sta. Iglesia: Highly useful descriptive research.
                           Y   5   6

3633. _____. Factors affecting costs and returns of palay production in Iloilo.
      PA 39, no. 6 (Nov. 1955), 365-368.
              Intengan: A discussion of factors affecting costs and returns of
                           palay production in a Philippine province.
                           C   3   6

3634. RAVENHOLT, ALBERT. Social yeast in the sugar industry; Jesuits organize the
      plantation workers. AUFSR. Southeast Asia Series 7, no. 4 (Apr. 1959),
      12p. (AR-3-59)
              Polson: An excellent case study of operational problems in rural
                           mobilization.
                           V   5   6

3635. SACAY, FRANCISCO M. and BLAS A. GAAC. The economic and social conditions of
      coconut farmers in Despujols, Romblon. PA 36, no. 4 (Sept. 1952), 225-229.
              Sta. Iglesia: Highly useful descriptive research.
                           Y(G)   5   6

3636. SALAZAR, MA PAZ GIL. Strengthening cooperation and coordination in community
      nutrition work in Cebu. Philippine Journal of Nutrition 20, no. 2 (Apr./June
      1967), 61-65.

Reprinted from DAP Bulletin 6, no. 2 (Apr. 1967).

3637. SCHUL, NORMAN W. Hacienda magnitude and Philippine sugar cane production. AS 5, no. 2 (Aug. 1967), 258-273.

3638. SELGA, MIGUEL. Father Francisco Ignacio Alzina, S.J.: an agricultural observer of the seventeenth century. PA 20, no. 6 (Nov. 1931), 367-369.
    Intengan: The article deals on some unpublished documents written by a 17th century agricultural observer and religious missionary.
    C   3   4

3639. SZANTON, DAVID L. The fishing industry of Estancia, Iloilo. (In: Modernization: its impact in the Philippines II. Guthrie, George M. and others, editors. Quezon City, Ateneo de Manila Univ. Press, 1967. IPC Papers, no. 5. p.4-34)

3640. TABLANTE, NATHANIEL B. Marketing cattle in the province of Masbate. PA 36, no. 1 (June 1952), 51-60.
    Intengan: The most important industry in Masbate is described giving size of ranch, market outlets, price of animal and cost of shipping per head.
    C   4   6
    Sta. Iglesia: Highly useful descriptive research.
    Y   5   6

3641. UMALI, AGUSTIN F. The fishery industries of southwestern Samar. PJS 54, no. 3 (July 1934), 365-392. 7 plates.
    Hart: Top-rate Filipino specialist on fishing.
    C   5   6
    Intengan: A survey of nine municipalities in Samar where fishing is the mainstay of the people. Fishing methods and fish preservation are cited.
    C   3   4

3642. VANDER MEER, CANUTE. Agricultural rituals for corn crops on Cebu Island, Philippines. PJS 96, no. 3 (Sept. 1967), 305-318.

3643. _____. Corn on the island of Cebu, the Philippines. Ann Arbor, 1962. 205p. Thesis (Ph.D.) - Univ. of Michigan.

3644. WERNSTEDT, FREDERICK L. Agricultural regionalism on Negros Island, Philippines. Los Angeles, 1953. 264p. Thesis (Ph.D.) - Univ. of California.

3645. _____. The role of corn in the agricultural economy of Negros Oriental. SJ 1, no. 1 (Jan. 1954), 59-67.
    Hart: Based on research done in 1950-51 for Philippine Islands dissertation.
    K   5   6
    Sibley: Wernstedt is a leading geographical analyst of Philippine Islands.
    K   5   6

ARCHAEOLOGY

3646.   AGA-OGLU, KAMER. Early blue and white wine pot excavated in the Philip-
        pines. Far Eastern Ceramic Bulletin 1/2, no. 10 (June 1950), 64-71. 1
        plate.
                Sibley: A   4   1

3647.   BERGER, RAINER. The Palawan Island series. California. Univ., Los Angeles.
        Dept. of Anthropology. Pacific Island Program, Los Angeles, 1968. no. 13,
        1-7.

3648.   BROECKER, W. S., J. L. KULP and C. S. TUCEK. Lamont natural radio-carbon
        measurements III. Science 124, no. 3213 (July 27, 1956), 154-165.
                Peterson: A listing of C-14 dates, including some from the Philip-
                                 pines.
                                 A   5   1
                Solheim: First C-14 date from the Philippines.
                                 N   3   1

3649.   FOX, ROBERT B. Ancient man in Palawan: a progress report of current exca-
        vations. Manila, National Museum (mimeographed). 1963.
                Hart: A   5   1
                Sibley: Principal excavator of Palawan materials.
                                 A   5   1
                Solheim: First report on the excavations in the most important
                                 prehistoric sites known in the Philippines.
                                 A/E   5   1

3650.   _____. Recent archaeological excavations in Palawan. U.P. Anthropology
        Bulletin 1, no. 1 (Sept. 1963), 6-7.
                Hart: A   5   1
                Sibley: Fox is main excavator of Palawan materials.
                                 A   5   1

3651.   GUTHE, CARL E. A burial site on the island of Samar, Philippine Islands.
        Michigan Academy of Science, Arts and Letters. Papers. 23, (1937), 29-35.
        2 plates.
                Hart: A   5   1
                Sibley: A   5   1
                Solheim: A brief site report.
                                 A   5   1

3652.   HUTTERER, CHARLES. Report on a preliminary exploration of some caves in
        southwestern Samar. Leyte-Samar Studies 2, no. 1 (1968), 123-143. 10
        figures. 1 plate.

3653.   RAHMANN, RUDOLPH and ROSA C. P. TENAZAS. A brief review of the archaeolog-
        ical field work undertaken by the Department of Anthropology, University of
        San Carlos, Philippines, during the years 1961-64. National Taiwan Univ.,
        Taipei. Dept. of Archaeology and Anthropology. Bulletin, no. 23/24, (Nov.
        1964), 46-51.
                Hart: M&A   3   7
                Sibley: M&A   4   7
                Solheim: M&A   3   7

3654. SIBLEY, WILLIS E. A discovery report: the Bongol San Miguel burial site, Guimbal, Iloilo. SR 6, nos. 7/8 (July/Aug. 1965), 31-36.
    Hart: Reprinted in Mario D. Zamora, ed. Studies in Philippine Anthropology.1967, p.273-298. 11 plates. Has wide research experience in Panay and Negros Occidental.
        E   5   1
    Sibley: Brief report of late Pre-Spanish burial site in Panay.
        E   3   1
    Solheim: E   5?   1

3655. SMITH, WARREN D. Ancient cave dwellers of Batwaan, Masbate, Philippine Islands. PJS 19, no. 2 (Aug. 1921), 233-241. 5 plates.

3656. SOLHEIM, WILHELM G.,II. The archaeology of the central Philippines; a study chiefly of the iron age and its relationships. Manila, Bureau of Printing, 1964. 235p. 45 plates. (Monographs of the National Institute of Science and Technology, 10)
    Solheim: A basic work presenting new data and new interpretation of the Philippine Iron Age; data primarily from the Visayan Islands.
        A   4/5   1/2

3657. _____. The Batungan cave sites, Masbate, Philippines. (In: Solheim, Wilhelm G., ed. Anthropology at the EighthPacific Science Congress of the Pacific Science Association and the Fourth Far-Eastern Prehistory Congress. Quezon City, Philippines, 1953. Honolulu, Social Science Research Institute, Univ. of Hawaii, 1968, p.21-62. 6 plates.
    Solheim: A   5   1

3658. _____. Further notes on the Kalanay pottery complex in the Philippines. AP 3, no. 2 (Winter 1959), 157-165. 7 plates.
    Solheim: Important data on a Late Neolithic--Early Iron Age pottery complex in the Philippines.
        A   4/5   1

3659. _____. Further relationships of the Sa-Huynh-Kalanay pottery tradition. AP 8, no. 1 (Summer 1964), 196-211. 7 plates.
    Solheim: New data on Philippine prehistoric pottery and on pottery found in Thailand which is clearly related to the Philippine prehistoric pottery.
        A   4/5   1

3660. _____. Jar burial in the Babuyan and Batanes Islands and in Central Philippines, and its relationship to jar burial elsewhere in the Far East. PJS 89, no. 1 (Mar. 1960), 115-148. 10 plates.
    Maher: A   5   1
    Scheans: Beyerian diffusionist study.
        A   4/5   1
    Solheim: New data and reinterpretation of jar burials found in the Philippines and elsewhere in Asia.
        A   4/5   1

3661. _____. The Kulanay pottery complex in the Philippines. Artibus Asiae 20, no. 4 (1957), 279-288.
    Solheim: Of historical interest.
        A   3   1

3662. _____. The Makabog burial - jar site. PJS 83, no. 1 (Mar. 1954), 57-68.
10 plates.
   Solheim: Site report.
         A 5   1

3663. _____. Notes on the archaeology of Masbate. JEAS 4, no. 1 (Jan. 1955),
47-50.
   Solheim: A 3   1

3664. _____. The Philippine iron age. 1959. 453p. Thesis (Ph.D.) - Univ. of
Arizona.
   Peterson, W.: Descriptive portions of this work are excellent.
         A 5   1
   Solheim: A basic work presenting new data and new interpretation
         of the Philippine Iron Age; data primarily from the Visa-
         yan Islands.
         A 4/5 1/2

3665. _____. Pottery manufacturing in the islands of Masbate and Batan, Philippines. JEAS 1, no. 3 (1952), 49-53. plates.

3666. _____. The Sa-Huynh-Kalanay pottery tradition: past and future research.
(In: Zamora, Mario D., ed. Studies in Philippine anthropology (In honor of
H. Otley Beyer). Quezon City, Alemar-Phoenix, 1967. p.151-174)

3667. _____ and TERRY SHULER. Further notes on Philippine pottery manufacture:
Mountain Province and Panay. JEAS 8, nos. 1/2 (Jan./Apr. 1959), 1-10.
   Hart: A 5   7
   Maher: A 5   7
   Sibley: A 5   7

3668. TENAZAS, ROSA C. P. A brief report on protohistoric trade potteries from
burial sites in Puerto Galera, Oriental Mindoro. PSR 12, nos. 1/2 (Jan./
Apr. 1964), 114-121.
   Solheim: A 5?   1/2

ARMED FORCES AND WAR

3669. HART, DONN V. Guerrilla warfare and the Filipino resistance on Negros Island
in the Bisayas, 1942-1945: a bibliographical essay. JSEAH 5 (Mar. 1964),
101-125.

3670. LEAR, ELMER N. The western Leyte guerrilla warfare forces: a case study in
the non-legitimation of a guerrilla organization. JSEAH 9, no. 1 (Mar.
1968), 69-94.

BEHAVIOR PROCESS AND PERSONALITY

3671. CEBU PSYCHOLOGICAL AND RESEARCH CENTER and UNIVERSITY OF SAN CARLOS. An analytical study of the personality, leadership patterns, mental abilities and problems of college student leaders in Cebu City, Philippines; a joint research project. Cebu City, the Center, 1967. 150p.

3672. JOCANO, F. LANDA. Variation in Philippine values: a western Bisayan case-study. Southeast Asia Quarterly 1, no. 1 (July 1966), 49-74.

3673. [KEPNER, WILLIAM ALLISON]. Observations on color perception among the Visayans of Leyte Island, P.I. Science 22, no. 569 (Nov. 24, 1905), 680-683.

3674. SIBLEY, WILLIS E. The definition and operation of **Hiya** in Manalad and environs. 1955. 5p. Ms. Philippine Studies Program, Univ. of Chicago.

Hart:	E	4	6
Sibley:	Description of major sanctioning force of shame in Philippine Islands.		
	E	5	6
Warren:	E	5	6

BUILDINGS, TOOLS AND EQUIPMENT

3675. HART, DONN V. The Cebuan Filipino dwelling in Caticugan: its construction and cultural aspects. New Haven, Yale Univ., 1958. 148p. (Southeast Asia Studies. Cultural report series no. 7)

Hart:	E	5	7
Polson:	Very comprehensive.		
	E	5	6
Sibley:	Detailed material culture analysis.		
	E	5	6

3676. MACEDA, MARCELINO N. A visit to the Ati of Iloilo. Carolinian 19, no. 2 (1955), 18, 35.
Cited in Lynch and Hollnsteiner. Sixty years of Philippine ethnology...(In: Philippines (Republic) National Sciences Development Board. Area VI-Social Sciences. Manila, 1963.)

Hart:	Anthropologist trained in Switzerland and at Univ. of San Carlos--worked with Rahmann.		
	E	4	6
Sibley:	E	3	6

3677. TALAVERA, FLORENCIO and HERACLIO R. MONTALBAN. Fishing appliances of Panay, Negros and Cebu. PJS 48, no. 3 (July 1932), 429-483. 15 plates.

Hart:	C	5	7

CLOTHING, ADORNMENT AND MATERIALS

3678. ARENS, RICHARD. The ready-made garment industry in Minglanilla, Cebu. Quezon City, Community Development Research Council, U.P. 1960. 135p. (Study series, no. 6)
    Hart: M/E   5   7

COMMUNITY DEVELOPMENT AND TERRITORIAL ORGANIZATION

3679. CANTERO-PASTRANO, CECELIA L. A report on a Visayan fishing barrio. PSR 3, no. 4 (Nov. 1955), 15-22.
    Polson: A good discussion of interactive norms and processes.
                    -      5   6

3680. COLLER, RICHARD W. Barrio Gacao; a study of village ecology and the schistosomiasis problem. Quezon City, Community Development Research Council, U.P. 1960. 123p. (Study series no. 9)
    Coller: Basic survey of a total village - socio-economic aspects plus health material.   Z   5   6
    Tiglao: Z   5   6
    Villanueva: Very insightful.
                    Z   5   6

3681. CUTSHALL, ALDEN. Dumaguete: an urban study of a Philippine community. PGJ 5, nos. 1/2 (Jan./June 1957), 8-13.
    Hart: Wide field research in the Philippines plus residence in Dumaguete.
                    K   3   5/6
    Sibley: G   5   6

3682. EALDAMA, EUGENIO. Alameda. 3d ed., Manila, University Pub. Co., 1952. 146p.
    Hart: A devoted "amateur" who writes fondly and often wisely about his childhood days.
                    X   4   7
    Sibley: Q   5   4

3683. FIRMALINO, TITO C. Political activities of barrio citizens in Iloilo as they affect community development. Quezon City, Community Development Research Council, U.P. 1959. 266p. (Study series no. 4)
    Grossholtz: Survey data on political communication and local, provincial and national linkages.
                    V   3   6
    Polson: Useful survey data on political attitudes and activities.
                    V   5   6
    Sibley: V   3   6
    Villanueva: Very insightful.
                    V   5   6

3684. HART, DONN V. Barrio Caticugan: a Visayan Filipino community. Syracuse, 1954. 769p. Thesis (Doctor of Social Science) - Syracuse Univ.
    Hart: Based on 13 months research in South Negros (Siaton municipality).

Polson: Good data on barrio economic practices including a brief
local history.

E   5   7

E   5   6

Sibley: Very detailed on material culture, geography, etc.; less
good on social organization.

E   5   6

3685. _____. The Philippine plaza complex; a focal point in culture change. New
Haven, Yale Univ. Southeast Asia Studies, 1955. 57p. (Cultural report series no. 3)

Hart: Based on field research, available literature and inter-
viewing Filipinos in the United States.

E   4   7

Polson: The role of the Spanish plaza in Filipino town life. Comparisons with Mexico.

E   5   6

Sibley: E   5/4   6

3686. HUKE, ROBERT. Maloco: a representative Aklan barrio. PSR 4, nos. 2/3
(Apr./July 1956), 23-29.

Hart: Geographer with extensive field research experience in
Philippine Islands.   K   4   6

Polson: Statistics and observations on land use based on a brief
survey.

K   5   6

Sibley: K   3   6

3687. JOCANO, F. LANDA. Malitbog: a Philippine barrio in transition. Unpublished Community Development Research Council Monograph no. 39.
Cited by F. Landa Jocano in PSR 14, no. 4 (Oct. 1966), p.287.

Sibley: Jocano is a leading young Philippine anthropologist.

E   5   6

3688. PAL, AGATON P. Dumaguete City, Central Philippines. (In: Spoehr, Alexander,
ed., Pacific port towns and cities; a symposium. 10th Pacific Science Congress, Honolulu, 1961. Honolulu, Bishop Museum Press, 1963. p.13-16)

Hart: Somewhat superficial but best existing source.

Z   3   6

3689. _____. A Philippine barrio: a study of social organizations in relation
to planned cultural change. Ithaca, New York, 1956. 400p. Thesis (Ph.D.) -
Cornell Univ.
Part II (Chapters 4-11) published under the same title in JEAS 5, no. 4
(Oct. 1956), 333-486.

Coller: Careful and comprehensive field study of a village in
Southern Leyte. Economics and communications are partic-
ularly well-covered.

Z   5   6

McMillan: A careful analysis of rural social organization.

Z   4   6

Polson: The most comprehensive description of a Visayan barrio.

Z   5   6

3690. _____. The resources, levels of living, and aspirations of rural households in Negros Oriental. Quezon City, Community Development Research Council, U.P. 1963. 429p. (Study series,no. 15)

Hart: Based on extensive field research.
               Z   5   6

Polson: Excellent survey data (1958) on the economic and social status of rural households. Comments on relation of data to development programs.
               Z   5   6

Sibley: Pal is a reliable sociologist who has published widely on Philippine Islands social organization.
               Z   5   6

3691. _____. Rural sociology in the Philippines. Current Sociology 8, no. 1 (1959), 16-23.

Hart: Basic summary of research done since World War II.
               Z   4   7

Sibley: Z   4   6

3692. POLSON, ROBERT A. and AGATON P. PAL. The status of rural life in the Dumaguete City trade area, Philippines 1952. Ithaca, N. Y., Southeast Asia Program, Dept. of Far Eastern Studies, Cornell Univ., 1956. 108p. (Data paper no. 21)

Hart: Z&Z   5   6

Polson: Economic and social survey data on rural households. Includes information on acceptance of information.
               Z&Z   5   6

Sibley: Z&Z   5   6

3693. SIBLEY, WILLIS E. Field notes, especially from Manalad, Negros Occidental. Ms., 1955. Philippine Studies Program, Univ. of Chicago, Chicago. Cited in Univ. of Chicago. Philippine Studies Program. Selected bibliography of the Philippines. p.47.

Sibley: These are notes from 1954-55 village study in W. Negros.
               E   5   6

Warren: E   5   6

3694. _____. Manalad: the maintenance of unity and distinctiveness in a Philippine village. Chicago, 1958. 233p. Thesis (Ph.D.) - Univ. of Chicago.

Polson: A good study based on kinship analysis.
               E   5   6

3695. _____. Social structures and planned change: a case study from the Philippines. HO 19, no. 4 (Winter 1960/1961), 209-211.

3696. SILLIMAN UNIVERSITY, DUMAGUETE. COMMUNITY DEVELOPMENT PROGRAM. Community development program, account of the planning, implementation, and training of workers of a community development program: the people's responses, perceptions of the roles of workers and the experiences of each worker [by] Agaton P. Pal and co-workers. Dumaguete City, 1959. 142p. (Its 1st report)

Hart: Z   4   6

Polson: A candid report of success and failure in an experimental community development program.
               Z   5   6

Sibley: Discussion of Silliman University Development Program.
               Z   5   6

3697. SMYTHE, LEWIS S. C. Community development at Silliman University. Philippine Christian Advance 11, no. 11 (Nov. 1959), 41-43.
   Hart: Z   4   6

3698. _____ and AGATON P. PAL. Community development program. SJ 4, no. 3 (July/Sept. 1957), 161-175.
   Hart: Z   4   6

3699. _____. Experimental design in the Silliman University Community Development Program. Dumaguete City, Silliman Univ., 1958. 92p.
   Hart: Z   4   6
   Polson: Exposition of selected aspects of the design of an experimental action-research community development program.
                      Z   5   6

3700. WELLS, STEPHEN and A. PAUL HARE, eds. Studies in regional development. Bicol Development Planning Board. 1968. 111p.

DRINK, DRUGS AND INDULGENCE

3701. HART, DONN V. "Tambal para sa uhaw"; the ethnography of the buri palm in barrio Caticugan Negros, Philippines. PJS 94, no. 3 (Sept. 1965), 339-370. 2 plates.

ECONOMICS

3702. MCINTYRE, MICHAEL P. Leyte and Samar: a geographical analysis of the rural economics of the eastern Visayans. Columbus, 1951. 426p. Thesis (Ph.D.) - Ohio State Univ.

3703. NURGE, ETHEL. Land ownership, occupation, and income in a Leyte barrio. PSR 4, nos. 2/3 (Apr./July 1956), 15-22.
   Hart: Based on field work done in a village in East Leyte.
                      E   5   6
   Sibley: E   5   6

3704. SIBLEY, WILLIS E. Work partner choice in a Philippine village. SJ 4, no. 3 (July/Sept. 1957), 196-206.
   Hart: Based on research in Southern Negros Occidental.
                      E   5   6
   Sibley: Study of criteria used in forming working parties in rural settlements.
                      E   5   6

EDUCATION

3705. CASTRO, TOMAS DE. The community schools of Negros Oriental - their influence on barrio and rural life. PJE 32, (1954), 432-434, 486.
Cited in Bibliography of Asian Studies. 1954, p.700.
Hart: Y   3   5

3706. FISHER, J. ELLIOTT. Patterns of interaction between religious and educational institutions. SJ 2, no. 4 (Oct. 1955), 312-325.
Hart: Taught many years at Silliman University.
Z   3   6

3707. ORATA, PEDRO T. Unesco associated projects - II. The Iloilo community school experiment: the vernacular as medium of instruction. Fundamental and Adult Education 8, no. 3 (1956), 173-178.

3708. TUMBAGAHAN, TIBURCIO J. The first forty years: a history of Silliman University, 1901-1941. 1948? 107p. Thesis (Ph.D.) - Stanford Univ. [Washington, Library of Congress Photoduplication Service] 1948.

ETHNIC INFLUENCES

3709. KUIZON, JOSE G. The Sanskrit loan-words in the Cebuano-Bisayan language and the Indian element in Cebuano-Bisayan culture. 1962. 144p. Thesis (M.A.) - Univ. of San Carlos.
Hart: B   3   7
Ward: Culture history as reflected in languages.
L   3   1

3710. LEAR, ELMER N. Collaboration, resistance, and liberation: a study of society and education in Leyte, The Philippines, under Japanese occupation. New York. 1951. 720p. Thesis (Ph.D.) - Columbia Univ.
Goodman: An early example of an attempt to analyze the wartime Philippine scene.
H   3   5

3711. _____. The Japanese occupation of the Philippines, Leyte, 1941-1945. Ithaca, N.Y., Southeast Asia Program, Dept. of Far Eastern Studies, Cornell Univ., 1961. 246p. (Data paper no. 42)
Goodman: Revised Ph.D. thesis but lacking in Japanese sources.
H   3   5
Wickberg: H   3   5

FAMILY AND KINSHIP

3712. GONZALEZ, MARY A. The Ilongo kinship system and terminology. PSR 13, no. 1 (Jan. 1965), 23-31.

Hart: E   3   6

3713. QUIJANO, IGNACIO T. Cebuano-Visayan kinship terms. PM 34, no. 8 (Aug. 1937), 359-360.
Hart: -   4   7

FINE ARTS

3714. CRUZ, BEATO A. DE LA. The Hinal-o or Pestle dance. JEAS 4, no. 3 (July 1955), 441-442.
Trimillos: Dance from Aklan, Capiz.
J   5   4

3715. FAJARDO, LIBERTAD V. Visayan folk dances. With foreword by Serafin Aquino. Manila, 1961. 1v.
Trimillos: Music, illustrations.
Y   5   6

3716. FRANCISCO, JUAN R. A note on the Pa'gang: a Tagbanuwa bamboo musical instrument. AS 5, no. 1 (Apr. 1967), 33-41. 3 plates.

3717. HEINE-GELDERN, ROBERT. Trommelsprachen ohne Trommeln. Anthropos 28, nos. 3/4 (May/Aug. 1933), 485-487.

GEOGRAPHY AND DEMOGRAPHY

3718. BARRERA, ALFREDO. Ursula Island. PGJ 3, no. 3 (July/Sept. 1955), 143-147.
Spencer: 'Notes on' an uninhabited island off Palawan.
C   4/5   6

3719. BLUMENTRITT, FERDINAND. Die Inseln Mindoro und Marinduque. Petermanns Geographische Mitteilungen 30, (1884), 89-92.
Spencer: Rather thin descriptive notes only and pretty out of date.
N   3   3

3720. CONCEPCION, MERCEDES B. Migration differentials in the Visayas, 1960. PSR 11, nos. 1/2 (Jan./Apr. 1963), 68-75.
Hart: Z   4   7
Sibley: One of leading Philippine Island demographers.
Z   5/4   6
Wernstedt: Z   4   6/7

3721. CREDO, FLAVIANO P. Emigration from the barrio of Malongcay, Zamboanguita, Negros Oriental since 1948: its causes and consequences. 1967. Thesis (M.A.) - Silliman Univ.

3722. MCINTYRE, MIKE. Geographic regionalism in Leyte. PGJ 3, no. 1 (Jan./Mar.

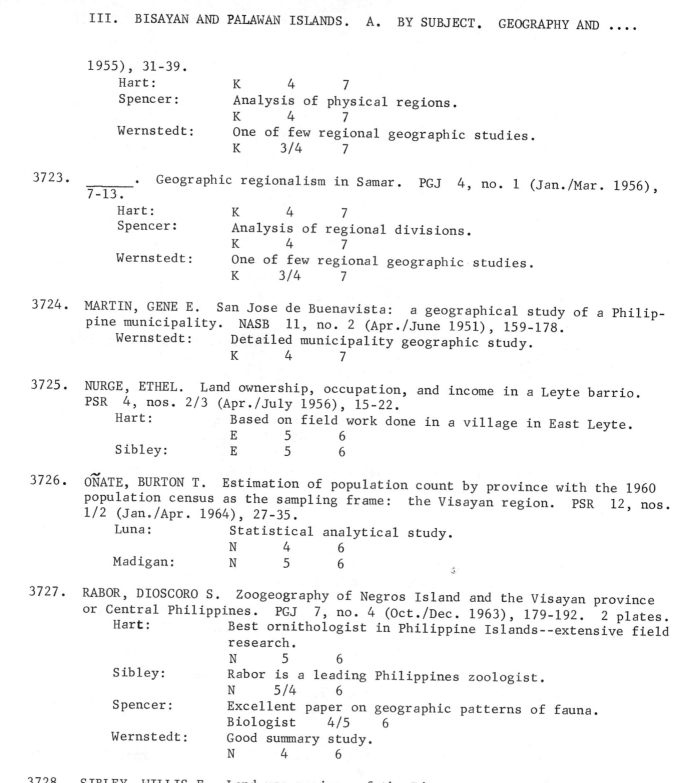

1955), 31-39.
    Hart: K   4   7
    Spencer: Analysis of physical regions.
                 K   4   7
    Wernstedt: One of few regional geographic studies.
                 K   3/4   7

3723. _____. Geographic regionalism in Samar. PGJ 4, no. 1 (Jan./Mar. 1956),
    7-13.
    Hart: K   4   7
    Spencer: Analysis of regional divisions.
                 K   4   7
    Wernstedt: One of few regional geographic studies.
                 K   3/4   7

3724. MARTIN, GENE E. San Jose de Buenavista: a geographical study of a Philip-
    pine municipality. NASB 11, no. 2 (Apr./June 1951), 159-178.
        Wernstedt: Detailed municipality geographic study.
                     K   4   7

3725. NURGE, ETHEL. Land ownership, occupation, and income in a Leyte barrio.
    PSR 4, nos. 2/3 (Apr./July 1956), 15-22.
        Hart: Based on field work done in a village in East Leyte.
                     E   5   6
        Sibley: E   5   6

3726. OÑATE, BURTON T. Estimation of population count by province with the 1960
    population census as the sampling frame: the Visayan region. PSR 12, nos.
    1/2 (Jan./Apr. 1964), 27-35.
        Luna: Statistical analytical study.
                     N   4   6
        Madigan: N   5   6

3727. RABOR, DIOSCORO S. Zoogeography of Negros Island and the Visayan province
    or Central Philippines. PGJ 7, no. 4 (Oct./Dec. 1963), 179-192. 2 plates.
        Hart: Best ornithologist in Philippine Islands--extensive field
                     research.
                     N   5   6
        Sibley: Rabor is a leading Philippines zoologist.
                     N   5/4   6
        Spencer: Excellent paper on geographic patterns of fauna.
                     Biologist   4/5   6
        Wernstedt: Good summary study.
                     N   4   6

3728. SIBLEY, WILLIS E. Land-use regions of the Bisayan areas. Chicago, Philip-
    pine Studies Program, Univ. of Chicago. 34p. Ms.
    Cited in Univ. of Chicago. Philippine Studies Program. Sixth Annual Report
    (1958/59).
        Sibley: Studies based mainly on 1950 P.I. census data.
                     E   4   6
        Warren: E   5   6

3729. VANDERMEER, CANUTE. Population patterns on the island of Cebu, the Philip-
    pines: 1500 to 1900. Association of American Geographers. Annals 57,

no. 2 (June 1967), 315-337.

3730. WERNSTEDT, FREDERICK L. Agricultural regionalism on Negros Island, Philippines. Los Angeles, 1953. 264p. Thesis (Ph.D.) - UCLA.
      Hart: Research done in 1950-51.
                   K   5   7
      Sibley: Excellent work of a leading student of Philippines geog-
                   raphy.
                   G   5/4   7
      Spencer: Comprehensive study of agriculture on Negros Island.
                   K   4/5   7

HEALTH AND SICKNESS

3731. APARECE, FRANCISCO T. The care of the sick and the burial of the dead in
the rural areas of Bohol and their educational implications. 1960. 196p.
Thesis (M.A.) - Univ. of San Carlos.
      Hart: Based, in large part, on interviews, mainly elementary
                   school teachers.
                   Z   4   6

3732. ARENS, RICHARD. The Tambalan and his medical practices in Leyte and Samar
Islands, Philippines. PJS 86, no. 1 (Mar. 1957), 121-130.
      Hart: M/E   4   6
      Sibley: M   5   6
      Tiglao: Excellent study of the practices of indigenous health
                   workers and why people patronize them.
                   M   5   6

3733. BAILEN, JEROME B. The Pala'wan Babaylan's views on disease-causation. U.P.
Anthropology Bulletin 3, no. 1 (First Semester 1967/1968), 6-9.

3734. COLLER, RICHARD W. Barrio Gacao; a study of village ecology and the schistosomiasis problem. Quezon City, Community Development Research Council,
U.P. 1960. 123p. (Study series no. 9)
      Coller: Basic survey of a total village - socio-economic aspects
                   plus health material.
                   Z   5   6
      Tiglao: Z   5   6
      Villanueva: Very insightful.
                   Z   5   6

3735. LIEBAN, RICHARD W. Cebuano sorcery; malign magic in the Philippines.
Berkeley Univ. of California Press, 1967. 163p.
      Sibley: Lieban has done extensive and excellent work on sorcery
                   and folk medical practice in Central Philippine Islands.
                   E   5   6

3736. _____. Fatalism and medicine in Cebuano areas of the Philippines. AQ 39,
no. 3 (July 1966), 171-179.
      Hart: E   5   6

Sibley: E   5   6

3737. _____. Qualification for folk medical practice in Sibulan, Negros Oriental, Philippines. PJS 91, no. 4 (Dec. 1962), 511-521.
    Hart: E   5   6
    Sibley: E   5   6
    Tiglao: A short but informative essay on cultural factors that
    validate an individual's qualifications as a healer of
    and conditions peoples' acceptance of modern medicine.
    E   5   6

3738. _____. Sorcery, illness, and social control in a Philippine municipality.
SWJA 16, no. 2 (Summer 1960), 127-143.
    Hart: E   5   6
    Nurge: E   5   6
    Sibley: E   5   6

3739. NURGE, ETHEL. Etiology of illness in Guinhangdan. AA 60, no. 6, pt. 1
(Dec. 1958), 1158-1172.
    Hart: Eastern Leyte.
    E   5   6
    Nurge: E   5   6
    Sibley: Part of a larger study of Guinhangdan, Leyte.
    E   5   6
    Tiglao: On theories of health and illness in a Philippine Commu-
    nity that will be useful for public health workers.
    E   5   6

3740. SILLIMAN UNIVERSITY. CULTURAL RESEARCH CENTER. Sorcery in a folk medicine
framework on Siquijor island: a preliminary report (abstract). PSR 16,
nos. 3/4 (July/Oct. 1968), 197-198.

HISTORY AND CULTURE CHANGE

3741. ALZINA, FRANCISCO INGANCIO. Historia de las islas e indios de las Bisayas,...
1668. Ms.
Cited in Frank Lynch, East Cultural Studies, March 1965 and John Phelan, The
Hispanization of the Philippines...p.179.
    Sibley: A major early work--not yet available in English.
    M   5   7
    "By far the most scholarly and detailed survey of Bisayan
    culture is the unpublished manuscript of Francisco Igna-
    cio Alcina (1610-74)....Alcina provided an account equally
    rich in ethnographic material...." John Phelan, The His-
    panization of the Philippines. 1959. p.179.

3742. ANGELES, FRANCISCO DELOR. Mindanao, the story of an island. Davao City,
San Pedro Press, 1964. 107p.

3743. CARLSON, ALVAR WARD. A geographical inquiry: sixteenth century Cebu city.
PGJ 12, nos. 3/4 (July/Dec. 1968), 38-47.

3744. HART, DONN V. Change in a Philippine village. Eastern World 10, no. 7
        (July 10, 1956), 14-15.

3745. _____. The Philippine plaza complex: a focal point in culture change.
        New Haven, Yale University, Southeast Asia Studies, 1955. 57p. (Cultural
        Report Series no. 3)
            Hart: Based on field research, available literature and inter-
                             viewing Filipinos in the United States.
                             E   4   7
            Polson: The role of the Spanish plaza in Filipino town life.
                             Comparisons with Mexico.
                             E   5   6
            Sibley: E   5/4   6

3746. HESTER, EVETT D. Notes on the texts of Bisayan accounts of early Bornean
        settlements in the Philippines. SMJ 7, no. 7 (June 1956), 23-24.
            Warren: C   5   7

3747. IGNACIO, REBECCA. An annotated translation of the Provedano manuscript
        (1578). 1951. Thesis (M.A.) - Far Eastern Univ.
        Reproduced by the Philippine Studies Program, Univ. of Chicago, Transcript
        No. 3.
        Cited in Compilation of graduate theses...p.286.
            Scott: "... appear to be deliberate fabrications with no historic
                             validity." Prehispanic source materials for the study of
                             Philippine history. 1968, p. 136.

3748. JOCANO, F. LANDA. Social structure and programs of directed change: a case
        study from Western Visayas. (In: Conference on the Relevance of the Social
        Sciences in Contemporary Asia. The Relevance of the social sciences in con-
        temporary Asia: university teachers in dialogue. Tokyo, 1968. p.157-166)
        Cited in Bibliography of Asian Studies, 1969, p.189.

3749. _____. Social structure and the program of directed change: a case study
        from Western Visayas, Philippines. SR 4, no. 11 (Nov. 1963), 8-13.
            Hart: Research done mainly in Central Panay.
                             E   5   6
            Sibley: E   5   6

3750. _____. The structure of social relations and its implication for social
        change: a conceptual analysis. PSR 11, nos. 3/4 (July/Oct. 1963), 206-215.
            Hart: E   5   6
            Sibley: E   4   6

3751. PAL, AGATON P. A Philippine barrio: a study of social organizations in re-
        lation to planned cultural change. Ithaca, New York, 1956. 400p. Thesis
        (Ph.D.) - Cornell Univ. Part II (Chapters 4-11) published under the same
        title in JEAS 5, no. 4 (Oct. 1956), 333-486.
            Coller: Careful and comprehensive field study of a village in
                             Southern Leyte. Economics and communications are partic-
                             ularly well-covered.
                             Z   5   6
            McMillan: A careful analysis of rural social organization.
                             Z   4   6
            Polson: The most comprehensive description of a Visayan barrio.
                             Z   5   6

3752. _____. A planned cultural change: improving chicken raising. SJ 4, no. 2 (Apr./June 1957), 81-89.
        Hart: Z   3   6
        Polson: Description of a strategy to promote adoption of new practices. Does not include measurement of results.
                      Z   3   6
        Sibley: Z   5/4   6

3753. POLSON, ROBERT A. and AGATON P. PAL. The influence of isolation on the acceptance of technological changes in the Dumaguete city trade area, Philippines. SJ 2, no. 2 (Apr. 1955), 149-159.
        Hart: Z&Z   4   6
        Polson: Data on relationship of geographic isolation to innovation adoption.
                      Z&Z   5   6
        Sibley: Z&Z   5   6

3754. _____. Social change in the Dumaguete trade area, Philippines, 1951-1958. Ithaca, N.Y., Dept. of Rural Sociology, New York State College of Agriculture at Cornell Univ. [1959?], 1964. 106p.
        Hart: Z&Z   5   6
        Polson: A comparison of 1952 and 1958 survey data on rural households.
                      Z&Z   5   6
        Sibley: Z&Z   5/4   6

3755. RIXHON, GERARD. Parte natural of Alzina's manuscript of 1668, a source of anthropological data. AS 6, no. 2 (Aug. 1968), 183-197.

3756. SANTAREN, TOMAS. Bisayan accounts of early Bornean settlements in the Philippines, recorded by Father Santaren [with an] introductory note [by] Fred Eggan; note on texts [by] E. D. Hester, translated by Mrs. Enriqueta Fox. SMJ 7, no. 7 (June 1956), 22-42.

3757. SIBLEY, WILLIS E. Persistence, variety and change in Visayan social organization: a brief research report. PSR 13, no. 3 (July 1965), 139-144.
        Hart: Based on research in Manalad--Negros Occidental.
                      E   5   6
        Polson: Description of the research plan and preliminary results of a comparative study on an upland and a lowland barrio.
                      E   3   6
        Sibley: Review of author's progress in 1964-65 fieldwork in Negros and Panay settlements.
                      E   5   6

3758. SZANTON, DAVID L. Estancia, Iloilo: town in transition. (In: Bello, Walden F., and Maria Clara Roldan, eds. Modernization: its impact in the Philippines. Quezon City, Institute of Philippine Culture, Ateneo de Manila Univ. Press, 1967. IPC Papers no. 4. p.64-86)

INDUSTRIES

3759. SOLHEIM, WILHELM G., II. Pottery manufacturing in the islands of Masbate and Batan, Philippines. JEAS 1, no. 3 (Apr. 1952), 49-53.

3760. _____ and TERRY SHULER. Further notes on Philippine pottery manufacture: Mountain Province and Panay. JEAS 8, nos. 1/2 (Jan./Apr. 1959), 1-10.

Hart:	A	5	7
Maher:	A	5	7
Sibley:	A	5	7

INFANCY AND CHILDHOOD

3761. NURGE, ETHEL. Infant feeding: the suckling and weaning. SJ 3, no. 2 (Apr./ June 1956), 127-138. Also published in Journal of Tropical Pediatrics, 3, no. 2 (Sept. 1957), 89-96, Infant feeding in the village of Guinhangdan, Leyte, Philippines.

INTERPERSONAL RELATIONS

3762. VEYRA, JAIME C. DE The Lagda. PSSHR 18, no. 3 (Sept. 1953), 287-326.

Hart:	Y	3	7

LABOR

3763. Philippines (Republic) Special Committee Appointed to Conduct a Survey of Employment Conditions of Workers in the Sugar Industry in Negros Occidental with Special Reference to Migrant Workers Commonly Known as "Sacadas". Report to the Honorable Secretary of Labor.... A survey by the Dept. Labor, Republic of the Philippines, conducted with the cooperation of the Labor Division, U.S. Operations Mission to the Philippines (ICA). Manila, 1956. 99p.

LANGUAGE AND LITERATURE

3764. ARANETA, FRANCISCO and MIGUEL A. BERNAD. "Bisayans" of Borneo and the "Tagalogs" and "Visayans" of the Philippines. SMJ 9, nos. 15/16 (July/Dec. 1960), 542-564.

Hart:	M&Q	3	7
Llamzon:	Popular, journalistic description of situation.		

<table>
<tr><td></td><td>M&Q</td><td>3</td><td>7</td></tr>
<tr><td>Ward:</td><td colspan="3">Comparative study with a fair amount of words presented.</td></tr>
<tr><td></td><td>M&Q</td><td>3</td><td>7</td></tr>
</table>

3765. CARROLL, JOHN. The word Bisaya in the Philippines and Borneo. SMJ 9, nos. 15/16 (July/Dec. 1960), 499-541.
      Hart: X   3   9

3766. KUIZON, JOSE G. The Sanskrit loan-words in the Cebuano-Bisayan language and the Indian element in Cebuano-Bisayan culture. 1962. 144p. Thesis (M.A.) - Univ. of San Carlos.
      Hart: B   3   7
      Ward: Culture history as reflected in languages.
                   L   3   7

3767. MEYER, ADOLF B. and A. SCHADENBERG. ... Die Mangianenschrift von Mindoro. Berlin, R. Friedlander & Sohn, 1895. 33p. 4 plates. (Abhandlungen und berichte des Koniglichen zoologischen und anthropologish-ethnographischen museums zu Dresden, 1894/1895, no. 15) 34p.
      Ward: An early attempt by European scholars to present data on the pre-Spanish writing system.
               A and E   3   1-3

3768. WOLFF, JOHN U. Cebuano Visayan syntax. New Haven, 1965. 269p. Thesis (Ph.D.) - Yale Univ.

3769. _____. History of the dialect of the Camotes Islands, Philippines, and the spread of Cebuano Bisayan. Oceanic Linguistics 6, no. 2 (Winter 1967), 63-79.

MARRIAGE

3770. NURGE, ETHEL. Factors operative in mate selection in a Philippine village. Eugenics Quarterly 5, (Sept. 1958), 162-168.

3771. QUISUMBING, LOURDES. Marriage customs in rural Cebu. Cebu City,Univ. of San Carlos, 1965. 77p. (San Carlos Publications, Series A: Humanities No. 3.) Manila: Catholic Trade School, 1965, 77p.
      Hart: E   4   6

3772. _____. A study of the marriage customs of the rural population of the Province of Cebu. Cebu, Philippines, 1956. 178p. Thesis (M.A.) - Univ. of San Carlos.
      Hart: E   4   6

POLITICAL ORGANIZATION AND BEHAVIOR

3773. AGPALO, REMIGIO E. Pandanggo-sa-Ilaw: the politics of Occidental Mindoro.
PJPA 8, no. 2 (Apr. 1964), 83-111.
Grossholtz: Useful but not well documented or explained.
V   3   6

3774. ARENS, RICHARD. The early Pulahan movement in Samar and Leyte. JH 7, no.
4 (Dec. 1959), 303-371.
Hart: Author resided in Leyte-Samar in 1950's.
M/E   3   3/4

3775. CAOILI, MANUEL A. Real property tax administration in the province of
Leyte. PJPA 12, no. 3 (July 1968), 316-326.

3776. FIRMALINO, TITO C. Political activities of barrio citizens in Iloilo as
they affect community development; ... Quezon City, Community Development
Research Council, U.P., 1959. 266p. (Study series, no. 4)
Grossholtz: Survey data on political communication and local, provin-
cial and national linkages.
V   3   6
Polson: Useful survey data on political attitudes and activities.
V   5   6
Sibley: V   3   6
Villanueva: Very insightful.
V   5   6

3777. GOWING, PETER G. Muslim-American relations in the Philippines, 1899-1920.
AS 6, no. 3 (Dec. 1968), 372-382.

3778. HUNT, CHESTER L. Iwahig penal colony: freedom as a social therapy. PSR
9, nos. 1/2 (Jan./Apr. 1961), 35-41.
Hart: Sociologist with extensive field experience in Philippine
Islands.
Z   4   6

3779. PAL, AGATON P. Leadership in a rural community. SJ 3, no. 3 (July/Sept.
1956), 185-206.
Hart: Z   4   6
Sibley: Z   5   6

3780. SIBLEY, WILLIS E. Filipino culture and Filipino politics - a preliminary
anthropological review. Southeast Asia Quarterly (Central Philippines Univ.)
1, no. 3 (Jan. 1967), 1-11.

3781. _____. Leadership in a Philippine barrio. PJPA 1, (1957), 154-159.

3782. TAN, SAMUEL K. Sulu under American military rule, 1899-1913. PSSHR 32,
no. 1 (Mar. 1967), 1-187.

PROPERTY AND EXCHANGE

3783. WERNSTEDT, FREDERICK L. Cebu: focus of Philippine interisland trade. Economic Geography 32, no. 4 (Oct. 1956), 336-346.
      Hart: K   5   6
      Sibley: K   4   6

RELIGIOUS BELIEFS AND PRACTICES

3784. APARECE, FRANCISCO T. The care of the sick and the burial of the dead in the rural areas of Bohol and their educational implications. 1960. 196p. Thesis (M.A.) - Univ. of San Carlos.
      Hart: Based, in large part, on interviews, mainly elementary school teachers.
                     Z   4   6

3785. ARENS, RICHARD. Animism in the rice ritual of Leyte and Samar. PSR 4, no. 1 (Jan. 1956), 2-6.
      Hart: The nine articles by Arens are based on interviewing informants and extensive travel in Leyte and Samar when the author was associated with St. Paul College in Tacloban.
                     M/E   5   6
      Sibley: M   5   6

3786. _____. Animistic fishing ritual in Leyte and Samar. PSR 4, no. 4 (Oct. 1956), 24-28.
      Hart: M/E   5   6
      Sibley: M   5   6

3787. _____. Camote ritual in Leyte and Samar. East and West (Istituto Italiano Per IL medio Ed Estremo Oriente) 7 (July 1956), 173-176.
      Hart: M/E   5   6
      Nurge: M   5   6
      Sibley: M   5   6

3788. _____. The corn ritual in Leyte and Samar. PSR 4, nos. 2/3 (Apr./July 1956), 29-31.
      Hart: M/E   5   6
      Nurge: M   5   6
      Sibley: M   5   6

3789. _____. The Lo-on or fumigation ceremony in Leyte and Samar. PSR 5, nos. 3/4 (July/Oct. 1957), 69-72.
      Hart: M/E   5   6
      Sibley: M   5   6

3790. _____. Notes on camote rituals in Leyte and Samar Islands. PJS 85, no. 3 (Sept. 1956), 343-347. 2 plates.
      Hart: M/E   5   6
      Nurge: M   5   6
      Sibley: M   5   6

3791. _____. The rice ritual in the East Visayan Islands, Philippines. Folklore Studies (Society of the Divine World. Tokyo) 16 (1957), 268-290.
12 photos.
    Hart: M/E   5   6
    Sibley: M   5   6

3792. _____. The use of amulets and talismans in Leyte and Samar. JEAS 6, no.
2 (Apr. 1957), 115-126.
    Hart: M/E   5   6
    Sibley: M   5   6
    Warren: M   5   6

3793. _____. Witches and witchcraft in Leyte and Samar Islands, Philippines.
PJS 85, no. 4 (Dec. 1956), 451-465.
    Hart: M/E   5   6
    Sibley: M   5   6

3794. DEMETRIO, FRANCISCO. Towards a classification of Bisayan folk beliefs and
customs. PS 16, no. 4 (Oct. 1968), 663-689.

3795. FISHER, J. ELLIOTT. Patterns of interaction between religious and educational institutions. SJ 2, no. 4 (Oct. 1955), 312-325.
    Hart: Taught many years at Silliman University.
              Z   3   6

3796. HARRISSON, TOM. "Bisaya": Borneo - Philippine impacts of Islam. SMJ 7,
no. 7 (June 1956), 43-47.
    Hart: E   3   7

3797. HART, DONN V. Buhawi of the Bisayas: the revitalization process and legend-
making in the Philippines. (In: Zamora, Mario D., ed. Studies in Philippine anthropology (In honor of H. Otley Beyer). Quezon City, Alemar-Phoenix,
1967. p.366-396)

3798. _____. The Filipino villager and his spirits. Solidarity 1, no. 4 (Oct./
Dec. 1966), 65-71.

3799. _____. Riddles in Filipino folklore; an anthropological analysis. Syracuse, New York, Syracuse Univ. Press, 1964. 318p.
    Hart: Based on field research and study of Philippine Island
              sources, printed and manuscripts.
              E   5   7
    Pfeiffer: E   5   7
    Polson: An extensive collection with a suggestive introduction.
              E   5   7
    Sibley: One of most complete studies of Philippine Island rid-
              dles.
              E   5/4   7

3800. _____ and HARRIET C. HART. Cinderella in the Eastern Bisayas. With a summary of the Philippine folktale. Journal of American Folklore 79, no. 312
(Apr./June 1966), 307-337.

3801. _____. Collecting folktales in Eastern Samar, Philippines. Appendix A.
An annotated bibliography of published and manuscript materials primarily

on Bisayan folktales,riddles and proverbs. SJ 3, no. 3 (Third Quarter 1956), 207-236.

3802. _____. "Maka-andog"; a reconstructed myth from eastern Samar, Philippines. Journal of American Folklore 79, no. 311 (Jan./Mar. 1966), 84-108.

3803. _____. A Philippine version of "The Two Brothers and the Dragon Slayer's Tale ".Western Folklore 19, (Oct. 1960), 263-275.

3804. JOCANO, F. LANDA. Agricultural rituals in a Philippine barrio. PSR 15, nos. 1/2 (Jan./Apr. 1967), 48-56.

3805. _____. Conversion and the patterning of Christian experience in Malitbog, Central Panay, Philippines. PSR 13, no. 2 (Apr. 1965), 96-119.
    Hart: E   5   6
    Gowing: Certainly will be regarded as a pioneering and classical treatment of the "religious acculturation" in the Philippines.
                   E   5   6
    Sibley: E   5   6

3806. _____. The epic of Labaw Donggon. PSSHR 29, no. 1 (Mar. 1964), 1-103.

3807. _____. Twenty-three place-name legends from Antique province, Philippines. AS 3, no. 1 (Apr. 1965), 16-40.
    Hart: E   5   7
    Sibley: E   4   7

3808. LIEBAN, RICHARD W. Cebuano sorcery; malign magic in the Philippines. Berkeley, Univ. of California Press, 1967. 163p.
    Sibley: Lieban has done extensive and excellent work on sorcery and folk medical practice in Central Philippine Islands.
                   E   5   7

3809. _____. Shamanism and social control in a Philippine city. Indiana Univ. Folklore Institute. Journal 2, no. 1 (June 1965), 43-54.
    Hart: E   5   7
    Sibley: E   5   6

3810. _____. Sorcery, illness, and social control in a Philippine municipality. SWJA 16, no. 2 (Summer 1960), 127-143.
    Hart: E   5   6
    Nurge: E   5   6
    Sibley: E   5   6

3811. NURGE, ETHEL D. A myth from Guinhangdan. SJ 5, no. 3 (July/Sept. 1958), 252-271.
    Hart: These excellent articles are based on extensive field research done in eastern Leyte in 1955-56.
                   E   5   6

3812. _____. A second myth from Guinhangdan. SJ 6, no. 3 (July/Sept. 1959), 217-238.
    Hart: E   5   6

3813. _____. The third myth from Guinhangdan. SJ 7, no. 3 (July/Sept. 1960),

219-235.
        Hart: E   5   6

3814. _____. The nature of the supernatural in four myths from Guinhangdan,
       Leyte, Philippines. SJ 8, no. 2 (Apr./June 1961), 78-97.
            Gowing: The last in a series of SJ articles on the subject.
                           E   4   6
            Hart: E   5   6
            Nurge: E   5   6
            Sibley: E   5/4   6
            Warren: E   5   6

3815. SILLIMAN UNIVERSITY. CULTURAL RESEARCH CENTER. Sorcery in a folk medicine
       framework on Siquijor island: a preliminary report (abstract). PSR 16,
       nos. 3/4 (July/Oct. 1968), 197-198.

3816. TAN, CRISPINA A. A study of popular beliefs and practices on death and bur-
       ial in rural Cebu. Cebu City, 1962. 202p. Thesis (M.A.) - Univ. of San
       Carlos.
            Hart: Z   4   6

3817. VENCER, CIRILO A., JR. The Belasyon: a post-burial rite among the people
       of Batad. U.P. Anthropology Bulletin 3, no. 1 (First Semester 1967/1968),
       10-11.

3818. VILLEGAS, MARIA G. Superstitious beliefs and practices in the coastal towns
       of eastern Leyte. Leyte-Samar Studies 2, no. 2 (1968), 221-233.

SEX AND REPRODUCTION

3819. HART, DONN V. From pregnancy through birth in a Bisayan Filipino village.
       (In: Hart, Donn V., Phya Anuman Rajadhon, and Richard J. Coughlin. South-
       east Asian birth customs: three studies in human reproduction. New Haven,
       Human Relations Area Files, 1965. p.1-113)
            Hart: Includes extensive data for other Christian Filipino
                           groups.
                           E   5   7
            Nurge: E   5   7
            Sibley: E   5/4   7

3820. _____. Homosexuality and transvestism in the Philippines: the Cebuan Fili-
       pino bayot and lakin-on. Behavior Science Notes 3, no. 4 (1968), 211-248.

3821. LAING, JOHN E. The Silliman University action-research family-planning proj-
       ect. (Abstract) SLQ 5, nos. 1/2 (Mar./June 1967), 192-194.

3822. PAL, AGATON P. Family planning project at Silliman University: experiences
       and insights. SJ 15, no. 3 (Third Quarter 1968), 371-384.

3823. RODIL-MARTIRES, CONCEPCION. Attitudes and opinions towards family planning.
       EQ 14, no. 4 (Apr. 1967), 65-69.

STANDARD OF LIVING AND RECREATION

3824. BALANE, JUAN I. The fiestas of the coastal towns of Southern Bohol: an evaluation of their socio-educational significance---1954. 156p. Thesis (M.A.) - Univ. of San Carlos.
    Hart: Z   4   7

3825. CESAR, LORENZO GA. A socio-educational study of the town fiestas of Tacloban City and neighboring towns (Palo, Tanauan, Tolosa, Dagamit, Pastrana, Alangalang, and Jaro). 1953. 175p. Thesis (M.A.) - Univ. of San Carlos. Cited in Compilation of graduate theses ... p.107.
    Hart: Z   4   7

3826. HART, DONN V. Preliminary notes on the rural Philippine fiesta complex (Negros Oriental province). SJ 1, no. 2 (Apr. 1954), 25-40.
    Hart: Southern Negros Oriental is locale.
                     E   5   7
    Sibley: E   5/4   7

3827. _____. Riddles in Filipino folklore; an anthropological analysis. Syracuse, New York, Syracuse Univ. Press, 1964. 318p.
    Hart: Based on field research and study of Philippine Island sources, printed and manuscripts.
                     E   5   7
    Pfeiffer: E   5   7
    Polson: An extensive collection with a suggestive introduction.
                     E   5   7
    Sibley: One of most complete studies of Philippine Island riddles.
                     E   5/4   7

3828. PAL, AGATON P. The resources, levels of living, and aspirations of rural households in Negros Oriental. Quezon City, Community Development Research Council, U.P., 1963. 429p. (Study series, no. 15)

TOTAL CULTURE

3829. GUTIERREZ, MARIA C. The Cebuano balitao and how it mirrors Visayan culture and folklore. 1955. 152p. Thesis (M.A.) - Univ. of San Carlos. Cited in Compilation of graduate theses ... p.262.
    Hart: B   4   6

3830. JOCANO, F. LANDA. Social structure and programs of directed change: a case study from Western Visayas. (In: Conference on the Relevance of the Social Sciences in Contemporary Asia. The relevance of the social sciences in contemporary Asia: university teachers in dialogue. Tokyo, 1968. p.157-166) Cited in Bibliography of Asian Studies, 1969. p.189.

3831. SIBLEY, WILLIS E. The maintenance of unity and distinctiveness by a Philippine peasant village. (In: Men and cultures. Selected papers of the Fifth International Congress of Anthropological and Ethnological Sciences, Philadelphia, 1956. Philadelphia, 1960. p.506-512)

B.   BY CULTURAL-LINGUISTIC GROUP

AKLAN

3832. TUASON, ROMEO R. Kinship terms among the Aklanon. PM 34, no. 12 (Dec. 1937), 552, 571.

BATAK - GENERAL

3833. MILLER, EDWARD Y. The Bataks of Palawan. (In: Scheerer, Otto. The Naba-loi dialect. Manila, Bureau of Public Printing, 1905. p.179-189. Philippine Islands. Ethnological Survey. Publications. vol. II, Parts II and III)
       Warren: G   3   4

3834. MORALES, EUGENIO and MANUEL HUGO VENTURELLO. Additional information on the Batak people. (In: Miller, E. Y.: The Bataks of Palawan. p.185-189) Philippine Islands. Ethnological Survey Publications. v.2, parts 2 and 3. 1905.
       Warren: G   3   4

3835. SAMSON, JOSE A. The Bataks of Sumurod and Kalakuasan. Unitas 40, no. 1 (Mar. 1967), 194-206.
       Tweddell: Somewhat thin but useful sketch of Bataks of Palawan.
                       P   5   6

3836. The vanishing islanders: Tagbanua and the Batacs. This Week, Sunday Supplement of the Manila Chronicle. (Dec. 19, 1954), 8-14.
       Suggested by Tweddell.
       Tweddell: Superficial but perceptive report on current situation from a lowland newspaperman's viewpoint.
                       Q   3   6

3837. VENTURELLO, MANUEL H. The "Batacs" of the island of Palawan, Philippine Islands. Translated from the Spanish by Mrs. E. Y. Miller. International Archives of Ethnography 18, (1908), 137-144.
       Warren: G   3   4

3838. WARREN, CHARLES P. The Batak of Palawan: a culture in transition. Philippine Studies Program, Dept. of Anthropology, Univ. of Chicago. 1964. 130p. Multilithed. (Research series, no. 3)
       Warren: E   5   4

3839. _____. Division of labor by sex among the Batak of Palawan. Chicago, Philippine Studies Program, Dept. of Anthropology, Univ. of Chicago, 1957. 53p. Unpublished typescript manuscript.
       Cited in Charles Warren, Negrito groups in the Philippines: preliminary bibliography. Chicago, Philippine Studies Program, Univ. of Chicago, 1959.
       Warren: E   5   6

3840. _____. Field-Notes on the Batak of Palawan. Chicago, Philippine Studies

Program, Dept.of Anthropology, Univ. of Chicago, 1956. 97p. Unpublished
manuscript.
Cited in Univ. of Chicago. Philippine Studies Program. Selected bibliography of the Philippines. p.48.
    Warren: E   5   6

3841.   _____. Marriage and associated customs among the Batak of Palawan (Philippines). 15p. Proceedings of the Eighth Pacific Science Congress. Quezon
City, Philippines. 1953.
Cited in Charles P. Warren, Negrito groups in the Philippines: preliminary
bibliography. Chicago, Philippine Studies Program, Univ. of Chicago, 1959.
    Warren: E   5   6

BATAK - LANGUAGE AND LITERATURE

3842. MOREY, VIRGINIA. Some particles and pronouns in Batak. PJS 90, no. 2
(June 1961), 263-270.
Suggested by Warren.
    Tweddell: Brief and competent phonemic statement of Batak.
                   L   4   6
    Warren: L   5   6

3843. RODDA, ROSEMARY. Phonemes of Batak. PJS 90, no. 2 (June 1961), 259-262.
Suggested by Warren.
    Tweddell: Competent outline of Batak particles and pronouns.
                   L   4   6
    Warren: L   5   6

3844. WARREN, CHARLES P. A vocabulary of the Batak of Palawan. Chicago, Philippine Studies Program, Dept. of Anthropology, Univ. of Chicago, 1959. 48p.
(Transcript no. 7)
    Warren: E   5   6

BUHID

3845. CONKLIN, HAROLD C. Buhíd pottery. JEAS 3, no. 1 (Oct. 1953), 1-12.
    Tweddell: Meticulous description of pottery-making techniques with
                   excellent drawings.
                   E   5   6

3846. GAWRYLETZ, NICK and IVY. Background history of O.M.F. work, Oriental Mindoro, Philippines. Private printing. Overseas Missionary Fellowship, Bong-
abon, Mindoro, 1968.
Suggested by Tweddell.
    Tweddell: Firsthand ethnographic, general, and missionary informa-
                   tion. Brief. Location map.
                   M   3   6

BUKIDNON

3847. ORACION, TIMOTEO S. Kaingin agriculture among the Bukidnons of southeastern
Negros, Philippines. Journal of Tropical Geography 17, (1963), 213-224.
    Spencer: First hand field study.
                E   5   6

3848. _____. A preliminary report on some culture aspects of the Bukidnons on
Southeastern Negros Island, Philippines. Unitas 40, no. 1 (Mar. 1967),
156-181.

3849. _____. The Southeastern Negros Bukidnon territory and people. PGJ 8,
nos. 1/2 (Jan./June 1964), 12-20.
    Spencer: Regional summary on tribal peoples.
                E   4   6

3850. TIEMPO, EDILBERTO K. The Bukidnons of Negros Oriental. PM 33, no. 4 (Apr.
1936), 187, 194, 196, 198.

CEBUANO

3851. HART, DONN V. Halfway to uncertainty: a short autobiography of a Cebuano
Filipino. JEAS 5, no. 3 (July 1956), 255-277.
    Sibley: One of few autobiographical documents from Central Phil-
                    ippines area.
                E   5   6

3852. LIU, WILLIAM T. and SIOK-HUE YU. The lower class Cebuano family: a preliminary profile analysis. PSR 16, nos. 3/4 (July/Oct. 1968), 114-123.

3853. QUISUMBING, LOURDES R. Characteristic features of Cebuano family life
amidst a changing society. PSR 11, nos. 1/2 (Jan./Apr. 1963), 135-141.

3854. _____. Child-rearing practices in the Cebuano extended family. PSR 12,
nos. 1/2 (Jan./Apr. 1964), 109-114.

3855. _____. Interlocking relationships in a Cebuano mountain sitio and their
implication for child-rearing. PSR 13, no. 4 (Oct. 1965), 281-284.

CUYONON

3856. LACKOWSKI, PETER. Verb inflection in Cuyonon. Oceanic Linguistics 7, no.
2 (Winter 1968), 92-103.
Suggested by Tweddell.
    Tweddell: Competent but brief sketch of phonology and verb system.
                L   4   6

3857. TWEDDELL, COLIN E. Proposal for Cuyonon orthography. Distributed by Division Supt., Division of Public Schools, Palawan, 1963. **Mimeo**graphed. Suggested by Tweddell.
  Tweddell: Scientific phonemic and orthographic statement designed
               for teacher information and classroom use.
               L   4   6

3858. VRIES, VIRGINIA DE and G. RICHARD ROE. Semivowels in the Cuyono alphabet. PJS **95, no.** 2 (June 1966), 267-274.
  Suggested by Tweddell.
  Tweddell: Competent analytic presentation of place and function of
               o/w and i/y in Cuyonon orthography.
               M and L   4   6

HANUNÓO - GENERAL

3859. CONKLIN, HAROLD C. Preliminary report on field work on the islands of Mindoro and Palawan, Philippines. AA 51, no. 2 (Apr./June 1949), 268-273.
  Hart: L   5   6
  Sibley: E   5   6
  Tweddell: First generally reliable report of identity and distri-
               bution of Mangyan tribes; subject to later correction.
               E   3   6
  Ward: Cultural linguistic groups are identified and located.
               E   3   6

3860. DICHOSO, FERMIN. Some notes on Hanunóo-Mangyan culture (abstract). PSR 16, nos. 3/4 (July/Oct. 1968), 193-195.

HANUNÓO - AGRICULTURE AND FOOD

3861. CONKLIN, HAROLD C. The cultural significance of land resources among the Hanunóo. Philadelphia Anthropological Society. Bulletin 13, no. 2 (1960), 38-42.
  Tweddell: Perceptive firsthand comments on unique system of 'real
               estate' ownership: of plant/tree stems, not of land or
               fruitage.
               E   5   6

3862. _____. Hanunóo agriculture: a report on an integral system of shifting cultivation in the Philippines. AA 60, no. 5 (Oct. 1958), 968-969.
  Tweddell: E   4   6

3863. _____. Hanunóo agriculture in the Philippines; a report on an integral system of shifting cultivation in the Philippines. Rome, Food and Agriculture Organization of the United Nations. 1957. 209p. (FAO series on shifting cultivation, no. 2)

Polson: Excellent study of the least resource damaging form of shifting agriculture.

                  E   5   6

Tweddell: Foundation study of Hanunóo swidden agriculture, meticulous illustrations with bibliography.

                  E   5   6

3864.   _____. The relation of Hanunóo culture to the plant world. 1954. 471p. Thesis (Ph.D.) - Yale Univ.

Tweddell: Cross-disciplinary analysis of ecological, botanical, cultural, and linguistic factors.

                  E   4   6

3865.   _____. Shifting cultivation and succession to grassland climax. Pacific Science Congress. 9th, Bangkok, 1957. Proceedings. Bangkok, 1959. 7:60-62.

3866.   _____. The study of shifting cultivation. Current Anthropology 2, no. 1 (Feb. 1961), 27-61.

Tweddell: An analytic model, an exhaustive topical outline, and a 1200 item bibliography.

                  E   4   6

HANUNÓO - BEHAVIOR PROCESS AND PERSONALITY

3867.   CONKLIN, HAROLD C. Hanunóo color categories. SWJA 11, no. 4 (Winter 1955), 339-344.

Tweddell: A basic analysis of field study in color categories.

                  E   4   6

HANUNÓO - DRINK, DRUGS AND INDULGENCE

3868.   CONKLIN, HAROLD C. Betel chewing among the Hanunóo. Diliman, Quezon City, Published by the National Research Council of the Philippines, U.P., 1958. 41p.

HANUNÓO - FAMILY AND KINSHIP

3869.   CONKLIN, HAROLD C. Ethnogenealogical method. (In: Goodenough, Ward H., ed. Explorations in cultural anthropology; essays in honor of George Peter Murdock. New York, McGraw-Hill Book Co., 1964. p.25-55)

Tweddell: Detailed theoretical analysis of Hanunóo kinship as example of ethnogenealogical research.

                  E   4   6

HANUNÓO - HISTORY AND CULTURE CHANGE

3870. PAZ, EMETERIO DE LA. A survey of the Hanunóo Mangyan culture and barriers to change. Unitas 41, no. 1 (Mar. 1968), 3-63. 27 photos.

HANUNÓO - INFANCY AND CHILDHOOD

3871. CONKLIN, HAROLD C. Maling, Hanunóo girl from the Philippines. (In: Casagrande, Joseph B., ed. In the company of man. New York, Harper, 1960. p.101-125)
    Tweddell: Good example of participant observer role in a dibble-stick society.
                 E   5   6

HANUNÓO - LANGUAGE AND LITERATURE

3872. CONKLIN, HAROLD C. Bamboo literacy on Mindoro. Pacific Discovery 2, no. 4 (July/Aug. 1949), 4-11.
    Pfeiffer: E   5   6
    Tweddell: Excellent, illustrated, ethnographic description centuring on their use of ancient Indic script.
                 E   5   6
    Ward: Details of use and retention of the pre-Spanish syllable script.
                 E   5   6

3873. _____. Hanunóo-English vocabulary. Berkeley, Univ. of California Press, 1953. 290p. (Publications in Linguistics. v.9)
    Tweddell: Basic Hanunóo dictionary; ethnographic introduction, bibliography.
                 E   5   6

3874. _____. Linguistic play in its cultural context. Language 35, no. 4 (Oct./Dec. 1959), 631-636.
    Tweddell: Perceptive and meticulous example of methodology in correlating diverse cultural phenomena. A striking and pertinent addition to descriptions of secondarily developed argots from standard speech.
                 E   4   6

3875. GARDNER, FLETCHER. Three contemporary incised bamboo manuscripts from Hampangan Mangyan, Mindoro, P.I. American Oriental Society. Journal. 59, (1939), 496-502.
    Tweddell: Early collection and analysis and identification of Hanunoo Indic script.
                 G   4   4

3876. POSTMA, ANTON. The <u>ambahan</u> of the Hanunóo-Mangyans of Southern Mindoro. Anthropos 60, fas. 1/6 (1965), 359-368.
      Tweddell: Competent description of features and usages of Hanunoo ambahan poetry.
                    -     5   6

IRAYA

3877. The Irayas, Ygorrotes, and Manobos of the Philippines. Journal of Anthropology 1, no. 3 (Jan. 1871), 296-307.

3878. MACEDA, MARCELINO N. A brief report on some Mangyans in northern Oriental Mindoro. Unitas 40, no. 1 (Mar. 1967), 102-155.
      Tweddell: General ethnographic survey of Iraya and Alangan of Northern Mindoro. Information is from reliable informants.
                    E   5   6

3879. TWEDDELL, COLIN E. The Iraya (Mangyan) language of Mindoro, Philippines phonology and morphology. Seattle, Washington, 1958. 171p. Thesis (Ph.D.) - Univ. of Washington.
      Tweddell: One of few modern analyses of Philippine languages.
                    E   4   6

MAGAHAT (NEGROS)

3880. ORACION, TIMOTEO S. Ceremonial customs and beliefs connected with Magahat kaingin agriculture. SJ 2, no. 3 (July 1955), 222-236.

3881. _____. Economic and social organization of the Magahats. PSSHR 19, (Mar. 1954), 77-86.

3882. _____. An introduction to the culture of the Magahats of the upper Tayabanan river valley, Tolong, Negros, Philippines. Chicago, 1952. 171p. Thesis (M.A.) - Univ. of Chicago.

3883. _____. An introduction to the culture of the Magahats of the upper Tayabanan river valley, Tolong, Negros Oriental, Philippines. SJ 1, no. 2 (Apr. 1954), 1-17. 6 plates.

3884. _____. Magahat: shelter, clothing and implements. SJ 5, no. 3 (July/Sept. 1958), 273-285.

3885. _____. Magahat food quest. SJ 3, no. 2 (Apr./June 1956), 110-126.

3886. _____. Magahat marriage practices. PSR 12, nos. 1/2 (Jan./Apr. 1964), 101-109.

3887. _____. Magahat pregnancy and births practices. PSR 13, no. 4 (Oct. 1965), 268-274.

MANGYAN - GENERAL

3888. BEAN, R. B. Filipino ears: IV. Ilongot and Mangyan. PJS 8D, no. 5 (Oct. 1913), 357-368. 20 plates.
    Tweddell: Anatomical and philosophic discussion of ear types; illustrated.
                    -      4   6

3889. BLUMENTRITT, FERDINAND. Die Mangianenschrift von Mindoro. Globus 69, no. 11 (Mar. 1896), 165-166.
    Suggested by Tweddell.
        Tweddell: Summary of existing information.
                        N   4   3

3890. COOK, ALBERT. Manggyan of Sablayan, Occidental Mindoro (Philippines). Anthropos 56, nos. 1/2 (1961), 280. 1 plate.

3891. MACEDA, MARCELINO N. A brief report on some Mangyans in Northern Oriental Mindoro. Unitas 40, no. 1 (Mar. 1967), 102-155.

3892. MILLER, MERTON L. The Mangyans of Mindoro. PJS 7D, no. 3 (June 1912), 135-156. 10 plates.
        Tweddell: Observation plus collation of records of Mangyan ethnology; brief, reliable as of 1912.
                        E   5   4

3893. TWEDDELL, COLIN E. Three reports concerning Mindoro tribal distributions observed on cross-island journeys. International Headquarters, Overseas Missionary Fellowship, Singapore, 1956-1957. Manuscript.
    Suggested by Tweddell.
        Tweddell: Firsthand details of terrain, tribes, population estimates, locations; map.
                        E   5   6

3894. WORM, ALFREDO. The Mangyan of Lake Naujan. Philippine Education Magazine 23, no. 11 (Apr. 1927), 669, 674.

MANGYAN - AGRICULTURE AND FOOD

3895. BARTLETT, HARLEY HARRIS. The geographic distribution, migration, and dialectical mutation of certain plant names in the Philippines and Netherlands India, with special reference to the materia medica of a Mangyan mediquillo. Sixth Pacific Science Congress of the Pacific Science Association. Proceedings 4:85-109. Berkeley and Los Angeles. Univ. of California Press. 1940.

3896. CONKLIN, HAROLD C. An ethnoecological approach to shifting agriculture. New York Academy of Sciences. Transactions. Series 2, 17, no. 2 (Dec. 1954), 133-142.

      Luna: E   5   6

      Tweddell: Excellent discussion of multiple aspects of swidden farming, based on detailed description of Hanunóo practices.

                  E   4/5   6

3897. _____. Hanunóo agriculture in the Philippines; a report on an integral system of shifting cultivation in the Philippines. Rome, Food and Agriculture Organization of the United Nations. 1957. 209p. (FAO series on shifting cultivation, no. 2)

      Polson: Excellent study of the least resource damaging form of shifting agriculture.

                  E   5   6

      Tweddell: Foundation study of Hanunóo swidden agriculture; meticulous illustrations with bibliography.

                  E   5   6

MANGYAN - EDUCATION

3898. BAGUITAN, FLORENTINO. More experiences of a Mangyan teacher. PJE 44, no. 5 (Nov. 1965), 392-393.

3899. _____. The story of a "Mangyan Teacher". PJE 44, no. 1 (July 1965), 68-69.

MANGYAN - HEALTH AND SICKNESS

3900. VEITH, ILZA. Health and disease among the Mangyans. Bulletin of the History of Medicine 17, no. 4 (Apr. 1945), 377-384.

      Tweddell: A topical collation of information quoted from Gardner's Indic writings of the Mindoro Palawan Axis, 1939.

                  D   5   3

MANGYAN - LANGUAGE AND LITERATURE

3901. CONKLIN, HAROLD C. Preliminary report on field work on the islands of Mindoro and Palawan, Philippines. AA 51, no. 2 (Apr./June 1949), 268-273.

      Hart: E   5   6

      Sibley: E   5   6

      Tweddell: First generally reliable report of identity and distribution of Mangyan tribes; subject to later correction.

E   3   6

Ward: Cultural linguistic groups are identified and located.

E   3   6

3902. GARDNER, FLETCHER. Philippine Indic studies. San Antonio, Texas, Witte Memorial Museum, 1943. 105p. (Witte Memorial Museum, San Antonio. Indic Bulletin, no. 1)

Tweddell: Meticulous historical account of Indic scripts in the Philippines; authentic ethnographic texts; plates; bibliography.

G   4/5   7

3903. _____ and ILDEFONSO MALIWANAG. Indic writings of the Mindoro-Palawan axis. San Antonio, Texas, Witte Memorial Museum, 1939-1940. 3v. (Witte Memorial Museum, San Antonio, Bulletin no. 1, v.1-3)

v.1 Hampangan-Hanono-o scripts, by Gardner and Maliwanag.

v.2 Mangyan prose and songs, by Gardner and Maliwanag.

v.3 Mangyan grammar and vocabulary, by Gardner.

Hart: Old-timer in Philippine Islands.

G   4   7

Tweddell: Mimeographed reproductions of ethnographic notations in Indic scripts (principally Hanunoo) on bamboo; translations in Tagalog and English.

G   4   7

Ward: An early attempt by an American scholar to study the pre-Spanish syllabic script.

G   3   7

3904. SCHNEIDER, E. E. Notes on the Mangyan language. PJS 7D, no. 3 (June 1912), 157-158.

Tweddell: Brief, comparative word list of Iraya, Hanunoo, and Tadyawan (Nauhan); phonetics are recognizable.

C   3   6

NEGRITO

3905. MANZANO, FELISA O. The Negritos of Panay. Unpublished paper. 1937. (In: Beyer Philippine Ethnographic Series, Manila)

Maceda: This better known as a part of "Negrito Papers".

-       4   4

3906. The negritos of the Philippines. Journal of Anthropology 1, no. 2 (Oct. 1870), 131-144.

3907. ORACION, TIMOTEO S. The Bais forest preserve Negritos: some notes on their rituals and ceremonials. (In: Zamora, Mario D., ed. Studies in Philippine anthropology (In honor of H. Otley Beyer). Quezon City, Alemar-Phoenix, 1967. p.419-442)

3908. _____. Notes on the culture of Negritos on Negros island. SJ 7, no. 3

(July/Sept. 1960), 201-218.
     Maceda: This is a field work report and analysis.
              E   5   6

3909.   _____. Notes on the social structure and the social change of the Negritos on Negros Islands. PSR 11, nos. 1/2 (Jan./Apr. 1963), 57-67.
     Maceda: Fieldwork report and analysis.
              E   5   6

3910. POVEDANO, DIEGO L. The Robertson text and translation of the Povedano manuscript of 1572, edited by E. D. Hester, with notes on Kabunian by Fred Eggan and on the Bisayan syllabary by Robert Fox. Chicago [1954] Philippine Studies Program, Dept. of Anthropology, Univ. of Chicago, 1954. 63p. (Phillipine Studies Program Transcript no. 2)
     Scott: "... appear to be deliberate fabrications with no historic validity." Prehispanic source materials for the study of Philippine history. 1968. p.136.

3911. RAHMANN, RUDOLF and MARCELINO N. MACEDA. Bow and arrow of the Visayan Negritos. PJS 84, no. 3 (Sept. 1955), 323-333. 6 plates.
     Maceda: Field report and comparative data.
              E   5   6

3912.   _____. Notes on the Negritos of Antique, Island of Panay, Philippines. Anthropos 57, fasc. 3/6 (1962), 626-643.
     Maceda: E   5   6

3913.   _____. Some notes on the Negritos of Iloilo, Island of Panay, Philippines. Anthropos 53, nos. 5/6 (1958), 864-876.
     Maceda: This is to a great part a field report.
              E   5   7

3914. SERRANO, CIRIACO. Gambling among the Negritos of Panay. Primitive Man 14, nos. 1/2 (Jan./Apr. 1941), 31-32.
     Maceda: A report on Negrito acculturation.
              M   5   7

SULOD

3915. JOCANO, F. LANDA. Corn and rice rituals among the Sulod of Central Panay, Philippines. PJS 87, no. 4 (Dec. 1958), 455-472.
     Jocano: Primary data based on field work.
              E   5   6

3916.   _____. Cultural context of Sulod "Calls". Anthropology Tomorrow 8 (1962), 58-69.
     Jocano: Primary data based on field work.
              E   5   6

3917.   _____. Death, bone-wishing and jar burial among the Sulod of Central Panay, Philippines. 1965. Manuscript.

Cited by Evangelista in Zamora. Studies in Philippine anthropology. 1967. p.87.
     Jocano: Primary data based on field work.
                   E   5   6

3918. _____. Notes on some medicinal plants used by the Sulod of Central Panay, Philippines. Anthropology Tomorrow 6, no. 4 (Dec. 1960), 51-64.
     Jocano: Primary data based on field work.
                   E   5   6

3919. _____. Notes on the Sulod concept of death, the soul, and the region of the dead. PS 12, no. 1 (Jan. 1964), 51-62.
     Jocano: Primary data based on field work.
                   E   5   6

3920. _____. The Sulod: a mountain people in central Panay, Philippines. PS 6, no. 4 (Nov. 1958), 401-436.
     Jocano: E   5   6

3921. _____. Sulod society; a study in the kinship system and social organization of a mountain people of central Panay. Quezon City, U.P. Press, 1968. 303p. Based on his Ph.D. thesis, Kinship system and social organization of the Sulod of central Panay, Philippines, Univ. of Chicago, 1963.
     Jocano: Primary data based on field work.
                   E   5   6

TAGBANUWA

3922. FOX, ROBERT B. Religion and society among the Tagbanuwa of Palawan Island, Philippines. Chicago, 1954. 383p. Thesis (Ph.D.) - Univ. of Chicago.
     Warren: E   5   6

3923. GARDNER, FLETCHER. Philippine Indic studies. San Antonio, Texas, Witte Memorial Museum, 1943. 105p. (Witte Memorial Museum, San Antonio Indic Bulletin, no. 1)
     Tweddell: Meticulous historical account of Indic scripts in the Philippines; authentic ethnographic texts; plates; bibliography.
                   G   4/5   7

3924. MARCHE, ALFRED. Études ethnographiques sur les Tagbanuas de L'Île de Palawan (Philippines). Revue d'Ethnographie 3 (1884), 424-429.
     Warren: T   5   3

3925. ROMUALDEZ, NORBERTO. Tagbanuwa alphabet; with some reforms proposed. Manila, Imprenta Cultura Filipina, 1914. 24 [i.e. 23p.]

3926. The vanishing islanders: Tagbanua and the Batacs. This Week, Sunday Supplement of the Manila Chronicle. (Dec. 19, 1954), 8-14.
     Suggested by Tweddell.
     Tweddell: Superficial but perceptive report on current situation

from a lowland newspaperman's viewpoint.
Q   3   6

3927. VENTURELLO, MANUEL H. Manners and customs of the Tagbanuas and other tribes
of the island of Palawan, Philippines. Translated from the original Spanish
by Mrs. Edw. Y. Miller. Smithsonian miscellaneous collections 48 (1907),
514-558.
      Tweddell: Personal observational account at time of early American
                  contact.
                  G   4   4
      Warren: G   5   4

3928. WARREN, CHARLES P. Dream interpretations of the Tagbanuwa. Anthropology
Tomorrow 4, no. 4 (1956), 50-61.
Cited in Antonio and Tan. A preliminary bibliography of Philippine cultural
minorities. 1967.
      Warren: E   5   6

3929. WORCESTER, DEAN C. The Philippine islands and their people. New York, Macmillan, 1899. 529p.
Suggested by Tweddell.
      Tweddell: Chapter 5: 94-122. Second visit to Palawan. Regarding
                  the Tagbanuas of Palawan: probably first American report
                  on Palawan and the Tagbanuas; thin, popular.
                  N   5   4
                  Chapter 20: 483-502. Culion and Busuanga
                  Early observation report; thin but competent.
                  N   5   4

PART IV

MINDANAO AND SULU

A. BY SUBJECT

GENERAL

3930. AFABLE, LOURDES B. The Muslims as an ethnic minority in the Philippines.
PSR 8, nos. 1/2 (Jan./Apr. 1960), 16-33.
<pre>
          Gowing: A good general description.
                           Z   3   6
          Stone: Z   4   6
</pre>

3931. ALGUÉ, JOSÉ. Album de las diferentes razas de Mindanao. Fototopias de
Marty. Album II, Serie E. Manila, Fototipografía de Marty? 1899?

3932. ALI, ABDURRAHAMAN A. A Moro speaks out. PM 35, no. 2 (Feb. 1938), 94, 99.

3933. ALONTO, HADJI MADKI. Islam in the Philippines. FTY (1960), 239, 241, 243.
<pre>
          Gowing: G   3   7
</pre>

3934. BUFFUM, KATHARINE G. and CHARLES LYNCH. Joloano Moro. Manila, Philippine
Islands, E. C. McCullough & Co., 1914. 138p.
<pre>
          Gowing: A text used for making Moros literature in their own
                           tongue.
                           Y   5   4
</pre>

3935. BURDETT, CAPT. FRED D. Camiguin island - home of a lost race. PM 33, no.
1 (Jan. 1936), 28-29, 34-36.

3936. CHICAGO. UNIVERSITY. PHILIPPINE STUDIES PROGRAM. MINDANAO CONFERENCE.
CHICAGO, 1955. 12 papers.
      [1] Cultural relations between Mindanao...and islands to the south,
         F. C. Cole.
      [2] Preliminary linguistic survey, H. C. Conklin.
      [3] Notes on the Tawsug of Siasi..., J. F. Ewing.
      [4] Sindangan social groups, C. O. Frake.
      [5] Ethnic stratification and integration in Cotabato, C. L. Hunt.
      [6] Mindanao, future perspectives, F. M. Keesing.
      [7] Mindanao in the 19th century, Paul Lietz.
      [8] Bukidnon in 1889, F. Lynch.
      [9] Bukidnons...1945-55, R. E. Lynch.
    [10] Spanish penetration into the southern Philippines, 1578-1662,
         J. L. Phelan.
    [11] Geographic foundations of Mindanao, F. L. Wernstedt.
    [12] The Tiruray, Grace L. Wood.
University of Chicago, Dept. of Anthropology. 1v. (various pagings). "A
series of papers prepared by participants in the Conference on Mindanao held
under the auspices of the Philippine Studies Program of the Univ. of Chicago
in May 1955", Fred Eggan, Director.
<pre>
          Frake: E   5   7
          Gowing: E   4/5   7
</pre>

3937. CLOMAN, SYDNEY A. Myself and a few Moros. Garden City, N.Y., Doubleday,
Page and Co. 1923. 180p.
<pre>
          Gowing: G   5   4
</pre>

3938. COLE, FAY-COOPER. Central Mindanao; the country and its people. Far Eastern

Quarterly 4, no. 2 (Feb. 1945), 109-118.
    Madigan: E   4   4

3939. _____. Cultural relations between Mindanao regions and islands to the South. (In: Chicago. Univ. Philippine Studies Program. Mindanao Conference. Chicago, 1955. 19p. Dittoed)
    Gowing: E   4/5   7

3940. _____. The wild tribes of the Davao district, Mindanao. Chicago. 1913. p. 49-203. (Field Museum of Natural History. Publication 170. Anthropological series. v.12, no. 2)
    Frake: E   5   4
    Nimmo: E   3   4
    Yengoyan: A good survey of Davao with emphasis on material culture.
                    E   3   4

3941. COMBÉS, FRANCISCO. The natives of the southern islands. (In: Blair and Robertson. v.40: 99-182)
    Frake: M/H   4/5   7
    Gowing: Basic source for the Spanish period.
                    M   4   7

3942. COSTA, HORACIO DE LA. Muhammad Alimuddin I, Sultan of Sulu, 1735-1773. Royal Asiatic Society. Malayan Branch. Journal. 38 (July 1965), 43-76.
    Wickberg: H   4   7

3943. DAMPIER, WILLIAM. A new voyage round the world. London, Printed for J. Knapton, 1729. (In: Blair and Robertson. v.38: 266-285 on Mindanao. v.39: 21-121 on Mindanao)
    Frake: T   5   1

3944. EGGAN, FRED. History, ethnology, social life and customs of Mindanao. (In: Chicago. Univ. Philippine Studies Program. Mindanao Conference. Chicago, 1955)
    Gowing: E   4/5   7

3945. EWING, J. FRANKLIN. Notes on the Tawsug of Siasi in particular, and the Moros of the Southern Philippines in general. (In: Chicago. Univ. Philippine Studies Program. Mindanao Conference. Chicago, 1955. 151p. Mimeographed)
    Arce: E   5   4/5
    Frake: E   5   4/5
    Gowing: E/M   4/5   7
    Stone: E/M   5   7

3946. FOLLETT, HELEN. Men of the Sulu Sea. New York, Charles Scribner's Sons, 1945. 250p.
    Gowing: A popular description.
                    Q   3   7
    Stone: Journalistic account--useful for attitudes of pre-war United States.
                    Q   4   4

3947. FORREST, THOMAS. A voyage to New Guinea and the Moluccas from Balambangan: including an account of Magindano, Sooloo and other islands. London,

J. Robson, 1779. 388p.
    Frake: T   5   2/3
    Gowing: A valuable source for the period.
                 G/T   5   3

3948. FOX, ROBERT B. A consideration of theories concerning possible affiliations of Mindanao cultures with Borneo, the Celebes, and other regions of the Philippines. (In: Chicago. Univ. Philippine Studies Program. Mindanao Conference. Chicago, 1955)
Published in PSR 5, no. 1 (Jan. 1957), 2-12.
    Frake: E   4   7
    Gowing: A   4   7

3949. GOODMAN, MAURICE. A reconnaissance from Davao, Mindanao, over the divide of the Sahug River to Butuan, including a survey from Davao to Mati: Narrative of the expedition. PJS 3A, no. 6 (Dec. 1908), 501-511. 2 plates.

3950. GOWING, PETER G. Islam: the contemporary scene. PS 12, no. 4 (Oct. 1964), 639-647.
    Stone: The following six works are uniformly excellent accounts and commentary by insightful teacher and student of Islam.
                 M/Y   5   6

3951. _____. Mosque and Moro: a study of Muslims in the Philippines. Manila, Philippine Islands, Philippine Federation of Christian Churches, 1964. 120p.
    Arce: M/Y   3   7
    Gowing: Y   3   7
    Nimmo: E   3   7
    Stone: M/Y   5   6

3952. _____. Muslim Filipinos - Present condition and future prospects. SJ 9, no. 4 (Oct./Dec. 1962), 305-316.
    Stone: M/Y   5   6

3953. _____. Muslim Filipinos today. Muslim World 54, no. 1 (Jan. 1964), 39-48; (Apr. 1964), 112-121.
    Stone: M/Y   5   6

3954. _____. Muslims in the Philippines. Muslimnews International 2, no. 7 (Jan. 1964), 30-32.
Cited in Kiefer and Schlegel, Selected bibliography: Philippine Moslems. Chicago, Univ. of Chicago, 1965.
    Stone: M/Y   5   6

3955. _____. Resurgent Islam and the Moro problem in the Philippines. South East Asia Journal of Theology 4, no. 1 (July 1962), 57-65.
    Stone: M/Y   5   6

3956. HERRE, ALBERT W. C. T. Lanao - lovely land of romance. Scientific Monthly 38, (June 1934), 534-542.

3957. _____. The Sibutu Islands. Scientific Monthly 28, (Apr. 1929), 304-317.
    Nimmo: N   3   4

3958. HOBBS, HORACE POTTS. Kris and Krag; adventures among the Moros of the Southern Philippine Islands. n.p., 1962. 191p.
    Gowing: A soldier's account of the initial clashes between Moros and Americans.
    G   3   4

3959. HUKE, ROBERT E. Mindanao--pioneer frontier? PGJ 7, no. 2 (Apr./June 1963), 74-83.
    Spencer: Prospects of development of a frontier area.
    K 4/5 6
    Stone: K 5 6
    Yengoyan: K 4 6

3960. HURLEY, VICTOR. Southeast of Zamboanga. With an introduction by Max Miller. 1st ed., New York, E. P. Dutton & Co., Inc., 1935. 237p.
    Stone: Colorful, somewhat biased travelogues, but with useful information.
    J 4 4

3961. _____. Swish of the Kris; the story of the Moros. New York, E. P. Dutton & Co., Inc., 1936. 301p.
    Gowing: A good general account in journalistic style.
    F/Q 4 7
    Stone: J 4 7

3962. JESUITS. LETTERS FROM MISSIONS (PHILIPPINE ISLANDS). Cartas de los radres de la Compañía de Jesús de la Mision de Filipines ... Manila, Impr. de los Amigos de país, 1877-1895. 10v. Imprint varies.
Contents analyzed in Streit, Bibliotheca Missionum. v.9: p.186-187, 192-194, 200-202, 217-219, 229-232, 256-259, 260-263, 275-279, 293-299, 350-359. For anthropological index to Cartas de los padres..., see Frank Lynch, The Jesuit letters of Mindanao as a source of anthropological data. PS, v.4, no.2 (June 1956), 247-272.
    Frake: M 5 3
    Gowing: Invaluable source of ethnographic data for the second half of the 19th century.
    M 5 3
    Yengoyan: Excellent primary source for Eastern Mindanao.
    M 5 3

3963. KEATS, JOHN. The fierce Moros. Holiday 34, no. 6 (Dec. 1963), 124, 126-128, 130, 133-135.
    Stone: Captures flavor and feeling of Sulu, but sensational in approach.
    J 4 6

3964. KEESING, FELIX M. Mindanao: future perspectives. (In: Papers Read at the Mindanao Conference. Chicago, Philippine Studies Program, Univ. of Chicago, May 1955. 20p. Dittoed)

3965. KUDER, EDWARD M. The Moros in the Philippines. Far Eastern Quarterly 4, no. 2 (Feb. 1945), 119-126.
    Frake: G 4 7
    Gowing: G 4 4/5

3966. LIETZ, PAUL. Mindanao in the nineteenth century. (In: Papers Read at the Mindanao Conference. Chicago, Philippine Studies Program, Univ. of Chicago,

May 1955. 10p. Dittoed)

3967. LYNCH, FRANK. Ateneo expedition to Sulu. PS 10, no. 2 (Apr. 1962), 314-316.

3968. _____. The Jesuit letters of Mindanao as a source of anthropological data.
PS 4, no. 2 (June 1956), 247-272.
      Arce: E   4   2/3
      Frake: E   4   3
      Gowing: E   4   3
      Stone: Excellent interpretation of ethnohistorical sources.
                    E   5   3

3969. _____, ed.   Sulu's people and their art. Quezon City, Ateneo de Manila
Univ. Press, 1963. 66p. (IPC Papers, no. 3)
Contents: Social organization of the Muslim peoples of Sulu, by W. F. Arce.
Art in Sulu, by David Szanton.
    Geoghegan: A fairly complete account of the art forms among the Sa-
                    mal and Badjaw of Sulu. Set of good to excellent photo-
                    graphs.
                    E and E   3   6
    Gowing: Two valuable studies of Sulu social organization and art.
                    E and E   5   6
    Nimmo: E and E   3   6
    Rixhon: E and E   5   6
    Stone: Pioneer paper on Muslim social organization. Excellent
                    photographic study of indigenous art of Sulu.
                    E and E   5   6
    Trimillos: Reproduction fuzzy.
                    E and E   5   6

3970. MADIGAN, FRANCIS C. Research in the Visayas-Mindanao area. PSR 11, nos.
1/2 (Jan./Apr. 1963), 125-130.

3971. _____. Social science research in the Mindanao area. SR 5, no. 2 (Feb.
1964), 5-8.

3972. MAJUL, CESAR ADIB. Islam in Philippines. Muslimnews International 6, (Dec.
1967), 29-34.

3973. MEDNICK, MELVIN. "The Moros." (In: Human Relations Area Files, Inc. Area
handbook on the Philippines. 1956. v.4, Chapter 24. p.1729-1774)
      Arce: E   4   7
      Frake: E   5   7
      Gowing: A helpful general description of Philippine Moros.
                E   4   7
      Nimmo: E   4   7
      Stone: E   5   7

3974. MUSLIM ASSOCIATION OF THE PHILIPPINES. Yearbook, 1956- v.for 1956 issued
without title. Published in connection with the 2d - Filipino Muslim National Conference, held in 1956-, and includes Conference Proceedings, 1st-,
1955-
Cited in Peter Gowing, Islam and Muslims in the Philippines, a bibliography
of materials in English. n.d. Mimeographed.

          Gowing: A useful source of information on Moros and their prob-
                          lems.
          W   3   6

3975. The Muslim minority in the Philippines. Cebu City, June 11, 1962, 27p.
      Mimeographed.
      Cited in Kiefer and Schlegel. Selected bibliography: Philippine Moslems.
      Chicago, Univ. of Chicago, 1965.
          Gowing: A general survey of the past and present conditions of
                          the Moros.
          G   3   7

3976. OROSA, SIXTO Y. The Sulu archipelago and its people. Yonkers-on-Hudson,
      N.Y., World Book Company, 1923. 134p.
          Arce: G   3   4
          Frake: G   3   7
          Gowing: G/D   3   7

3977. NATIONAL MUSLIM FILIPINO CONFERENCE, 2D, DANSALAN, PHILIPPINES, 1956.
      Second National Muslim Filipino Conference, Oct. 11-16, 1956, sponsored by
      the Muslim Association of the Philippines and other Muslim religious organ-
      izations in Lanao Province, City of Marawi, Lanao, Mindanao, Philippines.
      Dansalan, 1956. 162p.
          Gowing: A useful source of information on how Moros see them-
                          selves and their problems.
          W   3   6

3978. PHILIPPINE ISLANDS. ETHNOLOGICAL SURVEY. (4th) report (for year ended Sept.
      1, 1905). (In: Philippine Commission. 6th report, (Nov. 1904-Oct. 1905)
      (with reports of department, bureau officers, 1905, etc.) 1906. pt. 2,
      p. 417-427)
          Frake: G   4   3/4

3979. _____. GOVERNOR GENERAL. Report of Department of Mindanao and Sulu. (Re-
      port of department governor, year ending Dec. 31, 1918.) (Report, 1918.
      1919. p.49-101.)
          Gowing: Good for insights into what the American regime was at-
                          tempting to do among the "pacified" Moros.
          G   3   4

3980. PHILIPPINES (REPUBLIC) CONGRESS. HOUSE OF REPRESENTATIVES. Report of the
      Special Committee to investigate the Moro problem, especially with regard
      to peace and order in Mindanao and Sulu. By Congressmen Domocao Alonto,
      Q. Anilbangsa and L. Mangelen. 3rd Congress, 2nd Session. Manila, 1954. 93p.

3981. RAVENHOLT, ALBERT. The Amir Mindalano - profile of a Filipino Mohammedan
      leader. American Universities Field Staff AR-6-56. 1956. 11p.

3982. RIXHON, GERARD. The Philippines. Muslim World 56, no. 4 (Oct. 1966), 307-
      311.
          Stone: E   5   6

3983. SABER, MAMITUA. [Four papers. Marawi City? 196-] 1v. (various pagings)
      Contents: - Spanish fleet on Lake Lanao. - Muslim social organization in re-
      lation to the problems and possibilities of community development. - The

Muslim minority in the Philippines. - Some observations on Maranao social
and cultural transition.
    Gowing: Valuable papers by a competent, well trained Moro ethnol-
                ogist.
                E   4/5   7

3984. ST. JOHN, SPENSER. Life in the forests of the Far East. London, Smith,
Elder and Co., 1862. 2v.
v.2 Chapter 8. The Sulu Archipelago. p.165-185.
v.2 Chapter 9. The Sulu Islands. p.186-207.
    Spencer: Good travel account in 19th century manner.
               T   5   3

3985. SANTOS, ALEJO S. The Sulu problem. PSR 8, nos. 1/2 (Jan./Apr. 1960), 34-
38.
    Gowing: Valuable for insights into policies of Philippine society
                towards the Sulu Moros.
               G   3   7

3986. SCHADENBERG, ALEXANDER. Die Bewohner von Süd-Mindanao und der Insel Samal.
ZE 17, (1885), 8-37, 45-57. Bagobo vocabulary, p.33-36.
    Tangco: "Among his (Schadenberg) numerous publications dealing
                with Philippine ethnography, the most noteworthy are ...
                Die Bewohner von Süd-Mindanao..." PSSHR, Aug. 1940,
                p.195-196.

3987. SOPHER, DAVID E. The sea nomads; a study based on the literature of the
maritime boat people of Southeast Asia. Singapore, Government Printer,
1965. 422p. (Memoirs of the National Museum, no. 5) (His Ph.D. Thesis -
Univ. of California, Berkeley, 1954)
    Frake: K   3   7
    Geoghegan: An amazing collection of information on the Badjaw of
                Southeast Asia. Extremely valuable.
               K   4   7
    Gowing: Describes the Bajaw and some groups of Philippine Samals
                in a general description of Southeast Asian boat peoples.
               K   5   7
    Nimmo: K   4   7
    Stone: Library study of boat-dwellers throughout Malaysia. Pro-
                vides baseline.
               K   4   7

3988. WILKES, CHARLES. Narrative of the United States exploring expedition. During the years 1838, 1839, 1840, 1841, 1842. Philadelphia, Lea and Blanchard,
1845. V.5, Chapter 9. Sooloo (1842). p.323-367.
    Anderson: A short but succinct characterization of the physical out-
                lay of particularly Manila and the Sulu archipelago as
                well as a description of the social, political and eco-
                nomic life of their respective inhabitants as observed
                by the author during the few days of his stay.
               T/G   5   3
    Arce: T/G   3   2/3
    Nimmo: T/G   3   2/3

3989. _____. Sulu in 1842. (In: Craig, Austin, ed. The former Philippines

thru foreign eyes. New York, Appleton, 1916. p.493-529)
    Gowing: A valuable source of first-hand information from the pe-
                         riod.
                         T/G   5   3

3990. WULFF, INGER. Muhammedanske kvinder i det sydlige Philippinerne. (Copenhagen. Nationalmuseet, Nationalmuseets Arbejdsmark. 1967. København,
1967. p.31-42)

AGRICULTURE AND FOOD

3991. AQUINO, MARCELO V. Some aspects of agricultural loans granted by five rural
banks in the Visayas and Mindanao, 1953. PA 39, no. 9 (Feb. 1956), 510-
515.
    Sta. Iglesia: Highly useful descriptive research.
                  G   5   6

3992. BONGGA, DEMETRIA. Strengthening cooperation and coordination in community
nutrition work in the Muslim region. Philippine Journal of Nutrition 20,
no. 2 (Apr./June 1967), 52-60.

3993. CAINTIC, CRISOGONO U. Abaca marketing practices in Compostela, Davao. PA
43, no. 6 (Nov. 1959), 415-429.
    Sta. Iglesia: Highly useful descriptive research.
                  Y   5   6

3994. LUNA, TELESFORO W. Some aspects of agricultural development and settlement
in Basilan Island, southern Philippines. Pacific Viewpoint 4, no. 1 (Mar.
1963), 17-24.

3995. MADIGAN, FRANCIS C. The harvest ritual in north central Mindanao. Sociological Analysis 25, no. 4 (Winter 1964), 231-237.

3996. PELZER, KARL J. Pioneer settlement in the Asiatic tropics; studies in land
utilization and agricultural colonization in Southeastern Asia. New York,
American Geographical Society, 1945. 290p. (Special Publication, No. 29)
Chapter 5. Mindanao, the frontier. p.127-159.
        Frake: K   4   7
        Madigan: K   3/4   7
        Spencer: Excellent study.
                  K   4/5   7
        Wernstedt: Excellent study of settlement in Mindanao and Indonesia.
                  K   5   7
        Yengoyan: Good source.
                  K   4   7

3997. PENDLETON, ROBERT L. Glimpses of Cotabato province. PA 23, no. 9 (Feb.
1935), 733-741.

3998. _____. Land utilization and agriculture of Mindanao, Philippine Islands.
Geographical Review 32, (1942), 180-210.

Frake: K   3   4
Madigan: K   3/4   4
Spencer: Excellent study.
              K   4   4
Wernstedt: An excellent geographic land utilization study.
              K   5   4

3999. RAVENHOLT, ALBERT. Moro Bay Lumber Company case. AUFSR. Southeast Asia Series 4, no. 2 (Feb. 17, 1956), 13p. (AR-2-'56)

4000. SANDOVAL, PEDRO R. Socio-economic conditions of settlers in Kidapawan, Mindanao. PA 40, no. 9 (Feb. 1957), 498-518.
     Sta. Iglesia: Highly useful descriptive research.
              Y   5   6

4001. TORRES, REMIGIO D. Farm prices in Bukidnon. PA 47, no. 5 (Oct. 1963), 238-256.
     Sta. Iglesia: Highly useful descriptive research.
              Y   5   6

ARCHAEOLOGY

4002. EWING, J. FRANKLIN and FRANK LYNCH. A neolithic adze from Mindanao. PJS 81, no. 1 (Mar. 1952), 49-51. 1 plate.
     Solheim: E and E   3   1

4003. FRANCISCO, JUAN R. The golden image of Agusan - a new identification. AS 1, (1963), 31-39. 1 plate.

4004. _____. A note on the Golden Image of Agusan. PS 11, no. 3 (July 1963), 390-400. 1 plate.

4005. LYNCH, FRANK X. and J. FRANKLIN EWING. Twelve ground-stone implements from Mindanao, Philippine Islands. (In: Solheim, William G., ed. Anthropology at the Eighth Pacific Science Congress of the Pacific Science Association and the Fourth Far-Eastern Prehistory Congress. Quezon City, Philippines, 1953. Honolulu, Social Science Research Institute, Univ. of Hawaii, 1968. p.7-18) (In:Asian and Pacific archaeology series, no. 2)

4006. MACEDA, MARCELINO. Archaeological and socio-anthropological field work in Kulaman plateau, Southeastern Cotabato. SR 7, no. 9 (Sept. 1966), 12-20.

4007. _____. Preliminary report on ethnographic and archaeological field work in the Kulaman Plateau, Island of Mindanao, Philippines. Anthropos 59, (1964), 75-82. 3 plates.
     Solheim: E   3   7

4008. _____. A preliminary report on the Fenefe cave excavation Kulaman Plateau, Mindanao. (In: Zamora, Mario D., ed. Studies in Philippine anthropology (In honor of H. Otley Beyer). Quezon City, Alemar-Phoenix, 1967. p.265-272)

4009. _____. Second preliminary report on the archaeological excavation in the Kulaman Plateau (Cotabato), Island of Mindanao, Philippines. Anthropos 60, fas. 1/6 (1965), 237-240.

4010. _____. Preliminary studies of the figures and ornamentation of some selected jar covers from Kulaman Plateau (southwestern Cotabato), Island of Mindanao, Philippines. Anthropos 62, fas. 3/4 (1967), 509-532.

4011. SPOEHR, ALEXANDER. Archaeological survey of southern Zamboanga and the Sulu Archipelago. AP 11, (1968), 177-185.

ARMED FORCES AND WAR

4012. BARRANTES Y MORENO, VICENTE. Guerras piráticas de Filipinas contra Mindanaos y Joloanos. (Biblioteca hispano-ultramarina [t. III]) Madrid, Imprenta de Manuel G. Hernandez, 1878. 448p.

4013. BERNAD, MIGUEL A. Father Ducós and the Muslim wars, 1752-1759. PS 16, no. 4 (Oct. 1968), 690-728.

4014. KOBBE, WILLIAM A. Annual report of Brig. Gen. W. A. Kobbe, Commanding Dept. of Mindanao and Jolo. Sept. 10, 1900. (In: Annual reports of the War Dept.for the fiscal year ended June 30, 1900. Dept.of the Lt.-Gen. Commanding the Army. Part 3 (House of Representatives. 56th Congress. 2d Session, Document no. 2, 1900. p.255-271)
    Gowing: Reports period of initial Moro-American contacts of 1899-1900.
                G   3   4

4015. MONTERO Y VIDAL, JOSÉ. Historia de la piratería malayo-mahometana en Mindanao, Joló y Borneo. Madrid, M. Tello, 1888. 2v.
    Frake: H   4   2/3
    Geoghegan: An excellent, detailed collection of secondary data on piracy. Includes important historical documents.
                H   4   2/3
    Madigan: H   3   2/3

4016. WORCESTER, DEAN C. The Malay pirates of the Philippines. Century Magazine 56, no. 5 (Sept. 1898), 690-702.

BEHAVIOR PROCESS AND PERSONALITY

4017. BERNARDO, ANGELO G. Matigsalug color categories. U.P. Anthropology Bulletin 3, no. 1 (First Semester 1967/1968), 11-13.

4018. MASA, JORGE O. Comments on "ethnic relationships in Cotabato". PSSHR 19, no. 1 (Mar. 1954), 73-76.

CLOTHING, ADORNMENT AND MATERIALS

4019. GALANG, RICARDO E. Filing and blackening of teeth among some Philippine ethnic groups. PJS 75, no. 4 (Aug. 1941), 425-431. 2 plates.
        Intengan: C   3   5

4020. MASON, OTIS T. Basketry bolo case from Basilan Island. U.S. National Museum. Smithsonian Institution. Proceedings 33, (1908), 193-196.

COMMUNITY DEVELOPMENT AND TERRITORIAL ORGANIZATION

4021. DUCOMMUN, DOLORES. Sisangat: a Sulu fishing community. PSR 10, nos. 3/4 (July/Oct. 1962), 91-107.
        Arce: E   5   6
        Geoghegan: Thin in general, but useful because of the lack of information on this group.
                     E   2/3   6
        Madigan: E   3/5   6
        Nimmo: E   3   6
        Stone: Not expertly written but contains basic information.
                     E/F   5   6

4022. MADIGAN, FRANCIS C. The farmer said no; a study of background factors associated with dispositions to cooperate with or be resistant to community development projects. Quezon City, Community Development Research Council, U.P., 1962. 359p. (Study Series, no. 14)
        Madigan: Z   5   6

4023. _____ . Predicting receptivity to community development innovations. Current Anthropology 3, no. 2 (Apr. 1962), 207-208.
        Madigan: Z   5   6

4024. MEDNICK, MELVIN. Development programs and the Moslems of the Philippines. (In: Kaut, Charles R., ed. Community Development in the Philippines, Southern Illinois Univ., 18p. 1960. Mimeographed)
        Madigan: E   5   6

4025. SABER, MAMITUA and MAUYAG M. TAMANO. Decision-making and social change in rural Moroland, an investigation of socio-economic problems in community development. Quezon City, Community Development Research Council, U.P. 1961. (Study Series no. 16, unpublished paper)
Cited by Charles K. Warriner in PSR 12, nos. 3/4 (July/Oct. 1964), p.175.
        Madigan: Z   3/5   6

ECONOMICS

4026. JAYME, VICENTE R. The Mindanao development authority: a new concept in Philippine economic development. PJPA 5, no. 4 (Oct. 1961), 321-339.

447

4027. MANALAYSAY, M. O. Quantifying the growth potentials and economy of the Mindanao region. Phil. Stat. 15, nos. 3/4 (Sept./Dec. 1966), 49-60.

4028. MINTON, FRANK LEWIS. The pirate turns planter: a story of the economic development of Sulu. Philippine Education Magazine 25, no. 4 (Sept. 1928), 204-206.
Reprinted in JEAS 4, no. 1 (Jan. 1955), 85-87.

4029. REBOLOS, ZENAIDA. Promissory and dept (i.e., debt) aspects of the folk ritual in Misamis Oriental, by Zenaida Robolos (sic). PSR 12, nos. 1/2 (Jan./Apr. 1964), 95-101.
    Madigan: Z   5   6
    Rixhon: Z   4   6

4030. SACAY, FRANCISCO M., JAINARI S. KIBTIANI and MAJINDI K. ANUDDIN. A survey of economic and social conditions of farmers in Sulu. PA 34, no. 1 (July/Sept. 1950), 1-9.
    Sta. Iglesia: Highly useful descriptive research.
    Y   5   6

4031. SPOEHR, ALEXANDER. Technical innovation and economic development: Basnig fishing boats of Zamboanga, Mindanao. PSJ 97, no. 1 (Mar. 1968), 77-92.

4032. TORIBIO, CORAZON ARCEO. The economy of the province of Davao. Quezon City, College of Business Administration, U.P., 1955. 66p.

EDUCATION

4033. ALEGADO, GRACIANO I. A survey of the Notre Dame Schools of Tawi-Tawi. Cebu City, 1967. 124p. Thesis (M.A.) - Univ. of San Carlos.
Suggested by Rixhon.
    Rixhon: Y   4   6

4034. CAINGLET, EMETERIO B. The marriage customs among the Muslims in Bongcao, Sulu and their educational significance. Cebu City, 1966. 96p. Thesis (M.A.) - Univ. of San Carlos.
Suggested by Rixhon.
    Rixhon: Y   3   6

4035. ISIDRO Y SANTOS, ANTONIO. Mindanao State University: its development plan. Marawi City, Philippines, 1964. 80 p.

4036. MADIGAN, FRANCIS C. and MANUEL M. GAPUZ. Screening for college aptitude: predicting success in a Mindanao college by objective tests. Cagayan de Oro City, Research Institute for Mindanao Culture, Xavier Univ., 1968. 65p. (Xavier Univ. Studies, no. 2)
Suggested by Madigan.
    Madigan: Correlates scores on entrance exams with college grades for first and second year college. Multiple correlation and regression employed.
    Z and Y   5   6

4037. MEDINA, RICARDO C. The extent and causes of dropouts of Mohammedan pupils in Zamboanga City. Quezon City, 1961. 111p. Thesis (M.Ed.) - U.P.

4038. MIRAVITE, Q. F. A bold experiment in higher education. Exchange no. 36 (Third Quarter 1965), 6-13.
        Rixhon: Exposition of the aims, programs of education at the Mindanao State University, from an official standpoint.
                          Y   3   6

4039. MITCHELL, HUDSON. Growth in a frontier region. Exchange no. 36 (Third Quarter 1965), 2-5.
        Rixhon: Description of the effort of a Jesuit (Xavier) University in facing the economic development challenges in rural Mindanao.
                          Y   3   6

4040. RIXHON, GERARD. Educational work in Sulu. SJ 11, nos. 1/2 (Mar./June 1964), 49-56.

4041. SAN AGUSTIN, ARACELI (SEBASTIAN). The Moro way of life and the Philippine Public School System. 1959. 201p. Thesis (M.A.) - U.P.
Cited in U.P. theses and dissertations ... p.182.

4042. SANTOS, RUFINO DE LOS. Developing a revised program for the Dansalan Junior College High School, on Marawi City, Philippines on the discovered Maranaw needs. 1962. Thesis (Ed.D.) - Columbia (Teachers College).
        Rixhon: Y   4   6

4043. _____. Moslem values: a challenge to education. PSR 14, no. 2 (Apr. 1966), 76-82.

4044. TORRANCE, ARTHUR F. The Philippine Moro; a study in social and race pedagogy. New York, 1917. 202p. Thesis (Ph.D.) - New York Univ.
        Gowing: Y   3   7

ETHNIC INFLUENCES

4045. CODY, CECIL E. The consolidation of the Japanese in Davao. Comment, (Third Quarter 1958), 23-36.
Suggested by Goodman.
        Goodman: Objective, scholarly account based on research in Japanese sources.
                          H   4   4

4046. _____. The Japanese way of life in prewar Davao. PS 7, no. 2 (Apr. 1959), 172-186.
        Goodman: A careful and insightful study including work in Japanese sources.
                          H   4   4
        Wickberg: H   3   4

4047. GOODMAN, GRANT K. Davao: a case study in Japanese-Philippine relations.
[Lawrence] Center for East Asian Studies, University of Kansas [1967]
117p. (Center for East Asian Studies, University of Kansas. International
studies, East Asian series research publication, no. 1)

4048. _____. Davaokuo? Japan in Philippine politics, 1931-1941. (In: Studies
on Asia, 1963. Ed. by Robert K. Sakai. Lincoln, Univ. of Nebraska Press,
1963. p.185-196)

4049. KEMP, ELEANOR C. Moro-Chinese Mestizos. Eugenical News 8, no. 5 (May 1923),
42-43.
    Weightman: Dated; limited.
                    D   4   1

4050. KOLB, ALBERT. Die Japanische Ackerbaukolonie in Davao, Philippinen. Kolo-
niale Rundschau 29, (1938), 209-218.
    Frake: K   4   4
    Weightman: Kolb--a painstaking, exacting scientist.
                    K   5   4

4051. MAJUL, CESAR. Chinese relationship with the Sultanate of Sulu. (In: Felix,
Alfonso, ed. The Chinese in the Philippines, 1570-1770. Manila, Solidaridad
Publishing House, 1966. 143-159)
    Frake: H   4   2/3
    Wickberg: H   3   2

4052. _____. Islamic and Arab cultural influences in the south of the Philippines.
JSEAH 7, no. 2 (Sept. 1966), 61-73.
    Frake: H   4   7
    Stone: Excellent documentation by foremost Filipino student of
                  Muslim history.
                  H   5   7

4053. MALAYANG, JOSÉ. Filipino-Chinese relations in a small city. CC 7, no. 3
(May/June 1967), 25-30.

4054. PELZER, KARL JOSEF. Pioneer settlement in the Asiatic tropics; studies in
land utilization and agricultural colonization in Southeastern Asia. New
York, New York.American Geographical Society, 1945. 200p. (Special Publication No. 29) Chapter 4. Landless Filipinos. p.81-114.
    Goodman: Geographer's interpretation of such emigrant settlements
                  as that of the Japanese at Davao.
                  K   4   4
    Luna: Descriptive analytical study with maps and tables.
                  K   4   4
    Spencer: Excellent study of settlement activities in Mindanao.
                  K   5   4
    Wernstedt: Survey of resettlement programs in Philippines and Indo-
                  nesia.
                  K   5   4/5

4055. QUIASON, SERAFIN D. The Japanese colony in Davao, 1904-1941. PSSHR 23,
nos. 2/4 (June/Dec. 1958), 215-230.
    Goodman: A useful overview by a young Filipino historian.
                  H   3   4

Weightman: One of the few historic works done by Filipinos on this subject.

          H   3   4

4056. SANIEL, JOSEFA M. The Japanese minority in the Philippines before Pearl Harbor; social organization in Davao. AS 4, no. 1 (Apr. 1966), 103-126.

4057. TALLOW, ADAMIN. The Muslim problem. Manila, 1957. 38p.

FINE ARTS

4058. BARADAS, DAVID B. Some implications of the Okir Motif in Lanao and Sulu art. AS 6, no. 2 (Aug. 1968), 129-168. 27 figs.

4059. BERNAL, RAFAEL. The "Moro-moro": a possibility for folkloric theater. Comment, no. 15 (1962), 115-123.

      Trimillos: Good general description.

          R   4   7

4060. CASIÑO, ERIC. Muslim folk art in the Philippines. Manila, 1967. 20p. (Aspects of Philippine Culture, 4) "Fourth in a series of lectures presented by the National Museum and sponsored by Ambassador and Mrs. William McC. Blair, Jr."

4061. DACANAY, JULIAN E., JR. The Okil in Muslim art: a view from the drawing board. (In: Manuud, Antonio G., ed. Brown heritage: essays on Philippine cultural tradition and literature. Quezon City, Ateneo de Manila Univ. Press, 1967. p.149-162)

4062. HARTENDORP, A. V. H. The art of the Lanao Moros. Philippines Quarterly 2, no. 2 (1953), 8-13.

      Maher: X   5   7

4063. _____. The applied art of the Lanao Moros.

      PM 29, no. 10 (Mar. 1933), 437-440.

          29, no. 11 (Apr. 1933), 488-489.

          29, no. 12 (May 1933), 528-529.

      Trimillos: Good illustrations.

          J   5   4

4064. IMAO, ABDULMARI A. Okkil. University College Journal, no. 4 (1962/1963), 105-108.

4065. OCAMPO, GALO B. Muslim Filipino art. (In: Philippines (Republic) National Museum. Glimpses of Philippine Culture. Pedro F. Abella, ed. Manila, 1964. p.56-65)

4066. SOLLER, ROBERT. Three centuries of 'Moro-Moro'. Exchange News, no. 14 (First Quarter 1960), 16-19.

      Pfeiffer: R   3   6

4067. SZANTON, DAVID. Art in Sulu. PS 11, no. 3 (July 1963), 463-502. 86 figures.
        Geoghegan: A fairly complete account of the art forms among the Samal and Badjaw of Sulu. Set of good to excellent photographs.
                    E   3   6
        Nimmo: E   5   6
        Rixhon: First systematic study of the Sulu's art forms in wood and stone.
                    E   5   6
        Stone: Excellent photographic study of indigenous art of Sulu.
                    E   5   6
        Trimillos: Good reproduction general survey.
                    E   5   6

GEOGRAPHY AND DEMOGRAPHY

4068. BALABA, TERESA PILAR L. Mortality levels in Cagayan: a study of the death rates and expectations of life by sex and age in a medium-sized Philippine city (Cagayan de Oro City). 1967. 83p. Thesis (M.A.) - Xavier Univ.

4069. HUNT, CHESTER L. Cotabato: melting pot of the Philippines. PSSHR 19, no. 1 (Mar. 1954), 40-72.
        Madigan: Z   3/5   6
        Rixhon: Z   5   6
        Wernstedt: Excellent study of Colabato city and racial/ethnic/religious integration.
                    Z   4/5   6

4070. LOPEZ, FRANCISCO B. Geographical sketch of Camiguin island. PGJ 3, no. 4 (Oct./Dec. 1955), 170-176.
        Spencer: Summary notes.
                    C   4   6

4071. MADIGAN, FRANCIS C. Estimated trends of fertility, mortality, and natural increase in the north Mindanao region of the Philippine Islands, 1960-1970. PSR 13, no. 4 (Oct. 1965), 260-267.
        Madigan: Z   4   6
        Rixhon: Z   4   6
        Wernstedt: Good data sources.
                    Z   4   6

4072. _____. The facts of life in Misamis Oriental. PSR 11, nos. 1/2 (Jan./Apr. 1963), 98-106.
        Madigan: Z   4/5   6
        Rixhon: Z   4   6

4073. _____. Some population characteristics of Cagayan de Oro City. PSR 10, nos. 3/4 (July/Oct. 1962), 171-176.
        Madigan: Z   5   6
        Rixhon: Z   4   6

Wernstedt: Z   4   6

4074.   _____ and ROSALIA O. AVANCEÑA. Philippine fertility and mortality with
special reference to the North Mindanao region: a critique of recent estimates. PSR 12, nos. 1/2 (Jan./Apr. 1964). Part I: The Philippines in general. p.35-42. Part II: The North Mindanao Region. p.43-53.
    Madigan: Z   4   6
    Rixhon: Z   4   6
    Wernstedt: Good data sources.
                   Z   4   6

4075.   PELZER, KARL J. Pioneer settlement in the Asiatic tropics; studies in land
utilization and agricultural colonization in Southeastern Asia. New York,
American Geographical Society, 1945. 290p. (Special Publication No. 29)
Chapter 5. Mindanao, the frontier. p.127-159.
    Frake: K   4   7
    Madigan: K   3/4 7
    Spencer: Excellent study.
                   K   4/5 7
    Wernstedt: Excellent study of settlement in Mindanao and Indonesia.
                   K   5   7
    Yengoyan: Good source.
                   K   4   7

4076.   PENDLETON, ROBERT L. Land utilization and agriculture of Mindanao, Philippine Islands. Geographical Review 32, (1942), 180-210.
    Frake: K   3   4
    Madigan: K   3/4 4
    Spencer: Excellent study.
                   K   4   4
    Wernstedt: An excellent geographic land utilization study.
                   K   5   4

4077.   PIDO, ANTONIO J. A. Differential fertility patterns in Cagayan de Oro city.
PSR 11, nos. 1/2 (Jan./Apr. 1963), 91-98.
Based on his M.A. Thesis - Xavier Univ. 1961. 94p.
    Luna: Pilot study: descriptive statistical.
                   Z   4   6
    Madigan: Excellent pilot-study of differential fertility in one
                   Philippine city.
                   Z   3/4 6

4078.   ROSELL, DOMINADOR Z. The Koronadal Valley, Cotabato. PM 36, no. 12 (Dec.
1939), 493, 507-508.
    Wernstedt: K   3   5

4079.   STITT, ROBERT E. Mindanao: key to the Philippines future. Journal of
Geography 48, no. 4 (Apr. 1949), 150-160.
    Spencer: Fair popularized summary.
                   K   4   6

4080.   VANDERMEER, CANUTE and BERNARDO C. AGALOOS. Twentieth century settlement
of Mindanao. Michigan Academy of Science, Arts and Letters, Papers 47
(1961), 537-548.
    Spencer: Study of migration and settlement.
                   K   4   7

Wernstedt: Survey of road building periods.

K   3   7

4081. WARRINER, C. K. 1958 Census of Marawi City, Philippines. Lanao Community
and Leadership Studies, Report No. 1. Mimeographed. Marawi City,
1959.
Cited in Kiefer and Schlegel, Selected bibliography: Philippine Moslems.
Chicago, Univ. of Chicago, 1965.
    Madigan: Carefully done study.

Z   5   6
    Rixhon: Z   4   6

4082. WERNSTEDT, FREDERICK L. Geographic foundations of Mindanao. (In: Chicago.
Univ. Philippine Studies Program. Mindanao Conference. Chicago, 1955.
21p. Mimeographed)
    Spencer: K   4   7

4083. _____ and PAUL D. SIMKINS. Migrations and the settlement of Mindanao.
Journal of Asian Studies 25, no. 1 (Nov. 1965), 83-103.
    Madigan: Carefully done study. Survey data.

K   5   6/7

    Rixhon: So far the only authoritative study of the population in-
crease in Mindanao through migration as compared to the
whole of the Philippines.
K   4   7
    Spencer: Detailed study, migration and settlement.
K   5   7
    Yengoyan: Migration pattern and differential--excellent.
K   5   6

HEALTH AND SICKNESS

4084. GOMEZ, LIBORIO. Mohammedan medical practice in Cotabato province. PJS 12B,
no. 6 (Nov. 1917), 261-279. 1 plate. 7 text figures.

HISTORY AND CULTURE CHANGE

4085. [ALENÇON, FERDINAND PHILIPPE MARIE D'ORLEANS, DUC D'] Lucon et Mindanao.
Extraits d'un journal de voyage dans l'Extrême Orient. ...Paris, Michel
Lévy frères, 1870. 222p.

4086. COMBÉS, FRANCISCO. Historia de Mindanao y Joló...Obra publicada en Madrid
en 1667, y que ahora con la colaboración del p. Pablo Pastells...saca nue-
vamente á luz W. E. Retana. Madrid,[Viuda de M. Minuesa de los Rios] 1897.
800 cols.
    Madigan: H/M   5   2

Rixhon: M   4   2

4087. HAMM, DAVID L. and BATUA A. MACARAYA. Acculturation survey of the Dansalan Junior College. Practical Anthropology 6, no. 6 (Nov./Dec. 1959), 262-272. Also published in SJ 6, no. 2 (Apr./June 1959), 95-108.
          Hart: Senior author resided in Marawi City (Dansalan) area for many years.
                         M and Y   4   7

4088. HUNT, CHESTER L. Cotabato: melting pot of the Philippines. PSSHR 19, no. 1 (Mar. 1954), 40-72.
          Madigan: Z   3/5   6
          Rixhon: Z   5   6
          Wernstedt: Excellent study of Cotabato city and racial/ethnic/religious integration.
                            Z   4/5   6

4089. LYNCH, RALPH. Some changes in Bukidnon between 1910 and 1950. AQ 28, no. 3 (July 1955), 95-115.
          Madigan: E/M   3   7

4090. MADIGAN, FRANCIS C. The early history of Cagayan de Oro. PS 11, no. 1 (Jan. 1963), 76-130.
          Madigan: Z   3/4   7
          Rixhon: Z   4   7

4091. MAJUL, CESAR ADIB. The role of Islam in the history of the Filipino people. AS 4, no. 2 (Aug. 1966), 303-315.

4092. MONTERO Y VIDAL, JOSÉ. Historia de la piratería malayo-mahometana en Mindanao, Joló y Borneo. Madrid, M. Tello, 1888. 2v.
          Frake: H   4   2/3
          Geoghegan: An excellent, detailed collection of secondary data on piracy. Includes important historical documents.
                            H   4   2/3
          Madigan: H   3   2/3

4093. QUIASON, SERAFIN D. Early contacts of the English East India company with Mindanao. PSSHR 26, no. 2 (June 1961), 175-186.

4094. ROGERS, DOROTHY M. A history of American occupation and administration of the Sulu archipelago, 1899-1920. 1959. 137p. Thesis (M.A.) - Univ. of San Francisco.
       Cited in Robert Youngblood, A Study of the 1963 Mayoralty Election in Jolo, Philippines. Thesis (M.A.) - Univ. of Hawaii. p. 260.
          Arce: H   3   4
          Madigan: H   3/4   4
          Rixhon: H   3   4
          Stone: Excellent study by daughter of last American governor of Sulu.
                            H   5   4

4095. SALEEBY, NAJEEB M. The history of Sulu. Manila, Bureau of Printing, 1908. 283p. Bureau of Science. Division of Ethnology. Publications. v.4, pt. 2.

Frake: G   4/5   1-3
Geoghegan: Important contribution to the history of the Tau Sug
              (primarily) and the Sultanate of Sulu.
                      G   4   7
Madigan: G   3/5   7
Nimmo: G   3   7
Rixhon: Includes interesting 'tarsilas' or genealogies of the
              Sulu Sultanate.
                      G   4   7

4096. _____. Studies in Moro history, law and religion. Manila, Bureau of Public Printing, 1905. 107p. 16 plates. (Philippine Islands. Ethnological
Survey. Publications vol. 4, pt. 1)
        Frake: G   4/5   1-3
        Gowing: Virtually the only study of its kind on the Moros.
                          G/D   5   7
        Madigan: G   3/5   7
        Nimmo: G   3   7
        Rixhon: Compilation of old Muslim codes of the Southern Philip-
                  pines which are no longer extant.
                          G   5   7
        Stone: Pioneer study. Baseline for any work.
                          G   5   7

4097. SANTAYANA, AGUSTIN. La isla de Mindanao, su historia y su estado presente...
Madrid, Impr. de Alhambra y Co., 1862. 127p.

4098. SCAFF, ALVIN H. Cultural factors in ecological change on Mindanao in the
Philippines. Social Forces 27, no. 1 (Dec. 1948), 119-123.
        Madigan: Z   3   7

4099. SMITH, C. N. The history of the Moros: a study in conquest and colonial
government. 1948. Thesis (M.A.) - Univ. of Chicago.

4100. WALLACE, WILLIAM M. Condition of Moro affairs in Sulu group (annual report
of Col. William M. Wallace, p.354-364; Moros of Philippines, by Rev. Pio Pi,
p.365-378; Brief Summary of historical accounts respecting the Spanish military operations against Moros, from the year 1578 to 1898 ... compiled
Lt. William E. McKinley, p.379-398. U.S. War Dept. Report, 1903, v.3.
House of Representatives. 58th Congress. 2d Session. Document no. 2.
        Madigan: G   3   7

INFANCY AND CHILDHOOD

4101. FLORES, ENYA P. Child rearing among a Moslem group in the Sulu archipelago,
Philippines. 1967. Thesis (Ph.D.) - Catholic Univ.
Suggested by Rixhon.
        Rixhon: E   4   6

4102. TEMPORAL, ALMA M. Some Filipino child-rearing practices and personality
development. SJ 15, no. 3 (Third Quarter 1968), 385-398.

LABOR

4103. FIERRO, ALFONSO C. DEL, JR. Economic impact of labor mobility on the city
of Cagayan de Oro. PSR 16, nos. 3/4 (July/Oct. 1968), 184-189.

LANGUAGE AND LITERATURE

4104. CAMERON, CHARLES R...Sulu writing, an explanation of the Sulu-Arabic script
as employed in writing the Sulu language of the southern Philippines. Zamboanga, P.I., Sulu press, 1917. 161p.
    Frake: An excellent manual for learning Sulu writing.
                  G   4/5   7
    Rixhon: G   4   4
    Ward: A manual for teaching the Arabic script.
                  G   5   4

4105. CONKLIN, HAROLD C. Preliminary linguistic survey of Mindanao. (In: Chicago. University. Philippine Studies Program. Mindanao Conference. Chicago,
1955. 10p. Mimeographed)
    Frake: E/L   4   7
    Ward: E   5   6

4106. MEYER, A. B. Ein Beitrage zu der Kenntniss der Sprachen auf Mindanao, Solog
und Sian, der Papuas der Astrolabe-Bay auf New-Guinea, der Negritos der Philippinen, und einige Bemerkungen über Herrn Riedel's Uebersetzungen ins Taga-
lische und Visayasche. Bijdragen tot de Taal-, Land- en Volkenkunde van Ne-
derlandsch- Indië. 20 (1871), 441-470.

4107. SALEEBY, NAJEEB M. Sulu reader for the public schools of the Moro Province.
Prepared by the Provincial Supt. of Schools, Zamboanga, Mindanao Herald
Press, 1905. 134p.
    Ward: Arabic script text with a primer for school use.
                  Y   3   4

MARRIAGE

4108. CAINGLET, EMETERIO B. The marriage customs among the Muslims in Bongcao,
Sulu and their educational significance. Cebu City, 1966. 96p. Thesis
(M.A.) - Univ. of San Carlos.
    Rixhon: Y   3   6

4109. GALANG, RICARDO C. Bukidnon marriage. PM 31, no. 5 (May 1934), 195, 209-
212.
Reprinted in JEAS 4, no. 2 (Apr. 1955), 260-264.

4110. MANUEL, E. ARSENIO. Manuvu marriage. U.P. Anthropology Bulletin 1, no. 1
(Sept. 1963), 8-9, 12.

Rixhon: E   4   6

4111. PAÑGATO, HUSSAIN S. Muslim divorce customs and practices as recognized by law. Far Eastern Law Review 8 (Dec. 1960), 481-505.

4112. SATHER, CLIFFORD. Social rank and marriage payments in an immigrant Moro community in Malaysia. Ethnology 6, no. 1 (Jan. 1967), 97-102.
Rixhon: E   4   6

MOBILITY AND SOCIAL STRATIFICATION

4113. HUNT, CHESTER L. Ethnic stratification and integration in Cotabato. (In: Chicago. Univ. Philippine Studies Program. Mindanao Conference. Chicago, 1955)
Published in PSR 5, no. 1 (Jan. 1957), 13-38.
Rixhon: Z   4   6

POLITICAL ORGANIZATION AND BEHAVIOR

4114. ARCE, WILFREDO FLORENDA. Leadership in a Muslim-Christian community in the Philippines. 1968. 220p. Thesis (Ph.D.) - Cornell Univ.

4115. GOWING, PETER G. Mandate in Moroland: the American government of Muslim Filipinos, 1899-1920. Syracuse, New York, 1968. 915p. Thesis (Ph.D.) - Syracuse Univ.

4116. _____. Muslim-American relations in the Philippines, 1899-1920. AS 6, no. 3 (Dec. 1968), 372-382.

4117. HAYDEN, JOSEPH RALSTON. What next for the Moro? Foreign Affairs 6, no. 4 (July 1928), 633-644.

4118. MAJUL, CESAR ADIB. Political and historical notes on the old Sulu Sultanate. Abstract and paper presented at International Conference on Asian History, Hong Kong, Aug. 30-Sept. 5, 1964. Paper no. 30. 14p.
Frake: H   4   7
Rixhon: H   3   7

4119. MEDNICK, MELVIN. Some problems of Moro history and political organization. (In: Chicago. Univ. Philippine Studies Program. Mindanao Conference. Chicago, 1955)
Published in PSR 5, no. 1 (Jan. 1957), 39-52.
Arce: E   4   7
Rixhon: E   4   6

4120. _____. Sultans and mayors: the relation of a national to an indigenous political system. IL Politico; revista di Scienze Politiche 26, no. 1

(Mar. 1961), 142-147.
        Rixhon: E   4   6

4121. O'SHAUGHNESSY, THOMAS J. Islamic law and non-Muslim governments. PS 12,
       no. 3 (July 1964), 439-445.
        Rixhon: M   4   6

4122. RAVENHOLT, ALBERT. The Amir Mindalano--profile of a Filipino Mohammedan
       leader. AUFSR. Southeast Asia Series 4, no. 10 (July 26, 1956), 11p.
       (AR-6-'56)

4123. SABER, MAMITUA DESARIP. The transition from a traditional to a legal au-
       thority system: a Philippine case. 1967. 220p. Thesis (Ph.D.) - Univ.
       of Kansas.

4124. SALEEBY, NAJEEB M. The Moro problem; an academic discussion of the history
       and solution of the problem of the government of the Moros of the Philip-
       pine Islands. Manila, P.I., Press of E. C. McCullough & Co., 1913. 31p.

4125. _____. Studies in Moro history, law and religion. Manila, Bureau of Pub-
       lic Printing, 1905. 107p. 16 plates. (Philippine Islands.Ethnological
       Survey. Publications. v.4, pt. 1)
        Frake: G   4/5   1-3
        Gowing: Virtually the only study of its kind on the Moros.
                         G/D   5   7
        Madigan: G   3/5   7
        Nimmo: G   3   7
        Rixhon: Compilation of old Muslim codes of the Southern Philip-
                         pines which are no longer extant.
                         G   5   7
        Stone: Pioneer study. Baseline for any work.
                         G   5   7

4126. SMITH, C. N. The history of the Moros. A study in conquest and colonial
       government. 1948. Thesis (M.A.), Univ. of Chicago.

4127. YOUNGBLOOD, ROBERT L. A study of the 1963 mayoralty election in Joló, Phil-
       ippines. Honolulu, 1966. 260p. Thesis (M.A.) - Univ. of Hawaii.
        Arce: V   5   6
        Grossholtz: Documents changes in the political elite of Sulu from
                         American period to present.
                         V   3   6
        Nimmo: V   3   6
        Rixhon: Factual and accurate.
                         V   4   6

PROPERTY AND EXCHANGE

4128. REBOLOS, ZENAIDA. Promissory and dept (i.e., debt) aspects of the folk
       ritual in Misamis Oriental, by Zenaida Robolos (sic). PSR 12, nos. 1/2
       (Jan./Apr. 1964), 95-101.

Madigan: Z   5   6
Rixhon: Z   4   6

RELIGIOUS BELIEFS AND PRACTICES

4129. BILLMAN, CUTHBERT. Islam in Sulu. PS 8, no. 1 (Jan. 1960), 51-57.
    Gowing: Good general description by a veteran missionary educator
                     in Sulu.
                     M/Y   4   6
    Madigan: Y/M   3/5   6
    Stone: M/Y   5   6

4130. CHAVES, SISTER MARIA ASUNCION. A survey of religious instruction in Misamis
    and Bukidnon. 1963. 129p. Thesis (M.A.) - Xavier Univ.
    Madigan: M/Y   5   6

4131. COLE, FAY-COOPER. Central Mindanao; the country and its people. Far Eastern
    Quarterly 4, no. 2 (Feb. 1945), 109-118.
    Madigan: E   4   4

4132. CUSHNER, NICOLÁS. Las fiestas de "Moros y Cristianos" en las Islas Filipinas.
    Revista de Historia de América, no. 52 (Diciembre 1961), 518-520.
    Madigan: H   5   7

4133. GRISHAM, GLEN. Benguet cañaos. PM 27, no. 12 (May 1931), 724, 748-749.

4134. HUNT, CHESTER L. Moslem and Christian in the Philippines. Pacific Affairs
    28, no. 4 (Dec. 1955), 331-349.
    Gowing: Good summary of major problems.
                     Z   4   6
    Madigan: Z   3   7

4135. JESUITS. LETTERS FROM MISSIONS (PHILIPPINE ISLANDS). Cartas de los padres
    de la Compañía de Jesús de la Mision de Filipinas...Manila, Impr. de los
    Amigos de país, 1877-1895. 10v. Imprint varies.
    Contents analyzed in Streit. Bibliotheca Missionum. v.9:
         p.186-187, 192-194, 200-202, 217-219, 229-232, 256-259, 260-263, 275-279,
         293-299, 350-359.
    For anthropological index to Cartas de los padres..., see Frank Lynch, The
    Jesuit letters of Mindanao as a source of anthropological data. PS 4,
    no. 2 (June 1956), 247-272.
    Frake: M   5   3
    Gowing: Invaluable source of ethnographic data for the second
                     half of 19th century.
                     M   5   3
    Yengoyan: Excellent primary source for Eastern Mindanao.
                     M   5   3

4136. LAUBACH, FRANK C. Christianity and Islam in Lanao. Moslem World 25, no. 1
    (Jan. 1935), 45-49.
    Gowing: Reportorial in character.

460

	M/D	3	4
Madigan:	M/D	3	4

4137. MADIGAN, FRANCIS C. The harvest ritual in North Central Mindanao. Sociological Analysis 25, no. 4 (Winter 1964), 231-237.

Madigan:	Z	5	6

4138. _____ and NICHOLAS P. CUSHNER. Tamontaka reduction: a community approach to Mission work. Neue Zeitschrift für Missionswissenschaft 17, no. 2 (1961), 81-94.

Madigan:	Z and H	4/5	3

4139. _____ and ZENAIDA N. REBOLOS. Folk-rituals of the Misamis-Bukidnon area: a preliminary report. PSR 11, nos. 1/2 (Jan./Apr. 1963), 155-159.

Madigan:	Z and Z	5	6

4140. O'SHAUGHNESSY, THOMAS J. Islam - surrender to God. PS 15, no. 1 (Jan. 1967), 108-129.

4141. REBOLOS, ZENAIDA N. Promissory and dept (i.e., debt) aspects of the folk ritual in Misamis Oriental, by Zenaida Robolos (sic). PSR 12, nos. 1/2 (Jan./Apr. 1964), 95-101.

Madigan:	Z	5	6
Rixhon:	Z	4	6

4142. SALEEBY, NAJEEB M. Studies in Moro history, law and religion. Manila, Bureau of Public Printing, 1905. 107p. 16 plates. (Philippine Islands. Ethnological Survey. Publications vol. 4, pt. 1)

Frake:	G	4/5	7
Gowing:	Virtually the only study of its kind on the Moros.		
	G/D	5	7
Madigan:	G	3/5	7
Nimmo:	G	3	7
Rixhon:	Compilation of old Muslim codes of the Southern Philippines which are no longer extant.		
	G	5	7
Stone:	Pioneer study. Baseline for any work.		
	G	5	7

4143. SCHLEGEL, STUART A. The Upi Espiritistas: a case study in cultural adjustment. Journal for the Scientific Study of Religion 4, no. 2 (Apr. 1965), 198-212.

4144. STOFFEL, JOSEPH I. Historical background of the Lamitan Parish (in Basilan Island) n.d. Privately printed? 27p.
Verified in Alfredo T. Tiamson, Mindanao-Sulu Bibliography. 1970. p.207.

Madigan:	M	4/5	7

4145. SUMMER, G. V., JR. Customs of the Lanao tribe of Moros. (In: H. Otley Beyer and F. D. Holleman. A collection of source material for the study of Philippine customary law. v.5, ser. I, no. 3, #29)

Gowing:	G	3	4

SOCIAL PROBLEMS

4146. EWING, J. FRANKLIN. Juramentado: institutionalized suicide among the Moros of the Philippines. AQ 28, no. 4 (Oct. 1955), 148-155.
    Gowing: First-rate treatment of the subject.
                  M/E   4   7
    Madigan: E/D   4   4

STANDARD OF LIVING AND RECREATION

4147. CUSHNER, NICOLÁS. Las fiestas de "Moros y Cristianos" en las Islas Filipinas. Revista de Historia de América, no. 52 (Diciembre 1961), 518-520.
    Madigan: H   5   7

TOTAL CULTURE

4148. ARCE, WILFREDO F. Social organization of the Muslim peoples of Sulu. PS 11, no. 2 (Apr. 1963), 242-266.
        Frake: E   5   6
        Gowing: Clear, helpful description.
                  Z   5   6
        Nimmo: E   3   6
        Stone: Pioneer paper on Muslim social organization.
                  E   5   6

4149. MADIGAN, FRANCIS and NICHOLAS P. CUSHNER. Tamontaka: a sociological experiment. American Catholic Sociological Review 19, no. 4 (Dec. 1958), 322-336.
    Madigan: Z and H   4/5   3

4150. STONE, RICHARD L. Some aspects of Muslim social organization. (In: Manuud, Antonio G., ed. Brown heritage: essays on Philippine cultural tradition and literature. Quezon City, Ateneo de Manila Univ. Press, 1967. p.90-133)

TRANSPORTATION

4151. TAYLOR, CARL N. Sailing the Sulu sea with the Moros. Travel 60, no. 1 (Nov. 1932), 7-12, 41.

4152. _____. The sea gypsies of Sulu. Asia (New York) 31 (Aug. 1931), 476-483, 534-535.
    Gowing: -   3   4

B. BY CULTURAL-LINGUISTIC GROUP

BAGOBO

4153. BENEDICT, LAURA WATSON. Bagobo fine art collection. American Museum Journal 11, (1911), 164-171.

4154. _____. People who have two souls, [a belief of the Bagobo]. (In: Mead, Margaret, ed. Primitive heritage, an anthropological anthology. New York, Random House, 1953. p.577-583)

4155. _____. A study of Bagobo ceremonial, magic and myth. [New York, 1916] 308p. Thesis (Ph.D.) - Columbia Univ.
"Reprinted from the Annals of the New York Academy of Sciences, v.25 ... 1916."

4156. COLE, FAY C. The Bagobos of Davao Gulf. PJS 6D, no. 3 (June 1911), 127-138. 4 plates.

4157. HALL, HENRY U. The Bagobo; some notes on a lately acquired collection. Pennsylvania. University. Univ. Museum Journal 7, no. 3 (1916), 182-194.

4158. KALAW, MAXIMO M. The Moro Bugaboo. The Philippine Question, an analysis. PSSHR 3, no. 4 (Sept. 1931), 368-379.

4159. METCALF, ELIZABETH H. The people of Sandao-a. AA 14, no. 1 (Jan./Mar. 1912), 161-163.

4160. MEYER, A. B. Album of the Filipino-types. III. Negritos, Manguianes, Bagobos. About 190 figures on 37 plates in heliptype. Dresden, W. Hoffman, 1904. Text in German and English.

4161. PRICE, WILLARD. The mysterious land of the Bagobos. Natural History 60, no. 8 (Oct. 1951), 344-351, 383.

4162. SCHADENBERG, ALEXANDER. Die Bewohner von Süd-Mindanao und der Insel Samal. ZE 17 (1885), 8-37, 45-57. Bagobo vocabulary, p.33-36.
      Tangco: "Among his (Schadenberg) numerous publications dealing with Philippine ethnography, the most noteworthy are ... Die Bewohner von Sud-Mindanao..." PSSHR, Aug. 1940, p.195-196.

4163. SMITH, WARREN D. An account of a human sacrifice held by the Bagobos, district of Davao, Mindanao, P.I. PJS 3A, no. 3 (June 1908), 188-196. 3 plates.

4164. WILLOUGHBY, C. C. The Peabody museum Bagobo collection. Harvard Alumni Bulletin 19, no. 19 (Feb. 8, 1917), 368-369.

BADJAW - GENERAL

4165. ARONG, JOSE R. The Badjaw of Sulu. PSR 10, nos. 3/4 (July/Oct. 1962), 134-147.
      Nimmo: E   3   6

4166. NIMMO, H. ARLO. The Bajau of Sulu--fiction and fact. PS 16, no. 4 (Oct. 1968), 771-776.

4167. _____. Reflections on Bajau history. PS 16, no. 1 (Jan. 1968), 32-59. Suggested by Rixhon.
      Rixhon   E   4   6

4168. STONE, RICHARD L. Intergroup relations among the Taosug, Samal, and Badjaw of the Sulu archipelago. 1965. 153p. Thesis (M.A.) - Univ. of Hawaii.
      Frake: E   5   6
      Nimmo: E   3   6
      Stone: Single community study of group stereotypes and interactions.
                         E   5   6
      Trimillos: E   5   6

4169. TAYLOR, CARL N. The sea gypsies of Sulu. Asia (New York) 31, no. 8 (Aug. 1931), 476-483, 534-535.
      Gowing: -   3   4

BADJAW - BEHAVIOR PROCESS AND PERSONALITY

4170. NIMMO, HARRY A. Themes in Badjaw dreams. PSR 14, no. 1 (Jan. 1966), 49-56.
      Nimmo: E   3   6

4171. STONE, RICHARD L. Intergroup relations among the Taosug, Samal, and Badjaw of Sulu. PSR 10, nos. 3/4 (July/Oct. 1962), 107-133.
      Arce: E   5   6
      Frake: E   5   6
      Nimmo: E   3   6
      Stone: Basic survey paper on Sulu groups.
                         E   5   6
      Trimillos: E   5   6

BADJAW - EDUCATION

4172. CABRERA, AGUSTIN A. Status of the education of the Badjaos of Sulu. Manila, 1967. 99p. Thesis (M.A.) - Univ. of Santo Tomas. Suggested by Rixhon.
      Rixhon: Y   4   6

BADJAW - FAMILY AND KINSHIP

4173. NIMMO, HARRY. Social organization of the Tawi-Tawi Badjaw. Ethnology 4,
no. 4 (Oct. 1965), 421-439.
       Geoghegan: Much useful information, but there are many errors with
                     regard to kinship terminology and social organization.
                     E   2/3   6
       Nimmo: E   3   6

BADJAW - FINE ARTS

4174. NIMMO, HARRY ARLO. Songs of the Sulu sea. Etc.: A Review of General Seman-
tics 25, no. 4 (Dec. 1968), 489-494.

4175. SZANTON, DAVID. Art in Sulu. PS 11, no. 3 (July 1963), 463-502. 86 figures.
       Geoghegan: A fairly complete account of the art forms among the Samal
                     and Badjaw of Sulu. Set of good to excellent photographs.
                     E   3   6
       Nimmo: E   5   6
       Rixhon: First systematic study of the Sulu's art forms in wood and
                     stone.
                     E   5   6
       Stone: Excellent photographic study of indigenous art of Sulu.
                     E   5   6
       Trimillos: Good reproduction general survey.
                     E   5   6

BADJAW - LANGUAGE AND LITERATURE

4176. SATHER, CLIFFORD A. Bajau numbers and adjectives of quantity. Sabah Society
Journal 2, no. 4 (July 1965), 194-197.

BADJAW - TOTAL CULTURE

4177. NIMMO, HARRY. Social organization of the Tawi-Tawi Badjaw. Honolulu, 1965.
169p. Thesis (M.A.) - Univ. of Hawaii.
       Nimmo: E   3   6

BILAAN

4178. ALANO, SEGUNDO. The Bila-ans of Cotabato. PM 33, no. 5 (May 1936), 237-238, 270-271.

4179. CABRERA, SANTIAGO B. The origin, folkways and customs of the Bilaans of Southern Cotabato. Unitas 40, no. 1 (Mar. 1967), 182-193.

4180. DEAN, JAMES and GLADYS DEAN. The phonemes of Bilaan. PJS 84, no. 3 (Sept. 1955), 311-322.

4181. GENOTIVA, LORENZO C. Bilaan religious beliefs and practices. SJ 13, no. 1 (First Quarter 1966), 56-74.
    Yengoyan: Useful as a starting point.
            -    3   6

BUKIDNON GROUPS

4182. CLOTET, JOSÉ MARÍA. The Bukidnon of North-Central Mindanao in 1889. Translated by Frank Lynch. PS 15, no. 3 (July 1967), 464-482.

4183. COLE, FAY-COOPER. The Bukidnon of Mindanao. [Chicago] Chicago Natural History Museum, 1956. 140p. ([Chicago. Natural History Museum] Publication 792)

4184. CULLON [i.e. CULLEN], VINCENT G. The spirit world of the Bukidnon. Asian Folklore Studies 27, pt. 2 (1968), 17-25.

4185. GALANG, RICARDO C. Bukidnon marriage. PM 31, no. 5 (May 1934), 195, 209-212.
    Reprinted in JEAS 4, no. 2 (Apr. 1955), 260-264.

4186. _____. Pamuhat - the Bukidnon's religious sacrifice. PM 34, no. 2 (Feb. 1937), 71, 80, 82.
    Madigan: J   2/3   4

4187. LYNCH, FRANK (translator). The Bukidnon of North-Central Mindanao in 1889. Annotated translation of a Spanish source prepared for the participants in the Mindanao Conference...Letter of Father José María Clotet to the Rev. Father Rector of the Ateneo Municipal. (In: Chicago. University. Philippine Studies Program. Conference on Mindanao. Proceedings. Chicago, May 13-15, 1955. Chicago, 1955. 12p. Dittoed)
    Warren: Most complete single document on Bukidnon published during Spanish regime.
            M   5   3

4188. LYNCH, RALPH E. The Bukidnons of northern Mindanao: 1945-1955. (In: Chicago. University. Philippine Studies Program. Conference on Mindanao. Proceedings. Chicago, May 13-15, 1955. Chicago, 1955. 81p. Mimeographed)

4189. SITOY, TRANQUILINO. The Bukidnon ascension to heaven. PM 34, no. 10 (Oct.

1937), 445-446, 465-466.

4190. SITOY, T. VALENTINO, JR. The encounter between Christianity and Bukidnon animism. Southeast Asia Journal of Theology 10, nos. 2/3 (Oct. 1968/Jan. 1969), 53-79.

JAMA MAPUN

4191. CASIÑO, ERIC S. Folk-Islam in the life cycle of the Jama Mapun. PSR 15, nos. 1/2 (Jan./Apr. 1967), 34-48.

4192. _____. Jama Mapun ethnoecology: economic and symbolic (of grains, winds, and stars). AS 5, no. 1 (Apr. 1967), 1-32.

4193. _____. Lunsay: song-dance of the Jama Mapun of Sulu. AS 4, no. 2 (Aug. 1966), 316-323.
    Rixhon: E   5   6
    Trimillos: E   3   6

4194. _____. Stars over the Philippines. SR 8, no. 1 (Jan. 1967), 3-5.

MAGINDANAO

4195. COSTA, HORACIO DE LA. A Spanish Jesuit among the Magindanaus. Comment 12 (First Quarter 1961), 19-41.

4196. ENOC, PASANDALAN. Marriage among the Magindanaws. Philippines Today 9, no. 3 (1963), 13-15.

4197. LEE, ERNEST W. On non-syllabic high vocoids in Maguindanao. Studies in Linguistics 16, nos. 3/4 (Fall 1962), 65-72.

4198. LEWIS-MINTON, FRANK. Indarapatra and Sulayman; an epic of Magindanao. PM 26, no. 4 (Sept. 1929), 200-202, 236.

4199. MACEDA, JOSÉ. Magindanao music. PS 9, no. 4 (Oct. 1961), 666-671.
    Rixhon: R/E   4   6
    Trimillos: R/E   3   6

4200. _____. The music of the Magindanao in the Philippines. Los Angeles, 1963. 2 vols. Thesis (Ph.D.) - Univ. of California, Los Angeles.
    Spencer: Professor of Music in Philippines. Dissertation. Recorded scores of musical tunes of Moros.
                   R/E   5   6
    Trimillos: Most definitive study to date on Magindanao.
                   R/E   5   6
    Warren: R/E   5   6

4201. _____. The setting of Magindanao music. DR 7, no. 3 (July 1959), 308-316.

MAMANWA

4202. BLUMENTRITT, FERDINAND. Die Nachrichten der Jesuitenmissionäre P. Francisco
Sanchez, P. Llovera und P. Peruga: Ueber die Negritos von Mindanao oder die
Mamanuas. Internationales Archiv für Ethnographie 9 (1896), 251-252.
    Maceda: Evaluation of reports by the Jesuit missionaries.
    E   4   7

4203. COOPER, JOHN M. Andamanese-Semang-Eta cultural relations. Primitive Man 13,
no. 2 (Apr. 1940), 29-47.

4204. MACEDA, MARCELINO N. The culture of the Mamanua (Northeast Mindanao) as compared with that of the other negritos of Southeast Asia. Cebu City, 1964.
148p. (San Carlos Univ. Publications. Series A: Humanities. no. 1) His
Ph.D. Thesis - Univ. of Fribourg. 1959.
    Maceda: Comparative data with sizable bibliography.
    E   5   6

4205. _____. The full-moon prayer-ceremony of the Mamanuas of northeastern Mindanao. Anthropos 52, (1957), 277-284.
    Maceda: A description of full-moon ceremony.
    E   5   6

4206. _____. Some medicinal plants known to the Mamanua of northeastern Mindanao,
Philippines. (In: Festschrift Paul Schebesta zum 75. Geburtstag. Wien-
Mödling, 1963. p.133-136) (Studia Instituti Anthropos, v.18)
    Maceda: An early attempt for recording useful plants for the Mama-
                nua.
    E   5   6

4207. _____. A survey of the socio-economic, religious, and educational conditions of the Mamanuas of Northeast Mindanao. Cebu City, 1954. 169p. Thesis
(M.A.) - Univ. of San Carlos.
    Maceda: An early attempt to study the Mamanua.
    E   5   6

4208. _____. Urgent research among the Negritos of the Philippines, especially
among the southern groups. International Committee on Urgent Anthropological
and Ethnological Research. Bulletin no. 5 (1962), 29-31.

4209. _____. Utilization of a poisonous root by the Mamanuas. Carolinian (Cebu
City) 19, no. 4 (1956), 15-35.
Cited in Lynch and Hollnsteiner. Sixty years of Philippine ethnology. (In:
Philippines (Republic) National Science Development Board. Area VI-Social
Sciences. Manila, 1963)
    Maceda: A short report on plant utilization.
    E   5   6

4210. QUATREFAGES DE BRÉAU, ARMAND DE. The pygmies. London. (Translation of Les
       Pygmées, by Frederick Starr. 1887.) New York, D. Appleton, 1895. 255p.
       Chapter 5. Aetas of Luzon, and Mamanuas of Mindanao.
           Maceda: A small part of the work treats about the Negritos.
                           E   4   7
           Warren: -   5   3

4211. RAHMANN, RUDOLF. A thunderstorm blood-offering of the Mamanua Negritos of
       northeastern Mindanao. (In: Haekel, Josef. Die wiener schule der völker-
       kunde. Horn-Wien, 1956. p.369-371)
           Maceda: A comparison of the phenomenon of blood sacrifice.
                           E   5   6

4212. VERSTRAELEN, EUGENE. Some elementary data of the Mamanua language. Anthro-
       pos 60, fas. 1/6 (1965), 803-815.

MANDAYA - MANSAKA

4213. GARVAN, JOHN M. Report on drinks and drinking among the Mandaya, Manobo, and
       Mangguangan tribes. (In: The Alcohol Industry of the Philippine Islands.
       Part III, by H. D. Gibbs and F. Agcaoili. PJS 7A, no. 2 (Apr. 1912), 106-
       117)
           Yengoyan: Acute observation.
                           G/Y 5   4

4214. YENGOYAN, ARAM A. Aspects of ecological succession among Mandaya populations
       in Eastern Davao Province, Philippines. Michigan Academy of Science, Arts
       and Letters. Papers. 50, (1964), 437-443.
           Yengoyan: Description of population shift and differences, and so-
                           cial organizational differences.
                           E   5   6

4215. _____. Baptism and "Bisayanization" among the Mandaya of Eastern Mindanao,
       Philippines. AS 4, no. 2 (Aug. 1966), 324-327.
           Yengoyan: E   5   6

4216. _____. Environment, shifting cultivation, and social organization among the
       Mandaya of Eastern Mindanao, Philippines. 1964. 214p. Thesis (Ph.D.) -
       Univ. of Chicago.
           Yengoyan: Work on shifting cultivation and social organization and
                           ecological implications.
                           E   5   6

4217. _____. Marketing networks and economic processes among the abaca cultivating
       Mandaya of eastern Mindanao, Philippines. New York, Agricultural Development
       Council, 1966. 35p.
       Reprinted and abstracted in: Borton, Raymond E., ed. Selected readings to
       accompany getting agriculture moving. New York, Agricultural Development
       Council, 1966. v.2. p.689-701.
       Suggested by Yengoyan.
           Yengoyan: E   5   6

4218. _____. Survey reports to Ford Foundation. 1960-1962.
    1. Mandaya-Manobe communities in northeast Davao Province, Surigao del
       Sur, and southeast Agusan. Dec. 31, 1960. 11p. Mimeographed.
    2-3. Mandaya-Mansaka communities in eastern Davao Province. Mar. 26, 1961.
       15p. Mimeographed.
    4-6. Status of fieldwork among the Mandaya of upper Manay and Caraga, Davao
       Province. Sept. 26, 1961, Jan. 10, 1962, and June 7, 1962. 9p. Mimeo-
       graphed.
    Yengoyan: General reports.
               E   3   6

MANGGUANGAN

4219. GARVAN, JOHN M. Report on drinks and drinking among the Mandaya, Manobo, and
Mangguangan tribes. (In: The Alcohol Industry of the Philippine Islands.
Part III, by H. D. Gibbs and F. Agcaoili. PJS 7A, no. 2 (Apr. 1912), 106-
117)
    Yengoyan: Acute observation.
           G/Y   5   4

MANOBO GROUPS - GENERAL

4220. AUSTIN, VIRGINIA MOREY. Attention, emphasis, and focus in Ata Manobo. 1966.
149p. Thesis (M.A.) - Hartford Seminary Foundation. (Hartford studies in
linguistics, no. 20)

4221. BARNARD, MYRA L., ALICE LINDQUIST and VIVIAN FORSBERG. Cotabato Manobo survey. PSSHR 20, no. 2 (June 1955), 121-136.
    Pfeiffer: A brief but significant autobiographical travel monograph.
          L   5   6

4222. BORNEMANN, FRITZ. J. M. Garvans Materialien über die Negrito der Philippinen
und P. W. Schmidts Notizen dazu. Anthropos 50, (1955), 899-930.

4223. GARVAN, JOHN M. The manóbos of Mindanáo. Washington, U.S. Government Printing Office, 1931. 265p. 14 plates. (Memoirs of the National Academy of
Sciences, v.23, no. 1)
    Pfeiffer: Based on field notes taken ca. 1912.
          G/Y   5   4

4224. _____. A survey of the material and sociological culture of the Manobo of
eastern Mindanao. AA 29, no. 4 (Oct./Dec. 1927), 567-604.

4225. The Irayas, Ygorrotes, and Manobos of the Philippines. Journal of Anthropology 1, no. 3 (Jan. 1871), 296-307.

4226. MARTIN-ROQUERO, CORAZON TENORIO. The culture of the Central Mindanao Manobos. CEU. GFS 19 (1968), 33-47.

4227. OLSON, WILLIAM H. Beyond the plains; a study of the northern Cotabato Manobos. Manila, Christian Institute for the Study of Ethnic Communities, United
Church of Christ, 1967. 49p.

4228. REYNOLDS, HUBERT. The multi-level house of the Manobo in Salangsang and its
inter-relations with other aspects of culture. SJ 13, no. 4 (Fourth Quarter 1966), 581-593.

4229. SVELMOE, GORDON and NORMAN ABRAMS. A brief field trip among the Bukidnon
Tigwa people and the Davao Salug people. PSSHR 18, no. 2 (June 1953), 141-
185.

4230. VAN ODIJK, A. Ethnographische Gegevens over de Manobo's van Mindanao, Phil-
ippijnen. Anthropos 20, fas. 3/4 (May/Aug. 1925), 981-1000. 1 plate.

4231. YENGOYAN, ARAM A. Survey reports to Ford Foundation. 1960-1962. 1. Man-
daya-Manobo communities in Northeast Davao Province, Surigao del Sur, and
southeast Agusan. Dec. 31, 1960. 11p. Mimeographed.
        Yengoyan: General reports.
                       E   3   6

MANOBO GROUPS - ARCHAEOLOGY

4232. MACEDA, MARCELINO N. Preliminary report on ethnographic and archaeological
field work in the Kulaman Plateau, Island of Mindanao, Philippines. Anthropos 59, fas. 1/2 (1964), 75-82.

MANOBO GROUPS - DRINK, DRUGS AND INDULGENCE

4233. GARVAN, JOHN M. Report on drinks and drinking among the Mandaya, Manobo, and
Mangguangan tribes. (In: The Alcohol Industry of the Philippine Islands.
Part III, by H. D. Gibbs and F. Agcaoili. PJS 7A, no. 2 (Apr. 1912), 106-
117)
        Yengoyan: Acute observation.
                       G/Y   5   4

MANOBO GROUPS - FAMILY AND KINSHIP

4234. ELKINS, RICHARD E. A matrix display of Western Bukidnon Manobo kinship.
PSR 12, nos. 1/2 (Jan./Apr. 1964), 122-129.

Pfeiffer: L   5   6

4235. _____. Three models of western Bukidnon Manobo kinship. Ethnology 7, no. 2 (Apr. 1968), 171-189.

MANOBO GROUPS - FINE ARTS

4236. PFEIFFER, WILLIAM R. A musical analysis of some ritual songs of the Manobo of north central Cotabato on Mindanao Island in the Philippines. Honolulu, 1965. 636p. Thesis (M.A.) - Univ. of Hawaii.
      Pfeiffer: R   3   6
      Trimillos: Did not do his own fieldwork; analysis is (5) but social context is (4).
                E/R   4/5   6

MANOBO GROUPS - LANGUAGE AND LITERATURE

4237. BARNARD, MYRA L. Dibabawon nonverbal clauses. (In: Zamora, Mario D., ed. Studies in Philippine anthropology (In honor of H. Otley Beyer). Quezon City, Philippines, 1967. p.559-566)

4238. ELKINS, RICHARD E. Major grammatical patterns of Western Bukidnon Manobo. Honolulu, 1967. 136p. Thesis (Ph.D.) - Univ. of Hawaii.

4239. _____. Manobo - English dictionary. Honolulu, Univ. of Hawaii Press, 1968. 356p. (Oceanic linguistics. Special publication, no. 3)

4240. KERR, HARLAND B. The case-marking and classifying function of Cotabato Manobo voice affixes. Oceanic Linguistics 4, nos. 1/2 (1965), 15-47.

4241. VERSTRAELEN, EUGENE. Some elementary data of the Manobo language. Anthropos 63/64, fas. 5/6 (1968/1969), 808-817.

MANOBO GROUPS - MARRIAGE

4242. MCELROY, BARTON L. The ideal and the practical in Manobo marriage. U.P. Anthropology Bulletin 3, no. 1 (First Semester 1967/1968), 3-5.

MANOBO GROUPS - RELIGIOUS BELIEFS AND PRACTICES

4243. ELKINS, RICHARD. The Anit taboo: a Manobo cultural unit. Practical Anthropology 11, no. 4 (July/Aug. 1964), 185-188.

4244. KUIZON, JOSE G. The social significance of the Agusan Manobo myths. PSR 11, nos. 1/2 (Jan./Apr. 1963), 130-134.

MARANAO - GENERAL

4245. HOSILLOS, LUCILA. A concept of Maranaw culture change. Exchange no. 35 (Second Quarter 1965), 38-40.

4246. RIVERA, GENEROSO F. The Maranao Muslims in Lumbayao, Lanao. PSR 14, no. 3 (July 1966), 127-134.

4247. SABER, MAMITUA, MAUYAG TAMANO and CHARLES WARRINER. The Maratabat of the Maranao. PSR 8, nos. 1/2 (Jan./Apr. 1960), 10-15.

MARANAO - AGRICULTURE AND FOOD

4248. MCKAUGHAN, HOWARD P. and BATUA A. MACARAYA. Maranao plant names. Oceanic Linguistics 4, nos. 1/2 (1965), 48-112.

4249. RAMOS, MAXIMO. The Maranao Bansulat. PM 36, no. 4 (Apr. 1939), 168, 175.

MARANAO - COMMUNITY DEVELOPMENT AND TERRITORIAL ORGANIZATION

4250. SABER, MAMITUA. Problems of community development among cultural minorities. PSR 8, nos. 3/4 (July/Oct. 1960), 52-59.

MARANAO - EDUCATION

4251. LAUBACH, FRANK. The Lanao system of teaching illiterates. PM 29, no. 1 (June 1932), 16, 41-45.

4252. MADALE, ABDULLAH T. A preliminary study of Maranaw customs, practices, and beliefs and how they affect the administration and supervision of public

elementary schools in Lanao del Sur and Marawi City. 1966. Thesis (M.A.) -
Philippine Normal College.
Source: Rosalina Miravite. Philippine Muslims: a preliminary history and
bibliography. Paper prepared for Asian Studies 699, Univ. of Hawaii. 1967.
    Stone: I/E   3   6

MARANAO - FINE ARTS

4253. DENSMORE, FRANCES. Scale formation in primitive music. AA n.s. 11, no. 1
(Jan./Mar. 1909), 1-12.
    Stone: B/R   5   4
    Trimillos: Her musical conclusions are not entirely valid.
                E   3   4

4254. HARTENDORP, A. V. H. The art of the Lanao Moros. PQ 2, no. 2 (Sept. 1953),
8-13.
    Trimillos: Good illustrations.
                J   3   4

4255. LAUBACH, FRANK. Songs of my seven lovers. PM 31, no. 7 (July 1934), 295-
297.
    Trimillos: Song texts only; no music.
                M   5   4

4256. MERCADO, MARIO A. The Maranaos and their art. PQ 1, no. 1 (Oct./Dec. 1960),
26-29.
    Trimillos: Secondary sources.
                -     3   6

4257. RAMOS, MAXIMO. The Maranao Kutiapi. PM 36, no. 7 (July 1939), 296, 298-299.

MARANAO - LANGUAGE AND LITERATURE

4258. MCKAUGHAN, HOWARD P. The inflection and syntax of Maranao verbs. Ithaca,
N.Y. 1957. 99p. Thesis (Ph.D.) - Cornell Univ.

4259. _____. Relation markers in Maranao verbs. Pacific Science Congress. 9th,
Bangkok, 1957. Proceedings. Bangkok, 1963. 3: 81-83.

4260. VOEGELIN, CHARLES F. and F. M. VOEGELIN. Languages of the world: Indo-
Pacific. Fas. 4 - "Maranao". Anthropological Linguistics 7, no. 2 (Feb.
1965), 227-264.

4261. WARD, ROBERT G. and JANNETTE FORSTER. Verb stem classes in Maranao transitive
clauses. Anthropological Linguistics 9, no. 6 (June 1967), 30-42.

4262. SABER, MAMITUA. Marginal leadership in a culture-contact situation. 1957.
Thesis (M.A.) - Univ. of Kansas.
Cited in PSR, July/Oct. 64, p. 175.

4263. SANTOS, RUFINO DE LOS. A program to bring the Maranaws within the body pol-
itic of the Republic of the Philippines. 1950. Thesis (M.A.) - Silliman
Univ.

4264. WARRINER, CHARLES K. Traditional authority and the modern state: the case
of the Maranao of the Philippines. Social Problems 12, no. 1 (Summer 1964),
51-56. Also in PSR 12, nos. 3/4 (July/Oct. 1964), 172-177.

MARANAO - RELIGIOUS BELIEFS AND PRACTICES

4265. MCAMIS, ROBERT D. An introduction to the folk tales of the Marano Muslims
of Mindanao in the Southern Philippines. Chicago, Philippine Studies Program,
Dept. of Anthropology, Univ. of Chicago, 1966. 103p. (Transcript series
no. 9)

4266. MADALE, ABDULLAH T. A preliminary study of Maranaw customs, practices, and
beliefs and how they affect the administration and supervision of public elementary schools in Lanao del Sur and Marawi City. 1966. Thesis (M.A.) -
Philippine Normal College.
Source: Rosalina Miravite. Philippine Muslims: a preliminary history and
bibliography. Paper prepared for Asian Studies 699, Univ. of Hawaii. 1967.
    Stone: I/E   3   6

4267. WARRINER, CHARLES K. Myths, Moros and the Maranao. Exchange News Quarterly,
no. 10 (Jan./Mar. 1959), 2-3, 20.

MARANAO - TOTAL CULTURE

4268. MEDNICK, MELVIN. Encampment of the lake; the social organization of a Moslem-
Philippine (Moro) people. Chicago, Philippine Studies Program, Dept. of An-
thropology, Univ. of Chicago, 1965. 380p. (Research series, no. 5) His
Ph.D. Thesis - Univ. of Chicago, 1965.
    Frake: E   5   6
    Gowing: A thorough study of Maranao society.
                    E   5   6
    Nimmo: E   5   6
    Stone: E   5   6

4269. BLUMENTRITT, FERDINAND. Yákanen und Sámal-laut der Insel Basilan (Philippinen). Ausland 65, no. 52 (Dec. 24, 1892), 818-821.
      Stone: N   5   3

4270. DENSMORE, FRANCES. Scale formation in primitive music. AA n.s. 11, no. 1 (Jan./Mar. 1909), 1-12.
      Stone: B/R   5   4
      Trimillos: Her musical conclusions are not entirely valid.
                  E   3   4

4271. DUCOMMUN, DOLORES. Sisangat: a Sulu fishing community. PSR 10, nos. 3/4 (July/Oct. 1962), 91-107.
      Arce: E   5   6
      Geoghegan: Thin in general, but useful because of the lack of information on this group.
                  E   2/3   6
      Madigan: E   3/5   6
      Nimmo: E   3   6
      Stone: Not expertly written but contains basic information.
                  E   5   6

4272. ESLAO, NENA B. Child-rearing among the Samal of Manubul, Siasi, Sulu. PSR 10, nos. 3/4 (July/Oct. 1962), 80-91.
      Arce: E   5   6
      Geoghegan: An interesting sketch of child-training practices in a little-studied area.
                  E   3   6
      Nimmo: E   3   6
      Stone: Excellent basic data on one Sulu ethnic group.
                  E   5   6

4273. STONE, RICHARD L. Intergroup relations among the Taosug, Samal and Badjaw of Sulu. PSR 10, nos. 3/4 (July/Oct. 1962), 107-133.
      Arce: E   5   6
      Frake: E   5   6
      Nimmo: E   3   6
      Stone: Basic survey paper on Sulu groups.
                  E   5   6
      Trimillos: E   5   6

4274. _____. Intergroup relations among the Taosug, Samal, and Badjaw of the Sulu archipelago. 1965. 153p. Thesis (M.A.) - Univ. of Hawaii.
      Frake: E   5   6
      Nimmo: E   3   6
      Stone: Single community study of group stereotypes and interactions.
                  E   5   6
      Trimillos: E   5   6

4275. SZANTON, DAVID. Art in Sulu. PS 11, no. 3 (July 1963), 463-502. 86 figures.
      Geoghegan: A fairly complete account of the art forms among the Samal and Badjaw of Sulu. Set of good to excellent photographs.
                  E   3   6

        Nimmo: E   5   6
        Rixhon: First systematic study of the Sulu's art forms in wood
                        and stone.
                        E   5   6
        Stone: Excellent photographic study of indigenous art of Sulu.
                        E   5   6
        Trimillos: Good reproduction general survey.
                        E   5   6

4276.   WENDOVER, R. F.   The Balangingi pirates.   PM 38, no. 8 (Aug. 1941), 323-325,
        337-338.
        Nimmo: E   3   2/3
        Stone: T   3   2/3

                        SUBANUN - GENERAL

4277.   BLUMENTRITT, FERDINAND.   Neue Nachrichten über die Subanon (Insel Mindanao).
        Nach P. Francisco Sanchez.   Zeitschrift der Gesellschaft für Erdkunde zu Ber-
        lin 31 (1896), 369-372.

4278.   CHRISTIE, EMERSON BREWER...The Subanuns of Sindangan Bay.   Manila, Bureau of
        Printing, 1909. 121p. (Bureau of Science. Division of ethnology publica-
        tions. v.VI, pt. 1)
        Frake: The only useful general account of the subanun published
                        before World War II.
                        E/G   5   3/4
        Wulff: Excellent primary data as far as the author's information
                        goes; not all aspects of the culture are covered.
                        E/G   5   3/4

4279.   FINLEY, J. P., and WILLIAM CHURCHILL.   The Subanu; studies of a sub-Visayan
        mountain folk of Mindanao.   Pt. I. Ethnographical and geographical sketch of
        land and people, by Lieut.-Col. John Park Finley...Pt. II. Discussion of the
        linguistic material, by William Churchill.   Pt. III. Vocabularies. Washing-
        ton, D.C., Carnegie institution of Washington, 1913. 236p. 2 maps.
        (Carnegie institution of Washington. Publication, no. 184.)

4280.   FRAKE, CHARLES O.   Cultural ecology and ethnography.   AA 64, no. 1, part I
        (Feb. 1962), 53-59.
        Frake: E/L   5   6
        Wulff: Theoretical discussion based on data from the Subanun.
                        E   5   6

4281.   _____.   The Eastern Subanun of Mindanao. (In: Murdock, George Peter, ed.
        Social structure in Southeast Asia. New York, 1960. p.51-64) (In Wenner-
        Gren Foundation for Anthropological Research, Inc., Viking Fund. Publica-
        tions in anthropology, no. 29.)
        Frake: E/L   5   6
        Wulff: E   5   6

4282.   _____.   Sindangan social groups.   PSR 5, no. 2 (Apr. 1957), 2-11.

```
            Frake:          E/L    5       6
            Wulff:          E      5       6
```

4283. MOJARES, F. S. The Subanos of Zamboanga. Filipino Teacher 15, no. 8 (Jan. 1961), 538-541.

SUBANUN - AGRICULTURE AND FOOD

4284. FRAKE, CHARLES O. Social organization and shifting cultivation among the Sindangan Subanun. 1955. 311p. Thesis (Ph.D.) - Yale Univ.
```
            Frake:          E/L    5       6
```


SUBANUN - DRINK, DRUGS AND INDULGENCE

4285. CHRISTIE, EMERSON B. Report on the drinking customs of the Subanuns. PJS 7A, no. 2 (Apr. 1912), 114-117.
```
            Frake:          E/G    5       3/4
```

4286. FRAKE, CHARLES O. How to ask for a drink in Subanun. (In: Gumperz, John J. and Hymes, Dell H., eds. The ethnography of communication. Menasha, Wis., 1964. p.127-132) AA 66, no. 6, pt. 2. Special publication (Dec. 1964).
```
            Frake:          E/L    5       6
            Wulff:          E      5       6
```


SUBANUN - EDUCATION

4287. GABRIEL, SISTER MA. OBDULIA. Educational implications of the religious beliefs and customs of the Subanuns of Labason, Zamboanga del Norte. 1964. 86p. Thesis (M.A.) - Xavier Univ.
```
            Madigan:        Y      5       6
```


SUBANUN - HEALTH AND SICKNESS

4288. FRAKE, CHARLES O. The diagnosis of disease among the Subanun of Mindanao. AA 63, no. 1 (Feb. 1961), 113-132.
Comments on Frake's Methodology, by Jules Henry. AA 66, no. 1 (Feb. 1964), 122-124.
```
            Frake:          E/L    5       6
            Wulff:          E      5       6
```

SUBANUN - POLITICAL ORGANIZATION AND BEHAVIOR

4289. FRAKE, CHARLES O. Litigation in Lipay: a study in Subanun law. Ninth Pacific Science Congress. 1957. Proceedings. v.3, 217-222. Bangkok, 1963.
        Frake: E/L   5   6

SUBANUN - RELIGIOUS BELIEFS AND PRACTICES

4290. FRAKE, CHARLES O. A structural description of Subanun "religious behavior ".
        (In: Goodenough, Ward H., ed. Explorations in cultural anthropology; essays
        in honor of George Peter Murdock. New York, McGraw-Hill, 1964. p.111-129)
        Frake: E/L   5   6
        Wulff: Primary data with short methodological statement.
                        E   5   6

4291. GABRIEL, SISTER MA. OBDULIA. Educational implications of the religious beliefs and customs of the Subanuns of Labason, Zamboanga del Norte. 1964.
        86p. Thesis (M.A.) - Xavier Univ.
        Madigan: Y   5   6

SUBANUN - SEX AND REPRODUCTION

4292. FRAKE, CHARLES O. and CAROLYN M. FRAKE. Post-natal care among the Eastern
        Subanun. SJ 4, no. 3 (July/Sept. 1957), 207-215.
        Frake: E/L   5   6

SUBANUN - TOTAL CULTURE

4293. FRAKE, CHARLES O. Social organization and shifting cultivation among the
        Sindangan Subanun. 1955. 311p. Thesis (Ph.D.) - Yale Univ.
        Frake: E/L   5   6

TAWSUG - GENERAL

4294. EWING, J. FRANKLIN. Notes on the Tawsug of Siasi in particular, and the Moros of the Southern Philippines in general. (In: Chicago. Univ. Philippine Studies Program. Mindanao Conference. Chicago, 1955) 151p. Mimeographed.

```
Arce:          E       5      4
Frake:         E       5      4/5
Gowing:        E      4/5     7
Stone:        E/M/Y    5      7
```

TAWSUG - AGRICULTURE AND FOOD

4295. EWING, J. FRANKLIN. Food and drink among the Tawsug. AQ 36, no. 2 (Apr.
1963), 60-70.
```
Frake:         D       5      4/5
Stone:        E/M/Y    5      7
```

4296. _____. Subsistence activities of the Tawsug with comparative notes. AQ
36, no. 4 (Oct. 1963), 183-202.
```
Frake:         D       5      4/5
Stone:        E/M/Y    5      7
```

TAWSUG - ARMED FORCES AND WAR

4297. KIEFER, THOMAS M. Institutionalized friendship and warfare among the Tawsug
of Jolo. Ethnology 7, no. 3 (July 1968), 225-244.
```
Rixhon:        E       4      6
```

4298. _____. Tawsug armed conflict: the social organization of military activity
in a Philippine Moslem society. Chicago, Philippine Studies Program, Univ.
of Chicago, 1968. 202p. (Research Series, 7)

TAWSUG - BUILDINGS, TOOLS AND EQUIPMENT

4299. EWING, J. FRANKLIN. Housing among the Tawsug of Siasi Island, Philippines,
with comparative notes. AQ 35, no. 1 (Jan. 1962), 10-23.
```
Frake:         D       5      4/5
Stone:        E/M/Y    5      7
```

TAWSUG - DRINK, DRUGS AND INDULGENCE

4300. EWING, J. FRANKLIN. Food and drink among the Tawsug, with comparative notes
from other Philippine and nearby groups. AQ 36, no. 2 (Apr. 1963), 60-70.

4301.   KIEFER, THOMAS M.   A note on cross-sex identification among musicians.   Ethnomusicology 12, no. 1 (Jan. 1968), 107-109.
        Rixhon: E   4   6

4302.   TRIMILLOS, RICARDO D.   Some social and musical aspects of the music of the
Taosug in Sulu, Philippines.   Honolulu, 1965.   200p.   Thesis (M.A.) - Univ.
of Hawaii.
        Stone: Baseline study of one aspect of aesthetics of indigenous
                         groups.
                         E   5   6
        Trimillos: E/R   5   6

TAWSUG   -   HEALTH AND SICKNESS

4303.   EWING, J. FRANKLIN.   Illness, death and burial in the Southern Philippines
with special reference to the Tawsug.
        Part I.   AQ 40, no. 1 (Jan. 1967), 13-25.
        Part II. AQ 40, no. 2 (Apr. 1967), 45-64.

TAWSUG   -   INTERPERSONAL RELATIONS

4304.   KIEFER, THOMAS M.   Institutionalized friendship and warfare among the Tausug
of Jolo.   Ethnology 7, no. 3 (July 1968), 225-244.
        Suggested by Rixhon.
        Rixhon: E   4   6

4305.   _____.   Reciprocity and revenge in the Philippines: some preliminary remarks about the Tausug of Jolo.   PSR 16, nos. 3/4 (July/Oct. 1968), 124-131.

4306.   STONE, RICHARD L.   Intergroup relations among the Taosug, Samal and Badjaw
of Sulu.   PSR 10, nos. 3/4 (July/Oct. 1962), 107-133.
        Arce: E   5   6
        Frake: E   5   6
        Nimmo: E   3   6
        Stone: Basic survey paper on Sulu groups.
                         E   5   6
        Trimillos: E   5   6

4307.   _____.   Intergroup relations among the Taosug, Samal, and Badjaw of the Sulu
archipelago.   1965.   153p.   Thesis (M.A.) - Univ. of Hawaii.
        Frake: E   5   6
        Nimmo: E   3   6
        Stone: Single community study of group stereotypes and inter-
                         actions.
                         E   5   6
        Trimillos: E   5   6

TAWSUG - POLITICAL ORGANIZATION AND BEHAVIOR

4308. KIEFER, THOMAS M. Power, politics and guns in Jolo: the influence of modern weapons on Tao-sug legal and economic institutions. PSR 15, nos. 1/2 (Jan./ Apr. 1967), 21-29.
Suggested by Rixhon.
    Rixhon: E   4   6

TAWSUG - RELIGIOUS BELIEFS AND PRACTICES

4309. EWING, J. FRANKLIN. Illness, death and burial in the Southern Philippines with special reference to the Tawsug.
    Part I. AQ 40, no. 1 (Jan. 1967), 13-25.
    Part II. AQ 40, no. 2 (Apr. 1967), 45-64.

4310. _____. Some rites of passage among the Tawsug of the Philippines. AQ 31, no. 2 (Apr. 1958), 33-41.
    Frake: D   5   4/5
    Stone: E/M/Y 5   7
    Trimillos: M   3   5/6

4311. INDIN, NOOH H. The religious heritage of the Tausugs. Research Journal 6, (Feb. 1966), 169-174.
    Source: Index to Periodicals (U.P. Library. Filipiniana Section)
    Trimillos: A Tausug who studied at U.P.
                 Y   5   6

4312. KASMAN, EDWARD SALKIYA. Birth and death rituals among the Tausugs of Siasi. Unitas 35, no. 3 (Sept. 1962), 291-340.

4313. KIEFER, THOMAS M. A note on Tausug (Suluk) gravemarkers from Jolo. SMJ 16, nos. 32/33, n.s. (July/Dec. 1968), 107-110. 12 plates.

TAWSUG - SEX AND REPRODUCTION

4314. EWING, J. FRANKLIN. Birth customs of the Tawsug, compared with those of other Philippine groups. AQ 33, no. 3 (July 1960), 129-133.
    Frake: D   5   4/5
    Stone: Fr. Ewing's work always uniformly excellent and informative.
                 E/M/Y 5   7
    Trimillos: M   3   5/6

4315. KASMAN, EDWARD SALKIYA. Birth and death rituals among the Tausugs of Siasi. Unitas 35, no. 3 (Sept. 1962), 291-340.

TIRURAY

4316. BLUMENTRITT, FERDINAND. Die Tiruray der Insel Mindanao. Globus 58, no. 9 (1890), 129-131.
    Moore: Secondary data primarily from missionaries among the Ti-
                    ruray around the mission at Tamontaka.
                    N   3   3

4317. POST, URSULA R. The phonology of Tiruray. PJS 94, no. 4 (Dec. 1966), 563-575.

4318. SCHLEGEL, STUART A. Repercussions of naive scholarship: the background of local furor. PSR 15, nos. 3/4 (July/Oct. 1967), 108-113.

4319. _____. Tiruray constellations: the agricultural astronomy of a Philippine hill people. PJS 96, no. 3 (Sept. 1967), 319-331.

4320. TENORIO, JOSE. Costumbres de los indios Tirurayes escritas...traducidas al español y anotadas por un padre misionero de la compañía de Jesus. Manila, Amigos del país, 1892. 91p.
    Moore: Interesting description of Tiruray customs by a young man
                    strongly influenced by Spanish missionaries.
                    I   5   3
    Schlegel: Fascinating general account of the customs of the Awang
                    variant of Tiruray, written by a member of the tribe.
                    I   3   3

4321. WOOD, GRACE L. The Tiruray. PSR 5, no. 2 (Apr. 1957), 12-39.
    Moore: E   5   6
    Schlegel: Brief survey of traditional Tiruray custom notable for
                    inclusion of mythical material. The myths are not the
                    general Tiruray version, as the article suggests, but are
                    a version in use among a now defunct nativist cult that
                    flourished in the '30s.
                    E   3   3/4

YAKAN

4322. BLUMENTRITT, FERDINAND. Yákanen und Sámal-laut der Insel Basilan (Philip-pinen). Ausland 65, no. 52 (Dec. 24, 1892), 818-821.
    Stone: N   5   3

4323. CAVALLERIA, PABLO. Letter from Father Pablo Cavalleria to Father Francisco Sanchez. (In: Blair and Robertson. v.43: 255-267)
    Frake: Ethnographic data on the Yakan are poor but a primary
                    document of importance for Yakan-Spanish relations.
                    M   5   3

4324. WULFF, INGER. Burial customs among the Yakan, a Muslim people in the South-ern Philippines. Folk 4, (1962), 111-122.

Frake: E   5   6

4325.   _____. Features of Yakan culture. Folk; Dansk Etnografisk Tidsskrift   6,
No. 2 (1964), 53-72.
Frake: E   5   6

4326.   _____. The Yakan graduation ceremony. Folk; Dansk Etnografisk Tidsskrift
5, (1963), 325-332.
Frake: E   5   6

4327.   _____. The Yakan Imam. Folk; Dansk Etnografisk Tidsskrift   8/9, (1966/
1967), 355-371.

4328.   _____. The Yakan maulud celebration. (In: Zamora, Mario D., ed. Studies
in Philippine anthropology (In honor of H. Otley Beyer). Quezon City,
Alemar-Phoenix, 1967. p.494-502)

CULTURAL-LINGUISTIC GROUP INDEX

The numbers refer to entries, not to pages.

485

AUTHOR INDEX

This index also includes titles without authors.

The numbers refer to entries, not to pages.

A

Abarientos, Ernesto P., 132
Abaya, Consuelo, 268, 2571
Abaya, Hernando J., 2095
Abelarde, Pedro E., 809
Abella, Domingo, 1214, 1646, 1807,
  2983
Abello, Amelia B., 2096
Abijay, Francisco, 64
Abraham, William I., 2260-2261
Abrams, Norman, 4229
Abrenica, Cesar B., 2097
Abreu, Antonio Alvarez de, See Alvarez
  de Abreu, Antonio
Abueva, Jose V., 536-538, 2098-2099
Acayan, Dolores S., 154
Achútegui, Pedro S. de, 2302-2303,
  3349
Aclop, Leonard, 3217, 3228
Adams, Dorothy Inez, 155
Adams, Edith, 647
Adams, Wallace, 1369
Addis, J. M., 269
Adriano, F. T., 156, 1370
Aduarte, Diego, 1572, 2304
Afable, Lourdes B., 3930
Africa, Angel A., 157
Agabin, Pacifico A., 2234
Agaloos, Bernardo C., 4080
Aga-Oglu, Kamer, 270-276, 3646
Agbanlog, Anselmo, 2906
Agbayani, Amefil, 2100
Agcaoili, F., 3103, 4213, 4233
Agcaoili, T. D., 2486
Ageo, Gabriel G., 1004
Aglibut, Andres P., 2826

Agoncillo, Teodoro A., 1181-1182,
  1573-1574, 1704, 1958, 2101
Agpalo, Remigio E., 810-811, 2102,
  2235, 3773
Agreda, C. C., 2930
Aguas, Juan S., 3421
Aguila, Concepcion A., 2572
Aguila, Dani D., 1283
Aguila, Norma Alampay, 372-373, 2305
Aguila, P. J., 1397
Aguilar, Jose V., 904-905, 1808-1809
Aguillon, Delfina B., 1371
Agustin, E. P., 2937
Ahlborn, Richard, 2887
Aiyar, M. S. Ramaswami, 1170
Akhtar, Muhammad I., 2915
Alano, Segundo, 4178
Alarcón, Ruperto, 2719, 3140
Albano, Virginia G., 3326
Albert Leo N. and Others, 514
Alcachupas, Ramon C., 2970
Alcantara, Adelaida and Others, 1575,
  2040
Alcantara, Remedios O., 1443
Alcázar, José de, 1576
Alconis, Maria S., 2408
Aldaba, Vicente C., 2798, 2916-2919
Aldaba-Baluyut, Diwata, 2895
Aldaba-Lim, Estefania J., 374-377,
  455-456, 812, 2420, 2493
Aldaba-Lim, Estefania and Others,
  2205
Aldana, Benigno V., 906-907
Alegado, Graciano I., 4033
Alejandro, Rufino, 1810
Alencon, Ferdinand Philippe Marie
  d'Orleans, duc'd, 2734, 4085

Alfonso, Julio G., 3374
Alfonso, Oscar M., 1215, 1574, 1577
Algué, José, 1, 277, 643, 3931
Ali, Abdurrahaman A., 3932
Alip, Eufronio M., 1005-1006, 1284,
   1811, 1922, 2262
Allee, Ralph H., 948
Allen, James S., 1758
Allison, William W., 65-66, 2103
Allred, Wells M., 2041
Almanzor, Angelina C., 2443
Almanzor, Angelina C. and Others,
   2444
Almendralo, R. A., 638
Alomia, A., 1501
Alonto, Hadji Madki, 3933
Alonzo, Manuel P., Jr., 2888
Alunan, Julio A., 67
Alvarez, Manuel Francisco, 2770
Alvarez de Abreu, Antonio, 813
Alviar, Fabiana E., 2938
Alzina, Francisco Ingancio, 3741
Alzona, Encarnacion, 908-910, 1705,
   1959, 2494, 2573-2579
Amurao, Isabelo A., 2943
Amyot, Jacques, 222, 1007-1008, 2342,
   2844
Amyot, Jacques and Others, 1968
Anatomy of Philippine psychology, 378
Ancheta, Constancio M., 763
Anderson, James N., 2831, 2853, 2885,
   3514-3515
Ando, Hirofumi, 2236
Andrews, Vernon L., 694
Ang, Gertrudes R., 252
Angeles, Francisco Delor, 3742
Angeles, Noli de los, 1923
Angeles, Sixto de los, 2421-2422
Angus, William R., 1009
Antonio, Celia M., 223
Antonio, Doroteo U., 68
Anuddin, Majindi K., 4030
Apacible, Alejandro R., 158-159
Aparece, Francisco T., 3731, 3784
Apostol, Jose P., 3277
Appleton, Sheldon, 1010, 1118
Aquino, Belinda A., 2423
Aquino, Benigno,Jr., 1759-1760
Aquino, Francisca R., 1285
Aquino, Marcelo V., 3595, 3991
Aquino, Simeon, 2617
Aragon, Yldefonso de, 617
Aragones, Santos G., 2799
Araneta, A. S., 2206

Araneta, Francisco, 814, 911, 997,
   2495, 3567, 3764
Araneta, Salvador, 815
Arbues, Lilia R., 3424
Arce, Wilfredo Florenda, 4114, 4148
Arcellana, Emerenciana Y., 2104
Arceo-Ortega, Angelina, 2580
Arcinas, Fe Rodriguez, 2832, 2878,
   2896
Arellano, C. S., 1906
Arellano, Lourdes, 1899
Arendonk, Joep Van, 816
Arens, Richard, 160-161, 764, 912,
   2306, 2365, 3596-3602, 3678, 3732,
   3774, 3785-3793
Argensola, Bartolomé Leonardo de,
   See Leonardo y Argensola, Bartolomé
   Juan
Arguilla, Lydia, 1286; *See also*
   Villanueva-Arguilla, Lydia
Arias, Magdalena, 1559
Ariona, Adoracion, 378
Arnaldo, Marcelo V., 1761, 3603
Aromin, Basilio B., 618-619, 648-
   650, 695, 795
Aron, Hans, 1372, 2800
Arong, Jose R., 4165
Arquiza, Lino Q., 1270
Artigas y Cuerva, Manuel, 1578, 2487
Ascalon, S. J., 1435
Ashburn, Franklin G., 2424, 2897
Asuncion, Daniel F., 2657
Asuncion, Diosdado R., 1171
Atabug, Lourdes C., 762
Atangan, Remedios, 1236
Ateneo de Manila, 978
Atienza, José C., 2920
Augustin, Demetrio R., 2889
Austin, Virginia Morey, 4220
Avanceña, Rosalia O., 701, 4074
Aycardo, Manuel Ma, 620-621, 1502
Aziz, Ungku A., 69
Azores, Fortunata M., 426

B

Bacdayan, Albert S., 3252
Bacon, Raymond F., 366, 747
Baguilat, Raymundo, 3125, 3176
Baguilat, Teodoro B., 2658-2659,
   3604
Baguitan, Florentino, 3898-3899
Bailen, Jerome B., 224, 3733

488

Baja, Emanuel A., 1907
Balaba, Teresa Pilar L., 4068
Balane, Juan I., 3824
Baldoria, Pedro L., 1445
Ballard, D. Lee, Jr., 3034
Balmaceda, Cornelio, 539-540
Banogon, Rodolfo C., 3605
Bantegui, B. C., 650
Bantegui, Bernardino G., 765, 1221, 1373-1374, 1681, 1722, 2263-2264
Bantug, Jose P., 2496
Baquirin, Bienvenido V., 367
Baradas, David B., 4058
Barber, Clarence L., 766, 2265-2266
Barker, R., 162
Barnard, Myra L., 4221, 4237
Barnett, Milton L., 225, 379, 1011, 3035
Barnett, Patricia G., 1012
Barney, Charles Norton, 494
Barranco, Vicente, 1013
Barrantes y Moreno, Vicente, 2, 4012
Barrera, Alfredo, 3606, 3718
Barretto, Felisa R., 1476
Barrows, David P., 226, 651, 913, 2107, 2497-2498, 2618-2619, 3048-3050, 3363, 3425
Bartlett, Harley Harris, 70, 2685, 2771, 3501, 3895
Bartolome, Candido C., 58, 2488
Bartolome, Rafael, 1375
Barton, Roy Franklin, 239, 3051-3055, 3058, 3078, 3104, 3111, 3123, 3127-3130, 3141-3150, 3153, 3180, 3381, 3395-3396
Basco, Carmen Vibar, 3223
Bass, Flora (Gardner), 2581
Batacan, Delfin F., 2499
Baterina, Virginia F., 2237
Bateson, Mary Catherine, 380
Batil, Amor, 3003, 3007
Batnag, Jaime, 1146
Batungbacal, Jose, 1908
Bautista, Alicia P., 1376, 1405
Bautista, Alicia P. and Others, 1377
Bautista, Basilio R., 163
Bautista, Danilo T., 2801, 2921
Bautista, Marcelino, 3225
Bauzon, Leslie E., 817
Bawagan, Margarita P., 3607
Bayani-Sioson, Pelagia S., 1519
Bazaco, Evergisto, 914, 2307
Bean, Robert Bennett, 278, 1969-1971, 2788, 3181, 3364, 3426-3429, 3888

Beardsley, J. W., 1723
Belarmino, Isagani C., 622
Belen, Hermogenes F., 495
Beleno, Eugenia, 2126
Belford, Samuel W., 1014
Bell, Daniel C., 897
Bello, Moises C., 2772, 3278, 3399-3400
Bello, Walden F., 3-4, 21
Beltran, Anita K. G., 1724, 2845
Benavides, Enriqueta R., 2582
Benedict, Laura Watson, 4153-4155
Benetua, Nestora L., 2445
Benitez, Conrado, 1597, 2467
Bennett, Don C., 652
Bergaño, Diego, 3422
Berger, Rainer, 3647
Bernabe, Daisy G., 2042
Bernad, Miguel A., 1646, 3349, 3567, 3764, 4013
Bernal, Enriqueta A., 1762
Bernal, Rafael, 1216-1217, 1812, 2846, 4059
Bernal-Torres, E., 71
Bernard, Miguel A., 2302-2303
Bernardino, Vitaliano, 915-917, 1682
Bernardo, Angelo G., 4017
Bernardo, Gabriel A., 484, 2489
Berreman, Gerald D., 5
Berreman, Joel V., 2500-2501
Best, Elsdon, 1579, 1972, 3505
Beurms, Charles J., 3253
Die Bevölkerung der Philippinen, 653
Beyer, H. Otley, 229, 279-297, 496, 623, 654-657, 1015-1016, 1580-1582, 1909, 1973-1974, 2502, 2620, 2660, 2695, 2815-2819, 2951-2952, 3056-3060, 3072, 3089-3090, 3103, 3151-3153, 3172, 3182-3185, 3279-3280, 3382, 3410-3411, 3430, 3502, 3568-3569
Beyer, William, 2720
Bhalla, A. S., 767
Bielouss, Eva Gabrielle, 1924
Biermann, B., 1813
Billiet, Francis, 3383, 3392
Billman, Cuthbert, 4129
Binamira, Ramon P., 541
Bingle, Ernest J., 2308-2309
Birket-Smith, Kaj, 3218
Blair, Emma H., 6, 485, 1583
Blake, Frank R., 1814
Blaker, James Roland, 1017
Blount, James Henderson, 998

Concepcion, Mercedes B., 665-668, 697, 829, 1245, 2106, 2370-2371, 2409-2411, 2827, 2855, 3720
Concepcion, Rodolfo F., 2238
Concepcion, Rosalina A., 611
Conference on population, 669
Congreso Penal y Penitenciario Hispano-Luso-Americano y Filipino, 1915
Conklin, Harold C., 1828-1830, 1992, 3065, 3092-3093, 3115, 3178, 3845, 3859, 3861-3869, 3871-3874, 3896-3897, 3901, 3936, 4105
Constantino, E. O., 922, 1831
Constantino, Josefina D., 2509-2510
Constantino, Karina R., 923
Constantino, Melchor F., 2814
Constantino, Renato, 2511
Cook, Albert, 3890
Cook, Hugh L., 1387
Cooper, John M., 3442, 4203
Copeland, Edwin B., 78
Coquia, Jorge R., 2239, 2314
Cordero, Felicidad V., 404, 549, 611, 2471, 2968, 2982, 2987
Cordero, Narciso, 3189
Cornish, Louis C., 2315
Cornwell, Warren H., 770
Corocoto, Simon P., 3614
Coronel, Hernando de los Rios, *See* Rios Coronel, Hernando de los
Corpus, Manuel T., 2044
Corpus, Severino F., 937, 2476
Corpuz, Eduardo G., 166
Corpuz, Onofre D., 925-926, 981, 1592-1593, 2111-2115, 2240
Cortes, Irene R., 2116
Cortez, Olimpio C., 405, 1246
Cortez, Rodolfo V., 3423
Corvera, A. Cesar, 2841
Costa, Horacio de la, 406-407, 1222, 1594-1595, 1646, 2316-2320, 2512, 3942, 4195
Costenoble, Hermann, 1832
Covar, Prospero R., 167, 408, 1247, 2321-2322
Cragin, Michael, 1357
Craig, Austin, 1596-1597
Crawford, Calvin C., 794
Credo, Flaviano P., 3721
Crespillo, Alberto, 3066
Cressey, Paul F., 1451-1452, 2045
Crisostomo, Noe Ra, 3335
Crookes, Spencer H., 2446
Crowe, Clifford H., 1561

Cruz, Amelita Reysio, 2513
Cruz, Andres Cristobal, 517
Cruz, Beato de la, 3574, 3714
Cruz, Cornelio Castor, 2724
Cruz, Dalmacio A., 168, 2922, 2964
Cruz, Santiago F. de la, 892
Cruz, Santiago R., 1453
Cuaderno, Miguel, Sr., 771, 2117
Cuerquis, Florencio R., 2323
Cuerva, Manuel Artigas y, *See* Artigas y Cuerva, Manuel
Culin, Stewart, 2490
Cullen, Vincent G., 615, 4184
Cunningham, Charles H., 1764, 2118, 2880
Cushner, Nicholas P., 1598, 1733, 2324, 4132, 4138, 4147, 4149
Cutshall, Alden, 79, 169-170, 830-831, 1765, 3681
Cuyugan, Ruben Santos, 409, 553, 927, 1509, 1599, 2472, 2514; *See also* Santos-Cuyugan, Ruben

D

Dacanay, Julian E., Jr., 4061
Dait, Juan B., 3067
Dalisay, Amando M., 80-81, 550, 832, 1766, 2663
Dalmau, Rafael Comenge y, *See* Comenge y Dalmau, Rafael
Dalton, J. Albert, 1510
Dalupan, Francisco, 892
Damian, Amazona, 3443
Dampier, William, 3943
Danielson, Albert L., 670
Daoas, John K. S., 3272
Daroy, Petronilo Bn., 2515
David, Grace S., 685
David, Isidoro P., 82
David, Randolf S., 1734
Davis, William G., 2696
Dawis, Rene V., 1740
Dawson, Owen L., 83
Dayyo, Silverio C., 2664, 3289
Dean, Gladys, 4180
Dean, James, 4180
Deats, Richard L., 2372, 2447
Decker, John L., 1519
De Dios, M. B., 171
Dee, Howard Q., 1124
Delgado, Juan Jose, 1600
Del-Rosario, Mariano V., 892

Demetrio, Francisco, 1358, 2373-2374, 3794

Densmore, Frances, 1290-1291, 4253, 4270

Deomampo, N. R., 2923

Depositario, Willie G., 84

Depre, Albert A., 2701

Deraedt, Jules, 2773

Deutschman, Zygmunt, 1511

De Young, John E., 518-519, 551-552, 2516

Dia, Manuel A., 85, 2119

Diaz, A., 2416

Diaz, Casimiro, 2328

Diaz, Ralph C., 2924

Diaz-Catapusan, Flora E., 1242-1243, 2469

Diaz-Pascual, Nery, 2120

Díaz-Trechuelo, Lourdes, 671, 1125; *See also* Díaz-Trechuelo Spínola, María Lourdes

Díaz-Trechuelo Spínola, María Lourdes, 489; *See also* Díaz-Trechuelo, Lourdes

Dichoso, Fermin, 497, 2890, 3860

Dickerson, Roy Ernest and Others, 1454

Dinwiddie, William, 3190, 3268

Diokno, Jose W., 2876

Dixon, Roland Burrage, 299, 3058

Dizon, Jacinto J., 1536

Doerr, Arthur H., 1455

Doherty, David H., 13

Doherty, John F., 672-673, 1735, 2325, 2375-2377, 2427, 2583, 2900

Domantay, Juanita P., 2412

Domingo, Maria Fe, 1683, 2856

Donahue, Elizabeth Ann, 410, 2378

Donoghue, John, 674, 1456

Dorn, Louis, 1833

Doty, Edith A., 1834

Douglas, Louis H., 1601, 2867

Dozier, Edward P., 2622, 2665, 2769, 3384-3385, 3393-3394

Dozier, Marianne F., 3390

Drilon, J. D., 172

Ducommun, Dolores, 4021, 4271

Duff, Roger S., 2623, 3155

Dulatre-Padilla, Luz, 2843, 2848

Dulawan, Lourdes S., 3068

Dumlao, Alejandro, 3342

Dupree, Louis B., 1457

Duque, Francisco Q., 1512-1513

Dwyer, D. J., 675

Dy, Huanchay, 1033

E

Ealdama, Eugenio, 3575, 3682

Echaúz, Robustiano, 3576

Echon, E. J., 2674

Edralin, Josefa S., 2121

Educational leadership . . ., 86

Eggan, Fred, 14, 236-239, 833, 1602, 2517, 2624, 2712, 2735-2738, 2757, 3191-3192, 3229, 3247, 3255-3256, 3273, 3282, 3328-3329, 3560, 3565, 3589, 3594, 3910, 3944

Eickstedt, E. von, 3444, 3491

Einsiedel, Luz A., 1248, 1458, 2448, 2961

Eitzen, D. Stanley, 1034

Ejercito, Ma. Josefa (Ferriols), 1388

Elequin, Eleanor T., 982

Elevazo, Aurelio O., 928

Elkins, Richard E., 1603, 4234-4235, 4238-4239, 4243

Ellinger, Tage U. H., 3577

Elliott, Charles B., 2122-2123

The elusive Filipino soul, 1292

Embree, John F., 3445

Emerson, J. P., 87

Encarnación, Jose, Jr., 772

Encarnacion, Vicente, Jr., 2124, 3401-3402

Enoc, Pasandalan, 4196

Enrile-Gutierrez, Belen, 2584

Entenberg, Barbara, 1767

Enverga, Tobias Y., 411

Erdberg-Consten, Eleanor von, 300

Eslao, Nena, 929, 1249, 4272

Espina, Luz R., 1736

Espiritu, Augusto Cesar, 790

Espiritu, Socorro C., 552a, 773, 930, 1709

Espiritu, Socorro C. and Others, 2473

The establishments of local governments, 2046

Estanislao, J., 88

Estel, Leo A., 3446

Estolas, Josefina V., 412

Estrada, Josefa G., 378

Estrella, Conrado F., 1768

Eubinag, Aurora F., 2971

Eufemio, Flora, 1250

Evangelista, Alfredo E., 301-311, 1646, 1993, 2833, 2953, 2955-2956

Evangelista, Oscar L., 2326

Galang, Ricardo E., 498, 1997, 2567, 2829, 3024, 3372, 4019
Galdon, Joseph A., 1296
Gale, Albert, 3559
Gallman, Jeff. D., 3135
Galvante, Jesus R., 1563
Galvey, Guillermo, 2625, 3039
Gamboa, Enriqueta T., 3025
Gamboa, Ma. Elena, 2131
Gamboa, Melquiades J., 2587
Gamboa, Wenceslao Emilio Retana y, *See* Retana y Gamboa, Wenceslao Emilio
Gannett, Lucy M. J., 2891
Gaon, B. V., 2813
Gapuz, Manuel M., 4036
Garcia, Carlos P., 1515
Garcia, Mauro, 18, 1184, 2398, 2980, 3532, 3535
García, Motos M., 3233
Garcia, Natividad V., 2666, 3290
Garcia, Paulino J., 1391, 1516-1517
Garcia, Roberto Y., 860
Garcia, Rosalinda M., 1392
Gardner, Fletcher, 1841, 3546, 3875, 3902-3903, 3923
Garvan, John M., 3172, 3449-3451, 3496, 3512, 4213, 4219, 4223-4224, 4233
Gaspar de San Agustin, 1609, 2328
Gates, John M., 368
Gatmaitan, Armando N., 768
Gatmaytan, Leon, 2467
Gatue, Belen Tan, *See* Tan-Gatue, Belen
Gavino, Jasmin A., 416
Gawryletz, Ivy, 3846
Gawryletz, Nick, 3846
Geeroms, Henry, 2775
Gellerman, Saul W., 837
Gemelli Careri, Giovanni Francesco, 17-18
Genet-Varcin, E., 3452-3453
Genotiva, Lorenzo C., 4181
Gervacio, Emmanuel T., 3615
Gibbs, H. D., 3103, 4213, 4233
Gibson, Ann J., 243
Gill, Robert L., 1041
Ginsburg, Norton S., 14
Gironière, Paul Proust de la, 31-32
Gloria, Manuel, 3454
Goduco-Aglular, C., 417
Golay, Frank H., 173, 775, 838-841, 1772
Goldman, Irving, 3105, 3179

Gomez, C. M. Fr. Antonio Vences, 2429
Gomez, Iluminada, 1685
Gomez, Liborio, 4084
Gonzales, Enrique, 2382
Gonzáles, Julio, 2626, 3375
Gonzales, Leon Ma, 677-678
Gonzales, Natividad A., 1393
Gonzalez, B. M., 93
Gonzalez, Mary A., 1998, 2383, 3712
Gonzalez, Michaela B., 1253
Gonzalez, Pilar A., 1256
Goodman, Grant K., 983, 1185-1192, 4047-4048
Goodman, Maurice, 3949
Goodstein, Marvin E., 173, 842
Goquinco, Leonor O., 1297-1298
Gorospe, Vitaliano R., 418-419, 1257
Gorvine, Albert, 2049
Gosiengfiao, Victor, 1193
Goson, Gregorio Sancianco y, *See* Sancianco y Goson, Gregorio
Gowing, Peter G., 2329- 2330, 3777, 3950-3955, 4115-4116
Gozon, Benjamin M., 1773
Gozum, Patricio C., 2830
Greene, F. V., 19
Griese, John William, Jr., 1218, 2849
Grisham, Glen, 2627, 2716, 2731, 2776, 3221, 3237, 4133
Grossholtz, (Thelma) Jean, 2132-2133, 2134
Grubb, Kenneth G., 2308-2309
Grunder, Garel A., 1610
Guansing, Benjamin I., 2348
Guazon, Maria Paz (Mendoza), *See* Mendoza-Guazón, Maria Paz
Guerrero, Amor C., 984
Guerrero, León Ma, 750-751
Guerrero, Milagros C., 1042, 1194, 2210, 2272
Guerrero, Renato Ma, 679
Guerrero, Sylvia H., 420, 2969
Guerrero-Nakpil, Carmen, *See* Nakpil, Carmen Guerrero
Guevara, Sulpicio, 843, 1774
Guiang, Honesta F., 421, 2522
Guinid, Martin, 3100, 3156
Guthe, Carl E., 326-327, 499, 3651
Guthrie, George M., 20-21, 422-428, 1258, 1394, 1686-1687, 2523-2524, 3117

Howard, Joseph T., 24
Howe, Frederic C., 1461
Hsieh, S. C., 109-110, 1412, 2813
Huanchay, Dy, *See* Dy, Huanchay
Huang, Chi-Lu, 1045
Hue, Nguyen Thi, *See* Nguyen, Thi Hue
Huke, Robert E., 101, 190, 1462, 3686, 3959
Hunt, Chester L., 440-442, 519, 552-552a, 561, 686, 778-779, 849-850, 937-939, 943, 1000, 1260, 1618, 1710, 1738, 1847, 1928, 1944-1946, 2332, 2386-2387, 2450, 2475-2476, 3778, 3936, 4069, 4088, 4113, 4134
Hunt, Chester L. and Others, 2477
Hurley, Victor, 3960-3961
Hutterer, Charles, 3652

I

Icasiano, Mariano C., 1524-1527
Icban, Crispulo J., Jr., 520-521
Ignacio, Rebecca, 3590, 3747
Ilag, Leodegario M., 3621-3622
Imao, Abdulmari A., 4064
Imatung, Pablo, 3157
The Indian community in the Philippines, 1176
Indin, Nooh H., 4311
Indolos, Maximo, 2276
Intengan, Carmen L1., 1401
Intengan, Carmen L1. and Others, 1402-1403
International Labor Office, 851
International Labour Organization, 1739, 2588
The Irayas, Ygorrotes, and Manobos of the Philippines, 3877, 4225
Irikura, James K., 1196
Irving, Earl M., 2699
Isidro, Antonio, 940-941, 1149; *See also* Isidro y Santos, Antonio
Isidro, Antonio and Others, 942
Isidro y Santos, Antonio, 4035; *See also* Isidro, Antonio
Iturralde, Julia, 2333
Iwao, Sei-Ichi, 1197

J

Jacinto, Carmelo P., 1528
Jacinto, Visitacion E., 2717, 3307

Jacobs, Pepita J., 427, 1687
Jacoby, Erich H., 102
Jagor, Fedor, 25-27, 2909
Jamias, Juan F., 103, 522, 780
Janse, Olov R. T., 331-333, 1046
Jara, Josefa, 1299
Jarmin, Martin V., 2939
Jaug, Jose O., 2726
Javier, Benedicto M., 3547
Javillonar, Gloria V., 377, 812
Jayme, Josefina B., 1393; *See also* Bulatao-Jayme, Josefina
Jayme, Vicente R., 4026
Jenkins, Shirley, 852
Jenks, Albert E., 104, 1947, 2000, 2491, 3193-3194, 3222, 3224
Jenks, Maud Huntley, 28
Jensen, Khin Myint, 1047
Jesuits. Letters From Missions (Philippine Islands), 3962, 4135
Jesus, Jose P. de, 443
Jiang, Joseph P. L., 1048
Jiménez, Francisco de Paula Cañamaque y, *See* Cañamaque y Jiménez, Francisco de Paula
Jimenez, Teresita T., 1529, 2863
Joaquin, Nick, 1848, 2093
Jocano, F. Landa, 241, 334-335, 615, 1361-1362, 1404, 1530, 1619-1620, 1646, 1711, 1849, 2001-2001a, 2388-2390, 2528, 3623, 3672, 3687, 3748-3750, 3804-3807, 3830, 3915-3921
Jordana y Morera, Ramon, 29, 1049, 1463
Jose, Sionil, 562, 3069
Joya, Jose T., Jr., 1292
Joya, Petra R. de, 2451
Ju, I-Hsiung, 1050
Juan, E. San, Jr., 1850
Juan de la Concepción, 1621, 2334
Juan de Plasencia, 3414, 3521
Juco, Jorge M., 1158, 1929
Julian, Elisa A., 1165
Jumagui, Juan O., 2963
Jumawan, Lucy, 1300
Jupp, Kathleen M., 687, 2414
Jurika, Stephen, 1464

K

Kalantiaw Code, *See* Code of Calantiao
Kalaw, Máximo M., 191, 1227, 2141, 2151, 4158

Kalaw, Moises M., 3624

Kalaw, Pura (Villanueva), 2589

Kalaw, Teodoro M., 2529

Kamacho, H. B., 3611

Kane, Samuel E., 3070, 3158, 3195

Kasilag, Lucrecia R., 1301-1303

Kasman, Edward Salkiya, 4312, 4315

Katigbak, Aida, 1304

Katigbak, Maria Kalaw, 2902

Katigbak-Tan, Purisima, 853

Katz, Arthur, 2452

Kaut, Charles, 1712, 2139, 2908,
    3528-3529, 3550

Kaut, Charles and Others, 105

Kavanagh, Joseph J., 2335

Kearl, C. Delmar, 106, 192, 2926

Keats, John, 3963

Keesing, Felix M., 1622-1623, 2628,
    2739, 2767, 2994, 3231, 3274, 3283,
    3403, 3936, 3964

Keesing, Marie, 2739, 2767

Kelsey, Lincoln D., 563

Kemp, Eleanor C., 4049

Kepner, William Allison, 3673

Kern, H., 3507

Kerr, Harland B., 4240

Kibtiani, Jainari S., 4030

Kiefer, Thomas M., 4297- 4298, 4301,
    4304-4305, 4308, 4313

Kim, C. I. Eugene, 943

Kirk, Dudley, 776

Kneeland, Samuel, 3455, 3522

Knowlton, Edgar C., Jr., 1851

Kobbe, William A., 4014

Koenigswald, G. H. R. von, 336,
    2686, 3159

Kolb, Albert, 30, 1465, 4050

Krapf, E. Eduardo, 444

Krause, Walter, 781

Krauss, Wilma R., 2834, 2879

Krieger, Herbert W., 370, 2002-2004

Kroeber, Alfred L., 227, 242, 1261,
    2391, 3044, 3196

Kroef, Justus M. van der, 1713, 2212;
    See also Van der Kroef, Justus M.

Kuder, Edward M., 3965

Kuhonta, P. C., 2674

Kuizon, Jose G., 3709, 3766, 4244

Kulp, J. L., 3648

Kunde, Thelma A., 1740

Kurihara, Kenneth, 854, 1741

L

Lackowski, Peter, 3856

Lactao, Luciano E., 2966

Lacuesta, Manuel G., 944

Lafond de Lurcy, Gabriel, 1466, 2005

Laing, John E., 3821

Lambrecht, Francis, 2006, 3071, 3094-
    3095, 3101-3102, 3112-3114, 3118,
    3124, 3126, 3132-3133, 3136-3138,
    3160-3170

Lambrecht, Godfrey, 3026-3028

Lande, Carl H., 945, 1228, 2142-2143,
    2243-2246

Lansang, Amado A., 2461

Lansang, Flora C., 2903

Lansang, Jose A., 1779

Lapicque, Louis, 3504

Lapuz, Lourdes V., 445, 463

Laquian, Aprodicio A., 2058, 2144,
    2423, 2430, 2835, 2882-2883

Lara, Alma F., 2864

Lardizabal, Felisa, 1305

Larkin, John A., 2872, 3419-3420

Larson, Donald N., 1852, 2392

Lasker, Bruno, 1742, 1948

Laubach, Frank C., 2336-2337, 4136,
    4251, 4255

Laufer, Berthold, 298, 1051

Laurel, José P., 2059

Lava, Horacio C., 2786, 3360

Lava, Jose, 2213

Lawas, Jose M., 1387

Lawless, Robert, 446, 564, 946, 1714

Leaño, Isabel, 3040-3041

Lear, Elmer N., 3670, 3710-3711

Ledesma, Antonio J., 855, 1780

Ledesma, Oscar, 892

Ledesma, Purita (Kalaw), 1306

Lee, Ernest W., 4197

Lee, Geo. S., 1467

Leebrick, Karl C., 1166

Legarda, Benito, Jr., 856-860, 1001,
    1646, 2453

Legarda, Trinidad F., 2145, 2590-2591

Legarda y Fernandez, Benito, 2691,
    2777

Legaspi, Avelino, 325, 2957

Le Gentil, M., 1930, 2789, 2869-2970

Le Gentil de la Galaisière, Guillaume
    J. H., 33- 34

Lenk, Siegfried E., 688

Lent, John A., 523-526

Leon, Primitivo R. de, 2884
Leon, Raymundo De, 3134
León of Kutûg, 3072
Leonardo y Argensola, Bartolomé Juan, 1624
Le Roy, James Alfred, 35-36, 1002, 2530
Lesaca, Reynaldo M., 1468
Levy, Emanuel, 861-862
Lewis, A. B., 2060
Lewis, Henry T., 3291, 3305, 3362
Lewis-Minton, Frank, 752, 4198; See also Minton, Frank L.
Li, Yih-Yuan, 3171
Liang, Dapen, 2247
Liao, S. H., 109-110
Liao, Shubert S. C., 1052, 1126-1129
Lieban, Richard W., 1531, 1552, 3735-3738, 3808-3810
Lietz, Paul, 3936, 3966
Lillo de Garcia, Maximino, 3404
Limuaco, Josefina A., 462
Lindemans, Leon, 3386
Lindquist, Alice, 4221
Lingao, Alicia L., 1405
Lipio, A. V., 2826
Liquete, L. Gonzalez, 1931
Liu, Chi-Tien, 1053
Liu, William T., 1054, 3852
Livezey, William E., 1610
Llamzon, Teodoro A., 1853-1855, 3536-3538
Llovera, P., 4202
Loarca, Miguel de, 3584
Lobingier, Charles Sumner, 1932
Locain, Leandro V., 1292
Locsin, Cecilia Y., 337
Locsin, Leandro V., 491
Locsin, Teodoro M., 1055
Lodge, Henry Cabot, 38
Loewenstein, John, 338
Loney, Nicholas, 1167
Loofs, Helmut H., 339-340, 3073-3074, 3097-3098
Lopez, Cecilio, 1646, 1856-1862, 3539-3541
Lopez, Francisco B., 4070
Lopez, Oscar J., 2214
Lopez, Salvador P., 2146
Lorica, Loreto Q., 3107
Lorimer, Frank W., 689-690, 782-783
Lorrin, Rosario de Santos B., 244
Low, Stephen, 691
Lowie, Robert H., 3075

Lozano, Alfredo, 1307
Lozano, Olimpia U., 2454
Lu, Hsueh-Yi, 193
Lumbera, Bienvenido, 447, 1308, 1863-1864
Luna, Telesforo W., Jr., 692-693, 1469-1470, 1564, 2727, 2874, 3324, 3994
Lutz, Edward A., 2061
Luykx, Nicolaas G. M., 2062
Lynch, Charles, 3934
Lynch, Frank, 21, 39, 245-246, 448-450, 565-566, 1229, 1262-1263, 1615, 1646, 1715-1716, 1949-1950, 2147, 2338-2342, 2690, 2821-2822, 2910, 2981, 2985, 3013, 3513, 3530, 3936, 3967-3969, 4002, 4005, 4187
Lynch, Frank and Others, 567
Lynch, Ralph E., 3936, 4089, 4188

M

McAmis, Robert D., 4265
McCarron, John, 1865
McCormick, J. Scott, 1963
McElroy, Barton L., 4242
McHale, Mary C., 2267
McHale, Thomas R., 194, 778-779, 784-791, 863, 938-939, 1412, 1625-1629, 2267
McIntyre, Michael P., 3702, 3722-3723
McIntyre, Wallace E., 2842, 2860
McKaughan, Howard P., 4248, 4258-4259
McKendry, James M., 568
McLaughlin, Allan J., 694
MacMicking, Robert, 40, 2793
McMillan, Robert T., 111-112, 569-571, 594, 1781, 2063, 2836
McPhelin, Michael, 792-793, 1056, 2277
McPhelin, Michael and Others, 2215
Mabbun, Pablo, 1778, 2667, 2927-2928
Mabunay, Leticia D., 2904
Macapagal, Diosdado P., 864, 1057
Macaraig, Serafin E., 2431, 2478-2480, 2531
Macaranas, Eduarda A., 1264
Macaraya, Batua A., 4087, 4248
Macaspac, Isidro S., 1782
Maceda, Generosa S., 502, 2823, 3017-3018, 3456

Maceda, Jose, 1208, 1309-1311, 1316, 2718, 4199-4201
Maceda, Marcelino N., 794, 3477, 3676, 3878, 3891, 3911-3913, 4006-4010, 4204-4209, 4232
Madale, Abdullah T., 311, 4252, 4266
Maddela, Inocencio B., 2629
Madigan, Francis C., 451, 572-573, 695-701, 795, 865, 3585, 3970-3971, 3995, 4022-4023, 4036, 4071-4074, 4090, 4137-4139, 4149
Madrid, Esther Samonte, 1312-1313
Madrid. Exposición General de las Islas Filipinas, 41
Magbag, Cresencio S., 3343
Magsaysay, Jose P., 527
Magsaysay, Ramon, 2592
Maguigad, L. C., 452
Majul, Cesar Adib, 1630-1631, 2148-2149, 3972, 4051-4052, 4091, 4118
Makanas, Elpidio D., 113, 702
Makil, Perla Q., 1229
Makiling, Juan, 1314
Malayang, José, 4053
Malcolm, George A., 2150-2151
Maliaman, Dalmacio, 3248, 3258, 3269, 3405
Maliwanag, Ildefonso, 3903
Mallari, Carmen B., 2007
Mallari, Ismael V., 2532-2533, 2828
Malumbres, Julian, 2630, 2631, 2632, 2633, 2634, 2740-2742, 3172, 3175, 3267
Maminta, Aurora S., 1569
Mamisao, Jesus P., 1471
Manahan, Manuel P., 1783
Manalang, Priscila S., 947
Manalaysay, M. O., 4027
Manalili, Alfredo Luis Cura, 2415
Manalo, Eugenio B., 1472
Manalo, Fernando D., 1532
Manawis, Mariano D., 492, 2635-2636, 2668-2671, 2732, 2752, 2760, 2778-2780
Mane, Andres, 1406
Mangahas, Mahar, 195
Mangahas, Ruby K., 1315-1316
Manglapus, Raul S., 2064-2066, 2152, 2534
Manila (Archdiocese), 625-626
Manis, Jerome G., 1632
Manuel, Canuto G., 114
Manuel, E. Arsenio, 230-231, 247, 1363-1364, 1866-1868, 3376, 3542, 4110
Manulat, Mario V., 3625
Manuud, Antonio G., 1317, 1869
Manzano, Felisa O., 3905
Maquiso, Elena G., 1318
Marasigan, J. M., 208
Marasigan, Petronila C., 2911
Marche, Alfred, 3457, 3586, 3924
Marcilla y Martin, Cipriano, 1870
Marcos, Mario P., 1130
Mariano, E. P., 207
Mariano, Leonardo, Jr., 2929
Mariano, Leonardo C., 2067-2069
Marquez, Antonio, 1198
Marsella, Joy, 2439
Martin, Cipriano Marcilla y, *See* Marcilla y Martin, Cipriano
Martin, Claro, 1369, 1407, 1409, 2808
Martin, Gene E., 3724
Martin-Roquero, Corazon Tenorio, 4226
Martinez, Antonio M. and Others, 2070
Martinez de Zúñiga, Joaquin, 42, 1663-1634; *See also* Zúñiga, Joaquin Martinez de
Martires, Myrna, 2343
Mas y Sans, Sinibaldo de, 43, 2153
Masa, Jorge O., 574, 4018
Maso, Miguel Saderra, *See* Saderra Maso, Miguel
Mason, Otis T., 1975, 2035, 4020
Masterson, William F., 948
Matela, Arcadio G., 2432-2433
Matthews, J., 341
Maulit, Dimas A., 196, 1387, 2278
Mayo, Katherine, 2154
Mayuga, Pedro N., 1533-1534
Mead, Hugh S., 796
Mead, Margaret, 3076
Meadows, Martin, 2248
Mechtraud, Sister M., 1951, 2481
Medina, Belen Tan-Gatue, 1159; *See also* Tan-Gatue, Belen
Medina, Juan de, 1635, 2344
Medina, Ricardo C., 4037
Mednick, Melvin, 1408, 3973, 4024, 4119-4120, 4268
Megino, Rogelio P., 2801, 2921
Meimban, Maximo, 3119
Melendez, Pedro, 248
Mendez, Paz P., 1265
Mendoza, Elvira P., 703; *See also* Mendoza-Pascual, Elvira; Pascual, Elvira M.

Mendoza, Guillermo, 509
Mendoza, Jose, 1399
Mendoza, Teofilo M., 1453
Mendoza-Guazón, Maria Paz, 2593-2595
Mendoza-Pascual, Elvira, 627; *See also* Mendoza, Elvira P.; Pascual, Elvira M.
Mercado, C. M., 2930
Mercado, G. C., 2672, 3292
Mercado, Julian D., 892
Mercado, Mario A., 4256
Mercado, Nestor J., 704
Merino, Jesus M., 378
Merino, Manuel Walls y, *See* Walls y Merino, Manuel
Merrill, Elmer D., 1473-1475, 3077, 3090, 3626
Metasociology: an editorial foreword, 2482
Metcalf, Elizabeth H., 4159
Metzger, John A., 44
Meyer, Adolf B., 705-707, 2008-2010, 2761-2763, 3458-3466, 3508, 3767, 4106, 4160
Meyer, Hans, 3197-3198, 3467
Miao, Emily, 61, 1266, 1691
Micor, Efren, 742
Miles, W. K., 342
Millán y Villanueva, Camilo, 2637, 3284
Millare, Florencio D., 3566
Miller, E. Y., 3627, 3833
Miller, Hugo H., 197, 503-504, 866-867, 2467
Miller, Hugo H. and Others, 505-506
Miller, Merton L., 2011, 2781, 2912, 3892
Miller, Oliver C., 2012
Mills, Vicente, 708
Milne, R. S., 1964, 2155, 2249
Miñano, Gerónimo M., 3620
Miñoza, Aurora Abear, 453, 949, 989, 1692-1693
Minton, Frank Lewis, 507, 2393, 4028; *See also* Lewis-Minton, Frank
Mirafuente, Buenaventura, 1131
Miravite, Q. F., 4038
Mitchell, Hudson, 4039
Mitchell, Thomas A., 2455
Mojares, F. S., 4283
Molina, Antonio J., 1294, 1319-1322
Molina, Antonio M., 2535
Mondonedo, Ernesto R., 1412
Monroe, Paul, 963

Montalban, Heraclio R., 1369, 1409, 3628, 3677
Montana, Severino, 1323
Montano, J., 2013
Montemayor, Jeremias U., 115-116, 1784-1785
Montero y Vidal, José, 45, 1636-1637, 4015, 4092
Montilla, Jose, 2673, 3293
Mora, Juan Caro y, *See* Caro y Mora, Juan
Morales, Alfredo T., 950-953, 990, 1871, 2536-2540
Morales, Eugenio, 3834
Moreno, Vicente Barrantes y, *See* Barrantes y Moreno, Vicente
Morera, Ramon Jordana y, *See* Jordana y Morera, Ramon
Morey, Virginia, 3842
Morga, Antonio de, 1638-1639
Morrison, Frank S., 628, 709
Morrow, Robert, 1786
Moss, Claude R., 3042-3044, 3259, 3406
Moyer, Raymond T., 97
Munarriz, Natividad, 2541
Munchow, John R., 1324
Munoz, Ma. Teresa, 1325
Murillo Velarde, Pedro, 2345
Muslim Association of the Philippines, 3974
The Muslim minority in the Philippines, 3975
Myers, William I., 117
Myrdal, Gunnar, 710

N

Naanep, Florendo R., 2694, 3304, 3308
Nabong, Juan, 2542
Nakpil, Carmen G., 2543, 2596-2597
Nano, José F., 118
Nasol, Ramon L., 119, 2931
National Academy of Sciences, Washington, D. C., 1230
National Conference of Social Workers, 2456
National Muslim Filipino Conference, 3977
Navarro, Jose S., 1535
Navarro, Maximina, 3014
Nazaret, Francisco V., 663, 1476, 2416-2417

Neal, Ernest E., 575, 948
Negado, Susano R., 1477
The negritos of the Philippines, 3906
Netzorg, Morton J., 2793
Newell, Leonard E., 3121-3122
Newton, Philip P., 3468
Nguyen, Thi Hue, 576
Nimmo, Harry Arlo, 4166- 4167, 4170,
    4173-4174, 4177
Niu, Paul, 954, 1150
Nolasco, J. A., 1536
Norbeck, Edward, 2014, 2497
Nuestro, Marcos M., 2944
Nurge, Ethel, 1694, 1933, 3587, 3629,
    3703, 3725, 3739, 3761, 3770, 3811-
    3814
Nyberg, Albert J., 162, 198-199
Nydegger, Corinne, 2713, 3317
Nydegger, William F., 2638, 2713, 2753,
    3285, 3317, 3338

O

Oakes, Christopher, 3199
Obayashi, Taro, 200
Ocampo, Esteban A. de, 1058, 1965
Ocampo, Felicisimo, 2457
Ocampo, Galo B., 46, 493, 1326-1328,
    2394, 4065
Ocampo, Lazaro A., 201
La Oceania Española, 1059
O'Connor, Lillian, 1872
Olayao, I., 1565
Olivar, Jose D., 2071
Olson, William H., 4227
Oñate, Burton T., 629, 711-712, 797-
    798, 1231, 1410-1411, 1743, 3726
Ong, Genaro V., 2483
Ong, Siong Cho, 1132
Onorato, Michael P., 1640-1641, 2156-
    2157
Oosterwal, Gottfried, 2395
Opiana, Gil O., 1565
Oppenfeld, Horst von, 2434, 2924,
    3612; *See also* Von Oppenfeld, Horst
Oppenfeld, Judith von, 2924
Oracion, Timoteo S., 120, 249, 2396,
    3509, 3847-3849, 3880-3887, 3907-
    3909
Orata, Pedro T., 955-956, 3707
Ordinario, Candido, 2279
Ordoñez, E. A., 3543
Ordoño, Eustaquio O., 2280

Oren, Paul, 577
Orendain, Juan Claro, 3200
Organization of educational planning,
    957
Orosa, Severina (Luna), 2598
Orosa, Sixto Y., 3976
Orr, Kenneth G., 2544, 3330, 3561
Orteza, Evelina M., 958
Ortigas, Irene, 24
O'Shaughnessy, Thomas J., 1646, 2346,
    4121, 4140
Osias, Camilo, 47, 959, 2015, 2545
Osmeña, Sergio, 2599
Osteria, Trinidad, 1267
Oteyza, Carmencita Cawed, 3275

P

Pabale, M. E., 2930
Pacana, Honesto Ch., 454
Pacheco, Antonio, 1267
Pacyaya, Alfredo G., 3201-3202, 3238-
    3239, 3249, 3255, 3260-3262
Padilla, Sinforoso G., 455-456
Padilla de Leon, Felipe, 1294, 1329-
    1330
Padua, Regino G., 2418
Pagaduan, A. N., 2926
Pait, Tuginai, 3185
Pajaro, Eliseo M., 1292, 1294, 1331
Pal, Agaton P., 528, 578-579, 868,
    1268-1270, 1412, 2158, 2546-2547,
    3588, 3630, 3688-3692, 3696, 3698-
    3699, 3751-3754, 3779, 3822, 3828
Palad, Jose Garcia and Others, 1413
Palazon, Juan, 43
Palma, Andres de Leon, 1642
Palma, Rafael, 1271, 2159, 2600
Paluskas, Stella, 674, 1332
Pamintuan, Catalina M., 1133
Pan, José Felipe del, 630
Panganiban, Antonia G., 713, 960
Panganiban, Consuelo Torres, 1873,
    3544
Panganiban, Jose Villa, 1874-1879
Pangato, Hussain S., 4111
Pangilinan, Marie Lou, 1060
Panizo, Alfredo, 1880, 3423, 3469
Panlasigui, Isidoro, 457, 1061-1062,
    1881
Panopio, Isabel S., 2471
Pao, Shih Tien, 1151-1153
Paraiso, Virginia A., 2458

502

Paras-Perez, Rodolfo, 1333-1334
Parco, Salvador A., 403, 568, 580,
    2093, 2426, 2962
Pardo de Tavera, Trinidad H., 753,
    1668, 1882-1883, 2016, 2548
Parker, Luther, 48, 508, 3470
Parson, Ruben L., 1478
The Participants in the cooperative
    leadership, 961
Pascasio, Emy M., 458, 1884-1887
Pascual, Conrado R., 1414, 1417
Pascual, Conrado R. and Others, 1415,
    2809
Pascual, Elvira M., 714-715; *See also*
    Mendoza, Elvira P.; Mendoza-Pascual,
    Elvira
Pascual, Neri Diaz, 2017
Pascual, Ricardo Roque, 2549
Pasion, Honorio D., 2977
Passmore, Fred, 3203
Pastells, Pablo, 1643
Patanñe, E. P., 1943, 2018, 2550
Paterno, Pedro Alejandro, 3471, 3523-
    3525
Paz, Consuelo J., 1831, 3373
Paz, Emeterio de la, 3870
Peabody, Dean, 459, 986
The Peasant war in the Philippines;...,
    1952, 2216
Peck, Cornelius J., 2160
Pecson, Geronima T., 962, 1695, 2601-
    2602
Pedroche, C. V., 529
Pehrson, Robert N., 1272
Pelaez, Emmanuel, 460
Pelayo, Jose O., 2459
Pelzer, Karl J., 121, 202, 581, 1479,
    3996, 4054, 4075
Pendleton, Robert L., 3997-3998, 4076
Peng, Yang Se, *See* Yang, Se-peng
Peredo, Benjamin D., 203, 207, 2674
Perez, Alejandrino Q., 3415
Pérez, Angel, 2347, 2551, 2639-2640,
    2782, 3204-3205
Perez, Bernardino A., 716, 1273, 1480,
    1722
Pérez, Manuel Herbella y, *See* Herbella
    y Pérez, Manuel
Perez, Presentacion T., 1744, 2603-
    2604
Perpiñan, Jesus E., 1154
Persons, R. C., 1537
Peruga, P., 4202
Pfeiffer, William R., 4236

Phelan, John Leddy, 1209, 1644-1645,
    1745, 1888, 2397, 2913, 3936
Philippine Association of University
    Women, 1274, 2605
Philippine Islands
    Board of Educational Survey, 963
    Bureau of Customs, 1063-1065
    Bureau of Justice, 1066
    Bureau of Non-Christian Tribes,
        2019
    Census Office, 631-633
    Dept. of the Interior, 1953
    Division of Ethnology, 250
    Ethnological Survey, 3978
    Exposition Board. Louisiana Pur-
        chase Exposition, 49
    Governor, 2161
    Governor General, 3979
    Independence Commission, 50
    Legislature. Philippine Assembly.
        Committee on Slavery and Peonage,
        1954
    Office of Public Welfare Commission-
        er, 2435
    Public Welfare Board, 1696, 2436
Philippine Mental Health Association,
    Inc., 2437
A Philippine middletown, 2072
Philippine perspective, 1646
Philippine Statistical Association.
    Task Committee "A" of the Research
    Committee, 2281
The Philippines, 717
Philippines Christian year book, 2348
Philippines (Commonwealth)
    Commission of the Census, 634
    Dept. of Agriculture and Commerce,
        122
    President, 2162
Philippines Historical Committee,
    2349
Philippines (Republic)
    Bureau of Public Libraries, 1647
    Bureau of Public Schools, 1648
    Bureau of the Census and Statistics,
        635-637, 2728, 2972
    Congress. House of Representatives,
        3980; *See also* House of Represen-
        tatives
    Dept. of Agriculture and Natural
        Resources. Bureau of Fisheries,
        1416
    Food and Nutrition Research Center,
        2675-2676, 2810-2811, 2932

503

Q

Qadir, Syed Abdul, 591, 1653
Quatrefages de Bréau, Armand de, 3472-
  3473, 4210
Quema, Jose C., 2699
Quesada, Carmencita C., 473
Quetchenbach, Raymond, 964
Quezon, Manuel L., 1654
Quezon, Philippines. University of
  the Philippines, See Philippines.
  University
Quiason, Serafin D., 1134-1135, 2292-
  2293, 4055, 4093
Quijano, Ignacio T., 3713
Quintana, Emilio U., 177, 206-209,
  3631-3633
Quintana, Vicente U., 124-125, 872,
  2677, 2965
Quintos, Jose Ma., 2463
Quintos, Rolando N., 126, 1966
Quiogue, Elena S., 1411, 1423, 2676
Quiogue, Elena S. and Others, 1424,
  2675-2676
Quirino, Carlos, 1168, 1646, 2398,
  2980
Quisumbing, Eduardo, 754-756, 1425-
  1427, 1481-1482
Quisumbing, Lourdes R., 615, 3771-3772,
  3853-3855

R

Rabin, A. I., 462
Rabor, Dioscoro S., 3727
Racelis, Maria, 962
Radin, Paul, 3139
Rafel, S. Stephen, 1275, 1934
Rahmann, Rudolf, 252, 345, 1789, 2021-
  2022, 2824, 3474-3477, 3510, 3592,
  3653, 3911-3913, 4211
Ramachandran, K. V., 638, 2416
Ramiro, Rolando R., 873
Ramos, Carlos P., 2905
Ramos, Maximo, 1365-1366, 1892, 2399-
  2401, 2608, 4249, 4257
Ramos, Narciso, 1069
Ramos, Paz G., 1538
Ramsay, Ansil, 2165
Ramsey, Charles E., 1751
Rañola, Andres, 3548
Rasay, Daniel, 3303
Rausa-Gomez, Lourdes, 1646

Ravenholt, Albert, 53, 127-129, 210,
  253, 530-531, 722, 799, 874-875,
  965-966, 991-993, 1136-1137, 1232,
  1567, 1748, 1790-1791, 1893, 2075-
  2076, 2166-2169, 2221-2223, 2250,
  2402, 2553, 3634, 3981, 3999, 4122
Raymundo, Domiciano E., 2933
Raymundo, Luz J., 1336
Reade, Charles C., 1483
Rebolos, Zenaida, 4029, 4128, 4139,
  4141
Recto, Aida E., 195, 211
Recto, Claro M., 2554
Reed, Robert R., 1484, 2873
Reed, William A., 3478-3479
Regala, Roberto, 2251
Regala-Angangco, Ofelia D., 1177-1178
Regalado, Felix, 24
Regudo, Adriana C., 2785, 2894, 2986
Reid, Lawrence A., 3173, 3234, 3241,
  3250, 3377
Relación verdadera del levantamien-
  to..., 1070
Respicio, Annie P., 723
Retana, W. E., 42
Retana y Gamboa, Wenceslao Emilio,
  1655, 1894
Reyes, B. N. de los, 208
Reyes, Baltazar, 463
Reyes, Conrado de los, 509
Reyes, Pedrito and Others, 1656
Reyes, Teofilo D., Sr., 1071
Reyes, Wilfredo L., 724-725
Reyes y Florentino, Isabelo de los,
  1657, 3331, 3353, 3557, 3593
Reyes-Juan, Isabel, 400
Reynaldo, Gonzales, 2049
Reyno, Rodolfo U., 3336, 3344
Reynolds, Harriet R., 1276-1278, 1935,
  2403, 2705-2709, 3005, 3310-3314
Reynolds, Hubert, 592, 1138, 1155,
  2710-2711, 3315-3316, 4228
Reynolds, Ira Hubert, See Reynolds,
  Hubert
Ribadeneira, Marcelo de, 1658, 2354
Rich, John, 2023-2024
Riggs, Fred W., 800, 876, 2077, 2170-
  2174, 2555-2556
Riguera, Florencio, 2722, 3354
Rios Coronel, Hernando de los, 1659
Rivera, Generoso F., 593-594, 2836,
  4246
Rivera, Juan A., 2355
Rivera, Juan Fañgon, 2078

Rivera, Lolita C., 2936
Rivera Castillet, Edvigio de, 2641
Rixhon, Gerard, 3755, 3982, 4040
Rizal y Alonso, Jose, 2404
Robb, Walter, 297, 1072, 2819, 3325
Robertson, James Alexander, 6, 51, 485, 1583, 1919, 2356, 3276
Robertson, L. S., 2661, 2934-2935, 2988-2989
Robinson, C. B., 510
Roces, Alejandro R., 1073-1074, 1210, 2557
Roces, Alfredo R., 346, 1337-1338
Rodda, Rosemary, 3843
Rodil- Martires, Concepcion, 3823
Rodriguez, E. S., 2558
Rodriguez, Filemon C., 212, 877, 2609
Rodriguez, Herminia Soller, 3294
Rodríguez, Mariano, 3187, 3206, 3516, 3518
Roe, G. Richard, 3858
Rogel, Amelia O., 313
Rogers, Dorothy M., 4094
Roginsky, J. J., 3078
Rojo, Trinidad A., 726, 1895
Rola, Bienvenido R., 801
Rola, Ceferino, 3355
Roldan, Maria Clara, 4
Rolla-Bustrillos, Nena, 1428; *See also* Bustrillos, Nena
Romani, John H., 595, 2079, 2175-2176
Romano, Felino B., 2678
Romero, Isidoro A., 2973
Romero, Redentor, 1294, 1339
Romualdez, Norberto, Jr., 464, 892, 1340, 3925
Romulo, Carlos P., 2559
Ronduen, Pedro, 596
Ronquillo, Bernardino, 1075
Roosevelt, Theodore, 1792
Rosales, Vicente J. A., 465, 727
Rosario, Alejandro del, 1341
Rosario, Fanny C. del., 1539
Rosario, Paz L. del, 757
Rosell, Dominador Z., 1485-1486, 4078
Roth, David F., 2177
Rotz, Henry W., 2357
Rowe, John H., 243
Rowe, L. S., 2178
Roxas, Sixto K., 728, 802-804, 878-880
Roxas-Lim, Aurora, 347, 1660
Roy, David P. and Others, 597
Rōyama, Masamichi, 1661

Rubio, Hilarion F., 1342
Ruiz, Leopoldo T., 1793
Runes, Ildefonso T., 1076, 1139, 2492
Ruttan, Vernon W., 130, 195

S

Saber, Mamitua, 598, 3983, 4025, 4123, 4247, 4250, 4262
Sacay, Francisco M., 213, 1429-1430, 2679, 2694, 2702, 2937-2939, 2966-2967, 3304, 3308-3309, 3635, 4030
Sacay, Francisco M. and Others, 2680, 3295, 3309
Sacay, Orlando J., 1794, 2940, 2988
Saderra Maso, Miguel, 643
Sady, Emil J., 2080
Saguiguit, Gil F., 2967
St. John, Spenser, 3984
Saito, Shiro, 487
Salamanca, Bonifacio S., 1662, 1795, 2729
Salas, Rafael M., 805
Salazar (Bishop of the Philippines), 1077
Salazar, Francisco G., 2974
Salazar, Ma Paz Gil, 3636
Salazar, Meliton, 1749
Salazar, Vicente de, 1663
Salazar, Z. A., 1179
Salcedo, Juan, Jr., 254, 729, 1431-1433, 1540-1543
Saleeby, Najeeb M., 2025, 4095-4096, 4107, 4124-4125, 4142
Salita, Domingo C., 131
Salonga, Jovito R., 1078
Sals, Florent Joseph, 3108-3110, 3174
Salvador, Gregorio D., 1563
Salvosa, Luis R., 639
Samonte, Abelardo G., 806, 2081, 2179
Samonte, Esther I., 1343
Samonte, Quirico S., 2861-2862
Samson, Elizabeth D., 881
Samson, Emmanuel V., 378, 466-468
Samson, Jose A., 378, 468-472, 1544, 3835
Samson, M. S., 2931
Samson, Pablo, Jr., 1434
San Agustin, Araceli (Sebastian), 4041
San Agustin, Gaspar de, *See* Gaspar de San Agustin